PLAYFAIR
FOOTBALL ANNUAL
2005–2006

58th edition

Editors: Glenda Rollin and

Jack Rollin

headline

First published in 2005
by HEADLINE BOOK PUBLISHING

1

Cover photographs Front and spine: Eidur Gudjohnsen (Chelsea) – *Action Images/Andrew Couldridge*; back: Alan Smith (Manchester U) – *Empics/Matthew Ashton.*

ISBN 0 7553 1386 0

Typeset by Wearset Ltd, Boldon, Tyne and Wear

Printed and bound in Great Britain by
Clays Ltd, St Ives plc

Headline's policy is to use papers that are natural, renewable and recyclable products and made from wood grown in sustainable forests. The logging and manufacturing processes are expected to conform to the environmental regulations of the country of origin.

HEADLINE BOOK PUBLISHING
A division of Hodder Headline
338 Euston Road
London NW1 3BH

www.headline.co.uk
www.hodderheadline.com

CONTENTS

European and International Football

Other Football

Information and Records

EDITORIAL

Football's popularity remains at a high level, but everyone involved in the game whether it be organising or playing, must be aware of the enormous responsibility they have to ensure that the sport's image remains untarnished. There are too many instances on and off the field of behaviour which risks destroying the reputation of the beautiful game.

Of course only a small percentage of those concerned in it can be accused of causing the damage, but they are the ones who are making it difficult for the majority and the national press, television and media in general inevitably highlights those whose conduct is less than exemplary.

Whether players like it or not, they are role models for young people. Administrators of football should also be aware that they need to show unblemished behaviour, too, in their own conduct.

In World Cup terms England may be alone among the home nations in reaching the finals next year in Germany, 40 years after the triumph at Wembley which provided us with our only major trophy. Both Wales and Northern Ireland are unlikely to join them and Scotland have their own uphill task. However, the Republic of Ireland stands an excellent chance of being among the finalists.

At club level the success of Liverpool in the Champions League was a tremendous boost to English football, though the manner of deciding any game with penalties is a flawed one and there has to be a better way of determining the outcome of games when the calendar is so crowded it does not allow for replays.

One shudders to imagine what the reaction would have been had that incredible comeback from being three goals down to draw level been ruined by losing on penalties. We know how AC Milan must have felt.

Playing to a finish is surely a better option particularly as the extra period of play often now represents going through the motions, relying on the lottery of the penalty shoot-out to get through. Golden goals and silver goals – sudden or slow death as it were – have been discarded. These days players are fitter than ever, so why not carry on regardless and let the fitter team prevail? Time taken sorting out who should take the penalty kicks could be used actively on the field by continuing after 90 minutes, the first team to score being the winner. In essence the return of sudden death.

The penalty kick is awarded as a punishment for transgression on the part of the defending team. The penalty shoot-out can be the prelude to considerable wealth and status with little or no regard to the rules which govern the spot kick.

While during normal play any attacking player can follow up on a partial save, this is forbidden in the shoot-out. Moreover the goalkeeper has *carte blanche* to employ whatever tricks he can get away with to stop the ball. It is a circus act and outside the spirit of the game – let alone the laws.

Controversy over technology to determine whether goals have been scored or not has been experimented with and the outcome must be viewed with interest. The tinkering with the offside law has done nothing to make it clear to anybody involved on the playing or watching side and has to be made easier to understand.

Many will consider the vast sums of money which are coming into the game at the top level fail to reach the lower echelons which are the life blood of the game's health. There is sufficient finance to benefit all, but it is certainly not being channelled to the right sources. Too many of those receiving it are not justifying the rewards they are getting from football.

It is also unsatisfactory when Liverpool have to struggle to be allowed into the Champions League after winning it, while Tottenham Hotspur must be wondering whether the fair play place they were hoping to be awarded as a route into the UEFA Cup was decided against them by drawing lots!

Liverpool were eventually granted a place at the earliest round, leaving them with an even longer season than anticipated. In days gone by the winners of the European Cup would have been expected to be allowed to defend their title. But that was when it was a simple affair, not a competition which started and finished before and after domestic football and took up weeks and weeks of the season.

Players need rest and must not be burdened by too many games, but the fact remains that there is a conflict between club and national interests with the proliferation of competitive fixtures at international level. Much to be determined but above all the integrity of the game must be preserved as a matter of priority.

CLUB AND OTHER RECORDS DURING 2004–2005

Arsenal	49 unbeaten Premier League matches.
	Jose Antonio Reyes second player to be sent off in an FA Cup final.
	Francesc Fabregas youngest League scorer 17 years, 113 days.
	Thierry Henry overtakes Ian Wright's 128 League goals.
	Most capped player: Patrick Vieira, 79, France.
Boston United	Most capped player: Andy Kirk, 1, Northern Ireland.
	Eight games in succession with goals scored.
Bournemouty	Most League appearances: Steve Fletcher, 425, 1992–.
Chelsea	Best points average record of any Premier League club: 2.50 per game.
	Most Premier League wins: 29.
	Fewest goals conceded: 15.
	29 games in succession without defeat.
	Goalkeeper Petr Cech completes 1025 minutes without conceding a goal.
Cheltenham Town	13 games in succession without a draw.
Crewe Alexandra	Most capped player: Clayton Ince, 38, Trinidad & Tobago.
Everton	James Vaughan at 16 years 271 days the youngest Premier League goalscorer and youngest Everton debutant.
Gretna	130 League goals Division Three record; 98 points, 32 wins, 2 defeats.
Grimsby Town	Most League appearances: John McDermott, 592.
Ipswich Town	31 successive matches with goals scored.
Liverpool	First European Cup/Champions League team to retrieve a three goal deficit in the final, then win on penalties.
Macclesfield Town	Six consecutive League wins.
Manchester United	Ruud Van Nistelrooy overhauls Denis Law's European cup goalscoring record of 28 goals.
	Record Premier League attendance: 67,989 v Portsmouth.
	Ryan Giggs completes his 600th appearance in all matches.
	Sir Alex Ferguson 1000th match in charge.
Newcastle United	Most capped player: Shay Given, 61 (70), Republic of Ireland.
	Alan Shearer, the first player to score 250 Premier League goals.
Rochdale	Most capped player: Leo Bertos, 6 (7) New Zealand.
Rotherham United	21 games in succession without a win; six games in succession without a goal scored.
Rushden & Diamonds	12 games in succession without a win; seven games in succession without scoring.
Shrewsbury Town	11 successive defeats; 18 matches in succession without a win (starting from their previous Football League season).
West Bromwich Albion	15 games in succession without a win.
	Record transfer fee paid for Robbie Earnshaw £3,000,000 from Cardiff City.
Wycombe Wanderers	15 games in succession with goals scored.
Yeovil Town	Seven successive wins; 22 games in succession with goals scored; seven undefeated matches in sequence.
England	Michael Owen with 32 goals, becomes the fifth most prolific scorer for his country.
Northern Ireland	David Healy record goalscorer with 17.
Republic of Ireland	Robbie Keane record goalscorer with 25.

LEAGUE REVIEW AND CLUB SECTION

The season started where it had left off in 2003–04 with the New Invincibles from Highbury continuing on their unbeaten run but ended with the New Pretenders staking the strongest of claims to become just as potent a force in the future.

For Chelsea it was fitting in their Centenary year to win the first League title in half a century, but Arsenal's effort in extending an undefeated run to 49 before being beaten 2-0 by Manchester United may never be overtaken. In the process they also overhauled the previous top flight record of 42 held by Nottingham Forest.

Not that Chelsea missed out on records either with the most wins (29) and fewest goals conceded (15). They also recorded 25 clean sheets. Of the 30 players called upon 22 were full internationals.

And while it has been said that the financial wealth of Roman Abramovich has been the root cause of Chelsea's achievement, the expertise of coach Jose Mourinho has been an even more important factor. Moreover the improvement of English players like John Terry, Frank Lampard and Joe Cole has borne testimony to his ability.

Thus Arsenal had to be content with runners-up position with Manchester United third. There was a surprise in fourth place as Everton confounded their critics who said the loss of Wayne Rooney to United would be their downfall. Bolton Wanderers also caused a few eyebrows to be raised in finishing sixth behind Liverpool who played below expectations domestically, but above themselves in Europe. Middlesbrough pipped Manchester City for a UEFA Cup place and Tottenham Hotspur lost a fair play draw to accompany them.

While it had been a forgone conclusion for many weeks that Chelsea were to lift the crown, the battle for survival at the other end was the most intense throughout the history of the Premier League. It came down to four teams: West Bromwich Albion, Norwich City, Crystal Palace and Southampton.

The struggle went right to the wire and the last day of the season saw fortunes fluctuate for the quartet. The outcome was that Albion broke with the tradition of the bottom team at the turn of the year being relegated and escaped. Norwich after a plucky late season fight back joined them along with Palace and Southampton one of the founder members of the Premiership.

Taking their places in 2005–06 will be Sunderland, Wigan Athletic and West Ham United. Sunderland chipped away throughout the season and consolidated matters in the last six weeks during which they beat both of the other promoted teams.

West Ham were in and out of the play-off bracket, but came good at the death, while Ipswich Town who had appeared likely automatic material disappointed in the end. Derby County and Preston North End had been the other two play-off contenders.

While Rotherham United were favourites to go down from the Championship, Nottingham Forest could not have been much longer odds. And on the last day Crewe Alexandra retrieved themselves while Gillingham were relegated.

Luton Town were off to a flier in League One, faltered and recovered to head off Hull City. Sheffield Wednesday emerged from the play-offs beating Brentford then Hartlepool United in the final; the north-easterners had accounted for Tranmere Rovers.

Torquay United, Wrexham, Peterborough United and Stockport County were the unfortunate ones to leave the division, Wrexham as a result of being deducted ten points for going into administration. Their consolation was to win the LDV Vans Trophy beating Southend United in the final.

Southend did, however, have more to shout about in League Two though having reached first place had to do it the hard way in the play-offs against Northampton Town and Lincoln City in the final. Lincoln lost out again having beaten Macclesfield Town in the semi-final.

But Yeovil Town were champions with Scunthorpe United and Swansea City the other automatically promoted teams. Yeovil only two seasons out of the Conference justified the progress they had striven for in recent years.

On the downward trail went Cambridge United and Kidderminster Harriers both of them recruited to the Football League in comparatively recent times respectively 1970 and 2000. Cambridge went into administration in the final stages though the ten-point reduction had no bearing on the outcome.

Back out of the Conference after just one season are Carlisle United who won through the play-offs beating Aldershot Town and Stevenage Borough who had accounted for Hereford United. But Barnet had been the runaway winners and return to the fold after an absence of four years.

FA Barclaycard Premiership

			Home					Away					Total						
		P	*W*	*D*	*L*	*F*	*A*	*W*	*D*	*L*	*F*	*A*	*W*	*D*	*L*	*F*	*A*	*Gd*	*Pts*
1	Chelsea	38	14	5	0	35	6	15	3	1	37	9	29	8	1	72	15	57	95
2	Arsenal	38	13	5	1	54	19	12	3	4	33	17	25	8	5	87	36	51	83
3	Manchester U	38	12	6	1	31	12	10	5	4	27	14	22	11	5	58	26	32	77
4	Everton	38	12	2	5	24	15	6	5	8	21	31	18	7	13	45	46	–1	61
5	Liverpool	38	12	4	3	31	15	5	3	11	21	26	17	7	14	52	41	11	58
6	Bolton W	38	9	5	5	25	18	7	5	7	24	26	16	10	12	49	44	5	58
7	Middlesbrough	38	9	6	4	29	19	5	7	7	24	27	14	13	11	53	46	7	55
8	Manchester C	38	8	6	5	24	14	5	7	7	23	25	13	13	12	47	39	8	52
9	Tottenham H	38	9	5	5	36	22	5	5	9	11	19	14	10	14	47	41	6	52
10	Aston Villa	38	8	6	5	26	17	4	5	10	19	35	12	11	15	45	52	–7	47
11	Charlton Ath	38	8	4	7	29	29	4	6	9	13	29	12	10	16	42	58	–16	46
12	Birmingham C	38	8	6	5	24	15	3	6	10	16	31	11	12	15	40	46	–6	45
13	Fulham	38	8	4	7	29	26	4	4	11	23	34	12	8	18	52	60	–8	44
14	Newcastle U	38	7	7	5	25	25	3	7	9	22	32	10	14	14	47	57	–10	44
15	Blackburn R	38	5	8	6	21	22	4	7	8	11	21	9	15	14	32	43	–11	42
16	Portsmouth	38	8	4	7	30	26	2	5	12	13	33	10	9	19	43	59	–16	39
17	WBA	38	5	8	6	17	24	1	8	10	19	37	6	16	16	36	61	–25	34
18	Crystal Palace	38	6	5	8	21	19	1	7	11	20	43	7	12	19	41	62	–21	33
19	Norwich C	38	7	5	7	29	32	0	7	12	13	45	7	12	19	42	77	–35	33
20	Southampton	38	5	9	5	30	30	1	5	13	15	36	6	14	18	45	66	–21	32

LEADING GOALSCORERS 2004–05

FA BARCLAYCARD PREMIERSHIP

Players in this competition scoring ten or more League goals are listed. Other leading scorers classified by total number of goals in all competitions.

	League	*Carling Cup*	*FA Cup*	*Other*	*Total*
Thierry Henry *(Arsenal)*	25	0	0	5	30
Andy Johnson *(Crystal Palace)*	21	0	0	0	21
Robert Pires *(Arsenal)*	14	0	2	1	17
Jermain Defoe *(Tottenham H)*	13	5	4	0	22
Frank Lampard *(Chelsea)*	13	2	0	4	19
Jimmy Floyd Hasselbaink *(Middlesbrough)*	13	0	0	3	16
Ayegbeni Yakubu *(Portsmouth)*	12	2	2	0	16
Peter Crouch *(Southampton)*	12	0	4	0	16
Eidur Gudjohnsen *(Chelsea)*	12	1	1	2	16
Andy Cole *(Fulham)*	12	1	0	0	13
Wayne Rooney *(Manchester U)*	11	0	3	3	17
Robbie Keane *(Tottenham H)*	11	3	3	0	17
Robert Earnshaw *(WBA)*	11	0	3	0	14
Robbie Fowler *(Manchester C)*	11	1	0	0	12
Didier Drogba *(Chelsea)*	10	1	0	5	16
Emile Heskey *(Birmingham C)*	10	0	1	0	11
Freddie Ljungberg *(Arsenal)*	10	0	2	2	14
Kevin Phillips *(Southampton)*	10	1	2	0	13
Shaun Wright-Phillips *(Manchester C)*	10	1	0	0	11
In order of total goals:					
Alan Shearer *(Newcastle U)*	7	0	1	11	19
Ruud Van Nistelrooy *(Manchester U)*	6	0	2	8	16

Other matches consist of European games, LDV Vans Trophy, Community Shield and Football League play-offs. Only goals scored in the respective divisions count in the table. Players listed in order of League goals total.

Coca-Cola Football League Championship

		Home					Away					Total						
	P	*W*	*D*	*L*	*F*	*A*	*W*	*D*	*L*	*F*	*A*	*W*	*D*	*L*	*F*	*A*	*Gd*	*Pts*
1 Sunderland	46	16	4	3	45	21	13	3	7	31	20	29	7	10	76	41	35	94
2 Wigan Ath	46	13	5	5	42	15	12	7	4	37	20	25	12	9	79	35	44	87
3 Ipswich T	46	17	3	3	53	26	7	10	6	32	30	24	13	9	85	56	29	85
4 Derby Co	46	10	7	6	38	30	12	3	8	33	30	22	10	14	71	60	11	76
5 Preston NE	46	14	7	2	44	22	7	5	11	23	36	21	12	13	67	58	9	75
6 West Ham U	46	12	5	6	36	24	9	5	9	30	32	21	10	15	66	56	10	73
7 Reading	46	13	7	3	33	15	6	6	11	18	29	19	13	14	51	44	7	70
8 Sheffield U	46	9	7	7	28	23	9	6	8	29	33	18	13	15	57	56	1	67
9 Wolverhampton W	46	9	11	3	40	26	6	10	7	32	33	15	21	10	72	59	13	66
10 Millwall	46	12	5	6	33	22	6	7	10	18	23	18	12	16	51	45	6	66
11 QPR	46	10	7	6	32	26	7	4	12	22	32	17	11	18	54	58	–4	62
12 Stoke C	46	11	2	10	22	18	6	8	9	14	20	17	10	19	36	38	–2	61
13 Burnley	46	10	7	6	26	19	5	8	10	12	20	15	15	16	38	39	–1	60
14 Leeds U	46	7	10	6	28	26	7	8	8	21	26	14	18	14	49	52	–3	60
15 Leicester C	46	8	8	7	24	20	4	13	6	25	26	12	21	13	49	46	3	57
16 Cardiff C	46	10	4	9	24	19	3	11	9	24	32	13	15	18	48	51	–3	54
17 Plymouth Arg	46	9	8	6	31	23	5	3	15	21	41	14	11	21	52	64	–12	53
18 Watford	46	5	10	8	25	25	7	6	10	27	34	12	16	18	52	59	–7	52
19 Coventry C	46	8	7	8	32	28	5	6	12	29	45	13	13	20	61	73	–12	52
20 Brighton & HA	46	7	7	9	24	29	6	5	12	16	36	13	12	21	40	65	–25	51
21 Crewe Alex	46	6	8	9	37	38	6	6	11	29	48	12	14	20	66	86	–20	50
22 Gillingham	46	10	6	7	22	23	2	8	13	23	43	12	14	20	45	66	–21	50
23 Nottingham F	46	7	10	6	26	28	2	7	14	16	38	9	17	20	42	66	–24	44
24 Rotherham U	46	2	7	14	17	34	3	7	13	18	35	5	14	27	35	69	–34	29

COCA-COLA FOOTBALL LEAGUE CHAMPIONSHIP

	League	*Carling Cup*	*FA Cup*	*Other*	*Total*
Nathan Ellington *(Wigan Ath)*	24	0	0	0	24
Jason Roberts *(Wigan Ath)*	21	0	0	0	21
Teddy Sheringham *(West Ham U)*	20	0	1	0	21
Darren Bent *(Ipswich T)*	20	0	0	0	20
Kenny Miller *(Wolverhampton W)*	19	1	0	0	20
Shefki Kuqi *(Ipswich T)*	19	0	0	1	20
Dave Kitson *(Reading)*	19	0	0	0	19
Paul Furlong *(QPR)*	18	0	0	0	18
Marlon Harewood *(West Ham U)*	17	2	2	1	22
Dean Ashton *(Crewe Alex*)*	17	2	0	0	19
Heidar Helguson *(Watford)*	16	3	1	0	20
Richard Cresswell *(Preston NE)*	16	4	0	1	21
Grzegorz Rasiak *(Derby Co)*	16	0	1	0	17
Marcus Stewart *(Sunderland)*	16	0	1	0	17
Andy Gray *(Sheffield U)*	15	2	1	0	18
Carl Cort *(Wolverhampton W)*	15	0	1	0	16
Stephen Elliott *(Sunderland)*	15	1	0	0	16
Tommy Miller *(Ipswich T)*	13	1	1	0	15
David Connolly *(Leicester C)*	13	0	0	0	13
Gifton Noel-Williams *(Stoke C)*	13	0	0	0	13

**now Norwich C.*

Coca-Cola Football League Division 1

			Home					Away					Total						
		P	*W*	*D*	*L*	*F*	*A*	*W*	*D*	*L*	*F*	*A*	*W*	*D*	*L*	*F*	*A*	*Gd*	*Pts*
1	Luton T	46	17	4	2	46	16	12	7	4	41	32	29	11	6	87	48	39	98
2	Hull C	46	16	5	2	42	17	10	3	10	38	36	26	8	12	80	53	27	86
3	Tranmere R	46	14	5	4	43	23	8	8	7	30	32	22	13	11	73	55	18	79
4	Brentford	46	15	4	4	34	22	7	5	11	23	38	22	9	15	57	60	–3	75
5	Sheffield W	46	10	6	7	34	28	9	9	5	43	31	19	15	12	77	59	18	72
6	Hartlepool U	46	15	3	5	51	30	6	5	12	25	36	21	8	17	76	66	10	71
7	Bristol C	46	9	8	6	42	25	9	8	6	32	32	18	16	12	74	57	17	70
8	Bournemouth	46	9	7	7	40	30	11	3	9	37	34	20	10	16	77	64	13	70
9	Huddersfield T	46	12	6	5	42	28	8	4	11	32	37	20	10	16	74	65	9	70
10	Doncaster R	46	10	11	2	35	20	6	7	10	30	40	16	18	12	65	60	5	66
11	Bradford C	46	9	6	8	40	35	8	8	7	24	27	17	14	15	64	62	2	65
12	Swindon T	46	12	5	6	40	30	5	7	11	26	38	17	12	17	66	68	–2	63
13	Barnsley	46	7	11	5	38	31	7	8	8	31	33	14	19	13	69	64	5	61
14	Walsall	46	11	7	5	40	28	5	5	13	25	41	16	12	18	65	69	–4	60
15	Colchester U	46	8	6	9	27	23	6	11	6	33	27	14	17	15	60	50	10	59
16	Blackpool	46	8	7	8	28	30	7	5	11	26	29	15	12	19	54	59	–5	57
17	Chesterfield	46	9	8	6	32	28	5	7	11	23	34	14	15	17	55	62	–7	57
18	Port Vale	46	13	2	8	33	23	4	3	16	16	36	17	5	24	49	59	–10	56
19	Oldham Ath	46	10	5	8	42	34	4	5	14	18	39	14	10	22	60	73	–13	52
20	Milton Keynes Dons	46	8	10	5	33	28	4	5	14	21	40	12	15	19	54	68	–14	51
21	Torquay U	46	8	5	10	27	36	4	10	9	28	43	12	15	19	55	79	–24	51
22	Wrexham	46	6	8	9	26	37	7	6	10	36	43	13	14	19	62	80	–18	43
23	Peterborough U	46	5	6	12	27	35	4	6	13	22	38	9	12	25	49	73	–24	39
24	Stockport Co	46	3	4	16	26	46	3	4	16	23	52	6	8	32	49	98	–49	26

Wrexham deducted 10 points after entering administration.

COCA-COLA FOOTBALL LEAGUE DIVISION 1

	League	*Carling Cup*	*FA Cup*	*Other*	*Total*
Stuart Elliott *(Hull C)*	27	0	1	1	29
Dean Windass *(Bradford C)*	27	1	0	0	28
Pawel Abbott *(Huddersfield T)*	26	0	1	0	27
Leroy Lita *(Bristol C)*	24	2	1	2	29
Sam Parkin *(Swindon T)*	23	0	0	1	24
Adam Boyd *(Hartlepool U)*	22	1	3	3	29
Steve Brooker *(Bristol C)*	21	0	0	0	21
(including 5 League goals for Port Vale)					
James Hayter *(Bournemouth)*	19	3	0	0	22
Luke Beckett *(Oldham Ath (on loan))*	19	0	0	0	19
(including 6 League goals for Huddersfield T (on loan) and 7 for Stockport Co)					
Steve Howard *(Luton T)*	18	0	4	0	22
Steve MacLean *(Sheffield W)*	18	0	0	2	20
Juan Ugarte *(Wrexham)*	17	0	0	6	23
Michael Chopra *(Barnsley (on loan))*	17	0	0	0	17
Izale McLeod *(Milton Keynes D)*	16	2	0	0	18

Coca-Cola Football League Division 2

			Home					*Away*					*Total*						
		P	*W*	*D*	*L*	*F*	*A*	*W*	*D*	*L*	*F*	*A*	*W*	*D*	*L*	*F*	*A*	*Gd*	*Pts*
1	Yeovil T	46	16	4	3	57	28	9	4	10	33	37	25	8	13	90	65	25	83
2	Scunthorpe U	46	16	5	2	43	16	6	9	8	26	26	22	14	10	69	42	27	80
3	Swansea C	46	15	5	3	36	16	9	3	11	26	27	24	8	14	62	43	19	80
4	Southend U	46	13	5	5	31	14	9	7	7	34	32	22	12	12	65	46	19	78
5	Macclesfield T	46	15	3	5	39	24	7	6	10	21	25	22	9	15	60	49	11	75
6	Lincoln C	46	11	8	4	37	22	9	4	10	27	25	20	12	14	64	47	17	72
7	Northampton T	46	11	9	3	35	20	9	3	11	27	31	20	12	14	62	51	11	72
8	Darlington	46	13	4	6	33	21	7	8	8	24	28	20	12	14	57	49	8	72
9	Rochdale	46	11	8	4	34	21	5	10	8	20	27	16	18	12	54	48	6	66
10	Wycombe W	46	8	7	8	28	26	9	7	7	30	26	17	14	15	58	52	6	65
11	Leyton Orient	46	10	8	5	40	30	6	7	10	25	37	16	15	15	65	67	−2	63
12	Bristol R	46	10	12	1	39	22	3	9	11	21	35	13	21	12	60	57	3	60
13	Mansfield T	46	9	8	6	29	24	6	7	10	27	32	15	15	16	56	56	0	60
14	Cheltenham T	46	10	5	8	27	23	6	7	10	24	31	16	12	18	51	54	−3	60
15	Oxford U	46	11	4	8	29	24	5	7	11	21	39	16	11	19	50	63	−13	59
16	Boston U	46	11	8	4	39	24	3	8	12	23	34	14	16	16	62	58	4	58
17	Bury	46	8	9	6	26	18	6	7	10	28	36	14	16	16	54	54	0	58
18	Grimsby T	46	8	10	5	28	19	6	6	11	23	33	14	16	16	51	52	−1	58
19	Notts Co	46	6	7	10	21	27	7	6	10	25	35	13	13	20	46	62	−16	52
20	Chester C	46	7	8	8	25	33	5	8	10	18	36	12	16	18	43	69	−26	52
21	Shrewsbury T	46	9	7	7	34	18	2	9	12	14	35	11	16	19	48	53	−5	49
22	Rushden & D	46	8	6	9	29	29	2	8	13	13	34	10	14	22	42	63	−21	44
23	Kidderminster H	46	6	6	11	21	39	4	2	17	18	46	10	8	28	39	85	−46	38
24	Cambridge U*	46	7	6	10	22	27	1	10	12	17	35	8	16	22	39	62	−23	30

**Cambridge U deducted 10 points after entering administration.*

COCA-COLA FOOTBALL LEAGUE DIVISION 2

	League	*Carling Cup*	*FA Cup*	*Other*	*Total*
Phil Jevons *(Yeovil T)*	27	0	2	0	29
Andy Kirk *(Northampton T)*	25	0	2	0	27
(including 18 League and 2 FA Cup goals for Boston U)					
Jon Parkin *(Macclesfield T)*	22	1	1	2	26
Lee Trundle *(Swansea C)*	22	0	1	0	23
Nathan Tyson *(Wycombe W)*	22	0	0	0	22
Simon Yeo *(Lincoln C)*	21	2	0	0	23
Freddy Eastwood *(Southend U)*	19	0	0	5	24
Junior Agogo *(Bristol R)*	19	0	0	2	21
Paul Hayes *(Scunthorpe U)*	18	0	2	0	20
Grant Holt *(Rochdale)*	17	1	5	1	24
Lee Steele *(Leyton Orient)*	16	1	0	0	17
Tommy Mooney *(Oxford U)*	15	0	0	0	15
Glynn Hurst *(Notts Co)*	14	0	0	1	15
Clive Wijnhard *(Darlington)*	14	0	0	0	14
Scott McGleish *(Northampton T)*	13	1	2	1	17

FA BARCLAYCARD PREMIERSHIP

HOME TEAM	Arsenal	Aston Villa	Birmingham C	Blackburn R	Bolton W	Charlton Ath	Chelsea	Crystal Palace	Everton	Fulham
Arsenal	—	3-1	3-0	3-0	2-2	4-0	2-2	5-1	7-0	2-0
Aston Villa	1-3	—	1-2	1-0	1-1	0-0	0-0	1-1	1-3	2-0
Birmingham C	2-1	2-0	—	2-1	1-2	1-1	0-1	0-1	0-1	1-2
Blackburn R	0-1	2-2	3-3	—	0-1	1-0	0-1	1-0	0-0	1-3
Bolton W	1-0	1-2	1-1	0-1	—	4-1	0-2	1-0	3-2	3-1
Charlton Ath	1-3	3-0	3-1	1-0	1-2	—	0-4	2-2	2-0	2-1
Chelsea	0-0	1-0	1-1	4-0	2-2	1-0	—	4-1	1-0	3-1
Crystal Palace	1-1	2-0	2-0	0-0	0-1	0-1	0-2	—	1-3	2-0
Everton	1-4	1-1	1-1	0-1	3-2	0-1	0-1	4-0	—	1-0
Fulham	0-3	1-1	2-3	0-2	2-0	0-0	1-4	3-1	2-0	—
Liverpool	2-1	2-1	0-1	0-0	1-0	2-0	0-1	3-2	2-1	3-1
Manchester C	0-1	2-0	3-0	1-1	0-1	4-0	1-0	3-1	0-1	1-1
Manchester U	2-0	3-1	2-0	0-0	2-0	2-0	1-3	5-2	0-0	1-0
Middlesbrough	0-1	3-0	2-1	1-0	1-1	2-2	0-1	2-1	1-1	1-1
Newcastle U	0-1	0-3	2-1	3-0	2-1	1-1	1-1	0-0	1-1	1-4
Norwich C	1-4	0-0	1-0	1-1	3-2	1-0	1-3	1-1	2-3	0-1
Portsmouth	0-1	1-2	1-1	0-1	1-1	4-2	0-2	3-1	0-1	4-3
Southampton	1-1	2-3	0-0	3-2	1-2	0-0	1-3	2-2	2-2	3-3
Tottenham H	4-5	5-1	1-0	0-0	1-2	2-3	0-2	1-1	5-2	2-0
WBA	0-2	1-1	2-0	1-1	2-1	0-1	1-4	2-2	1-0	1-1

2004–2005 RESULTS

Liverpool	Manchester C	Manchester U	Middlesbrough	Newcastle U	Norwich C	Portsmouth	Southampton	Tottenham H	WBA
3-1	1-1	2-4	5-3	1-0	4-1	3-0	2-2	1-0	1-1
1-1	1-2	0-1	2-0	4-2	3-0	3-0	2-0	1-0	1-1
2-0	1-0	0-0	2-0	2-2	1-1	0-0	2-1	1-1	4-0
2-2	0-0	1-1	0-4	2-2	3-0	1-0	3-0	0-1	1-1
1-0	0-1	2-2	0-0	2-1	1-0	0-1	1-1	3-1	1-1
1-2	2-2	0-4	1-2	1-1	4-0	2-1	0-0	2-0	1-4
1-0	0-0	1-0	2-0	4-0	4-0	3-0	2-1	0-0	1-0
1-0	1-2	0-0	0-1	0-2	3-3	0-1	2-2	3-0	3-0
1-0	2-1	1-0	1-0	2-0	1-0	2-1	1-0	0-1	2-1
2-4	1-1	1-1	0-2	1-3	6-0	3-1	1-0	2-0	1-0
—	2-1	0-1	1-1	3-1	3-0	1-1	1-0	2-2	3-0
1-0	—	0-2	1-1	1-1	1-1	2-0	2-1	0-1	1-1
2-1	0-0	—	1-1	2-1	2-1	2-1	3-0	0-0	1-1
2-0	3-2	0-2	—	2-2	2-0	1-1	1-3	1-0	4-0
1-0	4-3	1-3	0-0	—	2-2	1-1	2-1	0-1	3-1
1-2	2-3	2-0	4-4	2-1	—	2-2	2-1	0-2	3-2
1-2	1-3	2-0	2-1	1-1	1-1	—	4-1	1-0	3-2
2-0	0-0	1-2	2-2	1-2	4-3	2-1	—	1-0	2-2
1-1	2-1	0-1	2-0	1-0	0-0	3-1	5-1	—	1-1
0-5	2-0	0-3	1-2	0-0	0-0	2-0	0-0	1-1	—

COCA-COLA FOOTBALL LEAGUE

HOME TEAM	Brighton & HA	Burnley	Cardiff C	Coventry C	Crewe Alex	Derby Co	Gillingham	Ipswich T	Leeds U	Leicester C
Brighton & HA	—	0-1	1-1	1-1	1-3	2-3	2-1	1-1	1-0	1-1
Burnley	1-1	—	1-0	2-2	3-0	0-2	1-2	0-2	0-1	0-0
Cardiff C	2-0	2-0	—	2-1	1-1	0-2	3-1	0-1	0-0	0-0
Coventry C	2-1	0-2	1-1	—	0-1	6-2	2-2	1-2	1-2	1-1
Crewe Alex	3-1	1-1	2-2	2-1	—	1-2	4-1	2-2	2-2	2-2
Derby Co	3-0	1-1	0-1	2-2	2-4	—	2-0	3-2	2-0	1-2
Gillingham	0-1	1-0	1-1	3-1	1-1	0-2	—	0-0	2-1	0-2
Ipswich T	1-0	1-1	3-1	3-2	5-1	3-2	2-1	—	1-0	2-1
Leeds U	1-1	1-2	1-1	3-0	0-2	1-0	1-1	1-1	—	0-2
Leicester C	0-1	0-0	1-1	3-0	1-1	1-0	2-0	2-2	2-0	—
Millwall	2-0	0-0	2-2	1-1	4-3	3-1	2-1	3-1	1-1	2-0
Nottingham F	0-1	1-0	0-0	1-4	2-2	2-2	2-2	1-1	0-0	1-1
Plymouth Arg	5-1	1-0	1-1	1-1	3-0	0-2	2-1	1-2	0-1	0-0
Preston NE	3-0	1-0	3-0	3-2	1-0	3-0	1-1	1-1	2-4	1-1
QPR	0-0	3-0	1-0	4-1	1-2	0-2	1-1	2-4	1-1	3-2
Reading	3-2	0-0	2-1	1-2	4-0	0-1	3-1	1-1	1-1	0-0
Rotherham U	0-1	0-0	2-2	1-2	2-3	1-3	1-3	0-2	1-0	0-2
Sheffield U	1-2	2-1	2-1	1-1	4-0	0-1	0-0	0-2	2-0	2-0
Stoke C	2-0	0-1	1-3	1-0	1-0	1-0	2-0	3-2	0-1	3-2
Sunderland	2-0	2-1	2-1	1-0	3-1	0-0	1-1	2-0	2-3	2-1
Watford	1-1	0-1	0-0	2-3	3-1	2-2	2-0	2-2	1-2	2-2
West Ham U	0-1	1-0	1-0	3-0	1-1	1-2	3-1	1-1	1-1	2-2
Wigan Ath	3-0	0-0	2-1	4-1	4-1	1-2	2-0	1-0	3-0	0-0
Wolverhampton W	1-1	2-0	2-3	0-1	1-1	2-0	2-2	2-0	0-0	1-1

CHAMPIONSHIP 2004–2005 RESULTS

Millwall	Nottingham F	Plymouth Arg	Preston NE	QPR	Reading	Rotherham U	Sheffield U	Stoke C	Sunderland	Watford	West Ham U	Wigan Ath	Wolverhampton W
1-0	0-0	0-2	1-0	2-3	0-1	1-0	1-1	0-1	2-1	2-1	2-2	2-4	0-1
1-0	1-0	2-0	2-0	2-0	0-0	2-1	1-1	2-2	0-2	3-1	0-1	1-0	1-1
0-1	3-0	0-1	0-1	1-0	2-0	2-0	1-0	0-1	0-2	0-3	4-1	0-2	1-1
0-1	2-0	2-1	1-1	1-2	3-2	0-0	1-2	0-0	2-0	1-0	2-1	1-2	2-2
2-1	1-1	3-0	1-2	0-2	1-1	1-1	2-3	0-2	0-1	3-0	2-3	1-3	1-4
0-3	3-0	1-0	3-1	0-0	2-1	3-2	0-1	3-1	0-2	2-2	1-1	1-1	3-3
0-0	2-1	1-0	2-1	0-1	0-0	3-1	1-3	2-1	0-4	0-0	0-1	2-1	1-0
2-0	6-0	3-2	3-0	0-2	1-1	4-3	5-1	1-0	2-2	1-2	0-2	2-1	2-1
1-1	1-1	2-1	1-0	6-1	3-1	0-0	0-4	0-0	0-1	2-2	2-1	0-2	1-1
3-1	0-1	2-1	1-1	1-0	0-2	0-1	3-2	1-1	0-1	0-1	0-0	0-2	1-1
—	1-0	3-0	2-1	0-0	1-0	1-2	1-2	0-1	2-0	0-2	1-0	0-2	1-2
1-2	—	0-3	2-0	2-1	1-0	2-2	1-1	1-0	1-2	1-2	2-1	1-1	1-0
0-0	3-2	—	0-2	2-1	2-2	1-1	3-0	0-0	2-1	1-0	1-1	1-2	1-2
1-1	3-2	1-1	—	2-1	3-0	2-0	0-1	3-0	3-2	2-1	2-1	1-1	2-2
1-1	2-1	3-2	1-2	—	0-0	1-1	0-1	1-0	1-3	3-1	1-0	1-0	1-1
2-1	1-0	0-0	3-1	1-0	—	1-0	0-0	1-0	1-0	3-0	3-1	1-1	1-2
1-1	0-0	0-1	1-2	0-1	1-0	—	2-2	1-1	0-1	0-1	2-2	0-2	1-2
0-1	1-1	2-1	1-1	3-2	0-1	1-0	—	0-0	1-0	1-1	1-2	0-2	3-3
1-0	0-0	2-0	0-0	0-1	0-1	1-2	2-0	—	0-1	0-1	0-1	0-1	2-1
1-0	2-0	5-1	3-1	2-2	1-2	4-1	1-0	1-0	—	4-2	0-2	1-1	3-1
1-0	0-2	3-1	0-2	3-0	0-1	0-0	0-0	0-1	1-1	—	1-2	0-0	1-1
1-1	3-2	5-0	1-2	2-1	1-0	1-0	0-2	2-0	1-2	3-2	—	1-3	1-0
2-0	1-1	0-2	5-0	0-0	3-1	2-0	4-0	0-1	0-1	2-2	1-2	—	2-0
1-2	2-1	1-1	2-2	2-1	4-1	2-0	4-2	1-1	1-1	0-0	4-2	3-3	—

COCA-COLA FOOTBALL LEAGUE

HOME TEAM	Barnsley	Blackpool	Bournemouth	Bradford C	Brentford	Bristol C	Chesterfield	Colchester U	Doncaster R	Hartlepool U
Barnsley	—	1-0	0-1	2-2	0-0	2-1	1-0	1-1	1-3	0-0
Blackpool	0-2	—	3-3	2-1	2-1	1-1	1-0	1-1	1-1	2-2
Bournemouth	1-3	2-3	—	2-0	3-2	2-2	0-0	1-3	5-0	2-2
Bradford C	1-0	2-1	4-2	—	4-1	4-1	2-3	2-2	2-0	1-2
Brentford	1-1	0-3	2-1	1-2	—	1-0	2-2	1-0	4-3	2-1
Bristol C	0-0	1-1	0-2	0-0	4-1	—	2-3	0-0	2-2	0-0
Chesterfield	2-2	1-0	2-3	0-0	3-1	2-2	—	2-1	0-0	0-1
Colchester U	0-2	0-1	3-1	0-0	0-1	0-2	1-0	—	4-1	1-1
Doncaster R	4-0	2-0	1-1	1-1	0-0	1-1	0-1	1-1	—	2-0
Hartlepool U	1-1	1-1	3-2	2-1	3-1	2-1	3-2	2-1	2-1	—
Huddersfield T	0-2	1-0	3-2	0-1	1-1	2-2	0-0	2-2	3-1	0-2
Hull C	2-1	2-1	1-0	0-1	2-0	1-1	1-0	2-0	2-1	1-0
Luton T	1-3	1-0	1-0	4-0	4-2	5-0	1-0	2-2	1-1	3-0
Milton Keynes Dons	1-1	3-1	1-3	1-2	0-0	1-2	1-1	2-0	0-1	4-2
Oldham Ath	3-2	1-2	1-2	2-1	0-2	0-0	4-1	1-1	1-2	3-2
Peterborough U	1-3	0-0	0-1	2-2	3-0	0-1	1-2	0-3	0-2	3-0
Port Vale	5-0	0-3	2-1	0-1	0-1	3-0	1-0	0-0	2-0	0-1
Sheffield W	1-0	3-2	0-1	1-2	1-2	2-3	2-2	0-3	2-0	2-0
Stockport Co	2-2	0-1	2-2	0-1	1-2	1-2	1-2	1-2	2-4	1-0
Swindon T	2-1	2-2	0-3	1-0	3-0	0-0	1-1	0-3	1-1	3-0
Torquay U	0-1	2-0	1-2	0-0	2-2	0-4	2-2	1-3	2-1	1-2
Tranmere R	1-1	0-0	2-0	4-5	1-0	0-1	1-0	1-1	2-4	2-1
Walsall	2-2	3-2	1-2	1-1	0-1	1-2	3-0	2-1	1-1	2-1
Wrexham	2-1	1-2	1-2	1-0	1-2	1-3	3-1	2-2	0-0	1-5

DIVISION 1 2004–2005 RESULTS

Huddersfield T	Hull C	Luton T	Milton Keynes Dons	Oldham Ath	Peterborough U	Port Vale	Sheffield W	Stockport Co	Swindon T	Torquay U	Tranmere R	Walsall	Wrexham
4-2	1-2	3-4	1-1	2-2	4-0	1-2	0-0	3-3	2-2	4-1	0-0	3-2	2-2
1-1	0-2	1-3	1-0	2-0	0-1	0-2	1-2	0-4	1-1	4-0	0-1	2-0	2-1
2-2	0-4	0-1	0-1	4-0	0-1	4-0	1-1	2-1	2-1	3-0	1-1	2-2	1-0
2-0	0-2	0-1	1-4	1-3	2-2	0-2	3-1	3-1	1-2	2-2	1-1	1-1	1-1
0-1	2-1	2-0	1-0	2-0	0-0	1-0	3-3	3-0	2-1	1-3	1-0	1-0	1-0
3-3	3-1	1-2	4-1	5-1	2-0	2-0	1-4	5-0	1-2	1-1	4-0	0-1	1-0
2-1	1-1	0-1	2-2	1-0	1-3	1-0	1-3	4-0	1-0	1-1	2-2	1-0	2-4
0-0	1-2	0-0	0-1	0-0	2-1	2-1	1-1	3-2	0-1	2-1	1-2	5-0	1-2
2-1	1-0	3-3	3-0	1-1	2-1	2-0	0-4	3-1	1-1	2-2	0-0	3-1	0-0
0-1	2-0	2-3	5-0	2-1	2-2	1-0	3-0	3-1	3-0	4-1	0-1	1-3	4-6
—	4-0	1-1	3-1	2-1	2-1	2-1	1-0	5-3	4-0	1-1	1-3	3-1	1-2
2-1	—	3-0	3-2	2-0	2-2	2-2	1-2	0-0	0-0	2-0	6-1	3-1	2-1
1-2	1-0	—	1-0	2-1	2-1	1-0	1-1	3-0	3-1	1-0	1-1	1-0	5-1
2-1	1-1	1-4	—	1-1	1-1	1-1	2-2	2-1	1-1	1-0	2-1	1-1	3-0
2-1	1-0	2-2	3-0	—	2-1	3-0	1-1	1-2	1-2	1-2	2-2	5-3	2-3
1-2	2-3	2-2	0-3	1-2	—	4-0	1-1	2-1	0-2	1-1	1-0	0-2	2-2
0-3	3-2	3-1	3-2	3-1	1-0	—	0-2	0-0	1-0	1-2	3-1	2-0	0-2
1-0	2-4	0-0	1-1	1-1	2-1	1-0	—	0-0	2-0	2-2	1-2	3-2	4-0
2-3	1-3	1-3	3-1	1-2	1-0	1-2	0-3	—	3-3	0-2	1-1	0-1	1-4
1-2	4-2	2-3	2-1	1-0	0-1	1-0	3-2	3-0	—	3-3	2-1	1-2	4-2
2-1	0-3	1-4	1-0	2-0	2-1	1-0	2-4	1-2	2-2	—	1-2	0-0	1-0
3-0	1-3	1-1	2-0	2-0	5-0	1-0	4-2	1-0	2-1	4-1	—	2-1	1-1
4-3	3-0	2-0	0-0	0-1	2-1	3-2	1-1	3-0	3-2	1-1	0-2	—	2-2
0-1	2-2	1-2	0-0	1-0	1-1	1-1	0-3	2-1	2-1	1-1	1-5	1-1	—

COCA-COLA FOOTBALL LEAGUE

HOME TEAM	Boston U	Bristol R	Bury	Cambridge U	Cheltenham T	Chester C	Darlington	Grimsby T	Kidderminster H	Leyton Orient
Boston U	—	2-2	2-2	2-1	2-1	3-1	3-1	1-1	3-0	2-2
Bristol R	1-1	—	2-2	1-1	1-1	4-1	3-3	3-0	2-0	1-1
Bury	1-1	1-1	—	2-1	3-1	1-1	0-1	3-1	4-0	0-0
Cambridge U	0-1	1-0	1-1	—	1-0	0-0	3-1	0-2	1-3	1-1
Cheltenham T	1-0	1-1	1-0	2-1	—	0-0	0-2	2-3	2-0	1-2
Chester C	2-1	2-2	2-1	0-0	0-3	—	0-3	2-1	3-0	1-1
Darlington	1-0	0-1	1-2	1-1	3-1	1-0	—	1-0	0-2	3-0
Grimsby T	1-1	0-0	5-1	3-0	1-1	1-0	0-1	—	2-1	2-0
Kidderminster H	0-4	1-1	2-2	1-1	1-0	0-1	1-0	1-4	—	1-2
Leyton Orient	0-0	4-2	1-1	1-1	2-3	2-0	1-0	1-2	2-1	—
Lincoln C	2-2	1-1	1-0	2-1	0-0	1-1	0-0	0-0	3-0	3-4
Macclesfield T	1-1	2-1	2-1	1-1	0-2	1-2	1-0	3-1	2-0	3-1
Mansfield T	3-2	0-2	0-0	0-0	1-2	0-0	1-1	2-0	2-1	0-1
Northampton T	2-1	2-1	2-0	2-2	1-1	1-1	1-1	0-1	3-0	2-2
Notts Co	2-1	1-2	0-1	2-1	0-0	1-1	1-1	2-2	1-3	1-2
Oxford U	2-0	3-2	3-1	2-1	1-0	0-1	1-2	1-2	0-2	2-2
Rochdale	2-0	0-0	0-3	2-1	1-2	2-2	1-1	2-0	1-1	2-0
Rushden & D	4-2	0-0	3-0	0-1	1-0	0-1	1-2	1-0	0-0	2-0
Scunthorpe U	1-1	4-0	3-2	4-0	4-1	1-2	0-1	2-0	2-1	1-0
Shrewsbury T	0-0	2-0	2-2	0-0	2-0	5-0	4-0	1-1	4-2	4-1
Southend U	2-1	2-0	1-0	0-0	0-2	1-0	2-0	1-1	1-0	0-1
Swansea C	3-1	1-0	1-3	3-0	1-1	3-0	2-1	0-0	3-0	1-0
Wycombe W	1-2	1-0	1-2	2-1	1-1	4-2	1-1	2-0	3-0	3-2
Yeovil T	2-0	4-2	0-1	2-1	4-1	4-1	1-1	2-1	2-1	1-0

DIVISION 2 2004–2005 RESULTS

Lincoln C	Macclesfield T	Mansfield T	Northampton T	Notts Co	Oxford U	Rochdale	Rushden & D	Scunthorpe U	Shrewsbury T	Southend U	Swansea C	Wycombe W	Yeovil T
0-2	1-1	0-0	0-1	4-0	1-0	1-1	1-0	2-1	2-2	2-0	2-3	2-0	1-2
0-0	0-0	4-4	3-1	2-1	2-0	0-0	3-0	0-3	0-0	2-1	2-0	1-0	2-2
0-1	2-1	0-2	2-0	1-0	0-0	0-0	1-1	0-1	0-0	0-1	0-1	2-2	3-1
0-1	0-1	2-2	0-1	0-0	2-1	0-0	3-1	1-2	1-0	0-2	0-1	2-1	3-5
1-0	3-0	2-0	1-0	0-2	0-1	2-0	4-1	0-2	1-1	0-3	1-2	1-1	1-1
0-1	1-0	0-3	0-2	3-2	1-3	0-0	3-1	1-1	1-1	2-2	1-1	0-2	0-2
0-3	3-1	2-1	1-1	1-2	1-1	0-3	2-0	0-0	3-0	4-0	2-1	1-0	2-1
2-4	0-0	2-0	1-2	3-2	1-1	0-1	0-0	0-0	0-1	1-1	1-1	0-0	2-1
2-1	1-0	1-3	0-2	0-0	1-3	2-1	0-0	3-2	0-1	1-3	1-5	0-2	1-1
1-1	1-3	2-1	3-2	2-0	0-0	2-1	2-2	1-1	4-1	2-2	3-1	1-2	2-3
—	2-0	2-0	3-2	1-2	3-0	1-1	1-3	2-0	2-0	1-1	1-0	2-3	3-1
2-1	—	3-1	1-3	1-2	1-0	3-0	1-0	2-2	2-1	1-2	1-0	2-1	3-1
2-2	0-1	—	4-1	3-1	1-3	1-0	0-0	1-0	1-1	1-1	1-0	1-4	4-1
1-0	1-0	2-1	—	0-0	1-0	5-1	1-0	1-2	2-0	1-2	2-2	1-1	1-1
1-0	0-5	0-1	0-0	—	0-1	0-0	1-1	2-0	3-0	1-2	1-0	0-1	1-2
0-1	1-1	1-0	1-2	2-1	—	0-1	0-0	1-1	2-0	2-1	0-1	2-1	2-1
3-1	3-0	1-1	1-0	0-3	5-1	—	2-0	0-0	1-1	2-0	0-2	1-1	2-1
1-4	0-2	0-0	3-2	5-1	3-3	0-0	—	1-3	0-0	1-4	0-2	1-2	2-0
3-2	0-0	1-1	2-0	0-0	1-1	3-1	1-0	—	3-1	3-2	1-0	2-0	1-0
0-1	0-1	0-2	2-0	1-1	3-0	0-2	0-1	0-0	—	1-1	2-0	0-1	1-2
1-1	2-1	0-1	2-1	0-0	4-0	3-0	3-0	0-0	1-0	—	4-2	1-2	0-1
1-0	2-0	1-0	0-2	4-0	1-0	2-2	1-0	2-1	1-0	1-1	—	2-2	0-2
1-0	1-1	1-1	0-1	1-2	1-1	0-3	1-1	2-1	1-1	0-1	0-1	—	0-1
3-0	1-2	5-2	1-1	1-3	6-1	2-2	3-1	4-3	4-2	3-1	1-0	1-1	—

ARSENAL FA PREMIERSHIP

Player	Ht	Wt	Birthplace	D.O.B.	Source
Aliadiere Jeremie (F)	6 0	11 00	Rambouillet	30 3 83	Scholar
Almunia Manuel (G)	6 3	13 00	Pamplona	19 5 77	Celta Vigo
Bentley David (F)	5 10	11 03	Peterborough	27 8 84	Scholar
Bergkamp Dennis (F)	6 0	12 10	Amsterdam	18 5 69	Internazionale
Campbell Sol (D)	6 2	15 07	Newham	18 9 74	Tottenham H
Clichy Gael (D)	5 9	10 04	Toulouse	26 7 85	Cannes
Cole Ashley (D)	5 8	10 05	Stepney	20 12 80	Trainee
Cregg Patrick (M)	5 9	10 04	Dublin	21 2 86	Trainee
Cygan Pascal (D)	6 4	13 12	Lens	19 4 74	Lille
Djourou Johan (D)	6 3	13 01	Ivory Coast	18 1 87	Scholar
Eboue Emmanuel (D)	5 10	10 03	Abidjan	4 6 83	Beveren
Fabregas Francesc (M)	5 11	11 01	Vilessoc de Mar	4 5 87	Barcelona
Flamini Mathieu (M)	5 11	11 10	Marseille	7 3 84	Marseille
Henry Thierry (F)	6 2	13 05	Paris	17 8 77	Juventus
Hoyte Justin (D)	5 11	11 00	Waltham Forest	20 11 84	Scholar
Jordan Michael (G)	6 2	13 02	Enfield	7 4 86	Scholar
Larsson Sebastian (M)	5 10	11 00	Eskiltuna	6 6 85	Trainee
Lauren Etame-Mayer (D)	5 11	11 07	Londi Kribi	19 1 77	Mallorca
Lehmann Jens (G)	6 4	13 05	Essen	10 11 69	Borussia Dortmund
Ljungberg Frederik (M)	5 9	11 00	Vittsjo	16 4 77	Halmstad
Lupoli Arturo (F)	5 9	10 07	Brescia	24 6 87	Parma
Owusu-Abeyie Quincy (F)	5 11	11 10	Amsterdam	15 4 86	Scholar
Pires Robert (M)	6 1	12 09	Reims	29 10 73	Marseille
Reyes Jose Antonio (F)	5 9	12 01	Utrera	1 9 83	Sevilla
Senderos Philippe (D)	6 1	13 10	Geneva	14 2 85	Servette
Silva Gilberto (M)	6 3	12 04	Lagoa da Prata	7 10 76	Atletico Mineiro
Stack Graham (G)	6 2	13 02	Hampstead	26 9 81	Scholar
Svard Sebastian (M)	6 0	12 06	Hvidovre	15 1 83	FC Copenhagen
Taylor Stuart (G)	6 5	14 07	Romford	28 11 80	Trainee
Toure Kolo (D)	5 10	13 08	Ivory Coast	19 3 81	ASEC Mimosas
Van Persie Robin (F)	6 0	11 00	Rotterdam	6 8 83	Feyenoord
Vieira Patrick (M)	6 4	13 09	Dakar	23 6 76	AC Milan

League Appearances: Aliadiere, J. (4); Almunia, M. 10; Bergkamp, D. 20(9); Campbell, S. 16; Clichy, G. 7(8); Cole, A. 35; Cygan, P. 15; Eboue, E. (1); Edu, 6(6); Fabregas, F. 24(9); Flamini, M. 9(12); Henry, T. 31(1); Hoyte, J. 4(1); Lauren, E. 32(1); Lehmann, J. 28; Ljungberg, F. 24(2); Owusu-Abeyie, Q. 1; Pennant, J. 1(6); Pires, R. 26(7); Reyes, J. 25(5); Senderos, P. 12(1); Silva, G. 13; Toure, K. 35; Van Persie, R. 12(14); Vieira, P. 32.
Goals – League (87): Henry 25, Pires 14 (1 pen), Ljungberg 10, Reyes 9, Bergkamp 8, Vieira 6, Van Persie 5, Cole 2, Edu 2 (1 pen), Fabregas 2, Campbell 1, Flamini 1, Lauren 1 (pen), own goal 1.
Carling Cup (5): Lupoli 2, Karbassiyoon 1, Owusu-Abeyie 1, Van Persie 1.
FA Cup (9): Van Persie 3, Ljungberg 2, Pires 2, Reyes 1, Vieira 1 (pen).
Community Shield (3): Silva 1, Reyes 1, own goal 1.
Champions League (13): Henry 5 (1 pen), Ljungberg 2, Fabregas 1, Pires 1 (pen), Reyes 1, Toure 1, Van Persie 1, own goal 1.
Ground: Arsenal Stadium, Highbury, London N5 1BU. Telephone (020) 7704 4000.
Record Attendance: 73,295 v Sunderland, Div 1, 9 March 1935. **Capacity:** 38,500.
Manager: Arsène Wenger.
Secretary: David Miles.
Most League Goals: 127, Division 1, 1930–31.
Highest League Scorer in Season: Ted Drake, 42, 1934–35.

Most League Goals in Total Aggregate: Cliff Bastin, 150, 1930–47.
Most Capped Player: Patrick Vieira, 79, France.
Most League Appearances: David O'Leary, 558, 1975–93.
Honours – FA Premier League: Champions – 1997–98, 2001–02, 2003–04. **Football League:** Division 1 Champions – 1930–31, 1932–33, 1933–34, 1934–35, 1937–38, 1947–48, 1952–53, 1970–71, 1988–89, 1990–91. **FA Cup:** Winners – 1929–30, 1935–36, 1949–50, 1970–71, 1978–79, 1992–93, 1997–98, 2001–02, 2002–03, 2004–05. **Football League Cup:** Winners – 1986–87, 1992–93. **European Competitions: European Cup-Winners' Cup:** Winners – 1993–94. **Fairs Cup:** Winners – 1969–70.
Colours: Redcurrant shirts, white shorts, redcurrent stockings.

ASTON VILLA — FA PREMIERSHIP

Angel Juan Pablo (F)	6 0	12 10	Medellin	24 10 75	River Plate
Barry Gareth (D)	5 11	12 06	Hastings	23 2 81	Trainee
Berson Mathieu (M)	5 9	11 06	Vannes	23 2 80	Nantes
Cahill Gary (D)	6 2	12 06	Dronfield	19 12 85	Trainee
Davis Steven (M)	5 7	9 07	Ballymena	1 1 85	Scholar
De la Cruz Ulises (D)	5 8	12 10	Bolivar	8 2 74	Hibernian
Delaney Mark (D)	6 1	11 07	Haverfordwest	13 5 76	Carmarthen T
Djemba-Djemba Eric (M)	5 9	11 13	Douala	4 5 81	Manchester U
Grant Lee (M)	6 2	12 02	York	31 12 85	Trainee
Henderson Wayne (G)	5 11	12 02	Dublin	16 9 83	Scholar
Hendrie Lee (M)	5 10	11 00	Birmingham	18 5 77	Trainee
Laursen Martin (D)	6 2	12 05	Silkeborg	26 7 77	AC Milan
McCann Gavin (M)	5 11	11 00	Blackpool	10 1 78	Sunderland
Mellberg Olof (D)	6 1	12 10	Amncharad	3 9 77	Santander
Moore Luke (F)	5 11	11 13	Birmingham	13 2 86	Trainee
Moore Stefan (F)	5 10	10 12	Birmingham	28 9 83	Scholar
Postma Stefan (G)	6 4	15 04	Utrecht	6 10 76	De Graafschap
Ridgewell Liam (D)	5 10	10 03	Bexley	21 7 84	Scholar
Samuel J Lloyd (D)	5 11	11 04	Trinidad	29 3 81	Charlton Ath
Solano Nolberto (M)	5 9	11 06	Callao	12 12 74	Newcastle U
Sorensen Thomas (G)	6 4	13 10	Fredericia	12 6 76	Sunderland
Vassell Darius (F)	5 7	12 00	Birmingham	13 6 80	Trainee
Whittingham Peter (D)	5 10	9 13	Nuneaton	8 9 84	Trainee

League Appearances: Angel, J. 30(5); Barry, G. 33(1); Berson, M. 7(4); Cole, C. 18(9); Davis, S. 19(9); De la Cruz, U. 30(4); Delaney, M. 30; Djemba-Djemba, E. 4(2); Hendrie, L. 25(4); Hitzlsperger, T. 17(11); Laursen, M. 12; McCann, G. 20; Mellberg, O. 30; Moore, L. 5(20); Moore, S. (1); Postma, S. 2(1); Ridgewell, L. 12(3); Samuel, J. 34(1); Solano, N. 32(4); Sorensen, T. 36; Vassell, D. 17(4); Whittingham, P. 5(8).
Goals – League (45): Solano 8, Angel 7, Barry 7 (3 pens), Hendrie 5, Cole 3, Mellberg 3, Hitzlsperger 2, Vassell 2, Davis 1, Laursen 1, McCann 1, Moore L 1, Whittingham 1, own goals 3.
Carling Cup (4): Angel 2, Solano 1, Vassell 1.
FA Cup (1): Barry 1.
Ground: Villa Park, Trinity Road, Birmingham B6 6HE. Telephone (0121) 327 2299.
Record Attendance: 76,588 v Derby Co, FA Cup 6th rd, 2 March 1946.
Capacity: 42,573.
Manager: David O'Leary.
Secretary: Steven Stride.
Most League Goals: 128, Division 1, 1930–31.
Highest League Scorer in Season: 'Pongo' Waring, 49, Division 1, 1930–31.
Most League Goals in Total Aggregate: Harry Hampton, 215, 1904–15.
Most Capped Player: Steve Staunton 64 (102), Republic of Ireland.

Most League Appearances: Charlie Aitken, 561, 1961–76.
Honours – Football League: Division 1 Champions – 1893–94, 1895–96, 1896–97, 1898–99, 1899–1900, 1909–10, 1980–81. Division 2 Champions – 1937–38, 1959–60. Division 3 Champions – 1971–72. **FA Cup:** Winners – 1887, 1895, 1897, 1905, 1913, 1920, 1957. **Football League Cup:** Winners – 1961, 1975, 1977, 1994, 1996. **European Competitions: European Cup:** Winners – 1981–82. **European Super Cup:** Winners: – 1982–83. **Intertoto Cup:** Winners – 2001.
Colours: Claret and blue shirts, white shorts, sky blue stockings with claret top.

BARNET — FL CHAMPIONSHIP 2

Bailey Nicky (M)	5 10	12 08	Hammersmith	10 6 84	Sutton U
Batt Damien (D)			Welwyn	16 9 84	Norwich C
Champion Tom (D)			Barnet	15 5 86	Enfield
Charles Anthony (D)			Isleworth	11 3 81	Farnborough T
Clist Simon (D)	5 10	11 05	Bournemouth	13 6 81	Bristol C
Elmes James M)			Harlow	8 6 86	Broxbourne B
Gore Shane (G)	6 1	12 01	Ashford	28 10 81	Wimbledon
Graham Richard (F)	5 10	12 03	London	20 3 75	Bristol R
Hatch Liam (F)	6 4	13 01	Hitchin	3 4 82	Gravesend & Northfleet
Hendon Ian (D)	6 1	13 05	Ilford	5 12 71	Peterborough U
King Simon (D)	6 0	13 00	Oxford	11 4 83	Oxford U
Lee Dwane (M)			Hillingdon	26 11 79	Exeter C
Lopez Guy (M)			Senegal	19 5 79	
Maddix Danny (D)	5 11	12 07	Ashford	11 10 67	Sheffield W
McBean Warren (F)			London	13 2 86	Broxbourne B
Millard Ricky (G)	6 3	13 07	Dagenham	3 5 84	
Reilly Andy (D)	5 10	12 08	Luton	26 10 85	Wycombe W
Roache Lee (F)	5 8	11 00	Leytonstone	30 4 84	
Sinclair Dean (M)	5 10	11 00	St Albans	17 12 84	Norwich C
Strevens Ben (M)	6 2	12 00	Edgware	24 5 80	Wingate & Finchley
Tynan Scott (G)			Liverpool	27 11 83	Nottingham F
Yakubu Ishmail (D)	6 1	12 09	Nigeria	8 4 85	

League Appearances: Ada, 0(2); Bailey, 23(13); Batt, 8(7); Champion, 0(2); Charles, 8(1); Clist, 40; Dobson, 0(3); Elmes, 0(2); Gore, 7; Graham, 38(1); Grazioli, 37; Hatch, 32(4); Hendon, 37; King, 40; Lee, 35(2); Lopez, 2(11); McBean, 0(4); Millard, 8; Plummer, 3; Roache, 8(20); Sinclair, 39; Strevens, 35(4); Tynan, 27(1); Yakubu, 35.
Goals – League (90): Grazioli 29, Sinclair 11, Hatch 10, Roache 6, Strevens 6, Bailey 5, Hendon 5 (4 pens), Graham 4, King 4, Lee 4, Yakubu 2, Batt 1, own goals 3.
FA Cup (3): Graham 1, Hatch 1, Yakubu 1.
LDV Vans Trophy (3): Bailey 2 (1 pen), Roache 1.
FA Trophy (2): Bailey 2.
Ground: Underhill Stadium, Barnet Lane, Barnet, Herts EN5 2BE. Telephone (020) 8441 6932.
Record Attendance: 11,026 v Wycombe Wanderers, FA Amateur Cup 4th Round 1951–52.
Manager: Paul Fairclough.
Secretary: Andrew Adie.
Most League Goals: 81, Division 4, 1991–92
Highest League Scorer in Season: Dougie Freedman, 24, Division 3, 1994–95.
Most League Goals in Total Aggregate: Sean Devine, 47, 1995–99.
Most Capped Player: Ken Charlery, 4, St. Lucia.

Most League Appearances: Paul Wilson, 263, 1991–2000.
Honours – Football League: GMVC: Champions – 1990–91. **Football Conference:** Champions – 2004–05. **FA Amateur Cup:** Winners 1945–46.
Colours: Black and amber.

BARNSLEY — FL CHAMPIONSHIP 1

Atkinson Rob (M)	6 1	12 00	Beverley	29 4 87	Scholar
Austin Neil (D)	5 10	11 09	Barnsley	26 4 83	Trainee
Baker Tom (F)	5 5	9 02	Salford	28 3 85	Scholar
Burns Jacob (M)	5 10	11 08	Sydney	21 1 78	Leeds U
Carbon Matt (D)	6 2	11 13	Nottingham	8 6 75	Walsall
Colgan Nick (G)	6 1	13 06	Drogheda	19 9 73	Hibernian
Conlon Barry (F)	6 3	14 00	Drogheda	1 10 78	Darlington
Flinders Scott (G)	6 4	14 00	Rotherham	12 6 86	Scholar
Hassell Bobby (D)	5 10	12 00	Derby	4 6 80	Trainee
Jarman Nathan (F)	5 11	11 03	Scunthorpe	19 9 86	Scholar
Joynes Nathan (M)	6 1	12 00	Hoyland	7 8 85	Scholar
Kay Antony (D)	5 11	11 08	Barnsley	21 10 82	Trainee
McPhail Stephen (M)	5 8	11 04	Westminster	9 12 79	Leeds U
Reid Paul (D)	6 2	11 08	Carlisle	18 2 82	Northampton T
Shuker Chris (M)	5 5	9 03	Liverpool	9 5 82	Manchester C
Tonge Dale (D)	5 10	10 06	Doncaster	7 5 85	Scholar
Vaughan Tony (D)	6 1	11 02	Manchester	11 10 75	Mansfield T
Williams Robbie (D)	5 10	11 13	Pontefract	2 10 84	Scholar
Williams Tom (D)	5 11	12 05	Carshalton	8 7 80	Peterborough U
Wroe Nicky (M)	5 11	10 02	Sheffield	28 9 85	Scholar

League Appearances: Atkinson, R. (1); Austin, N. 9(6); Baker, T. (3); Boulding, M. 22(7); Burns, J. 33(1); Carbon, M. 16(10); Chopra, M. 38(1); Colgan, N. 12(1); Conlon, B. 17(7); Flinders, S. 11; Hassell, B. 37(2); Jarman, N. 1(5); Johnson, S. 10(1); Joynes, N. (1); Kay, A. 37(2); McPhail, S. 36; Nardiello, D. 11(17); Onibuje, F. (3); Reid, P. 38(3); Shuker, C. 39(6); Stallard, M. (5); Tonge, D. 14; Turnbull, R. 23; Vaughan, T. 25(1); Williams, R. 13(4); Williams, T. 38(1); Wroe, N. 26(5).
Goals – League (69): Chopra 17 (2 pens), Boulding 10, Nardiello 7, Shuker 7, Conlon 6 (2 pens), Kay 6, Vaughan 4, Reid 3, Burns 2, Johnson 2, McPhail 2, Williams R 1, own goals 2.
Carling Cup (3): Conlon 1, Reid 1 (pen), Shuker 1.
FA Cup (0).
LDV Vans Trophy (0).
Ground: Oakwell Ground, Grove St, Barnsley S71 1ET. Telephone (01226) 211211.
Record Attendance: 40,255 v Stoke C, FA Cup 5th rd, 15 February 1936. **Capacity:** 25,000.
Manager: Andy Ritchie.
Secretary: Chris Patzelt.
Most League Goals: 118, Division 3 (N), 1933–34.
Highest League Scorer in Season: Cecil McCormack, 33, Division 2, 1950–51.
Most League Goals in Total Aggregate: Ernest Hine, 123, 1921–26 and 1934–38.
Most Capped Player: Gerry Taggart, 35 (50), Northern Ireland.
Most League Appearances: Barry Murphy, 514, 1962–78.
Honours – Football League: Division 3 (N) Champions – 1933–34, 1938–39, 1954–55. **FA Cup:** Winners – 1912.
Colours: Red shirts, white shorts, red stockings.

Anderton Darren (M)	6 1	12 05	Southampton	3 3 72	Tottenham H
Blake Robbie (F)	5 7	12 07	Middlesbrough	4 3 76	Burnley
Bruce Alex (D)	6 0	11 06	Norwich	28 9 84	Blackburn R
Carter Darren (M)	6 2	12 11	Solihull	18 12 83	Scholar
Clapham Jamie (M)	5 9	11 09	Lincoln	7 12 75	Ipswich T
Clemence Stephen (M)	6 0	12 09	Liverpool	31 3 78	Tottenham H
Cunningham Kenny (D)	5 11	12 07	Dublin	28 6 71	Wimbledon
Doyle Colin (G)	6 5	14 05	Cork	12 8 85	Scholar
Dunn David (M)	5 9	12 03	Gt Harwood	27 12 79	Blackburn R
Gray Julian (M)	6 1	11 00	Lewisham	21 9 79	Crystal Palace
Heskey Emile (F)	6 2	13 12	Leicester	11 1 78	Liverpool
Izzet Muzzy (M)	5 10	10 03	Mile End	31 10 74	Leicester C
Johnson Damien (M)	5 9	11 09	Lisburn	18 11 78	Blackburn R
Kilkenny Neil (M)	5 8	10 08	Middlesex	19 12 85	Arsenal
Kuqi Njazi (F)	6 3	13 05	Vushtrri	25 3 83	Lahti
Lazaridis Stan (M)	5 9	11 12	Perth	16 8 72	West Ham U
Melchiot Mario (D)	6 2	11 09	Amsterdam	4 11 76	Chelsea
Morrison Clinton (F)	6 1	11 13	Tooting	14 5 79	Crystal Palace
Nafti Mehdi (M)	5 9	11 03	Toulouse	20 11 78	Santander
Oji Samuel (D)	6 0	14 05	Westminster	9 10 85	
Pandiani Walter (F)	6 0	11 09	Montevideo	27 4 76	La Coruna
Pennant Jermaine (M)	5 9	10 06	Nottingham	15 1 83	Arsenal
Sadler Matthew (D)	5 11	11 08	Birmingham	26 2 85	Scholar
Taylor Maik (G)	6 4	14 02	Hildeshein	4 9 71	Fulham
Taylor Martin (D)	6 4	15 00	Ashington	9 11 79	Blackburn R
Tebily Oliver (D)	6 0	13 05	Abidjan	19 12 75	Celtic
Upson Matthew (D)	6 1	11 04	Hartismere	18 4 79	Arsenal
Vaesen Nico (G)	6 3	12 13	Hasselt	28 9 69	Huddersfield T

League Appearances: Anderton, D. 9(11); Blake, R. 2(9); Carter, D. 12(3); Clapham, J. 18(9); Clemence, S. 13(9); Cunningham, K. 36; Diao, S. 2; Dunn, D. 9(2); Forssell, M. 4; Gray, J. 18(14); Gronkjaer, J. 13(3); Heskey, E. 34; Izzet, M. 10; John, S. (3); Johnson, D. 36; Lazaridis, S. 15(5); Melchiot, M. 33(1); Morrison, C. 13(13); Nafti, M. 7(3); Pandiani, W. 13(1); Pennant, J. 12; Savage, R. 18; Taylor, Maik 38; Taylor, Martin 4(3); Tebily, O. 9(6); Upson, M. 36; Yorke, D. 4(9).
Goals – League (40): Heskey 10, Morrison 4, Pandiani 4 (1 pen), Savage 4 (1 pen), Anderton 3, Blake 2 (1 pen), Carter 2, Dunn 2, Gray 2, Upson 2, Yorke 2, Izzet 1, Melchiot 1, own goal 1.
Carling Cup (3): Gronkjaer 1, Morrison 1, Savage 1 (pen).
FA Cup (3): Carter 2, Heskey 1.
Ground: St Andrews, Birmingham B9 4NH. Telephone (0870) 066 1875.
Record Attendance: 66,844 v Everton, FA Cup 5th rd, 11 February 1939. **Capacity:** 29,949.
Manager: Steve Bruce.
Secretary: Julia Shelton.
Most League Goals: 103, Division 2, 1893–94 (only 28 games).
Highest League Scorer in Season: Joe Bradford, 29, Division 1, 1927–28.
Most League Goals in Total Aggregate: Joe Bradford, 249, 1920–35.
Most Capped Player: Malcolm Page, 28, Wales.
Most League Appearances: Frank Womack, 491, 1908–28.
Honours – Football League: Division 2 Champions – 1892–93, 1920–21, 1947–48, 1954–55, 1994–95. **Football League Cup:** Winners – 1963. **Leyland Daf Cup:** Winners – 1991. **Auto Windscreens Shield:** Winners – 1995.
Colours: Blue shirts, white shorts, blue stockings.

BLACKBURN ROVERS FA PREMIERSHIP

Amoruso Lorenzo (D)	6 2	13 10	Palese	28 6 71	Rangers
De Pedro Javier (M)	5 11	12 03	Logrono	4 8 73	Real Sociedad
Derbyshire Matt (F)	5 10	11 01	Gt Harwood	14 4 86	Great Harwood T
Dickov Paul (F)	5 6	10 06	Livingston	1 11 72	Leicester C
Douglas Jonathan (M)	6 0	12 07	Clones	22 11 81	Blackpool
Emerton Brett (M)	6 1	13 05	Bankstown	22 2 79	Feyenoord
Enckelman Peter (G)	6 2	12 05	Turku	10 3 77	Aston Villa
Flitcroft Garry (M)	6 0	11 08	Bolton	6 11 72	Manchester C
Friedel Brad (G)	6 3	14 00	Lakewood	18 5 71	Liverpool
Gallagher Paul (F)	6 1	12 00	Glasgow	9 8 84	Trainee
Gray Michael (D)	5 8	10 07	Sunderland	3 8 74	Sunderland
Gresko Vratislav (D)	6 0	11 05	Bratislava	24 7 77	Parma
Jansen Matt (F)	5 11	11 03	Carlisle	20 10 77	Crystal Palace
Johnson Jemal (F)	5 8	11 09	New Jersey	3 5 84	
Matteo Dominic (D)	6 1	13 08	Dumfries	28 4 74	Leeds U
McEveley James (D)	6 1	13 03	Liverpool	11 2 85	Trainee
Mokoena Aaron (D)	6 2	14 00	Johannesburg	25 11 80	Genk
Neill Lucas (D)	6 0	12 03	Sydney	9 3 78	Millwall
Nelsen Ryan (D)	5 11	14 02	New Zealand	18 10 77	DC United
Pedersen Morten (F)	5 11	11 00	Vadso	8 9 81	Tromso
Reid Steven (M)	6 0	12 07	Kingston	10 3 81	Millwall
Savage Robbie (M)	5 11	11 00	Wrexham	18 10 74	Birmingham C
Stead Jon (F)	6 3	12 00	Huddersfield	7 4 83	Huddersfield T
Thompson David (M)	5 7	10 00	Birkenhead	12 9 77	Coventry C
Todd Andy (D)	5 11	13 04	Derby	21 9 74	Charlton Ath
Tugay Kerimoglu (M)	5 9	11 07	Istanbul	24 8 70	Rangers
Yelldell David (G)	6 5	12 11	Stuttgart	1 10 81	
Yorke Dwight (F)	5 10	12 04	Canaan	3 11 71	Manchester U

League Appearances: Amoruso, L. 5(1); Bothroyd, J. 6(5); De Pedro, J. 1(1); Derbyshire, M. (1); Dickov, P. 27(2); Djorkaeff, Y. 3; Douglas, J. (1); Emerton, B. 33(4); Ferguson, B. 21; Flitcroft, G. 17(2); Friedel, B. 38; Gallagher, P. 5(11); Gray, M. 9; Gresko, V. 2(1); Jansen, M. 3(4); Johansson, N. 18(4); Johnson, J. (3); Matteo, D. 25(3); McEveley, J. 5; Mokoena, A. 16; Neill, L. 34(2); Nelsen, R. 15; Pedersen, M. 19; Reid, S. 23(5); Savage, R. 9; Short, C. 13(1); Stead, J. 19(10); Thompson, D. 11(13); Todd, A. 26; Tugay, K. 13(8); Yorke, D. 2(2).
Goals – League (32): Dickov 9 (2 pens), Emerton 4, Pedersen 4, Ferguson 2, Gallagher 2, Jansen 2, Reid S 2, Stead 2, Bothroyd 1, Neill 1, Short 1, Todd 1, own goal 1.
Carling Cup (3): Emerton 1, Gallagher 1, Pedersen 1.
FA Cup (10): Pedersen 3, Thompson 2, Dickov 1 (pen), Johnson 1, Matteo 1, Tugay 1, own goal 1.
Ground: Ewood Park, Blackburn BB2 4JF. Telephone (08701) 113232.
Record Attendance: 61,783 v Bolton W, FA Cup 6th rd, 2 March, 1929. **Capacity:** 31,367.
Manager: Mark Hughes.
Secretary: Tom Finn.
Most League Goals: 114, Division 2, 1954–55.
Highest League Scorer in Season: Ted Harper, 43, Division 1, 1925–26.
Most League Goals in Total Aggregate: Simon Garner, 168, 1978–92.
Most Capped Player: Henning Berg, 58 (100), Norway.
Most League Appearances: Derek Fazackerley, 596, 1970–86.
Honours – FA Premier League: Champions – 1994–95. **Football League:** Division 1 Champions – 1911–12, 1913–14. Division 2 Champions – 1938–39. Division 3

Champions – 1974–75. **FA Cup:** Winners – 1884, 1885, 1886, 1890, 1891, 1928. **Football League Cup:** Winners – 2002. **Full Members' Cup:** Winners – 1986–87. **Colours:** Blue and white halved shirts, white shorts with navy blue strip, white stockings with navy blue trim.

BLACKPOOL FL CHAMPIONSHIP 1

Anderson Stuart (M)	6 0	11 09	Banff	22 4 86	Southampton
Blinkhorn Matthew (F)	5 11	10 10	Blackpool	2 3 85	Scholar
Boyack Steven (M)	5 10	10 07	Edinburgh	4 9 76	Boston U
Bullock Martin (M)	5 5	10 07	Derby	5 3 75	Barnsley
Burns Jamie (M)	5 9	10 11	Blackpool	6 3 84	Scholar
Butler Tony (D)	6 2	13 07	Stockport	28 9 72	Bristol C
Clare Rob (D)	6 1	11 07	Belper	28 2 83	Stockport Co
Clarke Peter (D)	6 0	12 00	Southport	3 1 82	Everton
Coid Danny (D)	5 11	11 07	Liverpool	3 10 81	Trainee
Donnelly Ciaran (M)	5 9	11 09	Blackpool	2 4 84	Blackburn R
Edwards Paul (M)	5 11	10 12	Manchester	1 1 80	Wrexham
Edwards Rob (D)	6 0	12 02	Kendal	1 7 73	Preston NE
Evans Gareth (D)	6 0	11 12	Leeds	15 2 81	Huddersficeld T
Grabovac Zarko (F)	6 5	14 09	Ruma	16 3 83	
Grayson Simon (D)	6 0	13 07	Ripon	16 12 69	Blackburn R
Jones Lee (G)	6 3	14 04	Pontypridd	9 8 70	Stockport Co
McGregor Mark (D)	5 11	11 05	Chester	16 2 77	Burnley
Murphy John (F)	6 2	14 00	Whiston	18 10 76	Chester C
Parker Keigan (F)	5 7	10 05	Livington	8 6 82	St Johnstone
Paterson Sean (M)	5 11	11 05	Greenock	26 3 87	Scholar
Richardson Leam (D)	5 7	11 04	Leeds	19 11 79	Bolton W
Shaw Matthew (F)	6 1	11 09	Blackpool	17 5 84	Wrexham
Southern Keith (M)	5 10	12 06	Gateshead	24 4 81	Everton
Wellens Richard (M)	5 9	11 06	Manchester	26 3 80	Manchester U
Wiles Simon (M)	5 11	11 04	Preston	22 4 85	Scholar

League Appearances: Anderson, S. 1(3); Barrowman, A. (2); Blinkhorn, M. 2(2); Boyack, S. (1); Bullock, M. 24(4); Burns, J. 19(4); Butler, T. 6(2); Clare, R. 19(4); Clarke, P. 38; Coid, D. 33(2); Donnelly, C. 4(4); Edwards, P. 22(6); Edwards, R. 24(2); Ellegaard, K. 2; Evans, G. 22; Flynn, Michael 6; Flynn, Mike 5(1); Gorre, D. (1); Grabovac, Z. 1(2); Grayson, S. 32(4); Ilic, S. 3; Jones, B. 12; Jones, L. 29; Livesey, D. 1; Lynch, S. 5(2); McGregor, M. 36(2); Murphy, J. 30(1); Parker, K. 26(9); Paterson, S. (2); Richardson, L. 20(3); Shaw, M. 2(8); Southern, K. 25(2); Taylor, S. 24; Vernon, S. 4; Warhurst, P. 2(2); Wellens, R. 27(1).
Goals – League (54): Taylor 12 (4 pens), Murphy 9, Parker 9, Southern 6 (1 pen), Clarke 5, Edwards P 3, Vernon 3, Wellens 3, Grayson 2, Edwards R 1, own goal 1.
Carling Cup (1): Taylor 1.
FA Cup (6): Wellens 2, Clarke 1, Parker 1, Southern 1, Taylor 1.
LDV Vans Trophy (9): Blinkhorn 3, Burns 2, Parker 2 (1 pen), Coid 1, Murphy 1.
Ground: Bloomfield Road Ground, Blackpool FY1 6JJ. Telephone (0870) 443 1953.
Record Attendance: 38,098 v Wolverhampton W, Division 1, 17 September 1955.
Capacity: 9,491.
Manager: Colin Hendry.
Secretary: Peter Collins.
Most League Goals: 98, Division 2, 1929–30.
Highest League Scorer in Season: Jimmy Hampson, 45, Division 2, 1929–30.
Most League Goals in Total Aggregate: Jimmy Hampson, 246, 1927–38.
Most Capped Player: Jimmy Armfield, 43, England.
Most League Appearances: Jimmy Armfield, 568, 1952–71.

Honours – Football League: Division 2 Champions – 1929–30. **FA Cup:** Winners – 1953. **Anglo-Italian Cup:** Winners – 1971. **LDV Vans Trophy:** Winners – 2002, 2004.
Colours: Tangerine shirts, white shorts, tangerine stockings.

BOLTON WANDERERS — FA PREMIERSHIP

Ben Haim Tal (D)	5 11	11 09	Rishon Le Zion	31 3 82	Maccabi Tel Aviv
Buval Bedi (F)	5 11	11 01	Domont	17 6 86	Scholar
Campo Ivan (M)	6 1	12 11	San Sebastian	21 2 74	Real Madrid
Davies Kevin (F)	6 0	12 10	Sheffield	26 3 77	Southampton
Fadiga Khalilou (F)	6 0	12 02	Dakar	30 12 74	Auxerre
Gardner Ricardo (D)	5 9	11 00	St Andrews	25 9 78	Harbour View
Giannakopoulos Stelios (M)	5 8	11 00	Athens	12 7 74	Olympiakos
Hunt Nicky (D)	6 1	13 08	Westhoughton	3 9 83	Scholar
Jaaskelainen Jussi (G)	6 3	12 10	Mikkeli	19 4 75	VPS
Jaidi Radhi (D)	6 4	14 00	Tunis	30 8 75	Esperance
Julio Cesar (D)	6 1	12 04	Sao Luis de Maranhao	18 11 78	Valladolid
Kaku Blessing (M)	5 11	12 04	Ughelli	5 3 78	Ashdod
N'Gotty Bruno (D)	6 1	13 08	Lyon	10 6 71	Marseille
Nolan Kevin (M)	6 0	14 00	Liverpool	24 6 82	Scholar
O'Brien Joey (M)	6 0	10 13	Dublin	17 2 86	Scholar
Pedersen Henrik (F)	6 1	13 03	Jutland	10 6 75	Silkeborg
Speed Gary (M)	5 10	12 11	Deeside	8 9 69	Newcastle U
Vaz Te Ricardo (F)	6 2	12 07	Lisbon	1 10 86	Scholar

League Appearances: Barness, A. 5(3); Ben Haim, T. 19(2); Campo, I. 20(7); Candela, V. 9(1); Davies, K. 33(2); Diouf, E. 23(4); Fadiga, K. (5); Ferdinand, L. 1(11); Gardner, R. 30(3); Giannakopoulos, S. 28(6); Hierro, F. 15(14); Hunt, N. 29; Jaaskelainen, J. 36; Jaidi, R. 20(7); Julio Cesar, 4(1); Kaku, B. (1); N'Gotty, B. 37; Nolan, K. 27(9); O'Brien, J. (1); Oakes, A. 1; Okocha, J. 29(2); Pedersen, H. 13(14); Poole, K. 1(1); Speed, G. 37(1); Vaz Te, R. 1(6).
Goals – League (49): Diouf 9 (1 pen), Davies 8, Giannakopoulos 7, Okocha 6 (4 pens), Pedersen 6, Jaidi 5, Nolan 4, Ben Haim 1, Ferdinand 1, Hierro 1, Speed 1.
Carling Cup (5): Julio Cesar 1, Ferdinand 1, Okocha 1 (pen), Pedersen 1, own goal 1.
FA Cup (5): Pedersen 2, Davies 1, Giannakopoulos 1, Vaz Te 1.
Ground: Reebok Stadium, Burnden Way, Lostock, Bolton BL6 6JW. Telephone Bolton (01204) 673673.
Record Attendance: 69,912 v Manchester C, FA Cup 5th rd, 18 February 1933. **Capacity:** 27,879.
Manager: Sam Allardyce.
Secretary: Simon Marland.
Most League Goals: 100, Division 1, 1996–97.
Highest League Scorer in Season: Joe Smith, 38, Division 1, 1920–21.
Most League Goals in Total Aggregate: Nat Lofthouse, 255, 1946–61.
Most Capped Player: Mark Fish, 34 (62), South Africa.
Most League Appearances: Eddie Hopkinson, 519, 1956–70.
Honours – Football League: Division 1 Champions – 1996–97. Division 2 Champions – 1908–09, 1977–78. Division 3 Champions – 1972–73. **FA Cup:** Winners – 1923, 1926, 1929, 1958. **Sherpa Van Trophy:** Winners – 1989.
Colours: All white.

Abbey Nathan (G)	6 0	11 03	Islington	11 7 78	Burnley
Brooks Lewis (M)	5 10	11 06	Boston	4 9 87	
Clare Daryl (F)	5 9	12 08	Jersey	1 8 78	Chester C
Ellender Paul (D)	6 1	12 07	Scunthorpe	21 10 74	Scarborough
Greaves Mark (D)	6 1	13 00	Hull	22 1 75	Hull C
Holland Chris (M)	5 9	12 13	Clitheroe	11 9 75	Huddersfield T
Hurst Tom (M)	6 1	11 00	Leicester	23 9 87	Scholar
Lee Jason (F)	6 3	13 03	Newham	9 5 71	Peterborough U
McCann Austin (D)	5 9	11 13	Alexandria	21 1 80	Clyde
Melton Steve (M)	5 11	12 03	Lincoln	3 10 78	Hull C
Noble David (M)	6 0	12 04	Hitchin	2 2 82	West Ham U
Norris Rob (M)	5 9	10 03	Nottingham	12 10 87	Scholar
O'Donnell Stephen (M)	5 11	12 02	Belshill	10 7 83	
Pitt Courtney (F)	5 7	10 08	Westminster	17 12 81	Oxford U
Rusk Simon (M)	5 11	12 08	Peterborough	17 12 81	Peterborough U
Staff David (F)	6 1	11 07	Market Harborough	8 11 79	Kings Lynn
Thomas Danny (M)	5 7	10 10	Leamington Spa	1 5 81	Bournemouth
Thompson Lee (F)	5 7	10 10	Sheffield	25 3 83	Sheffield U
White Alan (D)	6 3	12 05	Darlington	22 3 76	Leyton Orient

League Appearances: Abbey, N. 44; Abbey, Z. 3(2); Beevers, L. 31; Bennett, T. 11; Boyack, S. 2(2); Brooks, L. 1(1); Carruthers, M. 4(2); Clare, D. 14(5); Easter, J. 5(4); Ellender, P. 39; Gabrieli, E. 4; Gascoigne, P. 2(2); Greaves, M. 21(1); Holland, C. 30(2); Hurst, T. (1); James, K. 6; Jelleyman, G. 3; Kirk, A. 25; Lee, J. 32(7); Maylett, B. 8(1); McCann, A. 45; McCormick, L. 2; McManus, T. 5(3); Melton, S. 5(4); Noble, D. 30(2); Norris, R. 1(1); O'Donnell, S. 2(2); O'Halloran, M. 5(3); Pitt, C. 20(12); Roma, D. 2; Rusk, S. 22(9); Staff, D. (5); Strong, G. 8(1); Thomas, D. 32(7); Thompson, L. 8(37); West, D. 22(2); White, A. 11; Wiseman, S. 1(1).
Goals – League (62): Kirk 19 (3 pens), Lee 9, Pitt 4 (2 pens), Clare 3 (1 pen), Easter 3, Maylett 3, Noble 3 (1 pen), Rusk 3, Thomas 3, Thompson 3, Ellender 2, Abbey Z 1, Beevers 1, McCann 1, Melton 1, O'Halloran 1, own goals 2.
Carling Cup (5): Thompson 2, Beevers 1, Lee 1, Pitt 1.
FA Cup (8): Kirk 2, McManus 2, Ellender 1, Lee 1, Noble 1, Thompson 1.
LDV Vans Trophy (0).
Ground: York Street, Boston, Lincolnshire PE21 6HJ. Telephone (01205) 364406.
Record Attendance: 10,086 v Corby Town, Friendly, 1955.
Capacity: 6868.
Manager: Steve Evans.
Secretary: John Blackwell.
Most Capped Player: Andy Kirk, 1, Northern Ireland.
Honours – Nationwide Conference: Champions – 2001–02. **Dr. Martens:** Champions – 1999–2000. Runners-up – 1998–99. **Unibond League:** Runners-up – 1995–96, 1997–98. **Unibond Challenge Cup:** Runners-up – 1996–97. **FA Trophy:** Runners-up – 1984–85. **Northern Premier League:** Champions – 1972–73, 1973–74, 1976–77, 1977–78. **Northern Premier League Cup:** Winners – 1974, 1976. **Northern Premier League Challenge Shield:** Winners – 1974, 1975, 1977, 1978. **Lincolnshire Senior Cup:** Winners – 1935, 1937, 1938, 1946, 1950, 1955, 1956, 1960, 1977, 1979, 1986, 1988, 1989. **Non-League Champions of Champions Cup:** Winners – 1973, 1977. **East Anglian Cup:** – Winners 1961. **Central Alliance League:** Champions – 1961–62. **United Counties League:** Champions – 1965–66. **West Midlands League:** Champions – 1966–67, 1967–68. **Eastern Professional Floodlit Cup:** Winners – 1972.
Colours: Amber and black striped shirts, black shorts with amber stripe, black stockings with yellow top.

Broadhurst Karl (D)	6 1	11 07	Portsmouth	18 3 80	Trainee
Browning Marcus (M)	6 1	12 12	Bristol	22 4 71	Gillingham
Connell Alan (F)	6 0	10 10	Enfield	5 2 83	Ipswich T
Coutts James (M)	5 6	9 07	Weymouth	15 4 87	Trainee
Cummings Warren (D)	5 9	11 08	Aberdeen	15 10 80	Chelsea
Fletcher Steve (F)	6 2	14 09	Hartlepool	26 7 72	Hartlepool U
Hayter James (F)	5 9	10 13	Newport (IW)	9 4 79	Trainee
Howe Eddie (D)	5 11	11 07	Amersham	29 11 77	Portsmouth
Maher Shaun (D)	6 1	13 02	Dublin	20 6 78	Bohemians
Moss Neil (G)	6 2	13 10	New Milton	10 5 75	Southampton
Moss Ryan (M)	5 11	12 04	Dorchester	14 11 86	Trainee
O'Connor Gareth (F)	5 10	11 00	Dublin	10 11 78	Bohemians
O'Connor James (D)	5 10	12 05	Birmingham	20 11 84	Aston Villa
Purches Stephen (M)	5 11	11 09	Ilford	14 1 80	West Ham U
Rodrigues Dani (F)	5 11	12 00	Madeira	3 3 80	Yeovil T
Rowe James (M)	5 9	10 00	Frimley	10 3 87	Scholar
Spicer John (M)	5 11	11 08	Romford	13 9 83	Arsenal
Stewart Gareth (G)	6 0	12 08	Preston	3 2 80	Blackburn R
Stock Brian (M)	5 11	11 02	Winchester	24 12 81	Trainee
Tindall Jason (M)	6 1	12 13	Stepney	15 11 77	Charlton Ath
Young Neil (D)	5 9	12 00	Harlow	31 8 73	Tottenham H

League Appearances: Broadhurst, K. 29; Browning, M. 17(23); Connell, A. 7(27); Coutts, J. (1); Cranie, M. 2(1); Cummings, W. 30; Elliott, W. 43; Fletcher, C. 6; Fletcher, S. 30(6); Green, A. 3; Hayter, J. 37(2); Holmes, D. 8(15); Howe, E. 33(2); Maher, S. 29(7); Mills, M. 12; Moss, N. 46; Moss, R. (1); O'Connor, G. 39(1); O'Connor, J. 6; Purches, S. 10(4); Rodrigues, D. 10(13); Rowe, J. (2); Simek, F. 8; Spicer, J. 39; Stock, B. 39(2); Young, N. 23(7).

Goals – League (77): Hayter 19 (1 pen), O'Connor G 13 (2 pens), Fletcher S 9, Spicer 6, Stock 6, Elliott 4, Mills 3, Rodrigues 3, Connell 2, Cummings 2, Fletcher C 2, Holmes 2, Maher 2, Broadhurst 1, Howe 1, Purches S 1, own goal 1.

Carling Cup (9): Hayter 3, Broadhurst 1, Browning 1, Cummings 1, O'Connor G 1, Spicer 1, Stock 1.

FA Cup (8): Connell 2, Elliott 1, Fletcher S 1, Holmes 1, Maher 1, Rodrigues 1, Spicer 1.

LDV Vans Trophy (2): Stock 1, own goal 1.

Ground: The Fitness First Stadium at Dean Court, Bournemouth BH7 7AF. Telephone (01202) 726300.

Record Attendance: 28,799 v Manchester U, FA Cup 6th rd, 2 March 1957.

Capacity: 9300 rising to 12,000.

Manager: Sean O'Driscoll.

Secretary: K. R. J. MacAlister.

Most League Goals: 88, Division 3 (S), 1956–57.

Highest League Scorer in Season: Ted MacDougall, 42, 1970–71.

Most League Goals in Total Aggregate: Ron Eyre, 202, 1924–33.

Most Capped Player: Gerry Peyton, 7 (33), Republic of Ireland.

Most League Appearances: Steve Fletcher, 425, 1992–.

Honours – Football League: Division 3 Champions – 1986–87. **Associate Members' Cup:** Winners – 1984.

Colours: Red with black panel shirts, black shorts, black stockings.

Armstrong Craig (M)	5 11	12 09	South Shields	23 5 75	Sheffield W
Atherton Peter (D)	5 11	13 12	Wigan	6 4 70	Sheffield W
Bentham Craig (D)	5 9	11 06	Bingley	7 3 85	Scholar
Bower Mark (D)	5 10	11 00	Bradford	23 1 80	Trainee
Cooke Andy (F)	6 0	12 07	Shrewsbury	20 1 74	Pusan Icons
Crooks Lee (M)	6 2	13 01	Wakefield	14 1 78	Barnsley
Emanuel Lewis (D)	5 8	12 01	Bradford	14 10 83	Scholar
Forrest Danny (M)	5 10	11 07	Keighley	23 10 84	Trainee
Gavin Jason (D)	6 0	11 13	Dublin	14 3 80	Middlesbrough
Henderson Paul (G)	6 1	12 06	Sydney	22 4 76	
Holloway Darren (D)	6 0	12 05	Crook	3 10 77	Wimbledon
Jacobs Wayne (D)	5 9	11 02	Sheffield	3 2 69	Rotherham U
Jacobs Wayne (D)	5 9	11 02	Sheffield	3 2 69	Rotherham U
Kearney Tom (M)	5 11	10 08	Liverpool	7 10 81	Everton
Morrison Owen (M)	5 8	11 12	Derry	8 12 81	Stockport Co
Muirhead Ben (M)	5 9	11 02	Doncaster	5 1 83	Manchester U
Penford Thomas (M)	5 10	11 03	Leeds	5 1 85	Scholar
Ricketts Donovan (G)	6 1	11 05	St James	6 7 77	Village U
Sanasy Kevin (M)	5 8	10 05	Leeds	2 11 84	Scholar
Schumacher Steven (M)	5 10	11 00	Liverpool	30 4 84	Everton
Summerbee Nicky (M)	5 11	12 08	Altrincham	26 8 71	Leicester C
Swift John (M)	5 7	10 06	Leeds	20 9 84	Scholar
Symes Michael (F)	6 3	12 04	Gt Yarmouth	31 10 83	Everton
Wetherall David (D)	6 3	13 12	Sheffield	14 3 71	Leeds U
Windass Dean (F)	5 10	12 03	North Ferriby	1 4 69	Sheffield U

League Appearances: Abbey, Z. 6; Adebola, D. 14(1); Armstrong, C. 4(3); Atherton, P. 12(4); Bentham, C. (2); Bower, M. 46; Bridge-Wilkinson, M. 12; Cooke, A. 20; Crooks, L. 30(2); Emanuel, L. 28(8); Forrest, D. 4(16); Gavin, J. 1(2); Henderson, P. 40; Holloway, D. 33; Jacobs, W. 13(1); Kearney, T. 13; Morrison, O. 17(5); Muirhead, B. 26(14); Penford, T. (3); Ricketts, D. 4; Roberts, N. 3; Sanasy, K. (3); Schumacher, S. 42(1); Summerbee, N. 31(2); Swift, J. 2(3); Symes, M. 5(7); Tierney, P. 14(2); Turnbull, R. 2; Wetherall, D. 45; Windass, D. 39(2).
Goals – League (64): Windass 27 (2 pens), Schumacher 6, Cooke 4, Wetherall 4, Adebola 3, Bridge-Wilkinson 3, Summerbee 3, Bower 2, Forrest 2, Morrison 2, Symes 2, Abbey 1, Crooks 1, Holloway 1, Kearney 1, Muirhead 1, Roberts 1.
Carling Cup (1): Windass 1 (pen).
FA Cup (0).
LDV Vans Trophy (1): Adebola 1.
Ground: Valley Parade, Bradford BD8 7DY. Telephone (01274) 773355.
Record Attendance: 39,146 v Burnley, FA Cup 4th rd, 11 March 1911. **Capacity:** 25,136.
Manager: Colin Todd.
Secretary: Jon Pollard.
Most League Goals: 128, Division 3 (N), 1928–29.
Highest League Scorer in Season: David Layne, 34, Division 4, 1961–62.
Most League Goals in Total Aggregate: Bobby Campbell, 121, 1981–84, 1984–86.
Most Capped Player: Jamie Lawrence, Jamaica.
Most League Appearances: Cec Podd, 502, 1970–84.
Honours – Football League: Division 2 Champions – 1907–08. Division 3 Champions – 1984–85. Division 3 (N) Champions – 1928–29. **FA Cup:** Winners – 1911.
Colours: Claret and amber shirts, white shorts with claret and amber trim, claret stockings with amber and black trim.

Bankole Ademola (G)	6 3	14 00	Lagos	9 9 69	Crewe Alex
Charles Darius (M)	5 11	11 10	Ealing	10 12 87	Scholar
Dobson Michael (D)	5 11	12 04	Isleworth	9 4 81	Trainee
Fitzgerald Scott P (F)	5 11	12 00	Hillingdon	18 11 79	Watford
Frampton Andrew (D)	5 11	10 10	Wimbledon	3 9 79	Crystal Palace
Gayle Marcus (D)	6 3	14 03	Hammersmith	28 9 70	Watford
Hargreaves Chris (M)	5 11	13 02	Cleethorpes	12 5 72	Northampton T
Harrold Matt (F)	6 1	11 10	Leyton	24 7 84	Harlow T
Hunt Steve (M)	5 7	12 06	Port Laoise	1 8 80	Crystal Palace
Hutchinson Eddie (M)	6 1	12 07	Kingston	23 2 82	Sutton U
Ide Charlie (M)	5 8	10 06	Sunbury	10 5 88	Scholar
Moleski George (M)	5 6	10 08	Hillingdon	23 7 87	Scholar
Nelson Stuart (G)	6 1	12 12	Stroud	17 9 81	Hucknall T
O'Connor Kevin (F)	5 11	12 00	Blackburn	24 2 82	Trainee
Osborne Karleigh (M)	6 2	12 08	Southall	19 3 88	Scholar
Peters Ryan (F)	5 8	10 08	London	21 8 87	Scholar
Rankin Isiah (F)	5 10	11 00	London	22 5 78	Grimsby T
Rhodes Alex (F)	5 9	10 04	Cambridge	23 1 82	Newmarket T
Smith Jay (M)	5 11	11 07	Hammersmith	29 12 81	Trainee
Sodje Sam (D)	6 0	12 00	Greenwich	29 5 79	Margate
Tabb Jay (M)	5 5	9 07	Tooting	21 2 84	Trainee
Talbot Stuart (M)	6 0	13 12	Birmingham	14 6 73	Rotherham U
Turner Michael (D)	6 4	12 06	Lewisham	9 11 83	Charlton Ath
Watts Ryan (M)	5 9	10 10	Greenford	18 5 88	Scholar

League Appearances: Bankole, A. 3; Burton, D. 38(2); Charles, D. 1; Claridge, S. 3(1); Dobson, M. 13(5); Fitzgerald, S. 12; Fitzgerald, S. 7(5); Frampton, A. 34(1); Gayle, M. 4(2); Hargreaves, C. 30; Harrold, M. 6(13); Hunt, S. 13(6); Hutchinson, E. 14(1); Ide, C. (1); Lawrence, J. 8(6); May, B. 7(3); Moleski, G. (1); Myers, A. 6(4); Nelson, S. 43; O'Connor, K. 32(5); Osborne, K. 1; Pacquette, R. 1; Peters, R. 1(8); Pratley, D. 11(3); Rankin, I. 33(8); Rhodes, A. 4(18); Salako, J. 30(5); Smith, J. (2); Sobers, J. 1; Sodje, S. 40; Somner, M. 1(1); Tabb, J. 29(11); Talbot, S. 35(2); Turner, M. 45; Watts, R. (1).
Goals – League (57): Burton 10, Rankin 8, Sodje 7, Tabb 5, Fitzgerald S 4, Salako 4 (2 pens), Hunt 3 (1 pen), Rhodes 3, Hargreaves 2, O'Connor 2, Dobson 1, Hutchinson 1, May 1, Peters 1, Pratley 1, Sobers 1, Talbot 1, Turner 1, own goal 1.
Carling Cup (0).
FA Cup (10): Rankin 2, Frampton 1, Hargreaves 1, Hutchinson 1, Rhodes 1 (pen), Salako 1, Sodje 1, Tabb 1, Talbot 1.
LDV Vans Trophy (0).
Play-Offs (1): Frampton 1.
Ground: Griffin Park, Braemar Road, Brentford, Middlesex TW8 0NT. Telephone (0845) 3456 442.
Record Attendance: 39,626 v Preston NE, FA Cup 6th rd, 5 March 1938. **Capacity:** 12,763.
Manager: Martin Allen.
Secretary: Lisa Hall.
Most League Goals: 98, Division 4, 1962–63.
Highest League Scorer in Season: Jack Holliday, 38, Division 3 (S), 1932–33.
Most League Goals in Total Aggregate: Jim Towers, 153, 1954–61.
Most Capped Player: John Buttigieg, 22 (98), Malta.
Most League Appearances: Ken Coote, 514, 1949–64.

Honours – Football League: Division 2 Champions – 1934–35. Division 3 Champions – 1991–92, 1998–99. Division 3 (S) Champions – 1932–33. Division 4 Champions – 1962–63.
Colours: Red and white vertical striped shirts, black shorts, black stockings.

BRIGHTON & HOVE ALBION FL CHAMPIONSHIP

Butters Guy (D)	6 1	15 05	Hillingdon	30 10 69	Gillingham
Carpenter Richard (M)	6 0	13 03	Sheppey	30 9 72	Cardiff C
El-Abd Adam (D)	5 10	13 05	Brighton	11 9 84	Scholar
Hammond Dean (M)	6 1	11 02	Hastings	7 3 83	Scholar
Harding Daniel (D)	6 0	11 11	Gloucester	23 12 83	Scholar
Hart Gary (F)	5 9	12 07	Harlow	21 9 76	Stansted
Hinshelwood Adam (D)	5 11	13 00	Oxford	8 1 84	Scholar
Jarrett Albert (M)	5 11	11 02	Sierra Leone	23 10 84	Dulwich Hamlet
Jones Natham (M)	5 6	10 06	Rhondda	28 5 73	Southend U
Knight Leon (F)	5 5	10 02	Hackney	16 9 82	Chelsea
Kuipers Michels (G)	6 2	15 00	Amsterdam	26 6 74	Bristol R
May Christopher (G)	5 11	11 08	Wakefield	2 9 85	Scholar
Mayo Kerry (D)	5 9	13 10	Cuckfield	21 9 77	Trainee
McCammon Mark (F)	6 3	15 02	Barnet	7 8 78	Millwall
McPhee Christopher (F)	6 0	11 11	Eastbourne	20 3 83	Scholar
Molango Maheta (F)	6 1	12 00	St Imier	24 7 82	VS Burghausen
Nicolas Alexis (M)	5 8	9 13	Westminster	13 2 83	Chelsea
Oatway Charlie (M)	5 7	11 11	Hammersmith	28 11 73	Brentford
Reid Paul (M)	5 8	12 09	Sydney	6 7 79	Bradford C
Robinson Jake (F)	5 7	10 10	Brighton	23 10 86	Scholar
Shaaban Rami (G)	6 4	14 02	Sweden	30 6 75	Arsenal
Virgo Adam (D)	6 2	13 12	Brighton	25 1 83	Juniors
Watson Paul (D)	5 8	11 04	Hastings	4 1 75	Brentford

League Appearances: Blayney, A. 7; Butters, G. 41; Carpenter, R. 28(4); Claridge, S. 5; Cullip, D. 18; Currie, D. 21(1); Dolan, J. 3; El-Abd, A. 14(2); Hammond, D. 20(10); Harding, D. 39(4); Hart, G. 16(10); Hinshelwood, A. 37(1); Jarrett, A. 3(9); Jones, N. 3(16); Knight, L. 33(6); Kuipers, M. 30; May, C. (1); Mayo, K. 21(6); McCammon, M. 16(2); McPhee, C. 6(10); Molango, M. 4(1); Nicolas, A. 29(4); Oatway, C. 31(3); Piercy, J. 1(1); Reid, P. 33(1); Robinson, J. 1(9); Shaaban, R. 6; Virgo, A. 36; Watson, P. 1(3); Yelldell, D. 3.
Goals – League (40): Virgo 8, Hammond 4, Knight 4 (1 pen), Carpenter 3, McCammon 3, Butters 2, Currie 2, Hart 2, Reid 2, Harding 1, Hinshelwood 1, Jarrett 1, Mayo 1, Molango 1, Oatway 1, Robinson 1, own goals 3.
Carling Cup (1): Butters 1.
FA Cup (1): Carpenter 1.
Ground: Withdean Stadium, Tongdean Lane, Brighton. East Sussex BN1 5JD. Telephone (01273) 695400
Record Attendance: 36,747 v Fulham, Division 2, 27 December 1958 (at Goldstone Ground).
Capacity: 6973 (all seated).
Manager: Mark McGhee.
Secretary: Derek Allan.
Most League Goals: 112, Division 3 (S), 1955–56.
Highest League Scorer in Season: Peter Ward, 32, Division 3, 1976–77.
Most League Goals in Total Aggregate: Tommy Cook, 114, 1922–29.
Most Capped Player: Steve Penney, 17, Northern Ireland.
Most League Appearances: 'Tug' Wilson, 509, 1922–36.

Honours – Football League: Division 2 Champions – 2001–02. Division 3 Champions – 2000–01. Division 3 (S) Champions – 1957–58. Division 4 Champions – 1964–65.
Colours: Blue and white striped shirts, white shorts, white stockings.

BRISTOL CITY — FL CHAMPIONSHIP 1

Anyinsah Joseph (M)	5 8	11 00	Bristol	8 10 84	Scholar
Bell Mickey (M)	5 10	12 09	Newcastle	15 11 71	Wycombe W
Brooker Stephen (F)	5 11	13 13	Newport Pagnell	21 5 81	Port Vale
Brown Scott (M)	5 9	11 00	Runcorn	8 5 85	Scholar
Carey Louis (D)	5 10	12 09	Bristol	20 1 77	Trainee
Coles Daniel (D)	6 1	13 05	Bristol	31 10 81	Scholar
Cotterill David (F)	5 10	10 11	Cardiff	4 12 87	Scholar
Doherty Tom (M)	5 8	11 12	Bristol	17 3 79	Trainee
Fortune Clayton (D)	6 3	14 04	Forest Gate	10 11 82	Tottenham H
Gillespie Steven (F)	5 9	11 05	Liverpool	4 6 84	Liverpool
Golbourne Scott (M)	5 8	11 08	Bristol	29 2 88	Scholar
Goodfellow Marc (M)	5 7	11 00	Swadlincote	20 9 81	Stoke C
Gould Jonathan (G)	6 1	13 01	Paddington	18 7 68	Preston NE
Harley Ryan (M)	5 9	11 00	Bristol	22 1 85	Scholar
Hawkins Darren (M)	5 8	11 09	Bristol	25 4 84	Scholar
Heffernan Paul (F)	5 9	11 00	Dublin	29 12 81	Notts Co
Lita Leroy (F)	5 8	11 12	DR Congo	28 12 84	Scholar
Miller Lee (F)	6 0	11 07	Lanark	18 5 83	Falkirk
Murray Scott (M)	5 8	11 02	Aberdeen	26 5 74	Reading
Orr Bradley (M)	6 0	11 11	Liverpool	1 11 82	Newcastle U
Phillips Steve (G)	6 1	13 06	Bath	6 5 78	Paulton R
Skuse Cole (M)	6 1	11 05	Bristol	29 3 86	Scholar
Smith Jamie (M)	5 8	11 02	Birmingham	17 9 74	Crystal Palace
Tinnion Brian (M)	6 0	13 05	Stanley	23 3 68	Bradford C
Wilkshire Luke (M)	5 9	11 00	Wollongong	2 10 81	Middlesbrough
Woodman Craig (D)	5 8	11 00	Tiverton	22 12 82	Trainee
Wring Danny (M)	5 10	10 03	Portishead	26 10 86	Scholar

League Appearances: Amankwaah, K. 1(4); Anyinsah, J. 2(5); Bell, M. 26(5); Brooker, S. 33; Brown, S. 13(6); Butler, T. 22; Carey, L. 14; Coles, D. 37(1); Cotterill, D. 8(4); Dinning, T. 15(4); Doherty, T. 25(4); Fortune, C. 17(13); Gillespie, S. 1(7); Golbourne, S. 7(2); Goodfellow, M. 1(4); Harley, R. 1(1); Heffernan, P. 10(17); Hill, M. 23; Ireland, C. 5; Keith, J. 3; Lita, L. 42(2); Miller, L. 2(5); Murray, S. 31(11); Orr, B. 23(14); Phillips, S. 46; Roberts, C. 6(2); Skuse, C. 4(3); Smith, J. 35(4); Tinnion, B. 15(7); Wilkshire, L. 35(2); Woodman, C. 3; Wring, D. (1).
Goals – League (74): Lita 24 (1 pen), Brooker 16, Wilkshire 9 (2 pens), Murray 8, Heffernan 5, Butler 2, Smith 2, Bell 1 (pen), Coles 1, Doherty 1, Roberts 1, Tinnion 1, own goals 3.
Carling Cup (3): Lita 2, own goal 1.
FA Cup (2): Heffernan 1, Lita 1.
LDV Vans Trophy (3): Lita 2, Heffernan 1.
Ground: Ashton Gate, Bristol BS3 2EJ. Telephone (0117) 9630630.
Record Attendance: 43,335 v Preston NE, FA Cup 5th rd, 16 February 1935.
Capacity: 21,497.
Manager: Brian Tinnion.
Secretary: Michelle McDonald.
Most League Goals: 104, Division 3 (S), 1926–27.
Highest League Scorer in Season: Don Clark, 36, Division 3 (S), 1946–47.
Most League Goals in Total Aggregate: John Atyeo, 314, 1951–66.
Most Capped Player: Billy Wedlock, 26, England.

Most League Appearances: John Atyeo, 597, 1951–66.
Honours – Football League: Division 2 Champions – 1905–06. Division 3 (S) Champions – 1922–23, 1926–27, 1954–55. **Welsh Cup:** Winners – 1934. **Anglo-Scottish Cup:** Winners – 1977–78. **Freight Rover Trophy:** Winners – 1985–86. **LDV Vans Trophy:** Winners – 2002–03.
Colours: Red shirts, red shorts, red stockings.

BRISTOL ROVERS — FL CHAMPIONSHIP 2

Agogo Junior (F)	5 10	11 07	Accra	1 8 79	Barnet
Anderson John (D)	6 2	12 02	Greenock	2 10 72	Hull C
Bass Jon (D)	6 0	12 02	Weston-Super-Mare	1 1 76	Pahang
Campbell Stuart (M)	5 10	10 00	Corby	9 12 77	Grimsby T
Clarke Ryan (G)	6 3	13 00	Bristol	30 4 82	Trainee
Disley Craig (M)	5 10	10 13	Worksop	24 8 81	Mansfield T
Edwards Christian (D)	6 2	12 08	Caerphilly	23 11 75	Nottingham F
Elliott Steve (D)	6 1	14 00	Derby	29 10 78	Blackpool
Forrester Jamie (F)	5 7	11 00	Bradford	1 11 74	Hull C
Gibb Ali (M)	5 9	11 07	Salisbury	17 2 76	Stockport Co
Haldane Lewis (F)	6 0	11 03	Trowbridge	13 3 85	Scholar
Hinton Craig (D)	6 0	12 00	Wolverhampton	26 11 77	Kidderminster H
Hunt James (M)	5 8	10 03	Derby	17 12 76	Oxford U
Jeannin Alex (D)	6 0	11 06	Troyes	30 12 77	Exeter C
Lescott Aaron (M)	5 8	10 09	Birmingham	2 12 78	Stockport Co
Miller Kevin (G)	6 1	13 00	Falmouth	15 3 69	Exeter C
Parker Sonny (D)	5 11	11 11	Middlesbrough	28 2 83	Birmingham C
Ryan Robbie (D)	5 10	12 05	Dublin	16 5 77	Millwall
Savage David (M)	6 2	12 07	Dublin	30 7 73	Oxford U
Sinclair Scott (F)	5 10	10 00	Bath	26 3 89	
Trollope Paul (M)	6 0	12 06	Swindon	3 6 72	Northampton T
Walker Richard (F)	6 0	12 04	Sutton Coldfield	8 11 77	Oxford U
Williams Ryan (M)	5 5	11 04	Sutton-in-Ashfield	31 8 78	Hull C

League Appearances: Agogo, J. 37(6); Anderson, J. 28(6); Bass, J. 3; Burns, L. 3; Campbell, S. 21(4); Carruthers, C. 2(3); Cash, B. (1); Clarke, R. 18; Disley, C. 18(10); Edwards, C. 39(3); Elliott, S. 40(1); Forrester, J. 20(15); Gibb, A. 16(7); Haldane, L. 1(12); Hinton, C. 33(5); Hunt, J. 41; Jeannin, A. 1; Lescott, A. 24(2); Louis, J. 1; Miller, K. 28; Ryan, R. 39(1); Savage, D. 21(6); Shakes, R. (1); Sinclair, S. (2); Soares, L. (1); Thorpe, L. 17(8); Trollope, P. 26(4); Walker, R. 20(7); Ward, E. (3); Williams, R. 9(8).
Goals – League (60): Agogo 19 (2 pens), Walker 10 (1 pen), Forrester 7 (3 pens), Disley 4, Hunt 4, Thorpe 3, Williams 3, Edwards 2, Elliott 2, Trollope 2, Anderson J 1, Savage 1, own goals 2.
Carling Cup (2): Thorpe 1, Walker 1.
FA Cup (1): Walker 1.
LDV Vans Trophy (9): Agogo 2, Forrester 2, Walker 2, Disley 1, Haldane 1, Thorpe 1.
Ground: The Memorial Ground, Filton Avenue, Horfield, Bristol BS7 0BF. Telephone (0117) 9096648
Record Attendance: 9464 v Liverpool, FA Cup 4th rd, 8 February 1992 (Twerton Park). 38,472 v Preston NE, FA Cup 4th rd, 30 January 1960 (Eastville). 11,433 v Sunderland, League Cup 3rd rd, 31 October 2000 (Memorial Ground).
Capacity: 11,626.
Manager: Ian Atkins.
Secretary: Rod Wesson.
Most League Goals: 92, Division 3 (S), 1952–53.
Highest League Scorer in Season: Geoff Bradford, 33, Division 3 (S), 1952–53.

Most League Goals in Total Aggregate: Geoff Bradford, 242, 1949–64.
Most Capped Player: Vitalijs Astafjevs, 31 (105), Latvia.
Most League Appearances: Stuart Taylor, 546, 1966–80.
Honours – Football League: Division 3 (S) Champions – 1952–53. Division 3 Champions – 1989–90.
Colours: Blue and white quartered shirts, blue shorts, white stockings.

BURNLEY — FL CHAMPIONSHIP

Akinbiyi Ade (F)	6 1	13 08	Hackney	10 10 74	Stoke C
Branch Graham (M)	6 3	13 11	Liverpool	12 2 72	Stockport Co
Camara Mo (D)	5 11	11 03	Conakry	25 6 75	Wolverhampton W
Coyne Danny (G)	6 0	12 11	Prestatyn	27 8 83	Leicester C
Duff Michael (D)	6 3	12 10	Belfast	11 1 78	Cheltenham T
Grant Tony (M)	5 9	11 00	Liverpool	14 11 74	Manchester C
Hyde Micah (M)	5 11	12 03	Newham	10 11 74	Watford
Jensen Brian (G)	6 4	16 09	Copenhagen	8 6 75	WBA
McGreal John (D)	6 0	12 06	Birkenhead	2 6 72	Ipswich T
O'Connor James (M)	5 8	11 06	Dublin	1 9 79	WBA
O'Neill Matt (F)	5 10	10 11	Accrington	25 6 84	Scholar
Pilkington Joel (M)	5 7	11 00	Accrington	1 8 84	Scholar
Roche Lee (D)	5 11	12 00	Bolton	28 10 80	Manchester U
Sinclair Frank (D)	5 9	12 03	Lambeth	3 12 71	Leicester C

League Appearances: Akinbiyi, A. 9(1); Blake, R. 24; Bowditch, D. 8(2); Branch, G. 39(4); Cahill, G. 27; Camara, M. 45; Chaplow, R. 16(5); Coyne, D. 20; Duff, M. 37(5); Duffy, R. 3(4); Grant, T. 37(5); Hyde, M. 37(1); Jensen, B. 26(1); McGreal, J. 38(1); Moore, I. 30(5); O'Connor, J. 20(1); O'Neill, M. (2); Oster, J. 12(3); Pilkington, J. (1); Roche, L. 17(12); Sanokho, A. (3); Sinclair, F. 36; Valois, J. 18(12); Whittingham, P. 7.
Goals – League (38): Blake 10 (3 pens), Akinbiyi 4, Moore I 4, Branch 3, Valois 3 (1 pen), Chaplow 2, Grant 2, O'Connor 2, Bowditch 1, Cahill 1, Duffy 1, Hyde 1, McGreal 1, Oster 1, Roche 1, Sinclair 1.
Carling Cup (7): Blake 3 (1 pen), Branch 1, Camara 1, Valois 1, own goal 1.
FA Cup (4): Moore 2, Hyde 1, own goal 1.
Ground: Turf Moor, Burnley BB10 4BX. Telephone (0870) 4431882.
Record Attendance: 54,775 v Huddersfield T, FA Cup 3rd rd, 23 February 1924.
Capacity: 22,516.
Manager: Steve Cotterill.
Secretary: Cathy Pickup.
Most League Goals: 102, Division 1, 1960–61.
Highest League Scorer in Season: George Beel, 35, Division 1, 1927–28.
Most League Goals in Total Aggregate: George Beel, 178, 1923–32.
Most Capped Player: Jimmy McIlroy, 51 (55), Northern Ireland.
Most League Appearances: Jerry Dawson, 522, 1907–28.
Honours – Football League: Division 1 Champions – 1920–21, 1959–60. Division 2 Champions – 1897–98, 1972–73. Division 3 Champions – 1981–82. Division 4 Champions – 1991–92. **FA Cup:** Winners – 1913–14. **Anglo-Scottish Cup:** Winners – 1978–79.
Colours: Claret and blue shirts, white shorts, white stockings.

BURY — FL CHAMPIONSHIP 2

Barry-Murphy Brian (M)	6 1	13 01	Cork	27 7 78	Sheffield W
Buchanan David (M)	5 8	10 08	Rochdale	6 5 86	Scholar
Cartledge Jon (D)	6 2	13 00	Carshalton	27 11 84	Scholar

Challinor Dave (D)	6 1	12 06	Chester	2 10 75	Stockport Co
Dunfield Terry (M)	5 11	12 04	Vancouver	20 2 82	Manchester C
Flitcroft David (M)	5 11	14 05	Bolton	14 1 74	Macclesfield T
Kazim-Richards Colin (F)	6 1	10 10	Leyton	26 8 86	Scholar
Kennedy Tom (D)	5 10	11 01	Bury	24 6 85	Scholar
Mattis Dwayne (M)	6 1	11 12	Huddersfield	31 7 81	Huddersfield T
Newby Jon (F)	5 11	11 00	Warrington	28 11 78	Huddersfield T
Porter Chris (F)	6 1	12 08	Wigan	12 12 83	School
Scott Paul (D)	5 11	12 00	Wakefield	5 11 79	Huddersfield T
Unsworth Lee (D)	5 11	11 09	Eccles	25 2 73	Crewe Alex
Whaley Simon (F)	5 10	11 11	Bolton	7 6 85	Scholar

League Appearances: Barrass, M. 8(1); Barry-Murphy, B. 43(2); Boshell, D. 2(4); Buchanan, D. (3); Cartledge, J. 1(4); Challinor, D. 43; Dunfield, T. 7(8); Fitzgerald, J. 14; Flitcroft, D. 32(4); Garner, G. 27; Harkins, G. 4(1); Jones, G. 1(2); Kazim-Richards, C. 10(20); Kennedy, T. 46; Keogh, A. 4; Marriott, A. 19; Mattis, D. 39; Moore, D. (3); Newby, J. 17(19); Nugent, D. 26; Porter, C. 29(3); Savage, B. 5; Scott, P. 20(3); Shakes, R. 4(3); Swailes, D. 20; Unsworth, L. 34(2); Whaley, S. 22(16); Woodthorpe, C. 29(1).
Goals – League (54): Nugent 11, Porter 9, Barry-Murphy 6, Mattis 5, Newby 4, Flitcroft 3, Kazim-Richards 3, Whaley 3, Keogh 2, Shakes 2, Challinor 1, Dunfield 1, Jones 1, Kennedy 1 (pen), Swailes 1, Unsworth 1.
Carling Cup (2): Challinor 1, Mattis 1.
FA Cup (5): Mattis 2, Challinor 1, Nugent 1, Porter 1.
LDV Vans Trophy (1): Scott 1.
Ground: Gigg Lane, Bury BL9 9HR. Telephone (0161) 764 4881.
Record Attendance: 35,000 v Bolton W, FA Cup 3rd rd, 9 January 1960. **Capacity:** 11,669.
Manager: Graham Barrow.
Secretary: Jill Neville.
Most League Goals: 108, Division 3, 1960–61.
Highest League Scorer in Season: Craig Madden, 35, Division 4, 1981–82.
Most League Goals in Total Aggregate: Craig Madden, 129, 1978–86.
Most Capped Player: Bill Gorman, 11 (13), Republic of Ireland and (4), Northern Ireland.
Most League Appearances: Norman Bullock, 506, 1920–35.
Honours – Football League: Division 2 Champions – 1894–95, 1996–97. Division 3 Champions – 1960–61. **FA Cup:** Winners – 1900, 1903. **Auto Windscreens Shield:** Winners – 1997.
Colours: White shirts, royal blue shorts and stockings.

CAMBRIDGE UNITED — CONFERENCE

Angus Stevland (D)	6 0	12 00	Westminster	16 9 80	West Ham U
Bimson Stuart (D)	5 11	11 12	Liverpool	29 9 69	Lincoln C
Blackburn Lee (M)	5 8	10 07	Hornchurch	1 10 85	Norwich C
Chillingworth Daniel (F)	6 1	12 06	Cambridge	13 9 81	Scholar
Davies Adam (D)	6 2	13 05	Peterborough	27 3 87	Scholar
Duncan Andy (D)	5 11	13 00	Hexham	20 10 77	Manchester U
El Kholti Abdelhalim (M)	5 10	11 00	Annesse	17 10 80	Yeovil T
Fuller Ashley (M)	5 9	10 10	Bedford	14 11 86	Scholar
Gleeson Dan (M)	6 3	13 02	Cambridge	17 2 85	Scholar
Goodhind Warren (D)	5 11	11 02	Johannesburg	16 8 77	Barnet
Latte-Yedo Igor (D)	6 3	13 00	Dabou	14 12 78	Endourne
Marshall Shaun (G)	6 1	13 03	Fakenham	3 10 78	Trainee
Mbome Kingsley (M)	6 2	13 06	Yaounde	21 11 81	
Nicholls Ashley (M)	5 11	11 11	Ipswich	30 10 81	Darlington

Quinton Darren (M)	5 10	10 10	Romford	28 1 86	Scholar
Somner Matt (D)	6 0	13 00	Isleworth	8 12 82	Brentford
Tann Adam (D)	6 0	11 05	Fakenham	12 5 82	Scholar
Turner John (F)	5 10	11 00	Harrow	12 2 86	Scholar
Walker Justin (M)	5 11	12 04	Nottingham	6 9 75	Exeter C
Wardley Stuart (M)	5 11	13 00	Cambridge	10 9 75	Leyton Orient
Webb Daniel (F)	6 1	11 08	Poole	2 7 83	Hull C

League Appearances: Angus, S. 14; Anselin, C. 2; Beech, T. (4); Bimson, S. 16(3); Blackburn, L. (3); Bramble, T. 9; Carruthers, M. 5; Chillingworth, D. 22(6); Davies, A. (2); Duncan, A. 40(2); Easter, J. 15(9); El Kholti, A. 13(2); Fuller, A. (2); Gleeson, D. 21(9); Goodhind, W. 25(1); Guttridge, L. 14(3); Heath, C. 5(1); Hodgson, R. 9(1); Hutton, R. (2); Johnson, B. (1); Jowsey, J. 1; Konte, A. 6(3); Latte-Yedo, I. 5(6); Marshall, S. 1; Mbome, K. 12(1); Newey, T. 15(1); Nicholls, A. 25(3); Oli, D. 4; Price, L. 6; Quinton, D. 14(17); Rea, S. 4; Roberts, I. 11; Robinson, M. (4); Ruddy, J. 38; Somner, M. 24; Tann, A. 34(2); Toner, C. 6(2); Tudor, S. 22(4); Turner, J. 16(22); Walker, J. 36; Wardley, S. 1(2); Webb, D. 15(7).
Goals – League (39): Easter 6, Tudor 6, Turner 6, Chillingworth 4, Bramble 3 (1 pen), Konte 3, Roberts 3, Hodgson 2, Duncan 1, Mbome 1, Oli 1, Tann 1, Walker 1, Webb 1.
Carling Cup (0).
FA Cup (1): Tudor 1.
LDV Vans Trophy (1): Easter 1.
Ground: Abbey Stadium, Newmarket Road, Cambridge CB5 8LN. Telephone (01223) 566500. **Capacity:** 8696.
Record Attendance: 14,000 v Chelsea, Friendly, 1 May 1970.
Manager: Rob Newman.
Secretary: Andrew Pincher.
Most League Goals: 87, Division 4, 1976–77.
Highest League Scorer in Season: David Crown, 24, Division 4, 1985–86.
Most League Goals in Total Aggregate: John Taylor, 86, 1988–92; 1996–01.
Most Capped Player: Tom Finney, 7 (15), Northern Ireland.
Most League Appearances: Steve Spriggs, 416, 1975–87.
Honours – Football League: Division 3 Champions – 1990–91. Division 4 Champions – 1976–77.
Colours: Amber shirts, black shorts, amber stockings.

CARDIFF CITY — FL CHAMPIONSHIP

Alexander Neil (G)	6 1	12 08	Edinburgh	10 3 78	Livingston
Anthony Byron (D)	6 1	11 02	Newport	20 9 84	Scholar
Ardley Neal (M)	5 10	12 12	Epsom	1 9 72	Watford
Barker Chris (D)	6 2	13 08	Sheffield	2 3 80	Barnsley
Boland Willie (M)	5 9	12 01	Ennis	6 8 75	Coventry C
Bullock Lee (M)	6 0	13 01	Stockton	22 5 81	York C
Campbell Andy (F)	5 11	12 04	Middlesbrough	18 4 79	Middlesbrough
Collins James (D)	6 2	14 05	Newport	23 8 83	Scholar
Fish Nicky (M)	5 10	11 02	Cardiff	15 9 84	Scholar
Fleetwood Stuart (F)	5 10	12 07	Gloucester	23 4 86	Scholar
Gabbidon Daniel (D)	6 0	13 05	Cwmbran	8 8 79	WBA
Jerome Cameron (F)	6 1	13 06	Huddersfield	14 8 86	Trainee
Koskela Toni (M)	6 2	12 08	Finland	16 3 83	KTP
Langley Richard (M)	5 10	12 08	Harlesden	27 12 79	QPR
Ledley Joe (M)	6 0	11 07	Cardiff	23 1 87	Scholar
Lee Alan (F)	6 2	15 04	Galway	21 8 78	Rotherham U
Margetson Martyn (G)	6 0	14 00	West Neath	8 9 71	Huddersfield T
McAnuff Jobi (M)	5 11	10 12	Edmonton	9 11 81	West Ham U

Parry Paul (M)	5 11	12 12	Newport	19 8 80	Hereford U
Thorne Peter (F)	6 0	14 00	Manchester	21 6 73	Stoke C
Vidmar Tony (D)	6 1	13 00	Adelaide	15 4 69	Middlesbrough
Warner Tony (G)	6 4	15 06	Liverpool	11 5 74	Millwall
Weston Rhys (D)	6 1	12 12	Kingston	27 10 80	Arsenal
Williams Darren (D)	5 11	12 06	Middlesbrough	28 4 77	Sunderland

League Appearances: Alexander, N. 17; Ardley, N. 8; Barker, C. 38(1); Boland, W. 18(3); Boulding, M. (4); Bullock, L. 8(13); Campbell, A. 6(6); Collins, J. 32(2); Croft, G. (1); Earnshaw, R. 4; Fleetwood, S. 1(5); Gabbidon, D. 45; Harris, N. 1(2); Inamoto, J. 13(1); Jerome, C. 21(8); Kavanagh, G. 28; Koskela, T. (2); Langley, R. 24(1); Ledley, J. 20(8); Lee, A. 24(14); Margetson, M. 3(1); McAnuff, J. 42(1); O'Neil, G. 8(1); Page, R. 8(1); Parry, P. 12(12); Robinson, J. 8; Thomas, D. (1); Thorne, P. 28(3); Vidmar, T. 23(5); Warner, T. 26; Weston, R. 23(2); Williams, D. 17(3).
Goals – League (48): Thorne 12 (5 pens), Jerome 6, Lee 5 (1 pen), Parry 4, Bullock 3, Kavanagh 3, Ledley 3, Langley 2, McAnuff 2, Ardley 1, Collins 1, Earnshaw 1, Gabbidon 1, Harris 1, O'Neil 1, Robinson 1, Vidmar 1.
Carling Cup (8): Bullock 2, Thorne 2, Anthony 1, Earnshaw 1, Jerome 1, Lee 1.
FA Cup (3): Collins 1, Lee 1, McAnuff 1.
Ground: Ninian Park, Cardiff CF11 8SX. Telephone (029) 2022 1001.
Record Attendance: 61,566, Wales v England, 14 October 1961. **Capacity:** 21,432.
Manager: Dave Jones.
Secretary: Jason Turner.
Most League Goals: 95, Division 3, 2000–01.
Highest League Scorer in Season: Robert Earnshaw, 31, Division 2, 2002–03.
Most League Goals in Total Aggregate: Len Davies, 128, 1920–31.
Most Capped Player: Alf Sherwood, 39 (41), Wales.
Most League Appearances: Phil Dwyer, 471, 1972–85.
Honours – Football League: Division 3 (S) Champions – 1946–47. **FA Cup:** Winners – 1926–27 (only occasion the Cup has been won by a club outside England). **Welsh Cup:** Winners – 22 times.
Colours: All royal blue.

CARLISLE UNITED — FL CHAMPIONSHIP 2

Andrews Lee (D)	5 11	11 00	Carlisle	23 4 83	Scholar
Arnison Paul (D)	5 10	10 12	Hartlepool	18 9 77	Hartlepool U
Beech Chris (D)	5 10	11 12	Congleton	5 11 75	Doncaster R
Beharall David (D)	6 0	11 06	Newcastle	8 3 79	Oldham Ath
Billy Chris (M)	5 11	11 08	Huddersfield	2 1 73	Bury
Cowan Tom (D)	5 8	11 08	Bellshill	28 8 69	York C
Farrell Craig (F)	6 0	12 06	Middlesbrough	5 12 82	Leeds U
Glennon Matt (G)	6 2	13 11	Stockport	8 10 78	Hull C
Grand Simon (D)	6 0	10 03	Chorley	23 2 84	Rochdale
Gray Kevin (D)	6 0	14 00	Sheffield	7 1 72	Tranmere R
Hackney Simon (M)			Manchester	5 2 84	Woodley Sports
Hawley Karl (F)	5 8	12 02	Walsall	6 12 81	Walsall
Henderson Kevin (F)	5 11	13 02	Ashington	8 6 74	Hartlepool U
Holmes Derek (F)	6 2	13 00	Lanark	18 10 78	Bournemouth
Livesey Danny (D)	6 3	12 10	Salford	31 12 84	Bolton W
Lumsdon Chris (M)	5 11	10 06	Newcastle	15 12 79	Barnsley
McGill Brendan (M)	5 8	9 02	Dublin	22 3 81	Sunderland
Murphy Peter (M)	5 10	12 10	Dublin	27 10 80	Blackburn R
Murray Adam (M)	5 8	10 12	Solihull	30 9 81	Mansfield T
Murray Glen (F)			Maryport	25 9 83	
Roca Carlos (F)	5 4	10 07	Manchester	4 9 84	Oldham Ath

Shelley Brian (D)	6 0	13 00	Dublin	15 11 81	Bohemians
Simpson Paul (M)	5 8	11 11	Carlisle	26 7 66	Rochdale
Westwood Keiren (G)			Manchester	23 10 84	

League Appearances: Andrews, 12(2); Arnison, 15(10); Beech, 2; Beharall, 13(1); Billy, 37(1); Cowan, 29; Farrell, 3(15); Glennon, 38; Grand, 23; Gray, 30; Hackney, 0(2); Hawley, 36(4); Henderson, 2(11); Holmes, 13; Livesey, 20; Lumsdon, 38; McGill, 26(2); Murphy, 38; Murray, A. 8; Murray, G. 5(15); Preece, 10(5); Roca, 4(7); Shelley, 20(1); Simpson, 0(2); Tierney, 10; Vieira, 26(10); Westwood, 4.
Goals – League (74): Hawley 13, Vieira 10, Lumsdon 9 (3 pens), Murphy 7, Preece 7 (1 pen), Holmes 5, McGill 4, Billy 2, Cowan 2, Farrell 2, Grand 2, Gray 2, Henderson 2, Livesey 2, Murray G 2, Beharall 1, Murray A 1, own goal 1.
FA Cup (6): Farrell 1, Gray 1, Hawley 1, McGill 1, Preece 1, Viera 1.
LDV Vans Trophy (2): Grand 1, Henderson 1.
FA Trophy (7): Farrell 2, Viera 2, Hawley 1, Livesey 1, Preece 1.
Play-Offs (3): Billy 1, Livesey 1, Murphy 1.
Ground: Brunton Park, Warwick Road, Carlisle CA1 1LL. telephone (01228) 526 237
Record Attendance: 27,500 v Birmingham C, FA Cup 3rd rd, 5 January 1957 and v Middlesbrough, FA Cup 5th rd, 7 February 1970. **Capacity:** 16,063
Manager: Paul Simpson.
Secretary: Sarah McKnight.
Most League Goals: 113, Division 4, 1963–64.
Highest League Scorer in Season: Jimmy McConnell, 42, Division 3 (N), 1928–29.
Most League Goals in Total Aggregate: Jimmy McConnell, 126, 1928–32.
Most Capped Player: Eric Welsh, 4, Northern Ireland.
Most League Appearances: Allan Ross, 466, 1963–79.
Honours – Football League: Division 3 Champions – 1964–65, 1994–95.
Colours: Blue shirts, white shorts, blue stockings.

CHARLTON ATHLETIC — FA PREMIERSHIP

Andersen Stephan (G)	6 2	13 07	Copenhagen	26 11 81	AB Copenhagen
Bartlett Shaun (F)	6 0	12 06	Cape Town	31 10 72	Zurich
El Karkouri Talal (D)	6 1	12 03	Casablanca	8 7 76	Sunderland
Elliot Rob (G)	6 3	14 10	Chatham	30 4 86	Scholar
Euell Jason (F)	5 11	11 13	Lambeth	6 2 77	Wimbledon
Fish Mark (D)	6 4	12 11	Cape Town	14 3 74	Bolton W
Fortune Jon (D)	6 2	12 12	Islington	23 8 80	Trainee
Holland Matt (M)	5 10	12 03	Bury	11 4 74	Ipswich T
Hreidarsson Hermann (D)	6 3	12 12	Reykjavik	11 7 74	Ipswich T
Hughes Bryan (M)	5 10	11 08	Liverpool	19 6 76	Birmingham C
Jeffers Francis (F)	5 10	11 02	Liverpool	25 1 81	Arsenal
Johansson Jonatan (F)	6 2	12 08	Stockholm	16 8 75	Rangers
Kiely Dean (G)	6 1	13 10	Salford	10 10 70	Bury
Kishishev Radostin (D)	5 11	12 03	Bourgas	30 7 74	Litets Lovech
Konchesky Paul (D)	5 10	11 07	Barking	15 5 81	Trainee
Lisbie Kevin (F)	5 10	11 06	Hackney	17 10 78	Trainee
Murphy Danny (M)	5 10	11 09	Chester	18 3 77	Liverpool
Perry Chris (D)	5 8	11 03	Carshalton	26 4 73	Tottenham H
Rommedahl Dennis (F)	5 9	11 08	Copenhagen	22 7 78	PSV Eindhoven
Sam Lloyd (F)	5 8	10 00	Leeds	27 9 84	
Sankofa Osei (D)	6 0	12 04	London	19 3 85	Scholar
Thomas Jerome (M)	5 9	11 09	Brent	23 3 83	Arsenal
Varney Alex (F)			Farnborough	27 12 84	Trainee
Young Luke (D)	6 0	12 04	Harlow	19 7 79	Tottenham H

League Appearances: Andersen, S. 2; Bartlett, S. 25; El Karkouri, T. 28(4); Euell, J. 7(19); Fish, M. 6(1); Fortune, J. 28(3); Holland, M. 31(1); Hreidarsson, H. 33(1); Hughes, B. 10(7); Jeffers, F. 9(11); Johansson, J. 15(11); Kiely, D. 36; Kishishev, R. 27(4); Konchesky, P. 15(13); Lisbie, K. 12(5); Murphy, D. 37(1); Perry, C. 17(2); Rommedahl, D. 19(7); Sam, L. (1); Stuart, G. 4; Thomas, J. 21(3); Young, L. 36.
Goals – League (42): Bartlett 6, El Karkouri 5, Johansson 4, Holland 3, Jeffers 3, Murphy 3, Thomas 3, Euell 2, Fortune 2, Rommedahl 2, Young 2, Hreidarsson 1, Hughes B 1, Konchesky 1, Lisbie 1, Perry 1, own goals 2.
Carling Cup (3): Hreidarsson 1, Jeffers 1, Murphy 1.
FA Cup (8): Hughes 3, Bartlett 2, Fortune 1, Jeffers 1, Murphy 1.
Ground: The Valley, Floyd Road, Charlton, London SE7 8BL. Telephone (020) 8333 4000.
Record Attendance: 75,031 v Aston Villa, FA Cup 5th rd, 12 February 1938 (at The Valley). **Capacity:** 27,111.
Manager: Alan Curbishley.
Secretary: Chris Parkes.
Most League Goals: 107, Division 2, 1957–58.
Highest League Scorer in Season: Ralph Allen, 32, Division 3 (S), 1934–35.
Most League Goals in Total Aggregate: Stuart Leary, 153, 1953–62.
Most Capped Player: Mark Kinsella, 33 (48), Republic of Ireland.
Most League Appearances: Sam Bartram, 583, 1934–56.
Honours – Football League: Division 1 Champions – 1999–2000. Division 3 (S) Champions – 1928–29, 1934–35. **FA Cup:** Winners – 1947.
Colours: Red shirts, white shorts, red stockings.

CHELSEA — FA PREMIERSHIP

Name	Ht	Wt	Birthplace	Birthdate	Source
Bridge Wayne (D)	5 10	12 13	Southampton	5 8 80	Southampton
Cech Petr (G)	6 5	14 03	Plzen	20 5 82	Rennes
Cole Carlton (F)	6 3	13 10	Croydon	12 10 83	Scholar
Cole Joe (M)	5 9	11 07	Islington	8 11 81	West Ham U
Crespo Hernan (F)	6 0	12 13	Florida	5 7 75	Internazionale
Cudicini Carlo (G)	6 1	12 06	Milan	6 9 73	Castel di Sangro
Drogba Didier (F)	6 2	13 08	Abidjan	11 3 78	Marseille
Duff Damien (M)	5 9	12 03	Ballyboden	2 3 79	Blackburn R
Forssell Mikael (F)	6 0	13 08	Steinfurt	15 3 81	HJK Helsinki
Gallas William (D)	6 0	11 13	Asnieres	17 8 77	Marseille
Geremi (M)	5 10	13 05	Bafoussam	20 12 78	Middlesbrough
Grant Anthony (M)			Lambeth	4 6 87	Scholar
Gudjohnsen Eidur (F)	6 1	14 02	Reykjavik	15 9 78	Bolton W
Huth Robert (D)	6 3	14 01	Berlin	18 8 84	Scholar
Jarosik Jiri (M)	6 4	13 03	Usti Nad Lebem	27 10 77	CSKA Moscow
Johnson Glen (D)	6 0	12 13	Greenwich	23 8 84	West Ham U
Kezman Mateja (F)	5 11	11 09	Zemun	12 4 79	PSV Eindhoven
Lampard Frank (M)	6 0	14 01	Romford	20 6 78	West Ham U
Makelele Claude (M)	5 7	10 08	Kinshasa	18 2 73	Real Madrid
Nuno Morais (D)	6 0	12 05	Penafiel	29 1 84	Penafiel
Oliveira Filipe (F)	5 11	11 05	Braga	27 5 84	Porto
Paulo Ferreira (D)	6 0	11 13	Cascais	18 1 79	Porto
Pidgeley Lenny (G)	6 4	14 07	Isleworth	7 2 84	Scholar
Ricardo Carvalho (D)	6 0	12 06	Amarante	18 5 78	Porto
Robben Arjen (M)	5 11	12 08	Groningen	23 1 84	PSV Eindhoven
Smertin Alexei (M)	5 9	10 10	Barnaul	1 5 75	Bordeaux
Terry John (D)	6 1	13 08	Barking	7 12 80	Trainee
Tiago (M)	6 0	11 07	Viana do Costelo	2 5 81	Benfica
Veron Juan Sebastian (F)	5 11	12 04	La Plata	9 3 75	Manchester U
Watt Steven (D)	6 3	13 12	Aberdeen	1 5 85	Trainee

League Appearances: Babayaro, C. 3(1); Bridge, W. 12(3); Cech, P. 35; Cole, J. 19(9); Cudicini, C. 3; Drogba, D. 18(8); Duff, D. 28(2); Forssell, M. (1); Gallas, W. 28; Geremi, 6(7); Grant, A. (1); Gudjohnsen, E. 30(7); Huth, R. 6(4); Jarosik, J. 3(11); Johnson, G. 13(4); Kezman, M. 6(19); Lampard, F. 38; Makelele, C. 36; Mutu, A. (2); Nuno Morais, (2); Oliveira, F. (1); Parker, S. 1(3); Paulo Ferreira, 29; Pidgeley, L. (1); Ricardo Carvalho, 22(3); Robben, A. 14(4); Smertin, A. 11(5); Terry, J. 36; Tiago, 21(13); Watt, S. (1).
Goals – League (72): Lampard 13 (3 pens), Gudjohnsen 12 (1 pen), Drogba 10, Cole 8, Robben 7, Duff 6, Kezman 4 (1 pen), Tiago 4, Terry 3, Gallas 2, Makelele 1, Ricardo Carvalho 1, own goal 1.
Carling Cup (10): Duff 2, Kezman 2, Lampard 2, Drogba 1, Gudjohnsen 1, Robben 1, own goal 1.
FA Cup (5): Gudjohnsen 1, Huth 1, Kezman 1, Terry 1, own goal 1.
Champions League (21): Drogba 5, Lampard 4, Terry 4, Duff 2, Gudjohnsen 2, Robben 1, Smertin 1, own goals 2.
Ground: Stamford Bridge, London SW6 1HS. Telephone (0870) 300 1212.
Record Attendance: 82,905 v Arsenal, Division 1, 12 October 1935.
Capacity: 42,522.
Manager: Jose Mourinho.
Secretary: David Barnard.
Most League Goals: 98, Division 1, 1960–61.
Highest League Scorer in Season: Jimmy Greaves, 41, 1960–61.
Most League Goals in Total Aggregate: Bobby Tambling, 164, 1958–70.
Most Capped Player: Marcel Desailly, 67 (116), France.
Most League Appearances: Ron Harris, 655, 1962–80.
Honours – FA Premier League: Champions – 2004–05. **Football League:** Division 1 Champions – 1954–55. **FA Cup:** Winners – 1970, 1997, 2000. **Football League Cup:** Winners – 1964–65, 1997–98, 2004–05. **Full Members' Cup:** Winners – 1985–86. **Zenith Data Systems Cup:** Winners – 1989–90. **European Cup-Winners' Cup:** Winners – 1970–71, 1997–98. **Super Cup:** Winners – 1999.
Colours: Royal blue shirts and shorts, white stockings.

CHELTENHAM TOWN — FL CHAMPIONSHIP 2

Bird David (M)	5 9	12 00	Gloucester	26 12 84	Cinderford T
Corbett Luke (F)	6 0	11 06	Worcester	10 8 84	Juniors
Devaney Martin (F)	5 11	12 00	Cheltenham	1 6 80	Coventry C
Melligan John (M)	5 9	11 02	Dublin	11 2 82	Wolverhampton W
Duff Shane (D)	6 1	12 10	Wroughton	2 4 82	Juniors
Finnigan John (M)	5 8	10 09	Wakefield	29 3 76	Lincoln C
Fyfe Graham (M)	5 6	10 06	Dundee	7 12 82	Raith R
Higgs Shane (G)	6 3	14 06	Oxford	13 5 77	Bristol R
McCann Grant (M)	5 10	11 00	Belfast	14 4 80	West Ham U
Odejayi Kayode (F)	6 2	12 02	Ibadon	21 2 82	Bristol C
Spencer Damien (F)	6 1	14 00	Ascot	19 9 81	Bristol C
Victory Jamie (D)	5 10	12 13	Hackney	14 11 75	Bournemouth
Wilson Brian (D)	5 10	11 00	Manchester	9 5 83	Stoke C
Gill Jeremy (D)	5 11	12 00	Clevedon	8 9 70	Northampton T
Vincent Ashley (F)	5 10	11 08	Oldbury	26 5 85	Wolverhampton W
Guinan Stephen (F)	6 1	13 02	Birmingham	24 12 75	Shrewsbury T
Taylor Michael (D)	6 1	13 08	Liverpool	21 11 82	Blackburn R
Caines Gavin (D)	6 1	12 00	Birmingham	20 9 83	Scholar
Murphy Chris (M)	5 5	9 06	Leamington Spa	8 3 83	Shrewsbury T
Connolly Adam (M)	5 9	12 04	Manchester	10 4 86	Scholar
Townsend Michael (D)	6 1	13 12	Walsall	17 5 86	Wolverhampton W

League Appearances: Bird, D. 26(8); Brough, J. 11(2); Caines, G. 27(2); Connolly, A. 1(3); Devaney, M. 37(1); Duff, S. 45; Finnigan, J. 31(1); Fyfe, G. 1(2); Gill, J. 43(1); Gillespie, S. 10(2); Guinan, S. 35(8); Higgs, S. 46; McCann, G. 39; Melligan, J. 23(6); Morgan, A. 8; Murphy, C. (4); Odejayi, K. 10(22); Spencer, D. 14(27); Taylor, M. 10(3); Victory, J. 40(2); Vincent, A. 14(12); Ward, G. (2); Wilson, B. 35(8).
Goals – League (51): Devaney 10 (2 pens), Spencer 8, Guinan 6, Gillespie 5 (2 pens), McCann 4 (2 pens), Finnigan 3, Victory 3, Wilson 3, Caines 2, Melligan 2, Duff 1, Odejayi 1, Vincent 1, own goals 2.
Carling Cup (1): Devaney 1.
FA Cup (1): Spencer 1.
LDV Vans Trophy (7): Vincent 2, Brough 1, Finnigan 1, Guinan 1, McCann 1 (pen), Spencer 1.
Ground: Whaddon Road, Cheltenham, Gloucester GL52 5NA. Telephone (01242) 573558.
Record Attendance: at Whaddon Road: 8326 v Reading, FA Cup 1st rd, 17 November 1956; at Cheltenham Athletic Ground: 10,389 v Blackpool, FA Cup 3rd rd, 13 January 1934.
Capacity: 7289.
Manager: John Ward.
Secretary: Paul Godfrey.
Most League Goals: 115, Southern League, 1957–58.
Highest League Scorer in Season: Julian Alsop, 20, Division 3, 2001–02.
Most League Goals in Total Aggregate: Martin Devaney, 38, 1999–2005.
Most League Appearances: Jamie Victory, 226, 1999–.
Most Capped Player: Grant McCann, 4 (9), Northern Ireland.
Honours – Football Conference: Champions – 1998–99. **FA Trophy:** Winners – 1997–98.
Colours: Red and white striped shirts, black shorts, black stockings.

CHESTER CITY — FL CHAMPIONSHIP 2

Belle Cortez (F)	6 4	14 08	Newport	27 8 83	Merthyr T
Bolland Phil (D)	6 4	12 13	Liverpool	26 8 76	Oxford U
Booth Robbie (M)	5 7	11 08	Liverpool	30 12 85	
Branch Michael (F)	5 10	12 00	Liverpool	18 10 78	Bradford C
Brown Wayne (G)	6 0	13 11	Southampton	14 1 77	Weston S Mare
Carden Paul(M)	5 8	12 03	Liverpool	29 3 79	Doncaster R
Davies Ben (M)	5 7	11 09	Birmingham	27 5 81	Kidderminster H
Drummond Stuart (M)	6 2	13 00	Preston	11 12 75	Morecambe
Edmondson Darren (D)	6 0	12 12	Ulverston	4 11 71	York C
Harris Andy (D)	5 10	12 05	Springs (S Africa)	26 2 77	Leyton Orient
Hessey Sean (D)	6 1	12 09	Liverpool	19 9 78	Blackpool
Hope Richard (D)	6 3	13 13	Middlesbrough	22 6 78	York C
Lowe Ryan (M)	5 11	11 03	Liverpool	18 9 78	Shrewsbury T
Lynch Gavin (F)	5 8	10 10	Chester	7 9 85	
MacKenzie Chris (G)	6 0	13 05	Northampton	14 5 72	Leyton Orient
Rapley Kevin (F)	5 10	12 07	Reading	21 9 77	Colchester U
Regan Carl (D)	6 0	11 03	Liverpool	14 1 80	Hull C
Vaughan Stephen (D)	5 6	11 01	Liverpool	22 1 85	Liverpool
Walsh Mike (M)	5 9	10 05	Liverpool	30 5 86	
Whalley Shaun (F)	5 9	10 07	Prescot	7 8 87	

League Appearances: Atieno, T. 3(1); Bayliss, D. 9; Belle, C. 17(5); Bolland, P. 42; Booth, R. 7(4); Branch, M. 31(2); Brown, M. 11(7); Brown, W. 23; Carden, P. 36(4); Clare, D. 3(4); Collins, D. 12; Davies, B. 38(6); Drummond, S. 44(1); Edmondson, D. 26(1); Ellison, K. 24; Elokobi, G. 4(1); Foy, R. 13; Harris, A. 9(10); Hessey, S. 31(3); Hillier, I. 7(1); Hope, R. 26(2); Lowe, R. 8; Lynch, G. (1);

MacKenzie, C. 23(1); McIntyre, K. 9(1); Navarro, A. 3; Nicholas, A. 5; O'Neill, J. 5(6); Rapley, K. 12(9); Regan, C. 4(2); Sestanovich, A. 3(4); Stamp, D. 2(2); Vaughan, S. 14(7); Walsh, M. 2(3); Whalley, S. (3).
Goals – League (43): Branch 11 (3 pens), Ellison 9, Drummond 6, Lowe 4, Davies 2, Rapley 2, Atieno 1, Belle 1, Bolland 1, Booth 1, Clare 1 (pen), Collins 1, Hessey 1, O'Neill 1, Walsh 1.
Carling Cup (0).
FA Cup (6): Branch 2 (1 pen), Rapley 2, Belle 1, Ellison 1.
LDV Vans Trophy (3): Ellison 1, Hessey 1, Hope 1.
Ground: Deva Stadium, Bumpers Lane, Chester CH1 4LT. Telephone (01244) 371376
Record Attendance: 20,500 v Chelsea, FA Cup 3rd rd (replay), 16 January 1952 (at Sealand Rd)
Capacity: 6000.
Manager: Keith Curle.
Secretary: Tony Allan.
Most League Goals: 119, Division 4, 1964–65.
Highest League Scorer in Season: Dick Yates, 36, Division 3 (N), 1946–47.
Most League Goals in Total Aggregate: Stuart Rimmer, 135, 1985–88, 1991–98.
Most Capped Player: Trevor Eve, 35, Trinidad & Tobago.
Most League Appearances: Ray Gill, 406, 1951–62.
Honours – Conference: Champions – 2003–04. **Welsh Cup:** Winners – 1908, 1933, 1947.
Colours: Blue and white striped shirts, blue shorts, blue stockings.

CHESTERFIELD — FL CHAMPIONSHIP 1

Allison Wayne (F)	6 0	15 00	Huddersfield	16 10 68	Sheffield U
Allott Mark (M)	6 0	11 10	Manchester	3 10 77	Oldham Ath
Bailey Alex (D)	5 9	11 03	Newham	21 9 83	Arsenal
Blatherwick Steve (D)	6 2	14 06	Nottingham	20 9 73	Burnley
Davies Gareth (M)	6 0	12 00	Chesterfield	4 2 83	Trainee
Dawson Kevin (D)	5 11	13 10	Northallerton	18 6 81	Nottingham F
De Bolla Mark (F)	5 7	12 00	Greenwich	1 1 83	Charlton Ath
Downes Aaron (D)	6 3	13 00	Mudgee	15 5 85	Frickley C
Evatt Ian (D)	6 3	14 00	Coventry	19 11 81	Derby Co
Folan Caleb (F)	6 2	14 00	Leeds	26 10 82	Leeds U
Fox Michael (M)	5 11	11 00	Mansfield	7 9 85	Scholar
Hudson Mark (M)	5 11	12 00	Bishop Auckland	24 10 80	Middlesbrough
McMaster Jamie (M)	5 11	12 00	Sydney	29 11 82	Leeds U
Muggleton Carl (G)	6 2	14 12	Leicester	13 9 68	Cheltenham T
N'Toya Tcham (F)	5 11	12 11	Kinshasa	3 11 83	Troyes
Nicholson Shane (D)	5 11	12 06	Newark	3 6 70	Tranmere R
Niven Derek (M)	6 0	12 02	Falkirk	12 12 83	Bolton W
O'Hare Alan (D)	6 2	12 08	Drogheda	31 7 82	Bolton W
Smith Adam (M)	5 11	12 00	Huddersfield	20 2 85	Scholar
Thompson Glyn (G)	6 2	13 01	Telford	24 2 81	Walsall

League Appearances: Allison, W. 27(11); Allott, M. 45; Bailey, A. 45; Blatherwick, S. 33(2); Campbell-Ryce, J. 14; Clingan, S. 15; Davies, G. 9(10); Dawson, K. 1; De Bolla, M. 15(13); Downes, A. 7(2); Evatt, I. 41; Folan, C. 17(15); Fowler, J. 4(2); Fox, M. (1); Fulop, M. 7; Hudson, M. 32(2); Innes, M. 18(3); Logan, C. 6(3); McMaster, J. 6(2); Muggleton, C. 37; N'Toya, T. 18(20); Nicholson, S. 42(1); Niven, D. 38; O'Hare, A. 14(7); Richmond, A. 1; Smith, A. 6(10); Stallard, M. 7(2); Thompson, G. 1.

Goals – League (55): N'Toya 8, Nicholson 7 (6 pens), Allison 6, Folan 6, Blatherwick 4, Evatt 4, Hudson 4, De Bolla 3, Allott 2, Clingan 2, Downes 2, Stallard 2, Bailey 1, Davies 1, Logan 1, Niven 1, own goal 1.
Carling Cup (1): Allott 1.
FA Cup (0).
LDV Vans Trophy (1): Campbell-Ryce 1.
Ground: Recreation Ground, Chesterfield S40 4SX. Telephone (01246) 209765.
Record Attendance: 30,968 v Newcastle U, Division 2, 7 April 1939. **Capacity:** 8502.
Manager: Roy McFarland.
Secretary: Alan Walters.
Most League Goals: 102, Division 3 (N), 1930–31.
Highest League Scorer in Season: Jimmy Cookson, 44, Division 3 (N), 1925–26.
Most League Goals in Total Aggregate: Ernie Moss, 161, 1969–76, 1979–81 and 1984–86.
Most Capped Player: Walter McMillen, 4 (7), Northern Ireland; Mark Williams, 4 (30), Northern Ireland.
Most League Appearances: Dave Blakey, 613, 1948–67.
Honours – Football League: Division 3 (N) Champions – 1930–31, 1935–36. Division 4 Champions – 1969–70, 1984–85. **Anglo-Scottish Cup:** Winners – 1980–81.
Colours: Blue shirts, white shorts, blue stockings.

COLCHESTER UNITED — FL CHAMPIONSHIP 1

Baldwin Pat (D)	6 3	12 07	City of London	12 11 82	Chelsea
Brown Wayne (D)	6 0	12 06	Barking	20 8 77	Watford
Cade Jamie (F)	5 8	10 10	Durham	15 1 84	Middlesbrough
Chilvers Liam (D)	6 2	12 03	Chelmsford	6 11 81	Arsenal
Danns Neil (M)	5 8	10 12	Liverpool	23 11 82	Blackburn R
Davison Aidan (G)	6 1	13 12	Sedgefield	11 5 68	Grimsby T
Duguid Karl (M)	5 11	11 06	Hitchin	21 3 78	Trainee
Garcia Richard (F)	5 11	12 01	Perth	4 9 81	West Ham U
Gerken Dean (G)	6 1	12 08	Rochford	22 5 85	Scholar
Guy Jamie (M)	6 1	13 00	Barking	1 8 87	Scholar
Halford Greg (D)	6 4	12 10	Chelmsford	8 12 84	Scholar
Hunt Stephen (D)	6 1	13 00	Southampton	11 11 84	Southampton
Izzet Kem (M)	5 7	10 05	Mile End	29 9 80	Charlton Ath
Johnson Gavin (M)	5 11	11 12	Stowmarket	10 10 70	Dunfermline Ath
Keith Joe (M)	5 7	10 06	Plaistow	1 10 78	West Ham U
Keith Marino (F)	5 10	12 13	Peterhead	16 12 74	Plymouth Arg
N'Dumbu Nsungu Guylain (F)	6 1	12 08	Kinshasa	26 12 82	Sheffield W
Stockley Sam (D)	6 0	12 08	Tiverton	5 9 77	Oxford U
Watson Kevin (M)	6 0	12 06	Hackney	3 1 74	Reading
White John (M)	5 10	12 01	Maldon	26 7 86	Scholar
Williams Gareth (F)	5 10	11 13	Germiston	10 9 82	Crystal Palace

League Appearances: Andrews, W. 4(1); Baldwin, P. 35(3); Bowditch, B. (5); Bowry, B. 7(4); Brown, W. 38(2); Cade, J. 4(5); Chilvers, L. 40(1); Danns, N. 32; Davison, A. 33; Fagan, C. 25(1); Garcia, R. 20(4); Gerken, D. 13; Goodfellow, M. 4(1); Guy, J. (2); Halford, G. 43(1); Hunt, S. 16(4); Izzet, K. 3(1); Jarvis, R. 2(4); Johnson, G. 36(1); Keith, J. 27(4); Keith, M. 12; May, B. 5(9); N'Dumbu Nsungu, G. 2(6); Stockley, S. 33(4); Watson, K. 44; White, J. 16(4); Williams, G. 12(17).
Goals – League (60): Danns 11 (1 pen), Johnson 9, Fagan 8 (1 pen), Garcia 4, Halford 4, Keith J 4, Keith M 4 (1 pen), Williams 3, Andrews 2 (1 pen), Watson 2, Brown W 1, Chilvers 1, Goodfellow 1, Hunt 1, May 1, N'Dumbu Nsungu 1, Stockley 1, own goals 2.

Carling Cup (6): Fagan 2, Danns 1, Halford 1, Johnson 1, May 1.
FA Cup (12): Fagan 4 (1 pen), Halford 4, Williams 2 (1 pen), Garcia 1, own goal 1.
LDV Vans Trophy (1): Garcia 1.
Ground: Layer Road Ground, Colchester CO2 7JJ. Telephone (0871) 226 2161.
Record Attendance: 19,072 v Reading, FA Cup 1st rd, 27 Nov, 1948. **Capacity:** 6143.
Manager: Phil Parkinson.
Secretary: Caroline Pugh.
Most League Goals: 104, Division 4, 1961–62.
Highest League Scorer in Season: Bobby Hunt, 38, Division 4, 1961–62.
Most League Goals in Total Aggregate: Martyn King, 130, 1956–64.
Most Capped Player: None.
Most League Appearances: Micky Cook, 613, 1969–84.
Honours – GM Vauxhall Conference: Winners – 1991–92. **FA Trophy:** Winners: 1991–92.
Colours: Blue and white striped shirts, white shorts, white stockings.

COVENTRY CITY — FL CHAMPIONSHIP

Adebola Dele (F)	6 3	15 00	Lagos	23 6 75	Crystal Palace
Barrett Graham (F)	5 10	11 07	Dublin	6 10 81	Arsenal
Benjamin Trevor (F)	6 2	14 08	Kettering	8 2 79	Leicester C
Brush Richard (G)	6 1	12 00	Birmingham	26 11 84	Scholar
Doyle Micky (M)	5 8	11 00	Dublin	8 7 81	Celtic
Giddings Stuart (M)	6 0	11 08	Coventry	27 3 86	Scholar
Hall Marcus (D)	6 1	12 02	Coventry	24 3 76	Stoke C
Hughes Stephen (M)	5 9	12 12	Wokingham	18 9 76	Charlton Ath
John Stern (F)	6 0	12 11	Trinidad	30 10 76	Birmingham C
Jorgensen Claus (M)	5 11	11 00	Holstebro	27 4 76	Bradford C
McSheffrey Gary (F)	5 8	10 06	Coventry	13 8 82	Trainee
Morrell Andy (F)	5 11	11 06	Doncaster	28 9 74	Wrexham
Osbourne Isaac (M)	5 9	11 11	Birmingham	22 6 86	Scholar
Page Robert (D)	6 0	13 10	Llwynpia	3 9 74	Cardiff C
Reid Craig (F)	5 10	11 10	Coventry	17 12 85	Ipswich T
Shaw Richard (D)	5 9	12 08	Brentford	11 9 68	Crystal Palace
Shearer Scott (G)	6 3	14 08	Glasgow	15 2 81	Albion R
Staunton Steve (D)	6 0	12 12	Dundalk	19 1 69	Aston Villa
Suffo Patrick (F)	5 9	13 05	Ebolowa	17 1 78	Sheffield U
Whing Andrew (D)	6 0	12 00	Birmingham	20 9 84	Scholar
Williams Adrian (D)	6 2	13 02	Reading	16 8 71	Reading
Wood Neil (M)	5 10	13 02	Manchester	4 1 83	Trainee

League Appearances: Adebola, D. 18(7); Barrett, G. 12(12); Benjamin, T. 6(6); Bennett, I. 6; Carey, L. 23; Davenport, C. 6; Deloumeaux, E. 1(1); Doyle, M. 43(1); Duffy, R. 14; Dyer, L. 6; Giddings, S. 11(1); Goater, S. 4(2); Gudjonsson, B. 3(7); Hall, M. 10; Hughes, S. 39(1); John, S. 25(5); Johnson, E. 20(6); Jorgensen, C. 11(6); Laville, F. 5(1); Leacock, D. 12(1); McSheffrey, G. 31(6); Mills, M. 4; Morrell, A. 24(10); Negouai, C. 1; Osbourne, I. 7(2); Page, R. 9; Ricketts, R. 5(1); Shaw, R. 30(3); Shearer, S. 8; Sherwood, T. 10(1); Staunton, S. 32(3); Steele, L. 32; Suffo, P. 2(19); Whing, A. 9(7); Williams, A. 21; Wood, N. 6(7).
Goals – League (61): McSheffrey 12 (6 pens), John 11 (2 pens), Morrell 6, Adebola 5, Johnson 5, Barrett 4, Hughes 4, Jorgensen 3, Suffo 3 (2 pens), Doyle 2, Williams 2, Benjamin 1, Staunton 1, Whing 1, own goal 1.
Carling Cup (5): Suffo 2, Doyle 1, Hughes 1, Morrell 1.
FA Cup (4): McSheffrey 2, Adebola 1, John 1.
Ground: Ricoh Arena, Coventry CV6 6AQ. Telephone (0870) 421 1987
Record Attendance: 51,455 v Wolverhampton W, Division 2, 29 April 1967 (at Highfield Road). **Capacity:** 32,500.

Manager: Micky Adams.
Secretary: Graham Hover.
Most League Goals: 108, Division 3 (S), 1931–32.
Highest League Scorer in Season: Clarrie Bourton, 49, Division 3 (S), 1931–32.
Most League Goals in Total Aggregate: Clarrie Bourton, 171, 1931–37.
Most Capped Player: Magnus Hedman, 44 (56), Sweden.
Most League Appearances: Steve Ogrizovic, 507, 1984–2000.
Honours – Football League: Division 2 Champions – 1966–67. Division 3 Champions – 1963–64. Division 3 (S) Champions 1935–36. **FA Cup:** Winners – 1986–87.
Colours: Sky blue body shirts and shorts with white and navy side panel, sky blue stockings with white and navy turnover and centre white strip.

CREWE ALEXANDRA FL CHAMPIONSHIP

Bell Lee (M)	5 11	11 00	Crewe	26 1 83	Scholar
Bignot Paul (D)	6 1	12 03	Birmingham	14 2 86	Scholar
Cochrane Justin (M)	5 11	11 07	Hackney	26 1 82	QPR
Foster Stephen (D)	6 0	11 05	Warrington	10 9 80	Trainee
Higdon Michael (M)	6 2	11 05	Liverpool	2 9 83	School
Ince Clayton (G)	6 3	13 00	Trinidad	13 7 72	Defence Force
Jones Billy (D)	5 11	13 00	Shrewsbury	24 3 87	Scholar
Jones Steve (F)	5 10	10 05	Derry	25 10 76	Leigh RMI
Lunt Kenny (M)	5 10	10 05	Runcorn	20 11 79	Trainee
McCready Chris (D)	6 1	12 05	Ellesmere Port	5 9 81	Scholar
Morris Alex (M)	6 0	11 08	Stoke	5 10 82	Scholar
Moses Adi (D)	5 11	13 01	Doncaster	4 5 75	Huddersfield T
Moss Darren (D)	5 10	11 00	Wreham	24 5 81	Shrewsbury T
Murdock Colin (D)	6 3	13 05	Belfast	12 7 76	Hibernian
Rivers Mark (F)	5 10	11 04	Crewe	26 11 75	Norwich C
Rix Ben (M)	5 9	11 05	Wolverhampton	11 12 82	Scholar
Roberts Gary (M)	5 8	10 05	Chester	4 2 87	Scholar
Roberts Mark (D)	6 1	12 00	Northwich	16 10 83	Scholar
Sorvel Neil (M)	6 0	12 03	Widnes	2 3 73	Macclesfield T
Tomlinson Stuart (G)	6 1	11 02	Chester	10 5 85	Scholar
Tonkin Anthony (D)	5 11	12 02	Newlyn	19 1 80	Stockport Co
Varney Luke (F)	5 11	11 00	Leicester	28 9 82	Quorn
Vaughan David (M)	5 7	11 00	Abergele	18 2 83	Scholar
Walker Richard (D)	6 2	12 08	Bolton	17 9 80	Trainee
Williams Ben (G)	6 0	13 01	Manchester	27 8 82	Manchester U
Wills Karl (G)	6 2	11 05	Warrington	31 8 87	Juniors
Wilson Kyle (F)	5 10	11 05	Wirrall	14 11 85	Scholar

League Appearances: Ashton, D. 23(1); Bell, L. 17; Bignot, P. 3(2); Briggs, K. 3; Cochrane, J. 21(8); Foster, S. 34; Higdon, M. 1(19); Ince, C. 23; Jones, B. 20; Jones, S. 24(12); Lunt, K. 46; McCready, C. 19(1); Moses, A. 19(2); Moss, D. 6; Murdock, C. 15(1); Otsemobor, J. 14; Platt, M. (1); Rivers, M. 26(8); Roberts, G. 2; Roberts, M. 3(3); Sorvel, N. 45(1); Tonkin, A. 33(2); Varney, L. 17(9); Vaughan, D. 43(1); Walker, R. 15(8); White, A. 11(11); Williams, B. 23.
Goals – League (66): Ashton 17 (4 pens), Jones S 10, Rivers 7, Vaughan 6, Lunt 5 (2 pens), Varney 4, White 4, Higdon 3, Sorvel 3, Walker 2, Foster 1, Otsemobor 1, own goals 3.
Carling Cup (7): Jones S 3, Ashton 2, Foster 1, Rivers 1.
FA Cup (0).
Ground: Football Ground, Gresty Road, Crewe CW2 6EB. Telephone (01270) 213014.
Record Attendance: 20,000 v Tottenham H, FA Cup 4th rd, 30 January 1960.

Capacity: 10,046.
Manager: Dario Gradi MBE.
Secretary: Andrew Blakemore.
Most League Goals: 95, Division 3 (N), 1931–32.
Highest League Scorer in Season: Terry Harkin, 35, Division 4, 1964–65.
Most League Goals in Total Aggregate: Bert Swindells, 126, 1928–37.
Most Capped Player: Clayton Ince, 38, Trinidad & Tobago.
Most League Appearances: Tommy Lowry, 436, 1966–78.
Honours – Welsh Cup: Winners – 1936, 1937.
Colours: Red shirts, white shorts, red stockings.

CRYSTAL PALACE — FL CHAMPIONSHIP

Andrews Wayne (F)	5 10	11 06	Paddington	25 11 77	Colchester U
Berry Tyrone (F)	5 8	10 02	London	11 3 87	Scholar
Black Tommy (M)	5 7	11 10	Chigwell	26 11 79	Arsenal
Borrowdale Gary (D)	6 0	12 01	Sutton	16 7 85	Scholar
Boyce Emmerson (D)	6 0	12 03	Aylesbury	24 9 79	Luton T
Butterfield Danny (D)	5 10	11 06	Boston	21 11 79	Grimsby T
Danze Anthony (M)	6 0	12 00	Perth	15 3 84	
Hall Fitz (D)	6 3	13 00	Leytonstone	20 12 80	Southampton
Hudson Mark (D)	6 1	12 01	Guildford	30 3 82	Fulham
Hughes Michael (M)	5 6	10 08	Larne	2 8 71	Wimbledon
Johnson Andy (F)	5 7	10 09	Bedford	10 2 81	Birmingham C
Kaviedes Ivan (F)	6 0	11 09	Santo Domingo	24 10 77	Dep Quito
Kiraly Gabor (G)	6 3	13 06	Szombathely	1 4 76	Hertha Berlin
Kolkka Joonas (M)	5 9	11 08	Lahti	28 9 74	M'gladbach
Leigertwood Mikele (D)	6 1	11 04	Enfield	12 11 82	Wimbledon
Popovic Tony (D)	6 5	13 01	Australia	7 4 73	Sanfrecce
Riihilahti Aki (M)	5 11	12 06	Helsinki	9 9 76	Valerenga
Routledge Wayne (F)	5 6	10 07	Eltham	7 1 85	Scholar
Shipperley Neil (F)	6 0	13 00	Chatham	30 10 74	Wimbledon
Soares Tom (M)	6 0	11 04	Reading	10 7 86	Scholar
Sorondo Gonzalo (D)	5 11	12 08	Montevideo	9 10 79	Internazionale
Speroni Julian (G)	6 0	11 00	Buenos Aires	18 5 79	Dundee
Togwell Sam (D)	5 11	12 04	Beaconsfield	14 10 84	Scholar
Torghelle Sandor (F)	6 1	13 06	Budapest	5 5 82	MTK
Ventola Nicola (F)	6 3	12 13	Bari	24 5 78	Siena
Watson Ben (M)	5 10	10 11	Camberwell	9 7 85	Scholar

League Appearances: Andrews, W. (9); Borrowdale, G. 2(5); Boyce, E. 26(1); Butterfield, D. 7; Derry, S. 1(6); Freedman, D. 10(10); Granville, D. 35; Hall, F. 36; Hudson, M. 7; Hughes, M. 34(2); Johnson, A. 37; Kaviedes, I. 1(3); Kiraly, G. 32; Kolkka, J. 20(3); Lakis, V. 6(12); Leigertwood, M. 16(4); Popovic, T. 21(2); Powell, D. 4(2); Riihilahti, A. 28(4); Routledge, W. 38; Shipperley, N. (1); Soares, T. 16(6); Sorondo, G. 16(4); Speroni, J. 6; Torghelle, S. 3(9); Ventola, N. (3); Watson, B. 16(5).
Goals – League (41): Johnson 21 (11 pens), Riihilahti 4, Granville 3, Kolkka 3, Hall 2, Hughes 2, Freedman 1, Hudson 1, Leigertwood 1, Powell 1, Ventola 1, own goal 1.
Carling Cup (4): Freedman 2, Soares 1, Torghelle 1.
FA Cup (1): own goal 1.
Ground: Selhurst Park, London SE25 6PU. Telephone (020) 8768 6000.
Record Attendance: 51,482 v Burnley, Division 2, 11 May 1979. **Capacity:** 26,257.
Manager: Iain Dowie.
Assistant Secretary: Christine Dowdeswell.
Most League Goals: 110, Division 4, 1960–61.

Highest League Scorer in Season: Peter Simpson, 46, Division 3 (S), 1930–31.
Most League Goals in Total Aggregate: Peter Simpson, 153, 1930–36.
Most Capped Player: Aleksandrs Kolinko, 23 (51), Latvia.
Most League Appearances: Jim Cannon, 571, 1973–88.
Honours – Football League: Division 1 – Champions 1993–94. Division 2 Champions – 1978–79. Division 3 (S) 1920–21. **Zenith Data Systems Cup:** Winners – 1991.
Colours: Red and blue vertical striped shirts, royal blue shorts and stockings.

DARLINGTON FL CHAMPIONSHIP 2

Appleby Matty (M)	5 10	11 04	Middlesbrough	16 4 72	Oldham Ath
Armstrong Alun (F)	6 0	13 08	Gateshead	22 2 75	Ipswich T
Clark Ian (M)	5 11	11 07	Stockton	23 10 74	Hartlepool U
Clarke Matthew (D)	6 3	13 00	Leeds	18 12 80	Halifax T
Close Brian (D)	5 10	12 00	Belfast	27 1 82	Middlesbrough
Convery Mark (M)	5 6	10 05	Newcastle	29 5 81	Sunderland
Dickman Jonjo (M)	5 11	11 12	Hexham	22 9 81	Sunderland
Fleming Curtis (D)	5 10	12 09	Manchester	8 10 68	Crystal Palace
Gilroy Keith (F)	5 10	11 04	Sligo	8 7 83	Scarborough
Gregorio Adolfo (M)	5 9	10 12	Hilmar	1 10 82	ULCA
Hignett Craig (M)	5 9	12 06	Whiston	12 1 70	Leeds U
Hughes Chris (M)	5 11	10 10	Sunderland	5 3 84	Scholar
Hutchinson Jonathan (D)	5 11	11 11	Middlesbrough	2 4 82	Birmingham C
Keltie Clark (M)	6 0	11 08	Newcastle	31 8 83	Shildon
Kendrick Joseph (D)	6 0	11 05	Dublin	26 6 83	Newcastle U
Logan Richard (M)	6 0	11 12	Washington	18 2 88	Scholar
Maddison Neil (M)	5 10	12 00	Darlington	2 10 69	Middlesbrough
McGurk David (D)	6 0	11 10	Middlesbrough	30 9 82	Scholar
Petta Bobby (M)	5 7	11 05	Rotterdam	6 8 74	Celtic
Price Mike (G)	6 3	13 10	Ashington	3 4 83	Leicester C
Russell Craig (F)	5 10	12 06	Jarrow	4 2 74	Carlisle U
Russell Sam (G)	6 0	11 00	Middlesbrough	4 10 82	Middlesbrough
St'Juste Jason (M)	5 6	10 05	Leeds	21 9 85	
Thomas Steve (M)	5 10	11 07	Hartlepool	23 6 79	Wrexham
Valentine Ryan (D)	5 10	11 05	Wrexham	19 8 82	Everton
Wainwright Neil (M)	6 0	12 00	Warrington	4 11 77	Sunderland
Webster Adrian (M)	5 8	10 09	Hawkes Bay	11 10 80	Maidstone U
Wijnhard Clyde (F)	5 11	13 02	Paramaribo	1 11 73	Beira-Mar

League Appearances: Appleby, M. 10; Armstrong, A. 31(1); Bates, M. 4; Clark, I. 13(11); Clarke, M. 42(1); Close, B. 37(1); Convery, M. 10(13); Dickman, J. 8; Fleming, C. 24(3); Gilroy, K. 1(1); Gregorio, A. 19(5); Hignett, C. 17(2); Hughes, C. 5(10); Hutchinson, J. 8; Keltie, C. 10(11); Kendrick, J. 19(12); Liddle, C. 19(1); Logan, R. (1); Maddison, N. 21(3); McGurk, D. 9(1); Petta, B. 12; Russell, C. 15(13); Russell, S. 46; Sodje, A. 1(6); St'Juste, J. 9(6); Thomas, S. 11(1); Valentine, R. 32(4); Wainwright, N. 26(12); Webster, A. 16(6); Wijnhard, C. 31.
Goals – League (57): Wijnhard 14 (4 pens), Armstrong 9, Hignett 9 (2 pens), Wainwright 4, Clarke 3, Clark 2, Gregorio 2, McGurk 2, St'Juste 2, Dickman 1, Kendrick 1, Liddle 1, Maddison 1, Petta 1, Russell C 1, Sodje 1, Valentine 1, own goals 2.
Carling Cup (0).
FA Cup (3): Armstrong 2, Keltie 1.
LDV Vans Trophy (0).
Ground: New Stadium, Neasham Road, Hurworth Moor, Darlington DL2 1GR. Telephone (01325) 387000.
Record Attendance: 21,023 v Bolton W, League Cup 3rd rd, 14 November 1960.
Capacity: 25,000.

Manager: David Hodgson.
Secretary: Lisa Charlton.
Most League Goals: 108, Division 3 (N), 1929–30.
Highest League Scorer in Season: David Brown, 39, Division 3 (N), 1924–25.
Most League Goals in Total Aggregate: Alan Walsh, 90, 1978–84.
Most Capped Player: Jason Devos, 3 (46), Canada.
Most League Appearances: Ron Greener, 442, 1955–68.
Honours – Football League: Division 3 (N) Champions – 1924–25. Division 4 Champions – 1990–91.
Colours: Black and white hooped shirts, black shorts, black stockings.

DERBY COUNTY — FL CHAMPIONSHIP

Bisgaard Morten (M)	6 1	12 04	Randers	25 6 74	FC Copenhagen
Boertien Paul (D)	5 10	11 02	Haltwhistle	21 1 79	Carlisle U
Bolder Adam (M)	5 9	10 08	Hull	25 10 80	Hull C
Camp Lee (G)	5 11	11 11	Derby	22 8 84	Scholar
Doyle Nathan (M)	5 10	12 06	Derby	12 1 87	Scholar
Grant Lee (G)	6 3	13 01	Hemel Hempstead	27 1 83	Scholar
Holmes Lee (M)	5 8	10 06	Sutton-in-Ashfield	2 4 87	Scholar
Huddlestone Tom (M)	6 2	11 02	Nottingham	28 12 86	Scholar
Idiakez Inigo (M)	6 0	12 02	San Sebastian	8 11 73	Rayo Vallecano
Jackson Richard (D)	5 8	12 10	Whitby	18 4 80	Scarborough
Johnson Michael (D)	5 11	11 12	Nottingham	4 7 73	Birmingham C
Kenna Jeff (D)	5 11	12 12	Dublin	27 8 70	Birmingham C
Konjic Muhamed (D)	6 3	13 00	Bosnia	14 5 70	Coventry C
Mills Pablo (D)	5 9	11 04	Birmingham	27 5 84	Trainee
Peschisolido Paul (F)	5 7	10 12	Scarborough, Can	25 5 71	Sheffield U
Rasiak Grzegorz (F)	6 3	13 03	Szczecin	12 1 79	Siena
Reich Marco (M)	6 0	12 00	Meisenheim	30 12 77	Werder Bremen
Smith Tommy (F)	5 8	11 04	Hemel Hempstead	22 5 80	Sunderland
Tudgay Marcus (F)	5 10	12 04	Worthing	3 2 83	Trainee
Vincent Jamie (D)	5 10	11 08	Wimbledon	18 6 75	Portsmouth
Zavagno Luciano (D)	5 11	11 07	Rosario	6 8 77	Troyes

League Appearances: Bisgaard, M. 31(5); Bolder, A. 24(12); Camp, L. 45; Doyle, N. 3; Grant, L. 1(1); Holmes, L. (3); Huddlestone, T. 42(3); Idiakez, I. 41; Jackson, R. 18(1); Johnson, M. 35(1); Junior, 5(13); Kaku, B. 3(1); Kenna, J. 40; Konjic, M. 13(3); Makin, C. 13; Mills, P. 15(7); Peschisolido, P. 10(22); Rasiak, G. 35; Reich, M. 27(10); Smith, T. 41(1); Talbot, J. 2; Taylor, I. 25(14); Tudgay, M. 22(12); Vincent, J. 15.
Goals – League (71): Rasiak 16, Smith 11, Idiakez 9 (2 pens), Tudgay 9, Peschisolido 8, Reich 6, Bisgaard 4, Taylor 3, Bolder 2, Johnson 1, Vincent 1, own goal 1.
Carling Cup (1): Idiakez 1.
FA Cup (5): Idiakez 1, Junior 1, Peschisolido 1, Rasiak 1, Tudgay 1.
Play-Offs (0).
Ground: Pride Park Stadium, Derby DE24 8XL. Telephone (0870) 444 1884.
Record Attendance: 41,826 v Tottenham H, Division 1, 20 September 1969. **Capacity:** 33,597.
Manager: Phil Brown.
Secretary: Marian McMinn.
Most League Goals: 111, Division 3 (N), 1956–57.
Highest League Scorer in Season: Jack Bowers, 37, Division 1, 1930–31; Ray Straw, 37 Division 3 (N), 1956–57.
Most League Goals in Total Aggregate: Steve Bloomer, 292, 1892–1906 and 1910–14.

Most Capped Players: Deon Burton, 41 (48), Jamaica and Mart Poom, 41 (98), Estonia.
Most League Appearances: Kevin Hector, 486, 1966–78 and 1980–82.
Honours – Football League: Division 1 Champions – 1971–72, 1974–75. Division 2 Champions – 1911–12, 1914–15, 1968–69, 1986–87. Division 3 (N) 1956–57. **FA Cup:** Winners – 1945–46.
Colours: White shirts with black piping, black shorts, white stockings.

DONCASTER ROVERS FL CHAMPIONSHIP 1

Albrighton Mark (D)	6 1	12 07	Nuneaton	6 3 76	Telford U
Beech Chris (D)	5 10	11 12	Congleton	5 11 75	Rotherham U
Blundell Greg (F)	5 9	12 12	Liverpool	3 10 77	Northwich Vic
Brown Adam (M)	5 10	10 07	Sunderland	17 12 87	Scholar
Coppinger James (F)	5 7	10 03	Middlesbrough	10 1 81	Exeter C
Fenton Nick (D)	6 0	12 02	Preston	23 11 79	Notts Co
Fortune-West Leo (F)	6 3	13 10	Stratford	9 4 71	Cardiff C
Foster Steve (D)	6 1	12 00	Mansfield	3 12 74	Bristol R
Green Paul (M)	5 10	12 00	Pontefract	10 4 83	Trainee
Guy Lewis (F)	5 10	10 07	Penrith	27 8 85	Newcastle U
Jackson Ben (F)	5 9	11 07	Peterlee	20 10 85	Scholar
Jones Stuart (G)	6 1	14 00	Bristol	24 10 77	Brighton & HA
Maloney Jon (M)	6 0	11 12	Leeds	3 3 85	Trainee
Marples Simon (D)	5 10	11 00	Sheffield	30 7 75	Trainee
McIndoe Michael (M)	5 8	11 00	Edinburgh	2 12 79	Yeovil T
McSporran Jermaine (M)	5 10	10 12	Manchester	1 1 77	Walsall
Mulligan David (D)	5 8	9 13	Bootle	24 3 82	Barnsley
Nelthorpe Craig (M)	5 10	11 00	Doncaster	10 6 87	Scholar
Price Jamie (D)	5 10	11 00	Normanton	27 10 81	Trainee
Priet Nicolas (D)	6 4	12 10	Lyon	31 1 83	Leicester C
Ravenhill Ricky (M)	5 10	11 03	Doncaster	16 1 81	Barnsley
Rigoglioso Adriano (M)	6 1	12 07	Liverpool	28 5 79	Morecambe
Roberts Neil (F)	5 10	11 00	Wrexham	7 4 78	Wigan Ath
Ryan Tim (D)	5 10	11 00	Stockport	10 12 74	Southport
Warrington Andy (G)	6 3	12 13	Sheffield	10 6 76	York C

League Appearances: Albrighton, M. 15(2); Beardsley, C. 1(3); Beech, C. 2; Blundell, G. 33(8); Brown, A. (3); Campbell, A. 1(2); Coppinger, J. 27(4); Doolan, J. 32(6); Fenton, N. 37(1); Fortune-West, L. 16(8); Foster, S. 34; Green, P. 38(4); Guy, L. 4(5); Ingham, M. 1; Ipoua, G. 1(8); Jackson, B. (1); Johnson, S. 8(3); Jones, S. 3(1); Maloney, J. 1(1); Marples, S. 12; McIndoe, M. 43(1); McSporran, J. 15(11); Morley, D. 9; Mulligan, D. 27(4); Nelthorpe, C. (1); Price, J. 5(1); Priet, N. 7; Ravenhill, R. 21(14); Rigoglioso, A. 2(10); Roberts, N. 30(1); Ryan, T. 38(1); Turner, I. 8; Warrington, A. 34; Wilson, M. 1(2).
Goals – League (65): McIndoe 10 (2 pens), Blundell 9, Green 7, Fortune-West 6, Roberts 6, Ryan 4, Guy 3, Johnson 3, Ravenhill 3, Doolan 2, Albrighton 1, Brown 1, Fenton 1, Foster 1, McSporran 1, Mulligan 1, own goals 6.
Carling Cup (5): Doolan 1, Fortune-West 1, McIndoe 1, McSporran 1, Ravenhill 1.
FA Cup (4): Blundell 2, Fenton 1, McIndoe 1.
LDV Vans Trophy (2): Beardsley 1, Rigoglioso 1.
Ground: The Earth Stadium, Belle Vue, Doncaster DN4 5HT. Telephone (01302) 539441.
Record Attendance: 37,149 v Hull C, Division 3 (N), 2 October 1948. **Capacity:** 10,593.
Manager: Dave Penney.
Secretary: David Morris.
Most League Goals: 123, Division 3 (N), 1946–47.
Highest League Scorer in Season: Clarrie Jordan, 42, Division 3 (N) 1946–47.

Most League Goals in Total Aggregate: Tom Keetley, 180, 1923–29.
Most Capped Player: Len Graham, 14, Northern Ireland.
Most League Appearances: Fred Emery, 417, 1925–36.
Honours – Football League: Division 3 Champions – 2003–04. Division 3 (N) Champions – 1934–35, 1946–47, 1949–50. Division 4 Champions – 1965–66, 1968–69. **Football Conference:** Champions – 2002–03.
Colours: Red and white hooped shirts, red shorts and stockings.

EVERTON — FA PREMIERSHIP

Beattie James (F)	6 1	13 06	Lancaster	27 2 78	Southampton
Bent Marcus (F)	6 2	13 03	Hammersmith	19 5 78	Ipswich T
Cahill Tim (M)	5 10	10 12	Sydney	6 12 79	Millwall
Carsley Lee (M)	5 10	12 04	Birmingham	28 2 74	Coventry C
Ferguson Duncan (F)	6 4	13 07	Stirling	27 12 71	Newcastle U
Hibbert Tony (D)	5 9	11 05	Liverpool	20 2 81	Trainee
Kilbane Kevin (M)	6 1	13 05	Preston	1 2 77	Sunderland
Li Tie(M)	6 0	11 10	China	18 9 77	Lianing Bodao
Martyn Nigel (G)	6 1	15 11	St Austell	11 8 66	Leeds U
McFadden James (M)	6 0	12 11	Glasgow	14 4 83	Motherwell
Naysmith Gary (D)	5 9	12 01	Edinburgh	16 11 78	Hearts
Osman Leon (F)	5 8	10 09	Billinge	17 5 81	Trainee
Pistone Alessandro (D)	5 11	11 08	Milan	27 7 75	Newcastle U
Stubbs Alan (D)	6 2	13 12	Kirkby	6 10 71	Celtic
Turner Iain (G)	6 3	12 10	Stirling	26 1 84	Trainee
Vaughan James (F)	5 11	12 08	Birmingham	14 7 88	Scholar
Watson Steve (D)	6 0	12 07	North Shields	1 4 74	Aston Villa
Weir David (D)	6 5	14 03	Falkirk	10 5 70	Hearts
Wright Richard (G)	6 2	14 04	Ipswich	5 11 77	Arsenal
Yobo Joseph (D)	6 1	13 00	Kano	6 9 80	Marseille

League Appearances: Arteta, M. 10(2); Beattie, J. 7(4); Bent, M. 31(6); Cahill, T. 33; Campbell, K. 4(2); Carsley, L. 35(1); Chadwick, N. (1); Ferguson, D. 6(29); Gravesen, T. 20(1); Hibbert, T. 35(1); Kilbane, K. 37(1); Martyn, N. 32; McFadden, J. 7(16); Naysmith, G. 5(6); Osman, L. 24(5); Pistone, A. 32(1); Stubbs, A. 29(2); Vaughan, J. (2); Watson, S. 12(13); Weir, D. 34; Wright, R. 6(1); Yobo, J. 19(8).
Goals – League (45): Cahill 11, Bent 6, Osman 6, Ferguson 5, Carsley 4, Gravesen 4 (2 pens), Arteta 1, Beattie 1, Kilbane 1, McFadden 1, Stubbs 1, Vaughan 1, Weir 1, own goals 2.
Carling Cup (5): Bent 1, Carsley 1, Chadwick 1, Ferguson 1 (pen), Gravesen 1.
FA Cup (6): McFadden 2, Beattie 1, Cahill 1, Chadwick 1, Osman 1.
Ground: Goodison Park, Liverpool L4 4EL. Telephone (0151) 330 2200.
Record Attendance: 78,299 v Liverpool, Division 1, 18 September 1948. **Capacity:** 40,565.
Manager: David Moyes.
Secretary: David Harrison.
Most League Goals: 121, Division 2, 1930–31.
Highest League Scorer in Season: William Ralph 'Dixie' Dean, 60, Division 1, 1927–28 (All-time League record).
Most League Goals in Total Aggregate: William Ralph 'Dixie' Dean, 349, 1925–37.
Most Capped Player: Neville Southall, 92, Wales.
Most League Appearances: Neville Southall, 578, 1981–98.
Honours – Football League: Division 1 Champions – 1890–91, 1914–15, 1927–28, 1931–32, 1938–39, 1962–63, 1969–70, 1984–85, 1986–87. Division 2 Champions – 1930–31. **FA Cup:** Winners – 1906, 1933, 1966, 1984, 1995. **European Competitions: European Cup-Winners' Cup:** Winners – 1984–85.
Colours: Royal blue shirts, white shorts, white stockings.

Boa Morte Luis (F)	5 9	12 06	Lisbon	4 8 77	Southampton
Bocanegra Carlos (D)	5 11	12 07	Alta Loma	25 5 79	Chicago Fire
Cole Andy (F)	5 10	12 11	Nottingham	15 10 71	Blackburn R
Crossley Mark (G)	6 3	15 09	Barnsley	16 6 69	Middlesbrough
Diop Papa Bouba (M)	6 4	14 12	Dakar	28 1 78	Lens
Ehui Ismael (F)	5 7	10 10	Lille	10 12 86	Scholar
Fontaine Liam (D)	6 3	12 02	Beckenham	7 1 86	Trainee
Goma Alain (D)	6 0	13 01	Sault	5 10 72	Newcastle U
Green Adam (D)	5 9	10 08	Hillingdon	12 1 84	Scholar
Hammond Elvis (F)	5 10	11 02	Accra	6 10 80	Trainee
Jensen Claus (M)	6 0	13 01	Nykobing	29 4 77	Charlton Ath
John Collins (F)	5 11	12 13	Zwandru	17 10 85	Twente
Knight Zat (D)	6 6	15 02	Solihull	2 5 80	Rushall Olympic
Leacock Dean (D)	6 2	12 04	Croydon	10 6 84	Trainee
Legwinski Sylvain (M)	6 1	11 07	Clermont-Ferrand	6 10 73	Bordeaux
Malbranque Steed (M)	5 8	11 07	Mouscron	6 1 80	Lyon
Marlet Steve (F)	5 11	11 10	Pithiviers	10 1 74	Lyon
McBride Brian (F)	6 0	12 08	Chicago	19 6 72	Columbus Crew
Pearce Ian (D)	6 3	15 06	Bury St Edmunds	7 5 74	West Ham U
Pembridge Mark (M)	5 9	11 13	Merthyr	29 11 70	Everton
Pratley Darren (M)	61	11 05	Barking	22 4 85	Scholar
Radzinski Tomasz (F)	5 8	11 11	Poznan	14 12 73	Everton
Rehman Zesh (M)	6 2	12 08	Birmingham	14 10 83	Scholar
Rosenior Liam (M)	5 9	11 05	Wandsworth	9 7 84	Bristol C
Sava Facundo (F)	6 0	13 01	Ituzaingo	3 7 74	Gimnasia
Timlin Michael (M)	5 9	11 10	Lambeth	19 3 85	Trainee
Van der Sar Edwin (G)	6 5	13 01	Voorhout	29 10 70	Juventus
Volz Moritz (D)	5 8	11 07	Siegen	21 1 83	Arsenal
Watkins Robert (D)			Carshalton	14 10 85	Trainee

League Appearances: Boa Morte, L. 29(2); Bocanegra, C. 26(2); Clark, L. 15(2); Cole, A. 29(2); Crossley, M. 5(1); Diop, P. 29; Fontaine, L. (1); Goma, A. 15(1); Green, A. 4; Hammond, E. (1); Jensen, C. 10(2); John, C. 13(14); Knight, Z. 35; Legwinski, S. 13(2); Malbranque, S. 22(4); McBride, B. 15(16); McKinlay, B. 1(1); Pearce, I. 11; Pembridge, M. 26(2); Radzinski, T. 25(10); Rehman, Z. 15(2); Rosenior, L. 16(1); Van der Sar, E. 33(1); Volz, M. 31.
Goals – League (52): Cole 12 (1 pen), Boa Morte 8, Diop 6, Malbranque 6 (1 pen), McBride 6, Radzinski 6, John 4, Bocanegra 1, Clark 1, Knight 1, Legwinski 1.
Carling Cup (10): Radzinski 4, McBride 3, Cole 1, Malbranque 1, Pembridge 1.
FA Cup (8): John 2, Boa Morte 1, Diop 1 (pen), Jensen 1, Knight 1, Radzinski 1, Volz 1.
Ground: Craven Cottage, Stevenage Road, London SW6 6HH. Telephone: (0870) 442 1222.
Record Attendance: 49,335 v Millwall, Division 2, 8 October 1938. **Capacity:** 22,150.
Manager: Chris Coleman.
Secretary: Lee Hoos.
Most League Goals: 111, Division 3 (S), 1931–32.
Highest League Scorer in Season: Frank Newton, 43, Division 3 (S), 1931–32.
Most League Goals in Total Aggregate: Gordon Davies, 159, 1978–84, 1986–91.
Most Capped Player: Johnny Haynes, 56, England.
Most League Appearances: Johnny Haynes, 594, 1952–70.
Honours – Football League: Division 1 Champions – 2000–01. Division 2 Champions – 1948–49, 1998–99. Division 3 (S) Champions – 1931–32. **European**

Competitions: Intertoto Cup: Winners – 2002.
Colours: White shirts, black shorts, white stockings.

GILLINGHAM FL CHAMPIONSHIP 1

Ashby Barry (D)	6 3	14 06	Park Royal	2 11 70	Brentford
Awuah Jones (F)	5 11	12 00	Ghana	10 7 83	Scholar
Banks Steve (G)	6 0	14 01	Hillingdon	9 2 72	Wimbledon
Beckwith Dean (D)	6 3	13 04	Southwark	18 9 83	Scholar
Bodkin Matt (F)	5 6	11 05	Chatham	23 11 83	Nottingham F
Bossu Bertrand (G)	6 7	14 13	Calais	14 10 80	Barnet
Brown Jason (G)	6 0	16 01	Southwark	18 5 82	Charlton Ath
Byfield Darren (F)	5 11	12 07	Sutton Coldfield	29 9 76	Sundeland
Cox Ian (D)	6 1	12 05	Croydon	25 3 71	Burnley
Crofts Andrew (D)	5 10	11 13	Chatham	29 5 84	Trainee
Flynn Michael (M)	5 10	12 10	Newport	17 10 80	Wigan Ath
Henderson Darius (F)	6 2	13 11	Doncaster	7 9 81	Reading
Hessenthaler Andy (M)	5 8	11 06	Gravesend	17 6 65	Watford
Hills John (D)	5 8	12 13	St Annes-on-Sea	21 4 78	Blackpool
Hope Chris (D)	6 1	13 01	Sheffield	14 11 72	Scunthorpe U
Jarvis Matthew (M)	5 7	11 05	Middlesbrough	22 5 86	Scholar
Johnson Leon (M)	6 0	12 08	London	10 5 81	Southend U
Nosworthy Nayron (D)	6 0	13 00	Brixton	11 10 80	Trainee
Pouton Alan (M)	6 1	13 06	Newcastle	1 2 77	Grimsby T
Roberts Iwan (F)	6 4	14 08	Bangor	26 6 68	Norwich C
Rose Richard (D)	5 10	11 09	Tunbridge Wells	8 9 82	Trainee
Saunders Mark (M)	5 11	13 03	Reading	23 7 71	Plymouth Arg
Sidibe Mamady (F)	6 4	13 10	Mali	18 12 79	CA Paris
Smith Paul (M)	6 0	14 06	East Ham	18 9 71	Brentford
Southall Nicky (M)	5 11	12 04	Stockton	28 1 72	Bolton W
Spiller Danny (M)	5 8	10 12	Maidstone	10 10 81	Trainee

League Appearances: Agyemang, P. 9(4); Ashby, B. 22; Banks, S. 26; Beckwith, D. (1); Bodkin, M. (2); Bossu, B. 1(1); Brown, J. 16; Byfield, D. 27(11); Cox, I. 29(2); Crofts, A. 25(2); Douglas, J. 10; Flynn, M. 16; Gallacher, P. 3; Henderson, D. 27(5); Hessenthaler, A. 14(3); Hills, J. 20(3); Hope, C. 35(2); Jarvis, M. 12(18); Johnson, L. 6(2); Johnson, T. 2(6); Marney, D. 3; McEveley, J. 10; Nosworthy, N. 36(1); Nowland, A. 3; Perpetuini, D. 3; Pouton, A. 8(4); Roberts, I. 11(9); Robinson, J. 2(2); Rose, R. 16(2); Saunders, M. 3; Sidibe, M. 22(13); Smith, P. 40(1); Southall, N. 30(3); Spiller, D. 19(3).
Goals – League (45): Henderson 9 (1 pen), Byfield 6, Flynn 3, Jarvis 3, Roberts 3, Smith 3, Agyemang 2, Cox 2, Crofts 2, Hope 2, Johnson T 2, Sidibe 2, McEveley 1, Nowland 1, Southall 1, own goals 3.
Carling Cup (1): Sidibe 1.
FA Cup (0).
Ground: Priestfield Stadium, Gillingham ME7 4DD. Telephone (01634) 300000.
Record Attendance: 23,002 v QPR, FA Cup 3rd rd, 10 January 1948. **Capacity:** 11,400.
Manager: Neale Cooper.
Secretary: Mrs G. E. Poynter.
Most League Goals: 90, Division 4, 1973–74.
Highest League Scorer in Season: Ernie Morgan, 31, Division 3 (S), 1954–55; Brian Yeo, 31, Division 4, 1973–74.
Most League Goals in Total Aggregate: Brian Yeo, 135, 1963–75.
Most Capped Player: Mamady Sidibe 7, Mali.
Most League Appearances: John Simpson, 571, 1957–72.
Honours – Football League: Division 4 Champions – 1963–64.
Colours: All blue.

Bull Ronnie (D)	5 8	11 04	Hackney	26 12 80	Brentford
Coldicott Stacy (M)	5 8	12 08	Worcester	29 4 74	WBA
Crane Tony (D)	6 5	12 05	Liverpool	8 9 82	Sheffield W
Crowe Jason (D)	5 9	10 09	Sidcup	30 9 78	Portsmouth
Downey Glen (D)	6 1	13 00	Sunderland	20 9 78	Scarborough
Fleming Terry (M)	5 8	11 00	Marston Green	5 1 73	Cambridge U
Forbes Terrell (D)	6 0	12 05	Southwark	17 8 81	QPR
Gritton Martin (F)	6 3	13 10	Glasgow	1 6 78	Torquay U
Hegarty Nick (M)	5 10	11 00	Hemsworth	25 6 86	Scholar
Hockless Graham (M)	5 7	11 00	Hull	20 10 82	Juniors
Jones Rob (D)	6 7	13 07	Stockton	30 11 79	Stockport Co
McDermott John (D)	5 7	11 02	Middlesbrough	3 2 69	Trainee
North Danny (F)	5 9	12 08	Grimsby	7 9 87	Scholar
Parkinson Andy (F)	5 7	10 07	Liverpool	27 5 79	Sheffield U
Pinault Thomas (M)	5 10	12 00	Grasse	4 12 81	Colchester U
Ramsden Simon (D)	6 0	13 00	Bishop Auckland	17 12 81	Sunderland
Reddy Michael (F)	6 1	13 00	Kilkenny	24 3 80	Sunderland
Soames David (F)	5 5	10 08	Grimsby	10 2 84	Scholar
Whittle Justin (D)	6 1	13 00	Derby	18 3 71	Hull C
Williams Anthony (G)	6 2	13 07	Maesteg	20 9 77	Hartlepool U

League Appearances: Bull, R. 22(5); Coldicott, S. 20(12); Cramb, C. 7(4); Crane, T. 2(1); Crowe, J. 37; Daly, J. 3; Downey, G. (1); Fleming, T. 43; Forbes, T. 33; Gordon, D. 20; Gritton, M. 22(1); Harrold, M. 6; Hegarty, N. (1); Hockless, G. 3(3); Jones, R. 18(2); Mansaram, D. 3(5); Marcelle, C. (3); McDermott, J. 39; North, D. (1); Parkinson, A. 43(2); Pinault, T. 32(11); Ramsden, S. 23(2); Reddy, M. 24(16); Robinson, P. 1(1); Sestanovich, A. 17(5); Soames, D. (4); Whittle, J. 39(1); Williams, A. 46; Williams, C. 1(2); Young, G. 2(4).
Goals – League (51): Reddy 9, Parkinson 8, Pinault 7 (1 pen), Crowe 4, Gritton 4, Bull 2, Cramb 2, Fleming 2, Gordon 2, Harrold 2, McDermott 2, Sestanovich 2, Coldicott 1, Daly 1, Jones 1, Mansaram 1, Whittle 1.
Carling Cup (1): Parkinson 1.
FA Cup (0).
LDV Vans Trophy (1): Cramb 1.
Ground: Blundell Park, Cleethorpes, North-East Lincolnshire DN35 7PY. Telephone (01472) 605050.
Record Attendance: 31,651 v Wolverhampton W, FA Cup 5th rd, 20 February 1937. **Capacity:** 10,033.
Manager: Russell Slade.
Secretary: Ian Fleming.
Most League Goals: 103, Division 2, 1933–34.
Highest League Scorer in Season: Pat Glover, 42, Division 2, 1933–34.
Most League Goals in Total Aggregate: Pat Glover, 180, 1930–39.
Most Capped Player: Pat Glover, 7, Wales.
Most League Appearances: John McDermott, 592, 1987–.
Honours – Football League: Division 2 Champions – 1900–01, 1933–34. Division 3 (N) Champions – 1925–26, 1955–56. Division 3 Champions – 1979–80. Division 4 Champions – 1971-72. **League Group Cup:** Winners – 1981–82. **Auto Windscreens Shield:** Winners – 1997–98.
Colours: Black and white striped shirts, black shorts, black stockings.

Appleby Andy (M)	5 10	11 01	Seaham	11 10 85	Scholar
Barron Micky (D)	5 11	11 10	Lumley	22 12 74	Middlesbrough
Boyd Adam (F)	5 9	10 12	Hartlepool	25 5 82	Scholar
Brackstone John (D)	6 0	11 06	Hartlepool	9 2 85	Scholar
Butler Thomas (M)	5 7	10 06	Dublin	25 4 81	Sunderland
Clark Ben (D)	6 1	13 11	Shotley Bridge	24 1 83	Sunderland
Craddock Darren (D)	6 0	12 02	Bishop Auckland	23 2 85	Scholar
Daly Jon (F)	6 3	12 00	Dublin	8 1 83	Stockport Co
Foley David (F)	5 4	8 09	South Shields	12 5 87	Scholar
Howey Steve (D)	6 2	13 05	Sunderland	26 10 71	New England R
Humphreys Richie (M)	5 11	12 07	Sheffield	30 11 77	Cambridge U
Istead Steven (F)	5 8	11 06	South Shields	23 4 86	Scholar
Konstantopoulos Dimitrios (G)	6 4	14 02	Kalamata	29 11 78	
Maidens Michael (M)	5 11	11 04	Middlesbrough	7 5 87	Scholar
Nelson Michael (D)	6 2	13 03	Gateshead	15 3 82	Bury
Porter Joel (F)	5 9	11 13	Adelaide	25 12 78	Sydney Olympic
Provett Jim (G)	6 0	13 04	Stockton	22 12 82	Trainee
Robertson Hugh (D)	5 9	13 11	Aberdeen	19 3 75	Ross Co
Robson Matty (D)	5 10	11 02	Durham	23 1 85	Scholar
Ross Jack (D)	6 1	11 05	Falkirk	5 6 76	Clyde
Strachan Gavin (M)	5 10	11 07	Aberdeen	23 12 78	Southend U
Sweeney Anthony (M)	6 0	11 07	Stockton	5 9 83	Scholar
Tinkler Mark (M)	6 2	12 00	Bishop Auckland	24 10 74	Southend U
Turnbull Stephen (M)	5 10	11 00	South Shields	7 1 87	Scholar
Westwood Chris (D)	5 11	12 10	Dudley	13 2 77	Wolverhampton W
Wilkinson Jack (M)	5 8	10 08	Beverley	12 9 85	Scholar
Williams Eifion (F)	5 11	11 02	Bangor	15 11 75	Torquay U

League Appearances: Appleby, A. (15); Barron, M. 10(3); Betsy, K. 3(3); Boyd, A. 43(2); Brackstone, J. 8(1); Butler, T. 5(4); Clark, B. 21(4); Craddock, D. 9(1); Daly, J. 4(8); Foley, D. 1(1); Gobern, L. 1; Howey, S. (1); Humphreys, R. 46; Istead, S. (17); Konstantopoulos, D. 25; Maidens, M. (1); Nelson, M. 42(1); Porter, J. 36(3); Pouton, A. 5; Provett, J. 21; Robertson, H. 17(3); Robson, M. 22(5); Ross, J. 21(3); Strachan, G. 21(8); Sweeney, A. 44; Tinkler, M. 30(3); Turnbull, S. (2); Westwood, C. 36(1); Wilkinson, J. 1(2); Williams, E. 31(7); Woods, M. 3(3).
Goals – League (76): Boyd 22 (6 pens), Porter 14, Sweeney 13, Williams E 5, Westwood 4, Humphreys 3, Appleby 2, Robertson 2, Robson 2, Tinkler 2, Betsy 1, Butler 1, Daly 1, Nelson 1, Strachan 1, own goals 2.
Carling Cup (3): Boyd 1, Sweeney 1, Williams 1.
FA Cup (9): Boyd 3, Westwood 2, Porter 1, Robson 1, Tinkler 1, Williams 1.
LDV Vans Trophy (5): Boyd 1, Porter 1, Pouton 1, Strachan 1 (pen), Sweeney 1.
Play-Offs (4): Boyd 2, Daly 1, Williams 1.
Ground: Victoria Park, Clarence Road, Hartlepool TS24 8BZ. Telephone (01429) 272584.
Record Attendance: 17,426 v Manchester U, FA Cup 3rd rd, 5 January 1957.
Capacity: 7629.
Manager: Martin Scott.
Secretary: Maureen Smith.
Most League Goals: 90, Division 3 (N), 1956–57.
Highest League Scorer in Season: William Robinson, 28, Division 3 (N), 1927–28; Joe Allon, 28, Division 4, 1990–91.
Most League Goals in Total Aggregate: Ken Johnson, 98, 1949–64.
Most Capped Player: Ambrose Fogarty, 1 (11), Republic of Ireland.

Most League Appearances: Wattie Moore, 447, 1948–64.
Honours – Nil.
Colours: Blue and white striped shirts, blue shorts, white stockings.

HUDDERSFIELD TOWN — FL CHAMPIONSHIP 1

Abbott Pawel (F)	5 7	11 07	York	5 5 82	Preston NE
Adams Danny (D)	5 8	13 05	Manchester	3 1 76	Stockport Co
Ahmed Adnan (M)	5 10	11 12	Burnley	7 6 84	Scholar
Booth Andy (F)	6 1	13 00	Huddersfield	6 12 73	Sheffield W
Brandon Chris (M)	5 8	10 13	Bradford	7 4 76	Chesterfield
Brown Nat (F)	6 2	12 05	Sheffield	15 6 81	Trainee
Carss Tony (M)	5 11	11 13	Alnwick	31 3 76	Oldham Ath
Clarke Nathan (D)	6 2	12 00	Halifax	30 11 83	Scholar
Clarke Tom (D)	5 11	12 02	Halifax	21 12 87	Scholar
Collins Michael (M)	6 0	10 12	Halifax	30 4 86	Scholar
Edwards Rob (D)	5 8	12 01	Manchester	23 2 70	Chesterfield
Fowler Lee (M)	5 7	10 00	Cardiff	10 6 83	Coventry C
Holdsworth Andy (D)	5 9	11 02	Pontefract	29 1 84	Scholar
Lloyd Anthony (D)	5 7	11 00	Taunton	14 3 84	Scholar
McAliskey John (F)	6 5	12 07	Huddersfield	2 9 84	Scholar
McCombe John (D)	6 1	14 02	Pontefract	7 5 85	Scholar
Mendes Junior (F)	5 11	12 05	Balham	15 9 76	Mansfield T
Mirfin David (M)	6 2	14 05	Sheffield	18 4 85	Scholar
Rachubka Paul (G)	6 1	13 01	San Luis Opispo	21 5 81	Charlton Ath
Schofield Danny (F)	5 11	12 00	Doncaster	10 4 80	Brodsworth
Senior Philip (G)	5 11	11 00	Huddersfield	30 10 82	Trainee
Worthington Jon (M)	5 9	11 05	Dewsbury	16 4 83	Scholar
Yates Steve (D)	5 11	12 00	Bristol	29 1 70	Sheffield U

League Appearances: Abbott, P. 36(8); Adams, D. 5; Ahmed, A. 16(2); Beckett, L. 7; Booth, A. 25(4); Brandon, C. 42(2); Brown, N. 7(10); Carss, T. 23(4); Clarke, N. 37; Clarke, T. 12; Collins, M. 7(1); Edwards, R. 21(3); Facey, D. 4; Fowler, A. 8(12); Gray, I. 12; Holdsworth, A. 38(2); Lloyd, A. 10(1); McAliskey, J. 7(11); McCombe, J. 4(1); Mendes, J. 13(12); Mirfin, D. 38(3); Rachubka, P. 29; Schofield, D. 21(12); Senior, P. 5(1); Sodje, A. 1(6); Sodje, E. 24(4); Worthington, J. 39; Yates, S. 15(2).
Goals – League (74): Abbott 26 (3 pens), Booth 10, Beckett 6, Brandon 6, Mendes 5, Schofield 5, Mirfin 4, Worthington 3, Edwards 2, McAliskey 2, Ahmed 1, Carss 1, Sodje E 1, own goals 2.
Carling Cup (0).
FA Cup (1): Abbott 1.
LDV Vans Trophy (6): Ahmed 1, Fowler 1, McAliskey 1, Mendes 1 (pen), Mirfin 1, Schofield 1.
Ground: Galpharm Stadium, Leeds Road, Huddersfield HD1 6PX. Telephone (01484) 484100.
Record Attendance: 67,037 v Arsenal, FA Cup 6th rd, 27 February 1932.
Capacity: 24,500.
Manager: Peter Jackson.
Secretary: Ann Hough.
Most League Goals: 101, Division 4, 1979–80.
Highest League Scorer in Season: Sam Taylor, 35, Division 2, 1919–20; George Brown, 35, Division 1, 1925–26.
Most League Goals in Total Aggregate: George Brown, 142, 1921–29; Jimmy Glazzard, 142, 1946–56.
Most Capped Player: Jimmy Nicholson, 31 (41), Northern Ireland.
Most League Appearances: Billy Smith, 520, 1914–34.

Honours – Football League: Division 1 Champions – 1923–24, 1924–25, 1925–26. Division 2 Champions – 1969–70. Division 4 Champions – 1969–70. **FA Cup:** Winners – 1922.
Colours: Blue and white striped shirts, white shorts, white stockings with blue trim.

HULL CITY FL CHAMPIONSHIP

Allsopp Danny (F)	6 1	12 00	Melbourne	10 8 78	Notts Co
Ashbee Ian (M)	6 1	13 07	Birmingham	6 9 76	Cambridge U
Barmby Nick (M)	5 7	11 03	Hull	11 2 74	Leeds U
Burgess Ben (F)	6 4	14 04	Buxton	9 11 81	Stockport Co
Cort Leon (D)	6 3	13 01	Bermondsey	11 9 79	Southend U
Dawson Andy (D)	5 10	11 02	Northallerton	20 10 78	Scunthorpe U
Delaney Damien (D)	6 3	14 00	Cork	20 7 81	Leicester C
Duke Matt (G)	6 5	13 04	Sheffield	16 7 77	Sheffield U
Edge Roland (D)	5 9	11 07	Gillingham	25 11 78	Gillingham
Elliott Stuart (M)	5 10	11 09	Belfast	23 7 78	Motherwell
Ellison Kevin (M)	6 2	13 04	Liverpool	23 2 79	Chester C
Fagan Craig (F)	5 11	11 08	Birmingham	11 12 82	Colchester U
France Ryan (M)	5 11	11 11	Sheffield	13 12 80	Alfreton T
Fry Russell (M)	6 0	12 01	Hull	4 12 85	Scholar
Fry Russell (M)	6 0	12 01	Hull	4 12 85	Scholar
Green Stuart (M)	5 10	11 01	Whitehaven	15 6 81	Newcastle U
Joseph Marc (D)	6 0	12 05	Leicester	10 11 76	Peterborough U
Lewis Junior (M)	6 2	13 00	Wembley	9 10 73	Leicester C
Myhill Boaz (G)	6 3	14 06	Modesto	9 11 82	Aston Villa
Peat Nathan (M)	5 9	10 09	Hull	19 9 82	Scholar
Price Jason (M)	6 2	11 05	Pontypridd	12 4 77	Tranmere R
Stockdale Robbie (D)	5 11	12 04	Middlesbrough	30 11 79	Rotherham U
Thelwell Alton (D)	6 0	12 00	Islington	5 9 80	Tottenham H
Walters Jonathan (F)	6 1	12 00	Birkenhead	20 9 83	Crewe Alex
Wilbraham Aaron (F)	6 3	12 04	Knutsford	21 10 79	Stockport Co
Wiseman Scott (D)	6 0	11 06	Hull	9 10 85	Scholar

League Appearances: Allsopp, D. 14(14); Angus, S. 1(1); Ashbee, I. 40; Barmby, N. 38(1); Burgess, B. (2); Cort, L. 43(1); Dawson, A. 34; Delaney, D. 43; Duke, M. 1(1); Edge, R. 13(1); Elliott, S. 35(1); Ellison, K. 11(5); Facey, D. 12(9); Fagan, C. 11(1); France, R. 22(9); Fry, R. 1; Green, S. 26(3); Hessenthaler, A. 6(4); Hinds, R. 6; Joseph, M. 25(4); Keane, M. 12(8); Lewis, J. 31(8); Myhill, B. 45; Price, J. 6(21); Stockdale, R. 12(2); Thelwell, A. 2(1); Walters, J. 4(17); Wilbraham, A. 10(9); Wiseman, S. 2(1).
Goals – League (80): Elliott 27 (3 pens), Barmby 9, Green 8 (1 pen), Allsopp 7, Cort 6, Facey 4, Fagan 4 (2 pens), Keane 3 (1 pen), France 2, Lewis 2, Price 2, Wilbraham 2, Ashbee 1, Delaney 1, Ellison 1, Walters 1.
Carling Cup (2): France 1, Keane 1.
FA Cup (7): Facey 2, Elliott 1, France 1, Green 1, Keane 1, Walters 1.
LDV Vans Trophy (3): Elliott 1, Green 1, Price 1.
Ground: KC Stadium, The Circle, Walton Street, Hull HU3 6HU. Telephone (0870) 8370003.
Record Attendance: 55,019 v Manchester U, FA Cup 6th rd, 26 February 1949; 23,495 v Huddersfield T, Division 3, 24 April 2004 at KC Stadium.
Capacity: 25,404.
Manager: Peter Taylor.
Secretary: Phil Hough.
Most League Goals: 109, Division 3, 1965–66.
Highest League Scorer in Season: Bill McNaughton, 39, Division 3 (N), 1932–33.
Most League Goals in Total Aggregate: Chris Chilton, 195, 1960–71.

Most Capped Player: Theo Whitmore, Jamaica.
Most League Appearances: Andy Davidson, 520, 1952–67.
Honours – Football League: Division 3 (N) Champions – 1932–33, 1948–49. Division 3 Champions – 1965–66.
Colours: Black and amber striped shirts, black shorts, amber stockings.

IPSWICH TOWN — FL CHAMPIONSHIP

Bowditch Dean (F)	5 11	10 08	Bishop's Stortford	15 6 86	Trainee
Collins Aidan (D)	6 3	13 09	Harlow	18 10 86	
Counago Pablo (F)	5 11	11 06	Pontevedra	9 8 79	Celta Vigo
Currie Darren (M)	5 10	12 07	Hampstead	29 11 74	Brighton & HA
Davis Kelvin (G)	6 1	14 00	Bedford	29 9 76	Wimbledon
De Vos Jason (D)	6 4	13 07	London, Can	2 1 74	Wigan Ath
Diallo Drissa (D)	6 0	11 08	Nouadhibou	4 1 73	Burnley
Horlock Kevin (M)	6 0	12 00	Erith	1 11 72	West Ham U
Knights Darryl (F)	5 7	10 01	Ipswich	1 5 88	Scholar
Kuqi Shefki (F)	6 2	13 10	Kosovo	10 11 76	Sheffield W
Magilton Jim (M)	6 0	14 00	Belfast	6 5 69	Sheffield W
Miller Tommy (M)	6 1	11 12	Shotton Colliery	8 1 79	Hartlepool U
Mitchell Scott (M)	5 11	12 00	Ely	2 9 85	Scholar
Nash Gerard (D)	6 1	11 08	Dublin	11 7 86	Scholar
Naylor Richard (D)	6 1	13 07	Leeds	28 2 77	Trainee
Patten Ben (D)	6 1	12 08	London	16 2 86	Ford U
Price Lewis (G)	6 3	13 06	Poole	19 7 84	Academy
Richards Matt (D)	5 8	10 10	Harlow	26 12 84	Scholar
Sobers Jerome (D)	6 2	13 05	London	18 4 86	Ford U
Supple Shane (G)	5 11	11 07	Dublin	4 5 87	Scholar
Westlake Ian (M)	5 11	11 00	Clacton	10 11 83	Scholar
Wilnis Fabian (D)	5 8	12 06	Paramaribo	23 8 70	De Graafschap

League Appearances: Bent, D. 45; Bowditch, D. 6(15); Counago, P. 4(15); Currie, D. 19(5); Davis, K. 39; De Vos, J. 45; Diallo, D. 23(3); Dinning, T. 3(4); Horlock, K. 33(8); Karbassiyon, D. 3(2); Knights, D. (1); Kuqi, S. 40(3); Magilton, J. 33(6); Miller, T. 45; Naylor, R. 46; Price, L. 7(1); Richards, M. 15(9); Scowcroft, J. 3(6); Unsworth, D. 16; Westlake, I. 41(4); Wilnis, F. 40(1).
Goals – League (85): Bent 20, Kuqi 19, Miller 13 (6 pens), Westlake 7, Naylor 6, Bowditch 3, Counago 3, Currie 3 (1 pen), De Vos 3, Magilton 3, Richards 1, Unsworth 1, own goals 3.
Carling Cup (2): Miller 1, Westlake 1.
FA Cup (1): Miller 1.
Play-Offs (2): Kuqi 1, own goal 1.
Ground: Portman Road, Ipswich, Suffolk IP1 2DA. Telephone (01473) 400500.
Record Attendance: 38,010 v Leeds U, FA Cup 6th rd, 8 March 1975.
Capacity: 30,311.
Manager: Joe Royle.
Secretary: Sally Webb.
Most League Goals: 106, Division 3 (S), 1955–56.
Highest League Scorer in Season: Ted Phillips, 41, Division 3 (S), 1956–57.
Most League Goals in Total Aggregate: Ray Crawford, 203, 1958–63 and 1966–69.
Most Capped Player: Allan Hunter, 47 (53), Northern Ireland.
Most League Appearances: Mick Mills, 591, 1966–82.
Honours – Football League: Division 1 Champions – 1961–62. Division 2 Champions – 1960–61, 1967–68, 1991–92. Division 3 (S) Champions – 1953–54, 1956–57. **FA Cup:** Winners – 1977–78. **European Competitions: UEFA Cup:** Winners – 1980–81.
Colours: Blue shirts, white shorts, blue stockings.

KIDDERMINSTER HARRIERS — CONFERENCE

Beardsley Chris (F)	6 0	12 00	Derby	28 2 84	Doncaster R
Burton Steven (D)	6 1	11 05	Hull	10 10 82	Hull C
Chambers Adam (D)	5 10	11 12	Sandwell	20 11 80	WBA
Christiansen Jesper (F)	6 3	13 06	Denmark	18 6 80	Odense
Christie Iyseden (F)	5 10	12 02	Coventry	14 11 76	Mansfield T
Danby John (G)	6 2	14 06	Stoke	20 9 83	Juniors
Gleeson Jamie (F)	6 0	12 03	Poole	15 1 85	Trainee
Hatswell Wayne (D)	6 0	13 10	Swindon	8 2 75	Oxford U
Hollis Jermain (M)	5 10	11 00	Nottingham	7 10 86	
Jackson Mark (D)	5 11	12 00	Barnsley	30 9 77	Scunthorpe U
Jones Billy (D)	6 1	11 05	Chatham	26 3 83	Leyton Orient
Keates Dean (M)	5 6	10 10	Walsall	30 6 78	Hull C
Lewis Daniel (G)	6 1	14 00	Redditch	18 6 82	Studley
Matias Pedro (M)	6 0	12 00	Madrid	11 10 73	Bristol R
McGrath John (M)	5 10	10 04	Limerick	27 3 80	Doncaster R
McHale Chris (D)	6 0	12 00	Birmingham	4 11 82	Juniors
Rawle Mark (F)	5 11	12 11	Leicester	27 4 79	Oxford U
Russell Simon (M)	5 7	10 06	Beverley	19 3 85	Hull C

League Appearances: Advice-Desruisseaux, F. 9; Appleby, R. 6(3); Beardsley, C. 15(10); Bennett, T. 24; Beswetherick, J. 10; Birch, G. 11(3); Brown, S. 11(2); Burns, L. (1); Burton, S. 15(1); Chambers, A. 2; Christiansen, J. 11(6); Christie, I. 1(7); Clarke, R. 6; Cooper, S. 10; Cozic, B. 13(2); Danby, J. 37; Diop, Y. 7(3); Foster, B. 2; Foster, I. 15(12); Gleeson, J. 2(5); Hatswell, W. 38(2); Hollis, J. (1); Jackson, M. 13; Jenkins, L. 31(1); Jones, B. 10(2); Keates, D. 40(1); Keene, J. 5; Langmead, K. 9(1); Lewis, D. 1; Matias, P. 4(1); McGrath, J. 18(1); McHale, C. 11(3); McMahon, S. 3(2); Mellon, M. 5(2); Mullins, J. 21; Rawle, M. 5(6); Rickards, S. (4); Roberts, S. 4(1); Russell, S. 18(10); Sall, A. 13(1); Stamp, D. 4; Sturrock, B. 17(5); Viveash, A. 7; Weaver, S. 22(1).
Goals – League (39): Foster I 6 (2 pens), Beardsley 5, Keates 5 (2 pens), Sturrock 5, Birch 4, Rawle 3, Mullins 2, Russell 2, Appleby 1 (pen), Hatswell 1, Langmead 1, Matias 1, Roberts 1, Stamp 1, own goal 1.
Carling Cup (1): Brown 1.
FA Cup (1): Hatswell 1.
LDV Vans Trophy (0).
Ground: Aggborough Stadium, Hoo Road, Kidderminster DY10 1NB. Telephone (01562) 823 931.
Record Attendance: 9,155 v Hereford U, 27 November 1948.
Capacity: 6444.
Manager: Stuart Watkiss.
Football Secretary: Roger Barlow.
Honours – Conference: Champions – 1993–94, 1999–2000; Runners-up 1996–97. **FA Trophy:** 1986–87 (winners); 1990–91 (runners-up), 1994–95 (runners-up). **League Cup:** 1996–97 (winners). **Welsh FA Cup:** 1985–86 (runners-up), 1988–89 (runners-up). **Southern League Cup:** 1979–80 (winners). **Worcester Senior Cup:** (21). **Birmingham Senior Cup:** (7). **Staffordshire Senior Cup:** (4). **West Midland League Champions:** (6), Runners-up (3). **Southern Premier:** Runners-up (1). **West Midland League Cup:** Winners (7). **Keys Cup:** Winners (7). **Border Counties Floodlit League Champions:** (3). **Camkin Floodlit Cup:** Winners (3). **Bass County Vase:** Winners (1). **Conference Fair Play Trophy:** (5)
Colours: Red shirts, white shorts, red stockings.

Bakke Eirik (M)	6 2	12 10	Sogndal	13 9 77	Sogndal
Butler Paul (D)	6 2	15 04	Manchester	2 11 72	Wolverhampton W
Carlisle Clarke (D)	6 3	14 12	Preston	14 10 79	QPR
Constable Robert (D)	6 0	12 13	Pontefract	26 1 86	Trainee
Coyles William (G)	6 0	12 01	Co Antrim	20 12 84	Scholar
Crainey Stephen (D)	5 9	12 05	Glasgow	22 6 81	Southampton
Derry Shaun (M)	5 10	13 02	Nottingham	6 12 77	Crystal Palace
Einarsson Gylfi (M)	6 0	12 00	Iceland	27 10 78	Lille
Gregan Sean (M)	6 2	15 08	Guisborough	29 3 74	WBA
Healy David (F)	5 8	11 07	Downpatrick	5 8 79	Preston NE
Ilic Sasa (G)	6 4	14 12	Melbourne	18 7 72	Blackpool
Joachim Julian (F)	5 6	12 05	Boston	20 9 74	Coventry C
Johnson Seth (M)	5 10	13 03	Birmingham	12 3 79	Derby Co
Johnson Simon (F)	5 10	12 02	West Bromwich	9 3 83	Scholar
Keegan Paul (M)	5 11	11 05	Dublin	5 7 84	Scholar
Kelly Gary (D)	5 10	11 02	Drogheda	9 7 74	Home Farm
Kilgallon Matthew (D)	6 1	12 07	York	8 1 84	Scholar
Lennon Aaron (F)	5 5	10 06	Leeds	16 4 87	Trainee
Moore Ian (F)	5 11	12 00	Birkenhead	26 8 76	Burnley
Pugh Danny (M)	6 0	11 11	Manchester	19 10 82	Manchester U
Radebe Lucas (D)	6 0	13 01	Johannesburg	12 4 69	Kaiser Chiefs
Richardson Frazer (D)	5 11	12 04	Rotherham	29 10 82	Trainee
Ricketts Michael (F)	6 2	15 10	Birmingham	4 12 78	Middlesbrough
Singh Harpal (M)	5 7	10 02	Bradford	15 9 81	Trainee
Spring Matthew (M)	6 0	12 00	Harlow	17 11 79	Luton T
Sullivan Neil (G)	6 3	15 08	Sutton	24 2 70	Chelsea
Walton Simon (D)	6 1	13 05	Sherburn-in-Elmet	13 9 87	Scholar
Winter Jamie (M)	5 10	13 10	Dundee	4 8 85	Scholar
Woods Martin (M)	5 11	11 05	Airdrie	1 1 86	Trainee
Wright Jermaine (M)	5 10	13 00	Greenwich	21 10 75	Ipswich T

League Appearances: Bakke, E. (1); Blake, N. 2; Butler, P. 39; Carlisle, C. 29(6); Crainey, S. 9; Deane, B. 23(8); Derry, S. 7; Duberry, M. 4; Einarsson, G. 6(2); Gray, M. 10; Gregan, S. 34(1); Griffit, L. (1); Guppy, S. 1(2); Healy, D. 27(1); Hulse, R. 13; Joachim, J. 10(17); Johnson, Seth 4(2); Johnson, Simon 1(1); Kelly, G. 43; Kilgallon, M. 26; King, M. 4(5); Lennon, A. 19(8); McMaster, J. (7); Moore, I. 4(2); Ormerod, B. 6; Oster, J. 8; Pugh, D. 33(5); Radebe, L. 1(2); Richardson, F. 28(10); Ricketts, M. 9(12); Spring, M. 4(9); Sullivan, N. 46; Walton, S. 23(7); Woods, M. (1); Wright, J. 33(2).
Goals – League (49): Healy 7 (1 pen), Deane 6, Hulse 6, Pugh 5, Carlisle 4, Walton 3, Wright 3, Derry 2, Joachim 2, Blake 1, Einarsson 1, Guppy 1, Seth Johnson 1, Lennon 1, Oster 1, Richardson 1, Spring 1, own goals 3.
Carling Cup (3): Deane 1, Pugh 1, Ricketts 1.
FA Cup (0).
Ground: Elland Road, Leeds LS11 0ES. Telephone (0113) 367 6000.
Record Attendance: 57,892 v Sunderland, FA Cup 5th rd (replay), 15 March 1967.
Capacity: 40,232.
Manager: Kevin Blackwell.
Most League Goals: 98, Division 2, 1927–28.
Highest League Scorer in Season: John Charles, 42, Division 2, 1953–54.
Most League Goals in Total Aggregate: Peter Lorimer, 168, 1965–79 and 1983–86.
Most Capped Player: Lucas Radebe, 58 (70), South Africa.
Most League Appearances: Jack Charlton, 629, 1953–73.

Honours – Football League: Division 1 Champions – 1968–69, 1973–74, 1991–92. Division 2 Champions – 1923–24, 1963–64, 1989–90. **FA Cup:** Winners – 1972. **Football League Cup:** Winners – 1967–68. **European Competitions: European Fairs Cup:** Winners – 1967–68, 1970–71.
Colours: All white.

LEICESTER CITY — FL CHAMPIONSHIP

Canero Peter (D)	5 9	12 06	Glasgow	18 1 81	Kilmarnock
Connolly David (F)	5 9	11 00	Willesden	6 6 77	West Ham U
Dawson Stephen (M)	5 9	11 09	Dublin	4 12 85	Scholar
De Vries Mark (F)	6 3	12 01	Surinam	24 8 75	Hearts
Dublin Dion (F)	6 2	15 00	Leicester	22 4 69	Aston Villa
Elliott Matt (D)	6 3	15 00	Wandsworth	1 11 68	Oxford U
Gillespie Keith (M)	5 10	11 01	Larne	18 2 75	Blackburn R
Gudjonsson Joey (M)	5 9	12 04	Akranes	25 5 80	Wolverhampton W
Heath Matthew (D)	6 4	13 13	Leicester	1 11 81	Scholar
Hirschfeld Lars (G)	6 4	13 08	Edmonton	17 10 78	Tottenham H
Hughes Stephen (M)	5 11	9 06	Motherwell	14 11 82	Rangers
Logan Conrad (G)	6 0	14 09	Letterkenny	18 4 86	Scholar
Maybury Alan (D)	5 8	11 08	Dublin	8 8 78	Hearts
McCarthy Patrick (D)	6 2	13 07	Dublin	31 5 83	Manchester C
Morris Lee (F)	5 10	11 07	Driffield	30 4 80	Derby Co
Sheehan Alan (D)	5 11	11 02	Athlone	14 9 86	Scholar
Stearman Richard (D)	6 2	10 08	Wolverhampton	19 8 87	Scholar
Stewart Jordan (D)	5 11	12 08	Birmingham	3 3 82	Trainee
Tiatto Danny (D)	5 8	11 08	Melbourne	22 5 73	Manchester C
Wilcox Jason (M)	5 11	11 01	Bolton	15 7 71	Leeds U
Williams Gareth (M)	6 1	12 03	Glasgow	16 12 81	Nottingham F
Wright Tommy (F)	6 0	12 02	Leicester	28 9 84	Scholar

League Appearances: Benjamin, T. 2(8); Blake, N. 4(10); Canero, P. 6; Connolly, D. 43(1); Dabizas, N. 33; De Vries, M. 9(7); Dublin, D. 34(3); Elliott, M. 1(1); Gemmill, S. 11(6); Gillespie, K. 19(11); Gudjonsson, J. 26(9); Harper, K. 2; Heath, M. 17(5); Hirschfeld, L. 1; Hughes, S. 13(3); Kenton, D. 9(1); Keown, M. 16(1); Makin, C. 21; Maybury, A. 17; McCarthy, P. 12; Moore, S. 2(5); Morris, L. 2(8); Nalis, L. 32(7); Pressman, K. 13; Scowcroft, J. 30(1); Sheehan, A. 1; Stearman, R. 3(5); Stewart, J. 33(2); Taylor, S. 10; Tiatto, D. 25(5); Walker, I. 22; Wilcox, J. 11(3); Williams, G. 25(8); Wright, T. 1(6).
Goals – League (49): Connolly 13 (4 pens), Dublin 5, Nalis 5, Scowcroft 4, Heath 3, Benjamin 2, Gillespie 2, Gudjonsson 2, Maybury 2, Dabizas 1, De Vries 1, Hughes 1, Stearman 1, Stewart 1, Tiatto 1, Wilcox 1, Williams 1, own goals 3.
Carling Cup (2): Blake 1, Gudjonsson 1 (pen)
FA Cup (7): Williams 2, Dabizas 1, Dublin 1, Gudjonsson 1, Scowcroft 1, own goal 1.
Ground: The Walkers Stadium, Filbert Way, Leicester LE2 7GL. Telephone (0870) 040 6000
Record Attendance: 47,298 v Tottenham H, FA Cup 5th rd, 18 February 1928.
Capacity: 32,500.
Manager: Craig Levein.
Secretary: Andrew Neville.
Most League Goals: 109, Division 2, 1956–57.
Highest League Scorer in Season: Arthur Rowley, 44, Division 2, 1956–57.
Most League Goals in Total Aggregate: Arthur Chandler, 259, 1923–35.
Most Capped Player: John O'Neill, 39, Northern Ireland.
Most League Appearances: Adam Black, 528, 1920–35.

Honours – Football League: Division 2 Champions – 1924–25, 1936–37, 1953–54, 1956–57, 1970–71, 1979–80. **Football League Cup:** Winners – 1964, 1997, 2000.
Colours: Royal blue shirts, white shorts, blue stockings.

LEYTON ORIENT FL CHAMPIONSHIP 2

Alexander Gary (F)	6 0	12 00	Lambeth	15 8 79	Hull C
Barnard Donny (D)	5 9	10 10	Forest Gate	1 7 84	Trainee
Carlisle Wayne (M)	5 10	11 00	Lisburn	9 9 79	Bristol R
Duncan Derek (M)	5 9	10 12	Newham	23 4 87	Scholar
Echanomi Efe (M)	5 7	11 07	Nigeria	27 9 86	Scholar
Ibehre Jabo (F)	6 1	12 10	Islington	28 1 83	Trainee
Lockwood Matt (D)	6 0	11 06	Rochford	17 10 76	Bristol R
Mackie John (D)	6 1	12 00	Enfield	5 7 76	Reading
McMahon Daryl (M)	5 11	12 02	Dublin	10 10 83	Port Vale
Miller Justin (D)	6 1	11 07	Johannesburg	16 12 80	Ipswich T
Morris Glenn (G)	5 11	11 00	Woolwich	20 12 83	Scholar
Palmer Aiden (M)	5 8	10 04	Enfield	2 1 87	Scholar
Saah Brian (M)	6 1	11 05	Rush Green	16 12 86	Scholar
Scott Andy (F)	6 2	12 00	Epsom	2 8 72	Oxford U
Simpson Michael (M)	5 7	10 05	Nottingham	28 2 74	Wycombe W
Steele Lee (F)	5 8	11 08	Liverpool	2 12 73	Oxford U
Wallis Scott (M)	5 10	10 10	Enfield	28 6 88	Scholar
Youngs Tom (F)	5 9	11 13	Bury St Edmunds	31 8 79	Northampton T
Zakuani Gaby (D)	6 0	11 08	Zaire	31 5 86	Scholar

League Appearances: Alexander, G. 25(3); Barnard, D. 22(11); Barnard, L. 3(5); Carlisle, W. 24(4); Chillingworth, D. 8; Duncan, D. 6(9); Echanomi, E. 4(14); Fitzgerald, S. 1; Harrison, L. 34; Hunt, D. 22(5); Ibehre, J. 10(9); Lockwood, M. 42(1); Mackie, J. 26(1); McMahon, D. 22(2); Miller, J. 43; Morris, G. 12; Newey, T. 3(17); Palmer, A. 3(2); Peters, M. (2); Purser, W. (2); Saah, B. 9(3); Scott, A. 37(2); Simpson, M. 45; Steele, L. 37(2); Wallis, S. (3); Wardley, S. 4(2); White, A. 26; Youngs, T. 6(4); Zakuani, G. 32(1).
Goals – League (65): Steele 16, Alexander 9, Scott 9, Lockwood 6 (5 pens), Echanomi 5, Mackie 4, Carlisle 3, McMahon 3, Chillingworth 2, Ibehre 2, Simpson 2, Barnard D 1, Newey 1, Purser 1, Youngs 1.
Carling Cup (1): Steele 1.
FA Cup (3): Carlisle 1, Hunt 1, Lockwood 1.
LDV Vans Trophy (7): Ibehre 2, Alexander 1, Carlisle 1, Miller 1, Saah 1, own goal 1.
Ground: Matchroom Stadium, Brisbane Road, Leyton, London E10 5NE. Telephone (020) 8926 1111.
Record Attendance: 34,345 v West Ham U, FA Cup 4th rd, 25 January 1964. **Capacity:** 7804.
Manager: Martin Ling.
Secretary: Lindsey Freeman.
Most League Goals: 106, Division 3 (S), 1955–56.
Highest League Scorer in Season: Tom Johnston, 35, Division 2, 1957–58.
Most League Goals in Total Aggregate: Tom Johnston, 121, 1956–58, 1959–61.
Most Capped Players: Tunji Banjo, 7 (7), Nigeria; John Chiedozie, 7 (9), Nigeria; Tony Grealish, 7 (45), Eire.
Most League Appearances: Peter Allen, 432, 1965–78.
Honours – Football League: Division 3 Champions – 1969–70. Division 3 (S) Champions – 1955–56.
Colours: Red shirts with black panel, red shorts, red stockings.

LINCOLN CITY — FL CHAMPIONSHIP 2

Asamoah Derek (F)	5 6	10 12	Ghana	1 5 81	Mansfield T
Beevers Lee (D)	6 1	13 00	Doncaster	4 12 83	Boston U
Bloomer Matt (D)	6 0	11 08	Cleethorpes	3 11 78	Hull C
Frecklington Lee (M)	5 8	11 00	Lincoln	8 9 85	Scholar
Futcher Ben (D)	6 7	12 05	Bradford	20 2 81	Oldham Ath
Gain Peter (M)	6 0	11 07	Hammersmith	2 11 76	Tottenham H
Green Francis (F)	5 9	11 06	Derby	25 4 80	Peterborough U
Hobbs Jack (D)	6 0	12 00	Portsmouth	18 8 88	Scholar
Marriott Alan (G)	6 0	12 04	Bedford	3 9 78	Tottenham H
McAuley Gareth (D)	6 3	13 00	Larne	5 12 79	Coleraine
McCombe Jamie (D)	6 5	12 03	Pontefract	1 1 83	Scunthorpe U
McNamara Niall (M)	6 1	12 07	Limerick	26 1 82	Belper T
Morgan Paul (D)	6 0	11 03	Belfast	23 10 78	Preston NE
Rayner Simon (G)	6 4	15 00	Vancouver	8 7 83	Port Talbot
Ryan Oliver (M)	5 9	11 00	Boston	26 9 85	Scholar
Sandwith Kevin (D)	5 11	12 05	Workington	30 4 78	Halifax T
Taylor-Fletcher Gary (F)	6 0	11 00	Liverpool	4 6 81	Leyton Orient
Yeo Simon (F)	5 10	11 08	Stockport	20 10 73	Hyde U

League Appearances: Asamoah, D. 8(2); Beevers, L. 4(4); Bermingham, K. (2); Blackwood, M. 5(4); Bloomer, M. 31(6); Butcher, R. 46; Carruthers, M. 7(4); Frecklington, L. (3); Futcher, B. 35; Gain, P. 36(4); Green, F. 28(9); Hanlon, R. 6(6); Hobbs, J. (1); Ipoua, G. (6); Kerley, A. (1); Littlejohn, A. 1(7); Marriott, A. 45; McAuley, G. 32(5); McCombe, J. 37(4); McNamara, N. (1); Morgan, P. 39; Pearson, G. 1(2); Peat, N. 6(4); Rayner, S. 1; Richardson, M. 7(7); Ryan, O. (6); Sandwith, K. 34(3); Taylor-Fletcher, G. 35(3); Toner, C. 10(5); Weaver, S. 5; West, D. 4; Westcarr, C. 5(1); Yeo, S. 38(6).
Goals – League (64): Yeo 21 (3 pens), Taylor-Fletcher 11 (1 pen), Green 8, Richardson 4, Futcher 3, McAuley 3, McCombe 3, Bloomer 2, Butcher 2, Sandwith 2, Toner 2, Hanlon 1, Westcarr 1, own goal 1.
Carling Cup (4): Yeo 2 (1 pen), McCombe 1, Taylor-Fletcher 1 (pen).
FA Cup (0).
LDV Vans Trophy (0).
Play-Offs (2): McAuley 2.
Ground: Sincil Bank, Lincoln LN5 8LD. Telephone (0870) 899 2005.
Record Attendance: 23,196 v Derby Co, League Cup 4th rd, 15 November 1967.
Capacity: 10,127.
Manager: Keith Alexander.
Secretary: Fran Martin.
Most League Goals: 121, Division 3 (N), 1951–52.
Highest League Scorer in Season: Allan Hall, 41, Division 3 (N), 1931–32.
Most League Goals in Total Aggregate: Andy Graver, 144, 1950–55 and 1958–61.
Most Capped Player: David Pugh, 3 (7), Wales; George Moulson, 3, Republic of Ireland.
Most League Appearances: Grant Brown, 407, 1989–2002.
Honours – Football League: Division 3 (N) Champions – 1931–32, 1947–48, 1951–52. Division 4 Champions – 1975–76.
Colours: Red and white striped shirts, black shorts, red stockings.

LIVERPOOL — FA PREMIERSHIP

Alonso Xabi (M)	6 0	12 02	Tolosa	25 11 81	Real Sociedad
Baros Milan (F)	5 9	12 05	Valasske Mezirici	28 10 81	Banik Ostrava

Carragher Jamie (D)	5 9	12 01	Liverpool	28 1 78	Trainee
Carson Scott (G)	6 3	13 12	Whitehaven	3 9 85	Leeds U
Cheyrou Bruno (M)	6 1	13 03	Suresnes	10 5 78	Lille
Cisse Djibril (F)	6 0	13 00	Arles	12 8 81	Auxerre
Diao Salif (M)	6 1	12 08	Kedougou	10 2 77	Sedan
Diarra Alou (M)	6 1	12 03	Villepinte	15 7 81	Le Havre
Diouf El Hadji (F)	5 8	12 05	Dakar	15 1 81	Lens
Dudek Jerzy (G)	6 2	12 08	Ribnek	23 3 73	Feyenoord
Finnan Steve (M)	6 0	12 03	Limerick	24 4 76	Fulham
Foy Robbie (F)	5 6	9 09	Edinburgh	29 10 85	Trainee
Gerrard Steven (M)	6 0	12 05	Whiston	30 5 80	Trainee
Hamann Dietmar (M)	6 2	13 00	Waldasson	27 8 73	Newcastle U
Hyypia Sami (D)	6 3	13 09	Porvoo	7 10 73	Willem II
Josemi (D)	5 9	12 08	Malaga	15 11 79	Malaga
Kewell Harry (M)	5 9	12 06	Sydney	22 9 78	Leeds U
Kirkland Christopher (G)	6 5	14 08	Leicester	2 5 81	Coventry C
Le Tallec Anthony (M)	6 0	12 00	Hennebont	3 10 84	Le Havre
Luis Garcia (M)	5 6	10 05	Badalona	24 6 78	Barcelona
Luzi-Bernardi Patrice (G)	6 2	13 08	Ajaccio	8 7 80	Monaco
Medjani Carl (D)	6 0	13 04	Lyon	15 5 85	
Mellor Neil (F)	6 0	13 05	Manchester	4 11 82	Scholar
Morientes Fernando (F)	6 0	12 04	Caceres	5 4 76	Real Madrid
Nunez Antonio (M)	6 0	12 02	Madrid	15 1 79	Real Madrid
Potter Darren (M)	6 0	10 08	Liverpool	21 12 84	Scholar
Raven David (D)	6 0	11 04	Birkenhead	10 3 85	Scholar
Riise John Arne (M)	6 1	14 00	Molde	24 9 80	Monaco
Sinama-Pongolle Florent (F)	5 7	11 05	Saint-Pierre	20 10 84	Le Havre
Traore Djimi (D)	6 2	12 07	Saint-Ouen	1 3 80	Lens
Vignal Gregory (D)	5 9	11 06	Montpellier	19 7 81	Bastia
Warnock Stephen (M)	5 7	11 09	Ormskirk	12 12 81	Trainee
Welsh John (M)	5 7	12 02	Liverpool	10 1 84	Scholar
Whitbread Zak (D)	6 2	12 07	Houston	4 3 84	
Wilkie Ryan (M)			Glasgow	11 12 85	Trainee

League Appearances: Alonso, X. 20(4); Baros, M. 22(4); Biscan, I. 8(11); Carragher, J. 38; Carson, S. 4; Cisse, D. 10(6); Diao, S. 4(4); Dudek, J. 24; Finnan, S. 29(4); Gerrard, S. 28(2); Hamann, D. 23(7); Hyypia, S. 32; Josemi, 13(2); Kewell, H. 15(3); Kirkland, C. 10; Le Tallec, A. 2(2); Luis Garcia, 26(3); Mellor, N. 6(3); Morientes, F. 12(1); Nunez, A. 8(10); Pellegrino, M. 11(1); Potter, D. (2); Raven, D. (1); Riise, J. 34(3); Sinama-Pongolle, F. 6(10); Smicer, V. 2(8); Traore, D. 18(8); Warnock, S. 11(8); Welsh, J. 2(1).
Goals – League (52): Baros 9 (2 pens), Luis Garcia 8, Gerrard 7, Riise 6, Cisse 4 (1 pen), Morientes 3, Alonso 2, Biscan 2, Hyypia 2, Mellor 2, Sinama-Pongolle 2, Finnan 1, Kewell 1, own goals 3.
Carling Cup (10): Baros 2, Gerrard 2, Mellor 2, Diao 1, Nunez 1, Riise 1, Sinama-Pongolle 1 (pen).
FA Cup (0).
Champions League (20): Luis Garcia 5, Gerrard 4, Baros 2, Alonso 1, Cisse 1, Hamann 1, Hyypia 1, Mellor 1, Riise 1, Sinama-Pongolle 1, Smicer 1, own goal 1.
Ground: Anfield Road, Liverpool L4 0TH. Telephone (0151) 263 2361.
Record Attendance: 61,905 v Wolverhampton W, FA Cup 4th rd, 2 February 1952.
Capacity: 45,362.
Manager: Rafael Benitez.
Secretary: Bryce Morrison.
Most League Goals: 106, Division 2, 1895–96.
Highest League Scorer in Season: Roger Hunt, 41, Division 2, 1961–62.
Most League Goals in Total Aggregate: Roger Hunt, 245, 1959–69.

Most Capped Player: Ian Rush, 67 (73), Wales.
Most League Appearances: Ian Callaghan, 640, 1960–78.
Honours – Football League: Division 1 – Champions 1900–01, 1905–06, 1921–22, 1922–23, 1946–47, 1963–64, 1965–66, 1972–73, 1975–76, 1976–77, 1978–79, 1979–80, 1981–82, 1982–83, 1983–84, 1985–86, 1987–88, 1989–90 (Liverpool have a record number of 18 League Championship wins). Division 2 Champions – 1893–94, 1895–96, 1904–05, 1961–62. **FA Cup**: Winners – 1965, 1974, 1986, 1989, 1992, 2001. **League Cup:** Winners – 1981, 1982, 1983, 1984, 1995, 2001, 2003. Super Cup: Winners 1985–86. **European Competitions: European Cup:** Winners – 1976–77, 1977–78, 1980–81, 1983–84. **Champions League:** Winners – 2004–05. **UEFA Cup:** Winners – 1972–73, 1975–76, 2001. **Super Cup:** Winners – 1977.
Colours: All red.

LUTON TOWN — FL CHAMPIONSHIP

Andrew Calvin (F)	6 0	12 11	Luton	19 12 86	Scholar
Beresford Marlon (G)	6 1	13 05	Lincoln	2 9 69	Barnsley
Brkovic Ahmet (M)	5 8	11 11	Dubrovnik	23 9 74	Leyton Orient
Coyne Chris (D)	6 2	13 12	Brisbane	20 12 78	Dundee
Davies Curtis (D)	6 2	11 13	London	15 3 85	Scholar
Davis Sol (D)	5 8	11 13	Cheltenham	4 9 79	Swindon T
Feeney Warren (F)	5 10	11 03	Belfast	17 1 81	Stockport Co
Foley Kevin (M)	5 10	11 02	London	1 11 84	Scholar
Holmes Peter (M)	5 11	11 09	Bishop Auckland	18 11 80	Sheffield W
Howard Steve (F)	6 3	15 00	Durham	10 5 76	Northampton T
Keane Keith (M)	5 9	11 02	Luton	20 11 86	Scholar
Leary Michael (M)	6 0	11 11	Ealing	17 4 83	Scholar
Mansell Lee (M)	5 9	11 00	Gloucester	28 10 82	Scholar
Neilson Alan (D)	5 11	12 13	Wegburg	26 9 72	Fulham
Nicholls Kevin (M)	5 10	12 04	Newham	2 1 79	Wigan Ath
O'Leary Stephen (M)	6 0	11 09	Barnet	12 2 85	Scholar
Perrett Russell (D)	6 1	12 06	Barton-on-Sea	18 6 73	Cardiff C
Robinson Steve (M)	5 9	11 02	Lisburn	10 12 74	Preston NE
Seremet Dino (G)	6 4	14 09	Slovenia	16 8 80	Maribor
Showunmi Enoch (F)	6 3	14 10	Kilburn	21 4 82	Willesden Constantine
Underwood Paul (M)	5 11	12 11	Wimbledon	16 8 73	Rushden & D

League Appearances: Andrew, C. 2(6); Beresford, M. 38; Blinkhorn, M. (2); Brkovic, A. 39(3); Coyne, C. 39(1); Davies, C. 44; Davis, S. 45; Feeney, W. 1(5); Foley, K. 38(1); Holmes, P. 13(6); Howard, S. 40; Keane, K. 11(6); Leary, M. 1(7); Mansell, L. (1); McSheffrey, G. 1(4); Neilson, A. 6(3); Nicholls, K. 44; O'Leary, S. 12(5); Perrett, R. 9(3); Robinson, S. 28(3); Royce, S. 2; Seremet, D. 6(1); Showunmi, E. 7(28); Underwood, P. 37; Vine, R. 43(2).
Goals – League (87): Howard 18, Brkovic 15, Nicholls 12 (7 pens), Vine 9, Showunmi 6, Coyne 5, Underwood 5, Robinson 4, Holmes 3, Davis 2, Foley 2, Davies 1, McSheffrey 1, O'Leary 1, Perrett 1, own goals 2.
Carling Cup (3): Nicholls 1 (pen), Showunmi 1, own goal 1.
FA Cup (6): Howard 4, Brkovic 1, Nicholls 1.
LDV Vans Trophy (0).
Ground: Kenilworth Road Stadium, 1 Maple Road, Luton, Beds. LU4 8AW. Telephone (01582) 411622.
Record Attendance: 30,069 v Blackpool, FA Cup 6th rd replay, 4 March 1959.
Capacity: 10,155.
Manager: Mike Newell.
Secretary: Cherry Newbery.
Most League Goals: 103, Division 3 (S), 1936–37.

Highest League Scorer in Season: Joe Payne, 55, Division 3 (S), 1936–37.
Most League Goals in Total Aggregate: Gordon Turner, 243, 1949–64.
Most Capped Player: Mal Donaghy, 58 (91), Northern Ireland.
Most League Appearances: Bob Morton, 494, 1948–64.
Honours – Football League: Championship 1: Winners – 2004–05. Division 2 Champions – 1981–82. Division 4 Champions – 1967–68. Division 3 (S) Champions – 1936–37. **Football League Cup:** Winners – 1987–88.
Colours: White shirts with orange and black trim, black shorts with orange and white trim, black stockings with two white hoops.

MACCLESFIELD TOWN — FL CHAMPIONSHIP 2

Bailey Mark (D)	5 10	12 00	Stoke	12 8 76	Lincoln C
Barras Tony (D)	6 3	14 09	Billingham	29 3 71	Notts Co
Brightwell Ian (D)	5 10	12 08	Lutterworth	9 4 68	Port Vale
Briscoe Michael (D)	6 1	11 07	Northampton	4 7 83	Coventry C
Fettis Alan (G)	6 2	13 10	Belfast	1 2 71	Hull C
Harsley Paul (M)	5 9	11 10	Scunthorpe	29 5 78	Northampton T
MacKenzie Neil (M)	6 2	12 06	Birmingham	15 4 76	Mansfield T
McIntyre Kevin (M)	5 11	12 00	Liverpool	23 12 77	Chester C
Miles John (F)	5 10	12 09	Fazackerley	28 9 81	Crewe Alex
Morley Dave (D)	6 3	13 00	St Helens	25 9 77	Doncaster R
Parkin Jonathan (F)	6 4	13 12	Barnsley	30 12 81	York C
Payne Steve (D)	6 0	13 03	Castleford	1 8 75	Chesterfield
Potter Graham (D)	6 1	12 03	Solihull	20 5 75	Boston U
Swailes Danny (D)	6 3	13 07	Bolton	1 4 79	Bury
Teague Andrew (D)	6 2	12 00	Preston	5 2 86	Scholar
Welch Michael (D)	6 3	11 12	Winsford	11 1 82	Barnsley
Whitaker Danny (M)	5 10	11 02	Manchester	14 11 80	Wilmslow Sports
Wilson Steve (G)	6 0	11 02	Hull	24 4 74	Hull C

League Appearances: Bailey, M. 20(1); Barras, T. 22(2); Boyd, M. 4(1); Brightwell, I. 3(3); Briscoe, M. 12(2); Carragher, M. 26(5); Fettis, A. 28; Harsley, P. 44(2); MacKenzie, N. 16(2); McIntyre, K. 21(2); Miles, J. 14(16); Morley, D. 19; Navarro, A. 11; Parkin, J. 42; Potter, G. 39(2); Rooney, T. (1); Sheron, M. 14(12); Strong, G. 4; Swadi-Fayadh, J. (1); Swailes, D. 17; Teague, A. 5; Tipton, M. 40(4); Townson, K. 2(4); Weaver, S. 7; Welch, M. 31; Whitaker, D. 26(10); Widdrington, T. 21(2); Wilson, S. 18(1).
Goals – League (60): Parkin 22 (1 pen), Tipton 12 (2 pens), Potter 6, Harsley 3, Miles 3, Sheron 3, Bailey 2, Morley 2, Welch 2, Whitaker 2, Barras 1, Navarro 1, own goal 1.
Carling Cup (1): Parkin 1.
FA Cup (3): Parkin 1, Sheron 1, Whitaker 1.
LDV Vans Trophy (6): Parkin 2, Tipton 2, Barras 1, Whitaker 1.
Play-Offs (1): Harsley 1.
Ground: The Moss Rose Ground, London Road, Macclesfield, Cheshire SK11 7SP. Telephone (01625) 264686.
Record Attendance: 9008 v Winsford U, Cheshire Senior Cup 2nd rd, 4 February 1948. **Capacity:** 6208.
Manager: Brian Horton.
Secretary: Colin Garlick.
Most League Goals: 66, Division 3, 1999–2000.
Highest League Scorer in Season: Richard Barker, 16, Division 3, 1999–2000.
Most League Goals in Total Aggregate: John Askey, 31, 1997–.
Most Capped Player: George Abbey, 10, Nigeria.
Most League Appearances: Darren Tinson, 263, 1997–2003; Matt Tipton, 16, Division 3, 2003–04.

Honours – Nil.
Colours: Royal blue shirts, white shorts, blue stockings.

MANCHESTER CITY — FA PREMIERSHIP

Barton Joey (M)	5 11	11 09	Huyton	2 9 82	Scholar
Bermingham Karl (M)	5 10	12 07	Dublin	6 10 85	Scholar
Bischoff Mikkel (D)	6 3	13 11	Denmark	3 2 82	AB Copenhagen
Croft Lee (F)	5 9	13 01	Wigan	21 6 85	Scholar
D'Laryea Jonathan (M)	5 10	12 02	Manchester	3 9 85	Trainee
D'Laryea Nathan (D)			Manchester	3 9 85	Trainee
De Vlieger Geert (G)	6 2	14 00	Dendermonde	16 10 71	Willem II
Distin Sylvain (D)	6 3	14 08	Bagnolet	16 12 77	Newcastle U
Dunne Richard (D)	6 2	15 12	Dublin	21 9 79	Everton
Flood Willo (M)	5 6	9 11	Dublin	10 4 85	Trainee
Fowler Robbie (F)	5 10	12 05	Liverpool	9 4 75	Leeds U
James David (G)	6 5	14 02	Welwyn	1 8 70	West Ham U
Jihai Sun (D)	5 9	12 02	Dalian	30 9 77	Dalian Wanda
Jordan Stephen (D)	6 1	11 13	Warrington	6 3 82	Scholar
Mills Danny (D)	5 11	12 06	Norwich	18 5 77	Leeds U
Musampa Kiki (F)	5 11	12 00	Kinshasa	20 7 77	Atletico Madrid
Negouai Christian (M)	6 4	14 01	Fort-de-France	20 1 75	Charleroi
Onuoha Nedum (D)	6 2	12 04	Warri	12 11 86	Scholar
Reyna Claudio (M)	5 9	11 08	New Jersey	20 7 73	Sunderland
Sibierski Antoine (M)	6 2	12 04	Lille	5 8 74	Lens
Sinclair Trevor (M)	5 9	13 05	Dulwich	2 3 73	West Ham U
Sommeil David (D)	5 10	12 12	Ponte-a-Pitre	10 8 74	Bordeaux
Thatcher Ben (D)	5 10	12 07	Swindon	30 11 75	Leicester C
Weaver Nick (G)	6 4	14 07	Sheffield	2 3 79	Mansfield T
Wright-Phillips Bradley (M)	5 8	11 00	Lewisham	12 3 85	Scholar
Wright-Phillips Shaun (M)	5 5	9 12	Greenwich	25 10 81	Scholar

League Appearances: Anelka, N. 18(1); Barton, J. 28(3); Bosvelt, P. 28; Croft, L. (7); Distin, S. 38; Dunne, R. 35; Flood, W. 4(5); Fowler, R. 28(4); James, D. 38; Jihai, S. 4(2); Jordan, S. 19; Macken, J. 16(7); McManaman, S. 5(8); Mills, D. 29(3); Musampa, K. 14; Negouai, C. (1); Onuoha, N. 11(6); Reyna, C. 16(1); Sibierski, A. 34(1); Sinclair, T. 2(2); Sommeil, D. 1; Thatcher, B. 17(1); Weaver, N. (1); Wright-Phillips, B. (14); Wright-Phillips, S. 33(1).
Goals – League (47): Fowler 11 (2 pens), Wright-Phillips S 10, Anelka 7 (2 pens), Sibierski 4 (1 pen), Musampa 3, Bosvelt 2, Reyna 2, Barton 1, Distin 1, Dunne 2, Flood 1, Macken 1, Sinclair 1, Wright-Phillips B 1.
Carling Cup (8): Macken 2, Sibierski 2, Barton 1, Flood 1, Fowler 1, Wright-Phillips S 1.
FA Cup (0).
Ground: City of Manchester Stadium, Sport City, Manchester M11 3FF. Telephone (0870) 062 1894
Record Attendance: (at Maine Road) 84,569 v Stoke C, FA Cup 6th rd, 3 March 1934 (British record for any game outside London or Glasgow). **Capacity:** 48,000.
Manager: Stuart Pearce.
General Secretary: J. B. Halford.
Most League Goals: 108, Division 2, 1926–27, 108, Division 1, 2001–02.
Highest League Scorer in Season: Tommy Johnson, 38, Division 1, 1928–29.
Most League Goals in Total Aggregate: Tommy Johnson, 158, 1919–30.
Most Capped Player: Colin Bell, 48, England.
Most League Appearances: Alan Oakes, 565, 1959–76.

Honours – Football League: Division 1 Champions – 1936–37, 1967–68, 2001–02. Division 2 Champions – 1898–99, 1902–03, 1909–10, 1927–28, 1946–47, 1965–66. **FA Cup winners** 1904, 1934, 1956, 1969. **Football League Cup:** Winners – 1970, 1976. **European Competitions: European Cup-Winners' Cup:** Winners – 1969–70.
Colours: Sky blue shirts, white shorts, sky blue stockings.

MANCHESTER UNITED — FA PREMIERSHIP

Bardsley Phillip (D)	5 11	11 08	Salford	28 6 85	Trainee
Bellion David (F)	6 0	11 09	Sevres	27 11 82	Sunderland
Brown Wes (D)	6 1	13 11	Manchester	13 10 79	Trainee
Cooper Kenny (F)	6 3	14 01	Baltimore	21 10 84	
Eagles Chris (M)	6 0	10 08	Hemel Hempstead	19 11 85	Trainee
Ebanks-Blake Sylvan (F)	5 10	13 04	Cambridge	29 3 86	Scholar
Ferdinand Rio (D)	6 2	13 12	Peckham	7 11 78	Leeds U
Fletcher Darren (M)	6 0	13 01	Edinburgh	1 2 84	Scholar
Fortune Quinton (F)	5 9	11 09	Cape Town	21 5 77	Atletico Madrid B
Fox David (M)	5 9	12 02	Leek	13 12 83	Scholar
Giggs Ryan (F)	5 11	11 00	Cardiff	29 11 73	School
Heath Colin (F)	6 0	13 01	Matlock	31 12 83	Scholar
Heinze Gabriel (D)	5 10	12 04	Crespo	19 4 78	Paris St Germain
Howard Tim (G)	6 3	14 12	New Brunswick	6 3 79	NY/NJ MetroStars
Johnson Eddie (F)	5 10	13 05	Chester	20 9 84	Scholar
Jones David (M)	5 11	10 00	Southport	4 11 84	Trainee
Keane Roy (M)	5 11	11 10	Cork	10 8 71	Nottingham F
Kleberson Jose (M)	5 9	10 00	Urai	19 6 79	Atletico PR
McShane Paul (D)	5 11	11 05	Wicklow	6 1 86	Trainee
Miller Liam (M)	5 8	10 06	Cork	13 2 81	Celtic
N'Galula Floribert (D)			Brussels	7 3 87	Scholar
Neville Gary (D)	5 11	12 04	Bury	18 2 75	Trainee
Neville Phil (D)	5 11	12 00	Bury	21 1 77	Trainee
O'Shea John (D)	6 3	12 10	Waterford	30 4 81	Waterford
Pique Gerard (D)	6 3	12 10	Barcelona	2 2 87	Scholar
Richardson Kieran (M)	5 8	11 00	Greenwich	21 10 84	Scholar
Ronaldo Cristiano (M)	6 1	12 04	Funchal	5 2 85	Sporting Lisbon
Rooney Wayne (F)	5 10	12 04	Liverpool	24 10 85	Everton
Rossi Giuseppe (F)	5 9	11 03	New Jersey	1 2 87	Scholar
Saha Louis (F)	6 1	12 06	Paris	8 8 78	Fulham
Scholes Paul (M)	5 7	11 00	Salford	16 11 74	Trainee
Silvestre Mikael (D)	6 0	13 01	Chambray les Tours	9 8 77	Internazionale
Smith Alan (F)	5 10	12 01	Leeds	28 10 80	Leeds U
Solskjaer Ole Gunnar (F)	5 10	11 11	Kristiansund	26 2 73	Molde
Spector Jonathan (D)	6 0	12 08	Chicago	1 3 86	
Steele Luke (G)	6 2	12 00	Peterborough	24 9 84	Scholar
Van Nistelrooy Ruud (F)	6 2	12 13	Oss	1 7 76	PSV Eindhoven

League Appearances: Bellion, D. 1(9); Brown, W. 18(3); Carroll, R. 26; Djemba-Djemba, E. 3(2); Ferdinand, R. 31; Fletcher, D. 18; Forlan, D. (1); Fortune, Q. 12(5); Giggs, R. 26(6); Heinze, G. 26; Howard, T. 12; Keane, R. 28(3); Kleberson, J. 6(2); Miller, L. 3(5); Neville, G. 22; Neville, P. 12(7); O'Shea, J. 16(7); Richardson, K. (2); Ronaldo, C. 25(8); Rooney, W. 24(5); Saha, L. 7(7); Scholes, P. 29(4); Silvestre, M. 33(2); Smith, A. 22(9); Spector, J. 2(1); Van Nistelrooy, R. 16(1).
Goals – League (58): Rooney 11, Scholes 9, Smith 6, Van Nistelrooy 6 (3 pens), Giggs 5, Ronaldo 5, Fletcher 3, O'Shea 2, Silvestre 2, Bellion 1, Brown 1, Heinze 1, Keane 1, Saha 1, own goals 4.
Carling Cup (7): Bellion 1, Giggs 1, Miller 1, Richardson 1, Saha 1, Smith 1, own goal 1.

FA Cup (15): Ronaldo 4, Rooney 3, Scholes 3, Van Nistelrooy 2, Fortune 1, Keane 1, O'Shea 1.
Champions League (19): Van Nistelrooy 8 (1 pen), Rooney 3, Bellion 2, Giggs 2, Smith 2, Neville G 1, own goal 1.
Community Shield (1): Smith 1.
Ground: Old Trafford, Sir Matt Busby Way, Manchester M16 0RA. Telephone (0161) 868 8000.
Record Attendance: 76,962 Wolverhampton W v Grimsby T, FA Cup semi-final. 25 March 1939. **Capacity:** 68,210.
Manager: Sir Alex Ferguson CBE.
Secretary: Kenneth Merrett.
Most League Goals: 103, Division 1, 1956–57 and 1958–59.
Highest League Scorer in Season: Dennis Viollet, 32, 1959–60.
Most League Goals in Total Aggregate: Bobby Charlton, 199, 1956–73.
Most Capped Player: Bobby Charlton, 106, England.
Most League Appearances: Bobby Charlton, 606, 1956–73.
Honours – FA Premier League: Champions – 1992–93, 1993–94, 1995–96, 1996–97, 1998–99, 1999–2000, 2000–01, 2002–03. **Football League:** Division 1 Champions – 1907–8, 1910–11, 1951–52, 1955–56, 1956–57, 1964–65, 1966–67. Division 2 Champions – 1935–36, 1974–75. **FA Cup:** Winners – 1909, 1948, 1963, 1977, 1983, 1985, 1990, 1994, 1996, 1999, 2004. **Football League Cup:** Winners – 1991–92. **European Competitions: European Cup:** Winners – 1967–68. **Champions League:** Winners – 1998–99. **European Cup-Winners' Cup:** Winners – 1990–91. **Super Cup:** Winners – 1991. **Inter-Continental Cup:** Winners – 1999.
Colours: Red shirts, white or black shorts, black or white stockings.

MANSFIELD TOWN — FL CHAMPIONSHIP 2

Artell Dave (D)	6 3	14 07	Rotherham	22 11 80	Rotherham U
Barker Richard (F)	6 1	14 06	Sheffield	30 5 75	Rotherham U
Barrowman Andrew (F)	5 11	11 06	Wishaw	27 11 84	Birmingham C
Brown Simon (F)	5 10	11 05	West Bromwich	18 9 83	WBA
Buxton Jake (D)	6 1	13 05	Sutton-in-Ashfield	4 3 85	Scholar
Coke Gilles (M)	6 0	11 11	London	3 6 86	Kingstonian
Curtis Tom (M)	5 10	11 13	Exeter	1 3 73	Portsmouth
Day Rhys (D)	6 2	13 12	Bridgend	31 8 82	Manchester C
Eaton Adam (D)	5 11	12 02	Wigan	2 5 88	Preston NE
Heron Daniel (M)	5 11	10 09	Cambridge	9 10 86	Scholar
Jelleyman Gareth (D)	5 10	11 05	Holywell	14 11 80	Peterborough U
John-Baptiste Alex (D)	5 11	11 11	Sutton-in-Ashfield	31 1 86	Scholar
Lambu Goma (M)	5 3	9 08	Ghana	10 11 84	Millwall
Lloyd Callum (M)	5 9	11 04	Nottingham	1 1 86	Scholar
Lonsdale Richard (M)	5 9	10 10	Burton	29 10 87	Scholar
Maxwell Leyton (M)	5 8	11 00	Rhyl	3 10 79	Cardiff C
McLachlan Fraser (M)	5 11	12 04	Knutsford	9 11 82	Stockport Co
Pilkington Kevin (G)	6 1	13 03	Hitchin	8 3 74	Wigan Ath
Rundle Adam (F)	5 8	11 02	Durham	8 7 84	Carlisle U
Smeltz Shane (F)	6 1	12 06	New Zealand	20 9 80	Adelaide U
White Jason (G)	6 2	12 13	Mansfield	28 1 83	Trainee
Wood Chris (M)	6 0	10 11	Worksop	24 1 87	Scholar

League Appearances: Artell, D. 19; Asamoah, D. 24(6); Barker, R. 28; Barrowman, A. 1(2); Brown, S. 16(5); Buxton, J. 29(1); Coke, G. 7(2); Corden, W. 19(5); Curtis, T. 26(6); Day, R. 11(7); Dimech, L. 19(6); Eaton, A. 2; Heron, D. 1(2); Ipoua, G. 4(1); Jelleyman, G. 14; John-Baptiste, A. 41; Kitamirike, J. 2; Lambu, G. 1; Larkin, C. 29(4); Lloyd, C. 7(3); MacKenzie, N. 9(6); Maxwell, L. 1; McIntosh, A. 1; McLachlan, F. 16(5); McNiven, S. 24(1); Murray, A. 27(5); Neil, A. 40(1);

O'Neill, J. 3(12); Pilkington, K. 42; Rundle, A. 18; Smeltz, S. 1(4); Talbot, J. 2; Tate, C. (4); Warne, P. 7; White, J. 4; Williamson, L. 3(1); Wood, C. (1); Woodman, C. 8.
Goals – League (56): Larkin 11 (2 pens), Barker 10, Asamoah 5, Murray 5, Lloyd 4, Rundle 4, Corden 3, Day 3 (1 pen), Artell 2, Brown 2, Buxton 1, John-Baptiste 1, MacKenzie 1, Neil 1, Warne 1, Woodman 1, own goal 1.
Carling Cup (0).
FA Cup (2): John-Baptiste 1, Neil 1.
LDV Vans Trophy (0).
Ground: Field Mill Ground, Quarry Lane, Mansfield NG18 5DA. Telephone (0870) 756 3160.
Record Attendance: 24,467 v Nottingham F, FA Cup 3rd rd, 10 January 1953.
Capacity: 9954.
Manager: Carlton Palmer.
Secretary: Rita Stringfellow.
Most League Goals: 108, Division 4, 1962–63.
Highest League Scorer in Season: Ted Harston, 55, Division 3 (N), 1936–37.
Most League Goals in Total Aggregate: Harry Johnson, 104, 1931–36.
Most Capped Player: John McClelland, 6 (53), Northern Ireland.
Most League Appearances: Rod Arnold, 440, 1970–83.
Honours – Football League: Division 3 Champions – 1976–77. Division 4 Champions – 1974–75. **Freight Rover Trophy:** Winners – 1986–87.
Colours: Amber shirts, blue shorts, blue stockings.

MIDDLESBROUGH — FA PREMIERSHIP

Name	Ht	Wt	Birthplace	Birthdate	Source
Bates Matthew (D)	5 10	12 03	Stockton	10 12 86	Scholar
Boateng George (M)	5 9	12 06	Nkawkaw	5 9 75	Aston Villa
Christie Malcolm (F)	6 0	12 06	Peterborough	11 4 79	Derby Co
Cooper Colin (D)	5 11	11 11	Sedgefield	28 2 67	Nottingham F
Davies Andrew (D)	6 3	14 08	Stockton	17 12 84	Scholar
Downing Stewart (M)	5 11	10 04	Middlesbrough	22 7 84	Scholar
Ehiogu Ugo (D)	6 2	14 10	Hackney	3 11 72	Aston Villa
Graham Danny (F)	5 11	12 05	Gateshead	12 8 85	Trainee
Hasselbaink Jimmy Floyd (F)	5 10	13 10	Paramaribo	27 3 72	Chelsea
Job Joseph-Desire (F)	5 11	11 00	Venissieux	1 12 77	Lens
Johnson Adam (M)	5 9	9 11	Sunderland	14 7 87	Scholar
Jones Brad (G)	6 3	12 01	Armadale	19 3 82	Trainee
Kennedy Jason (M)	6 1	11 10	Stockton	11 9 86	Scholar
Knight David (G)			Sunderland	15 1 87	Scholar
McMahon Anthony (D)	5 10	11 04	Bishop Auckland	24 3 86	Scholar
Mendieta Gaizka (M)	5 9	11 02	Bilbao	27 3 74	Barcelona
Morrison James (M)	5 10	10 06	Darlington	25 5 86	Trainee
Nemeth Szilard (F)	5 11	11 04	Komarno	8 8 77	Inter Bratislava
Parlour Ray (M)	5 10	11 12	Romford	7 3 73	Arsenal
Parnaby Stuart (M)	5 11	11 00	Durham City	19 7 82	Trainee
Queudrue Franck (D)	6 1	12 01	Paris	27 8 78	Lens
Reiziger Mikael (D)	5 7	11 07	Amsterdam	3 5 73	Barcelona
Riggott Chris (D)	6 2	13 09	Derby	1 9 80	Derby Co
Schwarzer Mark (G)	6 4	14 07	Sydney	6 10 72	Bradford C
Southgate Gareth (D)	6 0	12 03	Watford	3 9 70	Aston Villa
Taylor Andrew (D)	5 10	11 04	Hartlepool	1 8 86	Trainee
Turnbull Ross (G)	6 4	15 00	Bishop Auckland	4 1 85	Trainee
Viduka Mark (F)	6 2	15 01	Melbourne	9 10 75	Leeds U
Wheater David (D)	6 4	12 12	Redcar	14 2 87	Scholar

Wilson Mark (M)	5 10	12 07	Scunthorpe	9 2 79	Manchester U
Zenden Boudewijn (M)	5 8	11 11	Maastricht	15 8 76	Chelsea

League Appearances: Bates, M. (2); Boateng, G. 25; Christie, M. 2; Cooper, C. 11(4); Davies, A. 2(1); Doriva, 15(11); Downing, S. 28(7); Ehiogu, U. 9(1); Graham, D. (11); Hasselbaink, J. 36; Job, J. 10(13); Jones, B. 5; Kennedy, J. (1); McMahon, A. 12(1); Mendieta, G. 7; Morrison, J. 4(10); Nash, C. 2; Nemeth, S. 18(13); Parlour, R. 32(1); Parnaby, S. 16(3); Queudrue, F. 31; Reiziger, M. 15(3); Riggott, C. 20(1); Schwarzer, M. 31; Southgate, G. 36; Viduka, M. 15(1); Zenden, B. 36.
Goals – League (53): Hasselbaink 13, Downing 5, Queudrue 5, Viduka 5, Zenden 5 (1 pen), Job 4, Nemeth 4, Boateng 3, Riggott 2, Christie 1, Graham 1, Reiziger 1, own goals 4.
Carling Cup (3): Graham 1, Morrison 1, Nemeth 1.
FA Cup (2): Doriva 1, Job 1.
UEFA Cup (16): Hasselbaink 3, Morrison 3, Zenden 3, Job 2, Viduka 2, Downing 1, Nemeth 1, Riggott 1.
Ground: Riverside Stadium, Middlesbrough, Cleveland TS3 6RS. Telephone (0870) 421 1986
Record Attendance: 53,596 v Newcastle U, Division 1, 27 December 1949 (at Ayresome Park) and 34,800 v Leeds U, Premier League, 26 February 2000. **Capacity:** 35,120.
Manager: Steve McClaren.
Secretary: Karen Nelson.
Most League Goals: 122, Division 2, 1926–27.
Highest League Scorer in Season: George Camsell, 59, Division 2, 1926–27 (Second Division record).
Most League Goals in Total Aggregate: George Camsell, 325, 1925–39.
Most Capped Player: Wilf Mannion, 26, England.
Most League Appearances: Tim Williamson, 563, 1902–23.
Honours – Football League: Division 1 Champions 1994–95. Division 2 Champions 1926–27, 1928–29, 1973–74. **Football League Cup:** Winners – 2004. **Amateur Cup:** Winners – 1895, 1898, **Anglo-Scottish Cup:** Winners – 1975–76.
Colours: Red shirts with white chest band, red shorts, red stockings.

MILLWALL — FL CHAMPIONSHIP

Braniff Kevin (F)	5 11	10 03	Belfast	4 3 83	Scholar
Cogan Barry (F)	5 9	9 0	Sligo	4 11 84	Scholar
Craig Tony (D)	6 0	10 03	Greenwich	20 4 85	Scholar
Dichio Danny (F)	6 6	14 02	Hammersmith	19 10 74	WBA
Dolan Joe (D)	6 2	12 03	Harrow	27 5 80	Chelsea
Dunne Alan (D)	5 10	10 13	Dublin	23 8 82	Trainee
Elliott Marvin (M)	6 0	12 02	Wandsworth	15 9 84	Scholar
Hayles Barry (F)	5 10	12 11	Lambeth	17 5 72	Sheffield U
Healy Joe (F)	6 0	12 04	Sidcup	26 12 86	
Hearn Charley (M)	5 11	11 13	Ashford	5 11 83	School
Lawrence Matthew (D)	6 1	12 12	Northampton	19 6 74	Wycombe W
Livermore David (M)	5 11	12 02	Edmonton	20 5 80	Trainee
Marshall Andy (G)	6 3	14 08	Bury	14 4 75	Ipswich T
Masterson Terence (G)	6 2	11 04	Dublin	5 6 86	Scholar
May Ben (F)	6 3	12 12	Gravesend	10 3 84	Juniors
Morris Jody (F)	5 5	10 03	Hammersmith	22 12 78	Rotherham U
Muscat Kevin (D)	5 11	12 08	Crawley	7 8 73	Wolverhampton W
Peeters Bob (F)	6 5	13 12	Lier	28 1 72	Vitesse
Phillips Mark (D)	6 2	11 00	Lambeth	27 1 82	Scholar
Quigley Mark (M)	5 10	11 07	Dublin	27 10 85	Scholar

Robinson Paul (D)	6 1	11 09	Barnet	7 1 82	Scholar
Robinson Trevor (M)	5 9	12 11	Jamaica	20 9 84	Scholar
Serioux Adrian (D)	6 0	12 12	Scarborough, Can	12 5 79	Toronto Lynx
Simpson Josh (M)	5 10	12 02	Vancouver	15 5 83	
Sutton John (F)	6 2	13 11	Norwich	26 12 83	Swindon T
Sweeney Peter (F)	6 0	12 01	Glasgow	25 9 84	Scholar
Weston Curtis (M)	5 11	11 09	Greenwich	24 1 87	Scholar
Wise Dennis (M)	5 6	10 10	Kensington	16 12 66	Leicester C

League Appearances: Braniff, K. 1; Cogan, B. 2(5); Craig, T. 9(1); Dichio, D. 27(4); Dobie, S. 15(1); Dunne, A. 15(4); Elliott, M. 32(9); Harris, N. 5(7); Hayles, B. 28(4); Healy, J. (2); Ifill, P. 9(9); Impey, A. (5); Lawrence, M. 40(4); Livermore, D. 41; Marshall, A. 21(1); May, B. 4(4); McCammon, M. 5(3); Moore, S. 3(3); Morris, J. 35(2); Muscat, K. 25(1); Peeters, B. (3); Phillips, M. 25; Quigley, M. 4(4); Robinson, T. 8(1); Serioux, A. 10(9); Simpson, J. 22(8); Stack, G. 25(1); Sweeney, P. 23(1); Tessem, J. 11(1); Ward, D. 43; Weston, C. 2(1); Wise, D. 16(9).
Goals – League (51): Hayles 12, Dichio 10 (1 pen), Morris 5 (2 pens), Ifill 4, Dobie 3, Dunne 3, Wise 3 (2 pens), Livermore 2, Sweeney 2, Elliott 1, Harris 1, May 1 (pen), Phillips 1, Robinson T 1, Simpson 1, Tessem 1.
Carling Cup (0).
FA Cup (0).
UEFA Cup (2): Wise 2.
Ground: The Den, Zampa Road, Bermondsey SE16 3LN. Telephone (020) 7232 1222.
Record Attendance: 20,093 v Arsenal, FA Cup 3rd rd, 10 January 1994. **Capacity:** 20,146.
Manager: Steve Claridge.
Secretary: Yvonne Haines.
Most League Goals: 127, Division 3 (S), 1927–28.
Highest League Scorer in Season: Richard Parker, 37, Division 3 (S), 1926–27.
Most League Goals in Total Aggregate: Teddy Sheringham, 93, 1984–91.
Most Capped Player: Eamonn Dunphy, 22 (23), Republic of Ireland.
Most League Appearances: Barry Kitchener, 523, 1967–82.
Honours – Football League: Division 2 Champions – 1987–88, 2000–01. Division 3 (S) Champions – 1927–28, 1937–38. Division 4 Champions – 1961–62. **Football League Trophy:** Winners – 1982–83.
Colours: Blue and white shirts, blue shorts, blue stockings.

MILTON KEYNES DONS — FL CHAMPIONSHIP 1

Baker Matt (G)	6 0	14 00	Harrogate	18 12 79	Wrexham
Bevan Scott (G)	6 6	15 10	Southampton	16 9 79	Wycombe W
Chorley Ben (M)	6 3	13 02	Sidcup	30 9 82	Arsenal
Crooks Leon (M)	6 0	11 12	Greenwich	21 11 85	Scholar
Edds Gareth (D)	5 11	11 01	Sydney	3 2 81	Bradford C
Harding Ben (M)	5 10	11 02	Carshalton	6 9 84	Scholar
Heald Paul (G)	6 2	14 00	Wath-on-Dearne	20 9 68	Leyton Orient
Herve Laurent (M)	5 10	11 07	Quimper	19 6 76	Beauvais-Oise
Hornuss Julien (F)	5 10	11 00	Paris	12 6 86	Sedan
Kamara Malvin (M)	5 11	13 00	London	17 11 83	Scholar
Koo-Boothe Nathan (D)	6 4	13 12	London	18 7 84	Watford
Lewington Dean (D)	5 11	11 07	Kingston	18 5 84	Scholar
Makofo Serge (M)	5 11	12 06	Kinshasa	22 10 86	Scholar
Martin David (G)	6 1	13 04	Romford	22 1 86	Scholar
McLeod Izale (F)	6 1	11 02	Perry Bar	15 10 84	Derby Co
Ntimban-Zeh Harry (D)	6 1	12 07	Aubervilliers	26 9 73	SC Espinho
Oyedele Shola (D)	5 11	12 07	Kano	14 9 84	Scholar

Palmer Steve (D)	6 1	12 13	Brighton	31 3 68	QPR
Pensee-Bilong Michel (D)	6 4	14 02	Cameroon	16 6 73	Sanfrecce
Platt Clive (F)	6 4	12 07	Wolverhampton	27 10 77	Peterborough U
Puncheon Jason (M)	5 9	12 05	Croydon	26 6 86	Scholar
Rizzo Nicky (M)	5 10	12 00	Sydney	9 6 79	Prato
Small Wade (M)	5 8	11 05	Croydon	23 2 84	Scholar
Smith Gary (M)	5 8	10 09	Middlesbrough	30 1 84	Middlesbrough
Tapp Alex (M)	5 8	10 13	Redhill	7 6 82	Trainee

League Appearances: Baker, M. 20; Bevan, S. 7; Chorley, B. 41; Crooks, L. 15(2); Danze, A. 2; Edds, G. 37(2); Harding, B. 21(5); Herve, L. 15(5); Hornuss, J. (3); Johnson, R. 2; Kamara, M. 16(9); Koo-Boothe, N. 1; Lewington, D. 43; Mackie, J. (3); Makofo, S. (1); Martin, D. 15; McClenahan, T. 7(1); McLeod, I. 39(4); Mitchell, P. 13; Ntimban-Zeh, H. 11; Oyedele, S. 18(7); Pacquette, R. 1(4); Palmer, S. 27(5); Pensee-Bilong, M. 18; Platt, C. 20; Puncheon, J. 8(17); Rachubka, P. 4; Rizzo, N. 13(5); Small, W. 41(3); Smart, A. 15(3); Smith, G. 20(3); Tapp, A. 5(7); Westcarr, C. (4); Williams, M. 11(2).
Goals – League (54): McLeod 16, Small 10, Edds 5, Harding 4, Smart 4 (2 pens), Platt 3, Chorley 2 (1 pen), Lewington 2, Rizzo 2, Kamara 1, Palmer 1, Pensee-Bilong 1, Puncheon 1, Smith 1 (pen), Tapp 1.
Carling Cup (4): McLeod 2, Kamara 1, Smart 1.
FA Cup (2): Small 1, Smart 1.
LDV Vans Trophy (4): Lewington 1, Makofo 1, Pacquette 1, Small 1.
Ground: The National Hockey Stadium, Silbury Boulevard, Central Milton Keynes, Buckinghamshire MK9 1FA. Telephone (01908) 607090.
Record Attendance: 30,115 v Manchester U, FA Premier League, 9 May 1993 (at Selhurst Park). **Capacity:** 8500.
Manager: Danny Wilson.
Football Operations Manager: Kirstine Nicholson.
Most League Goals: 97, Division 3, 1983–84.
Highest League Scorer in Season: Alan Cork, 29, 1983–84.
Most League Goals in Total Aggregate: Alan Cork, 145, 1977–92.
Most Capped Player: Kenny Cunningham, 40 (68), Republic of Ireland.
Most League Appearances: Alan Cork, 430, 1977–92.
Honours – Football League: Division 4 Champions – 1982–83. **FA Cup:** Winners – 1987–88.
Colours: All white with gold trim.

NEWCASTLE UNITED — FA PREMIERSHIP

Ambrose Darren (M)	6 0	11 00	Harlow	29 2 84	Ipswich T
Ameobi Foluwashola (F)	6 3	11 13	Zaria	12 10 81	Trainee
Babayaro Celestine (D)	5 9	12 06	Kaduna	29 8 78	Chelsea
Bellamy Craig (F)	5 8	10 05	Cardiff	13 7 79	Coventry C
Boumsong Jean-Alain (D)	6 3	13 03	Douala	14 12 79	Rangers
Bramble Titus (D)	6 2	13 10	Ipswich	31 7 81	Ipswich T
Brittain Martin (M)	5 8	10 08	Newcastle	29 12 84	Trainee
Butt Nicky (M)	5 10	11 05	Manchester	21 1 75	Manchester U
Caig Tony (G)	6 0	13 03	Whitehaven	11 4 74	Hibernian
Carr Stephen (D)	5 9	12 02	Dublin	29 8 76	Tottenham H
Chopra Michael (F)	5 9	10 03	Newcastle	23 12 83	Scholar
Dyer Kieron (M)	5 8	10 00	Ipswich	29 12 78	Ipswich T
Elliott Robbie (D)	5 10	10 12	Gosforth	25 12 73	Bolton W
Faye Amdy (M)	6 1	12 04	Dakar	12 3 77	Portsmouth
Given Shay (G)	6 0	13 03	Lifford	20 4 76	Blackburn R
Harper Steve (G)	6 2	13 10	Easington	14 3 75	Seaham Red Star
Jenas Jermaine (M)	5 10	11 13	Nottingham	18 2 83	Nottingham F

Johnsen Ronny (D)	6 2	13 05	Sandefjord	10 6 69	Manchester U
Milner James (M)	5 10	11 00	Leeds	4 1 86	Leeds U
N'Zogbia Charles (M)	5 9	11 00	France	28 5 86	Le Havre
O'Brien Andy (D)	6 2	11 13	Harrogate	29 6 79	Bradford C
Ramage Peter (D)	6 1	11 03	Whitley Bay	22 11 83	Trainee
Robert Laurent (M)	5 8	10 12	Saint-Benoit	21 5 75	Paris St Germain
Shanks Chris (D)	6 0	11 00	Ashington	16 10 86	Scholar
Shearer Alan (F)	5 11	12 06	Newcastle	13 8 70	Blackburn R
Taylor Steven (D)	6 1	13 01	Greenwich	23 1 86	Trainee
Viana Hugo (M)	5 9	11 09	Barcelos	15 1 83	Sporting Lisbon

League Appearances: Ambrose, D. 8(4); Ameobi, F. 17(14); Babayaro, C. 7; Bellamy, C. 21; Bernard, O. 19(2); Boumsong, J. 14; Bowyer, L. 26(1); Bramble, T. 18(1); Butt, N. 16(2); Carr, S. 26; Chopra, M. (1); Dyer, K. 20(3); Elliott, R. 15(2); Faye, A. 8(1); Given, S. 36; Harper, S. 2; Hughes, A. 18(4); Jenas, J. 28(3); Johnsen, R. 3; Kluivert, P. 15(10); Milner, J. 13(12); N'Zogbia, C. 8(6); O'Brien, A. 21(2); Ramage, P. 2(2); Robert, L. 20(11); Shearer, A. 26(2); Taylor, S. 11(2).
Goals – League (47): Bellamy 7, Shearer 7 (3 pens), Kluivert 6, Dyer 4, Ambrose 3, Bowyer 3, Robert 3, Ameobi 2, O'Brien 2, Bramble 1, Butt 1, Carr 1, Elliott 1, Hughes 1, Jenas 1, Milner 1, own goals 3.
Carling Cup (2): Ameobi 1 (pen), Jenas 1.
FA Cup (8): Ameobi 3, Kluivert 2, Babayaro 1, Bowyer 1, Shearer 1,
UEFA Cup (28): Shearer 11 (3 pens), Kluiver 5, Bellamy 3, Bowyer 3, Dyer 2, Robert 2, Ameobi 1, own goal 1.
Ground: St James' Park, Newcastle-upon-Tyne NE1 4ST. Telephone (0191) 201 8400.
Record Attendance: 68,386 v Chelsea, Division 1, 3 Sept 1930. **Capacity:** 52,387.
Manager: Graeme Souness.
Secretary: Russell Cushing.
Most League Goals: 98, Division 1, 1951–52.
Highest League Scorer in Season: Hughie Gallacher, 36, Division 1, 1926–27.
Most League Goals in Total Aggregate: Jackie Milburn, 177, 1946–57.
Most Capped Player: Shay Given, 61 (70), Republic of Ireland.
Most League Appearances: Jim Lawrence, 432, 1904–22.
Honours – Football League: Division 1 – Champions 1904–05, 1906–07, 1908–09, 1926–27, 1992–93. Division 2 Champions – 1964–65. **FA Cup:** Winners – 1910, 1924, 1932, 1951, 1952, 1955. **Texaco Cup:** Winners – 1973–74, 1974–75. **European Competitions: European Fairs Cup:** Winners – 1968–69. **Anglo-Italian Cup:** Winners – 1973.
Colours: Black and white striped shirts, black shorts, black stockings.

NORTHAMPTON TOWN — FL CHAMPIONSHIP 2

Bojic Pedj (D)	5 11	11 12	Sydney	9 4 84	Sydney Olympic
Bunn Mark (G)	6 0	12 02	Camden	16 11 84	Scholar
Carruthers Chris (D)	5 10	12 03	Kettering	19 8 83	Scholar
Chambers Luke (D)	6 1	11 13	Kettering	29 8 85	Scholar
Galbraith David (M)	5 8	11 00	Luton	21 12 83	Tottenham H
Harper Lee (G)	6 1	15 06	Chelsea	30 10 71	Walsall
Hunt David (D)	5 10	11 08	Dulwich	10 9 82	Leyton Orient
Jaszczun Tommy (D)	5 10	10 10	Kettering	16 9 77	Blackpool
Kirk Andy (F)	5 11	11 07	Belfast	29 5 79	Boston U
Low Josh (F)	6 2	14 03	Bristol	15 2 79	Oldham Ath
McGleish Scott (F)	5 9	11 09	Barnet	10 2 74	Colchester U
Murray Fred (D)	5 10	11 12	Tipperary	22 5 82	Cambridge U
Ngoyi Greg (F)			Zaire	20 7 87	Scholar
Richards Marc (F)	6 0	13 04	Wolverhampton	8 7 82	Blackburn R

Sabin Eric (F)	6 1	12 04	Sarcelles	22 1 75	QPR
Smith Martin (F)	5 11	12 07	Sunderland	13 11 74	Huddersfield T
Westwood Ashley (D)	6 0	12 09	Bridgnorth	31 8 76	Sheffield W
Williamson Lee (M)	5 10	11 13	Derby	7 6 82	Mansfield T

League Appearances: Alsop, J. 1(6); Amoo, R. 2(3); Barnard, L. 3(2); Benjamin, T. 5; Bojic, P. 25(11); Carruthers, C. (1); Chambers, L. 19(8); Cozic, B. 8(6); Cross, S. (1); Crow, D. 4(6); Galbraith, D. 9(16); Harper, L. 36; Haslam, S. 2(1); Hearn, C. 21(3); Hicks, D. 1(2); Hughes, M. 3; Hunt, D. 2(2); Jaszczun, T. 24(8); Kirk, A. 8; Low, J. 33(1); McGleish, S. 43(1); Morison, S. 1(3); Murray, F. 38; Noble, S. (4); Rachubka, P. 10; Reeves, M. (1); Richards, M. 8(4); Rowson, D. 35(2); Sabin, E. 28(12); Smith, M. 31(3); Togwell, S. 7(1); Westwood, A. 19; Williamson, L. 31(6); Willmott, C. 45; Youngs, T. 4(5).
Goals – League (62): McGleish 13, Smith 10 (1 pen), Sabin 8, Kirk 7, Low 7, Benjamin 2, Crow 2, Richards 2, Rowson 2, Westwood 2, Alsop 1, Galbraith 1, Hearn 1, Morison 1, own goals 3.
Carling Cup (2): McGleish 1, Sabin 1.
FA Cup (3): McGleish 2, Williamson 1.
LDV Vans Trophy (3): Alsop 1, McGleish 1, Williamson 1.
Play-Offs (0).
Ground: Sixfields Stadium, Upton Way, Northampton NN5 5QA. Telephone (01604) 757773.
Record Attendance: 24,523 v Fulham, Division 1, 23 April 1966. **Capacity:** 7653.
Manager: Colin Calderwood.
Secretary: Norman Howells.
Most League Goals: 109, Division 3, 1962–63 and Division 3 (S), 1952–53.
Highest League Scorer in Season: Cliff Holton, 36, Division 3, 1961–62.
Most League Goals in Total Aggregate: Jack English, 135, 1947–60.
Most Capped Player: E. Lloyd Davies, 12 (16), Wales.
Most League Appearances: Tommy Fowler, 521, 1946–61.
Honours – Football League: Division 3 Champions – 1962–63. Division 4 Champions – 1986–87.
Colours: Claret shirts with white trim, white shorts, claret stockings.

NORWICH CITY — FL CHAMPIONSHIP

Ashton Dean (F)	6 2	12 08	Swindon	24 11 83	Crewe Alex
Brennan Jim (D)	5 11	12 12	Toronto	8 5 77	Nottingham F
Charlton Simon (D)	5 8	11 05	Huddersfield	25 10 71	Bolton W
Doherty Gary (D)	6 2	13 04	Carndonagh	31 1 80	Tottenham H
Drury Adam (D)	5 10	11 08	Cottenham	29 8 78	Peterborough U
Edworthy Marc (D)	5 8	10 05	Barnstaple	24 12 72	Wolverhampton W
Fleming Craig (D)	5 11	12 05	Halifax	6 10 71	Oldham Ath
Francis Damien (M)	6 0	11 10	Wandsworth	27 2 79	Wimbledon
Gallacher Paul (G)	6 0	12 00	Glasgow	16 8 79	Dundee U
Green Robert (G)	6 3	13 01	Chertsey	18 1 80	Trainee
Helveg Thomas (D)	5 10	12 04	Odense	24 6 71	Internazionale
Henderson Ian (F)	5 9	10 12	Thetford	24 1 85	Scholar
Holt Gary (M)	6 0	12 00	Irvine	9 3 73	Kilmarnock
Huckerby Darren (F)	5 10	12 02	Nottingham	23 4 76	Manchester C
Jarvis Ryan (F)	6 0	11 05	Fakenham	11 7 86	Scholar
Jonson Mattias (M)	5 10	11 09	Orebro	16 1 74	Brondby
Lewis Joe (G)	6 5	11 12	Bury St Edmunds	6 10 87	Scholar
McKenzie Leon (F)	5 10	10 06	Croydon	17 5 78	Peterborough U
McVeigh Paul (F)	5 6	10 12	Belfast	6 12 77	Tottenham H
Mulryne Phil (M)	5 9	11 03	Belfast	1 1 78	Manchester U
Safri Youseff (M)	5 8	11 00	Casablanca	13 1 77	Coventry C

Shackell Jason (D)	6 3	12 09	Hitchin	27 9 83	Scholar
Stuart Graham (M)	5 9	12 01	Tooting	24 10 70	Charlton Ath
Svensson Mathias (F)	6 1	12 07	Boras	24 9 74	Charlton Ath
Ward Darren (G)	6 0	13 03	Worksop	11 5 74	Nottingham F

League Appearances: Ashton, D. 16; Bentley, D. 22(4); Brennan, J. 6(4); Charlton, S. 22(2); Crow, D. (3); Doherty, G. 17(3); Drury, A. 31(2); Edworthy, M. 27(1); Fleming, C. 38; Francis, D. 32; Green, R. 38; Helveg, T. 16(4); Henderson, I. (3); Holt, G. 21(6); Huckerby, D. 36(1); Jarvis, R. 1(3); Jonson, M. 19(9); McKenzie, L. 24(13); McVeigh, P. 3(14); Mulryne, P. 8(2); Safri, Y. 13(5); Shackell, J. 11; Stuart, G. 7(1); Svensson, M. 10(12); Ward, D. (1).
Goals – League (42): Ashton 7 (1 pen), Francis 7, McKenzie 7, Huckerby 6 (2 pens), Svensson 4, Bentley 2, Doherty 2, Charlton 1, Drury 1, Fleming 1, Jarvis 1, McVeigh 1, Safri 1, own goal 1.
Carling Cup (2): Huckerby 1 (pen), Safri 1.
FA Cup (0).
Ground: Carrow Road, Norwich NR1 1JE. Telephone (01603) 760760.
Record Attendance: 43,984 v Leicester C, FA Cup 6th rd, 30 March 1963.
Capacity: 26,034.
Manager: Nigel Worthington.
Secretary: Kevan Platt.
Most League Goals: 99, Division 3 (S), 1952–53.
Highest League Scorer in Season: Ralph Hunt, 31, Division 3 (S), 1955–56.
Most League Goals in Total Aggregate: Johnny Gavin, 122, 1945–54, 1955–58.
Most Capped Player: Mark Bowen, 35 (41), Wales.
Most League Appearances: Ron Ashman, 592, 1947–64.
Honours – Football League: Division 1 Champions – 2003–04. Division 2 Champions – 1971–72, 1985–86. Division 3 (S) Champions – 1933–34. **Football League Cup:** Winners – 1962, 1985.
Colours: Yellow shirts, green shorts, yellow stockings.

NOTTINGHAM FOREST — FL CHAMPIONSHIP 1

Beaumont James (M)	5 7	10 10	Stockton	11 11 84	Newcastle U
Bopp Eugene (M)	5 11	12 03	Kiev	5 9 83	Bayern Munich
Commons Kris (M)	5 6	9 08	Nottingham	30 8 83	Stoke C
Curtis John (D)	5 10	11 07	Nuneaton	3 9 78	Portsmouth
Dobie Scott (F)	6 1	12 05	Workington	10 10 78	Millwall
Evans Paul (M)	5 8	12 06	Oswestry	1 9 74	Bradford C
Friio David (M)	6 0	11 05	Thionville	17 2 73	Plymouth Arg
Gardner Ross (M)	5 8	10 06	South Shields	15 12 85	Newcastle U
Gerrard Paul (G)	6 2	13 11	Heywood	22 1 73	Everton
Harris Neil (F)	5 11	12 00	Orsett	12 7 77	Millwall
James Kevin (M)	5 7	11 12	Southwark	3 1 80	Gillingham
Johnson David (F)	5 6	12 00	Kingston, Jam	15 8 76	Ipswich T
King Marlon (F)	6 0	12 10	Dulwich	26 4 80	Gillingham
Lester Jack (F)	5 9	12 08	Sheffield	8 10 75	Sheffield U
Louis-Jean Mathieu (D)	5 9	11 03	Mont-St-Aignan	22 2 76	Le Havre
Morgan Wes (D)	6 2	14 00	Nottingham	21 1 84	Scholar
Nowland Adam (M)	5 11	11 06	Preston	6 7 81	West Ham U
Perch James (D)	5 11	11 05	Mansfield	29 9 85	Scholar
Rogers Alan (D)	5 9	12 10	Liverpool	3 1 77	Leicester C
Taylor Gareth (F)	6 2	13 07	Weston-Super-Mare	25 2 73	Burnley
Thompson John (D)	6 0	12 01	Dublin	12 10 81	Home Farm

League Appearances: Bopp, E. 6(12); Commons, K. 19(11); Curtis, J. 11; Dawson, M. 13(1); Derry, S. 7; Dobie, S. 11(1); Doig, C. 20(1); Doyle, C. 2(1); Evans, P.

34(5); Folly, Y. (1); Friio, D. 5; Gardner, R. 9(5); Gerrard, P. 42; Harris, N. 5(8); Hjelde, J. 13(1); Impey, A. 18(2); James, K. 2(5); Jess, E. 16(4); Johnson, D. 24(7); King, M. 17(9); Lester, J. 3; Louis-Jean, M. 22(3); Melville, A. 13; Morgan, W. 42(1); Nowland, A. 5; Perch, J. 17(5); Powell, D. 11; Reid, A. 25; Robertson, G. 13(7); Roche, B. 2; Rogers, A. 32(1); Taylor, G. 33(3); Thompson, J. 14(6); Walker, D. (1); Westcarr, C. (1).
Goals – League (42): Taylor G 7, Commons 6, Johnson 6, King 5 (1 pen), Reid 5 (1 pen), Evans 4 (1 pen), Bopp 3, Jess 2, Dawson 1, Dobie 1, Lester 1, Morgan 1.
Carling Cup (8): King 3, Taylor 3, Perch 1, Reid 1.
FA Cup (5): Commons 1, Folly 1, King 1, Reid 1, Taylor 1.
Ground: City Ground, Nottingham NG2 5FJ. Telephone (0115) 9824444.
Record Attendance: 49,945 v Manchester U, Division 1, 28 October 1967.
Capacity: 30,602.
Manager: Gary Megson.
Secretary: Paul White.
Most League Goals: 110, Division 3 (S), 1950–51.
Highest League Scorer in Season: Wally Ardron, 36, Division 3 (S), 1950–51.
Most League Goals in Total Aggregate: Grenville Morris, 199, 1898–1913.
Most Capped Player: Stuart Pearce, 76 (78), England.
Most League Appearances: Bob McKinlay, 614, 1951–70.
Honours – Football League: Division 1 – Champions 1977–78, 1997–98. Division 2 Champions – 1906–07, 1921–22. Division 3 (S) Champions – 1950–51. **FA Cup:** Winners – 1898, 1959. **Football League Cup:** Winners – 1977–78, 1978–79, 1988–89, 1989–90. **Anglo-Scottish Cup:** Winners 1– 976–77. **Simod Cup:** Winners – 1989. **Zenith Data Systems Cup:** Winners – 1991–92. **European Competitions: European Cup:** Winners – 1978–79, 1979–80. **Super Cup:** Winners – 1979–80.
Colours: Red shirts, white shorts, red stockings.

NOTTS COUNTY — FL CHAMPIONSHIP 2

Baudet Julien (D)	6 3	15 03	St Martin D'heres	13 1 79	Rotherham U
Bolland Paul (M)	6 0	12 05	Bradford	23 12 79	Bradford C
Deeney Saul (G)	6 0	12 13	Londonderry	12 3 83	Scholar
Edwards Mike (D)	6 1	13 01	North Ferriby	25 4 80	Grimsby T
Gill Matthew (M)	5 10	11 05	Cambridge	8 11 80	Peterborough U
Gordon Gavin (F)	6 2	13 01	Manchester	24 6 79	Cardiff C
Harrad Shaun (F)	5 10	12 04	Nottingham	11 12 84	Scholar
Hurst Glynn (F)	5 10	11 11	Barnsley	17 1 76	Chesterfield
McFaul Shane (M)	6 1	11 11	Dublin	23 5 86	Scholar
Palmer Chris (M)	5 7	10 12	Derby	16 10 83	Derby Co
Pipe David (M)	5 10	12 04	Caerphilly	5 11 83	Coventry C
Richardson Ian (D)	5 11	12 04	Barking	22 10 70	Dagenham & Redbridge
Scoffham Steve (F)	5 11	12 13	Germany	12 7 83	Gedling
Scully Tony (M)	5 8	11 11	Dublin	12 6 76	Peterborough U
Ullathorne Robert (D)	5 7	11 07	Wakefield	11 10 71	Northampton T
Whitlow Mike (D)	6 0	13 03	Northwich	13 1 68	Sheffield U
Williams Matthew (F)	5 8	10 10	St Asaph	5 11 82	Manchester U
Wilson Kelvin (D)	6 1	11 13	Nottingham	3 9 85	Scholar
Zadkovich Ruben (M)	5 10	11 07	Australia	23 5 86	QPR

League Appearances: Baudet, J. 38(1); Bolland, P. 38(2); Deeney, S. 31(1); Edwards, M. 8(1); Elliot, R. 3(1); Friars, E. 4(5); Gill, M. 38(5); Gordon, G. 23(4); Harrad, S. 4(12); Henderson, W. 11; Hurst, G. 36(5); Kuduzovic, F. (3); McFaul, S. 17(7); Mildenhall, S. 1; O'Grady, C. 3(6); Oakes, S. 28(3); Palmer, C. 23(2); Pead, C. 4(1); Pipe, D. 38(3); Richardson, I. 10; Robinson, M. 1(1); Scoffham, S. 3(4);

Scully, T. 20(11); Sofiane, Y. 2(2); Stallard, M. 16; Ullathorne, R. 34(2); Whitlow, M. 22(2); Williams, M. 8(10); Wilson, K. 36(5); Zadkovich, R. 6(2).
Goals – League (46): Hurst 14, Baudet 5 (4 pens), Gordon 5, Oakes 5, Palmer 4, Stallard 3, Pipe 2, Scully 2, Wilson 2, Bolland 1, Harrad 1, Williams 1, Zadkovich 1.
Carling Cup (4): Richardson 2, Ullathorne 1, Wilson 1.
FA Cup (6): Gordon 3, Baudet 1 (pen), Oakes 1, Scully 1.
LDV Vans Trophy (2): Hurst 1, Sofiane 1.
Ground: County Ground, Meadow Lane, Nottingham NG2 3HJ. Telephone (0115) 952 9000.
Record Attendance: 47,310 v York C, FA Cup 6th rd, 12 March 1955. **Capacity:** 20,300.
Manager: Gudjon Thordason.
Secretary: Tony Cuthbert.
Most League Goals: 107, Division 4, 1959–60.
Highest League Scorer in Season: Tom Keetley, 39, Division 3 (S), 1930–31.
Most League Goals in Total Aggregate: Les Bradd, 124, 1967–78.
Most Capped Player: Kevin Wilson, 15 (42), Northern Ireland.
Most League Appearances: Albert Iremonger, 564, 1904–26.
Honours – Football League: Division 2 Champions – 1896–97, 1913–14, 1922–23. Division 3 Champions – 1997–98. Division 3 (S) Champions – 1930–31, 1949–50. Division 4 Champions – 1970–71. **FA Cup:** Winners – 1893–94. **Anglo-Italian Cup:** Winners – 1995.
Colours: Black and white striped shirts, white shorts, white stockings.

OLDHAM ATHLETIC — FL CHAMPIONSHIP 1

Betsy Kevin (M)	6 1	12 00	Seychelles	20 3 78	Barnsley
Bonner Mark (M)	5 10	11 00	Ormskirk	7 6 74	Cardiff C
Boshell Danny (M)	5 11	11 08	Bradford	30 5 81	Trainee
Branston Guy (D)	6 1	15 03	Leicester	9 1 79	Sheffield W
Eyres David (M)	5 11	11 06	Liverpool	26 2 64	Preston NE
Griffin Adam (D)	5 7	10 03	Manchester	26 8 84	Scholar
Haining Will (D)	6 0	11 00	Glasgow	2 10 82	Scholar
Hall Chris (F)	6 1	11 04	Manchester	27 11 86	Scholar
Hall Danny (D)	6 0	12 01	Tameside	14 11 83	Scholar
Holden Dean (D)	6 1	12 05	Salford	15 9 79	Bolton W
Jack Rodney (F)	5 7	10 05	Kingston, Jam	28 9 72	Rushden & D
Killen Chris (F)	6 0	11 05	Wellington	8 10 81	Manchester C
Lomax Kelvin (D)	5 11	12 03	Bury	12 11 86	Scholar
Pogliacomi Les (G)	6 4	13 02	Sydney	3 5 76	Parramatta Power
Sanokho Amadou (M)	6 3	12 06	Paris	1 9 79	Burnley
Stam Stefan (D)	6 2	13 00	Amersfoort	14 9 79	
Tierney Marc (D)	5 11	11 02	Manchester	7 9 86	Trainee
Vernon Scott (F)	6 0	11 10	Manchester	8 7 84	Scholar
Wilkinson Wes (F)	5 10	11 01	Wythenshawe	1 5 84	Nantwich T
Winn Ashley (M)	5 11	11 02	Stockton	1 12 85	Scholar
Wolfenden Matthew (M)	5 9	11 01	Oldham	23 7 87	Scholar

League Appearances: Appleby, M. 9(8); Arber, M. 13(1); Barlow, M. 1(8); Beckett, L. 9; Beharall, D. 3; Betsy, K. 34(2); Bonner, M. 15(4); Boshell, D. 10(6); Branston, G. 6(1); Bruce, A. 8(4); Cooksey, E. 1; Cooper, K. 5(2); Croft, L. 11(1); Eyre, J. 18(6); Eyres, D. 40(2); Facey, D. 1(5); Griffin, A. 33(2); Haining, W. 34(1); Hall, C. 2(4); Hall, D. 20(1); Holden, D. 39(1); Hughes, M. 25(2); Jack, R. 5(5); Johnson, J. 13(6); Kilkenny, N. 24(3); Killen, C. 25(1); Lee, D. 5(2); Lomax, K. 7(2); Mawson, C. 3(1); Mildenhall, S. 6; Owen, G. 9; Pogliacomi, L. 37; Sanokho, A. (1); Stam, S. 11(2); Tierney, M. 7(4); Vernon, S. 13(9); Wilbraham, A. 4; Wilkinson, W. (1); Winn, A. (2); Wolfenden, M. (1).
Goals – League (60): Killen 10 (1 pen), Vernon 7 (1 pen), Beckett 6, Betsy 5, Hain-

ing 5, Eyres 4, Johnson 4, Kilkenny 4, Cooper 3, Griffin 2, Holden 2, Jack 2, Wilbraham 2, Arber 1, Boshell 1, Branston 1, Eyre 1.
Carling Cup (2): Eyre 1 (pen), Eyres 1.
FA Cup (6): Killen 4 (2 pens), Croft 1, Vernon 1.
LDV Vans Trophy (10): Eyres 2, Vernon 2 (1 pen), Appleby 1 (pen), Croft 1, Griffin 1, Holden 1, Kilkenny 1, Killen 1 (pen).
Ground: Boundary Park, Oldham OL1 2PA. Telephone (0871) 226 2235
Record Attendance: 46,471 v Sheffield W, FA Cup 4th rd. 25 January 1930.
Capacity: 13,624.
Manager: Ronnie Moore.
Secretary: Alan Hardy.
Most League Goals: 95, Division 4, 1962–63.
Highest League Scorer in Season: Tom Davis, 33, Division 3 (N), 1936–37.
Most League Goals in Total Aggregate: Roger Palmer, 141, 1980–94.
Most Capped Player: Gunnar Halle, 24 (64), Norway.
Most League Appearances: Ian Wood, 525, 1966–80.
Honours – Football League: Division 2 Champions – 1990–91, Division 3 (N) Champions – 1952–53. Division 3 Champions – 1973–74.
Colours: Royal blue shirts with white piping, royal blue shorts, white stockings.

OXFORD UNITED — FL CHAMPIONSHIP 2

Ashton Jon (D)	6 2	13 12	Nuneaton	4 10 82	Leicester C
Basham Steve (F)	5 11	12 04	Southampton	2 12 77	Preston NE
Beechers Billy (M)	5 9	11 10	Oxford	1 6 87	Scholar
Bradbury Lee (F)	6 0	13 12	Isle of Wight	3 7 75	Walsall
Brooks Jamie (M)	5 10	11 05	Oxford	12 8 83	Scholar
Brown Danny (M)	6 0	13 01	Bethnal Green	12 9 80	Barnet
Burton Paul (M)	6 0	11 12	London	30 11 85	Scholar
Clarke Bradie (G)	6 2	13 10	Cambridge	26 5 86	Scholar
Cox Simon (G)	6 1	11 09	Clapham	23 3 84	Scholar
Davies Craig (F)	6 2	13 05	Burton-on-Trent	9 1 86	Manchester C
E'Beyer Mark (M)	5 11	11 05	Stevenage	21 9 84	Milton Keynes D
Hackett Chris (M)	6 0	12 00	Oxford	1 3 83	Scholar
Mackay David (D)	6 0	13 03	Rutherglen	2 5 81	Dundee U
Molyneaux Lee (D)	6 0	12 00	Portsmouth	16 1 83	Portsmouth
Morgan Danny (F)	6 0	14 00	Stepney	4 11 84	Milton Keynes D
Parker Terry (D)	5 9	11 11	Southampton	20 12 83	Portsmouth
Quinn Barry (M)	6 0	13 01	Dublin	9 5 79	Coventry C
Robinson Matt (D)	5 11	11 02	Exeter	23 12 74	Reading
Roget Leo (D)	6 2	13 05	Ilford	1 8 77	Rushden & D
Tardif Chris (G)	6 1	13 03	Guernsey	19 9 79	Portsmouth
Winters Tom (M)	5 9	10 10	Banbury	11 12 85	Scholar
Woozley David (D)	6 3	15 00	Ascot	6 12 79	Torquay U

League Appearances: Alsop, J. 3(2); Ashton, J. 30; Basham, S. 29(10); Beechers, B. (3); Bradbury, L. 39(2); Brooks, J. 6(6); Brown, D. 3(1); Burton, P. (1); Clarke, B. 3(1); Cominelli, L. 11(5); Corbo, M. 13; Cox, S. 2(1); Davies, C. 13(15); Diaz, E. 2(5); Dodou, E. (1); E'Beyer, M. 6(4); Hackett, C. 31(6); Hand, J. 11; Judge, A. 1; Karam, A. (2); Louis, J. (1); Mackay, D. 44; Molyneaux, L. 6(10); Mooney, T. 42; Morgan, D. (3); Parker, T. 6(2); Quinn, B. 34(2); Raponi, J. 5(5); Rawle, M. (6); Robinson, M. 45; Roget, L. 35; Tardif, C. 40; Togwell, S. 3(1); Wanless, P. 18(9); Winters, T. (4); Wolleaston, R. 14(6); Woozley, D. 11(2).
Goals – League (50): Mooney 15 (2 pens), Basham 9, Davies 6, Bradbury 4 (2 pens), Hackett 4, Brooks 2, E'Beyer 2, Robinson 2, Roget 2, Cominelli 1, Wanless 1, Woozley 1, own goal 1

Carling Cup (0).
FA Cup (1): Bradbury 1.
LDV Vans Trophy (2): Hand 1, Winters 1.
Ground: The Kassam Stadium, Grenoble Road, Oxford OX4 4XP. Telephone (01865) 337500.
Record Attendance: 22,750 (at Manor Ground) v Preston NE, FA Cup 6th rd, 29 February 1964. **Capacity:** 12,450.
Manager: Brian Talbot.
Secretary: Mick Brown.
Most League Goals: 91, Division 3, 1983–84.
Highest League Scorer in Season: John Aldridge, 30, Division 2, 1984–85.
Most League Goals in Total Aggregate: Graham Atkinson, 77, 1962–73.
Most Capped Player: Jim Magilton, 18 (52), Northern Ireland.
Most League Appearances: John Shuker, 478, 1962–77.
Honours – Football League: Division 2 Champions – 1984–85. Division 3 Champions – 1967–68, 1983–84. **Football League Cup:** Winners – 1985–86.
Colours: Yellow shirts, navy shorts and stockings.

PETERBOROUGH UNITED FL CHAMPIONSHIP 2

Arber Mark (D)	6 1	12 11	Johannesburg	8 10 77	Oldham Ath
Boucaud Andre (M)	5 10	11 04	Enfield	9 10 84	Reading
Burton Sagi (D)	6 2	13 06	Birmingham	25 11 77	Crewe Alex
Clarke Andy (F)	5 10	11 07	Islington	22 7 67	Wimbledon
Coulson Mark (M)	5 8	10 03	Huntingdon	11 2 86	Scholar
Day Jamie (M)	5 9	10 06	Wycombe	7 5 86	Scholar
Deen Ahmed (M)	5 9	11 05	Sierra Leone	30 6 85	Leicester C
Farrell Dave (M)	5·11	11 08	Birmingham	11 11 71	Wycombe W
Fry Adam (M)	5 8	10 07	Bedford	9 2 85	Scholar
Huke Shane (M)	5 11	12 07	Reading	2 10 85	Scholar
Ireland Craig (D)	6 3	13 09	Dundee	29 11 75	Barnsley
Kanu Chris (D)	5 8	11 04	Owerri	4 12 79	TOP Oss
Kennedy Peter (D)	5 11	11 11	Lisburn	10 9 73	Wigan Ath
Logan Richard (F)	6 0	12 05	Bury St Edmunds	4 1 82	Boston U
McShane Luke (G)	6 1	10 09	Peterborough	6 11 85	Scholar
Newton Adam (M)	5 10	11 00	Ascot	4 12 80	West Ham U
Nolan Matt (F)	6 0	12 00	Hitchin	25 2 82	Hitchin T
Onibuje Fola (F)	6 7	12 00	Lagos	25 9 84	Barnsley
Plummer Chris (D)	6 2	12 12	Isleworth	12 10 76	QPR
Purser Wayne (F)	5 8	12 05	Basildon	13 4 80	Hornchurch
Rea Simon (D)	6 1	13 00	Coventry	20 9 76	Birmingham C
Semple Ryan (M)	5 11	10 11	Belfast	4 7 85	Scholar
St Ledger-Hall Sean (D)	6 0	11 09	Solihull	28 12 84	Scholar
Thomson Steve (M)	5 8	10 04	Glasgow	23 1 78	Crystal Palace
Tyler Mark (G)	5 11	12 00	Norwich	2 4 77	Trainee
Willock Calum (F)	6 0	12 09	Lambeth	29 10 81	Fulham

League Appearances: Arber, M. 21; Boucaud, A. 13(9); Branston, G. 4; Burton, S. 16; Caskey, D. 2(2); Clarke, A. 13(20); Constantine, L. 5(6); Coulson, M. 2(5); Day, J. (1); Deen, A. 4(1); Farrell, D. 22(9); Fry, A. 3; Huke, S. 6(2); Ireland, C. 22(1); Jelleyman, G. 11(3); Jenkins, S. 5(1); Kanu, C. 9(4); Kennedy, P. 15(2); Legg, A. 38(1); Logan, R. 15(11); McMaster, J. 3; Newton, A. 27(3); Onibuje, F. (2); Platt, C. 18(1); Plummer, C. 21; Purser, W. 15(11); Rea, S. 13(1); Semple, R. 2(6); Sonner, D. 11(4); St Ledger-Hall, S. 33; Thomson, S. 30(1); Tyler, M. 46; Willock, C. 29(6); Woodhouse, C. 32(2).

Goals – League (49): Willock 12, Purser 6, Legg 5, Logan 4, Platt 4, Woodhouse 4 (2 pens), Clarke 3, Farrell 2, Kennedy 2, Thomson 2, Boucaud 1, Branston 1, Burton 1, Constantine 1, Jenkins 1.
Carling Cup (0).
FA Cup (6): Willock 2, Arber 1, Kennedy 1, Logan 1, Woodhouse 1.
LDV Vans Trophy (0).
Ground: London Road Ground, Peterborough PE2 8AL. Telephone (01733) 563 947
Record Attendance: 30,096 v Swansea T, FA Cup 5th rd, 20 February 1965.
Capacity: 15,460.
Manager: Mark Wright.
Secretary: Julie Etherington.
Most League Goals: 134, Division 4, 1960–61.
Highest League Scorer in Season: Terry Bly, 52, Division 4, 1960–61.
Most League Goals in Total Aggregate: Jim Hall, 122, 1967–75.
Most Capped Player: Tony Millington, 8 (21), Wales.
Most League Appearances: Tommy Robson, 482, 1968–81.
Honours – Football League: Division 4 Champions – 1960–61, 1973–74.
Colours: All blue.

PLYMOUTH ARGYLE — FL CHAMPIONSHIP

Aljofree Hasney (D)	6 0	12 03	Manchester	11 7 78	Dundee U
Capaldi Tony (M)	6 0	12 00	Porsgrunn	12 8 81	Birmingham C
Chadwick Nick (F)	5 11	10 09	Stoke	26 10 82	Everton
Connolly Paul (D)	6 0	11 10	Liverpool	29 9 83	Scholar
Coughlan Graham (D)	6 2	13 04	Dublin	18 11 74	Livingston
Dickson Ryan (M)	5 10	11 05	Saltash	14 12 86	Scholar
Doumbe Stephen (D)	6 1	12 05	Paris	28 0 79	Hibernian
Evans Micky (F)	6 0	13 04	Plymouth	1 1 73	Bristol R
Gilbert Peter (D)	5 11	12 13	Newcastle	31 7 83	Birmingham C
Gudjonsson Bjarni (M)	5 7	11 02	Reykjavik	26 2 79	Coventry C
Hodges Lee (M)	6 0	12 01	Epping	4 9 73	Reading
Larrieu Romain (G)	6 2	13 00	Mont-de-Marsan	31 8 76	ASOA Valence
Lasley Keith (M)	5 8	10 07	Glasgow	21 9 79	Motherwell
McCormick Luke (G)	6 0	13 12	Coventry	15 8 83	Scholar
Milne Steven (F)	5 7	10 00	Dundee	5 5 80	Dundee
Norris David (M)	5 7	11 06	Peterborough	22 2 81	Bolton W
Summerfield Luke (M)	6 0	11 00	Ivybridge	6 12 87	Scholar
Taylor Scott (F)	5 10	11 04	Chertsey	5 5 76	Blackpool
Villis Matt (D)	6 3	12 07	Bridgwater	13 4 84	
Worrell David (D)	5 11	11 08	Dublin	12 1 78	Dundee U
Wotton Paul (D)	5 11	11 01	Plymouth	17 8 77	Trainee

League Appearances: Adams, S. 17(3); Aljofree, H. 12, Blackstock, D. 10(4); Buzsaky, A. 14(1), Capaldi, T. 24(11); Chadwick, N. 11(4); Connolly, P. 19; Coughlan, G. 43; Crawford, S. 19(7); Dickson, R. 2(1); Dodd, J. 4; Doumbe, S. 24(2); Evans, M. 33(9); Friio, D. 23(5); Gilbert, P. 38; Gudjonsson, B. 12(3); Hodges, L. 11(8); Keith, M. 6(11); Larrieu, R. 23; Lasley, K. 14(10); Lowndes, N. 1(3); Makel, L. 13(6); McCormick, L. 23; Milne, S. (12); Norris, D. 33(2); Summerfield, L. (1); Taylor, S. 9(7); Worrell, D. 30; Wotton, P. 38(2); Yetton, S. (1).
Goals – League (52): Wotton 12 (5 pens), Crawford 6, Friio 6, Blackstock 4, Evans 4, Norris 3, Taylor 3, Capaldi 2, Coughlan 2, Doumbe 2, Adams 1, Aljofree 1, Buzsaky 1, Chadwick 1, Keith 1, own goals 3.
Carling Cup (2): Crawford 1, Wotton 1 (pen).
FA Cup (1): Gudjonsson 1.
Ground: Home Park, Plymouth, Devon PL2 3DQ. Telephone (01752) 562561.
Record Attendance: 43,596 v Aston Villa, Division 2, 10 October 1936.

Capacity: 20,922.
Manager: Bobby Williamson.
Secretary: Carole Rowntree.
Most League Goals: 107, Division 3 (S), 1925–26 and 1951–52.
Highest League Scorer in Season: Jack Cock, 32, Division 3 (S), 1926–27.
Most League Goals in Total Aggregate: Sammy Black, 180, 1924–38.
Most Capped Player: Moses Russell, 20 (23), Wales.
Most League Appearances: Kevin Hodges, 530, 1978–92.
Honours – Football League: Division 2 Champions – 2003–04. Division 3 (S) Champions – 1929–30, 1951–52. Division 3 Champions – 1958–59, 2001–02.
Colours: Green shirts, white shorts, green stockings.

PORTSMOUTH — FA PREMIERSHIP

Ashdown Jamie (G)	6 1	13 05	Reading	30 11 80	Reading
Berkovic Eyal (M)	5 9	10 13	Haifa	2 4 72	Manchester C
Chalkias Kostas (G)	6 6	15 03	Larrisa	30 5 74	Panathinaikos
Cisse Aliou (M)	5 9	12 02	Zinguichor	24 3 76	Birmingham C
De Zeeuw Arjan (D)	6 0	13 06	Castricum	16 4 70	Wigan Ath
Duffy Richard (D)	5 10	9 05	Swansea	30 8 85	Swansea C
Fuller Ricardo (F)	6 3	13 13	Kingston, Jam	31 10 79	Preston NE
Griffin Andy (D)	5 9	10 10	Billinge	7 3 79	Newcastle U
Guatelli Andrea (G)	6 0	12 00	Parma	5 5 84	Parma
Hughes Richard (M)	6 0	13 03	Glasgow	25 6 79	Bournemouth
Kamara Diomansy (F)	6 0	11 05	Paris	8 11 80	Modena
Lua-Lua Lomano (F)	5 8	12 00	Kinshasa	28 12 80	Newcastle U
Mezague Valery (M)	6 1	13 00	Marseille	8 12 83	Montpellier
Mornar Ivica (F)	6 2	13 01	Split	12 1 74	Anderlecht
O'Neil Gary (M)	5 10	11 00	Beckenham	18 5 83	Trainee
Pericard Vincent de Paul (F)	6 1	13 08	Efko	3 10 82	Juventus
Primus Linvoy (D)	5 10	12 04	Forest Gate	14 9 73	Reading
Rodic Alexsander (F)	6 2	12 11	Serbia	26 12 79	
Schemmel Sebastian (D)	5 8	11 13	Nancy	2 6 75	West Ham U
Silk Gary (M)	5 9	13 07	Newport (IW)	13 9 84	Scholar
Skopelitis Giannis (M)	5 11	11 12	Greece	2 3 78	Aigaleo
Stefanovic Dejan (D)	6 2	13 01	Belgrade	28 10 74	Vitesse
Taylor Matthew (D)	5 11	12 03	Oxford	27 11 81	Luton T
Todorov Svetoslav (F)	6 0	12 02	Dobrich	30 8 78	West Ham U
Unsworth Dave (D)	6 1	15 02	Chorley	16 10 73	Everton
Vine Rowan (F)	6 1	11 12	Basingstoke	21 9 82	Scholar
Wapenaar Harald (G)	6 1	13 07	Vlaardingen	10 4 70	Utrecht

League Appearances: Ashdown, J. 16; Berger, P. 30(2); Berkovic, E. 6(5); Chalkias, K. 5; Cisse, A. 12(8); Curtis, J. (1); De Zeeuw, A. 32; Faye, A. 17(3); Fuller, R. 13(18); Griffin, A. 18(4); Hislop, S. 17; Hughes, R. 13(3); Kamara, D. 15(10); Keene, J. 1(1); Lua-Lua, L. 20(5); Mezague, V. 3(8); O'Neil, G. 21(3); Primus, L. 31(4); Quashie, N. 19; Rodic, A. 1(3); Skopelitis, G. 9(4); Stefanovic, D. 32; Stone, S. 22(1); Taylor, M. 21(11); Unsworth, D. 15; Yakubu, A. 29(1).
Goals – League (43): Yakubu 12 (4 pens), Lua-Lua 6, Kamara 4, Berger 3, De Zeeuw 3, Stone 3, O'Neil 2, Unsworth 2 (2 pens), Berkovic 1, Fuller 1, Primus 1, Taylor 1, own goals 4.
Carling Cup (5): Kamara 2, Yakubu 2 (1 pen), Berkovic 1 (pen).
FA Cup (2): Yakubu 2.
Ground: Fratton Park, Frogmore Road, Portsmouth PO4 8RA. Telephone (023) 9273 1204.
Record Attendance: 51,385 v Derby Co, FA Cup 6th rd, 26 February 1949.

Capacity: 20,288.
Manager: Alain Perrin.
Secretary: Paul Weld.
Most League Goals: 97, Division 1, 2002–03.
Highest League Scorer in Season: Guy Whittingham, 42, Division 1, 1992–93.
Most League Goals in Total Aggregate: Peter Harris, 194, 1946–60.
Most Capped Player: Jimmy Dickinson, 48, England.
Most League Appearances: Jimmy Dickinson, 764, 1946–65.
Honours – Football League: Division 1 Champions – 1948–49, 1949–50, 2002–03. Division 3 (S) Champions – 1923–24. Division 3 Champions – 1961–62, 1982–83.
FA Cup: Winners – 1939.
Colours: Blue shirts, white shorts, red stockings.

PORT VALE — FL CHAMPIONSHIP 1

Abbey George (D)	5 9	10 08	Port Harcourt	20 10 78	Macclesfield T
Birchall Chris (M)	5 9	13 02	Stafford	5 5 84	Scholar
Brain Jonny (G)	6 3	13 05	Carlisle	11 2 83	Newcastle U
Collins Sam (D)	6 3	13 11	Pontefract	5 6 77	Bury
Cummins Michael (M)	5 11	13 10	Dublin	1 6 78	Middlesbrough
Eldershaw Simon (F)	5 11	11 04	Stoke	2 12 83	Scholar
Goodlad Mark (G)	6 2	14 00	Barnsley	9 9 79	Nottingham F
Hibbert David (M)	6 2	12 06	Eccleshall	28 1 86	Scholar
Hulbert Robin (M)	5 10	11 10	Plymouth	14 3 80	Bristol C
Innes Mark (M)	5 11	12 01	Bellshill	27 9 78	Chesterfield
James Craig (D)	6 2	13 03	Middlesbrough	15 11 82	Sunderland
Lowndes Nathan (F)	5 10	12 06	Salford	2 6 77	Plymouth Arg
Matthews Lee (F)	6 2	14 00	Middlesbrough	16 1 79	Bristol C
Paynter Billy (F)	6 0	13 08	Liverpool	13 7 84	Schoolboy
Pilkington George (D)	5 11	12 00	Rugeley	7 11 81	Everton
Rowland Stephen (D)	5 10	11 12	Wrexham	2 11 81	Scholar
Smith Jeff (M)	5 11	11 05	Middlesbrough	28 6 80	Preston NE
Walsh Michael (D)	6 0	13 10	Rotherham	5 8 77	Scunthorpe U
Widdrington Tommy (M)	5 10	12 07	Newcastle	1 10 71	Macclesfield T

League Appearances: Abbey, G. 16(2); Armstrong, I. 6(3); Birchall, C. 29(5); Brain, J. 26(1); Brooker, S. 9; Brown, R. 16(4); Collins, S. 33; Cummins, M. 39; Dinning, T. 7; Eldershaw, S. 5(8); Goodfellow, M. 4(1); Goodlad, M. 20; Hanson, C. 3(2); Hibbert, D. 2(7); Hulbert, R. 23(1); Innes, M. 2(3); James, C. 23(7); Lipa, A. (2); Loran, T. 6; Lowndes, N. 7(5); Matthews, L. 21(10); McMahon, D. 1(4); O'Connor, J. 13; Paynter, B. 43(2); Pilkington, G. 42(1); Porter, A. (2); Reid, L. 21(9); Rowland, S. 17(7); Smith, D. 12(1); Smith, J. 23(11); Sonner, D. 13; Walsh, M. 22(1); Widdrington, T. 2(4).
Goals – League (49): Matthews 11 (2 pens), Paynter 10, Birchall 6, Brooker 5, Armstrong 3, Dinning 3, Cummins 2, Hibbert 2, Collins 1, Eldershaw 1, James 1, Lowndes 1, Smith J 1, own goals 2.
Carling Cup (1): Smith D 1.
FA Cup (3): Paynter 2, Reid 1.
LDV Vans Trophy (2): Birchall 1, Paynter 1 (pen).
Ground: Vale Park, Burslem, Stoke-on-Trent ST6 1AW. Telephone (01782) 655 800.
Record Attendance: 50,000 v Aston Villa, FA Cup 5th rd, 20 February 1960.
Capacity: 19,892
Manager: Martin Foyle.
Secretary: Bill Lodey.
Most League Goals: 110, Division 4, 1958–59.
Highest League Scorer in Season: Wilf Kirkham 38, Division 2, 1926–27.

Most League Goals in Total Aggregate: Wilf Kirkham, 154, 1923–29, 1931–33.
Most Capped Player: Tony Rougier, Trinidad and Tobago.
Most League Appearances: Roy Sproson, 761, 1950–72.
Honours – Football League: Division 3 (N) Champions – 1929–30, 1953–54. Division 4 Champions – 1958–59. **LDV Vans Trophy:** Winners – 2001
Colours: White shirts with black trim, black shorts, black stockings.

PRESTON NORTH END — FL CHAMPIONSHIP

Agyemang Patrick (F)	6 1	13 10	Walthamstow	29 9 80	Gillingham
Alexander Graham (D)	5 10	12 02	Coventry	10 10 71	Luton T
Broomes Marlon (D)	6 1	12 12	Meriden	28 11 77	Sheffield W
Cresswell Richard (F)	6 0	11 05	Bridlington	20 9 77	Leicester C
Davidson Callum (D)	5 10	11 00	Stirling	25 6 76	Leicester C
Davis Claude (D)	6 2	13 09	Jamaica	6 3 79	Portmore U
Etuhu Dixon (M)	6 2	13 00	Kano	8 6 82	Manchester C
Hill Matt (D)	5 8	11 13	Bristol	26 3 81	Bristol C
Jackson Mark (F)	5 11	10 09	Preston	3 2 86	Scholar
Lewis Eddie (M)	5 10	11 05	Cerritos	17 5 74	Fulham
Lonergan Andrew (G)	6 2	13 00	Preston	19 10 83	Scholar
Lucketti Chris (D)	6 1	13 00	Littleborough	28 9 71	Huddersfield T
Mawene Youl (D)	6 1	13 00	Caen	16 7 79	Derby Co
McKenna Paul (M)	5 8	11 00	Eccleston	20 10 77	Trainee
Mears Tyrone (D)	6 1	11 10	Stockport	18 2 83	Manchester C
Nash Carlo (G)	6 3	15 03	Bolton	13 9 73	Middlesbrough
Neal Chris (G)	6 2	12 04	St Albans	23 10 85	Scholar
Nugent Dave (F)	5 11	12 00	Liverpool	2 5 85	Bury
O'Neil Brian (M)	6 1	12 04	Paisley	6 9 72	Derby Co
O'Neill Joe (F)	6 0	10 05	Blackburn	28 10 82	Scholar
Sedgwick Chris (M)	6 0	12 01	Sheffield	28 4 80	Rotherham U
Skora Eric (M)	5 11	12 00	Metz	20 8 81	Nancy
Smith Andy (F)	5 11	11 10	Lisburn	25 9 80	Glentoran
Ward Gavin (G)	6 3	14 00	Sutton Coldfield	30 6 70	Coventry C

League Appearances: Agyemang, P. 15(12); Alexander, G. 41(1); Broomes, M. 8(3); Cresswell, R. 46; Curtis, J. 12; Daley, O. 1(13); Davidson, C. 16(3); Davis, C. 21(11); Day, C. 6; Etuhu, D. 22(13); Folly, Y. (2); Fuller, R. 2; Gould, J. 4; Healy, D. 11; Hill, M. 11(3); Jackson, M. (2); Kozluk, R. (1); Langmead, K. (1); Lewis, E. 37(3); Lonergan, A. 23; Lucketti, C. 41; Lynch, S. 2(7); Mawene, Y. 46; McCormack, A. (3); McKenna, P. 37(2); Mears, T. 1(3); N'Dumbu Nsungu, G. 4(2); Nash, C. 7; Neal, C. (1); Nugent, D. 13(5); O'Neil, B. 40(3); O'Neill, J. (2); Oliveira, F. 1(4); Sedgwick, C. 24; Skora, E. 5(4); Smith, A. 3(11); Ward, G. 6(1).
Goals – League (67): Cresswell 16 (1 pen), Nugent 8, Alexander 7 (6 pens), Healy 5 (1 pen), Agyemang 4, Lewis 4, Lucketti 4, Etuhu 3, McKenna 3, O'Neil 3, Sedgwick 3, Mawene 2, Davidson 1, Fuller 1, Lonergan 1, own goals 2.
Carling Cup (7): Cresswell 4 (1 pen), Alexander 1, Daley 1, Lynch 1.
FA Cup (0).
Play-Offs (2): Cresswell 1, Nugent 1.
Ground: Deepdale, Sir Tom Finney Way, Preston PR1 6RU. Telephone (0870) 442 1964.
Record Attendance: 42,684 v Arsenal, Division 1, 23 April 1938. **Capacity:** 20,600.
Manager: Billy Davies.
Secretary: Janet Parr.
Most League Goals: 100, Division 2, 1927–28 and Division 1, 1957–58.
Highest League Scorer in Season: Ted Harper, 37, Division 2, 1932–33.
Most League Goals in Total Aggregate: Tom Finney, 187, 1946–60.
Most Capped Player: Tom Finney, 76, England.

Most League Appearances: Alan Kelly, 447, 1961–75.
Honours – Football League: Division 1 Champions – 1888–89 (first champions), 1889–90. Division 2 Champions – 1903–04, 1912–13, 1950–51, 1999–2000. Division 3 Champions – 1970–71, 1995–96. **FA Cup:** Winners – 1889, 1938.
Colours: White shirts, navy shorts, white stockings.

QUEENS PARK RANGERS — FL CHAMPIONSHIP

Ainsworth Gareth (M)	5 10	12 05	Blackburn	10 5 73	Cardiff C
Baidoo Shabazz (M)	5 8	10 07	Hackney	13 4 88	Scholar
Bailey Stefan (M)	5 11	12 08	London	10 11 87	Scholar
Bignot Marcus (D)	5 7	11 04	Birmingham	22 8 74	Rushden & D
Bircham Marc (M)	5 11	11 06	Hammersmith	11 5 78	Millwall
Brown Aaron (M)	5 11	12 13	Bristol	14 3 80	Bristol C
Cook Lee (M)	5 8	11 10	Hammersmith	3 8 82	Watford
Culkin Nick (G)	6 2	13 07	York	6 7 78	Manchester U
Cureton Jamie (F)	5 8	12 08	Bristol	28 8 75	Reading
Day Chris (G)	6 2	13 06	Whipps Cross	28 7 75	Watford
Donnelly Scott (M)	5 8	11 10	Hammersmith	25 12 87	Scholar
Furlong Paul (F)	6 0	13 11	London	1 10 68	Birmingham C
Gallen Kevin (F)	5 11	13 05	Hammersmith	21 9 75	Barnsley
Hamilton Lewis (D)	6 0	11 08	Derby	21 11 84	Derby Co
Kanyuka Patrick (D)	6 0	12 06	Kinshasa	19 7 87	
Miller Adam (M)	5 11	11 06	London	19 2 82	Aldershot T
Mulholland Scott (M)	5 8	10 05	Bexley Heath	7 9 86	Scholar
Padula Gino (D)	5 9	12 11	Buenos Aires	11 7 76	Wigan Ath
Perry Jack (M)			Islington	26 10 84	Juniors
Rose Matthew (D)	5 11	12 02	Dartford	24 9 75	Arsenal
Rossi Generoso (G)	6 3	13 05	Naples	3 1 79	Siena
Rowlands Martin (M)	5 9	10 10	Hammersmith	8 2 79	Brentford
Santos Georges (M)	6 3	14 00	Marseille	15 8 70	Ipswich T
Shittu Dan (D)	6 2	16 03	Lagos	2 9 80	Charlton Ath
Sturridge Dean (F)	5 8	12 02	Birmingham	27 7 73	Wolverhampton W
Thorpe Tony (F)	5 9	12 01	Leicester	10 4 74	Luton T
Townsend Luke (M)	6 0	11 10	Guildford	28 9 86	Scholar

League Appearances: Ainsworth, G. 14(8); Baidoo, S. 2(2); Bailey, S. 1(1); Bean, M. 13(7); Best, L. 2(3); Bignot, M. 41(2); Bircham, M. 32(3); Branco, S. 3(4); Brown, A. (1); Cook, L. 38(4); Cureton, J. 18(12); Davies, A. 9; Day, C. 30; Donnelly, S. (2); Edghill, R. 13(7); Forbes, T. 2(1); Furlong, P. 39(1); Gallen, K. 46; Gnohere, A. 3; Hamilton, L. (1); Johnson, R. 6; Kanyuka, P. 1; McLeod, K. 4(20); Miller, A. 9(5); Mulholland, S. (1); Padula, G. 28(5); Rose, M. 24(4); Rossi, G. 3; Rowlands, M. 31(4); Royce, S. 13; Santos, G. 39(4); Shittu, D. 33(1); Simek, F. 5; Sturridge, D. (2); Thorpe, T. 4(6); Townsend, L. (2).
Goals – League (54): Furlong 18, Gallen 10 (1 pen), Santos 5, Cureton 4, Shittu 4, Rowlands 3, Ainsworth 2, Cook 2, Rose 2, Bean 1, Bircham 1, McLeod 1, own goal 1.
Carling Cup (4): Cureton 1, Gallen 1, McLeod 1, Rowlands 1.
FA Cup (0).
Ground: Loftus Road Stadium, South Africa Road, W12 7PA. Telephone (020) 8743 0262.
Record Attendance: 35,353 v Leeds U, Division 1, 27 April 1974. **Capacity:** 18,200.
Manager: Ian Holloway.
Secretary: Sheila Marson.
Most League Goals: 111, Division 3, 1961–62.
Highest League Scorer in Season: George Goddard, 37, Division 3 (S), 1929–30.
Most League Goals in Total Aggregate: George Goddard, 172, 1926–34.

Most Capped Player: Alan McDonald, 52, Northern Ireland.
Most League Appearances: Tony Ingham, 519, 1950–63.
Honours – Football League: Division 2 Champions – 1982–83. Division 3 (S) Champions – 1947–48. Division 3 Champions – 1966–67. **Football League Cup:** Winners – 1966–67.
Colours: Blue and white hooped shirts, white shorts, white stockings.

READING — FL CHAMPIONSHIP

Brooker Paul (M)	5 8	10 06	Hammersmith	25 11 76	Leicester C
Campbell Darren (M)	5 5	10 00	Huntingdon	16 4 86	Scholar
Castle Peter (D)	6 0	12 02	Southampton	12 3 87	Scholar
Convey Bobby (M)	5 9	11 04	Philadelphia	27 5 83	DC United
Forster Nicky (F)	5 8	11 05	Caterham	8 9 73	Birmingham C
Goater Shaun (F)	6 1	11 10	Bermuda	25 2 70	Manchester C
Hahnemann Marcus (G)	6 3	16 04	Seattle	15 6 72	Fulham
Harper James (M)	5 10	11 02	Chelmsford	9 11 80	Arsenal
Hughes Andy (M)	5 11	12 01	Stockport	2 1 78	Notts Co
Ingimarsson Ivar (D)	6 0	12 07	Reykjavik	20 8 77	Wolverhampton W
Kitson Dave (F)	6 3	13 00	Hitchin	21 1 80	Cambridge U
Little Glen (M)	6 3	13 00	Wimbledon	15 10 75	Burnley
Morgan Dean (F)	6 0	12 02	Enfield	3 10 83	Colchester U
Mullins John (D)	5 11	12 07	Hampstead	6 11 85	Scholar
Murty Graeme (D)	5 10	11 10	Saltburn	13 11 74	York C
Owusu Lloyd (F)	6 1	13 07	Slough	12 12 76	Sheffield W
Rifat Ahmet (D)	6 3	11 08	London	3 1 86	Scholar
Shorey Nicky (D)	5 9	10 10	Romford	19 2 81	Leyton Orient
Sidwell Steven (M)	5 10	11 00	Wandsworth	14 12 82	Arsenal
Sonko Ibrahima (D)	6 3	13 07	Bignola	22 1 81	Brentford
Young Jamie (G)	5 11	13 01	Brisbane	25 8 85	Scholar

League Appearances: Brooker, P. 22(9); Convey, B. 4(14); Ferdinand, L. 4(8); Forster, N. 27(3); Goater, S. 2(7); Hahnemann, M. 46; Harper, J. 39(2); Hughes, A. 40(1); Ingimarsson, I. 43(1); Keown, M. 3(2); Kitson, D. 37; Little, G. 29(6); Morgan, D. 10(8); Murty, G. 41; Newman, R. 11(6); Owusu, L. 14(11); Shorey, N. 44; Sidwell, S. 44; Sonko, I. 35(4); Williams, A. 11.
Goals – League (51): Kitson 19 (4 pens), Forster 7, Owusu 6, Sidwell 5, Harper 3, Ingimarsson 3, Shorey 3, Morgan 2, Ferdinand 1, Sonko 1, own goal 1.
Carling Cup (2): Goater 1, Hughes 1.
FA Cup (3): Forster 2, Ingimarsson 1.
Ground: Madejski Stadium, Junction 11, M4, Reading, Berks RG2 0FL. Telephone (0118) 968 1100.
Record Attendance: 33,042 v Brentford, FA Cup 5th rd, 19 February 1927. **Capacity:** 24,200.
Manager: Steve Coppell.
Secretary: Sue Hewett.
Most League Goals: 112, Division 3 (S), 1951–52.
Highest League Scorer in Season: Ronnie Blackman, 39, Division 3 (S), 1951–52.
Most League Goals in Total Aggregate: Ronnie Blackman, 158, 1947–54.
Most Capped Player: Jimmy Quinn, 17 (46), Northern Ireland.
Most League Appearances: Martin Hicks, 500, 1978–91.
Honours – Football League: Division 2 Champions – 1993–94. Division 3 Champions – 1985–86. Division 3 (S) Champions – 1925–26. Division 4 Champions – 1978–79. **Simod Cup:** Winners – 1987–88.
Colours: Royal blue and white hooped shirts, royal blue shorts and stockings.

ROCHDALE — FL CHAMPIONSHIP 2

Brisco Neil (M)	5 11	13 05	Billinge	26 1 78	Port Vale
Clarke Jamie (M)	6 2	13 02	Sunderland	18 9 82	Mansfield T
Cooksey Ernie (M)	5 9	11 12	Bishops Stortford	17 9 78	Oldham Ath
Edwards Neil (G)	5 9	12 11	Aberdare	5 12 70	Stockport Co
Gallimore Tony (D)	5 10	13 02	Nantwich	21 2 72	Barnsley
Gilks Matthew (G)	6 3	13 09	Rochdale	4 6 82	Scholar
Goodall Alan (D)	5 9	11 06	Birkenhead	2 12 81	Bangor C
Griffiths Gareth (D)	6 4	13 11	Winsford	10 4 70	Wigan Ath
Heald Greg (D)	6 1	12 07	Enfield	26 9 71	Leyton Orient
Holt Grant (F)	6 1	13 09	Carlisle	12 4 81	Sheffield W
Lambert Ricky (M)	6 2	12 01	Liverpool	16 2 82	Stockport Co
McCourt Patrick (F)	6 0	11 10	Derry	16 12 83	Scholar
Tait Paul (F)	6 2	12 00	Newcastle	24 10 74	Bristol R
Warner Scott (M)	5 11	12 06	Rochdale	3 12 83	Scholar

League Appearances: Atieno, T. 6(7); Bertos, L. 33(9); Brisco, N. 6(5); Brown, G. 1; Burgess, D. 19(2); Cash, B. 6; Clarke, J. 32(9); Cooksey, E. 27(7); Edwards, N. 16; Evans, W. 40; Gallimore, T. 32(2); Gilks, M. 30; Goodall, A. 27(7); Griffiths, G. 36(3); Heald, G. 29; Holt, G. 40; Jones, G. 39; Kitchen, B. (1); Lambert, R. 15; McCourt, P. 3(3); McGivern, L. 2(23); Probets, A. 4(5); Richards, M. 4(1); Richardson, M. 1(1); Tait, P. 27(9); Townson, K. 1; Warner, S. 25(3); Weller, P. 5; Williams, M. (1).
Goals – League (54): Holt 17, Jones 8 (4 pens), Lambert 6, Cooksey 5, Bertos 4 (1 pen), Atieno 2, Goodall 2, Heald 2, Richards 2, Tait 2, Clarke 1, Griffiths 1, McGivern 1, own goal 1.
Carling Cup (2): Holt 1, Tait 1.
FA Cup (5): Holt 5.
LDV Vans Trophy (4): Griffiths 3 (1 pen), Holt 1.
Ground: Spotland, Sandy Lane, Rochdale OL11 5DS. Telephone (01706) 644648.
Record Attendance: 24,231 v Notts Co, FA Cup 2nd rd, 10 December 1949.
Capacity: 10,200.
Manager: Steve Parkin.
Secretary: Hilary Molyneux Dearden.
Most League Goals: 105, Division 3 (N), 1926–27.
Highest League Scorer in Season: Albert Whitehurst, 44, Division 3 (N), 1926–27.
Most League Goals in Total Aggregate: Reg Jenkins, 119, 1964–73.
Most Capped Player: Leo Bertos, 6 (7), New Zealand.
Most League Appearances: Graham Smith, 317, 1966–74.
Honours – Nil.
Colours: Blue shirts with white trim, blue shorts, blue stockings with white hoop on turnover.

ROTHERHAM UNITED — FL CHAMPIONSHIP 1

Barker Shaun (D)	6 3	12 09	Nottingham	19 9 82	Scholar
Butler Martin (F)	5 11	12 09	Wordsley	15 9 74	Reading
Campbell-Ryce Jamal (F)	5 7	11 10	Lambeth	6 4 83	Charlton Ath
Duncum Sam (M)	5 9	11 02	Sheffield	18 2 87	Scholar
Gilchrist Phil (D)	6 0	14 07	Stockton	25 8 73	WBA
Hoskins Will (F)	5 11	11 08	Nottingham	6 5 86	Scholar
Hurst Paul (D)	5 5	10 03	Sheffield	25 9 74	Trainee
Keane Michael (M)	5 7	13 07	Dublin	29 12 82	Hull C
McIntosh Martin (D)	6 2	13 02	East Kilbride	19 3 71	Hibernian

Minto Scott (D)	5 10	12 10	Bromborough	6 8 71	West Ham U
Monkhouse Andy (M)	6 2	13 00	Leeds	23 10 80	Trainee
Montgomery Gary (G)	6 2	13 06	Leamington Spa	8 10 82	Coventry C
Mullin John (M)	6 1	12 09	Bury	11 8 75	Burnley
Newsham Mark (M)	5 10	9 11	Hatfield	24 3 87	Scholar
Pollitt Mike (G)	6 4	15 03	Farnworth	29 2 72	Chesterfield
Proctor Michael (F)	6 0	12 13	Sunderland	3 10 80	Sunderland
Swailes Chris (D)	6 2	13 07	Gateshead	19 10 70	Bury
Vernazza Paulo (M)	5 11	12 03	Islington	1 11 79	Watford
Warne Paul (M)	5 10	11 07	Norwich	8 5 73	Wigan Ath

League Appearances: Barker, R. 16(1); Barker, S. 30(3); Burchill, M. 3; Butler, M. 21; Campbell-Ryce, J. 23(1); Duncum, S. 1(1); Garner, D. 17(1); Gilchrist, P. 21(3); Griffit, L. 1(1); Hoskins, W. 6(16); Hurst, P. 38(1); Junior, 12; Keane, M. 9(1); McIntosh, M. 23; McLaren, P. 32(1); Minto, S. 13(1); Monkhouse, A. 11(3); Montgomery, G. 1; Mullin, J. 26(5); Newsham, M. (4); Pollitt, M. 45; Proctor, M. 16(12); Scott, R. 17(7); Sedgwick, C. 19(1); Shaw, P. 9; Stockdale, R. 27; Swailes, C. 37; Thorpe, T. 5; Vernazza, P. 14(13); Warne, P. 13(11).
Goals – League (35): Butler 6 (1 pen), McIntosh 5, Barker S 2, Hoskins 2, Junior 2, Monkhouse 2, Scott 2, Sedgwick 2, Shaw 2, Swailes 2, Burchill 1, Gilchrist 1, McLaren 1, Mullin 1, Proctor 1, Thorpe 1, Warne 1, own goal 1.
Carling Cup (3): Barker R 1, Proctor 1, Sedgwick 1.
FA Cup (0).
Ground: Millmoor Ground, Rotherham S60 1RH. Telephone (01709) 512434.
Record Attendance: 25,137 v Sheffield U, Division 2, 13 December 1952. **Capacity:** 9624.
Manager: Mick Harford.
Most League Goals: 114, Division 3 (N), 1946–47.
Highest League Scorer in Season: Wally Ardron, 38, Division 3 (N), 1946–47.
Most League Goals in Total Aggregate: Gladstone Guest, 130, 1946–56.
Most Capped Player: Shaun Goater, 14 (19), Bermuda.
Most League Appearances: Danny Williams, 459, 1946–62.
Honours – Football League: Division 3 Champions – 1980–81. Division 3 (N) Champions – 1950–51. Division 4 Champions – 1988–89. **Auto Windscreens Shield:** Winners – 1996
Colours: Red shirts with white trim, white shorts, red stockings.

RUSHDEN & DIAMONDS FL CHAMPIONSHIP 2

Allen Graham (D)	6 1	13 00	Bolton	8 4 77	Tranmere R
Bell David (M)	5 10	12 01	Kettering	21 1 84	Trainee
Broughton Drewe (F)	6 2	13 06	Hitchin	25 10 78	Southend U
Burgess Andy (M)	6 2	11 12	Bedford	10 8 81	Juniors
Dempster John (D)	6 0	12 05	Kettering	1 4 83	Trainee
Duffy Robert (F)	6 1	13 01	Swansea	2 12 82	Juniors
Gier Rob (D)	5 10	11 00	Ascot	6 1 80	Wimbledon
Gray Stuart (M)	5 10	13 07	Harrogate	18 12 73	Reading
Gulliver Phil (D)	6 2	14 09	Bishop Auckland	12 9 82	Middlesbrough
Hawkins Peter (D)	6 0	12 04	Maidstone	19 9 78	Wimbledon
Hunter Barry (D)	6 4	12 06	Coleraine	18 11 68	Reading
Jackson Simeon (M)	5 8	11 00	Kingston, Jam	28 3 87	Scholar
Kelly Marcus (M)	5 7	10 00	Ketteringham	16 3 86	Juniors
Kennedy Luke (M)	6 1	11 03	Peterborough	22 5 86	Scholar
Mills Gary (M)	5 9	11 11	Sheppey	20 5 81	Juniors
Okuonghae Magnus (F)	6 3	13 04	Nigeria	16 2 86	Scholar
Sambrook Andrew (D)	5 10	11 09	Chatham	13 7 79	Gillingham
Taylor Jason (M)	6 2	12 00	Burgess Hill	28 1 87	Scholar

Turley Billy (G)	6 3	15 11	Wolverhampton	15 7 73	Northampton T
Wark Scott (M)	6 3	13 04	Glasgow	9 6 87	Scholar

League Appearances: Allen, G. 25(1); Bell, David 39(1); Blayney, A. 4; Braniff, K. 11(1); Broughton, D. 20(1); Burgess, A. 42; Connelly, S. 40(2); Dempster, J. 9(6); Dove, C. 31(5); Duffy, R. (1); Gier, R. 30(2); Gray, S. 37(1); Gulliver, P. 29(3); Hawkins, P. 41; Hay, A. 29(13); Hunter, B. (1); Jackson, S. (3); Kelly, M. 3(8); Kennedy, L. 1(2); Littlejohn, A. 8(7); McCafferty, N. 16; Mills, G. 7; Mulligan, G. 12(1); Robinson, M. (2); Sambrook, A. 3(5); Sharp, B. 16; Shearer, S. 13; Taylor, J. 4(16); Turley, B. 22; Wark, S. (1); Williams, M. 7; Worgan, L. 7.
Goals – League (42): Sharp 9, Broughton 6 (2 pens), Dove 6, David Bell 3, Braniff 3, Hay 3, Mulligan 3, Gier 2, Taylor 2, Allen 1, Burgess 1, Gray 1, Hawkins 1, Mills 1.
Carling Cup (0).
FA Cup (3): Broughton 1, Gray 1, Robinson 1.
LDV Vans Trophy (0).
Ground: Nene Park, Diamond Way, Irthlingborough, Northants NN9 5QF. Telephone (01933) 652 000.
Record Attendance: 6431 v Leeds U, F.A. Cup 3rd rd, 2 January 1999.
Capacity: 6441
Manager: Barry Hunter.
Secretary: David Joyce.
Most League Goals: 109, Southern League Midland Division, 1993–94.
Most capped player: Onandi Lowe, 9, Jamaica.
Honours – Football League: Division 3 Champions – 2002–03. **Conference:** Champions – 2000–01. **Southern League Midland Division:** Champions – 1993–94. **Premier Division:** Champions – 1995–96. **FA Trophy:** Semi-finalists – 1994. **Northants FA Hillier Senior Cup:** Winners – 1993–94, 1998–99. **Maunsell Premier Cup:** Winners – 1994–95, 1998–99.
Colours: All red.

SCUNTHORPE UNITED FL CHAMPIONSHIP 1

Baraclough Ian (M)	6 1	12 02	Leicester	4 12 70	Notts Co
Beagrie Peter (M)	5 8	12 00	Middlesbrough	28 11 65	Wigan Ath
Butler Andy (D)	6 2	14 02	Doncaster	4 11 83	Scholar
Byrne Cliff (D)	6 0	12 11	Dublin	27 4 82	Sunderland
Corden Wayne (M)	5 10	12 04	Leek	1 11 75	Mansfield T
Crosby Andy (D)	6 2	13 07	Rotherham	3 3 73	Oxford U
Evans Tom (G)	6 0	13 02	Doncaster	31 12 76	Crystal Palace
Featherstone Lee (M)	6 0	12 08	Chesterfield	20 7 83	Sheffield U
Keogh Andrew (F)	6 0	11 06	Dublin	16 5 86	Leeds U
Musselwhite Paul (G)	6 2	14 02	Portsmouth	22 12 68	Hull C
Parton Andy (F)	5 10	12 00	Doncaster	29 9 83	Scholar
Rankine Michael (F)	6 1	14 12	Doncaster	15 1 85	
Ridley Lee (D)	5 9	11 09	Scunthorpe	5 12 81	Scholar
Sparrow Matt (M)	5 11	11 06	Wembley	3 10 81	Scholar
Stanton Nathan (D)	5 9	11 03	Nottingham	6 5 81	Trainee
Taylor Cleveland (M)	5 8	10 07	Leicester	9 9 83	Bolton W
Torpey Steve (F)	6 3	14 13	Islington	8 12 70	Bristol C
Williams Marcus (D)	5 10	10 07	Doncaster	8 4 86	Scholar

League Appearances: Angus, S. 9; Bailey, M. 2(2); Baraclough, I. 45; Beagrie, P. 36; Brighton, T. 2(3); Butler, A. 36(1); Byrne, C. 24(5); Corden, W. 3(5); Crosby, A. 43(1); Featherstone, L. (1); Hayes, P. 41(5); Hinds, R. 6(1); Jackson, M. 1(2); Kell, R. 43; Keogh, A. 13(12); Musselwhite, P. 46, Parton, A. (1); Rankine, M.

1(20); Ridley, L. 43(1); Sharp, K. 4(2); Sparrow, M. 35(9); Stanton, N. 18(3); Taylor, C. 18(26); Teggart, N. 1; Torpey, S. 33(1); Walters, J. 3; Williams, M. (4).
Goals – League (69): Hayes 18, Torpey 12, Butler 10, Taylor 6, Kell 5, Sparrow 5, Baraclough 3, Crosby 3 (2 pens), Keogh 3, Beagrie 2 (1 pen), Byrne 1, Rankine 1.
Carling Cup (0).
FA Cup (5): Hayes 2, Baraclough 1, Ridley 1, Sparrow 1.
LDV Vans Trophy (1): Torpey 1.
Ground: Glanford Park, Scunthorpe, South Humberside DN15 8TD. Telephone (01724) 848 077.
Record Attendance: Old Showground: 23,935 v Portsmouth, FA Cup 4th rd, 30 January 1954. Glanford Park: 8775 v Rotherham U, Division 4, 1 May 1989.
Capacity: 9088.
Manager: Brian Laws.
Secretary: J. Hammond.
Most League Goals: 88, Division 3 (N), 1957–58.
Highest League Scorer in Season: Barrie Thomas, 31, Division 2, 1961–62.
Most League Goals in Total Aggregate: Steve Cammack, 110, 1979–81, 1981–86.
Most Capped Player: None.
Most League Appearances: Jack Brownsword, 595, 1950–65.
Honours – Football League: Division 3 (N) Champions – 1957–58.
Colours: Claret shirts, blue shorts, white stockings.

SHEFFIELD UNITED — FL CHAMPIONSHIP

Barnes Phil (G)	6 2	15 04	Sheffield	2 3 79	Blackpool
Beckett Luke (F)	5 11	11 02	Sheffield	25 11 76	Stockport Co
Bromby Leigh (D)	6 0	12 04	Dewsbury	2 6 80	Sheffield W
Cullip Danny (D)	6 0	12 12	Ascot	17 9 76	Brighton & HA
Forte Jonathan (M)	6 0	12 06	Sheffield	25 7 86	Scholar
Francis Simon (D)	6 0	14 09	Nottingham	16 2 85	Bradford C
Geary Derek (D)	5 6	10 08	Dublin	19 6 80	Sheffield W
Gray Andy (F)	6 2	14 02	Harrogate	15 11 77	Bradford C
Harley Jon (D)	5 8	11 09	Maidstone	26 9 79	Fulham
Haystead Daniel (G)	6 1	11 09	Chesterfield	13 2 86	Scholar
Horwood Evan (D)	6 0	10 06	Billingham	10 3 86	Scholar
Jagielka Phil (D)	5 11	14 00	Manchester	17 8 82	Scholar
Kabba Steven (F)	5 8	12 06	Lambeth	7 3 81	Crystal Palace
Kenny Paddy (G)	6 0	15 10	Halifax	17 5 78	Bury
Kozluk Rob (D)	5 8	11 07	Sutton-in-Ashfield	5 7 77	Derby Co
Liddell Andy (M)	5 7	11 11	Leeds	28 6 73	Wigan Ath
Montgomery Nick (M)	5 8	12 08	Leeds	28 10 81	Scholar
Morgan Chris (D)	6 0	13 06	Barnsley	9 11 77	Barnsley
Quinn Alan (M)	5 9	11 09	Dublin	13 6 79	Sheffield W
Sharp Billy (F)	5 8	12 02	Sheffield	5 2 86	Scholar
Shaw Paul (F)	5 10	13 01	Burnham	4 9 73	Gillingham
Thirlwell Paul (M)	6 2	12 02	Springwell	13 2 79	Sunderland
Tonge Michael (M)	5 10	12 06	Manchester	7 4 83	Scholar
Ward Ashley (F)	6 0	13 10	Manchester	24 11 70	Bradford C
Wright Alan (D)	5 3	9 13	Ashton-under-Lyme	28 9 71	Middlesbrough

League Appearances: Barnes, P. 1; Beckett, L. 1(4); Bennett, I. 5; Black, T. 3(1); Bromby, L. 46; Cadamarteri, D. 14(7); Cullip, D. 11; Forte, J. 1(21); Francis, S. 2(4); Gabrieli, E. (1); Geary, D. 15(4); Gray, A. 41(2); Harley, J. 44; Hayles, B. 4; Hurst, K. (1); Jagielka, P. 46; Johnson, T. 1(4); Kabba, S. 6(5); Kenny, P. 40; Kozluk, R. 9; Lester, J. 1(11); Liddell, A. 26(7); Montgomery, N. 16(9); Morgan, C. 40(1); Quinn, A. 38(5); Sharp, B. (2); Shaw, P. 16(5); Thirlwell, P. 24(6); Tonge, M. 33(1); Ward, A. 5(5); Webber, D. 6(1); Wright, A. 11(3).

Goals – League (57): Gray 15 (1 pen), Quinn A 7, Shaw 7, Bromby 5, Liddell 3, Webber 3, Harley 2, Kabba 2, Morgan 2, Tonge 2, Black 1, Cadamarteri 1, Forte 1, Geary 1, Montgomery 1, Thirlwell 1, Ward 1, own goals 2.
Carling Cup (7): Gray 2, Jagielka 1, Lester 1, Morgan 1, Tonge 1, own goal 1.
FA Cup (6): Liddell 3, Cullip 1, Gray 1 (pen), Jagielka 1.
Ground: Bramall Lane Ground, Sheffield S2 4SU. Telephone (0870) 787 1960.
Record Attendance: 68,287 v Leeds U, FA Cup 5th rd, 15 February 1936.
Capacity: 28,000.
Manager: Neil Warnock.
Secretary: Donna Fletcher.
Most League Goals: 102, Division 1, 1925–26.
Highest League Scorer in Season: Jimmy Dunne, 41, Division 1, 1930–31.
Most League Goals in Total Aggregate: Harry Johnson, 205, 1919–30.
Most Capped Player: Billy Gillespie, 25, Northern Ireland.
Most League Appearances: Joe Shaw, 629, 1948–66.
Honours – Football League: Division 1 Champions – 1897–98. Division 2 Champions – 1952–53. Division 4 Champions – 1981–82. **FA Cup:** Winners – 1899, 1902, 1915, 1925.
Colours: Red and white striped shirts with white trim, red shorts and red stockings.

SHEFFIELD WEDNESDAY FL CHAMPIONSHIP

Adams Steve (M)	6 0	12 01	Plymouth	25 9 80	Plymouth Arg
Brunt Chris (M)	6 1	13 02	Belfast	14 12 84	Middlesbrough
Bullen Lee (D)	6 1	12 08	Edinburgh	29 3 71	Dunfermline Ath
Carr Chris (D)	6 1	12 07	Newcastle	14 12 84	Newcastle U
Collins Patrick (D)	6 2	12 07	Newcastle	4 2 85	Sunderland
Evans Richard (M)	5 10	12 05	Cardiff	19 6 83	Birmingham C
Heckingbottom Paul (D)	6 0	12 12	Barnsley	17 7 77	Bradford C
Lee Graeme (D)	6 2	13 07	Middlesbrough	31 5 78	Hartlepool U
Lucas David (G)	6 1	13 06	Preston	23 11 77	Preston NE
MacLean Steve (F)	5 10	12 01	Edinburgh	23 8 82	Scunthorpe U
McGovern John-Paul (M)	5 8	11 11	Glasgow	3 10 80	Celtic
Olsen Kim (F)	6 4	13 07	Herning	11 2 79	Midtjylland
Peacock Lee (F)	6 0	13 00	Paisley	9 10 76	Bristol C
Proudlock Adam (F)	6 0	13 12	Wellington	9 5 81	Wolverhampton W
Quinn James (M)	6 1	12 10	Coventry	15 12 74	WBA
Rocastle Craig (M)	6 1	12 13	Lewisham	17 8 81	Chelsea
Talbot Drew (F)	5 10	11 00	Barnsley	19 7 86	Trainee
Whelan Glenn (M)	5 11	12 07	Dublin	13 1 84	Manchester C
Wood Richard (D)	6 3	12 03	Ossett	5 7 85	Scholar

League Appearances: Adams, S. 8(1); Adamson, C. 1(1); Aljofree, H. 2; Aranalde, Z. 1(1); Barrett, G. 5(1); Branston, G. 10(1); Bruce, A. 5(1); Brunt, C. 27(15); Bullen, L. 46; Collins, P. 25(3); Gallacher, P. 8; Green, A. 3; Greenwood, R. (2); Hamshaw, M. 9(11); Heckingbottom, P. 37(1); Jones, K. 7; Lee, G. 19(3); Lucas, D. 34; MacLean, S. 36; Marsden, C. 15; McGovern, J. 46; McMahon, L. 13(2); N'Dumbu Nsungu, G. 4(7); O'Brien, J. 14(1); Peacock, L. 18(11); Proudlock, A. 11(3); Quinn, J. 10(5); Rocastle, C. 9(2); Shaw, J. 1(2); Smith, P. 7(1); Talbot, D. 3(18); Tidman, O. 3(1); Whelan, G. 36; Wood, R. 33(1).
Goals – League (77): MacLean 18 (6 pens), Bullen 7, Jones 7, McGovern 6, Proudlock 6, Brunt 4 (1 pen), Heckingbottom 4, Peacock 4, Talbot 4, McMahon 2, O'Brien 2, Quinn 2, Whelan 2, Barrett 1, Collins 1, Hamshaw 1, Lee 1, N'Dumbu Nsungu 1, Rocastle 1, Wood 1, own goals 2.
Carling Cup (1): Peacock 1.
FA Cup (1): Whelan 1.
LDV Vans Trophy (1): MacLean 1.

Play-Offs (7): McGovern 2, Brunt 1, MacLean 1 (pen), Peacock 1, Talbot 1, Whelan 1.
Ground: Hillsborough, Sheffield, S6 1SW. Telephone (0114) 2212121
Record Attendance: 72,841 v Manchester C, FA Cup 5th rd, 17 February 1934.
Capacity: 39,814
Manager: Paul Sturrock.
Chief Executive: Kaven Walker.
Most League Goals: 106, Division 2, 1958–59.
Highest League Scorer in Season: Derek Dooley, 46, Division 2, 1951–52.
Most League Goals in Total Aggregate: Andy Wilson, 199, 1900–20.
Most Capped Player: Nigel Worthington, 50 (66), Northern Ireland.
Most League Appearances: Andy Wilson, 501, 1900–20.
Honours – Football League: Division 1 Champions – 1902–03, 1903–04, 1928–29, 1929–30. Division 2 Champions – 1899–1900, 1925–26, 1951–52, 1955–56, 1958–59.
FA Cup: Winners – 1896, 1907, 1935. **Football League Cup:** Winners – 1990–91.
Colours: Blue and white striped shirts, black shorts, blue stockings.

SHREWSBURY TOWN — FL CHAMPIONSHIP 2

Adaggio Marco (F)	5 8	12 04	Malaga	6 10 87	
Aiston Sam (M)	6 1	12 10	Newcastle	21 11 76	Sunderland
Cowan Gavin (D)	6 4	12 06	Hanover	24 5 81	Canvey Island
Darby Duane (F)	5 11	12 06	Birmingham	17 10 73	Rushden & D
Edwards Dave (M)	5 11	11 05	Shrewsbury	3 2 86	Trainee
Hart Joe (G)	6 3	13 03	Shrewsbury	19 4 87	Trainee
Howie Scott (G)	6 2	13 07	Motherwell	4 1 72	Bristol R
Langmead Kelvin (F)	6 1	12 00	Coventry	23 3 85	Preston NE
Rodgers Luke (F)	5 7	11 00	Birmingham	1 1 82	Trainee
Sheron Mike (F)	5 10	12 07	St Helens	11 1 72	Macclesfield T
Tolley Jamie (M)	6 0	11 03	Ludlow	12 5 83	Trainee
Walton David (D)	6 2	14 08	Bedlington	10 4 73	Derby Co
Whitehead Stuart (D)	6 0	12 02	Bromsgrove	17 7 77	Darlington

League Appearances: Adaggio, M. (5); Aiston, S. 26(9); Ashton, N. 22(2); Burns, L. 1(1); Challis, T. 38; Cowan, G. 5; Cramb, C. (2); Darby, D. 8(8); Edwards, D. 16(11); Fox, D. 2(2); Grant, J. 10(9); Hart, J. 6; Howie, S. 40; Langmead, K. 24(4); Logan, R. 5; Lowe, R. 19(11); Lyng, C. (4); McGrath, J. 7(1); Moss, D. 26; O'Connor, M. 13(8); Ridler, D. 6(3); Rodgers, L. 35(1); Sedgemore, J. 25(6); Sheron, M. 6(1); Smith, B. 10(2); Stephens, R. (2); Street, K. 15(6); Tinson, D. 42(1); Tolley, J. 33(3); Walton, D. 20(2); Whitehead, S. 37(3); Wilkinson, A. 9.
Goals – League (48): Moss 6, Rodgers 6, Edwards 5, Sedgemore 5 (2 pens), Tolley J 4, Langmead 3, Lowe 3, Smith 3, Grant 2, Sheron 2 (1 pen), Walton 2, Aiston 1, Darby 1, Fox 1, Logan 1, Street 1, own goals 2.
Carling Cup (1): Rodgers 1.
FA Cup (0).
LDV Vans Trophy (4): Logan 1, Rodgers 1, Tolley 1, own goal 1.
Ground: Gay Meadow, Abbey Foregate, Shrewsbury SY2 6AB. Telephone (01743) 360111.
Record Attendance: 18,917 v Walsall, Division 3, 26 April 1961. **Capacity:** 8000.
Manager: Gary Peters.
Secretary: Mrs Judy Shone.
Most League Goals: 101, Division 4, 1958–59.
Highest League Scorer in Season: Arthur Rowley, 38, Division 4, 1958–59.
Most League Goals in Total Aggregate: Arthur Rowley, 152, 1958–65 (completing his League record of 434 goals).

Most Capped Player: Jimmy McLaughlin, 5 (12), Northern Ireland; Bernard McNally, 5, Northern Ireland.
Most League Appearances: Mickey Brown, 418, 1986–91; 1992–94; 1996–2001.
Honours – Football League: Division 3 Champions – 1978–79, 1993–94. **Welsh Cup:** Winners – 1891, 1938, 1977, 1979, 1984, 1985.
Colours: Amber and blue shirts, blue shorts, blue stockings with amber trim.

SOUTHAMPTON — FL CHAMPIONSHIP

Anaclet Edward (F)	5 9	10 00	Tanzania	31 8 85	Scholar
Baird Chris (D)	5 10	11 11	Ballymoney	25 2 82	Scholar
Best Leon (F)	6 1	13 03	Nottingham	19 9 86	Scholar
Blackstock Dexter (F)	6 2	13 00	Oxford	20 5 86	Scholar
Blayney Alan (G)	6 2	13 12	Belfast	9 10 81	Scholar
Crouch Peter (F)	6 7	13 03	Macclesfield	30 1 81	Aston Villa
Delap Rory (M)	6 3	13 00	Sutton Coldfield	6 7 76	Derby Co
Fernandes Fabrice (M)	5 8	10 07	Aubervilliers	29 10 79	Rennes
Folly Yoann (M)	5 9	11 04	Togo	6 6 85	St Etienne
Griffit Leandre (M)	5 8	11 04	Maubeuge	21 5 84	Amiens
Higginbotham Danny (D)	6 2	12 01	Manchester	29 12 78	Derby Co
Jakobsson Andreas (D)	6 2	13 00	Utanfor	6 10 72	Brondby
Jones Kenwyne (F)	6 2	13 06	Trinidad & Tobago	5 10 84	W Connection
Kenton Darren (D)	5 10	12 06	Wandsworth	13 9 78	Norwich C
Lundekvam Claus (D)	6 3	13 05	Austevoll	22 2 73	Brann
McCann Neil (M)	5 10	11 00	Greenock	11 8 74	Rangers
Mills Matthew (D)	6 3	12 12	Swindon	14 7 86	Scholar
Niemi Antti (G)	6 1	12 04	Oulu	31 5 72	Hearts
Nilsson Mikael (M)	5 10	12 00	Kristianstad	24 6 78	Halmstad
Oakley Matthew (M)	5 10	12 06	Peterborough	17 8 77	Trainee
Ormerod Brett (F)	5 10	11 12	Blackburn	18 10 76	Blackpool
Pahars Marian (F)	5 8	10 08	Latvia	5 8 76	Skonto Riga
Phillips Kevin (F)	5 7	12 00	Hitchin	25 7 73	Sunderland
Poke Michael (G)	6 1	13 12	Spelthorne	21 11 85	Trainee
Prutton David (M)	5 10	13 00	Hull	12 9 81	Nottingham F
Quashie Nigel (M)	5 9	12 08	Nunhead	10 7 78	Portsmouth
Smith Paul (G)	6 3	14 00	Epsom	17 12 79	Brentford
Surman Andrew (M)	6 0	11 09	Johannesburg	20 8 86	Trainee
Svensson Michael (D)	6 2	12 02	Sweden	25 11 75	Troyes
Telfer Paul (D)	5 10	11 13	Edinburgh	21 10 71	Coventry C
Van Damme Jelle (D)	6 4	13 01	Lokeren	10 10 83	Ajax

League Appearances: Beattie, J. 11; Bernard, O. 12(1); Best, L. 1(2); Blackstock, D. 8(1); Blayney, A. 1; Camara, H. 10(3); Cranie, M. 3; Crouch, P. 18(9); Davenport, C. 5(2); Delap, R. 31(3); Dodd, J. 4(1); Fernandes, F. 14(2); Folly, Y. 1(2); Griffit, L. (2); Higginbotham, D. 20(1); Jakobsson, A. 24(3); Jones, K. 1(1); Keller, K. 4; Kenton, D. 9; Le Saux, G. 24(1); Lundekvam, C. 33(1); McCann, N. 5(6); Niemi, A. 28; Nilsson, M. 12(4); Oakley, M. 6(1); Ormerod, B. 5(4); Phillips, K. 21(9); Prutton, D. 19(4); Quashie, N. 13; Redknapp, J. 16; Smith, P. 5(1); Svensson, A. 21(9); Telfer, P. 26(4); Van Damme, J. 4(2).
Goals – League (45): Crouch 12 (1 pen), Phillips 10 (1 pen), Camara 4, Beattie 3 (1 pen), Svensson A 3, Delap 2, Jakobsson 2, Blackstock 1, Higginbotham 1, Le Saux 1, Oakley 1, Prutton 1, Quashie 1, own goals 3.
Carling Cup (8): Blackstock 4, McCann 1, Ormerod 1, Phillips 1, Prutton 1.
FA Cup (10): Crouch 4 (1 pen), Camara 2, Phillips 2, Oakley 1, Redknapp 1.
Ground: The Friends Provident St Mary's Stadium, Britannia Road, Southampton SO14 5FP. Telephone (0870) 220 0000.

Record Attendance: 32,104 v Liverpool, FA Premier League, 18 January 2003.
Capacity: 32,689.
Manager: Harry Redknapp.
Secretary: Liz Coley.
Most League Goals: 112, Division 3 (S), 1957–58.
Highest League Scorer in Season: Derek Reeves, 39, Division 3, 1959–60.
Most League Goals in Total Aggregate: Mike Channon, 185, 1966–77, 1979–82.
Most Capped Player: Peter Shilton, 49 (125), England.
Most League Appearances: Terry Paine, 713, 1956–74.
Honours – Football League: Division 3 (S) Champions – 1921–22. Division 3 Champions – 1959–60. **FA Cup:** Winners – 1975–76.
Colours: Red and white striped shirts, black shorts, white stockings.

SOUTHEND UNITED — FL CHAMPIONSHIP 1

Barrett Adam (D)	6 1	12 09	Dagenham	29 11 79	Bristol R
Bentley Mark (M)	6 2	13 04	Hertford	7 1 78	Dagenham & R
Dudfield Lawrie (F)	6 1	13 00	Southwark	7 5 80	Northampton T
Eastwood Freddy (F)	5 11	12 00	Epsom	29 10 83	Grays Ath
Edwards Andy (D)	6 4	13 09	Epping	17 9 71	Rushden & D
Flahavan Darryl (G)	5 11	12 06	Southampton	28 11 78	Woking
Gower Mark (M)	5 8	12 02	Edmonton	5 10 78	Barnet
Gray Wayne (F)	5 10	13 05	Dulwich	7 11 80	Wimbledon
Griemink Bart (G)	6 3	14 06	Holland	29 3 72	Swindon T
Guttridge Luke (M)	5 5	8 06	Barnstaple	27 3 82	Cambridge U
Hunt Lewis (D)	5 11	12 09	Birmingham	25 8 82	Derby Co
Husbands Michael (F)	5 8	10 10	Birmingham	13 11 83	Aston Villa
Jupp Duncan (D)	6 1	12 12	Guildford	25 1 75	Luton T
Lawson James (M)	5 9	10 03	Basildon	21 1 87	Scholar
Maher Kevin (M)	6 0	12 00	Ilford	17 10 76	Tottenham H
Nicolau Nicky (D)	5 7	10 03	Camden	12 10 83	Arsenal
Pettefer Carl (M)	5 8	10 06	Burnham	22 3 81	Portsmouth
Prior Spencer (D)	6 3	13 00	Rochford	22 4 71	Cardiff C
Smith Jay (M)	5 7	10 11	London	24 9 81	Aston Villa
Wilson Che (D)	5 9	12 01	Ely	17 1 79	Cambridge C

League Appearances: Barrett, A. 42(1); Bentley, M. 35(4); Blewitt, D. (1); Bramble, T. 10(10); Broughton, D. 4(5); Clarke, R. 1; Corbett, J. 1(5); Dudfield, L. 16(20); Eastwood, F. 31(2); Edwards, A. 9(3); Flahavan, D. 26(2); Gower, M. 32(6); Gray, W. 33(11); Griemink, B. 19; Guttridge, L. 3(2); Hunt, L. 27(4); Husbands, M. (2); Jupp, D. 28(3); Kightly, M. (1); Lawson, J. (1); Maher, K. 42; McCormack, A. 5(2); Nicolau, N. 15(7); Pettefer, C. 46; Prior, S. 41; Wilson, C. 40.
Goals – League (65): Eastwood 19 (1 pen), Barrett 11, Gray 11 (3 pens), Gower 6, Bentley 5, Dudfield 4 (2 pens), McCormack 2, Prior 2, Bramble 1, Corbett 1, Edwards 1, Maher 1, Nicolau 1.
Carling Cup (0).
FA Cup (0).
LDV Vans Trophy (13): Dudfield 3, Eastwood 3, Gray 2 (1 pen), Bentley 1, Bramble 1, Gower 1, Nicolau 1, Pettefer 1.
Play-Offs (3): Eastwood 2 (1 pen), Jupp 1.
Ground: Roots Hall Football Ground, Victoria Avenue, Southend-on-Sea SS2 6NQ. Telephone (0870) 304 050.
Record Attendance: 31,090 v Liverpool FA Cup 3rd rd, 10 January 1979. **Capacity:** 12,343.
Manager: Steve Tilson.
Secretary: Helen Norbury.
Most League Goals: 92, Division 3 (S), 1950–51.

Highest League Scorer in Season: Jim Shankly, 31, 1928–29; Sammy McCrory, 1957–58, both in Division 3 (S).
Most League Goals in Total Aggregate: Roy Hollis, 122, 1953–60.
Most Capped Player: George Mackenzie, 9, Eire.
Most League Appearances: Sandy Anderson, 452, 1950–63.
Honours – Football League: Division 4 Champions – 1980–81.
Colours: All navy blue with white trim.

STOCKPORT COUNTY FL CHAMPIONSHIP 2

Allen Damien (M)	5 11	11 04	Cheadle	1 8 86	
Briggs Keith (M)	6 0	11 05	Glossop	11 12 81	Norwich C
Cartwright Lee (M)	5 10	11 00	Rawtenstall	19 9 72	Preston NE
Cutler Neil (G)	6 4	12 00	Birmingham	3 9 76	Stoke C
Dje Ludovic (M)	6 4	14 06	Paris	22 7 77	
Goodwin Jim (M)	5 9	12 01	Waterford	20 11 81	Celtic
Griffin Danny (D)	5 11	12 05	Belfast	10 8 77	Dundee U
Hadfield Jordan (M)	5 10	11 04	Swinton	12 8 87	
Hardiker John (M)	5 11	11 01	Preston	17 7 82	Morecambe
Jackman Danny (D)	5 4	9 00	Worcester	3 1 83	Aston Villa
Le Fondre Adam (F)	5 9	11 04	Stockport	2 12 86	
Raynes Michael (M)	6 2	12 02	Wythenshawe	15 10 87	Scholar
Robertson Mark (M)	5 9	12 04	Sydney	6 4 77	St Johnstone
Robinson Marvin (F)	6 0	12 03	Crewe	11 4 80	Walsall
Spencer James (G)	6 3	15 04	Stockport	11 4 85	Trainee
Tomlinson Ezekiel (M)	5 9	11 02	Birmingham	9 11 85	Scholar
Turnbull Paul (F)	5 10	11 07	Stockport	23 1 89	Scholar
Williams Ashley (D)	6 0	11 02	Wolverhampton	23 8 84	Hednesford T
Williams Chris (F)	5 7	9 00	Manchester	2 2 85	Scholar

League Appearances: Adams, D. 27; Allen, D. 14(7); Armstrong, C. 9(2); Bailey, M. (1); Barlow, S. 11(20); Beckett, L. 15; Bridge-Wilkinson, M. 19(3); Briggs, K. 14(2); Cartwright, L. 18(1); Clarke, D. 1; Cutler, N. 22; Daly, J. 10(4); Dje, L. 2(1); Dolan, J. 11; Feeney, W. 31; Geary, D. 12(1); Goodwin, J. 30(6); Griffin, D. 16; Hadfield, J. 1; Hardiker, J. 26(3); Horwood, E. 10; Hurst, K. 14; Jackman, D. 24(9); Lambert, R. 27(2); Le Fondre, A. 11(9); Mair, L. 9(5); Morrison, O. (1); Raynes, M. 15(4); Robertson, M. 18(2); Robinson, M. 3; Singh, H. 5(1); Smith, A. 1; Spencer, J. 24; Tomlinson, E. 2(3); Turnbull, P. (1); Welsh, A. 4(9); Williams, A. 44; Williams, C. 6(3).
Goals – League (49): Feeney 15 (2 pens), Beckett 7, Lambert 4 (1 pen), Le Fondre 4 (1 pen), Barlow 3, Daly 3, Bridge-Wilkinson 2, Briggs 2, Jackman 2, Adams 1, Allen 1, Armstrong 1, Cartwright 1, Dolan 1, Hurst 1, Williams A 1.
Carling Cup (1): own goal 1.
FA Cup (4): Feeney 2, Griffin 1, Williams A 1.
LDV Vans Trophy (3): Barlow 1, Daly 1, Le Fondre 1.
Ground: Edgeley Park, Hardcastle Road, Stockport, Cheshire SK3 9DD. Telephone (0161) 286 8888.
Record Attendance: 27,833 v Liverpool, FA Cup 5th rd, 11 February 1950.
Capacity: 10,817.
Manager: Chris Turner.
Secretary: Kevan Taylor.
Most League Goals: 115, Division 3 (N), 1933–34.
Highest League Scorer in Season: Alf Lythgoe, 46, Division 3 (N), 1933–34.
Most League Goals in Total Aggregate: Jack Connor, 132, 1951–56.
Most Capped Player: Jarkko Wiss, 9 (36), Finland.
Most League Appearances: Andy Thorpe, 489, 1978–86, 1988–92.
Honours – Football League: Division 3 (N) Champions – 1921–22, 1936–37. Division 4 Champions – 1966–67.
Colours: Blue shirts and shorts, white stockings.

Asaba Carl (F)	6 2	13 00	London	28 1 73	Sheffield U
Bremmer Dave (M)	5 10	12 00	Bromborough	28 2 75	Crewe Alex
Buxton Lewis (D)	6 1	13 10	Newport (IW)	10 12 83	Portsmouth
Clarke Clive (D)	5 11	12 03	Dublin	14 1 80	Trainee
De Goey Ed (G)	6 6	12 00	Gouda	20 12 66	Chelsea
Dickinson Carl (D)	6 0	12 00	Swadlincote	31 3 87	Scholar
Duberry Michael (D)	6 1	14 09	Enfield	14 10 75	Leeds U
Eustace John (M)	5 11	11 12	Solihull	3 11 79	Coventry C
Foster Ben (G)	6 2	12 00	Leamington Spa	3 4 83	Racing Club Warwick
Greenacre Chris (F)	5 11	12 08	Halifax	23 12 77	Mansfield T
Gudjonsson Thordur (M)	5 10	11 06	Reykjavik	23 1 73	Bochum
Halls John (M)	6 0	11 00	Islington	14 2 82	Arsenal
Harper Kevin (F)	5 6	12 00	Oldham	15 1 76	Portsmouth
Henry Karl (M)	6 0	12 00	Wolverhampton	26 11 82	Trainee
Hill Clint (D)	6 0	11 06	Liverpool	19 10 78	Oldham Ath
Neal Lewis (M)	5 10	10 11	Leicester	14 7 81	Juniors
Noel-Williams Gifton (F)	6 1	13 06	Islington	21 1 80	Watford
Owen Gareth (D)	6 1	11 07	Stoke	21 9 82	Scholar
Palmer Jermaine (F)	6 1	11 03	Nottingham	28 8 86	Scholar
Paterson Mark (M)	5 9	11 05	Tunstall	13 5 87	Scholar
Pulis Anthony (M)	5 10	11 10	Bristol	21 7 84	Portsmouth
Russell Darel (M)	6 0	11 09	Mile End	22 10 80	Norwich C
Simonsen Steve (G)	6 2	12 00	South Shields	3 4 79	Everton
Taggart Gerry (D)	6 2	14 00	Belfast	18 10 70	Leicester C
Thomas Wayne (D)	5 11	11 12	Gloucester	17 5 79	Torquay U
Wilkinson Andy (D)	5 11	11 00	Stone	6 8 84	Scholar

League Appearances: Akinbiyi, A. 29; Asaba, C. 14(19); Barker, C. 4; Brammer, D. 42(1); Buxton, L. 14(2); Clark, C. (2); Clarke, C. 42; De Goey, E. 17; Dickinson, C. (1); Duberry, M. 25; Eustace, J. 2(5); Greenacre, C. 18(14); Gudjonsson, T. (2); Guppy, S. (4); Hall, M. 19(1); Halls, J. 20(2); Harper, K. 8(1); Henry, K. 14(20); Hill, C. 31(1); Jarrett, J. 2; Jones, K. 13; Neal, L. 10(13); Noel-Williams, G. 41(5); Owen, G. (2); Palmer, J. (1); Paterson, M. (3); Ricketts, M. 1(10); Russell, D. 45; Simonsen, S. 29(2); Taggart, G. 31; Thomas, W. 35; Wilkinson, A. (1).
Goals – League (36): Noel-Williams 13 (2 pens), Akinbiyi 7, Jones 3, Russell 2, Taggart 2, Thomas 2, Asaba 1, Brammer 1, Clarke 1 (pen), Greenacre 1, Hall 1, Hill 1, Neal 1.
Carling Cup (1): Asaba 1.
FA Cup (1): Thomas 1.
Ground: Britannia Stadium, Stoke-on-Trent ST4 4EG. Telephone (01782) 592222.
Record Attendance: 51,380 v Arsenal, Division 1, 29 March 1937. **Capacity:** 28,218.
Manager: Johan Boskamp.
Secretary: Diane Richardson.
Most League Goals: 92, Division 3 (N), 1926–27.
Highest League Scorer in Season: Freddie Steele, 33, Division 1, 1936–37.
Most League Goals in Total Aggregate: Freddie Steele, 142, 1934–49.
Most Capped Player: Gordon Banks, 36 (73), England.
Most League Appearances: Eric Skeels, 506, 1958–76.
Honours – Football League: Division 2 Champions – 1932–33, 1962–63, 1992–93. Division 3 (N) Champions – 1926–27. **Football League Cup:** Winners – 1971–72. **Autoglass Trophy:** Winners – 1992. **Auto Windscreens Shield:** Winners – 2000.
Colours: Red and white striped shirts, white shorts, white stockings.

Alnwick Ben (G)	6 2	13 12	Prudhoe	1 1 87	Scholar
Arca Julio (M)	5 9	11 13	Quilmes	31 1 81	Argentinos Juniors
Bell Ryan (D)	6 1	13 06	Ashington	30 3 86	Trainee
Breen Gary (D)	6 3	13 03	Hendon	12 12 73	West Ham U
Brown Chris (F)	6 3	13 08	Doncaster	11 12 84	Trainee
Caldwell Steven (D)	6 2	13 13	Stirling	12 9 80	Newcastle U
Collins Danny (D)	6 2	12 00	Buckley	6 8 80	Chester C
Collins Neil (D)	6 3	13 00	Irvine	2 9 83	
Deane Brian (F)	6 3	14 02	Leeds	7 2 68	Leeds U
Dodds Lewis (D)	5 8	11 02	Spennymoor	14 12 85	Trainee
Elliott Stephen (F)	5 8	11 08	Dublin	6 1 84	Manchester C
Flynn Niall (M)	5 7	10 03	Dublin	22 1 86	Trainee
Healy Colin (M)	6 1	12 13	Cork	14 3 80	Celtic
Ingham Michael (G)	6 4	14 06	Preston	7 9 80	Cliftonville
Kingsberry Chris (M)	5 7	9 02	Lisburn	10 9 85	Trainee
Kyle Kevin (F)	6 3	14 08	Stranraer	7 6 81	Ayr Boswell
Lawrence Liam (M)	5 11	12 06	Retford	14 12 81	Mansfield T
Leadbitter Grant (M)	5 9	11 06	Sunderland	7 1 86	Trainee
Lynch Mark (D)	5 11	11 03	Manchester	2 9 81	Manchester U
McCartney George (D)	5 11	11 03	Belfast	29 4 81	Trainee
Myhre Thomas (G)	6 4	14 02	Sarpsborg	16 10 73	Besiktas
Piper Matt (M)	6 1	13 00	Leicester	29 9 81	Leicester C
Poom Mart (G)	6 4	13 13	Tallinn	3 2 72	Derby Co
Robinson Carl (M)	5 11	12 08	Llandrindod Wells	13 10 76	Portsmouth
Ryan Richie (M)	5 10	11 09	Kilkenny	6 1 85	Scholar
Smith Daniel (D)	5 9	10 10	Sunderland	5 10 86	Scholar
Taylor Sean (D)	5 7	11 00	Amble	9 12 85	Trainee
Teggart Neil (F)	6 2	12 06	Downpatrick	16 9 84	Scholar
Thornton Sean (M)	5 11	13 11	Drogheda	18 5 83	Scholar
Welsh Andy (F)	5 8	9 06	Manchester	24 11 83	Stockport Co
Whitehead Dean (M)	5 11	12 06	Oxford	12 1 82	Oxford U
Wright Stephen (D)	6 0	12 00	Liverpool	8 2 80	Liverpool

League Appearances: Alnwick, B. 3; Arca, J. 39(1); Breen, G. 40; Bridges, M. 5(14); Brown, C. 13(24); Caldwell, S. 41; Carter, D. 8(2); Clark, B. 1(1); Collins, D. 6(8); Collins, N. 8(3); Deane, B. (4); Elliott, S. 29(13); Ingham, M. 1(1); Johnson, S. 1(4); Kyle, K. 5(1); Lawrence, L. 20(12); Lynch, M. 5(6); McCartney, G. 35(1); Myhre, T. 31; Oster, J. 6(3); Piper, M. 1(1); Poom, M. 11; Robinson, C. 40; Stewart, M. 40(3); Thornton, S. 3(13); Welsh, A. 3(4); Whitehead, D. 39(3); Whitley, J. 32(3); Williams, D. 1; Wright, S. 39.

Goals – League (76): Stewart 16 (2 pens), Elliott 15, Arca 9, Lawrence 7 (2 pens), Brown 5, Whitehead 5, Caldwell 4, Robinson 4, Thornton 4, Breen 2, Bridges 1, Carter 1, Welsh 1, Wright 1, own goal 1.

Carling Cup (6): Brown 2, Caldwell 1, Elliott 1, Kyle 1, own goal 1.

FA Cup (2): Stewart 1 (pen), Welsh 1.

Ground: Stadium of Light, Sunderland, Tyne and Wear SR5 1SU. Telephone (0191) 551 5000.

Record Attendance: 75,118 v Derby Co, FA Cup 6th rd replay, 8 March 1933 (Roker Park). 48,353 v Liverpool, FA Premier League, 13 April 2002 (Stadium of Light). **Capacity:** 49,000.

Manager: Mick McCarthy.

Secretary: Jane Purdon.

Most League Goals: 109, Division 1, 1935–36.

Highest League Scorer in Season: Dave Halliday, 43, Division 1, 1928–29.

Most League Goals in Total Aggregate: Charlie Buchan, 209, 1911–25.
Most Capped Player: Charlie Hurley, 38 (40), Republic of Ireland.
Most League Appearances: Jim Montgomery, 537, 1962–77.
Honours – Football League: Championship – Winners – 2004–05. Division 1 Champions – 1891–92, 1892–93, 1894–95, 1901–02, 1912–13, 1935–36, 1995–96, 1998–99. Division 2 Champions – 1975–76. Division 3 Champions – 1987–88. **FA Cup:** Winners – 1937, 1973.
Colours: Red and white striped shirts, black shorts, black stockings.

SWANSEA CITY FL CHAMPIONSHIP 1

Anderson Ijah (D)	5 8	10 06	Hackney	30 12 75	Bristol R
Austin Kevin (D)	6 2	15 00	Hackney	12 2 73	Bristol R
Britton Leon (M)	5 6	10 00	Merton	16 9 82	West Ham U
Connor Paul (F)	6 2	11 08	Bishop Auckland	12 1 79	Rochdale
Corbisiero Antonio (M)	5 8	11 04	Reading	17 11 84	Scholar
Fisken Gary (M)	5 11	12 10	Watford	27 10 81	Watford
Forbes Adrian (F)	5 9	12 06	Greenford	23 1 79	Luton T
Gueret Willy (G)	6 2	14 01	Saint Claude	3 8 73	Millwall
Gurney Andy (D)	6 0	13 04	Bristol	25 1 74	Swindon T
Iriekpen Ezomo (D)	6 1	12 02	East London	14 5 82	West Ham U
Jones Stuart (D)	6 0	11 08	Aberystwyth	14 3 84	Scholar
Martinez Roberto (M)	5 9	12 02	Balaguer	13 7 73	Walsall
Maylett Brad (M)	5 10	10 04	Manchester	24 12 80	Burnley
McLeod Kevin (M)	5 11	12 00	Liverpool	12 9 80	QPR
Monk Garry (D)	6 1	13 00	Bedford	6 3 79	Barnsley
Murphy Brian (G)	6 0	13 00	Waterford	7 5 83	Manchester C
Nugent Kevin (F)	6 1	13 03	Edmonton	10 4 69	Leyton Orient
O'Leary Kristian (M)	6 0	12 09	Port Talbot	30 8 77	Trainee
Pritchard Mark (F)	5 10	12 04	Tredegar	23 11 85	Scholar
Ricketts Sam (D)	6 0	12 11	Aylesbury	11 10 81	Oxford U
Robinson Andy (M)	5 8	11 04	Birkenhead	3 11 79	Cammell Laird
Tate Alan (D)	6 1	13 05	Easington	2 9 82	Manchester U
Thomas James (F)	6 0	13 05	Swansea	16 1 79	Blackburn R
Thorpe Lee (F)	6 1	12 07	Wolverhampton	14 12 75	Bristol R
Trundle Lee (F)	6 0	13 03	Liverpool	10 10 76	Wrexham

League Appearances: Anderson, I. 8(5); Austin, K. 41(1); Bean, M. 6(2); Britton, L. 16(14); Connor, P. 34(6); Fisken, G. 1(4); Fitzgerald, S. (3); Forbes, A. 36(4); Goodfellow, M. 6; Gueret, W. 44; Gurney, A. 25(3); Iriekpen, E. 29; Jones, S. 2(2); Martinez, R. 34(3); Maylett, B. 4(12); McLeod, K. 7(4); Monk, G. 34; Murphy, B. 2; Nugent, K. 7(12); O'Leary, K. 32; Oli, D. (1); Ricketts, S. 42; Robinson, A. 29(8); Tate, A. 17(6); Thomas, J. (2); Thorpe, L. 9(6); Trundle, L. 41(1).
Goals – League (62): Trundle 22 (7 pens), Connor 10, Robinson 8 (1 pen), Forbes 7, Goodfellow 3, Nugent 3, Thorpe 3, Iriekpen 2, Britton 1, Gurney 1, O'Leary 1, own goal 1.
Carling Cup (0).
FA Cup (6): Connor 3, Goodfellow 1, O'Leary 1, Trundle 1.
LDV Vans Trophy (2): Nugent 1, Ricketts 1.
Ground: The New Stadium, Landure, Swansea SA1 2FA. Telephone (01792) 616 600.
Record Attendance: 32,796 v Arsenal, FA Cup 4th rd, 17 February 1968 (at Vetch Field). **Capacity:** 20,000.
Director of Football: Kenny Jackett.
Secretary: Jackie Rockey.
Most League Goals: 90, Division 2, 1956–57.
Highest League Scorer in Season: Cyril Pearce, 35, Division 2, 1931–32.

Most League Goals in Total Aggregate: Ivor Allchurch, 166, 1949–58, 1965–68.
Most Capped Player: Ivor Allchurch, 42 (68), Wales.
Most League Appearances: Wilfred Milne, 585, 1919–37.
Honours – Football League: Division 3 Champions – 1999–2000. Division 3 (S) Champions – 1924–25, 1948–49. **Autoglass Trophy:** Winners – 1994. **Welsh Cup:** Winners – 10 times.
Colours: All white.

SWINDON TOWN — FL CHAMPIONSHIP 1

Book Steve (G)	5 11	11 01	Bournemouth	7 7 69	Cheltenham T
Duke David (M)	5 10	11 03	Inverness	7 11 78	Sunderland
Evans Rhys (G)	6 1	12 02	Swindon	27 1 82	Chelsea
Fallon Rory (F)	6 2	11 10	Gisbourne	20 3 82	Barnsley
Hewlett Matt (M)	6 2	11 03	Bristol	25 2 76	Bristol C
Holgate Ashan (F)	6 2	12 00	Swindon	9 11 86	Scholar
Ifil Jerel (D)	6 1	12 11	Wembley	27 6 82	Watford
Igoe Sammy (M)	5 6	10 00	Staines	30 9 75	Reading
Jenkins Steve (D)	5 11	12 12	Merthyr	16 7 72	Peterborough U
Lapham Kyle (D)	5 11	11 00	Swindon	5 1 86	Scholar
Miglioranzi Stefani (M)	6 0	11 12	Pacos de Caldas	20 9 77	Portsmouth
Nicholas Andrew (D)	6 0	12 10	Liverpool	10 10 83	Liverpool
O'Hanlon Sean (D)	6 1	12 05	Southport	2 1 83	Everton
Parkin Sam (F)	6 2	13 00	Roehampton	14 3 81	Chelsea
Pook Michael (M)	5 11	11 10	Swindon	22 10 85	Scholar
Reeves Alan (D)	6 0	12 00	Birkenhead	19 11 67	Wimbledon
Roberts Chris (F)	5 9	13 02	Cardiff	22 10 79	Bristol C
Robinson Steve (M)	5 9	11 03	Nottingham	17 1 75	Birmingham C

League Appearances: Book, S. 1(1); Caton, A. 1(7); Duke, D. 42(2); Evans, R. 45; Fallon, R. 12(19); Garrard, L. 8(1); Gurney, A. 6; Henderson, D. 6; Hewlett, M. 30(1); Heywood, M. 28(4); Holgate, A. (2); Holmes, L. 14(1); Howard, B. 28(7); Ifil, J. 31(4); Igoe, S. 42(1); Jenkins, S. 24; Lapham, K. 2; McMaster, J. 2(2); Miglioranzi, S. 16(5); Mitchell, P. 7; Nicholas, A. 8(8); O'Hanlon, S. 40; Parkin, S. 41; Pook, M. 3(2); Proctor, M. 4; Reeves, A. 6(2); Roberts, C. 18(3); Robinson, M. 11(7); Slabber, J. 4(5); Smith, G. 23(7); Wells, B. (1); Yeates, M. 3(1).
Goals – League (66): Parkin 23 (2 pens), Smith G 10, Henderson 5, Howard 5, Igoe 4, Fallon 3, O'Hanlon 3, Roberts 3, Proctor 2, Caton 1, Duke 1, Hewlett 1, Heywood 1, Holmes 1, McMaster 1, Reeves 1, own goal 1.
Carling Cup (1): Hewlett 1.
FA Cup (5): Duke 1, Howard 1, Jenkins 1, O'Hanlon 1, Roberts 1.
LDV Vans Trophy (3): Fallon 1, Nicholas 1, Parkin 1.
Ground: County Ground, Swindon, Wiltshire SN1 2ED. Telephone (0870) 443 1969.
Record Attendance: 32,000 v Arsenal, FA Cup 3rd rd, 15 January 1972. **Capacity:** 14,540.
Manager: Andy King.
Secretary: Linda Birrell.
Most League Goals: 100, Division 3 (S), 1926–27.
Highest League Scorer in Season: Harry Morris, 47, Division 3 (S), 1926–27.
Most League Goals in Total Aggregate: Harry Morris, 216, 1926–33.
Most Capped Player: Rod Thomas, 30 (50), Wales.
Most League Appearances: John Trollope, 770, 1960–80.
Honours – Football League: Division 2 Champions – 1995–96. Division 4 Champions – 1985–86. **Football League Cup:** Winners – 1968–69. **Anglo-Italian Cup:** Winners – 1970.
Colours: Red and white shirts, white shorts, red stockings, with white turnover.

TORQUAY UNITED — FL CHAMPIONSHIP 2

Akinfenwa Adebayo (F)	6 0	15 04	Nigeria	10 5 82	Doncaster R
Bedeau Anthony (F)	5 9	12 00	Hammersmith	24 3 79	Trainee
Boardley Stuart (M)			Ipswich	14 2 85	Ipswich T
Bond Kain (F)	5 8	11 03	Torquay	19 6 85	Scholar
Canoville Lee (D)	6 1	12 08	Ealing	14 3 81	Arsenal
Constantine Leon (F)	6 2	11 10	Hackney	24 2 78	Peterborough U
Dearden Kevin (G)	5 11	14 00	Luton	8 3 70	Wrexham
Gottskalksson Olafur (G)	6 3	13 12	Keflavik	12 3 68	
Hill Kevin (F)	5 11	11 00	Exeter	6 3 76	Torrington
Hockley Matthew (D)	5 10	12 07	Paignton	5 6 82	Trainee
Lopes Osvaldo (M)	5 10	11 07	France	6 4 80	Cork C
Marriott Andy (G)	6 0	12 04	Sutton-in-Ashfield	11 10 70	Bury
McGlinchey Brian (D)	5 9	11 07	Derry	26 10 77	Plymouth Arg
Osei-Kuffour Jo (F)	5 8	12 00	Edmonton	17 11 81	Arsenal
Phillips Martin (M)	5 8	10 03	Exeter	13 3 76	Plymouth Arg
Russell Alex (M)	5 10	11 10	Crosby	17 3 73	Cambridge U
Taylor Craig (D)	6 1	13 00	Plymouth	24 1 74	Plymouth Arg
Woods Steve (D)	6 0	12 05	Northwich	15 12 76	Chesterfield

League Appearances: Abbey, Z. 2(4); Akinfenwa, A. 28(9); Barnes, P. 5; Bedeau, A. 31(4); Boardley, S. 2(4); Bond, K. (1); Bossu, B. 2; Brown, A. 5; Canoville, L. 29(2); Constantine, L. 24(3); Dearden, K. 5; Fowler, J. 7(5); Garner, D. 8(1); Gosling, J. 6(1); Gottskalksson, O. 15; Gritton, M. 16(3); Hill, K. 36(3); Hockley, M. 20(14); Jarvie, P. 1; Lopes, O. 1; Marriott, A. 11; McGlinchey, B. 32(1); Meirelles, B. 5(4); Noble, S. 2(1); Osei-Kuffour, J. 26(8); Owen, G. 2(3); Phillips, M. 19(11); Pulis, A. 1(2); Robinson, P. 12; Russell, A. 38; Story, O. (2); Taylor, C. 35(1); Van Heusden, A. 7; Villis, M. 12(10); Wardley, S. 5(2); Woodman, C. 20(2); Woods, S. 36.
Goals – League (55): Akinfenwa 14, Constantine 9 (1 pen), Gritton 6 (1 pen), Osei-Kuffour 6, Hill 5, Russell 3, Bedeau 2, Phillips 2, Wardley 2, Woods 2 (1 pen), Abbey 1, Gosling 1, Hockley 1, Woodman 1.
Carling Cup (1): Osei-Kuffour 1.
FA Cup (0).
LDV Vans Trophy (5): Akinfenwa 2, Bedeau 1, Osei-Kuffour 1, Taylor 1.
Ground: Plainmoor Ground, Torquay, Devon TQ1 3PS. Telephone (01803) 328666.
Record Attendance: 21,908 v Huddersfield T, FA Cup 4th rd, 29 January 1955.
Capacity: 6104.
Manager: Leroy Rosenior.
Secretary: Deborah Hancox.
Most League Goals: 89, Division 3 (S), 1956–57.
Highest League Scorer in Season: Sammy Collins, 40, Division 3 (S), 1955–56.
Most League Goals in Total Aggregate: Sammy Collins, 204, 1948–58.
Most Capped Player: Rodney Jack, St Vincent.
Most League Appearances: Dennis Lewis, 443, 1947–59.
Honours – Nil.
Colours: Yellow shirts, royal blue shorts, yellow stockings.

TOTTENHAM HOTSPUR — FA PREMIERSHIP

Atouba Thimothee (M)	6 3	12 06	Douala	17 2 82	Basle
Barnard Lee (F)	5 10	10 10	Romford	18 7 84	Trainee

Brown Michael (M)	5 9	12 04	Hartlepool	25 1 77	Sheffield U
Bunjevcevic Goran (D)	6 3	12 02	Karlovac	17 2 73	Red Star Belgrade
Burch Rob (G)	6 2	12 13	Yeovil	8 10 83	Trainee
Carrick Michael (M)	6 1	11 10	Wallsend	28 7 81	West Ham U
Davenport Calum (D)	6 4	14 00	Bedford	1 1 83	Coventry C
Dawson Michael (D)	6 2	12 02	Northallerton	18 11 83	Nottingham F
Defoe Jermain (F)	5 7	10 04	Beckton	7 10 82	West Ham U
Edman Erik (D)	5 10	12 04	Huskvarna	11 11 78	Heerenveen
Fulop Marton (G)	6 3	12 08	Budapest	3 5 83	MTK
Gardner Anthony (D)	6 3	14 00	Stafford	19 9 80	Port Vale
Hallfredsson Emil (M)	6 1	13 01	Iceland	29 6 84	FH
Hughes Mark (M)	5 10	12 04	Dungannon	16 9 83	Scholar
Ifil Phil (D)	5 9	10 08	Willesden	18 11 86	Scholar
Jackson Johnnie (M)	6 1	12 00	Camden	15 8 82	Trainee
Kanoute Frederic (F)	6 3	13 08	Ste. Foy-Les-Lyon	2 9 77	West Ham U
Keane Robbie (F)	5 9	12 06	Dublin	8 7 80	Leeds U
Kelly Stephen (D)	6 1	12 01	Dublin	6 9 83	Juniors
King Ledley (D)	6 2	14 05	Bow	12 10 80	Trainee
Marney Dean (D)	5 9	11 04	Barking	31 1 84	Scholar
Mido (F)	6 3	12 11	Cairo	23 2 83	Roma
Naybet Nourredine (D)	6 0	11 11	Casablanca	10 2 70	La Coruna
Pamarot Noe (D)	5 11	13 08	Fontenay-sous-Bois	14 4 79	Nice
Pedro Mendes (M)	5 10	12 02	Guimaraes	26 2 79	Porto
Reid Andy (F)	5 8	11 02	Dublin	29 7 82	Nottingham F
Robinson Paul (G)	6 4	15 07	Beverley	15 10 79	Leeds U
Yeates Mark (F)	5 9	10 07	Dublin	11 1 85	Trainee
Ziegler Reto (M)	6 0	12 06	Nyon	16 1 86	Grasshoppers

League Appearances: Atouba, T. 15(3); Brown, M. 20(4); Bunjevcevic, G. 2(1); Carrick, M. 26(3); Cerny, R. 2(1); Davenport, C. (1); Davies, S. 17(4); Davis, S. 11(4); Dawson, M. 5; Defoe, J. 28(7); Doherty, G. (1); Edman, E. 28; Gardner, A. 8(9); Ifil, P. 2; Jackson, J. 3(5); Kanoute, F. 22(10); Keane, R. 23(12); Kelly, S. 13(4); King, L. 38; Mabizela, M. 1; Marney, D. 3(2); Mido, 4(5); Naybet, N. 27; Pamarot, N. 23; Pedro Mendes, 22(2); Redknapp, J. 9(5); Reid, A. 13; Ricketts, R. 5(1); Robinson, P. 36; Yeates, M. (2); Ziegler, R. 12(11).
Goals – League (47): Defoe 13, Keane 11 (1 pen), Kanoute 7, Kelly 2, King 2, Marney 2, Mido 2, Atouba 1, Brown 1, Edman 1, Naybet 1, Pamarot 1, Pedro Mendes 1, Reid 1, Ziegler 1.
Carling Cup (14): Defoe 5, Keane 3, Bunjevcevic 2, Kanoute 2, Brown 1, Gardner 1.
FA Cup (10): Defoe 4 (1 pen), Keane 3, King 1, Mido 1, Pamarot 1.
Ground: White Hart Lane, Bill Nicholson Way, 748 High Road, Tottenham, London N17 0AP. Telephone (0870) 420 5000.
Record Attendance: 75,038 v Sunderland, FA Cup 6th rd, 5 March 1938. **Capacity:** 36,237.
Manager: Martin Jol.
Secretary: John Alexander.
Most League Goals: 115, Division 1, 1960–61.
Highest League Scorer in Season: Jimmy Greaves, 37, Division 1, 1962–63.
Most League Goals in Total Aggregate: Jimmy Greaves, 220, 1961–70.
Most Capped Player: Pat Jennings, 74 (119), Northern Ireland.
Most League Appearances: Steve Perryman, 655, 1969–86.
Honours – Football League: Division 1 Champions – 1950–51, 1960–61. Division 2 Champions – 1919–20, 1949–50. **FA Cup:** Winners – 1901 (as non-League club), 1921, 1961, 1962, 1967, 1981, 1982, 1991. **Football League Cup:** Winners – 1970–71, 1972–73, 1998–99. **European Competitions: European Cup-Winners' Cup:** Winners – 1962–63. **UEFA Cup:** Winners – 1971–72, 1983–84.
Colours: White shirts, navy blue shorts, white stockings.

Achterberg John (G)	6 1	13 00	Utrecht	8 7 71	Eindhoven
Ashton Neil (M)	5 7	12 03	Liverpool	15 1 85	Scholar
Brown Paul (M)	5 8	12 02	Liverpool	10 9 84	Scholar
Dadi Eugene (F)	6 2	12 11	Abidjan	20 8 73	Livingston
Dagnall Chris (F)	5 8	11 11	Liverpool	15 4 86	Scholar
Goodison Ian (D)	6 1	12 06	St James, Jam	21 11 72	Seba U
Hall Paul (M)	5 9	10 04	Manchester	3 7 72	Rushden & D
Harrison Danny (M)	5 11	12 04	Liverpool	4 11 82	Scholar
Haworth Simon (F)	6 1	13 08	Cardiff	30 3 77	Wigan Ath
Hume Iain (F)	5 7	11 02	Brampton	31 10 83	Juniors
Jackson Michael (D)	6 0	13 08	Runcorn	4 12 73	Preston NE
Jennings Steven (M)	5 7	11 07	Liverpool	28 10 84	Scholar
Jones Gary (M)	6 3	15 02	Chester	10 5 75	Nottingham F
Linwood Paul (D)	6 2	13 04	Birkenhead	24 10 83	Scholar
McAteer Jason (M)	5 9	11 05	Birkenhead	18 6 71	Sunderland
Navarro Alan (M)	5 10	11 07	Liverpool	31 5 81	Liverpool
Palethorpe Philip (G)	6 2	11 08	Wallasey	17 9 86	Scholar
Rankine Mark (M)	5 10	11 01	Doncaster	30 9 69	Sheffield U
Roberts Gareth (D)	5 8	11 00	Wrexham	6 2 78	Liverpool
Sharps Ian (D)	6 3	13 05	Warrington	23 10 80	Trainee
Taylor Ryan (D)	5 8	10 04	Liverpool	19 8 84	Scholar
Tremarco Carl (D)	5 10	12 02	Liverpool	11 10 85	Scholar
Whitmore Theo (M)	6 2	12 10	Montego Bay	5 8 72	Hull C
Zola Makongo Calvin (F)	6 3	13 07	Kinshasa	31 12 84	Newcastle U

League Appearances: Achterberg, J. 39; Beresford, D. 8(11); Brown, P. 1(3); Dadi, E. 15(16); Dagnall, C. 13(10); Goodison, I. 43(1); Hall, P. 40(6); Harrison, D. 16(16); Haworth, S. 2(1); Howarth, R. 7(1); Hume, I. 40(2); Jackson, M. 43; Jennings, S. 4(7); Jones, G. 5(5); Linwood, P. 4(6); Loran, T. (2); McAteer, J. 32(2); Rankine, M. 41; Roberts, G. 40; Sharps, I. 44; Taylor, R. 43; Tremarco, C. 2(1); Whitmore, T. 17(16); Zola Makongo, C. 7(8).
Goals – League (73): Hume 15, Hall 11, Dadi 9, Taylor 8 (4 pens), Dagnall 6, Jackson 5, Whitmore 5, McAteer 4, Roberts 3, Beresford 2, Zola Makongo 2, Goodison 1, Jones 1, Sharps 1.
Carling Cup (2): McAteer 1, Zola 1.
FA Cup (1): Taylor 1.
LDV Vans Trophy (4): Hall 1, Hume 1, Roberts 1, Zola 1.
Play-Offs (2): Beresford 1, Taylor 1.
Ground: Prenton Park, Prenton Road West, Birkenhead, Wirral CH42 9PY. Telephone (0870) 460 3333.
Record Attendance: 24,424 v Stoke C, FA Cup 4th rd, 5 February 1972.
Capacity: 16,789.
Manager: Brian Little.
Secretary: Mick Horton.
Most League Goals: 111, Division 3 (N), 1930–31.
Highest League Scorer in Season: Bunny Bell, 35, Division 3 (N), 1933–34.
Most League Goals in Total Aggregate: Ian Muir, 142, 1985–95.
Most Capped Player: John Aldridge, 30 (69), Republic of Ireland.
Most League Appearances: Harold Bell, 595, 1946–64 (incl. League record 401 consecutive appearances).
Honours – Football League: Division 3 (N) Champions – 1937–38. **Welsh Cup:** Winners – 1935. **Leyland Daf Cup:** Winners – 1990.
Colours: All white.

Atieno Taiwo (F)	6 2	12 13	Brixton	6 8 85	Scholar
Bradley Mark (D)	6 0	11 05	Dudley	14 1 88	
Broad Joseph (M)	5 11	12 07	Bristol	24 8 82	Torquay U
Coleman Dean (G)	6 1	14 03	Dudley	18 9 85	
Dann Scott (D)	6 2	12 00	Liverpool	14 2 87	Scholar
Emblen Neil (D)	6 1	13 11	Bromley	19 6 71	Norwich C
Fryatt Matty (F)	5 10	11 00	Nuneaton	5 3 86	Scholar
Kinsella Mark (M)	5 8	11 04	Dublin	12 8 72	WBA
Leitao Jorge (F)	5 11	13 04	Oporto	14 1 74	Feirense
McDermott David (M)	5 5	10 00	Stourbridge	6 2 88	Scholar
McKinney Richard (G)	6 2	13 06	Ballymoney	18 5 79	Colchester U
Merson Paul (M)	6 0	13 02	Harlesden	20 3 68	Portsmouth
Oakes Andy (G)	6 3	12 04	Crewe	11 1 77	Derby Co
Osborn Simon (M)	5 9	11 04	New Addington	19 1 72	Gillingham
Roper Ian (D)	6 3	14 00	Nuneaton	20 6 77	Trainee
Standing Michael (M)	5 10	10 07	Shoreham	20 3 81	Bradford C
Taylor Daryl (F)	5 10	11 03	Birmingham	14 11 84	Scholar
Taylor Kris (M)	5 9	11 05	Stafford	12 1 84	Manchester U
Wrack Darren (M)	5 9	12 02	Cleethorpes	5 5 76	Grimsby T
Wright Mark (M)	5 11	11 00	Wolverhampton	24 2 82	Scholar

League Appearances: Aranalde, Z. 28(2); Atieno, T. (3); Bazeley, D. 7; Bennett, J. 30(1); Bewers, J. 1; Birch, G. 11(2); Bradley, M. 1; Broad, J. 5(5); Coleman, D. 1(1); Dakinah, K. 1; Dann, S. (1); Emblen, N. 34(2); Fryatt, M. 22(14); Gerrard, A. 8; Harkness, J. 1; Herivelto, H. (1); Joachim, J. 8; Kinsella, M. 21(1); Leitao, J. 34(8); McKinney, R. 3; McShane, P. 3(1); Merson, P. 31(5); Murphy, J. 25; Oakes, A. 9; Osborn, S. 32(6); Paston, M. 8(1); Pead, C. 8; Perpetuini, D. 7; Robinson, M. 4(6); Roper, I. 25(1); Standing, M. 27(5); Surman, A. 10(4); Taylor, D. 10(9); Taylor, K. 11(1); Williams, L. 2(5); Wrack, D. 43; Wright, M. 35(2).
Goals – League (65): Fryatt 15 (4 pens), Leitao 8, Wrack 7, Joachim 6, Robinson 4, Standing 4, Taylor D 3, Bennett 2, Birch 2, Emblen 2, Merson 2, Surman 2, Taylor K 2, Wright 2, McShane 1, Williams 1, own goals 2.
Carling Cup (0).
FA Cup (1): Wrack 1.
LDV Vans Trophy (3): Leitao 3.
Ground: Bescot Stadium, Bescot Cresent, Walsall WS1 4SA. Telephone (0870) 442 0442.
Record Attendance: 10,628 B International, England v Switzerland, 20 May 1991.
Capacity: 11,200.
Manager: Paul Merson.
Secretary/Commercial Manager: Roy Whalley.
Most League Goals: 102, Division 4, 1959–60.
Highest League Scorer in Season: Gilbert Alsop, 40, Division 3 (N), 1933–34 and 1934–35.
Most League Goals in Total Aggregate: Tony Richards, 184, 1954–63; Colin Taylor, 184, 1958–63, 1964–68, 1969–73.
Most Capped Player: Mick Kearns, 15 (18), Republic of Ireland.
Most League Appearances: Colin Harrison, 467, 1964–82.
Honours – Football League: Division 4 Champions – 1959–60.
Colours: Red shirts, white shorts, red stockings.

Bangura Al Hassan (M)	5 8	10 07	Sierra Leone	24 1 88	Scholar
Blizzard Dominic (M)	6 2	13 05	High Wycombe	2 9 83	Scholar
Bouazza Hameur (F)	5 11	12 01	Evry	22 2 85	Scholar
Chamberlain Alec (G)	6 2	14 00	March	20 6 64	Sunderland
Chambers James (D)	5 10	12 05	Sandwell	20 11 80	WBA
Cox Neil (D)	5 11	13 08	Scunthorpe	8 10 71	Bolton W
Darlington Jermaine (D)	5 8	11 05	Hackney	11 4 74	Wimbledon
De Merit Jay (D)	6 1	13 05	Wisconsin	4 12 79	
Devlin Paul (M)	5 7	11 13	Birmingham	14 4 72	Birmingham C
Doyley Lloyd (D)	5 10	12 05	Whitechapel	1 12 82	Scholar
Dyche Sean (D)	6 1	13 12	Kettering	28 6 71	Millwall
Dyer Bruce (F)	5 11	12 11	Ilford	13 4 75	Barnsley
Gunnarsson Brynjar (M)	6 2	12 12	Reykjavik	16 10 75	Nottingham F
Helguson Heidar (F)	5 10	12 09	Akureyri	22 8 77	Lillestrom
Herd Ben (D)	5 9	10 12	Welwyn	21 6 85	Scholar
Lee Richard (G)	6 0	13 03	Oxford	5 10 82	Scholar
Mahon Gavin (M)	6 0	13 00	Birmingham	2 1 77	Brentford
Mayo Paul (D)	6 0	12 11	Lincoln	13 10 81	Lincoln C
McNamee Anthony (M)	5 6	9 11	Lambeth	13 7 84	Scholar
Norville Jason (F)	6 0	11 07	Trinidad & Tobago	9 9 83	Scholar
Osborne Junior (M)	5 10	12 03	Watford	12 2 88	Scholar
Smith Jack (D)	5 10	11 05	Hemel Hempstead	14 11 83	Scholar
Young Ashley (M)	5 9	9 13	Stevenage	9 7 85	Juniors

League Appearances: Ardley, N. 28(2); Bangura, A. 1(1); Blizzard, D. 12(5); Bouazza, H. 10(18); Chamberlain, A. 4(1); Chambers, J. 40; Cox, N. 38(1); Cullip, D. 4; Darlington, J. 25(1); Demerit, J. 22(2); Devlin, P. 15(2); Doyley, L. 25(4); Dyche, S. 23; Dyer, B. 21(15); Eagles, C. 10(3); Fitzgerald, S. (7); Gayle, M. (3); Gunnarsson, B. 34(2); Helguson, H. 36(3); Jackson, J. 14(1); Jones, P. 9; Lee, R. 33; Mahon, G. 42(1); Mayo, P. 13; McNamee, A. 1(13); Osborne, J. (1); Smith, J. 7; Webber, D. 24(4); Young, A. 15(19).
Goals – League (52): Helguson 16 (1 pen), Webber 12 (1 pen), Dyer 9, Ardley 4, Demerit 3, Gunnarsson 3, Blizzard 1, Bouazza 1, Devlin 1, Eagles 1, own goal 1.
Carling Cup (12): Helguson 3, Bouazza 2, Chambers 2, Dyer 2, Cox 1 (pen), Ferrell 1, own goal 1.
FA Cup (1): Helguson 1 (pen).
Ground: Vicarage Road Stadium, Watford WD18 0ER. Telephone (0870) 111 1881.
Record Attendance: 34,099 v Manchester U, FA Cup 4th rd (replay), 3 February 1969. **Capacity:** 19,500.
Manager: Adrian Boothroyd.
Secretary: Michelle Ives.
Most League Goals: 92, Division 4, 1959–60.
Highest League Scorer in Season: Cliff Holton, 42, Division 4, 1959–60.
Most League Goals in Total Aggregate: Luther Blissett, 148, 1976–83, 1984–88, 1991–92.
Most Capped Player: John Barnes, 31 (79), England and Kenny Jackett, 31, Wales.
Most League Appearances: Luther Blissett, 415, 1976–83, 1984–88, 1991–92.
Honours – Football League: Division 3 Champions – 1968–69. Division 2 Champions – 1997–98. Division 4 Champions – 1977–78.
Colours: Yellow shirts, black shorts, black stockings.

WEST BROMWICH ALBION FA PREMIERSHIP

Albrechtsen Martin (D)	6 1	12 13	Copenhagen	30 3 80	FC Copenhagen
Campbell Kevin (F)	6 0	13 08	Lambeth	4 2 70	Everton
Chaplow Richard (M)	5 9	9 03	Accrington	2 2 85	Burnley
Clement Neil (D)	6 0	12 03	Reading	3 10 78	Chelsea
Dyer Lloyd (M)	5 10	11 04	Aston	13 9 82	Aston Villa
Earnshaw Robert (F)	5 6	9 09	Mulfulira	6 4 81	Cardiff C
Gaardsoe Thomas (D)	6 2	12 08	Randers	23 11 79	Ipswich T
Gera Zoltan (M)	6 0	11 11	Pecs	22 4 79	Ferencvaros
Greening Jonathan (M)	5 11	11 00	Scarborough	2 1 79	Middlesbrough
Horsfield Geoff (F)	5 10	11 02	Barnsley	1 11 73	Wigan Ath
Hoult Russell (G)	6 3	14 09	Ashby	22 11 72	Portsmouth
Inamoto Junichi (M)	6 0	11 11	Cogoshima	18 9 79	Fulham
Johnson Andy (M)	6 0	13 00	Bristol	2 5 74	Nottingham F
Kanu Nwankwo (F)	6 5	12 08	Owerri	1 8 76	Arsenal
Koumas Jason (M)	5 10	11 02	Wrexham	25 9 79	Tranmere R
Kuszczak Tomasz (G)	6 3	13 03	Krosno Odrzansia	20 3 82	Hertha Berlin
Moore Darren (D)	6 2	15 07	Birmingham	22 4 74	Portsmouth
Murphy Joe (G)	6 2	13 06	Dublin	21 8 81	Tranmere R
Purse Darren (D)	6 2	12 08	Stepney	14 2 77	Birmingham C
Robinson Paul (D)	5 9	11 12	Watford	14 12 78	Watford
Scimeca Riccardo (D)	6 1	12 09	Leamington Spa	13 6 75	Leicester C
Wallwork Ronnie (M)	5 10	12 09	Manchester	10 9 77	Manchester U

League Appearances: Albrechtsen, M. 20(4); Campbell, K. 16; Chaplow, R. 3(1); Clement, N. 35; Contra, C. 5; Dobie, S. 1(4); Dyer, L. (4); Earnshaw, R. 18(13); Gaardsoe, T. 25(4); Gera, Z. 31(7); Greening, J. 32(2); Haas, B. 9(1); Horsfield, G. 18(11); Hoult, R. 36; Hulse, R. (5); Inamoto, J. (3); Johnson, A. 22; Kanu, N. 21(7); Koumas, J. 5(5); Kuszczak, T. 2(1); Moore, D. 10(6); Purse, D. 22; Richardson, K. 11(1); Robinson, P. 28(2); Sakiri, A. 2(1); Scimeca, R. 27(6); Wallwork, R. 19(1).
Goals – League (36): Earnshaw 11 (2 pens), Gera 6, Campbell 3, Clement 3, Horsfield 3, Richardson 3, Kanu 2, Dobie 1, Robinson 1, Wallwork 1, own goals 2.
Carling Cup (1): Horsfield 1.
FA Cup (4): Earnshaw 3, Kanu 1.
Ground: The Hawthorns, West Bromwich B71 4LF. Telephone (0870) 066 8888
Record Attendance: 64,815 v Arsenal, FA Cup 6th rd, 6 March 1937. **Capacity:** 28,000.
Manager: Bryan Robson.
Secretary: Dr. John J. Evans BA, PHD.
Most League Goals: 105, Division 2, 1929–30.
Highest League Scorer in Season: William 'Ginger' Richardson, 39, Division 1, 1935–36.
Most League Goals in Total Aggregate: Tony Brown, 218, 1963–79.
Most Capped Player: Stuart Williams, 33 (43), Wales.
Most League Appearances: Tony Brown, 574, 1963–80.
Honours – Football League: Division 1 Champions – 1919–20. Division 2 Champions – 1901–02, 1910–11. **FA Cup:** Winners – 1888, 1892, 1931, 1954, 1968. **Football League Cup:** Winners – 1965–66.
Colours: Navy blue and white striped shirts, white shorts, navy blue stockings.

WEST HAM UNITED FA PREMIERSHIP

Ashikodi Moses (M)	6 0	11 09	Lagos	27 6 87	Millwall
Brevett Rufus (D)	5 9	11 13	Derby	24 9 69	Fulham
Bywater Steve (G)	6 2	12 00	Manchester	7 6 81	Trainee
Chadwick Luke (M)	5 11	11 08	Cambridge	18 11 80	Manchester U
Cohen Chris (M)	5 11	10 11	Norwich	5 3 87	Scholar
Dailly Christian (D)	6 1	12 10	Dundee	23 10 73	Blackburn R
Etherington Matthew (M)	5 10	10 12	Truro	14 8 81	Tottenham H
Ferdinand Anton (D)	6 2	11 00	Peckham	18 2 85	Trainee
Fletcher Carl (M)	5 10	11 07	Camberley	7 4 80	Bournemouth
Harewood Marlon (F)	6 1	13 07	Hampstead	25 8 79	Nottingham F
Hutchison Don (M)	6 2	11 08	Gateshead	9 5 71	Sunderland
Lomas Steve (M)	6 0	12 08	Hanover	18 1 74	Manchester C
MacKay Malky (D)	6 3	13 02	Bellshill	19 2 72	Norwich C
McClenahan Trent (D)	5 11	12 00	Australia	4 2 85	Scholar
Melville Andy (D)	6 2	12 13	Swansea	29 11 68	Fulham
Mullins Hayden (D)	5 11	11 12	Reading	27 3 79	Crystal Palace
Newton Shaun (M)	5 8	11 00	Camberwell	20 8 75	Wolverhampton W
Noble Mark (M)	5 11	12 00	West Ham	8 5 87	Scholar
Pearson Greg (F)	5 11	12 00	Birmingham	3 4 85	Trainee
Powell Chris (D)	5 11	11 12	Lambeth	8 9 69	Charlton Ath
Rebrov Sergei (F)	5 8	11 00	Gorlovka	3 6 74	Tottenham H
Reo-Coker Nigel (M)	5 8	12 03	Southwark	14 5 84	Wimbledon
Repka Tomas (D)	6 0	12 04	Slavicin Zlin	2 1 74	Fiorentina
Sheringham Teddy (F)	6 0	12 05	Highams Park	2 4 66	Portsmouth
Walker Jim (G)	5 11	13 04	Sutton-in-Ashfield	9 7 73	Walsall
Ward Elliott (D)	6 2	13 00	Harrow	19 1 85	Scholar
Williams Gavin (M)	5 10	11 05	Merthyr	20 6 80	Yeovil T
Zamora Bobby (F)	6 1	11 11	Barking	16 1 81	Tottenham H

League Appearances: Brevett, R. 10; Bywater, S. 36; Chadwick, L. 22(10); Cohen, C. 1(10); Dailly, C. 2(1); Davenport, C. 10; Etherington, M. 37(2); Ferdinand, A. 24(5); Fletcher, C. 26(6); Garcia, R. (1); Harewood, M. 45; Hutchison, D. 2(3); Lomas, S. 18(5); MacKay, M. 17(1); McAnuff, J. (1); McClenahan, T. (2); Melville, A. 3; Mullins, H. 32(5); Newton, S. 11; Noble, M. 10(3); Nowland, A. 3(1); Powell, C. 35(1); Powell, D. 5; Rebrov, S. 12(14); Reo-Coker, N. 34(5); Repka, T. 42; Sheringham, T. 26(7); Taricco, M. 1; Walker, J. 10; Ward, E. 10(1); Williams, G. 7(3); Zamora, B. 15(19).
Goals – League (66): Sheringham 20 (3 pens), Harewood 17 (5 pens), Zamora 7, Etherington 4, Reo-Coker 3, Fletcher 2, MacKay 2, Brevett 1, Chadwick 1, Ferdinand 1, Lomas 1, Mullins 1, Nowland 1, Powell D 1, Rebrov 1, Williams 1, own goals 2.
Carling Cup (5): Harewood 2, Zamora 2, Rebrov 1.
FA Cup (3): Harewood 2, Sheringham 1 (pen).
Play-Offs (5): Zamora 4, Harewood 1.
Ground: Boleyn Ground, Green Street, Upton Park, London E13 9AZ. Telephone (020) 8548 2748.
Record Attendance: 42,322 v Tottenham H, Division 1, 17 October 1970. **Capacity:** 34,500.
Manager: Alan Pardew.
Secretary: Peter Barnes.
Most League Goals: 101, Division 2, 1957–58.
Highest League Scorer in Season: Vic Watson, 42, Division 1, 1929–30.
Most League Goals in Total Aggregate: Vic Watson, 298, 1920–35.
Most Capped Player: Bobby Moore, 108, England.
Most League Appearances: Billy Bonds, 663, 1967–88.

Honours – Football League: Division 2 Champions – 1957–58, 1980–81. **FA Cup:** Winners – 1964, 1975, 1980. **European Competitions: European Cup-Winners' Cup:** Winners – 1964–65. **Intertoto Cup:** Winners – 1999.
Colours: Claret shirts with sky blue sleeves, white shorts and stockings.

WIGAN ATHLETIC — FA PREMIERSHIP

Baines Leighton (D)	5 8	11 10	Liverpool	11 12 84	Trainee
Breckin Ian (D)	6 2	13 05	Rotherham	24 2 75	Chesterfield
Bullard Jimmy (M)	5 10	11 07	Newham	23 10 78	Peterborough U
Eaden Nicky (D)	5 9	12 02	Sheffield	12 12 72	Birmingham C
Ellington Nathan (F)	5 10	13 01	Bradford	2 7 81	Bristol R
Emerson (D)	6 2	13 04	Porto Alegre	30 3 72	Bolton W
Filan John (G)	6 2	14 06	Sydney	8 2 70	Blackburn R
Graham David (F)	5 11	12 01	Edinburgh	6 10 78	Torquay U
Jackson Matt (D)	6 1	14 00	Leeds	19 10 71	Norwich C
Jarrett Jason (M)	6 1	13 01	Bury	14 9 79	Bury
Johansson Andreas (M)	5 11	12 05	Vanersborg	5 7 78	Djurgaarden
Kavanagh Graham (M)	5 10	13 02	Dublin	2 12 73	Cardiff C
Mahon Alan (M)	5 8	11 10	Dublin	4 4 78	Blackburn R
McCulloch Lee (F)	6 1	13 00	Bellshill	14 5 78	Motherwell
McMillan Steve (D)	5 9	11 12	Edinburgh	19 1 76	Motherwell
Mitchell Paul (D)	5 9	11 12	Manchester	26 8 81	Scholar
Roberts Jason (F)	6 0	12 06	Park Royal	25 1 78	WBA
Salisbury James (G)	6 1	14 01	Preston	10 3 84	Burnley
Teale Gary (F)	5 11	12 00	Glasgow	21 7 78	Ayr U
Traynor Greg (M)	5 10	11 00	Salford	17 10 74	Scholar
Vieira Magno (F)	5 9	11 00	Brazil	13 2 85	Juniors
Walsh Gary (G)	6 3	14 13	Wigan	21 3 68	Bradford C
Whalley Gareth (M)	5 10	11 00	Manchester	19 12 73	Crewe Alex
Wright David (D)	5 11	11 00	Warrington	1 5 80	Crewe Alex

League Appearances: Baines, L. 41; Breckin, I. 42; Bullard, J. 46; Eaden, N. 33(6); Ellington, N. 43(2); Emerson, 11(4); Filan, J. 46; Flynn, M. 1(12); Frandsen, P. 9; Graham, D. 13(17); Jackson, M. 35(1); Jarrett, J. 4(10); Johansson, A. (1); Kavanagh, G. 11; Mahon, A. 21(6); McCulloch, L. 42; McMillan, S. 5(3); Mitchell, P. (1); Ormerod, B. 3(3); Roberts, J. 45; Teale, G. 29(8); Whalley, G. 7(1); Wright, D. 19(12).
Goals – League (79): Ellington 24 (5 pens), Roberts 21 (2 pens), McCulloch 14, Mahon 7, Bullard 3, Teale 3, Ormerod 2, Baines 1, Flynn 1, Frandsen 1, Graham 1, Jackson 1.
Carling Cup (0).
FA Cup (1): Mahon 1.
Ground: JJB Stadium, Robin Park, Newtown, Wigan WN5 OU2. Telephone (01942) 774 000
Record Attendance: 27,500 v Hereford U, FA Cup 2nd rd, 12 December 1953 (at Springfield Park). **Capacity:** 25,000
Manager: Paul Jewell.
Secretary: Stuart Hayton.
Most League Goals: 84, Division 3, 1996–97.
Highest League Scorer in Season: Graeme Jones, 31, Division 3, 1996–97.
Most League Goals in Total Aggregate: Andy Liddell, 70, 1998–2004.
Most Capped Player: Roy Carroll, 9 (17), Northern Ireland.
Most League Appearances: Kevin Langley, 317, 1981–86, 1990–94.
Honours – Football League: Division 2 Champions – 2002–03. Division 3 Champions – 1996–97. **Freight Rover Trophy:** Winners – 1984–85. **Auto Windscreens Shield:** Winners – 1998–99.
Colours: Blue shirts and shorts, white stockings.

WOLVERHAMPTON WANDERERS FL CHAMPIONSHIP

Bjorklund Joachim (D)	5 11	12 08	Vaxjo	15 3 71	Sunderland
Camara Henri (F)	5 9	10 08	Dakar	10 5 77	Sedan
Cameron Colin (M)	5 8	11 00	Kirkcaldy	23 10 72	Hearts
Clarke Leon (F)	6 2	14 02	Birmingham	10 2 85	Trainee
Clingan Sammy (M)	5 11	11 06	Belfast	13 1 84	Scholar
Clyde Mark (D)	6 2	12 04	Limavady	27 12 82	Scholar
Cooper Kevin (M)	5 8	10 04	Derby	8 2 75	Wimbledon
Cornes Christopher (M)			Worcester	20 12 86	Scholar
Cort Carl (F)	6 4	12 07	Southwark	1 11 77	Newcastle U
Craddock Jody (D)	6 2	12 00	Bromsgrove	25 7 75	Sunderland
Edwards Rob (D)	6 1	11 10	Telford	25 12 82	Aston Villa
Ganea Viorel (F)	5 10	12 06	Fagaras	10 8 73	Bursa
Gobern Lewis (M)	5 10	11 07	Birmingham	28 1 85	Scholar
Ince Paul (M)	5 10	12 04	Ilford	21 10 67	Middlesbrough
Jones Paul (G)	6 3	15 02	Chirk	18 4 67	Southampton
Kennedy Mark (M)	5 11	11 09	Dublin	15 5 76	Manchester C
Lescott Jolean (D)	6 2	14 00	Birmingham	16 8 82	Trainee
Lowe Keith (D)	6 2	13 03	Wolverhampton	13 9 85	Scholar
Miller Kenny (F)	5 10	11 04	Edinburgh	23 12 79	Rangers
Murray Matt (G)	6 4	13 10	Solihull	2 5 81	Trainee
Naylor Lee (D)	5 10	12 00	Bloxwich	19 3 80	Trainee
Ndah George (F)	6 1	12 06	Dulwich	23 12 74	Swindon T
Oakes Michael (G)	6 2	14 00	Northwich	30 10 73	Aston Villa
Olofinjana Seyi (M)	6 2	13 05	Nigeria	30 6 80	Brann
Seol Ki-Hyun (F)	6 2	12 08	South Korea	18 1 79	Anderlecht

League Appearances: Andrews, K. 14(6); Bischoff, M. 9(2); Bjorklund, J. 2(1); Cameron, C. 24(13); Clarke, L. 11(17); Clyde, M. 17(1); Cooper, K. 15(15); Cort, C. 34(3); Craddock, J. 40(2); Edwards, R. 15(2); Ince, P. 25(3); Jones, P. 10; Kennedy, M. 27(3); Lescott, J. 41; Lowe, K. 11; Miller, K. 41(3); Mulligan, G. (1); Murray, M. 1; Naylor, L. 36(2); Newton, S. 21(3); Oakes, M. 35; Olofinjana, S. 41(1); Ricketts, R. 3(4); Seol, K. 28(9); Sturridge, D. 5(6).
Goals – League (72): Miller 19 (2 pens), Cort 15 (1 pen), Clarke 7, Cooper 6 (3 pens), Olofinjana 5, Lescott 4, Seol 4, Cameron 3, Ince 3, Bischoff 1, Craddock 1, Naylor 1, Newton 1, Ricketts 1, Sturridge 1.
Carling Cup (5): Andrews 1, Clarke 1, Ince 1, Miller 1, Seol 1.
FA Cup (2): Cort 1, Seol 1.
Ground: Molineux, Waterloo Road, Wolverhampton WV1 4QR. Telephone (0870) 442 0123.
Record Attendance: 61,315 v Liverpool, FA Cup 5th rd, 11 February 1939.
Capacity: 29,277.
Manager: Glenn Hoddle.
Secretary: Richard Skirrow.
Most League Goals: 115, Division 2, 1931–32.
Highest League Scorer in Season: Dennis Westcott, 38, Division 1, 1946–47.
Most League Goals in Total Aggregate: Steve Bull, 250, 1986–99.
Most Capped Player: Billy Wright, 105, England (70 consecutive).
Most League Appearances: Derek Parkin, 501, 1967–82.
Honours – Football League: Division 1 Champions – 1953–54, 1957–58, 1958–59. Division 2 Champions – 1931–32, 1976–77. Division 3 (N) Champions – 1923–24. Division 3 Champions – 1988–89. Division 4 Champions – 1987–88. **FA Cup:** Winners – 1893, 1908, 1949, 1960. **Football League Cup:** Winners – 1973–74, 1979–80. **Sherpa Van Trophy:** Winners – 1988.
Colours: Gold shirts with black trim, black shorts, black stockings.

Armstrong Chris (F)	6 0	13 03	Newcastle	19 6 71	Bolton W
Bennett Dean (M)	5 11	11 00	Wolverhampton	13 12 77	Kidderminster H
Carey Brian (D)	6 3	13 02	Cork	31 5 68	Leicester C
Crowell Matt (M)	5 11	10 10	Bridgend	3 7 84	Southampton
Edwards Carlos (M)	5 11	11 01	Trinidad	24 10 78	Defence Force
Evans Danny (G)	6 0	13 00	Wrexham	11 3 86	Scholar
Ferguson Darren (M)	6 0	11 10	Glasgow	9 2 72	Wolverhampton W
Holt Andy (M)	6 1	12 07	Stockport	21 5 78	Hull C
Jones Mark (M)	5 11	10 12	Wrexham	15 8 83	Scholar
Jones Michael (M)	6 3	13 00	Liverpool	3 12 87	Scholar
Lawrence Dennis (D)	6 7	11 13	Trinidad	1 8 74	Defence Force
Llewellyn Chris (F)	6 0	11 06	Merthyr	29 8 79	Norwich C
Mackin Levi (M)	6 1	12 00	Chester	4 4 86	Scholar
Morgan Craig (D)	6 0	11 12	St Asaph	18 6 85	Scholar
Pejic Shaun (D)	6 0	11 07	Hereford	16 11 82	Trainee
Quinn Kieran (M)	5 10	10 00	Liverpool	20 3 86	Scholar
Roberts Steve (D)	6 2	11 06	Wrexham	24 2 80	Trainee
Sam Hector (F)	5 9	11 05	Trinidad	25 2 78	San Juan Jabloteh
Smith Alex (M)	5 8	10 09	Liverpool	15 2 76	Reading
Spender Simon (D)	5 11	11 00	Mold	15 11 85	Scholar
Ugarte Juan (F)	5 10	11 11	San Sebastian	7 11 80	Real Sociedad
Whitley Jim (M)	5 9	10 12	Zambia	14 4 75	Manchester C
Williams Danny (M)	6 1	13 00	Wrexham	12 7 79	Bristol R

League Appearances: Armstrong, C. 18(15); Baker, M. 11(2); Bennett, D. 7(7); Carey, B. 10; Crowell, M. 22(6); Dibble, A. 15; Edwards, C. 18; Ferguson, D. 40; Foster, B. 17; Green, S. 5(7); Holt, A. 45; Jones, Mark 17(9); Jones, Michael (1); Lawrence, D. 44; Llewellyn, C. 45; Mackin, L. 5(5); Morgan, C. 18(8); Pejic, S. 30(5); Roberts, S. 34; Sam, H. 19(19); Shaw, M. (1); Smith, A. 17(7); Spender, S. 9(4); Ugarte, J. 23(7); Valero, V. 3; Whitley, J. 13(3); Williams, D. 21.
Goals – League (62): Ugarte 17 (1 pen), Sam 9, Armstrong 8 (3 pens), Llewellyn 7, Holt 6, Lawrence 4, Ferguson 3, Mark Jones 3, Roberts 3, Edwards C 1, own goal 1.
Carling Cup (4): Ferguson 1, Llewellyn 1, Morgan 1, Sam 1.
FA Cup (4): Holt 1, Lawrence 1, Llewellyn 1, Sam 1.
LDV Vans Trophy (16): Ugarte 6, Llewellyn 3, Ferguson 2, Mark Jones 1, Lawrence 1, Pejic 1, Sam 1, Williams 1.
Ground: Racecourse Ground, Mold Road, Wrexham LL11 2AH. Telephone (01978) 262 190.
Record Attendance: 34,445 v Manchester U, FA Cup 4th rd, 26 January 1957.
Capacity: 15,500.
Manager: Denis Smith.
Secretary: Geraint Parry.
Most League Goals: 106, Division 3 (N), 1932–33.
Highest League Scorer in Season: Tom Bamford, 44, Division 3 (N), 1933–34.
Most League Goals in Total Aggregate: Tom Bamford, 175, 1928–34.
Most Capped Player: Joey Jones, 29 (72), Wales.
Most League Appearances: Arfon Griffiths, 592, 1959–61, 1962–79.
Honours – Football League: Division 3 Champions – 1977–78. **LDV Vans Trophy:** Winners – 2004–05. **Welsh Cup:** Winners – 22 times.
Colours: Red shirts, white shorts, red stockings.

WYCOMBE WANDERERS FL CHAMPIONSHIP 2

Ahmed Shahed (M)	5 10	11 02	East Ham	13 9 85	MK Dons
Anya Ikechi (M)	5 5	11 04	Glasgow	3 1 88	Scholar
Bloomfield Matt (M)	5 9	11 00	Ipswich	8 2 84	Ipswich T
Burnell Joe (M)	5 8	12 00	Bristol	10 10 80	Bristol C
Dixon Jonny (F)	5 9	11 01	Murcia	16 1 84	Scholar
Easton Clint (M)	5 11	11 00	Barking	1 10 77	Norwich C
Faulconbridge Craig (F)	6 1	13 00	Nuneaton	20 4 78	Wrexham
Johnson Roger (D)	6 3	11 00	Ashford	28 4 83	Trainee
Lee Robert (M)	5 10	11 10	Plaistow	1 2 66	Oldham Ath
Martin Russell (M)	6 0	11 08	Brighton	4 1 86	
Philo Mark (M)	5 11	11 05	Bracknell	5 10 84	Scholar
Ryan Keith (M)	5 10	12 06	Northampton	25 6 70	Berkhamsted T
Senda Danny (M)	5 10	10 02	Harrow	17 4 81	Southampton
Stonebridge Ian (F)	6 0	11 04	Lewisham	30 8 81	Plymouth Arg
Talia Frank (G)	6 1	13 06	Melbourne	20 7 72	Reading
Tyson Nathan (F)	5 10	10 02	Reading	4 5 82	Reading
Williams Steve (G)	6 6	13 10	Oxford	21 4 83	Scholar

League Appearances: Abbey, Z. 3(2); Ahmed, S. (4); Anya, I. (3); Birchall, A. 11(1); Bloomfield, M. 20(6); Broughton, D. 2(1); Burnell, J. 23(1); Caceres, A. 1(2); Claridge, S. 14(5); Comyn-Platt, C. 3(1); Cooke, S. 4(2); Craig, T. 14; Cronin, L. 1; Dixon, J. 4(12); Easton, C. 29(4); Faulconbridge, C. 6(2); Guppy, S. 12(2); Johnson, R. 40(2); Lee, R. 6(1); Martin, R. 1(6); Nethercott, S. 27(2); Perpetuini, D. 1(1); Philo, M. 2(3); Ryan, K. 35(3); Savage, B. 2(2); Senda, D. 42(2); Silk, G. 19(3); Stonebridge, I. 31(7); Talia, F. 45; Tyson, N. 40(2); Uhlenbeek, G. 36(6); Williams, S. (1); Williamson, M. 32(5).
Goals – League (58): Tyson 22 (3 pens), Johnson 6, Birchall 4, Claridge 4 (1 pen), Senda 4 (1 pen), Stonebridge 4, Uhlenbeek 4, Bloomfield 2, Ryan 2, Williamson 2, Ahmed 1, Dixon 1 (pen), Easton 1, Guppy 1.
Carling Cup (0).
FA Cup (1): Johnson 1.
LDV Vans Trophy (2): Birchall 1, Dixon 1.
Ground: Adams Park, Hillbottom Road, Sands, High Wycombe HP12 4HJ. Telephone (01494) 472100.
Record Attendance: 9002 v West Ham U, FA Cup 3rd rd, 7 January 1995.
Capacity: 10,000 (7350 seats).
Manager: John Gorman.
Secretary: Keith J. Allen.
Most League Goals: 67, Division 3, 1993–94.
Highest League Goalscorer in Season: Sean Devine, 23, 1999–2000.
Most League Goals in Total Aggregate: Dave Carroll, 41, 1993–2002.
Most Capped Player: Mark Rogers, 7, Canada.
Most League Appearances: Steve Brown, 371, 1994–2004.
Honours – GM Vauxhall Conference: Winners – 1993. **FA Trophy:** Winners – 1991, 1993.
Colours: Sky and navy blue quartered shirts, navy shorts, sky blue stockings.

YEOVIL TOWN FL CHAMPIONSHIP 1

Amankwaah Kevin (D)	6 1	12 12	Harrow	19 5 82	Bristol C
Brown Marvin (F)	5 9	11 12	Bristol	6 7 83	Tamworth
Collis Steve (G)	6 3	12 05	Harrow	18 3 81	Nottingham F

Davies Arron (M)	5 9	11 00	Cardiff	22 6 84	Southampton
Gall Kevin (F)	5 9	10 08	Merthyr	4 2 82	Bristol R
Guyett Scott (D)	6 2	13 06	Ascot	20 1 76	Chester C
Ibe Kesie (F)	5 10	12 00	London	6 12 82	Staines T
Jevons Phil (F)	5 11	12 00	Liverpool	1 8 79	Grimsby T
Johnson Lee (M)	5 6	10 07	Newmarket	7 6 81	Brentford
Lindegaard Andy (F)	5 8	11 04	Taunton	10 9 80	Westland Sport
Lockwood Adam (D)	6 0	12 07	Wakefield	26 10 81	Reading
Miles Colin (D)	6 0	13 10	Edmonton	6 9 78	Morton
Reed Steve (D)	5 8	12 02	Barnstaple	18 6 85	Juniors
Richardson Marcus (F)	6 3	12 05	Reading	31 8 77	Lincoln C
Rose Michael (D)	5 10	11 02	Salford	28 7 82	Manchester U
Skiverton Terry (D)	6 1	13 06	Mile End	26 6 75	Wycombe W
Sodje Efe (D)	6 1	12 00	Greenwich	5 12 72	Huddersfield T
Stolcers Andrejs (F)	5 8	11 02	Riga	8 7 74	Fulham
Tarachulski Bartosz (F)	6 3	13 06	Gliwice	14 5 75	Polonia
Terry Paul (M)	5 10	12 06	Barking	3 4 79	Dagenham & R
Way Darren (M)	5 6	10 00	Plymouth	21 11 79	Norwich C
Weale Chris (G)	6 2	13 03	Yeovil	9 2 82	Juniors
Williams Dale (M)	6 0	11 04	Swansea	26 3 87	Scholar

League Appearances: Amankwaah, K. 10(5); Brown, M. (2); Caceres, A. 7(14); Collis, S. 9; Davies, A. 15(8); Fallon, R. 2(4); Fontaine, L. 15; Gall, K. 30(13); Guyett, S. 13(5); Ibe, K. (3); Jevons, P. 45(1); Johnson, L. 44; Lindegaard, A. 19(10); Lockwood, A. 6(4); Miles, C. 20(1); Mirza, N. (3); O'Brien, R. 10(4); Odubade, Y. (4); Reed, S. 1(2); Richardson, M. 2(2); Rose, M. 37(3); Skiverton, T. 36(2); Sodje, E. 6; Stolcers, A. 23(13); Tarachulski, B. 27(15); Terry, P. 35(4); Way, D. 45; Weale, C. 37(1); Weatherstone, S. (6); Williams, G. 12(1); Woozley, D. (1).
Goals – League (90): Jevons 27 (10 pens), Tarachulski 10, Davies 8, Johnson 7 (1 pen), Way 7, Terry 6, Stolcers 5, Skiverton 4, Caceres 3, Gall 3, Guyett 2, Sodje 2, Williams 2 (1 pen), Fallon 1, Lindegaard 1, Rose 1, own goal 1.
Carling Cup (3): Johnson 3.
FA Cup (12): Jevons 2 (2 pens), Tarachulski 2, Way 2, Davies 1, Johnson 1, Miles 1, Odubade 1, Stolcers 1, Terry 1.
LDV Vans Trophy (3): Caceres 1, Stolcers 1, Tarachulski 1.
Ground: Huish Park, Lufton Way, Yeovil, Somerset, BA22 8YF. Telephone (01935) 423662.
Record Attendance: 8612 v Arsenal, FA Cup 3rd rd, 2 January 1993 (16,318 v Sunderland at Huish). **Capacity:** 9634.
Manager: Gary Johnson.
Secretary: Jean Cotton.
Most League Goals: 90, FL Championship 2, 2004–05.
Highest League Goalscorer in Season: Phil Jevons, 27, 2004–05.
Most League Goals in Total Aggregate: Phil Jevons, 27, 2004–05.
Most Capped Player: None.
Most League Appearances: Lee Johnson, 89, 2003–05.
Honours – Football League: Championship 2 – Winners 2004–05. **Football Conference:** Champions – 2002–03. **FA Trophy:** Winners 2001–02.
Colours: Green and white hooped shirts, white shorts, white stockings.

LEAGUE POSITIONS: FA PREMIER from 1992–93 and DIVISION 1 1979–80 to 1991–92

	2003–04	2002–03	2001–02	2000–01	1999–2000	1998–99	1997–98	1996–97	1995–96	1994–95	1993–94	1992–93	1991–92
Arsenal	1	2	1	2	2	2	1	3	5	12	4	10	4
Aston Villa	6	16	8	8	6	6	7	5	4	18	10	2	7
Barnsley	–	–	–	–	–	–	19	–	–	–	–	–	–
Birmingham C	10	13	–	–	–	–	–	–	–	–	–	–	–
Blackburn R	15	6	10	–	–	19	6	13	7	1	2	4	–
Bolton W	8	17	16	–	–	–	18	–	20	–	–	–	–
Bradford C	–	–	–	20	17	–	–	–	–	–	–	–	–
Brighton & HA	–	–	–	–	–	–	–	–	–	–	–	–	–
Bristol C	–	–	–	–	–	–	–	–	–	–	–	–	–
Charlton Ath	7	12	14	9	–	18	–	–	–	–	–	–	–
Chelsea	2	4	6	6	5	3	4	6	11	11	14	11	14
Coventry C	–	–	–	19	14	15	11	17	16	16	11	15	19
Crystal Palace	–	–	–	–	–	–	20	–	–	19	–	20	10
Derby Co	–	–	19	17	16	8	9	12	–	–	–	–	–
Everton	17	7	15	16	13	14	17	15	6	15	17	13	12
Fulham	9	14	13	–	–	–	–	–	–	–	–	–	–
Ipswich T	–	–	18	5	–	–	–	–	–	22	19	16	–
Leeds U	19	15	5	4	3	4	5	11	13	5	5	17	1
Leicester C	18	–	20	13	8	10	10	9	–	21	–	–	–
Liverpool	4	5	2	3	4	7	3	4	3	4	8	6	6
Luton T	–	–	–	–	–	–	–	–	–	–	–	–	20
Manchester C	16	9	–	18	–	–	–	–	18	17	16	9	5
Manchester U	3	1	3	1	1	1	2	1	1	2	1	1	2
Middlesbrough	11	11	12	14	12	9	–	19	12	–	–	21	–
Millwall	–	–	–	–	–	–	–	–	–	–	–	–	–
Newcastle U	5	3	4	11	11	13	13	2	2	6	3	–	–
Norwich C	–	–	–	–	–	–	–	–	–	20	12	3	18
Nottingham F	–	–	–	–	–	20	–	20	9	3	–	22	8
Notts Co	–	–	–	–	–	–	–	–	–	–	–	–	21
Oldham Ath	–	–	–	–	–	–	–	–	–	–	21	19	17
Oxford U	–	–	–	–	–	–	–	–	–	–	–	–	–
Portsmouth	13	–	–	–	–	–	–	–	–	–	–	–	–
QPR	–	–	–	–	–	–	–	–	19	8	9	5	11
Sheffield U	–	–	–	–	–	–	–	–	–	–	20	14	9
Sheffield W	–	–	–	–	19	12	16	7	15	13	7	7	3
Southampton	12	8	11	10	15	17	12	16	17	10	18	18	16
Stoke C	–	–	–	–	–	–	–	–	–	–	–	–	–
Sunderland	–	20	17	7	7	–	–	18	–	–	–	–	–
Swansea C	–	–	–	–	–	–	–	–	–	–	–	–	–
Swindon T	–	–	–	–	–	–	–	–	–	–	22	–	–
Tottenham H	14	10	9	12	10	11	14	10	8	7	15	8	15
Watford	–	–	–	–	20	–	–	–	–	–	–	–	–
WBA	–	19	–	–	–	–	–	–	–	–	–	–	–
West Ham U	–	18	7	15	9	5	8	14	10	14	13	–	22
Wimbledon	–	–	–	–	18	16	15	8	14	9	6	12	13
Wolv'hampton W	20	–	–	–	–	–	–	–	–	–	–	–	–

1990–91	1989–90	1988–89	1987–88	1986–87	1985–86	1984–85	1983–84	1982–83	1981–82	1980–81	1979–80	
1	4	1	6	4	7	7	6	10	5	3	4	Arsenal
17	2	17	–	22	16	10	10	6	11	1	7	Aston Villa
–	–	–	–	–	–	–	–	–	–	–	–	Barnsley
–	–	–	–	–	21	–	20	17	16	13	–	Birmingham C
–	–	–	–	–	–	–	–	–	–	–	–	Blackburn R
–	–	–	–	–	–	–	–	–	–	22	17	Bolton W
–	–	–	–	–	–	–	–	–	–	–	–	Bradford C
–	–	–	–	–	–	–	–	22	13	19	16	Brighton & HA
–	–	–	–	–	–	–	–	–	–	–	20	Bristol C
–	19	14	17	19	–	–	–	–	–	–	–	Charlton Ath
11	5	–	18	14	6	6	–	–	–	–	–	Chelsea
16	12	7	10	10	17	18	19	19	14	16	15	Coventry C
3	15	–	–	–	–	–	–	–	–	22	13	Crystal Palace
20	16	5	15	–	–	–	–	–	–	–	21	Derby Co
9	6	8	4	1	2	1	7	7	8	15	19	Everton
–	–	–	–	–	–	–	–	–	–	–	–	Fulham
–	–	–	–	–	20	17	12	9	2	2	3	Ipswich T
4	–	–	–	–	–	–	–	–	20	9	11	Leeds U
–	–	–	–	20	19	15	15	–	–	21	–	Leicester C
2	1	2	1	2	1	2	1	1	1	5	1	Liverpool
18	17	16	9	7	9	13	16	18	–	–	–	Luton T
5	14	–	–	21	15	–	–	20	10	12	17	Manchester C
6	13	11	2	11	4	4	4	3	3	8	2	Manchester U
–	–	18	–	–	–	–	–	–	22	14	9	Middlesbrough
–	20	10	–	–	–	–	–	–	–	–	–	Millwall
–	–	20	8	17	11	14	–	–	–	–	–	Newcastle U
15	10	4	14	5	–	20	14	14	–	20	12	Norwich C
8	9	3	3	8	8	9	3	5	12	7	5	Nottingham F
–	–	–	–	–	–	–	21	15	15	–	–	Notts Co
–	–	–	–	–	–	–	–	–	–	–	–	Oldham Ath
–	–	–	21	18	18	–	–	–	–	–	–	Oxford U
–	–	–	19	–	–	–	–	–	–	–	–	Portsmouth
12	11	9	5	16	13	19	5	–	–	–	–	QPR
13	–	–	–	–	–	–	–	–	–	–	–	Sheffield U
–	18	15	11	13	5	8	–	–	–	–	–	Sheffield W
14	7	13	12	12	14	5	2	12	7	6	8	Southampton
						22	18	13	18	11	18	Stoke C
19	–	–	–	–	–	21	13	16	19	17	–	Sunderland
–	–	–	–	–	–	–	–	21	6	–	–	Swansea C
–	–	–	–	–	–	–	–	–	–	–	–	Swindon T
10	3	6	13	3	10	3	8	4	4	10	14	Tottenham H
–	–	–	20	9	12	11	11	2	–	–	–	Watford
–	–	–	–	–	22	12	17	11	17	4	10	WBA
–	–	19	16	15	3	16	9	8	9	–	–	West Ham U
7	8	12	7	6	–	–	–	–	–	–	–	Wimbledon
–	–	–	–	–	–	–	22	–	21	18	6	Wolv'hampton W

LEAGUE POSITIONS: DIVISION 1 from 1992–93 and DIVISION 2 1979–80 to 1991–92

	2003–04	2002–03	2001–02	2000–01	1999–2000	1998–99	1997–98	1996–97	1995–96	1994–95	1993–94	1992–93	1991–92
Aston Villa	–	–	–	–	–	–	–	–	–	–	–	–	–
Barnsley	–	–	23	16	4	13	–	2	10	6	18	13	16
Birmingham C	–	–	5	5	5	4	7	10	15	–	22	19	–
Blackburn R	–	–	–	2	11	–	–	–	–	–	–	–	6
Bolton W	–	–	–	3	6	6	–	1	–	3	14	–	–
Bournemouth	–	–	–	–	–	–	–	–	–	–	–	–	–
Bradford C	23	19	15	–	–	2	13	21	–	–	–	–	–
Brentford	–	–	–	–	–	–	–	–	–	–	–	22	–
Brighton & HA	–	23	–	–	–	–	–	–	–	–	–	–	23
Bristol C	–	–	–	–	–	24	–	–	–	23	13	15	17
Bristol R	–	–	–	–	–	–	–	–	–	–	–	24	13
Burnley	19	16	7	7	–	–	–	–	–	22	–	–	–
Bury	–	–	–	–	–	22	17	–	–	–	–	–	–
Cambridge U	–	–	–	–	–	–	–	–	–	–	–	23	5
Cardiff C	13	–	–	–	–	–	–	–	–	–	–	–	–
Carlisle U	–	–	–	–	–	–	–	–	–	–	–	–	–
Charlton Ath	–	–	–	–	1	–	4	15	6	15	11	12	7
Chelsea	–	–	–	–	–	–	–	–	–	–	–	–	–
Coventry C	12	20	11	–	–	–	–	–	–	–	–	–	–
Crewe Alex	18	–	22	14	19	18	11	–	–	–	–	–	–
Crystal Palace	6	14	10	21	15	14	–	6	3	–	1	–	–
Derby Co	20	18	–	–	–	–	–	–	2	9	6	8	3
Fulham	–	–	–	1	9	–	–	–	–	–	–	–	–
Gillingham	21	11	12	13	–	–	–	–	–	–	–	–	–
Grimsby T	–	24	19	18	20	11	–	22	17	10	16	9	19
Huddersfield T	–	–	–	22	8	10	16	20	8	–	–	–	–
Hull C	–	–	–	–	–	–	–	–	–	–	–	–	–
Ipswich T	5	7	–	–	3	3	5	4	7	–	–	–	1
Leeds U	–	–	–	–	–	–	–	–	–	–	–	–	–
Leicester C	–	2	–	–	–	–	–	–	5	–	4	6	4
Leyton Orient	–	–	–	–	–	–	–	–	–	–	–	–	–
Luton T	–	–	–	–	–	–	–	–	24	16	20	20	–
Manchester C	–	–	1	–	2	–	22	14	–	–	–	–	–
Mansfield T	–	–	–	–	–	–	–	–	–	–	–	–	–
Middlesbrough	–	–	–	–	–	–	2	–	–	1	9	–	2
Millwall	10	9	4	–	–	–	–	–	22	12	3	7	15
Newcastle U	–	–	–	–	–	–	–	–	–	–	–	1	20
Norwich C	1	8	6	15	12	9	15	13	16	–	–	–	–
Nottingham F	14	6	16	11	14	–	1	–	–	–	2	–	–
Notts Co	–	–	–	–	–	–	–	–	–	24	7	17	–
Oldham Ath	–	–	–	–	–	–	–	23	18	14	–	–	–
Oxford U	–	–	–	–	–	23	12	17	–	–	23	14	21
Peterborough U	–	–	–	–	–	–	–	–	–	–	24	10	–
Plymouth Arg	–	–	–	–	–	–	–	–	–	–	–	–	22
Port Vale	–	–	–	–	23	21	19	8	12	17	–	–	24
Portsmouth	–	1	17	20	18	19	20	7	21	18	17	3	9
Preston NE	15	12	8	4	–	–	–	–	–	–	–	–	–
QPR	–	–	–	23	10	20	21	9	–	–	–	–	–
Reading	9	4	–	–	–	–	24	18	19	2	–	–	–

1990–91	1989–90	1988–89	1987–88	1986–87	1985–86	1984–85	1983–84	1982–83	1981–82	1980–81	1979–80	
–	–	–	2	–	–	–	–	–	–	–	–	Aston Villa
8	19	7	14	11	12	11	14	10	6	–	–	Barnsley
–	–	23	19	19	–	2	–	–	–	–	3	Birmingham C
19	5	5	5	12	19	5	6	11	10	4	–	Blackburn R
–	–	–	–	–	–	–	–	22	19	18	–	Bolton W
–	22	12	17	–	–	–	–	–	–	–	–	Bournemouth
–	23	14	4	10	13	–	–	–	–	–	–	Bradford C
–	–	–	–	–	–	–	–	–	–	–	–	Brentford
6	18	19	–	22	11	6	9	–	–	–	–	Brighton & HA
9	–	–	–	–	–	–	–	–	–	21	–	Bristol C
13	–	–	–	–	–	–	–	–	–	22	19	Bristol R
–	–	–	–	–	–	–	–	21	–	–	21	Burnley
–	–	–	–	–	–	–	–	–	–	–	–	Bury
–	–	–	–	–	–	–	22	12	14	13	8	Cambridge U
–	–	–	–	–	–	21	15	–	20	19	15	Cardiff C
–	–	–	–	–	20	16	7	14	–	–	–	Carlisle U
16	–	–	–	–	2	17	13	17	13	–	22	Charlton Ath
–	–	1	–	–	–	–	1	18	12	12	4	Chelsea
–	–	–	–	–	–	–	–	–	–	–	–	Coventry C
–	–	–	–	–	–	–	–	–	–	–	–	Crewe Alex
–	–	3	6	6	5	15	18	15	15	–	–	Crystal Palace
–	–	–	–	1	–	–	20	13	16	6	–	Derby Co
–	–	–	–	–	22	9	11	4	–	–	20	Fulham
–	–	–	–	–	–	–	–	–	–	–	–	Gillingham
–	–	–	–	21	15	10	5	19	17	7	–	Grimsby T
–	–	–	23	17	16	13	12	–	–	–	–	Huddersfield T
24	14	21	15	14	6	–	–	–	–	–	–	Hull C
14	9	8	8	5	–	–	–	–	–	–	–	Ipswich T
–	1	10	7	4	14	7	10	8	–	–	–	Leeds U
22	13	15	13	–	–	–	–	3	8	–	1	Leicester C
–	–	–	–	–	–	–	–	–	22	17	14	Leyton Orient
–	–	–	–	–	–	–	–	–	1	5	6	Luton T
–	–	2	9	–	–	3	4	–	–	–	–	Manchester C
–	–	–	–	–	–	–	–	–	–	–	–	Mansfield T
7	21	–	3	–	21	19	17	16	–	–	–	Middlesbrough
5	–	–	1	16	9	–	–	–	–	–	–	Millwall
11	3	–	–	–	–	–	3	5	9	11	9	Newcastle U
–	–	–	–	–	1	–	–	–	3	–	–	Norwich C
–	–	–	–	–	–	–	–	–	–	–	–	Nottingham F
4	–	–	–	–	–	20	–	–	–	2	17	Notts Co
1	8	16	10	3	8	14	19	7	11	15	11	Oldham Ath
10	17	17	–	–	–	1	–	–	–	–	–	Oxford U
–	–	–	–	–	–	–	–	–	–	–	–	Peterborough U
18	16	18	16	7	–	–	–	–	–	–	–	Plymouth Arg
15	11	–	–	–	–	–	–	–	–	–	–	Port Vale
17	12	20	–	2	4	4	16	–	–	–	–	Portsmouth
–	–	–	–	–	–	–	–	–	–	20	10	Preston NE
–	–	–	–	–	–	–	–	1	5	8	5	QPR
–	–	–	22	13	–	–	–	20	7	–	–	Reading

LEAGUE POSITIONS: DIVISION 1 from 1992–93 and DIVISION 2 1979–80 to 1991–92 (cont.)

	2003–04	2002–03	2001–02	2000–01	1999–2000	1998–99	1997–98	1996–97	1995–96	1994–95	1993–94	1992–93	1991–92
Rotherham U	17	15	21	–	–	–	–	–	–	–	–	–	–
Sheffield U	8	3	13	10	16	8	6	5	9	8	–	–	–
Sheffield W	–	22	20	17	–	–	–	–	–	–	–	–	–
Shrewsbury T	–	–	–	–	–	–	–	–	–	–	–	–	–
Southend U	–	–	–	–	–	–	–	24	14	13	15	18	12
Stockport Co	–	–	24	19	17	16	8	–	–	–	–	–	–
Stoke C	11	21	–	–	–	–	23	12	4	11	10	–	–
Sunderland	3	–	–	–	–	1	3	–	1	20	12	21	18
Swansea C	–	–	–	–	–	–	–	–	–	–	–	–	–
Swindon T	–	–	–	–	24	17	18	19	–	21	–	5	8
Tranmere R	–	–	–	24	13	15	14	11	13	5	5	4	14
Walsall	22	17	18	–	22	–	–	–	–	–	–	–	–
Watford	16	13	14	9	–	5	–	–	23	7	19	16	10
WBA	2	–	2	6	21	12	10	16	11	19	21	–	–
West Ham U	4	–	–	–	–	–	–	–	–	–	–	2	–
Wigan Ath	7		–	–	–	–	–	–	–	–	–	–	–
Wimbledon	24	10	9	8	–	–	–	–	–	–	–	–	–
Wolv'hampton W	–	5	3	12	7	7	9	3	20	4	8	11	11
Wrexham	–	–	–	–	–	–	–	–	–	–	–	–	–

LEAGUE POSITIONS: DIVISION 2 from 1992–93 and DIVISION 3 1979–80 to 1991–92

	2003–04	2002–03	2001–02	2000–01	1999–2000	1998–99	1997–98	1996–97	1995–96	1994–95	1993–94	1992–93	1991–92
Aldershot	–	–	–	–	–	–	–	–	–	–	–	–	–
Barnet	–	–	–	–	–	–	–	–	–	–	24	–	–
Barnsley	12	19	–	–	–	–	–	–	–	–	–	–	–
Birmingham C	–	–	–	–	–	–	–	–	–	1	–	–	2
Blackburn R	–	–	–	–	–	–	–	–	–	–	–	–	–
Blackpool	14	12	16	–	22	14	12	7	3	12	20	18	–
Bolton W	–	–	–	–	–	–	–	–	–	–	–	2	13
Bournemouth	9	–	21	7	16	7	9	16	14	19	17	17	8
Bradford C	–	–	–	–	–	–	–	–	6	14	7	10	16
Brentford	17	16	3	14	17	–	21	4	15	2	16	–	1
Brighton & HA	4	–	1	–	–	–	–	–	23	16	14	9	–
Bristol C	3	3	7	9	9	–	2	5	13	–	–	–	–
Bristol R	–	–	–	21	7	13	5	17	10	4	8	–	–
Burnley	–	–	–	–	2	15	20	9	17	–	6	13	–
Bury	–	–	22	16	15	–	–	1	–	–	–	–	21
Cambridge U	–	–	24	19	19	–	–	–	–	20	10	–	–
Cardiff C	–	6	4	–	21	–	–	–	–	22	19	–	–
Carlisle U	–	–	–	–	–	–	23	–	21	–	–	–	–

1990–91	1989–90	1988–89	1987–88	1986–87	1985–86	1984–85	1983–84	1982–83	1981–82	1980–81	1979–80	
–	–	–	–	–	–	–	–	20	7	–	–	Rotherham U
–	2	–	21	9	7	18	–	–	–	–	–	Sheffield U
3	–	–	–	–	–	–	2	6	4	10	–	Sheffield W
–	–	22	18	18	17	8	8	9	18	14	13	Shrewsbury T
–	–	–	–	–	–	–	–	–	–	–	–	Southend U
–	–	–	–	–	–	–	–	–	–	–	–	Stockport Co
–	24	13	11	8	10	–	–	–	–	–	–	Stoke C
–	6	11	–	20	18	–	–	–	–	–	2	Sunderland
–	–	–	–	–	–	–	21	–	–	3	12	Swansea C
21	4	6	12	–	–	–	–	–	–	–	–	Swindon T
–	–	–	–	–	–	–	–	–	–	–	–	Tranmere R
–	–	24	–	–	–	–	–	–	–	–	–	Walsall
20	15	4	–	–	–	–	–	–	2	9	18	Watford
23	20	9	20	15	–	–	–	–	–	–	–	WBA
2	7	–	–	–	–	–	–	–	–	1	7	West Ham U
–	–	–	–	–	–	–	–	–	–	–	–	Wigan Ath
–	–	–	–	–	3	12	–	–	–	–	–	Wimbledon
12	10	–	–	–	–	22	–	2	–	–	–	Wolv'hampton W
–	–	–	–	–	–	–	–	–	21	16	16	Wrexham

1990–91	1989–90	1988–89	1987–88	1986–87	1985–86	1984–85	1983–84	1982–83	1981–82	1980–81	1979–80	
–	–	24	20	–	–	–	–	–	–	–	–	Aldershot
–	–	–	–	–	–	–	–	–	–	–	–	Barnet
–	–	–	–	–	–	–	–	–	–	2	11	Barnsley
12	7					–	–	–	–	–	–	Birmingham C
–	–	–	–	–	–	–	–	–	–	–	2	Blackburn R
–	23	19	10	9	12	–	–	–	–	23	18	Blackpool
4	6	10	–	21	18	17	10	–	–	–	–	Bolton W
9	–	–	–	1	15	10	17	14	–	–	–	Bournemouth
8	–	–	–	–	–	1	7	12	–	–	–	Bradford C
6	13	7	12	11	10	13	20	9	8	9	19	Brentford
–	–	–	2	–	–	–	–	–	–	–	–	Brighton & HA
–	2	11	5	6	9	5	–	–	23	–	–	Bristol C
–	1	5	8	19	16	6	5	7	15	–	–	Bristol R
–	–	–	–	–	–	21	12	–	1	8	–	Burnley
7	5	13	14	16	20	–	–	–	–	–	21	Bury
1	–	–	–	–	–	24	–	–	–	–	–	Cambridge U
	21	16			22	–	–	?	–	–	–	Cardiff C
–	–	–	–	22	–	–	–	–	2	19	6	Carlisle U

LEAGUE POSITIONS: DIVISION 2 from 1992–93 and DIVISION 3 1979–80 to 1991–92 (cont.)

	2003–04	2002–03	2001–02	2000–01	1999–2000	1998–99	1997–98	1996–97	1995–96	1994–95	1993–94	1992–93	1991–92
Charlton Ath	–	–	–	–	–	–	–	–	–	–	–	–	–
Cheltenham T	–	21	–	–	–	–	–	–	–	–	–	–	–
Chester C	–	–	–	–	–	–	–	–	–	23	–	24	18
Chesterfield	20	20	18	–	24	9	10	10	7	–	–	–	–
Colchester U	11	12	15	17	18	18	–	–	–	–	–	–	–
Crewe Alex	–	2	–	–	–	–	–	6	5	3	–	–	–
Darlington	–	–	–	–	–	–	–	–	–	–	–	–	24
Derby Co	–	–	–	–	–	–	–	–	–	–	–	–	–
Doncaster R	–	–	–	–	–	–	–	–	–	–	–	–	–
Exeter C	–	–	–	–	–	–	–	–	–	–	22	19	20
Fulham	–	–	–	–	–	1	6	–	–	–	21	12	9
Gillingham	–	–	–	–	3	4	8	11	–	–	–	–	–
Grimsby T	21	–	–	–	–	–	3	–	–	–	–	–	3
Hartlepool U	6	–	–	–	–	–	–	–	–	–	23	16	11
Huddersfield T	–	22	6	–	–	–	–	–	–	5	11	15	3
Hull C	–	–	–	–	–	–	–	–	24	8	9	20	14
Leyton Orient	–	–	–	–	–	–	–	–	–	24	18	7	10
Lincoln C	–	–	–	–	–	23	–	–	–	–	–	–	–
Luton T	10	9	–	22	13	12	17	3	–	–	–	–	–
Macclesfield T	–	–	–	–	–	24	–	–	–	–	–	–	–
Manchester C	–	–	–	–	–	3	–	–	–	–	–	–	–
Mansfield T	–	23	–	–	–	–	–	–	–	–	–	22	–
Middlesbrough	–	–	–	–	–	–	–	–	–	–	–	–	–
Millwall	–	–	–	1	5	10	18	14	–	–	–	–	–
Newport Co	–	–	–	–	–	–	–	–	–	–	–	–	–
Northampton T	–	24	20	18	–	22	4	–	–	–	–	–	–
Notts Co	23	15	19	8	8	16	–	24	4	–	–	–	–
Oldham Ath	15	5	9	15	14	20	13	–	–	–	–	–	–
Oxford U	–	–	–	24	20	–	–	–	2	7	–	–	–
Peterborough U	18	11	17	12	–	–	–	21	19	15	–	–	6
Plymouth Arg	1	8	–	–	–	–	22	19	–	21	3	14	–
Portsmouth	–	–	–	–	–	–	–	–	–	–	–	–	–
Port Vale	7	17	14	11	–	–	–	–	–	–	2	3	–
Preston NE	–	–	–	–	1	5	15	15	–	–	–	21	17
QPR	2	4	8	–	–	–	–	–	–	–	–	–	–
Reading	–	–	2	3	10	11	–	–	–	–	1	8	12
Rotherham U	–	–	–	2	–	–	–	23	16	17	15	11	–
Rushden & D	22	–	–	–	–	–	–	–	–	–	–	–	–
Scunthorpe U	–	–	–	–	23	–	–	–	–	–	–	–	–
Sheffield U	–	–	–	–	–	–	–	–	–	–	–	–	–
Sheffield W	16	–	–	–	–	–	–	–	–	–	–	–	–
Shrewsbury T	–	–	–	–	–	–	–	22	18	18	–	–	22
Southend U	–	–	–	–	–	–	24	–	–	–	–	–	–
Stockport Co	19	14	–	–	–	–	–	2	9	11	4	6	5
Stoke C	–	–	5	5	6	8	–	–	–	–	–	1	4
Sunderland	–	–	–	–	–	–	–	–	–	–	–	–	–
Swansea C	–	–	–	23	–	–	–	–	22	10	13	5	19
Swindon T	5	10	13	20	–	–	–	–	1	–	–	–	–
Torquay U	–	–	–	–	–	–	–	–	–	–	–	–	23
Tranmere R	8	7	12	–	–	–	–	–	–	–	–	–	–

1990–91	1989–90	1988–89	1987–88	1986–87	1985–86	1984–85	1983–84	1982–83	1981–82	1980–81	1979–80	
–	–	–	–	–	–	–	–	–	–	3	–	Charlton Ath
–	–	–	–	–	–	–	–	–	–	–	–	Cheltenham T
19	16	8	15	15	–	–	–	–	24	18	9	Chester C
–	–	22	18	17	17	–	–	24	11	5	4	Chesterfield
–	–	–	–	–	–	–	–	–	–	22	5	Colchester U
22	12	–	–	–	–	–	–	–	–	–	–	Crewe Alex
–	–	–	–	22	13	–	–	–	–	–	–	Darlington
–	–	–	–	–	3	7	–	–	–	–	–	Derby Co
–	–	–	24	13	11	14	–	23	19	–	–	Doncaster R
16	–	–	–	–	–	–	24	19	18	11	8	Exeter C
21	20	4	9	18	–	–	–	–	3	13	–	Fulham
–	–	23	13	5	5	4	8	13	6	15	16	Gillingham
–	–	22	–	–	–	–	–	–	–	–	1	Grimsby T
–	–	–	–	–	–	–	–	–	–	–	–	Hartlepool U
11	8	14	–	–	–	–	–	3	17	4	–	Huddersfield T
–	–	–	–	–	–	3	4	–	–	24	20	Hull C
13	14	–	–	–	–	22	11	20	–	–	–	Leyton Orient
–	–	–	–	21	19	14	6	4	–	–	–	Lincoln C
–	–	–	–	–	–	–	–	–	–	–	–	Luton T
–	–	–	–	–	–	–	–	–	–	–	–	Macclesfield T
–	–	–	–	–	–	–	–	–	–	–	–	Manchester C
24	15	15	19	10	–	–	–	–	–	–	23	Mansfield T
–	–	–	–	2	–	–	–	–	–	–	–	Middlesbrough
–	–	–	–	–	–	2	9	17	9	16	14	Millwall
–	–	–	–	23	19	18	13	4	16	12	–	Newport Co
–	22	20	6	–	–	–	–	–	–	–	–	Northampton T
–	3	9	4	7	8	–	–	–	–	–	–	Notts Co
–	–	–	–	–	–	–	–	–	–	–	–	Oldham Ath
–	–	–	–	–	–	–	1	5	5	14	17	Oxford U
–	–	–	–	–	–	–	–	–	–	–	–	Peterborough U
–	–	–	–	–	2	15	19	8	10	7	15	Plymouth Arg
–	–	–	–	–	–	–	–	1	13	6	–	Portsmouth
–	–	3	11	12	–	–	23	–	–	–	–	Port Vale
17	19	6	16	–	–	23	16	16	14	–	–	Preston NE
–	–	–	–	–	–	–	–	–	–	–	–	QPR
15	10	18	–	–	1	9	–	21	12	10	7	Reading
23	9	–	21	14	14	12	18	–	–	1	13	Rotherham U
–	–	–	–	–	–	–	–	–	–	–	–	Rushden & D
–	–	–	–	–	–	–	21	–	–	–	–	Scunthorpe U
–	–	2	–	–	–	–	3	11	–	21	12	Sheffield U
–	–	–	–	–	–	–	–	–	–	–	3	Sheffield W
18	11	–	–	–	–	–	–	–	–	–	–	Shrewsbury T
2	–	21	17	–	–	–	22	15	7	–	22	Southend U
–	–	–	–	–	–	–	–	–	–	–	–	Stockport Co
14	–	–	–	–	–	–	–	–	–	–	–	Stoke C
–	–	–	1	–	–	–	–	–	–	–	–	Sunderland
20	17	12	–	–	24	20	–	–	–	–	–	Swansea C
–	–	–	–	3	–	–	–	–	22	17	10	Swindon T
–	–	–	–	–	–	–	–	–	–	–	–	Torquay U
5	4	–	–	–	–	–	–	–	–	–	–	Tranmere R

LEAGUE POSITIONS: DIVISION 2 from 1992–93 and DIVISION 3 1979–80 to 1991–92 (cont.)

	2003–04	2002–03	2001–02	2000–01	1999–2000	1998–99	1997–98	1996–97	1995–96	1994–95	1993–94	1992–93	1991–92
Walsall	–	–	–	4	–	2	19	12	11	–	–	5	–
Watford	–	–	–	–	–	–	1	13	–	–	–	–	–
WBA	–	–	–	–	–	–	–	–	–	–	–	4	7
Wigan Ath	–	1	10	6	4	6	11	–	–	–	–	23	15
Wimbledon	–	–	–	–	–	–	–	–	–	–	–	–	–
Wolv'hampton W	–	–	–	–	–	–	–	–	–	–	–	–	–
Wrexham	13	–	23	10	11	17	7	8	8	13	12	–	–
Wycombe W	24	18	11	13	12	19	14	18	12	6	–	–	–
York C	–	–	–	–	–	21	16	20	20	9	5	–	–

LEAGUE POSITIONS: DIVISION 3 from 1992–93 and DIVISION 4 1979–80 to 1991–92

	2003–04	2002–03	2001–02	2000–01	1999–2000	1998–99	1997–98	1996–97	1995–96	1994–95	1993–94	1992–93	1991–92
Aldershot	–	–	–	–	–	–	–	–	–	–	–	–	*
Barnet	–	–	–	24	6	16	7	15	9	11	–	3	7
Blackpool	–	–	–	7	–	–	–	–	–	–	–	–	4
Bolton W	–	–	–	–	–	–	–	–	–	–	–	–	–
Boston U	11	15	–	–	–	–	–	–	–	–	–	–	–
Bournemouth	–	4	–	–	–	–	–	–	–	–	–	–	–
Bradford C	–	–	–	–	–	–	–	–	–	–	–	–	–
Brighton & HA	–	–	–	1	11	17	23	23	–	–	–	–	–
Bristol C	–	–	–	–	–	–	–	–	–	–	–	–	–
Bristol R	15	20	23	–	–	–	–	–	–	–	–	–	–
Burnley	–	–	–	–	–	15	–	–	–	–	–	–	1
Bury	12	7	–	–	–	–	–	–	3	4	13	7	–
Cambridge U	13	12	–	–	–	2	16	10	16	–	–	–	–
Cardiff C	–	–	–	2	–	3	21	7	22	–	–	1	9
Carlisle U	23	22	17	22	23	23	–	3	–	1	7	18	22
Cheltenham T	14	–	4	9	8	–	–	–	–	–	–	–	–
Chester C	–	–	–	–	24	14	14	6	8	–	2	–	–
Chesterfield	–	–	–	3	–	–	–	–	–	3	8	12	13
Colchester U	–	–	–	–	–	–	4	8	7	10	17	10	–
Crewe Alex	–	–	–	–	–	–	–	–	–	–	3	6	6
Darlington	18	14	15	20	4	11	19	18	5	20	21	15	–
Doncaster R	1	–	–	–	–	–	24	19	13	9	15	16	21
Exeter C	–	23	16	19	21	12	15	22	14	22	–	–	–
Fulham	–	–	–	–	–	–	–	2	17	8	–	–	–
Gillingham	–	–	–	–	–	–	–	–	2	19	16	21	11

*Record expunged

1990–91	1989–90	1988–89	1987–88	1986–87	1985–86	1984–85	1983–84	1982–83	1981–82	1980–81	1979–80	
–	24	–	3	8	6	11	6	10	20	20	–	Walsall
–	–	–	–	–	–	–	–	–	–	–	–	Watford
–	–	–	–	–	–	–	–	–	–	–	–	WBA
10	18	17	7	4	4	16	15	18	–	–	–	Wigan Ath
–	–	–	–	–	–	–	2	–	21	–	24	Wimbledon
–	–	1	–	–	23	–	–	–	–	–	–	Wolv'hampton W
–	–	–	–	–	–	–	–	22	–	–	–	Wrexham
–	–	–	–	–	–	–	–	–	–	–	–	Wycombe W
–	–	–	23	20	7	8	–	–	–	–	–	York C

1990–91	1989–90	1988–89	1987–88	1986–87	1985–86	1984–85	1983–84	1982–83	1981–82	1980–81	1979–80	
23	22	–	–	6	16	13	5	18	16	6	10	Aldershot
–	–	–	–	–	–	–	–	–	–	–	–	Barnet
5	–	–	–	–	–	2	6	21	12	–	–	Blackpool
–	–	–	3	–	–	–	–	–	–	–	–	Bolton W
–	–	–	–	–	–	–	–	–	–	–	–	Boston U
–	–	–	–	–	–	–	–	–	4	13	11	Bournemouth
–	–	–	–	–	–	–	–	–	2	14	5	Bradford C
–	–	–	–	–	–	–	–	–	–	–	–	Brighton & HA
–	–	–	–	–	–	–	4	14	–	–	–	Bristol C
–	–	–	–	–	–	–	–	–	–	–	–	Bristol R
6	16	16	10	22	14	–	–	–	–	–	–	Burnley
–	–	–	–	–	–	4	15	5	9	12	–	Bury
–	6	8	15	11	22	–	–	–	–	–	–	Cambridge U
13	–	–	2	13	–	–	–	–	–	–	–	Cardiff C
20	8	12	23	–	–		–	–	–	–	–	Carlisle U
–	–	–	–	–	–	–	–	–	–	–	–	Cheltenham T
–	–	–	–	–	2	16	24	13	9	–	–	Chester C
18	7	–	–	–	–	1	13	–	–	–	–	Chesterfield
–	24	22	9	5	6	7	8	6	6	–	–	Colchester U
–	–	3	17	17	12	10	16	23	24	18	23	Crewe Alex
1	–	24	13	–	–	3	14	17	3	8	22	Darlington
11	20	23	–	–	–	–	2	–	–	3	12	Doncaster R
–	1	13	22	14	21	18	–	–	–			Exeter C
–	–	–	–	–	–	–	–	–	–	–	–	Fulham
15	14	–	–	–	–	–	–	–	–	–	–	Gillingham

LEAGUE POSITIONS: DIVISION 3 from 1992–93 and DIVISION 4 1979–80 to 1991–92 (cont.)

	2003–04	2002–03	2001–02	2000–01	1999–2000	1998–99	1997–98	1996–97	1995–96	1994–95	1993–94	1992–93	1991–92
Grimsby T	–	–	–	–	–	–	–	–	–	–	–	–	–
Halifax T	–	–	24	23	18	10	–	–	–	–	–	22	20
Hartlepool U	–	2	7	4	7	22	17	20	20	18	–	–	–
Hereford U	–	–	–	–	–	–	–	24	6	16	20	17	17
Huddersfield T	4	–	–	–	–	–	–	–	–	–	–	–	–
Hull C	2	13	11	6	14	21	22	17	–	–	–	–	–
Kidderminster H	16	11	10	16	–	–	–	–	–	–	–	–	–
Leyton Orient	19	18	18	5	19	6	11	16	21	–	–	–	–
Lincoln C	7	6	22	18	15	–	3	9	18	12	18	8	10
Luton T	–	–	2	–	–	–	–	–	–	–	–	–	–
Macclesfield T	20	16	13	14	13	–	2	–	–	–	–	–	–
Maidstone U	–	–	–	–	–	–	–	–	–	–	–	–	18
Mansfield T	5	–	3	13	17	8	12	11	19	6	12	–	3
Newport Co	–	–	–	–	–	–	–	–	–	–	–	–	–
Northampton T	6	–	–	–	3	–	–	4	11	17	22	20	16
Notts Co	–	–	–	–	–	–	1	–	–	–	–	–	–
Oxford U	9	8	21	–	–	–	–	–	–	–	–	–	–
Peterborough U	–	–	–	–	5	9	10	–	–	–	–	–	–
Plymouth Arg	–	–	1	12	12	13	–	–	4	–	–	–	–
Portsmouth	–	–	–	–	–	–	–	–	–	–	–	–	–
Port Vale	–	–	–	–	–	–	–	–	–	–	–	–	–
Preston NE	–	–	–	–	–	–	–	–	1	5	5	–	–
Reading	–	–	–	–	–	–	–	–	–	–	–	–	–
Rochdale	21	19	5	8	10	19	18	14	15	15	9	11	8
Rotherham U	–	–	–	–	2	5	9	–	–	–	–	–	2
Rushden & D	–	1	6	–	–	–	–	–	–	–	–	–	–
Scarborough	–	–	–	–	–	24	6	12	23	21	14	13	12
Scunthorpe U	22	5	8	10	–	4	8	13	12	7	11	14	5
Sheffield U	–	–	–	–	–	–	–	–	–	–	–	–	–
Shrewsbury T	–	24	9	15	22	15	13	–	–	–	1	9	–
Southend U	17	17	12	11	16	18	–	–	–	–	–	–	–
Stockport Co	–	–	–	–	–	–	–	–	–	–	–	–	–
Swansea C	10	21	20	–	1	7	20	5	–	–	–	–	–
Swindon T	–	–	–	–	–	–	–	–	–	–	–	–	–
Torquay U	3	9	19	21	9	20	5	21	24	13	6	19	–
Tranmere R	–	–	–	–	–	–	–	–	–	–	–	–	–
Walsall	–	–	–	–	–	–	–	–	–	2	10	5	15
Wigan Ath	–	–	–	–	–	–	–	1	10	14	19	–	–
Wimbledon	–	–	–	–	–	–	–	–	–	–	–	–	–
Wolv'hampton W	–	–	–	–	–	–	–	–	–	–	–	–	–
Wrexham	–	3	–	–	–	–	–	–	–	–	–	2	14
Wycombe W	–	–	–	–	–	–	–	–	–	–	4	–	–
Yeovil T	8	–	–	–	–	–	–	–	–	–	–	–	–
York C	24	10	14	17	20	–	–	–	–	–	–	4	19

1990–91	1989–90	1988–89	1987–88	1986–87	1985–86	1984–85	1983–84	1982–83	1981–82	1980–81	1979–80	
–	2	9	–	–	–	–	–	–	–	–	–	Grimsby T
22	23	21	18	15	20	21	21	11	19	23	18	Halifax T
3	19	19	16	18	7	19	23	22	14	9	19	Hartlepool U
17	17	15	19	16	10	5	11	24	10	22	21	Hereford U
–	–	–	–	–	–	–	–	–	–	–	1	Huddersfield T
–	–	–	–	–	–	–	–	2	8	–	–	Hull C
–	–	–	–	–	–	–	–	–	–	–	–	Kidderminster H
–	–	6	8	7	5	–	–	–	–	–	–	Leyton Orient
14	10	10	–	24	–	–	–	–	–	2	7	Lincoln C
–	–	–	–	–	–	–	–	–	–	–	–	Luton T
–	–	–	–	–	–	–	–	–	–	–	–	Macclesfield T
19	5	–	–	–	–	–	–	–	–	–	–	Maidstone U
–	–	–	–	–	3	14	19	10	20	7	–	Mansfield T
–	–	–	24	–	–	–	–	–	–	–	3	Newport Co
10	–	–	–	1	8	23	18	15	22	10	13	Northampton T
–	–	–	–	–	–	–	–	–	–	–	–	Notts Co
–	–	–	–	–	–	–	–	–	–	–	–	Oxford U
4	9	17	7	10	17	11	7	9	5	5	8	Peterborough U
–	–	–	–	–	–	–	–	–	–	–	–	Plymouth Arg
–	–	–	–	–	–	–	–	–	–	–	4	Portsmouth
–	–	–	–	–	4	12	–	3	7	19	20	Port Vale
–	–	–	–	2	23	–	–	–	–	–	–	Preston NE
–	–	–	–	–	–	–	3	–	–	–	–	Reading
12	12	18	21	21	18	17	22	20	21	15	24	Rochdale
–	–	1	–	–	–	–	–	–	–	–	–	Rotherham U
–	–	–	–	–	–	–	–	–	–	–	–	Rushden & D
9	18	5	12	–	–	–	–	–	–	–	–	Scarborough
8	11	4	4	8	15	9	–	4	23	16	14	Scunthorpe U
–	–	–	–	–	–	–	–	–	1	–	–	Sheffield U
–	–	–	–	–	–	–	–	–	–	–	–	Shrewsbury T
–	3	–	–	3	9	20	–	–	–	1	–	Southend U
2	4	20	20	19	11	22	12	16	18	20	16	Stockport Co
–	–	–	6	12	–	–	–	–	–	–	–	Swansea C
–	–	–	–	–	1	8	17	8	–	–	–	Swindon T
7	15	14	5	23	24	24	9	12	15	17	9	Torquay U
–	–	2	14	20	19	6	10	19	11	21	15	Tranmere R
16	–	–	–	–	–	–	–	–	–	–	2	Walsall
–	–	–	–	–	–	–	–	–	3	11	6	Wigan Ath
–	–	–	–	–	–	–	–	1	–	4	–	Wimbledon
–	–	–	1	4	–	–	–	–	–	–	–	Wolv'hampton W
24	21	7	11	9	13	15	20	–	–	–	–	Wrexham
–	–	–	–	–	–	–	–	–	–	–	–	Wycombe W
–	–	–	–	–	–	–	–	–	–	–	–	Yeovil T
21	13	11	–	–	–	–	1	7	17	24	17	York C

LEAGUE CHAMPIONSHIP HONOURS

FA PREMIER LEAGUE

Maximum points: 126

	First	*Pts*	*Second*	*Pts*	*Third*	*Pts*
1992–93	Manchester U	84	Aston Villa	74	Norwich C	72
1993–94	Manchester U	92	Blackburn R	84	Newcastle U	77
1994–95	Blackburn R	89	Manchester U	88	Nottingham F	77

Maximum points: 114

	First	*Pts*	*Second*	*Pts*	*Third*	*Pts*
1995–96	Manchester U	82	Newcastle U	78	Liverpool	71
1996–97	Manchester U	75	Newcastle U*	68	Arsenal*	68
1997–98	Arsenal	78	Manchester U	77	Liverpool	65
1998–99	Manchester U	79	Arsenal	78	Chelsea	75
1999–00	Manchester U	91	Arsenal	73	Leeds U	69
2000–01	Manchester U	80	Arsenal	70	Liverpool	69
2001–02	Arsenal	87	Liverpool	80	Manchester U	77
2002–03	Manchester U	83	Arsenal	78	Newcastle U	69
2003–04	Arsenal	90	Chelsea	79	Manchester U	75
2004–05	Chelsea	95	Arsenal	83	Manchester U	77

FOOTBALL LEAGUE CHAMPIONSHIP

Maximum points: 138

	First	*Pts*	*Second*	*Pts*	*Third*	*Pts*
2004–05	Sunderland	94	Wigan Ath	87	Ipswich T††	85

DIVISION 1

Maximum points: 138

	First	*Pts*	*Second*	*Pts*	*Third*	*Pts*
1992–93	Newcastle U	96	West Ham U*	88	Portsmouth††	88
1993–94	Crystal Palace	90	Nottingham F	83	Millwall††	74
1994–95	Middlesbrough	82	Reading††	79	Bolton W	77
1995–96	Sunderland	83	Derby Co	79	Crystal Palace††	75
1996–97	Bolton W	98	Barnsley	80	Wolverhampton W††	76
1997–98	Nottingham F	94	Middlesbrough	91	Sunderland††	90
1998–99	Sunderland	105	Bradford C	87	Ipswich T††	86
1999–00	Charlton Ath	91	Manchester C	89	Ipswich T	87
2000–01	Fulham	101	Blackburn R	91	Bolton W	87
2001–02	Manchester C	99	WBA	89	Wolverhampton W††	86
2002–03	Portsmouth	98	Leicester C	92	Sheffield U††	80
2003–04	Norwich C	94	WBA	86	Sunderland††	79

FOOTBALL LEAGUE CHAMPIONSHIP 1

Maximum points: 138

	First	*Pts*	*Second*	*Pts*	*Third*	*Pts*
2004–05	Luton T	98	Hull C	86	Tranmere R††	79

DIVISION 2

Maximum points: 138

	First	*Pts*	*Second*	*Pts*	*Third*	*Pts*
1992–93	Stoke C	93	Bolton W	90	Port Vale††	89
1993–94	Reading	89	Port Vale	88	Plymouth Arg††	85
1994–95	Birmingham C	89	Brentford††	85	Crewe Alex††	83
1995–96	Swindon T	92	Oxford U	83	Blackpool††	82
1996–97	Bury	84	Stockport Co	82	Luton T††	78
1997–98	Watford	88	Bristol C	85	Grimsby T	72
1998–99	Fulham	101	Walsall	87	Manchester C	82
1999–00	Preston NE	95	Burnley	88	Gillingham	85
2000–01	Millwall	93	Rotherham U	91	Reading††	86
2001–02	Brighton & HA	90	Reading	84	Brentford*††	83
2002–03	Wigan Ath	100	Crewe Alex	86	Bristol C††	83
2003–04	Plymouth Arg	90	QPR	83	Bristol C††	82

FOOTBALL LEAGUE CHAMPIONSHIP 2

Maximum points: 138

	First	*Pts*	*Second*	*Pts*	*Third*	*Pts*
2004–05	Yeovil T	83	Scunthorpe U*	80	Swansea C	80

DIVISION 3

Maximum points: 126

1992–93	Cardiff C	83	Wrexham	80	Barnet	79
1993–94	Shrewsbury T	79	Chester C	74	Crewe Alex	73
1994–95	Carlisle U	91	Walsall	83	Chesterfield	81

Maximum points: 138

1995–96	Preston NE	86	Gillingham	83	Bury	79
1996–97	Wigan Ath*	87	Fulham	87	Carlisle U	84
1997–98	Notts Co	99	Macclesfield T	82	Lincoln C	75
1998–99	Brentford	85	Cambridge U	81	Cardiff C	80
1999–00	Swansea C	85	Rotherham U	84	Northampton T	82
2000–01	Brighton & HA	92	Cardiff C	82	Chesterfield¶	80
2001–02	Plymouth Arg	102	Luton T	97	Mansfield T	79
2002–03	Rushden & D	87	Hartlepool U	85	Wrexham	84
2003–04	Doncaster R	92	Hull C	88	Torquay U*	81

* *Won or placed on goal average (ratio)/goal difference.*
†† *Not promoted after play-offs.* ¶ *9 pts deducted for irregularities.*

FOOTBALL LEAGUE

Maximum points: a 44; *b* 60

1888–89*a*	Preston NE	40	Aston Villa	29	Wolverhampton W	28
1889–90*a*	Preston NE	33	Everton	31	Blackburn R	27
1890–91*a*	Everton	29	Preston NE	27	Notts Co	26
1891–92*b*	Sunderland	42	Preston NE	37	Bolton W	36

DIVISION 1 to 1991–92

Maximum points: a 44; *b* 52; *c* 60; *d* 68; *e* 76; *f* 84; *g* 126; *h* 120; *k* 114.

1892–93*c*	Sunderland	48	Preston NE	37	Everton	36
1893–94*c*	Aston Villa	44	Sunderland	38	Derby Co	36
1894–95*c*	Sunderland	47	Everton	42	Aston Villa	39
1895–96*c*	Aston Villa	45	Derby Co	41	Everton	39
1896–97*c*	Aston Villa	47	Sheffield U*	36	Derby Co	36
1897–98*c*	Sheffield U	42	Sunderland	37	Wolverhampton W*	35
1898–99*d*	Aston Villa	45	Liverpool	43	Burnley	39
1899–1900*d*	Aston Villa	50	Sheffield U	48	Sunderland	41
1900–01*d*	Liverpool	45	Sunderland	43	Notts Co	40
1901–02*d*	Sunderland	44	Everton	41	Newcastle U	37
1902–03*d*	The Wednesday	42	Aston Villa*	41	Sunderland	41
1903–04*d*	The Wednesday	47	Manchester C	44	Everton	43
1904–05*d*	Newcastle U	48	Everton	47	Manchester C	46
1905–06*e*	Liverpool	51	Preston NE	47	The Wednesday	44
1906–07*e*	Newcastle U	51	Bristol C	48	Everton*	45
1907–08*e*	Manchester U	52	Aston Villa*	43	Manchester C	43
1908–09*e*	Newcastle U	53	Everton	46	Sunderland	44
1909–10*e*	Aston Villa	53	Liverpool	48	Blackburn R*	45
1910–11*e*	Manchester U	52	Aston Villa	51	Sunderland*	45
1911–12*e*	Blackburn R	49	Everton	46	Newcastle U	44
1912–13*e*	Sunderland	54	Aston Villa	50	Sheffield W	49
1913–14*e*	Blackburn R	51	Aston Villa	44	Middlesbrough*	43
1914–15*e*	Everton	46	Oldham Ath	45	Blackburn R*	43
1919–20*f*	WBA	60	Burnley	51	Chelsea	49
1920–21*f*	Burnley	59	Manchester C	54	Bolton W	52

	First	*Pts*	*Second*	*Pts*	*Third*	*Pts*
1921–22*f*	Liverpool	57	Tottenham H	51	Burnley	49
1922–23*f*	Liverpool	60	Sunderland	54	Huddersfield T	53
1923–24*f*	Huddersfield T*	57	Cardiff C	57	Sunderland	53
1924–25*f*	Huddersfield T	58	WBA	56	Bolton W	55
1925–26*f*	Huddersfield T	57	Arsenal	52	Sunderland	48
1926–27*f*	Newcastle U	56	Huddersfield T	51	Sunderland	49
1927–28*f*	Everton	53	Huddersfield T	51	Leicester C	48
1928–29*f*	Sheffield W	52	Leicester C	51	Aston Villa	50
1929–30*f*	Sheffield W	60	Derby Co	50	Manchester C*	47
1930–31*f*	Arsenal	66	Aston Villa	59	Sheffield W	52
1931–32*f*	Everton	56	Arsenal	54	Sheffield W	50
1932–33*f*	Arsenal	58	Aston Villa	54	Sheffield W	51
1933–34*f*	Arsenal	59	Huddersfield T	56	Tottenham H	49
1934–35*f*	Arsenal	58	Sunderland	54	Sheffield W	49
1935–36*f*	Sunderland	56	Derby Co*	48	Huddersfield T	48
1936–37*f*	Manchester C	57	Charlton Ath	54	Arsenal	52
1937–38*f*	Arsenal	52	Wolverhampton W	51	Preston NE	49
1938–39*f*	Everton	59	Wolverhampton W	55	Charlton Ath	50
1946–47*f*	Liverpool	57	Manchester U*	56	Wolverhampton W	56
1947–48*f*	Arsenal	59	Manchester U*	52	Burnley	52
1948–49*f*	Portsmouth	58	Manchester U*	53	Derby Co	53
1949–50*f*	Portsmouth*	53	Wolverhampton W	53	Sunderland	52
1950–51*f*	Tottenham H	60	Manchester U	56	Blackpool	50
1951–52*f*	Manchester U	57	Tottenham H*	53	Arsenal	53
1952–53*f*	Arsenal*	54	Preston NE	54	Wolverhampton W	51
1953–54*f*	Wolverhampton W	57	WBA	53	Huddersfield T	51
1954–55*f*	Chelsea	52	Wolverhampton W*	48	Portsmouth*	48
1955–56*f*	Manchester U	60	Blackpool*	49	Wolverhampton W	49
1956–57*f*	Manchester U	64	Tottenham H*	56	Preston NE	56
1957–58*f*	Wolverhampton W	64	Preston NE	59	Tottenham H	51
1958–59*f*	Wolverhampton W	61	Manchester U	55	Arsenal*	50
1959–60*f*	Burnley	55	Wolverhampton W	54	Tottenham H	53
1960–61*f*	Tottenham H	66	Sheffield W	58	Wolverhampton W	57
1961–62*f*	Ipswich T	56	Burnley	53	Tottenham H	52
1962–63*f*	Everton	61	Tottenham H	55	Burnley	54
1963–64*f*	Liverpool	57	Manchester U	53	Everton	52
1964–65*f*	Manchester U*	61	Leeds U	61	Chelsea	56
1965–66*f*	Liverpool	61	Leeds U*	55	Burnley	55
1966–67*f*	Manchester U	60	Nottingham F*	56	Tottenham H	56
1967–68*f*	Manchester C	58	Manchester U	56	Liverpool	55
1968–69*f*	Leeds U	67	Liverpool	61	Everton	57
1969–70*f*	Everton	66	Leeds U	57	Chelsea	55
1970–71*f*	Arsenal	65	Leeds U	64	Tottenham H*	52
1971–72*f*	Derby Co	58	Leeds U*	57	Liverpool*	57
1972–73*f*	Liverpool	60	Arsenal	57	Leeds U	53
1973–74*f*	Leeds U	62	Liverpool	57	Derby Co	48
1974–75*f*	Derby Co	53	Liverpool*	51	Ipswich T	51
1975–76*f*	Liverpool	60	QPR	59	Manchester U	56
1976–77*f*	Liverpool	57	Manchester C	56	Ipswich T	52
1977–78*f*	Nottingham F	64	Liverpool	57	Everton	55
1978–79*f*	Liverpool	68	Nottingham F	60	WBA	59
1979–80*f*	Liverpool	60	Manchester U	58	Ipswich T	53
1980–81*f*	Aston Villa	60	Ipswich T	56	Arsenal	53
1981–82*g*	Liverpool	87	Ipswich T	83	Manchester U	78
1982–83*g*	Liverpool	82	Watford	71	Manchester U	70
1983–84*g*	Liverpool	80	Southampton	77	Nottingham F*	74
1984–85*g*	Everton	90	Liverpool*	77	Tottenham H	77

	First	Pts	Second	Pts	Third	Pts
1985–86*g*	Liverpool	88	Everton	86	West Ham U	84
1986–87*g*	Everton	86	Liverpool	77	Tottenham H	71
1987–88*h*	Liverpool	90	Manchester U	81	Nottingham F	73
1988–89*k*	Arsenal*	76	Liverpool	76	Nottingham F	64
1989–90*k*	Liverpool	79	Aston Villa	70	Tottenham H	63
1990–91*k*	Arsenal†	83	Liverpool	76	Crystal Palace	69
1991–92*g*	Leeds U	82	Manchester U	78	Sheffield W	75

No official competition during 1915–19 and 1939–46; Regional Leagues operating.
** Won or placed on goal average (ratio)/goal difference.*
† 2 pts deducted

DIVISION 2 to 1991–92

Maximum points: a 44; *b* 56; *c* 60; *d* 68; *e* 76; *f* 84; *g* 126; *h* 132; *k* 138.

1892–93*a*	Small Heath	36	Sheffield U	35	Darwen	30
1893–94*b*	Liverpool	50	Small Heath	42	Notts Co	39
1894–95*c*	Bury	48	Notts Co	39	Newton Heath*	38
1895–96*c*	Liverpool*	46	Manchester C	46	Grimsby T*	42
1896–97*c*	Notts Co	42	Newton Heath	39	Grimsby T	38
1897–98*c*	Burnley	48	Newcastle U	45	Manchester C	39
1898–99*d*	Manchester C	52	Glossop NE	46	Leicester Fosse	45
1899–1900*d*	The Wednesday	54	Bolton W	52	Small Heath	46
1900–01*d*	Grimsby T	49	Small Heath	48	Burnley	44
1901–02*d*	WBA	55	Middlesbrough	51	Preston NE*	42
1902–03*d*	Manchester C	54	Small Heath	51	Woolwich A	48
1903–04*d*	Preston NE	50	Woolwich A	49	Manchester U	48
1904–05*d*	Liverpool	58	Bolton W	56	Manchester U	53
1905–06*e*	Bristol C	66	Manchester U	62	Chelsea	53
1906–07*e*	Nottingham F	60	Chelsea	57	Leicester Fosse	48
1907–08*e*	Bradford C	54	Leicester Fosse	52	Oldham Ath	50
1908–09*e*	Bolton W	52	Tottenham H*	51	WBA	51
1909–10*e*	Manchester C	54	Oldham Ath*	53	Hull C*	53
1910–11*e*	WBA	53	Bolton W	51	Chelsea	49
1911–12*e*	Derby Co*	54	Chelsea	54	Burnley	52
1912–13*e*	Preston NE	53	Burnley	50	Birmingham	46
1913–14*e*	Notts Co	53	Bradford PA*	49	Woolwich A	49
1914–15*e*	Derby Co	53	Preston NE	50	Barnsley	47
1919–20*f*	Tottenham H	70	Huddersfield T	64	Birmingham	56
1920–21*f*	Birmingham*	58	Cardiff C	58	Bristol C	51
1921–22*f*	Nottingham F	56	Stoke C*	52	Barnsley	52
1922–23*f*	Notts Co	53	West Ham U*	51	Leicester C	51
1923–24*f*	Leeds U	54	Bury*	51	Derby Co	51
1924–25*f*	Leicester C	59	Manchester U	57	Derby Co	55
1925–26*f*	Sheffield W	60	Derby Co	57	Chelsea	52
1926–27*f*	Middlesbrough	62	Portsmouth*	54	Manchester C	54
1927–28*f*	Manchester C	59	Leeds U	57	Chelsea	54
1928–29*f*	Middlesbrough	55	Grimsby T	53	Bradford PA*	48
1929–30*f*	Blackpool	58	Chelsea	55	Oldham Ath	53
1930–31*f*	Everton	61	WBA	54	Tottenham H	51
1931–32*f*	Wolverhampton W	56	Leeds U	54	Stoke C	52
1932–33*f*	Stoke C	56	Tottenham H	55	Fulham	50
1933–34*f*	Grimsby T	59	Preston NE	52	Bolton W*	51
1934–35*f*	Brentford	61	Bolton W*	56	West Ham U	56
1935–36*f*	Manchester U	56	Charlton Ath	55	Sheffield U*	52
1936–37*f*	Leicester C	56	Blackpool	55	Bury	52
1937–38*f*	Aston Villa	57	Manchester U*	53	Sheffield U	53
1938–39*f*	Blackburn R	55	Sheffield U	54	Sheffield W	53
1946–47*f*	Manchester C	62	Burnley	58	Birmingham C	55

	First	Pts	Second	Pts	Third	Pts
1947–48*f*	Birmingham C	59	Newcastle U	56	Southampton	52
1948–49*f*	Fulham	57	WBA	56	Southampton	55
1949–50*f*	Tottenham H	61	Sheffield W*	52	Sheffield U*	52
1950–51*f*	Preston NE	57	Manchester C	52	Cardiff C	50
1951–52*f*	Sheffield W	53	Cardiff C*	51	Birmingham C	51
1952–53*f*	Sheffield U	60	Huddersfield T	58	Luton T	52
1953–54*f*	Leicester C*	56	Everton	56	Blackburn R	55
1954–55*f*	Birmingham C*	54	Luton T*	54	Rotherham U	54
1955–56*f*	Sheffield W	55	Leeds U	52	Liverpool*	48
1956–57*f*	Leicester C	61	Nottingham F	54	Liverpool	53
1957–58*f*	West Ham U	57	Blackburn R	56	Charlton Ath	55
1958–59*f*	Sheffield W	62	Fulham	60	Sheffield U*	53
1959–60*f*	Aston Villa	59	Cardiff C	58	Liverpool*	50
1960–61*f*	Ipswich T	59	Sheffield U	58	Liverpool	52
1961–62*f*	Liverpool	62	Leyton Orient	54	Sunderland	53
1962–63*f*	Stoke C	53	Chelsea*	52	Sunderland	52
1963–64*f*	Leeds U	63	Sunderland	61	Preston NE	56
1964–65*f*	Newcastle U	57	Northampton T	56	Bolton W	50
1965–66*f*	Manchester C	59	Southampton	54	Coventry C	53
1966–67*f*	Coventry C	59	Wolverhampton W	58	Carlisle U	52
1967–68*f*	Ipswich T	59	QPR*	58	Blackpool	58
1968–69*f*	Derby Co	63	Crystal Palace	56	Charlton Ath	50
1969–70*f*	Huddersfield T	60	Blackpool	53	Leicester C	51
1970–71*f*	Leicester C	59	Sheffield U	56	Cardiff C*	53
1971–72*f*	Norwich C	57	Birmingham C	56	Millwall	55
1972–73*f*	Burnley	62	QPR	61	Aston Villa	50
1973–74*f*	Middlesbrough	65	Luton T	50	Carlisle U	49
1974–75*f*	Manchester U	61	Aston Villa	58	Norwich C	53
1975–76*f*	Sunderland	56	Bristol C*	53	WBA	53
1976–77*f*	Wolverhampton W	57	Chelsea	55	Nottingham F	52
1977–78*f*	Bolton W	58	Southampton	57	Tottenham H*	56
1978–79*f*	Crystal Palace	57	Brighton & HA*	56	Stoke C	56
1979–80*f*	Leicester C	55	Sunderland	54	Birmingham C*	53
1980–81*f*	West Ham U	66	Notts Co	53	Swansea C*	50
1981–82*g*	Luton T	88	Watford	80	Norwich C	71
1982–83*g*	QPR	85	Wolverhampton W	75	Leicester C	70
1983–84*g*	Chelsea*	88	Sheffield W	88	Newcastle U	80
1984–85*g*	Oxford U	84	Birmingham C	82	Manchester C	74
1985–86*g*	Norwich C	84	Charlton Ath	77	Wimbledon	76
1986–87*g*	Derby Co	84	Portsmouth	78	Oldham Ath††	75
1987–88*h*	Millwall	82	Aston Villa*	78	Middlesbrough	78
1988–89*k*	Chelsea	99	Manchester C	82	Crystal Palace	81
1989–90*k*	Leeds U*	85	Sheffield U	85	Newcastle U††	80
1990–91*k*	Oldham Ath	88	West Ham U	87	Sheffield W	82
1991–92*k*	Ipswich T	84	Middlesbrough	80	Derby Co	78

No official competition during 1915–19 and 1939–46; Regional Leagues operating.
** Won or placed on goal average (ratio)/goal difference.*
†† Not promoted after play-offs.

DIVISION 3 to 1991–92

Maximum points: 92; 138 from 1981–82.

	First	Pts	Second	Pts	Third	Pts
1958–59	Plymouth Arg	62	Hull C	61	Brentford*	57
1959–60	Southampton	61	Norwich C	59	Shrewsbury T*	52
1960–61	Bury	68	Walsall	62	QPR	60
1961–62	Portsmouth	65	Grimsby T	62	Bournemouth*	59
1962–63	Northampton T	62	Swindon T	58	Port Vale	54
1963–64	Coventry C*	60	Crystal Palace	60	Watford	58

	First	Pts	Second	Pts	Third	Pts
1964–65	Carlisle U	60	Bristol C*	59	Mansfield T	59
1965–66	Hull C	69	Millwall	65	QPR	57
1966–67	QPR	67	Middlesbrough	55	Watford	54
1967–68	Oxford U	57	Bury	56	Shrewsbury T	55
1968–69	Watford*	64	Swindon T	64	Luton T	61
1969–70	Orient	62	Luton T	60	Bristol R	56
1970–71	Preston NE	61	Fulham	60	Halifax T	56
1971–72	Aston Villa	70	Brighton & HA	65	Bournemouth*	62
1972–73	Bolton W	61	Notts Co	57	Blackburn R	55
1973–74	Oldham Ath	62	Bristol R*	61	York C	61
1974–75	Blackburn R	60	Plymouth Arg	59	Charlton Ath	55
1975–76	Hereford U	63	Cardiff C	57	Millwall	56
1976–77	Mansfield T	64	Brighton & HA	61	Crystal Palace*	59
1977–78	Wrexham	61	Cambridge U	58	Preston NE*	56
1978–79	Shrewsbury T	61	Watford*	60	Swansea C	60
1979–80	Grimsby T	62	Blackburn R	59	Sheffield W	58
1980–81	Rotherham U	61	Barnsley*	59	Charlton Ath	59
1981–82	Burnley*	80	Carlisle U	80	Fulham	78
1982–83	Portsmouth	91	Cardiff C	86	Huddersfield T	82
1983–84	Oxford U	95	Wimbledon	87	Sheffield U*	83
1984–85	Bradford C	94	Millwall	90	Hull C	87
1985–86	Reading	94	Plymouth Arg	87	Derby Co	84
1986–87	Bournemouth	97	Middlesbrough	94	Swindon T	87
1987–88	Sunderland	93	Brighton & HA	84	Walsall	82
1988–89	Wolverhampton W	92	Sheffield U*	84	Port Vale	84
1989–90	Bristol R	93	Bristol C	91	Notts Co	87
1990–91	Cambridge U	86	Southend U	85	Grimsby T*	83
1991–92	Brentford	82	Birmingham C	81	Huddersfield T	78

** Won or placed on goal average (ratio)/goal difference.*

DIVISION 4 (1958–1992)

Maximum points: 92; 138 from 1981–82.

1958–59	Port Vale	64	Coventry C*	60	York C	60
1959–60	Walsall	65	Notts Co*	60	Torquay U	60
1960–61	Peterborough U	66	Crystal Palace	64	Northampton T*	60
1961–62†	Millwall	56	Colchester U	55	Wrexham	53
1962–63	Brentford	62	Oldham Ath*	59	Crewe Alex	59
1963–64	Gillingham*	60	Carlisle U	60	Workington	59
1964–65	Brighton & HA	63	Millwall*	62	York C	62
1965–66	Doncaster R*	59	Darlington	59	Torquay U	58
1966–67	Stockport Co	64	Southport*	59	Barrow	59
1967–68	Luton T	66	Barnsley	61	Hartlepools U	60
1968–69	Doncaster R	59	Halifax T	57	Rochdale*	56
1969–70	Chesterfield	64	Wrexham	61	Swansea C	60
1970–71	Notts Co	69	Bournemouth	60	Oldham Ath	59
1971–72	Grimsby T	63	Southend U	60	Brentford	59
1972–73	Southport	62	Hereford U	58	Cambridge U	57
1973–74	Peterborough U	65	Gillingham	62	Colchester U	60
1974–75	Mansfield T	68	Shrewsbury T	62	Rotherham U	59
1975–76	Lincoln C	74	Northampton T	68	Reading	60
1976–77	Cambridge U	65	Exeter C	62	Colchester U*	59
1977–78	Watford	71	Southend U	60	Swansea C*	56
1978–79	Reading	65	Grimsby T*	61	Wimbledon*	61
1979–80	Huddersfield T	66	Walsall	64	Newport Co	61
1980–81	Southend U	67	Lincoln C	65	Doncaster R	56
1981–82	Sheffield U	96	Bradford C*	91	Wigan Ath	91
1982–83	Wimbledon	98	Hull C	90	Port Vale	88

	First	Pts	Second	Pts	Third	Pts
1983–84	York C	101	Doncaster R	85	Reading*	82
1984–85	Chesterfield	91	Blackpool	86	Darlington	85
1985–86	Swindon T	102	Chester C	84	Mansfield T	81
1986–87	Northampton T	99	Preston NE	90	Southend U	80
1987–88	Wolverhampton W	90	Cardiff C	85	Bolton W	78
1988–89	Rotherham U	82	Tranmere R	80	Crewe Alex	78
1989–90	Exeter C	89	Grimsby T	79	Southend U	75
1990–91	Darlington	83	Stockport Co*	82	Hartlepool U	82
1991–92§	Burnley	83	Rotherham U*	77	Mansfield T	77

* *Won or placed on goal average (ratio)/goal difference.*
†*Maximum points:* 88 owing to Accrington Stanley's resignation. ††*Not promoted after play-offs.*
§*Maximum points:* 126 owing to Aldershot being expelled.

DIVISION 3—SOUTH (1920–1958)

1920–21 Season as Division 3.
Maximum points: a 84; *b* 92.

1920–21*a*	Crystal Palace	59	Southampton	54	QPR	53
1921–22*a*	Southampton*	61	Plymouth Arg	61	Portsmouth	53
1922–23*a*	Bristol C	59	Plymouth Arg*	53	Swansea T	53
1923–24*a*	Portsmouth	59	Plymouth Arg	55	Millwall	54
1924–25*a*	Swansea T	57	Plymouth Arg	56	Bristol C	53
1925–26*a*	Reading	57	Plymouth Arg	56	Millwall	53
1926–27*a*	Bristol C	62	Plymouth Arg	60	Millwall	56
1927–28*a*	Millwall	65	Northampton T	55	Plymouth Arg	53
1928–29*a*	Charlton Ath*	54	Crystal Palace	54	Northampton T*	52
1929–30*a*	Plymouth Arg	68	Brentford	61	QPR	51
1930–31*a*	Notts Co	59	Crystal Palace	51	Brentford	50
1931–32*a*	Fulham	57	Reading	55	Southend U	53
1932–33*a*	Brentford	62	Exeter C	58	Norwich C	57
1933–34*a*	Norwich C	61	Coventry C*	54	Reading*	54
1934–35*a*	Charlton Ath	61	Reading	53	Coventry C	51
1935–36*a*	Coventry C	57	Luton T	56	Reading	54
1936–37*a*	Luton T	58	Notts Co	56	Brighton & HA	53
1937–38*a*	Millwall	56	Bristol C	55	QPR*	53
1938–39*a*	Newport Co	55	Crystal Palace	52	Brighton & HA	49
1939–46	Competition cancelled owing to war.					
1946–47*a*	Cardiff C	66	QPR	57	Bristol C	51
1947–48*a*	QPR	61	Bournemouth	57	Walsall	51
1948–49*a*	Swansea T	62	Reading	55	Bournemouth	52
1949–50*a*	Notts Co	58	Northampton T*	51	Southend U	51
1950–51*b*	Nottingham F	70	Norwich C	64	Reading*	57
1951–52*b*	Plymouth Arg	66	Reading*	61	Norwich C	61
1952–53*b*	Bristol R	64	Millwall*	62	Northampton T	62
1953–54*b*	Ipswich T	64	Brighton & HA	61	Bristol C	56
1954–55*b*	Bristol C	70	Leyton Orient	61	Southampton	59
1955–56*b*	Leyton Orient	66	Brighton & HA	65	Ipswich T	64
1956–57*b*	Ipswich T*	59	Torquay U	59	Colchester U	58
1957–58*b*	Brighton & HA	60	Brentford*	58	Plymouth Arg	58

* *Won or placed on goal average (ratio).*

DIVISION 3—NORTH (1921–1958)

Maximum points: a 76; *b* 84; *c* 80; *d* 92.

	First	Pts	Second	Pts	Third	Pts
1921–22*a*	Stockport Co	56	Darlington*	50	Grimsby T	50
1922–23*a*	Nelson	51	Bradford PA	47	Walsall	46
1923–24*b*	Wolverhampton W	63	Rochdale	62	Chesterfield	54

	First	*Pts*	*Second*	*Pts*	*Third*	*Pts*
1924–25*b*	Darlington	58	Nelson*	53	New Brighton	53
1925–26*b*	Grimsby T	61	Bradford PA	60	Rochdale	59
1926–27*b*	Stoke C	63	Rochdale	58	Bradford PA	55
1927–28*b*	Bradford PA	63	Lincoln C	55	Stockport Co	54
1928–29*g*	Bradford C	63	Stockport Co	62	Wrexham	52
1929–30*b*	Port Vale	67	Stockport Co	63	Darlington*	50
1930–31*b*	Chesterfield	58	Lincoln C	57	Wrexham*	54
1931–32*c*	Lincoln C*	57	Gateshead	57	Chester	50
1932–33*b*	Hull C	59	Wrexham	57	Stockport Co	54
1933–34*b*	Barnsley	62	Chesterfield	61	Stockport Co	59
1934–35*b*	Doncaster R	57	Halifax T	55	Chester	54
1935–36*b*	Chesterfield	60	Chester*	55	Tranmere R	55
1936–37*b*	Stockport Co	60	Lincoln C	57	Chester	53
1937–38*b*	Tranmere R	56	Doncaster R	54	Hull C	53
1938–39*b*	Barnsley	67	Doncaster R	56	Bradford C	52
1939–46	Competition cancelled owing to war.					
1946–47*b*	Doncaster R	72	Rotherham U	60	Chester	56
1947–48*b*	Lincoln C	60	Rotherham U	59	Wrexham	50
1948–49*b*	Hull C	65	Rotherham U	62	Doncaster R	50
1949–50*b*	Doncaster R	55	Gateshead	53	Rochdale*	51
1950–51*d*	Rotherham U	71	Mansfield T	64	Carlisle U	62
1951–52*d*	Lincoln C	69	Grimsby T	66	Stockport Co	59
1952–53*d*	Oldham Ath	59	Port Vale	58	Wrexham	56
1953–54*d*	Port Vale	69	Barnsley	58	Scunthorpe U	57
1954–55*d*	Barnsley	65	Accrington S	61	Scunthorpe U*	58
1955–56*d*	Grimsby T	68	Derby Co	63	Accrington S	59
1956–57*d*	Derby Co	63	Hartlepools U	59	Accrington S*	58
1957–58*d*	Scunthorpe U	66	Accrington S	59	Bradford C	57

** Won or placed on goal average (ratio).*

PROMOTED AFTER PLAY-OFFS

(Not accounted for in previous section)

1986–87 Aldershot to Division 3.
1987–88 Swansea C to Divison 3.
1988–89 Leyton Orient to Division 3.
1989–90 Cambridge U to Division 3; Notts Co to Division 2; Sunderland to Division 1.
1990–91 Notts Co to Division 1; Tranmere R to Division 2; Torquay U to Division 3.
1991–92 Blackburn R to Premier League; Peterborough U to Division 1.
1992–93 Swindon T to Premier League; WBA to Division 1; York C to Division 2.
1993–94 Leicester C to Premier League; Burnley to Division 1; Wycombe W to Division 2.
1994–95 Huddersfield T to Division 1.
1995–96 Leicester C to Premier League; Bradford C to Division 1; Plymouth Arg to Division 2.
1996–97 Crystal Palace to Premier League; Crewe Alex to Division 1; Northampton T to Division 2.
1997–98 Charlton Ath to Premier League; Colchester U to Division 2.
1998–99 Watford to Premier League; Scunthorpe to Division 2.
1999–00 Peterborough U to Division 2.
2000–01 Walsall to Division 1; Blackpool to Division 2.
2001–02 Birmingham C to Premier League; Stoke C to Division 1; Cheltenham T to Division 2.
2002–03 Wolverhampton W to Premier League; Cardiff C to Division 1; Bournemouth to Division 2.
2003–04 Crystal Palace to Premier League; Brighton & HA to Division 1; Huddersfield T to Division 2
2004–05 West Ham U to Premier League; Sheffield W to Football League Championship, Southend U to Football League Championship 1.

RELEGATED CLUBS

FA PREMIER LEAGUE TO DIVISION 1

1992–93 Crystal Palace, Middlesbrough, Nottingham F.
1993–94 Sheffield U, Oldham Ath, Swindon T.
1994–95 Crystal Palace, Norwich C, Leicester C, Ipswich T.
1995–96 Manchester C, QPR, Bolton W.
1996–97 Sunderland, Middlesbrough, Nottingham F.
1997–98 Bolton W, Barnsley, Crystal Palace.
1998–99 Charlton Ath, Blackburn R, Nottingham F.
1999–90 Wimbledon, Sheffield W, Watford.
2000–01 Manchester C, Coventry C, Bradford C.
2001–02 Ipswich T, Derby Co, Leicester C.
2002–03 West Ham U, WBA, Sunderland.
2003–04 Leicester C, Leeds U, Wolverhampton W.

FA PREMIER LEAGUE TO FOOTBALL LEAGUE CHAMPIONSHIP

2004–05 Crystal Palace, Norwich C, Southampton.

DIVISION 1 TO DIVISION 2

1898–99 Bolton W and Sheffield W
1899–1900 Burnley and Glossop
1900–01 Preston NE and WBA
1901–02 Small Heath and Manchester C
1902–03 Grimsby T and Bolton W
1903–04 Liverpool and WBA
1904–05 League extended. Bury and Notts Co, two bottom clubs in First Division, re-elected.
1905–06 Nottingham F and Wolverhampton W
1906–07 Derby Co and Stoke C
1907–08 Bolton W and Birmingham C
1908–09 Manchester C and Leicester Fosse
1909–10 Bolton W and Chelsea
1910–11 Bristol C and Nottingham F
1911–12 Preston NE and Bury
1912–13 Notts Co and Woolwich Arsenal
1913–14 Preston NE and Derby Co
1914–15 Tottenham H and Chelsea*
1919–20 Notts Co and Sheffield W
1920–21 Derby Co and Bradford PA
1921–22 Bradford C and Manchester U
1922–23 Stoke C and Oldham Ath
1923–24 Chelsea and Middlesbrough
1924–25 Preston NE and Nottingham F
1925–26 Manchester C and Notts Co
1926–27 Leeds U and WBA
1927–28 Tottenham H and Middlesbrough
1928–29 Bury and Cardiff C
1929–30 Burnley and Everton
1930–31 Leeds U and Manchester U
1931–32 Grimsby T and West Ham U
1932–33 Bolton W and Blackpool
1933–34 Newcastle U and Sheffield U
1934–35 Leicester C and Tottenham H
1935–36 Aston Villa and Blackburn R
1936–37 Manchester U and Sheffield W
1937–38 Manchester C and WBA
1938–39 Birmingham C and Leicester C
1946–47 Brentford and Leeds U
1947–48 Blackburn R and Grimsby T
1948–49 Preston NE and Sheffield U
1949–50 Manchester C and Birmingham C
1950–51 Sheffield W and Everton
1951–52 Huddersfield T and Fulham
1952–53 Stoke C and Derby Co
1953–54 Middlesbrough and Liverpool
1954–55 Leicester C and Sheffield W
1955–56 Huddersfield T and Sheffield U
1956–57 Charlton Ath and Cardiff C
1957–58 Sheffield W and Sunderland
1958–59 Portsmouth and Aston Villa
1959–60 Luton T and Leeds U
1960–61 Preston NE and Newcastle U
1961–62 Chelsea and Cardiff C
1962–63 Manchester C and Leyton Orient
1963–64 Bolton W and Ipswich T
1964–65 Wolverhampton W and Birmingham C
1965–66 Northampton T and Blackburn R
1966–67 Aston Villa and Blackpool
1967–68 Fulham and Sheffield U
1968–69 Leicester C and QPR
1969–70 Sunderland and Sheffield W
1970–71 Burnley and Blackpool
1971–72 Huddersfield T and Nottingham F
1972–73 Crystal Palace and WBA
1973–74 Southampton, Manchester U, Norwich C
1974–75 Luton T, Chelsea, Carlisle U
1975–76 Wolverhampton W, Burnley, Sheffield U

1976–77 Sunderland, Stoke C, Tottenham H
1977–78 West Ham U, Newcastle U, Leicester C
1978–79 QPR, Birmingham C, Chelsea
1979–80 Bristol C, Derby Co, Bolton W
1980–81 Norwich C, Leicester C, Crystal Palace
1981–82 Leeds U, Wolverhampton W, Middlesbrough
1982–83 Manchester C, Swansea C, Brighton & HA
1983–84 Birmingham C, Notts Co, Wolverhampton W
1984–85 Norwich C, Sunderland, Stoke C
1985–86 Ipswich T, Birmingham C, WBA
1986–87 Leicester C, Manchester C, Aston Villa
1987–88 Chelsea**, Portsmouth, Watford, Oxford U
1988–89 Middlesbrough, West Ham U, Newcastle U
1989–90 Sheffield W, Charlton Ath, Millwall
1990–91 Sunderland and Derby Co
1991–92 Luton T, Notts Co, West Ham U
1992–93 Brentford, Cambridge U, Bristol R
1993–94 Birmingham C, Oxford U, Peterborough U
1994–95 Swindon T, Burnley, Bristol C, Notts Co
1995–96 Millwall, Watford, Luton T
1996–97 Grimsby T, Oldham Ath, Southend U
1997–98 Manchester C, Stoke C, Reading
1998–99 Bury, Oxford U, Bristol C
1999–00 Walsall, Port Vale, Swindon T
2000–01 Huddersfield T, QPR, Tranmere R
2001–02 Crewe Alex, Barnsley, Stockport Co
2002–03 Sheffield W, Brighton & HA, Grimsby T
2003–04 Walsall, Bradford C, Wimbledon

***Relegated after play-offs.*
**Subsequently re-elected to Division 1 when League was extended after the War.*

FOOTBALL LEAGUE CHAMPIONSHIP TO FOOTBALL LEAGUE CHAMPIONSHIP 1

2004–05 Gillingham, Nottingham F, Rotherham U.

DIVISION 2 TO DIVISION 3

1920–21 Stockport Co
1921–22 Bradford PA and Bristol C
1922–23 Rotherham Co and Wolverhampton W
1923–24 Nelson and Bristol C
1924–25 Crystal Palace and Coventry C
1925–26 Stoke C and Stockport Co
1926–27 Darlington and Bradford C
1927–28 Fulham and South Shields
1928–29 Port Vale and Clapton Orient
1929–30 Hull C and Notts Co
1930–31 Reading and Cardiff C
1931–32 Barnsley and Bristol C
1932–33 Chesterfield and Charlton Ath
1933–34 Millwall and Lincoln C
1934–35 Oldham Ath and Notts Co
1935–36 Port Vale and Hull C
1936–37 Doncaster R and Bradford C
1937–38 Barnsley and Stockport Co
1938–39 Norwich C and Tranmere R
1946–47 Swansea T and Newport Co
1947–48 Doncaster R and Millwall
1948–49 Nottingham F and Lincoln C
1949–50 Plymouth Arg and Bradford PA
1950–51 Grimsby T and Chesterfield
1951–52 Coventry C and QPR
1952–53 Southampton and Barnsley
1953–54 Brentford and Oldham Ath
1954–55 Ipswich T and Derby Co
1955–56 Plymouth Arg and Hull C
1956–57 Port Vale and Bury
1957–58 Doncaster R and Notts Co
1958–59 Barnsley and Grimsby T
1959–60 Bristol C and Hull C
1960–61 Lincoln C and Portsmouth
1961–62 Brighton & HA and Bristol R
1962–63 Walsall and Luton T
1963–64 Grimsby T and Scunthorpe U
1964–65 Swindon T and Swansea T
1965–66 Middlesbrough and Leyton Orient
1966–67 Northampton T and Bury
1967–68 Plymouth Arg and Rotherham U
1968–69 Fulham and Bury
1969–70 Preston NE and Aston Villa
1970–71 Blackburn R and Bolton W
1971–72 Charlton Ath and Watford
1972–73 Huddersfield T and Brighton & HA

1973–74 Crystal Palace, Preston NE, Swindon T
1974–75 Millwall, Cardiff C, Sheffield W
1975–76 Oxford U, York C, Portsmouth
1976–77 Carlisle U, Plymouth Arg, Hereford U
1977–78 Blackpool, Mansfield T, Hull C
1978–79 Sheffield U, Millwall, Blackburn R
1979–80 Fulham, Burnley, Charlton Ath
1980–81 Preston NE, Bristol C, Bristol R
1981–82 Cardiff C, Wrexham, Orient
1982–83 Rotherham U, Burnley, Bolton W
1983–84 Derby Co, Swansea C, Cambridge U
1984–85 Notts Co, Cardiff C, Wolverhampton W
1985–86 Carlisle U, Middlesbrough, Fulham
1986–87 Sunderland**, Grimsby T, Brighton & HA
1987–88 Huddersfield T, Reading, Sheffield U**
1988–89 Shrewsbury T, Birmingham C, Walsall
1989–90 Bournemouth, Bradford C, Stoke C
1990–91 WBA and Hull C
1991–92 Plymouth Arg, Brighton & HA, Port Vale
1992–93 Preston NE, Mansfield T, Wigan Ath, Chester C
1993–94 Fulham, Exeter C, Hartlepool U, Barnet
1994–95 Cambridge U, Plymouth Arg, Cardiff C, Chester C, Leyton Orient
1995–96 Carlisle U, Swansea C, Brighton & HA, Hull C
1996–97 Peterborough U, Shrewsbury T, Rotherham U, Notts Co
1997–98 Brentford, Plymouth Arg, Carlisle U, Southend U
1998–99 York C, Northampton T, Lincoln C, Macclesfield T
1999–00 Cardiff C, Blackpool, Scunthorpe U, Chesterfield
2000–01 Bristol R, Luton T, Swansea C, Oxford U
2001–02 Bournemouth, Bury, Wrexham, Cambridge U
2002–03 Cheltenham T, Huddersfield T, Mansfield T, Northampton T
2003–04 Grimsby T, Rushden & D, Notts Co, Wycombe W

FOOTBALL LEAGUE CHAMPIONSHIP 1 TO FOOTBALL LEAGUE CHAMPIONSHIP 2

2004–05 Torquay U, Wrexham, Peterborough U, Stockport Co.

DIVISION 3 TO DIVISION 4

1958–59 Rochdale, Notts Co, Doncaster R, Stockport Co
1959–60 Accrington S, Wrexham, Mansfield T, York C
1960–61 Chesterfield, Colchester U, Bradford C, Tranmere R
1961–62 Newport Co, Brentford, Lincoln C, Torquay U
1962–63 Bradford PA, Brighton & HA, Carlisle U, Halifax T
1963–64 Millwall, Crewe Alex, Wrexham, Notts Co
1964–65 Luton T, Port Vale, Colchester U, Barnsley
1965–66 Southend U, Exeter C, Brentford, York C
1966–67 Doncaster R, Workington, Darlington, Swansea T
1967–68 Scunthorpe U, Colchester U, Grimsby T, Peterborough U (demoted)
1968–69 Oldham Ath, Crewe Alex, Hartlepool, Northampton T
1969–70 Bournemouth, Southport, Barrow, Stockport Co
1970–71 Reading, Bury, Doncaster R, Gillingham
1971–72 Mansfield T, Barnsley, Torquay U, Bradford C
1972–73 Rotherham U, Brentford, Swansea C, Scunthorpe U
1973–74 Cambridge U, Shrewsbury T, Southport, Rochdale
1974–75 Bournemouth, Tranmere R, Watford, Huddersfield T
1975–76 Aldershot, Colchester U, Southend U, Halifax T
1976–77 Reading, Northampton T, Grimsby T, York C
1977–78 Port Vale, Bradford C, Hereford U, Portsmouth
1978–79 Peterborough U, Walsall, Tranmere R, Lincoln C
1979–80 Bury, Southend U, Mansfield T, Wimbledon

1980–81	Sheffield U, Colchester U, Blackpool, Hull C	1986–87	Bolton W**, Carlisle U, Darlington, Newport Co
1981–82	Wimbledon, Swindon T, Bristol C, Chester	1987–88	Doncaster R, York C, Grimsby T, Rotherham U**
1982–83	Reading, Wrexham, Doncaster R, Chesterfield	1988–89	Southend U, Chesterfield, Gillingham, Aldershot
1983–84	Scunthorpe U, Southend U, Port Vale, Exeter C	1989–90	Cardiff C, Northampton T, Blackpool, Walsall
1984–85	Burnley, Orient, Preston NE, Cambridge U	1990–91	Crewe Alex, Rotherham U, Mansfield T
1985–86	Lincoln C, Cardiff C, Wolverhampton W, Swansea C	1991–92	Bury, Shrewsbury T, Torquay U, Darlington

***Relegated after play-offs.*

LEAGUE STATUS FROM 1986–87

	RELEGATED FROM LEAGUE	PROMOTED TO LEAGUE
1986–87	Lincoln C	Scarborough
1987–88	Newport Co	Lincoln C
1988–89	Darlington	Maidstone U
1989–90	Colchester U	Darlington
1990–91	—	Barnet
1991–92	—	Colchester U
1992–93	Halifax T	Wycombe W
1993–94	—	—
1994–95	—	—
1995–96	—	—
1996–97	Hereford U	Macclesfield T
1997–98	Doncaster R	Halifax T
1998–99	Scarborough	Cheltenham T
1999–2000	Chester C	Kidderminster H
2000–01	Barnet	Rushden & D
2001–02	Halifax T	Boston U
2002–03	Shrewsbury T, Exeter C	Yeovil T, Doncaster R
2003–04	Carlisle U, York C	Chester C, Shrewsbury T
2004–05	Kidderminster H, Cambridge U	Barnet, Carlisle U

LEAGUE TITLE WINS

FA PREMIER LEAGUE – Manchester U 8, Arsenal 3, Blackburn R 1.

FOOTBALL LEAGUE CHAMPIONSHIP – Sunderland 1

LEAGUE DIVISION 1 – Liverpool 18, Arsenal 10, Everton 9, Sunderland 8, Aston Villa 7, Manchester U 7, Newcastle U 5, Sheffield W 4, Huddersfield T 3, Leeds U 3, Manchester C 3, Portsmouth 3, Wolverhampton W 3, Blackburn R 2, Burnley 2, Derby Co 2, Nottingham F 2, Preston NE 2, Tottenham H 2; Bolton W, Charlton Ath, Chelsea, Crystal Palace, Fulham, Ipswich T, Middlesbrough, Norwich C, Sheffield U, WBA 1 each.

FOOTBALL LEAGUE CHAMPIONSHIP 1 – Luton T 1

LEAGUE DIVISION 2 – Leicester C 6, Manchester C 6, Birmingham C (one as Small Heath) 5, Sheffield W 5, Derby Co 4, Liverpool 4, Preston NE 4, Ipswich T 3, Leeds U 3, Middlesbrough 3, Notts Co 3, Stoke C 3, Aston Villa 2, Bolton W 2, Burnley 2, Bury 2, Chelsea 2, Fulham 2, Grimsby T 2, Manchester U 2, Millwall 2, Norwich C 2, Nottingham F 2, Tottenham H 2, WBA 2, West Ham U 2, Wolverhampton W 2; Blackburn R, Blackpool, Bradford C, Brentford, Brighton & HA, Bristol C, Coventry C, Crystal Palace, Everton, Huddersfield T, Luton T, Newcastle U, Plymouth Arg, QPR, Oldham Ath, Oxford U, Reading, Sheffield U, Sunderland, Swindon T, Watford, Wigan Ath 1 each.

FOOTBALL LEAGUE CHAMPIONSHIP 2 – Yeovil T 1

LEAGUE DIVISION 3 – Brentford 2, Carlisle U 2, Oxford U 2, Plymouth Arg 2, Portsmouth 2, Preston NE 2, Shrewsbury T 2; Aston Villa, Blackburn R, Bolton W, Bournemouth, Bradford C, Brighton & HA, Bristol R, Burnley, Bury, Cambridge U, Cardiff C, Coventry C, Doncaster R, Grimsby T, Hereford U, Hull C, Leyton Orient, Mansfield T, Northampton T, Notts Co, Oldham Ath, QPR, Reading, Rotherham U, Rushden & D Southampton, Sunderland, Swansea C, Watford, Wigan Ath, Wolverhampton W, Wrexham 1 each.

LEAGUE DIVISION 4 – Chesterfield 2, Doncaster R 2, Peterborough U 2; Brentford, Brighton & HA, Burnley, Cambridge U, Darlington, Exeter C, Gillingham, Grimsby T, Huddersfield T, Lincoln C, Luton T, Mansfield T, Millwall, Northampton T, Notts Co, Port Vale, Reading, Rotherham U, Sheffield U, Southend U, Southport, Stockport Co, Swindon T, Walsall, Watford, Wimbledon, Wolverhampton W, York C 1 each.

DIVISION 3 (South) – Bristol C 3, Charlton Ath 2, Ipswich T 2, Millwall 2, Notts Co 2, Plymouth Arg 2, Swansea T 2; Brentford, Brighton & HA, Bristol R, Cardiff C, Coventry C, Crystal Palace, Fulham, Leyton Orient, Luton T, Newport Co, Norwich C, Nottingham F, Portsmouth, QPR, Reading, Southampton 1 each.

DIVISION 3 (North) – Barnsley 3, Doncaster R 3, Lincoln C 3, Chesterfield 2, Grimsby T 2, Hull C 2, Port Vale 2, Stockport Co 2; Bradford C, Bradford PA, Darlington, Derby Co, Nelson, Oldham Ath, Rotherham U, Scunthorpe U, Stoke C, Tranmere R, Wolverhampton W 1 each.

FOOTBALL LEAGUE PLAY-OFFS 2004–05

CHAMPIONSHIP SEMI-FINALS FIRST LEG

West Ham U	(2) 2	Ipswich T	(1) 2
Preston NE	(1) 2	Derby Co	(0) 0

CHAMPIONSHIP SEMI-FINALS SECOND LEG

Ipswich T	(0) 0	West Ham U	(0) 2
Derby Co	(0) 0	Preston NE	(0) 0

CHAMPIONSHIP FINAL Monday, 30 May 2005 *(at Millennium Stadium)*

West Ham U (0) 1 *(Zamora 57)*

Preston NE (0) 0 70,275

West Ham U: Walker (Bywater); Repka, Powell, Mullins, Ferdinand, Ward, Newton (Noble), Reo-Coker, Harewood, Zamora (Dailly), Etherington.
Preston NE: Nash; Davis, Hill, O'Neil (Etuhu), Lucketti, Mawene (Alexander), Sedgwick (Agyemang), McKenna, Cresswell, Nugent, Lewis.
Referee: M. Riley (Yorkshire).

LEAGUE 1 SEMI-FINALS FIRST LEG

Sheffield W	(1) 1	Brentford	(0) 0
Hartlepool U	(1) 2	Tranmere R	(0) 0

LEAGUE 1 SEMI-FINALS SECOND LEG

Brentford	(0) 1	Sheffield W	(1) 2
Tranmere R	(0) 2	Hartlepool U	(0) 0

aet; Hartlepool U won 6-5 on penalties.

LEAGUE 1 FINAL Sunday, 29 May 2005 *(at Millennium Stadium)*

Hartlepool U (0) 2 *(Williams 47, Daly 71)*

Sheffield W (1) 4 *(McGovern 45, MacLean 82 (pen), Whelan 94, Talbot 120)* 59,808

Hartlepool U: Konstantopoulos; Barron (Craddock), Robson, Nelson, Westwood ■, Strachan, Butler (Williams), Sweeney, Porter (Daly), Boyd, Humphreys.
Sheffield W: Lucas; Bruce (Collins), Heckingbottom, Bullen, Wood, Whelan, Rocastle, McGovern, Peacock (Talbot), Quinn (MacLean), Brunt.
aet.
Referee: P. Crossley (Kent).

LEAGUE 2 SEMI-FINALS FIRST LEG

Lincoln C	(1) 1	Macclesfield T	(0) 0
Northampton T	(0) 0	Southend U	(0) 0

LEAGUE 2 SEMI-FINALS SECOND LEG

Macclesfield T	(0) 1	Lincoln C	(1) 1
Southend U	(0) 1	Northampton T	(0) 0

LEAGUE 2 FINAL Saturday, 28 May 2005 *(at Millennium Stadium)*

Lincoln C (0) 0

Southend U (0) 2 *(Eastwood 105, Jupp 110)* 19,653

Lincoln C: Marriott; McCombe, Sandwith, McAuley, Morgan, Futcher, Butcher, Green (Beevers), Taylor-Fletcher (Bloomer), Yeo (Asamoah), Gain.
Southend U: Flahavan; Jupp, Wilson, Maher, Barrett, Prior, Pettefer, Bentley, Gray (Dudfield), Eastwood (Edwards), Nicolau (Gower).
aet.
Referee: M. Atkinson (West Yorkshire).

LEAGUE ATTENDANCES 2004–2005

FA BARCLAYCARD PREMIERSHIP ATTENDANCES

	Average Gate			*Season 2004/05*	
	2003/04	2004/05	+/–%	Highest	Lowest
Arsenal	38,079	37,978	–0.27	38,164	37,010
Aston Villa	36,622	37,354	+2.00	42,593	31,312
Birmingham City	29,078	28,760	–1.09	29,382	27,177
Blackburn Rovers	24,376	22,314	–8.46	29,271	18,006
Bolton Wanderers	26,718	26,006	–2.66	27,880	23,692
Charlton Athletic	26,278	26,403	+0.48	27,104	24,263
Chelsea	41,272	41,870	+1.45	42,328	40,864
Crystal Palace	17,344	24,108	+39.00	26,193	20,705
Everton	38,837	36,834	–5.16	40,552	32,406
Fulham	16,240	19,838	+22.16	21,940	16,180
Liverpool	42,677	42,587	–0.21	44,224	35,064
Manchester City	46,830	45,192	–3.50	47,221	42,453
Manchester United	67,641	67,871	+0.34	67,989	67,704
Middlesbrough	30,395	31,965	+5.17	34,836	29,603
Newcastle United	51,966	51,844	–0.23	52,326	50,430
Norwich City	19,074	24,354	+27.68	25,522	23,549
Portsmouth	20,054	20,072	+0.09	20,210	19,620
Southampton	31,717	30,610	–3.49	32,066	27,343
Tottenham Hotspur	34,872	35,883	+2.90	36,254	35,105
West Bromwich Albion	24,765	25,987	+4.93	27,751	23,849

FOOTBALL LEAGUE CHAMPIONSHIP ATTENDANCES

	Average Gate			*Season 2004/05*	
	2003/04	2004/05	+/–%	Highest	Lowest
Brighton & Hove Albion	6,248	6,434	+3.0	6,848	5,996
Burnley	12,541	12,466	–0.6	17,789	7,200
Cardiff City	15,569	12,976	–16.7	17,006	10,007
Coventry City	14,816	16,048	+8.3	22,728	11,966
Crewe Alexandra	7,741	7,403	–4.4	9,269	5,409
Derby County	22,200	25,219	+13.6	31,237	22,096
Gillingham	8,517	8,528	+0.1	10,810	6,089
Ipswich Town	24,520	25,651	+4.6	30,003	21,246
Leeds United	36,666	29,207	–20.3	34,496	24,585
Leicester City	30,983	24,137	–22.1	30,231	21,249
Millwall	10,497	11,699	+11.5	15,603	8,835
Nottingham Forest	24,759	23,608	–4.6	28,887	19,209
Plymouth Argyle	12,654	16,428	+29.8	20,555	13,508
Preston North End	14,150	13,889	–1.8	20,221	10,339
Queens Park Rangers	14,785	16,056	+8.6	18,363	13,559
Reading	15,095	17,169	+13.7	23,203	11,404
Rotherham United	7,138	6,272	–12.1	9,050	3,804
Sheffield United	21,646	19,594	–9.5	22,959	16,079
Stoke City	14,425	16,456	+14.1	23,029	12,785
Sunderland	27,119	28,821	+6.3	47,350	22,267
Watford	14,856	14,290	–3.8	19,673	11,084
West Ham United	31,167	27,403	–12.1	33,482	22,031
Wigan Athletic	9,505	11,571	+21.7	20,745	7,547
Wolverhampton Wanderers	28,864	26,620	–7.8	28,516	24,336

Premiership and Football League attendance averages and highest crowd figures for 2004–05 are unofficial. The official Premiership total was 12,881,768.

FOOTBALL LEAGUE CHAMPIONSHIP 1 ATTENDANCES

	Average Gate			*Season 2004/05*	
	2003/04	2004/05	+/–%	Highest	Lowest
Barnsley	9,620	9,779	+1.7	19,659	7,466
Blackpool	6,326	6,032	–4.6	8,774	4,179
AFC Bournemouth	6,913	7,123	+3.0	9,058	5,390
Bradford City	11,377	8,839	–22.3	15,417	6,409
Brentford	5,542	6,082	+9.7	9,604	4,643
Bristol City	12,879	11,391	–11.6	14,852	8,267
Chesterfield	4,331	4,961	+14.5	7,831	3,715
Colchester United	3,536	3,534	–0.1	4,834	2,616
Doncaster Rovers	6,939	6,886	–0.8	10,131	5,209
Hartlepool United	5,419	5,182	–4.4	6,520	4,206
Huddersfield Town	10,528	11,905	+13.1	17,292	9,194
Hull City	16,847	18,027	+7.0	24,277	14,317
Luton Town	6,339	7,940	+25.3	9,500	6,603
Milton Keynes Dons FC	4,751	4,896	+3.1	7,620	3,015
Oldham Athletic	6,566	6,462	–1.6	9,645	4,291
Peterborough United	5,274	4,341	–17.7	7,662	3,048
Port Vale	5,810	4,973	–14.4	8,671	3,496
Sheffield Wednesday	22,336	23,100	+3.4	28,798	18,465
Stockport County	5,315	5,000	–5.9	7,473	3,850
Swindon Town	7,925	5,835	–26.4	8,275	4,484
Torquay United	3,460	3,511	+1.5	5,347	2,384
Tranmere Rovers	7,606	9,044	+18.9	12,684	7,613
Walsall	7,853	6,085	–22.5	8,225	4,966
Wrexham	4,440	4,751	+7.0	7,833	2,391

FOOTBALL LEAGUE CHAMPIONSHIP 2 ATTENDANCES

	Average Gate			*Season 2004/05*	
	2003/04	2004/05	+/–%	Highest	Lowest
Boston United	2,964	2,932	–1.1	6,445	2,053
Bristol Rovers	7,142	7,077	–0.9	9,295	5,294
Bury	2,892	3,032	+4.8	7,575	1,866
Cambridge United	3,919	3,616	–7.7	6,715	2,021
Cheltenham Town	4,116	3,648	–11.4	5,511	2,706
Chester City	3,065	2,812	–8.3	3,847	1,643
Darlington	5,023	4,245	–15.5	7,028	2,709
Grimsby Town	4,730	4,943	+4.5	7,941	3,144
Kidderminster Harriers	2,980	2,785	–6.5	4,288	2,082
Leyton Orient	4,157	3,712	–10.7	4,753	2,436
Lincoln City	4,910	4,927	+0.3	8,056	3,274
Macclesfield Town	2,385	2,272	–4.7	3,076	1,436
Mansfield Town	5,207	4,092	–21.4	7,682	2,497
Northampton Town	5,306	5,927	+11.7	7,107	4,373
Notts County	5,940	5,384	–9.4	10,005	3,586
Oxford United	6,296	5,347	–15.1	7,830	4,089
Rochdale	3,277	2,690	–17.9	3,912	2,107
Rushden & Diamonds	4,457	3,321	–25.5	5,520	1,803
Scunthorpe United	3,840	5,178	+34.8	8,054	3,402
Shrewsbury Town	4,007	4,251	+6.1	6,285	2,956
Southend United	4,535	6,077	+34.0	11,735	3,753
Swansea City	6,853	8,458	+23.4	11,469	6,462
Wycombe Wanderers	5,291	4,937	–6.7	8,124	3,844
Yeovil Town	6,197	6,320	+2.0	9,153	4,639

TRANSFERS 2004–2005

June 2004	*From*	*To*
30 Branch, Paul M.	Bradford City	Chester City
16 Dickov, Paul	Leicester City	Blackburn Rovers
2 Keane, Michael	Preston North End	Hull City
14 Lucas, David A.	Preston North End	Sheffield Wednesday
14 Paston, Mark	Bradford City	Walsall
18 Purse, Darren J.	Birmingham City	West Bromwich Albion
30 Thatcher, Benjamin D.	Leicester City	Manchester City
29 Wright, David	Crewe Alexandra	Wigan Athletic
Temporary transfers		
28 Bentley, David M.	Arsenal	Norwich City
July 2004		
19 Asamoah, Derek	Northampton Town	Mansfield Town
8 Bent, Marcus N.	Ipswich Town	Everton
8 Beresford, Marlon	Barnsley	Luton Town
2 Brooker, Paul	Leicester City	Reading
7 Burnell, Joseph M.	Bristol City	Wycombe Wanderers
30 Butt, Nicholas	Manchester United	Newcastle United
29 Cahill, Timothy	Millwall	Everton
13 Charton, Simon T.	Bolton Wanderers	Norwich City
2 Commons, Kristian A.	Stoke City	Nottingham Forest
22 Connolly, David J.	West Ham United	Leicester City
7 Cook, Lee	Watford	Queens Park Rangers
9 Coppinger, James	Exeter City	Doncaster Rovers
24 Coyne, Daniel	Leicester City	Burnley
14 Crouch, Peter J.	Aston Villa	Southampton
10 Davis, Sean	Fulham	Tottenham Hotspur
8 Duff, Michael J.	Cheltenham Town	Burnley
23 Duke, Matthew	Burton Albion	Hull City
29 Edds, Gareth J.	Bradford City	Milton Keynes Dons
26 Edwards, Robert O.	Aston Villa	Wolverhampton Wanderers
29 Feeney, Warren J.	AFC Bournemouth	Stockport County
26 Graham, David	Torquay United	Wigan Athletic
30 Greening, Jonathan	Middlesbrough	West Bromwich Albion
30 Gronkjaer, Jesper	Chelsea	Birmingham City
2 Heskey, Emile W.	Liverpool	Birmingham City
12 Hudson, Mark A.	Fulham	Crystal Palace
14 Ifil, Jerel C.	Watford	Swindon Town
27 Jensen, Claus W.	Charlton Athletic	Fulham
13 Lua-Lua, Lomano T.	Newcastle United	Portsmouth
26 Lynch, Mark J.	Manchester United	Sunderland
27 MacLean, Steven	Rangers	Sheffield Wednesday
5 McGovern, Jon P.	Livingston	Sheffield Wednesday
21 Melligan, John J.	Wolverhampton Wanderers	Cheltenham Town
7 Milner, James P.	Leeds United	Newcastle United
31 Murray, Adam D.	Kidderminster Harriers	Mansfield Town
20 Murray, Frederick A.	Cambridge United	Northampton Town
14 Opara, Lloyd	Grays Athletic	Swindon Town
30 Parlour, Raymond	Arsenal	Middlesbrough
20 Pugh, Daniel A.	Manchester United	Leeds United
19 Reid, Paul M.	Northampton Town	Barnsley
8 Ricketts, Michael B.	Middlesbrough	Leeds United
8 Robinson, Carl P.	Portsmouth	Sunderland
13 Safri, Youssef	Coventry City	Norwich City
21 Speed, Gary A.	Newcastle United	Bolton Wanderers
19 Stockdale, Robert K.	Middlesbrough	Rotherham United
8 Viduka, Mark A.	Leeds United	Middlesbrough
19 Wilbraham, Aaron T.	Stockport County	Hull City
12 Wolleaston, Robert A.	Bradford City	Oxford United
Temporary transfers		
30 Blinkhorn, Matthew D.	Blackpool	Luton Town
30 Braniff, Kevin	Millwall	Rushden & Diamonds

13 Cole, Carlton	Chelsea	Aston Villa
2 Forssell, Mikael K.	Chelsea	Birmingham City
16 Johnson, Edward W.	Manchester United	Coventry City
16 Nardiello, Daniel A.	Manchester United	Barnsley
15 Owen, Gareth J.	Stoke City	Torquay United
26 Peat, Nathan N.M.	Hull City	Lincoln City
1 Sestanovich, Ashley	Sheffield United	Grimsby Town
6 Silk, Gary L.	Portsmouth	Wycombe Wanderers
9 Stack, Graham	Arsenal	Millwall
15 Villis, Matthew	Plymouth Argyle	Torquay United
27 Ward, Elliott L.	West Ham United	Peterborough United
8 Williamson, Michael J.	Southampton	Wycombe Wanderers

August 2004

24 Carrick, Michael	West Ham United	Tottenham Hotspur
12 Carr, Stephen	Tottenham Hotspur	Newcastle United
6 Cisse, Aliou	Birmingham City	Portsmouth
13 Crainey, Stephen	Southampton	Leeds United
31 Davenport, Calum R.P.	Coventry City	Tottenham Hotspur
20 Doherty, Gary M.T.	Tottenham Hotspur	Norwich City
6 Elliott, Stephen W.	Manchester City	Sunderland
6 Fisken, Gary S.	Watford	Swansea City
31 Fletcher, Carl N.	AFC Bournemouth	West Ham United
27 Fuller, Ricardo	Preston North End	Portsmouth
12 Hall, Fitz	Southampton	Crystal Palace
31 Hayles, Barry	Sheffield United	Millwall
12 Jeffers, Francis	Arsenal	Charlton Athletic
5 Lawrence, Liam	Mansfield Town	Sunderland
13 McAnuff, Joel J.F.M.	West Ham United	Cardiff City
5 McAuley, Gareth	Coleraine	Lincoln City
4 McLeod, Izale M.	Derby County	Milton Keynes Dons
12 Murphy, Daniel B.	Liverpool	Charlton Athletic
11 Radzinski, Tomasz	Everton	Fulham
31 Rooney, Wayne	Everton	Manchester United
6 Smith, Gary S.	Middlesbrough	Milton Keynes Dons
5 Stonebridge, Ian R.	Plymouth Argyle	Wycombe Wanderers
6 Ward, Darren	Nottingham Forest	Norwich City
2 Whitehead, Dean	Oxford United	Sunderland
31 Yorke, Dwight E.	Blackburn Rovers	Birmingham City

Temporary transfers

26 Abbey, Zema	Norwich City	Boston United
13 Adebola, Bamberdele O.	Coventry City	Bradford City
6 Bailey, Matthew J.	Stockport County	Scunthorpe United
13 Banim, Jody	Shrewsbury Town	Accrington Stanley
6 Barker, Christopher A.	Cardiff City	Stoke City
3 Barrowman, Andrew	Birmingham City	Blackpool
13 Beck, Daniel G.	Brighton & Hove Albion	Bognor Regis Town
6 Betsy, Kevin	Barnsley	Hartlepool United
12 Bimson, Stuart J.	Cambridge United	Accrington Stanley
20 Birchall, Adam S.	Arsenal	Wycombe Wanderers
3 Bossu, Bertrand	Gillingham	Torquay United
6 Braniff, Kevin R.	Millwall	Rushden & Diamonds
5 Briggs, Keith	Norwich City	Crewe Alexandra
31 Brighton, Tom	Rangers	Scunthorpe United
6 Brown, Simon	West Bromwich Albion	Kidderminster Harriers
13 Budd, Darren L.	Brighton & Hove Albion	Bognor Regis Town
16 Burch, Robert K.	Tottenham Hotspur	Stevenage Borough
20 Campbell-Ryce, Jamal J.	Charlton Athletic	Chesterfield
20 Cash, Brian D.	Nottingham Forest	Rochdale
9 Chambers, James A.	West Bromwich Albion	Watford
27 Chopra, Rocky M.	Newcastle United	Barnsley
20 Commons, Spencer J.	Notts County	Grantham Town
6 Crainey, Stephen	Southampton	Leeds United
19 Daly, Wesley J.P.	Queens Park Rangers	Raith Rovers
9 Dinning, Tony	Wigan Athletic	Ipswich Town

20 Diouf, El Hadji O.	Liverpool	Bolton Wanderers
20 Flynn, Michael J.	Wigan Athletic	Blackpool
4 Folkes, Peter A.	Bradford City	Lincoln City
13 Fontaine, Liam V.H.	Fulham	Yeovil Town
13 Gould, Jonathan A.	Preston North End	Hereford United
27 Hand, Jamie	Watford	Oxford United
27 Hawkins, Darren M.	Bristol City	Bath City
20 Henderson, Darius A.	Gillingham	Swindon Town
9 Henderson, Wayne	Aston Villa	Notts County
6 Howe, Edward J.F.	Portsmouth	AFC Bournemouth
27 Hughes, Mark A.	Tottenham Hotspur	Northampton Town
6 Jelleyman, Gareth A.	Peterborough United	Boston United
6 Keogh, Andrew D.	Leeds United	Scunthorpe United
5 Livesey, Daniel	Bolton Wanderers	Blackpool
27 Louis, Jefferson L.	Oxford United	Gravesend & Northfleet
13 Martin, Marcus A.P.	Plymouth Argyle	Exeter City
13 Maxwell, Marcus A.	Plymouth Argyle	Exeter City
6 May, Ben S.	Millwall	Colchester United
31 McGrath, John M.	Doncaster Rovers	Shrewsbury Town
18 McGurk, David	Darlington	Bishop Auckland
27 McLachlan, Fraser M.	Stockport County	Northwich Victoria
31 McManus, Thomas K.	Hibernian	Boston United
6 Moore, Stefan	Aston Villa	Millwall
20 Navarro, Alan E.	Tranmere Rovers	Chester City
6 Nicolas, Alexis P.	Chelsea	Brighton & Hove Albion
24 Noble, Stuart W.	Fulham	Torquay United
31 Oakes, Andrew M.	Derby County	Bolton Wanderers
6 O'Neill, Joseph	Preston North End	Mansfield Town
20 Pearson, Gregory	West Ham United	Lincoln City
17 Perry, Jack J.	Queens Park Rangers	Raith Rovers
6 Rachubka, Paul S.	Charlton Athletic	Milton Keynes Dons
13 Ross, Neil J.	Macclesfield Town	Tamworth
13 Sawyer, Gary D.	Plymouth Argyle	Exeter City
6 Shaw, Paul	Sheffield United	Rotherham United
2 Silk, Gary L.	Portsmouth	Wycombe Wanderers
6 Smith, Jonathan	Accrington Stanley	Barrow
13 Thomas, Bradley M.	Peterborough United	Sutton United
6 Turnbull, Ross	Middlesbrough	Bradford City
6 Turner, Michael T.	Charlton Athletic	Brentford
19 Vieira, Magno S.	Wigan Athletic	Carlisle United
6 Vine, Rowan L.	Portsmouth	Luton Town
6 Viveash, Adrian L.	Swindon Town	Kidderminster Harriers
27 Yeates, Mark S.	Tottenham Hotspur	Swindon Town

September 2004

9 Andrews, Wayne M.H.	Colchester United	Crystal Palace
30 Brooker, Stephen M.L.	Port Vale	Bristol City
30 Cadamarteri, Daniel L.	Leeds United	Sheffield United
21 Carruthers, Martin G.	Boston United	Lincoln City
28 Chambers, James	West Bromwich Albion	Watford
17 Regan, Sean M.	West Bromwich Albion	Leeds United
1 Gurney, Andrew R.	Swindon Town	Swansea City
14 John, Stern	Birmingham City	Coventry City
24 Louis, Jefferson	Oxford United	Forest Green Rovers
10 Mackay, Malcolm	Norwich City	West Ham United
3 Plummer, Christopher S.	Barnet	Peterborough United
14 Weatherstone, Simon	Yeovil Town	Hornchurch
21 West, Dean	Lincoln City	Boston United
3 Williams, Gareth A.	Crystal Palace	Colchester United
9 Williamson, Lee T.	Mansfield Town	Northampton Town

Temporary transfers

12 Adebola, Bamidele O.	Coventry City	Bradford City
23 Aljofree, Hasney	Plymouth Argyle	Sheffield Wednesday
17 Beck, Daniel G.	Brighton & Hove Albion	Bognor Regis Town
10 Beckwith, Dean	Gillingham	Margate

21 Birchall, Adam S.	Arsenal	Wycombe Wanderers
30 Bischoff, Mikkel	Manchester City	Wolverhampton Wanderers
17 Black, Thomas R.	Crystal Palace	Sheffield United
24 Bridges, Michael	Bolton Wanderers	Sunderland
10 Brown, Simon	West Bromwich Albion	Kidderminster Harriers
24 Burchill, Mark J.	Portsmouth	Rotherham United
3 Byrne, Michael T.	Stockport County	Leigh RMI
17 Campbell-Ryce, Jamal	Charlton Athletic	Chesterfield
17 Carter, Darren A.	Birmingham City	Sunderland
24 Chambers, James A.	West Bromwich Albion	Watford
9 Clancy, Timothy	Millwall	Walton & Hersham
18 Clarke, Peter M.	Everton	Blackpool
18 Comyn-Platt, Charlie	Bolton Wanderers	Wycombe Wanderers
24 Cooper, Shaun D.	Portsmouth	Kidderminster Harriers
24 Crouch, Ross A.	Colchester United	Wivenhoe Town
10 Curtis, John C.K.	Portsmouth	Preston North End
9 Danns, Neil A.	Blackburn Rovers	Colchester United
9 Davenport, Calum R.P.	Tottenham Hotspur	West Ham United
20 Day, Jamie R.	Peterborough United	Crawley Town
9 Dolan, Joseph	Millwall	Walton & Hersham
17 Donaldson, Clayton A.	Hull City	Harrogate Town
24 Duffy, Richard M.	Portsmouth	Burnley
23 Edwards, Paul	Crewe Alexandra	Redditch United
28 Fitzgerald, Scott P.	Watford	Swansea City
17 Flynn, Michael J.	Wigan Athletic	Blackpool
12 Fontaine, Liam V.H.	Fulham	Yeovil Town
9 Gerrard, Anthony	Everton	Accrington Stanley
12 Gould, Jonathan A.	Preston North End	Hereford United
26 Hand, Jamie	Watford	Oxford United
9 Harper, Kevin P.	Portsmouth	Leicester City
24 Harrad, Shaun N.	Notts County	Tamworth
29 Hawkins, Darren M.	Bristol City	Bath City
7 Howe, Edward J.	Portsmouth	AFC Bournemouth
10 Huke, Shane	Peterborough United	Cambridge City
10 Johnson, Simon A.	Leeds United	Sunderland
5 Keogh, Andrew D.	Leeds United	Scunthorpe United
4 Langmead, Kelvin S.	Preston North End	Kidderminster Harriers
10 Leacock, Dean	Fulham	Coventry City
17 Logan, Richard J.	Peterborough United	Shrewsbury Town
20 MacNamara, Niall A.	Lincoln City	Eastwood Town
13 Mansaram, Darren	Grimsby Town	Halifax Town
13 Masterson, Terence P.	Millwall	Weymouth
17 McGurk, David	Darlington	York City
4 McMahon, Stephen J.	Blackpool	Kidderminster Harriers
28 McMaster, Jamie	Leeds United	Swindon Town
18 McSheffrey, Gary	Coventry City	Luton Town
24 McStay, Henry M.P.	Leeds United	Halifax Town
18 Mills, Matthew C.	Southampton	Coventry City
3 Mitchell, Paul A.	Wigan Athletic	Swindon Town
10 Moore, David L.	Wigan Athletic	Stalybridge Celtic
28 Ndumbu-Nsungu, Guylain	Sheffield Wednesday	Preston North End
29 Nowland, Adam C.	West Ham United	Gillingham
3 O'Connor, James F.E.	Aston Villa	Port Vale
24 O'Grady, Christopher J.	Leicester City	Notts County
24 O'Neil, Gary P.	Portsmouth	Cardiff City
23 Ormerod, Brett R.	Southampton	Leeds United
30 Otsemobor, Jon	Liverpool	Crewe Alexandra
10 Pead, Craig G.	Coventry City	Notts County
10 Pouton, Alan	Gillingham	Hartlepool United
10 Powell, Christopher G.	Charlton Athletic	West Ham United
11 Price, Jamie B.	Doncaster Rovers	Burton Albion
10 Pullen, James D.C.	Peterborough United	Hornchurch
3 Rachubka, Paul S.	Charlton Athletic	Northampton Town
22 Reilly, Philip B.	Stockport County	Bradford Park Avenue
4 Rickards, Scott	Kidderminster Harriers	Redditch United

17 Roberts, Neil W.	Wigan Athletic	Bradford City
4 Robinson, Paul	Tranmere Rovers	Grimsby Town
2 Savage, Basir M.	Reading	Wycombe Wanderers
30 Simpson, Sekani	Bristol City	Tamworth
10 Sofiane, Youssef	West Ham United	Notts County
10 Spicer, John W.	Arsenal	AFC Bournemouth
11 Steele, Luke D.	Manchester United	Coventry City
17 Symes, Michael	Bradford City	Darlington
25 Talbot, Jason C.	Bolton Wanderers	Derby County
30 Townson, Kevin	Rochdale	Scarborough
7 Turner, Michael T.	Charlton Athletic	Brentford
10 Vernon, Scott M.	Oldham Athletic	Blackpool
20 Vieira, Magno S.	Wigan Athletic	Carlisle United
7 Vine, Rowan	Portsmouth	Luton Town
13 Wheeler, Kirk	Grimsby Town	Barrow
4 Williams, Christopher J.	Stockport County	Grimsby Town
23 Williams, Darren	Sunderland	Cardiff City
2 Wilson, Mark A.	Middlesbrough	Doncaster Rovers
25 Woodman, Craig A.	Bristol City	Mansfield Town
10 Woods, Martin P.	Leeds United	Hartlepool United

October 2004

22 Clark, Benjamin	Sunderland	Hartlepool United
12 Collins, Daniel L.	Chester City	Sunderland
22 Geary, Derek P.	Stockport County	Sheffield United
29 Healy, David J.	Preston North End	Leeds United
28 Hodgson, Richard J.	Crawley Town	Cambridge United
22 Morison, Steve	Northampton Town	Bishop's Stortford
22 Nicolas, Alexis	Chelsea	Brighton & Hove Albion
15 Roberts, Christian J.	Bristol City	Swindon Town
7 Roberts, Neil W.	Wigan Athletic	Doncaster Rovers

Temporary transfers

13 Adebola, Bamidele O.	Coventry City	Bradford City
22 Atieno, Taiwo L.	Walsall	Rochdale
25 Birchall, Adam S.	Arsenal	Wycombe Wanderers
29 Bossu, Bertrand	Gillingham	Oldham Athletic
20 Brock, Stuart A.	AFC Telford United	Hull City
14 Broughton, Drewe O.	Southend United	Rushden & Diamonds
29 Brown, Simon	West Bromwich Albion	Kidderminster Harriers
25 Campbell-Ryce, Jamal	Charlton Athletic	Chesterfield
25 Chopra, Rocky M.	Newcastle United	Barnsley
14 Clarke, Ryan A.	Boston United	King's Lynn
14 Clarke, Ryan J.	Bristol Rovers	Southend United
8 Clingan, Samuel G.	Wolverhampton Wanderers	Chesterfield
29 Constantine, Leon	Peterborough United	Torquay United
29 Cooper, Shaun D.	Portsmouth	Kidderminster Harriers
22 Craig, Tony A.	Millwall	Wycombe Wanderers
29 Cranie, Martin J.	Southampton	AFC Bournemouth
22 Curtis, John C.K.	Portsmouth	Preston North End
22 Daly, Jonathan M.	Stockport County	Grimsby Town
11 Danns, Neil A.	Blackburn Rovers	Colchester United
28 Dinning, Tony	Wigan Athletic	Bristol City
15 Dolan, Joseph	Millwall	Crawley Town
14 Donaldson, Clayton A.	Hull City	Harrogate Town
22 Doyle, Colin	Birmingham City	Chester City
15 Duberry, Michael W.	Leeds United	Stoke City
25 Duffy, Richard	Portsmouth	Burnley
4 Eastwood, Freddy	Grays Athletic	Southend United
7 Eyre, Nicholas	Tottenham Hotspur	Grays Athletic
11 Featherstone, Lee	Scunthorpe United	Barrow
17 Fontaine, Liam V.H.	Fulham	Yeovil Town
29 Foster, Benjamin	Stoke City	Kidderminster Harriers
7 Fox, David L.	Manchester United	Shrewsbury Town
7 Gleeson, Jamie	Kidderminster Harriers	Eastleigh
6 Goodfellow, Marc D.	Bristol City	Port Vale

12 Gould, Jonathan A.	Preston North End	Hereford United
25 Guimaraes, Sanabio J.L.	Derby County	Rotherham United
12 Harper, Kevin P.	Portsmouth	Leicester City
29 Hildred, Ashley	Grimsby Town	Northwich Victoria
15 Hockless, Graham	Grimsby Town	Leigh RMI
14 Howe, Edward J.	Portsmouth	AFC Bournemouth
29 Hunt, Jonathan	Scunthorpe United	Guiseley
14 Ibe, Kezie	Yeovil Town	Tiverton Town
15 Ikeme, Carl	Wolverhampton Wanderers	Accrington Stanley
16 Ipoua, Guy	Doncaster Rovers	Mansfield Town
29 Jenkins, Stephen R.	Peterborough United	Swindon Town
27 Johnson, Richard M.	Queens Park Rangers	Milton Keynes Dons
8 Johnson, Simon A.	Leeds United	Sunderland
4 Keogh, Andrew D.	Leeds United	Scunthorpe United
22 Kightly, Michael J.	Southend United	Farnborough Town
8 Langmead, Kelvin S.	Preston North End	Kidderminster Harriers
29 Laville, Florent	Bolton Wanderers	Coventry City
11 Leacock, Dean	Fulham	Coventry City
2 Loxton, Craig A.	Bristol City	Forest Green Rovers
6 Mansaram, Darren	Grimsby Town	Halifax Town
6 May, Ben S.	Millwall	Colchester United
22 McCormick, Luke M.	Plymouth Argyle	Boston United
6 McMahon, Stephen J.	Blackpool	Kidderminster Harriers
22 McStay, Henry M.P.	Leeds United	Halifax Town
1 Meadowcroft, Daniel B.	Stockport County	Mossley
4 Mitchell, Paul A.	Wigan Athletic	Swindon Town
22 Moore, David L.	Wigan Athletic	Bradford Park Avenue
13 Mulligan, Gary	Wolverhampton Wanderers	Rushden & Diamonds
8 Murphy, Joseph	West Bromwich Albion	Walsall
1 Murphy, Paul	Manchester City	Mossley
4 O'Connor, James F.E.	Aston Villa	Port Vale
28 O'Connor, James	West Bromwich Albion	Burnley
25 O'Grady, Christopher	Leicester City	Notts County
22 Otsemobor, John	Liverpool	Crewe Alexandra
13 Peat, Nathan N.M.	Hull City	Lincoln City
7 Powell, Christopher G.	Charlton Athletic	West Ham United
21 Pullen, James	Peterborough United	Welling United
9 Rachubka, Paul S.	Charlton Athletic	Northampton Town
15 Reed, Steven	Yeovil Town	Forest Green Rovers
15 Ricketts, Rohan A.	Tottenham Hotspur	Coventry City
1 Rifat, Ahmet	Reading	Kingstonian
30 Royce, Simon E.	Charlton Athletic	Luton Town
19 Simek, Franklin M.	Arsenal	Queens Park Rangers
31 Simpson, Sekani	Bristol City	Tamworth
1 Spicer, John W.	Arsenal	AFC Bournemouth
14 Staff, David S.	Boston United	King's Lynn
1 Stallard, Mark	Barnsley	Chesterfield
22 Talbot, Daniel	Rushden & Diamonds	Cambridge City
1 Tessem, Jo	Southampton	Millwall
22 Thomas, Bradley M.	Peterborough United	Welling United
22 Togwell, Samuel J.	Crystal Palace	Oxford United
22 Traynor, Greg	Wigan Athletic	Bradford Park Avenue
6 Turnbull, Ross	Middlesbrough	Barnsley
5 Turner, Michael T.	Charlton Athletic	Brentford
25 Veira, Magno S.	Wigan Athletic	Carlisle United
15 Weaver, Simon D.	Lincoln City	Macclesfield Town
22 Wheeler, Kirk	Grimsby Town	Ossett Town
29 Wilbraham, Aaron	Hull City	Oldham Athletic
24 Woodman, Craig A.	Bristol City	Mansfield Town
13 Woods, Martin P.	Leeds United	Hartlepool United
7 Young, Gregory J.	Grimsby Town	Northwich Victoria

November 2004

17 Agyemang, Patrick	Gillingham	Preston North End
26 Barker, Richard I.	Rotherham United	Mansfield Town
15 Beckett, Luke J.	Stockport County	Sheffield United

30 Campbell-Ryce, Jamal	Charlton Athletic	Rotherham United
19 Clare, Daryl A.	Chester City	Boston United
9 Dobie, Scott	West Bromwich Albion	Millwall
4 Eastwood, Freddie	Grays Athletic	Southend United
26 Lester, Jack	Sheffield United	Nottingham Forest
5 Lowndes, Nathan P.	Plymouth Argyle	Port Vale
15 Miller, Adam E.	Aldershot Town	Queens Park Rangers
5 Nowland, Adam C.	West Ham United	Nottingham Forest
12 Purser, Wayne M.	Hornchurch	Peterborough United
24 Sedgwick, Christopher E.	Rotherham United	Preston North End
4 Turner, Michael T.	Charlton Athletic	Brentford
23 Welsh, Andrew	Stockport County	Sunderland

Temporary transfers

5 Barnard, Lee J.	Tottenham Hotspur	Leyton Orient
20 Barnett, Leon P.	Luton Town	Aylesbury United
3 Bischoff, Mikkel	Manchester City	Wolverhampton Wanderers
18 Brisco, Neil A.	Rochdale	Northwich Victoria
11 Broughton, Drewe O.	Southend United	Rushden & Diamonds
8 Cahill, Gary J.	Aston Villa	Burnley
28 Campbell-Ryce, Jamal	Charlton Athletic	Rotherham United
19 Carruthers, Christopher P.	Northampton Town	Hornchurch
29 Chopra, Rocky M.	Newcastle United	Barnsley
12 Clarke, Ryan J.	Bristol Rovers	Kidderminster Harriers
8 Clingan, Samuel G.	Wolverhampton Wanderers	Chesterfield
20 Coghlan, Michael	Darlington	Bishop Auckland
4 Corbett, Luke J.	Cheltenham Town	Weston-Super-Mare
19 Craig, Tony A.	Millwall	Wycombe Wanderers
11 Croft, Lee	Manchester City	Oldham Athletic
5 Dixon, Jonathan J.	Wycombe Wanderers	Aldershot Town
15 Dolan, Joseph	Millwall	Crawley Town
12 Forde, Daniel	Oldham Athletic	Mossley
1 Gobern, Lewis T.	Wolverhampton Wanderers	Hartlepool United
5 Grant, Lee	Aston Villa	York City
23 Guimaraes, Sanabio J.L.	Derby County	Rotherham United
25 Haystead, Daniel	Sheffield United	Scarborough
19 Hicks, David	Northampton Town	Hornchurch
19 Hughes, Mark A.	Tottenham Hotspur	Oldham Athletic
15 Ibe, Kezie	Yeovil Town	Tiverton Town
1 Ingham, Michael	Sunderland	Doncaster Rovers
4 Jones, Bradley	Middlesbrough	Blackpool
26 Kaku, Blessing	Bolton Wanderers	Derby County
12 Keller, Kasey C.	Tottenham Hotspur	Southampton
18 Kerley, Adam	Lincoln City	Lincoln United
23 Kightly, Michael J.	Southend United	Farnborough Town
19 Kilkenny, Neil M.	Birmingham City	Oldham Athletic
26 Langmead, Kelvin S.	Preston North End	Shrewsbury Town
30 Laville, Florent	Bolton Wanderers	Coventry City
26 MacKenzie, Neil	Mansfield Town	Macclesfield Town
5 Marney, Dean E.	Tottenham Hotspur	Gillingham
11 McLachlan, Fraser	Stockport County	Mansfield Town
11 Mulligan, Gary	Wolverhampton Wanderers	Rushden & Diamonds
12 Nolan, Matthew L.	Peterborough United	St Albans City
11 Oakes, Andrew M.	Derby County	Bolton Wanderers
3 O'Connor, James F.E.	Aston Villa	Port Vale
29 O'Connor, James	West Bromwich Albion	Burnley
5 Oster, John	Sunderland	Leeds United
23 Otsemobor, John	Liverpool	Crewe Alexandra
12 Peters, Mark	Leyton Orient	Aldershot Town
4 Powell, Christopher G.	Charlton Athletic	West Ham United
19 Powell, Darren	Crystal Palace	West Ham United
19 Price, Lewis P.	Ipswich Town	Cambridge United
5 Rachubka, Paul S.	Charlton Athletic	Huddersfield Town
15 Reed, Steven	Yeovil Town	Forest Green Rovers
1 Rifat, Ahmet	Reading	Kingstonian

29 Simpson, Sekani	Bristol City	Tamworth
12 Smith, Andrew W.	Preston North End	Stockport County
11 Spicer, John W.	Arsenal	AFC Bournemouth
15 Staff, David S.	Boston United	Kings Lynn
7 Stallard, Mark	Barnsley	Chesterfield
5 Stamp, Darryn	Chester City	Kidderminster Harriers
19 Talbot, Jason C.	Bolton Wanderers	Mansfield Town
18 Taylor, Stuart J.	Arsenal	Leicester City
1 Tessem, Jo	Southampton	Millwall
8 Turnbull, Ross	Middlesbrough	Barnsley
11 Vieira, Magno S.	Wigan Athletic	Carlisle United
26 Warne, Paul	Rotherham United	Mansfield Town
5 Watson, Andrew	Chester City	Forest Green Rovers
11 Weaver, Simon D.	Lincoln City	Macclesfield Town
22 Wheeler, Kirk	Grimsby Town	Ossett Town
3 Yetton, Stewart D.	Plymouth Argyle	Weymouth
December 2004		
17 Anderson, Stuart	Southampton	Blackpool
10 Beardsley, Christopher K.	Doncaster Rovers	Kidderminster Harriers
14 Birch, Gary S.	Walsall	Kidderminster Harriers
6 Brown, Simon	West Bromwich Albion	Mansfield Town
24 Buxton, Lewis E.	Portsmouth	Stoke City
10 Constantine, Leon	Peterborough United	Torquay United
17 Cullip, Daniel	Brighton & Hove Albion	Sheffield United
10 Currie, Darren	Brighton & Hove Albion	Ipswich Town
24 Danns, Neil A.	Blackburn Rovers	Colchester United
16 Davies, Arron R.	Southampton	Yeovil Town
24 Gritton, Martin	Torquay United	Grimsby Town
30 Langmead, Kelvin S.	Preston North End	Shrewsbury Town
23 Lyng, Ciaran	Preston North End	Shrewsbury Town
24 McIntyre, Kevin	Chester City	Macclesfield Town
20 Morrison, John O.	Stockport County	Bradford City
17 Powell, Christopher G.	Charlton Athletic	West Ham United
24 Pulis, Anthony J.	Portsmouth	Stoke City
6 Rachubka, Paul S.	Charlton Athletic	Huddersfield Town
17 Spicer, John W.	Arsenal	AFC Bournemouth
30 Taylor, Scott J.	Blackpool	Plymouth Argyle
9 Weaver, Simon D.	Lincoln City	Kidderminster Harriers
9 Williams, Gavin J.	Yeovil Town	West Ham United
Temporary transfers		
16 Angus, Stevland D.	Cambridge United	Hull City
21 Arber, Mark A.	Oldham Athletic	Peterborough United
9 Ashton, Neil J.	Tranmere Rovers	Shrewsbury Town
10 Awuah, Jones	Gillingham	Worthing
8 Barnard, Lee J.	Tottenham Hotspur	Leyton Orient
16 Bayliss, David A.	Luton Town	Chester City
31 Benjamin, Trevor J.	Leicester City	Northampton Town
10 Bennett, Ian M.	Birmingham City	Sheffield United
17 Best, Leon J.	Southampton	Queens Park Rangers
31 Blake, Nathan A.	Leicester City	Leeds United
3 Braniff, Kevin	Millwall	Canvey Island
30 Branston, Guy	Sheffield Wednesday	Peterborough United
31 Brisco, Neil A.	Rochdale	Northwich Victoria
17 Broughton, Drewe O	Southend United	Wycombe Wanderers
24 Brown, Michael	Preston North End	Chester City
23 Bruce, Alex	Blackburn Rovers	Oldham Athletic
9 Burch, Robert K.	Tottenham Hotspur	West Ham United
2 Cahill, Gary J.	Aston Villa	Burnley
6 Chillingworth, Daniel T.	Cambridge United	Leyton Orient
3 Clarke, Ryan A.	Boston United	Leigh RMI
16 Clarke, Ryan J.	Bristol Rovers	Kidderminster Harriers
21 Coghlan, Michael	Darlington	Bishop Auckland
10 Cooke, Stephen L.	Aston Villa	Wycombe Wanderers
31 Corbett, Luke J.	Cheltenham Town	Bath City

20 Craig, Tony A.	Millwall	Wycombe Wanderers
12 Croft, Lee	Manchester City	Oldham Athletic
23 Danze, Anthony	Crystal Palace	Milton Keynes Dons
16 De Oliveira, Filipe V.	Chelsea	Preston North End
24 Derry, Shaun	Crystal Palace	Nottingham Forest
17 Dixon, Jonathan J.	Wycombe Wanderers	Aldershot Town
20 Dolan, Joseph	Millwall	Crawley Town
24 Doyle, Colin	Birmingham City	Nottingham Forest
31 Ellegaard, Kevin S.	Manchester City	Blackpool
10 Gallacher, Paul	Norwich City	Gillingham
22 Graham, Luke	Northampton Town	Aylesbury United
5 Grant, Lee	Aston Villa	York City
27 Hamilton, Lewis E.	Queens Park Rangers	Kingstonian
17 Hanlon, Ritchie K.	Stevenage Borough	Lincoln City
18 Harrold, Matthew	Brentford	Dagenham & Redbridge
22 Haystead, Daniel	Sheffield United	Scarborough
26 Hearn, Charles R.	Millwall	Northampton Town
6 Heath, Colin	Manchester United	Cambridge United
3 Henderson, Wayne	Aston Villa	Notts County
16 Hillier, Ian M.	Luton Town	Chester City
22 Holmes, Lee D.	Derby County	Swindon Town
18 Hughes, Mark A.	Tottenham Hotspur	Oldham Athletic
24 Ibe, Kezie	Yeovil Town	Exeter City
23 Jackson, Johnnie	Tottenham Hotspur	Watford
30 James, Kevin E.	Nottingham Forest	Boston United
6 Johnson, Simon A.	Leeds United	Doncaster Rovers
17 Jones, Kenwyne J.	Southampton	Sheffield Wednesday
24 Jones, Paul S.	Wolverhampton Wanderers	Watford
21 Karbassiyon, Daniel	Arsenal	Ipswich Town
31 Kempson, Darren	Preston North End	Morecambe
24 Kightly, Michael J.	Southend United	Farnborough Town
30 Kilkenny, Neil M.	Birmingham City	Oldham Athletic
24 Livesey, Daniel	Bolton Wanderers	Carlisle United
3 Loran, Tyrone	Tranmere Rovers	Port Vale
16 Lynch, Simon	Preston North End	Blackpool
31 Maloney, Jonathan	Doncaster Rovers	York City
3 May, Ben S.	Millwall	Brentford
16 McCammon, Mark J.	Millwall	Brighton & Hove Albion
12 McLachlan, Fraser	Stockport County	Mansfield Town
23 McShane, Paul D.	Manchester United	Walsall
9 Mitchell, Paul A.	Wigan Athletic	Milton Keynes Dons
10 Morrison, John O.	Stockport County	Bradford City
13 Mulligan, Gary	Wolverhampton Wanderers	Rushden & Diamonds
17 Mullins, John	Reading	Kidderminster Harriers
31 Murphy, Joseph	West Bromwich Albion	Walsall
21 Nacca, Francesco	Cambridge United	Histon
17 Navarro, Alan E.	Tranmere Rovers	Macclesfield Town
3 O'Brien, Joseph M.	Bolton Wanderers	Sheffield Wednesday
3 O'Brien, Roy	Yeovil Town	Weymouth
31 O'Donoghue, Paul M.	Tottenham Hotspur	Hornchurch
6 Oster, John	Sunderland	Leeds United
10 Pearson, Gregory	West Ham United	Canvey Island
19 Price, Lewis P.	Ipswich Town	Cambridge United
24 Pulis, Anthony J.	Stoke City	Torquay United
23 Robinson, Paul M.J.	Millwall	Torquay United
31 Slabber, Jamie	Tottenham Hotspur	Swindon Town
3 Somner, Matthew J.	Brentford	Cambridge United
13 Steele, Luke	Manchester United	Coventry City
10 Strong, Greg	Boston United	Macclesfield Town
17 Taylor, Kris	Walsall	Burton Albion
18 Taylor, Stuart J.	Arsenal	Leicester City
31 Teggart, Neil	Sunderland	Scunthorpe United
10 Tierney, Marc	Oldham Athletic	Carlisle United
21 Tierney, Paul T.	Manchester United	Bradford City
3 Tomlinson, Stuart C.	Crewe Alexandra	Stafford Rangers

29 Ward, Elliott L.	West Ham United	Bristol Rovers
23 Warne, Paul	Rotherham United	Mansfield Town
6 Watson, Andrew	Chester City	Forest Green Rovers
31 Westcarr, Craig N.	Nottingham Forest	Lincoln City
22 Wheeler, Kirk	Grimsby Town	Ossett Town
10 Williams, Ryan N.	Bristol Rovers	Forest Green Rovers
6 Woodman, Craig A.	Bristol City	Torquay United
2 Young, Gregory J.	Grimsby Town	Northwich Victoria

January 2005

11 Ashton, Dean	Crewe Alexandra	Norwich City
1 Babayaro, Celestine	Chelsea	Newcastle United
5 Beattie, James S.	Southampton	Everton
5 Blake, Robert J.	Burnley	Birmingham City
26 Bruce, Alex	Blackburn Rovers	Birmingham City
21 Carson, Scott P.	Leeds United	Liverpool
31 Chaplow, Richard D.	Burnley	West Bromwich Albion
31 Dawson, Michael R.	Nottingham Forest	Tottenham Hotspur
31 Djemba-Djemba, Eric D.	Manchester United	Aston Villa
12 Ellison, Kevin	Chester City	Hull City
25 Faye, Amdy M.	Portsmouth	Newcastle United
10 Hill, Matthew C.	Bristol City	Preston North End
25 Jelleyman, Gareth A.	Peterborough United	Mansfield Town
25 Livesey, Daniel	Bolton Wanderers	Carlisle United
21 Mansaram, Darren	Grimsby Town	Halifax Town
14 McGrath, John M.	Doncaster Rovers	Kidderminster Harriers
7 McLachlan, Fraser	Stockport County	Mansfield Town
13 Morley, David T.	Doncaster Rovers	Macclesfield Town
11 Nugent, David J.	Bury	Preston North End
13 Platt, Clive L.	Peterborough United	Milton Keynes Dons
20 Quashie, Nigel F.	Portsmouth	Southampton
4 Redknapp, Jamie F.	Tottenham Hotspur	Southampton
31 Reid, Andrew M.	Nottingham Forest	Tottenham Hotspur
19 Savage, Robert W.	Birmingham City	Blackburn Rovers
31 Stockdale, Robert K.	Rotherham United	Hull City
31 Stuart, Graham C.	Charlton Athletic	Norwich City
13 Swailes, Daniel	Bury	Macclesfield Town

Temporary transfers

15 Angus, Stevland D.	Cambridge United	Hull City
13 Anyinsah, Joseph G.	Bristol City	Hereford United
14 Bayliss, David A.	Luton Town	Chester City
14 Beckett, Luke J.	Sheffield United	Huddersfield Town
7 Blayney, Alan	Southampton	Rushden & Diamonds
26 Brisco, Neil A.	Rochdale	Northwich Victoria
27 Bruce, Alex	Birmingham City	Oldham Athletic
7 Burch, Robert K.	Tottenham Hotspur	Stevenage Borough
31 Camara, Henri	Wolverhampton Wanderers	Southampton
26 Carruthers, Christopher P.	Northampton Town	Kettering Town
28 Carruthers, Martin G.	Lincoln City	Cambridge United
13 Claridge, Stephen E.	Brentford	Wycombe Wanderers
13 Clarke, Darrell J.	Hartlepool United	Stockport County
7 Clarke, Ryan A.	Boston United	Leigh RMI
20 Constable, Robert A.	Leeds United	York City
28 Cooper, Kenneth S.	Manchester United	Oldham Athletic
17 Croft, Lee	Manchester City	Oldham Athletic
17 Crouch, Ross A.	Colchester United	Redbridge
4 Davenport, Calum R.P.	Tottenham Hotspur	Southampton
12 Davies, Andrew	Middlesbrough	Queens Park Rangers
24 Derry, Shaun	Crystal Palace	Nottingham Forest
18 Diao, Salif	Liverpool	Birmingham City
21 Dolan, Joseph	Millwall	Stockport County
14 Doughty, Philip M.	Blackpool	Leigh RMI
26 Duffy, Richard	Portsmouth	Coventry City
13 Duffy, Robert J.	Rushden & Diamonds	Stamford AFC
21 Eagles, Christopher M.	Manchester United	Watford

28 Elliot, Robert	Charlton Athletic	Notts County
27 Elokobi, George N.	Colchester United	Chester City
7 Featherstone, Lee	Scunthorpe United	Harrogate Town
21 Fitzgerald, John	Blackburn Rovers	Bury
14 Fitzgerald, Scott	Watford	Leyton Orient
28 Flitney, Ross	Fulham	Doncaster Rovers
28 Flynn, Liam D.	Bradford City	Guiseley
7 Folly, Yoann	Southampton	Nottingham Forest
24 Fowler, Jordan	Arsenal	Chesterfield
11 Gillespie, Steven	Bristol City	Cheltenham Town
5 Grant, Lee	Aston Villa	York City
25 Green, Adam	Fulham	Sheffield Wednesday
6 Griffit, Leandre	Southampton	Leeds United
21 Harrison, Paul A.	Liverpool	Leeds United
14 Hillier, Ian M.	Luton Town	Chester City
21 Holloway, Craig D.	Farnborough Town	Southend United
24 Holmes, Lee D.	Derby County	Swindon Town
24 Hughes, Mark A.	Tottenham Hotspur	Oldham Athletic
10 Ireland, Craig	Peterborough United	Bristol City
7 Jarrett, Jason L.	Wigan Athletic	Stoke City
21 Jelleyman, Gareth A.	Peterborough United	Mansfield Town
5 Johnson, Simon A.	Leeds United	Doncaster Rovers
26 Jones, Paul S.	Wolverhampton Wanderers	Watford
23 Karbassiyon, Daniel	Arsenal	Ipswich Town
14 Keogh, Andrew D.	Leeds United	Bury
6 Kozluk, Robert	Sheffield United	Preston North End
17 Lynch, Simon	Preston North End	Blackpool
10 Maloney, Jonathan	Doncaster Rovers	York City
13 Marshall, Shaun A.	Cambridge United	Stevenage Borough
5 May, Ben S.	Millwall	Brentford
27 McCafferty, Neil	Charlton Athletic	Rushden & Diamonds
28 McCammon, Mark J.	Millwall	Brighton & Hove Albion
21 McMaster, Jamie	Leeds United	Peterborough United
20 Mirza, Nicolas	Yeovil Town	Weymouth
9 Mitchell, Paul A.	Wigan Athletic	Milton Keynes Dons
21 Moore, David L.	Wigan Athletic	Bury
17 Navarro, Alan E.	Tranmere Rovers	Macclesfield Town
7 Neal, Christopher M.	Preston North End	Tamworth
28 Negouai, Christian	Manchester City	Coventry City
21 Newey, Thomas	Leyton Orient	Cambridge United
4 O'Brien, Joseph M.	Bolton Wanderers	Sheffield Wednesday
4 O'Brien, Roy	Yeovil Town	Weymouth
27 O'Neill, Joseph	Preston North End	Chester City
31 Pennant, Jermaine	Arsenal	Birmingham City
28 Rapley, Kevin J.	Chester City	Forest Green Rovers
21 Rawle, Mark A.	Oxford United	Tamworth
7 Rea, Simon	Peterborough United	Cambridge United
31 Richardson, Kieran E.	Manchester United	West Bromwich Albion
23 Robinson, Paul M.J.	Millwall	Torquay United
13 Royce, Simon E.	Charlton Athletic	Queens Park Rangers
21 Sharp, William	Sheffield United	Rushden & Diamonds
5 Somner, Matthew J.	Brentford	Cambridge United
28 Surman, Andrew R.	Southampton	Walsall
14 Taylor, Kris	Walsall	Burton Albion
5 Thomas, Bradley M.	Peterborough United	Weymouth
5 Tierney, Marc	Oldham Athletic	Carlisle United
4 Tomlinson, Stuart C.	Crewe Alexandra	Stafford Rangers
21 Watkins, Robert J.	Fulham	Crawley Town
11 Williams, Ryan N.	Bristol Rovers	Forest Green Rovers
28 Yelldell, David R.	Blackburn Rovers	Brighton & Hove Albion
2 Young, Gregory J.	Grimsby Town	Northwich Victoria

February 2005

24 Akinbiyi, Adeola P.	Stoke City	Burnley
23 Beevers, Lee J.	Boston United	Lincoln City
16 Benjamin, Trevor J.	Northampton Town	Coventry City

18 Branston, Guy	Sheffield Wednesday	Oldham Athletic
9 Chadwick, Nicholas E.	Everton	Plymouth Argyle
10 Claridge, Stephen E.	Brentford	Wycombe Wanderers
11 Daly, Jonathan M.	Stockport County	Hartlepool United
18 Derry, Shaun	Crystal Palace	Leeds United
25 Dobie, Scott	Millwall	Nottingham Forest
28 Fagan, Craig	Colchester United	Hull City
3 Flynn, Michael J.	Wigan Athletic	Gillingham
14 Friio, David	Plymouth Argyle	Nottingham Forest
21 Hall, Marcus T.J.	Stoke City	Coventry City
2 Harper, Kevin P.	Portsmouth	Stoke City
23 Holmes, Derek	AFC Bournemouth	Carlisle United
15 Hughes, Mark A.	Tottenham Hotspur	Oldham Athletic
18 Jackson, Mark G.	Scunthorpe United	Kidderminster Harriers
14 Keogh, Andrew D.	Leeds United	Scunthorpe United
17 Lambert, Rickie L.	Stockport County	Rochdale
1 MacKenzie, Neil	Mansfield Town	Macclesfield Town
16 Makin, Christopher	Leicester City	Derby County
4 McCammon, Mark J.	Millwall	Brighton & Hove Albion
3 Rocastle, Craig A.	Chelsea	Sheffield Wednesday
2 Thomas, Bradley M.	Peterborough United	Weymouth
Temporary transfers		
3 Amankwaah, Kevin	Bristol City	Yeovil Town
1 Angus, Stevland D.	Cambridge United	Scunthorpe United
1 Atieno, Taiwo L.	Walsall	Chester City
3 Barnes, Philip K.	Sheffield United	Torquay United
14 Beckett, Luke J.	Sheffield United	Huddersfield Town
21 Beevers, Lee J.	Boston United	Lincoln City
17 Bennett, Ian M.	Birmingham City	Coventry City
11 Bermingham, Karl	Manchester City	Lincoln City
1 Blackstock, Dexter A.T.	Southampton	Plymouth Argyle
25 Bridge-Wilkinson, Marc	Stockport County	Bradford City
2 Clark, Christopher J.	Portsmouth	Stoke City
4 Clarke, Ryan A.	Boston United	Leigh RMI
4 Coulson, Mark D.	Peterborough United	Dunstable Town
15 Crow, Daniel	Norwich City	Northampton Town
21 Day, Christopher N.	Queens Park Rangers	Preston North End
20 Dolan, Joseph	Millwall	Stockport County
26 Facey, Delroy M.	Hull City	Huddersfield Town
22 Fallon, Rory	Swindon Town	Yeovil Town
22 Fitzgerald, John	Blackburn Rovers	Bury
24 Folkes, Peter A.	Lincoln City	Stamford AFC
27 Fowler, Jordan	Arsenal	Chesterfield
18 Foy, Robert A.	Liverpool	Chester City
26 Gillespie, Steven	Bristol City	Cheltenham Town
25 Graham, Luke	Northampton Town	Kettering Town
3 Gray, Michael	Blackburn Rovers	Leeds United
8 Harkins, Gary	Blackburn Rovers	Bury
18 Harris, Andrew D.D.	Chester City	Forest Green Rovers
15 Healy, Joe B.	Millwall	Crawley Town
1 Hessenthaler, Andrew	Gillingham	Hull City
24 Holmes, Lee D.	Derby County	Swindon Town
8 Hulse, Robert W.	West Bromwich Albion	Leeds United
18 Hurst, Kevan	Sheffield United	Stockport County
25 Ibe, Kezi	Yeovil Town	Weymouth
11 Ipoua, Guy	Doncaster Rovers	Lincoln City
7 Ireland, Craig	Peterborough United	Bristol City
1 Jackson, Johnnie	Tottenham Hotspur	Watford
4 Jackson, Nathan	Walsall	Bromsgrove Rovers
24 Johnson, Simon A.	Leeds United	Barnsley
14 Jones, Kenwyne J.	Southampton	Stoke City
3 Kempson, Darren	Preston North End	Morecambe
19 Kerley, Adam	Lincoln City	Spalding United
21 Lynch, Simon	Preston North End	Blackpool
24 Mackie, James	Milton Keynes Dons	Havant & Waterlooville

28 Maloney, Jonathan	Doncaster Rovers	York City
8 May, Ben S.	Millwall	Brentford
28 McCafferty, Neil	Charlton Athletic	Rushden & Diamonds
25 McHale, Christopher M.J.	Kidderminster Harriers	Redditch United
9 Melville, Andrew R.	West Ham United	Nottingham Forest
21 Mills, Matthew C.	Southampton	AFC Bournemouth
21 Mirza, Nicolas	Yeovil Town	Weymouth
10 Mitchell, Paul A.	Wigan Athletic	Milton Keynes Dons
21 Moore, David L.	Wigan Athletic	Bury
7 Neal, Christopher M.	Preston North End	Tamworth
24 Newey, Thomas	Leyton Orient	Cambridge United
3 Noble, Stuart W.	Fulham	Northampton Town
11 O'Brien, Joseph M.	Bolton Wanderers	Sheffield Wednesday
18 O'Connor, James F.E.	Aston Villa	AFC Bournemouth
21 O'Neill, Matthew	Burnley	Accrington Stanley
7 Paxton, Andrew	Scunthorpe United	Stalybridge Celtic
22 Pratley, Darren	Fulham	Brentford
21 Proctor, Michael A.	Rotherham United	Swindon Town
17 Richardson, Marcus G.	Lincoln City	Rochdale
22 Ricketts, Michael B.	Leeds United	Stoke City
24 Robinson, Jake D.	Brighton & Hove Albion	Aldershot Town
18 Roma, Dominic	Sheffield United	Boston United
14 Royce, Simon E.	Charlton Athletic	Queens Park Rangers
11 Savage, Basir M.	Reading	Bury
15 Scowcroft, James B.	Leicester City	Ipswich Town
19 Shakes, Ricky U.	Bolton Wanderers	Bristol Rovers
20 Sharp, William	Sheffield United	Rushden & Diamonds
18 Shearer, Scott	Coventry City	Rushden & Diamonds
18 Singh, Harpal	Leeds United	Stockport County
28 Soares, Louie P.	Reading	Tamworth
22 Sonner, Daniel J.	Peterborough United	Port Vale
4 Stallard, Mark	Barnsley	Notts County
3 Tierney, Marc	Oldham Athletic	Carlisle United
18 Tomlinson, Stuart C.	Crewe Alexandra	Stafford Rangers
3 Unsworth, David G.	Portsmouth	Ipswich Town
1 Walters, Jonathan R.	Hull City	Scunthorpe United
14 Whittingham, Peter	Aston Villa	Burnley
18 Wiseman, Scott N.K.	Hull City	Boston United

March 2005

9 Adams, Stephen	Plymouth Argyle	Sheffield Wednesday
24 Amankwaah, Kevin	Bristol City	Yeovil Town
11 Asamoah, Derek	Mansfield Town	Lincoln City
24 Deane, Brian C.	Leeds United	Sunderland
3 Duberry, Michael W.	Leeds United	Stoke City
15 Easter, Jermaine	Cambridge United	Boston United
24 Feeney, Warren J.	Stockport County	Luton Town
29 Fitzgerald, Scott	Watford	Brentford
18 Guttridge, Luke	Cambridge United	Southend United
23 Hunt, David	Leyton Orient	Northampton Town
24 Keane, Michael	Hull City	Rotherham United
2 Keith, Marino	Plymouth Argyle	Colchester United
11 Kirk, Andrew R.	Boston United	Northampton Town
3 McCarthy, Patrick	Manchester City	Leicester City
11 McMaster, Jamie	Leeds United	Chesterfield
24 Moore, Ian R.	Burnley	Leeds United
2 Moss, Darren M.	Shrewsbury Town	Crewe Alexandra
23 Murray, Adam D.	Mansfield Town	Carlisle United
23 Nash, Carlo J.	Middlesbrough	Preston North End
11 Newey, Thomas	Leyton Orient	Cambridge United
11 Newton, Shaun O.	Wolverhampton Wanderers	West Ham United
24 O'Connor, James	West Bromwich Albion	Burnley
24 O'Connor, James F.E.	Aston Villa	AFC Bournemouth
24 Perpetuini, David P.	Wycombe Wanderers	Walsall
24 Robinson, Marvin L. St.C	Walsall	Stockport County

29 Singh, Harpal	Leeds United	Stockport County
23 Sodje, Efteobore	Huddersfield Town	Yeovil Town
18 Sturridge, Dean	Wolverhampton Wanderers	Queens Park Rangers
18 Zadkovich, Ruben A.	Queens Park Rangers	Notts County
Temporary transfers		
6 Amankwaah, Kevin	Bristol City	Yeovil Town
6 Angus, Stevland D.	Cambridge United	Scunthorpe United
4 Barnard, Lee J.	Tottenham Hotspur	Northampton Town
24 Barrett, Graham	Coventry City	Sheffield Wednesday
4 Barrowman, Andrew	Birmingham City	Mansfield Town
24 Bates, Matthew D.	Middlesbrough	Darlington
18 Beckett, Luke J.	Sheffield United	Oldham Athletic
4 Beckwith, Robert	Luton Town	Rugby United
24 Bischoff, Mikkel	Manchester City	Wolverhampton Wanderers
6 Blackstock, Dexter A.T.	Southampton	Plymouth Argyle
24 Blayney, Alan	Southampton	Brighton & Hove Albion
16 Blewitt, Darren L.	West Ham United	Southend United
24 Boshell, Daniel	Oldham Athletic	Bury
9 Bowditch, Dean	Ipswich Town	Burnley
11 Bramble, Tesfaye	Southend United	Cambridge United
8 Briscoe, Michael J.	Macclesfield Town	Burton Albion
22 Brown, Aaron	Queens Park Rangers	Torquay United
10 Bruce, Alex	Birmingham City	Sheffield Wednesday
24 Carruthers, Christopher P.	Northampton Town	Bristol Rovers
7 Cooper, Kenneth S.	Manchester United	Oldham Athletic
24 Cornelly, Christopher	Lincoln City	Spalding United
2 Coulson, Mark D.	Peterborough United	Dunstable Town
31 Coyles, William A.	Leeds United	Carlisle United
18 Cronin, Lance	Crystal Palace	Wycombe Wanderers
22 Crow, Daniel	Norwich City	Northampton Town
24 Cullip, Daniel	Sheffield United	Watford
14 Davies, Andrew	Middlesbrough	Queens Park Rangers
23 Dinning, Tony	Bristol City	Port Vale
24 Dodd, Jason R.	Southampton	Plymouth Argyle
24 Dolan, Joseph	Millwall	Brighton & Hove Albion
27 Dolan, Joseph	Millwall	Stockport County
10 Dougals, Jonathan	Blackburn Rovers	Gillingham
22 Dyer, Lloyd	West Bromwich Albion	Coventry City
31 Elliot, Robert	Charlton Athletic	Notts County
22 Fitzgerald, John	Blackburn Rovers	Bury
4 Fitzgerald, Scott	Watford	Brentford
24 Flitney, Ross	Fulham	Yeading
14 Folly, Yoann	Southampton	Preston North End
21 Foy, Robert A.	Liverpool	Chester City
11 Fulop, Marton	Tottenham Hotspur	Chesterfield
18 Gallacher, Paul	Norwich City	Sheffield Wednesday
14 Garner, Darren	Rotherham United	Torquay United
24 Gerrard, Anthony	Everton	Walsall
23 Goater, Leonard S.	Reading	Coventry City
17 Goodfellow, Marc D.	Bristol City	Colchester United
28 Graham, Luke	Northampton Town	Kettering Town
11 Green, Adam	Fulham	AFC Bournemouth
11 Griffit, Leandre	Southampton	Rotherham United
31 Haldane, Lewis O.	Bristol Rovers	Forest Green Rovers
5 Hamilton, Lewis E.	Queens Park Rangers	AFC Wimbledon
22 Harris, Andrew D.D.	Chester City	Forest Green Rovers
4 Harrold, Matthew	Brentford	Grimsby Town
4 Hessenthaler, Andrew	Gillingham	Hull City
17 Hinds, Richard	Hull City	Scunthorpe United
24 Holloway, Craig D.	Farnborough Town	Southend United
18 Hurst, Kevan	Sheffield United	Stockport County
30 Ibe, Kezie	Yeovil Town	St Albans City
11 Impey, Andrew R.	Nottingham Forest	Millwall
4 Jackson, Ben	Doncaster Rovers	York City
6 Jackson, Johnnie	Tottenham Hotspur	Watford

24 Jarrett, Albert O.	Brighton & Hove Albion	Stevenage Borough
24 Jarvis, Ryan	Norwich City	Colchester United
24 Joachim, Julian K.	Leeds United	Walsall
10 Johnson, David A.	Nottingham Forest	Sheffield United
20 Jones, Kenwyne J.	Southampton	Stoke City
11 Keane, Michael	Hull City	Rotherham United
27 Keith, Joseph R.	Colchester United	Bristol City
3 Kenton, Darren E.	Southampton	Leicester City
24 Kerley, Adam	Lincoln City	Spalding United
4 King, Marlon F.	Nottingham Forest	Leeds United
3 Logan, Carlos S.	Manchester City	Chesterfield
30 McCafferty, Neil	Charlton Athletic	Rushden & Diamonds
24 McClenahan, Trent	West Ham United	Milton Keynes Dons
17 McCormack, Alan	Preston North End	Southend United
10 McEveley, James	Blackburn Rovers	Gillingham
28 McHale, Christopher M.J.	Kidderminster Harriers	Redditch United
4 McMaster, Jamie	Leeds United	Chesterfield
24 Miller, Kevin	Bristol Rovers	Derby County
21 Mills, Matthew C.	Southampton	AFC Bournemouth
11 Moore, Stefan	Aston Villa	Leicester City
24 Morgan, Alan	Blackburn Rovers	Cheltenham Town
18 Morgan, Daniel F.	Oxford United	Brackley Town
18 Nicholas, Andrew P.	Swindon Town	Chester City
20 O'Neill, Matthew	Burnley	Accrington Stanley
18 Ormerod, Brett R.	Southampton	Wigan Athletic
19 Owen, Gareth J.	Stoke City	Oldham Athletic
4 Parker, Terry J.	Oxford United	Farnborough Town
3 Parton, Andrew	Scunthorpe United	Stalybridge Celtic
23 Pead, Craig G.	Coventry City	Walsall
24 Perpetuini, David P.	Wycombe Wanderers	Walsall
25 Pratley, Darren	Fulham	Brentford
31 Rapley, Kevin J.	Chester City	Droylsden
24 Richards, Marc J.	Northampton Town	Rochdale
22 Ricketts, Michael B.	Leeds United	Stoke City
15 Ricketts, Rohan A.	Tottenham Hotspur	Wolverhampton Wanderers
1 Roberts, Iwan W.	Gillingham	Cambridge United
14 Royce, Simon E.	Charlton Athletic	Queens Park Rangers
24 Ryan, Richard	Sunderland	Scunthorpe United
11 Salisbury, James A.	Wigan Athletic	Halifax Town
24 Shakes, Ricky U.	Bolton Wanderers	Bury
21 Sharp, William	Sheffield United	Rushden & Diamonds
11 Shearer, Scott	Coventry City	Rushden & Diamonds
24 Simek, Franklin M.	Arsenal	AFC Bournemouth
24 Sobers, Jerome	Ipswich Town	Brentford
24 Sodje, Akpo	Huddersfield Town	Darlington
23 Sonner, Daniel J.	Peterborough United	Port Vale
4 Surman, Andrew R.	Southampton	Walsall
24 Taylor, Daryl S.	Walsall	Hereford United
14 Thorpe, Anthony L.	Queens Park Rangers	Rotherham United
24 Togwell, Samuel J.	Crystal Palace	Northampton Town
19 Toner, Ciaran	Lincoln City	Cambridge United
24 Townson, Kevin	Rochdale	Macclesfield Town
18 Turner, Iain R.	Everton	Doncaster Rovers
24 Ward, Graham W.	Cheltenham Town	Burton Albion
24 Webber, Daniel V.	Watford	Sheffield United
24 Westcarr, Craig N.	Nottingham Forest	Milton Keynes Dons
8 Wilkinson, Andrew G.	Stoke City	Shrewsbury Town
24 Williams, Leroy D.	Walsall	Hereford United
3 Williams, Mark S.	Milton Keynes Dons	Rushden & Diamonds
21 Woozley, David J.	Oxford United	Yeovil Town
April 2005		
27 Pennant, Jermaine	Arsenal	Birmingham City

Temporary transfers

1 Beckwith, Robert	Luton Town	Rugby United
10 Bowditch, Dean	Ipswich Town	Burnley
5 Cooney, Sean P.	Coventry City	Woking
10 Douglas, Jonathan	Blackburn Rovers	Gillingham
24 Flitney, Ross	Fulham	Yeading
18 Foy, Robert A.	Liverpool	Chester City
10 Fulop, Marton	Tottenham Hotspur	Chesterfield
14 Gallacher, Paul	Norwich City	Sheffield Wednesday
12 Garner, Darren	Rotherham United	Torquay United
13 Hinds, Richard	Hull City	Scunthorpe United
11 Horwood, Evan D.	Sheffield United	Stockport County
17 Hurst, Kevan	Sheffield United	Stockport County
4 Jackson, Ben	Doncaster Rovers	York City
25 Jarrett, Albert O.	Brighton & Hove Albion	Stevenage Borough
6 Kenton, Darren E.	Southampton	Leicester City
3 Logan, Carlos S.	Manchester City	Chesterfield
17 McCormack, Alan	Preston North End	Southend United
10 McEveley, James	Blackburn Rovers	Gillingham
26 Mills, Matthew C.	Southampton	AFC Bournemouth
21 Morgan, Alan W.	Blackburn Rovers	Cheltenham Town
1 O'Donoghue, Paul M.	Tottenham Hotspur	Heybridge Swifts
17 Ormerod, Brett R.	Southampton	Wigan Athletic
27 Owen, Gareth J.	Stoke City	Oldham Athletic
12 Ricketts, Rohan A.	Tottenham Hotspur	Wolverhampton Wanderers
3 Robinson, Jake D.	Brighton & Hove Albion	Aldershot Town
22 Ryan, Richard	Sunderland	Scunthorpe United
26 Simek, Franklin M.	Arsenal	AFC Bournemouth
21 Togwell, Samuel J.	Crystal Palace	Northampton Town
24 Vieira, Magno S.	Wigan Athletic	Carlisle United
5 Williams, Mark S.	Milton Keynes Dons	Rushden & Diamonds
24 Woozley, David J.	Oxford United	Yeovil Town

May 2005

11 Bailey, Matthew	Northwich Victoria	Crewe Alexandra
26 Davies, Simon	Tottenham Hotspur	Everton
24 Ifill, Paul E.	Millwall	Sheffield United
20 Ruddy, John T.G.	Cambridge United	Everton
31 Ward, Darren P.	Millwall	Crystal Palace
28 Woodhouse, Curtis	Peterborough United	Hull City

Temporary transfers

11 Blewitt, Darren L.	West Ham United	Southend United
5 Graham, Luke	Northampton Town	Kettering Town

FOREIGN TRANSFERS 2004–2005

June 2004	*From*	*To*
30 Albrechtsen, Martin	FC Copenhagen	West Bromwich Albion
8 Fulop, Marton	MTK	Tottenham Hotspur
July 2004		
19 Almunia, Manuel	Celta Vigo	Arsenal
6 Andersen, Stephan	AB Copenhagen	Charlton Athletic
30 Ben Haim, Tal	Maccabi Tel Aviv	Bolton Wanderers
9 Bisgaard, Morten	FC Copenhagen	Derby County
19 Cech, Petr	Rennes	Chelsea
16 Cisse, Djibril	Auxerre	Liverpool
16 Pedro Mendes	Porto	Tottenham Hotspur
16 De Pedro, Javi	Real Sociedad	Blackburn Rovers
13 De Vlieger, Geert	Willem II	Manchester City
30 Diop, Papa Bouba	Lens	Fulham
23 Drogba, Didier	Marseille	Chelsea
20 Paulo Ferreira	Porto	Chelsea
29 Josemi	Malaga	Liverpool
7 Heinze, Gabriel	Paris St Germain	Manchester United
28 Idiakez, Inigo	Rayo Vallecano	Derby County
14 Jaidi, Radhi	Esperance	Bolton Wanderers
20 Reiziger, Michael	Barcelona	Middlesbrough

22 Robben, Arjen	PSV Eindhoven	Chelsea
23 Rommedahl, Dennis	PSV Eindhoven	Charlton Athletic
30 Ricardo Carvalho	Porto	Chelsea
14 Speroni, Julian	Dundee	Crystal Palace
30 Tarachulski, Bartosz	Gornik Zabrze	Yeovil Town
5 Van Damme, Jelle	Ajax	Southampton
August 2004		
27 Xabi Alonso	Real Sociedad	Liverpool
13 Atouba, Timothee	Basle	Tottenham Hotspur
31 Nuno Morais	Penafiel	Chelsea
11 Berson, Mathieu	Nantes	Aston Villa
4 Bosnar, Eddy	Sturm Graz	Everton
31 Contra, Cosmin	Atletico Madrid	West Bromwich Albion
25 Defendi, Rodrigo	Cruzeiro	Tottenham Hotspur
11 Drobny, Vaclav	Strasbourg	Aston Villa
5 Edman, Erik	Heerenveen	Tottenham Hotspur
11 Flamini, Mathieu	Marseille	Arsenal
27 Luis Garcia	Barcelona	Liverpool
9 Gera, Zoltan	Ferencvaros	West Bromwich Albion
11 Guatelli, Andrea	Parma	Portsmouth
3 Helveg, Thomas	Internazionale	Norwich City
9 Hierro, Fernando	Al Rayyan	Bolton Wanderers
31 Jakobsson, Andreas	Brondby	Southampton
10 Jonson, Mattias	Brondby	Norwich City
13 Julio Cesar	Real Madrid	Bolton Wanderers
25 Kaku, Blessing	MS Ashdod	Bolton Wanderers
17 Kaviedes, Ivan	Barcelona (Guayaquil)	Crystal Palace
12 Kiraly, Gabor	Hertha Berlin	Crystal Palace
2 Kuszczak, Tomasz	Hertha Berlin	West Bromwich Albion
13 Naybet, Nourredine	La Coruna	Tottenham Hotspur
4 Nilsson, Mikael	Halmstad	Southampton
18 Nunez, Antonio	Real Madrid	Liverpool
14 Olofinjana, Seyi	Brann	Wolverhampton Wanderers
24 Pamarot, Noe	Nice	Tottenham Hotspur
27 Pedersen, Morten	Tromso	Blackburn Rovers
13 Silva, Edson	PSV Eindhoven	Tottenham Hotspur
10 Tiago	Benfica	Chelsea
6 Torghelle, Sandor	MTK	Crystal Palace
26 Waterreus, Ronald	PSV Eindhoven	Manchester City
31 Yahia, Alaeddine	Guingcamp	Southampton
31 Ziegler, Reto	Grasshoppers	Tottenham Hotspur
September 2004		
1 Kamara, Diomansy	Modena	Portsmouth
1 Seol, Ki-Hyeon	Anderlecht	Wolverhampton Wanderers
January 2005		
28 Mido	Roma	Tottenham Hotspur
31 Arteta, Mikel	Real Sociedad	Everton
4 Boumsong, Jean Alain	Rangers	Newcastle United
21 Buzsaky, Akos	Porto	Plymouth Argyle
31 Candela, Vincent	Roma	Bolton Wanderers
28 Cerny, Radek	Slavia Prague	Tottenham Hotspur
28 Chalkias, Konstantinos	Panathinaikos	Portsmouth
7 Eboue, Emmanuel	Beveren	Arsenal
1 Einarsson, Gylfi	Lillestrom	Leeds United
28 El Hamdaoui, Mounir	Excelsior	Tottenham Hotspur
28 Gudmundsson, Tryggvi	Hafnarfjordur	Stoke City
28 Haidong, Hao	Dalian Shide	Sheffield United
6 Hallfredsson, Emil	Hafnarfjordur	Tottenham Hotspur
6 Jarosik, Jiri	CSKA Moscow	Chelsea
13 Johansson, Andreas	Djurgaarden	Wigan Athletic
4 Kuqi, Njazi	Lahti	Birmingham City
6 Limbersky, David	Viktoria Plzen	Tottenham Hotspur
5 Mokoena, Aaron	Genk	Blackburn Rovers
13 Morientes, Fernando	Real Madrid	Liverpool
31 Musampa, Kiki	Atletico Madrid	Manchester City
31 Nafti, Mehdi	Santander	Birmingham City
10 Nelsen, Ryan	DC United	Blackburn Rovers
10 Pellegrino, Mauricio	Valencia	Liverpool
31 Plessis, Guillaume	Lens	Everton
31 Rodic, Aleksander	Gorica	Portsmouth
28 Skopelitis, Ioannis	Egaleo	Portsmouth

FA CUP REVIEW 2004–2005

As the only surviving major domestic cup competition still endowed with replays it is illogical that there is no provision for a replayed final. Thus for the first time in 133 years at the end of full-time and the extra period it was necessary to send Arsenal and Manchester United into the lottery of a penalty shoot-out.

Whether because of this reason or simply for the fact that the oldest cup competition in the world has now been reduced to the vagaries of spot kicks, there was more than the odd rumblings of discontent over this manner of deciding matches let alone finals.

That said after a goalless draw Arsenal who had had little or no attacking invention throughout 120 minutes won the game 5-4 on penalties. United who had missed several good opportunities to score during play must have felt poorly served by the fates. In statistical terms it was Arsenal's 10th title, just one behind United.

Quite naturally back in November when the surviving minnows were splashed into the first round proper pool, such thoughts did not exist. While Vauxhall Motors have become better known in the cup as have Thurrock, there were others like Coalville Town, Hornchurch and Alfreton Town of a less familiar nature at this level. Indeed Alfreton did well enough to hold Macclesfield Town to a draw before losing two late goals in the replay.

There were some surprises as expected. Exeter City took out Grimsby Town, Halifax Town disposed of Cambridge United convincingly as did Hinckley Athletic against Torquay United. Histon shook Shrewsbury Town recently restored to the Football League and Slough Town edged out Walsall. Yeading won an all-tiddlers clash against Halesowen.

Cambridge City who had beaten Leigh RMI in the first round then lost to MK Dons as the second round promised a few more upsets and saw Exeter send another recently repatriated League club Doncaster Rovers packing and Yeading winning comfortably at Slough. But the accolade went to Hinckley who showed their Sunday best by drawing with Brentford and only lost the replay 2-1.

On another occasion Oldham Athletic beating Premier neighbours Manchester City 1-0 would have been the chief talking point of the third round. But their outstanding performance was overshadowed by Exeter City hold Manchester United the holders to a goalless draw at Old Trafford in front of 67,551 spectators.

Out went Norwich City at West Ham United, Aston Villa at Sheffield United and Crystal Palace visiting Sunderland who thus revenged themselves for play-off failure the year before. Fulham needed a replay against Watford as did Blackburn Rovers over Cardiff City. And Yeading suffered no disgrace in losing 2-0 to Newcastle United. Then in a delayed tie, Burnley knocked out Liverpool 1-0. Arsenal managed to beat Stoke City 2-1.

Exeter put up an inspiring resistance to United in the replay and after recovering from an early Cristiano Ronaldo goal, kept United to just one other goal from Wayne Rooney three minutes from time.

Round four by comparison held fewer shocks. Manchester United with a Rooney double were relatively easy winners 3-0 over Middlesbrough and Arsenal broke Wolverhampton Wanderers' resolve with two late goals. Then shock horror there was room for three replays on a Saturday! Fulham needed extra time against Derby, then on the following day Sheffield United similarly accounted for West Ham United.

A last minute penalty earned Sheffield United a replay at ten-man Arsenal, Leicester City surprised Charlton Athletic 2-1 at The Valley with a Dion Dublin strike at the end and Brentford fought back from two down at Southampton to draw. The Sunday ties had struggling Nottingham Forest holding Tottenham Hotspur, Newcastle United ending Chelsea's hopes of a season foursome and Burnley goalless with Blackburn in round five.

The replays had Blackburn edging home, Spurs scoring three, Saints recovering and Arsenal needing penalties to go through to the sixth round. Arsenal won a difficult game at Bolton Wanderers with an early Freddie Ljungberg goal, Manchester United hit four at Southampton, Patrick Kluivert repeated his early goal strike against Spurs and a Paul Dickov penalty for Rovers dispensed with Leicester.

It was the Millennium Stadium which provided the semi-finals. A Robin Van Persie double helped Arsenal prise open Blackburn 3-0 and Manchester United had an equally satisfying 4-1 success over Newcastle. Goals which would become scarce enough in the final.

THE FA CUP 2004–2005

FIRST ROUND

Bristol C	(0) 1	Brentford	(1) 1
Port Vale	(0) 3	Kidderminster H	(1) 1
Southend U	(0) 0	Luton T	(3) 3
Aldershot T	(0) 4	Canvey Island	(0) 0
Alfreton T	(0) 1	Macclesfield T	(0) 1
Barnet	(0) 1	Bath C	(0) 2
Billericay T	(0) 0	Stevenage B	(0) 1
Blackpool	(1) 3	Tamworth	(0) 0
Boston U	(0) 5	Hornchurch	(1) 2
Bradford C	(0) 0	Rushden & D	(0) 1
Bristol R	(0) 1	Carlisle U	(0) 1
Bury	(4) 5	Vauxhall M	(0) 2
Cambridge C	(0) 2	Leigh RMI	(1) 1
Darlington	(1) 3	Yeovil T	(0) 3
Exeter C	(1) 1	Grimsby T	(0) 0
Forest Green R	(0) 1	Bournemouth	(1) 1
Halifax T	(1) 3	Cambridge U	(1) 1
Hartlepool U	(3) 3	Lincoln C	(0) 0
Hayes	(0) 0	Wrexham	(3) 4
Hinckley U	(1) 2	Torquay U	(0) 0
Histon	(1) 2	Shrewsbury T	(0) 0
Hull C	(1) 3	Morecambe	(1) 2
Leyton Orient	(2) 3	Dagenham & R	(0) 1
Mansfield T	(1) 1	Colchester U	(1) 1
Milton Keynes D	(0) 1	Lancaster C	(0) 0
Northampton T	(1) 1	Barnsley	(0) 0
Notts Co	(1) 2	Woking	(0) 0
Peterborough U	(1) 2	Tranmere R	(1) 1
Rochdale	(1) 2	Oxford U	(1) 1
Scunthorpe U	(1) 2	Chesterfield	(0) 0
Slough T	(1) 2	Walsall	(1) 1
Southport	(0) 1	Hereford U	(1) 3
Stafford R	(0) 0	Chester C	(1) 2
Stockport Co	(3) 3	Huddersfield T	(0) 1
Swindon T	(1) 4	Sheffield W	(0) 1
Tiverton T	(0) 1	Doncaster R	(2) 3
Wycombe W	(0) 1	Coalville T	(0) 0
Yeading	(2) 2	Halesowen T	(1) 1
Cheltenham T	(0) 1	Swansea C	(1) 3
Thurrock	(0) 0	Oldham Ath	(0) 1

FIRST ROUND REPLAYS

Carlisle U	(0) 1	Bristol R	(0) 0
(aet.)			
Colchester U	(2) 4	Mansfield T	(0) 1
Macclesfield T	(0) 2	Alfreton T	(0) 0
Yeovil T	(0) 1	Darlington	(0) 0
Bournemouth	(1) 3	Forest Green R	(0) 1
Brentford	(1) 1	Bristol C	(0) 1

(aet; Brentford won 4-3 on penalties.)

SECOND ROUND

Cambridge C	(0) 0	Milton Keynes D	(1) 1
Scunthorpe U	(1) 2	Wrexham	(0) 0
Blackpool	(0) 1	Port Vale	(0) 0

Bournemouth	(0) 2	Carlisle U	(0) 1
Exeter C	(1) 2	Doncaster R	(0) 1
Halifax T	(0) 1	Chester C	(1) 3
Hartlepool U	(2) 5	Aldershot T	(1) 1
Hereford U	(1) 2	Boston U	(1) 3
Histon	(0) 1	Yeovil T	(0) 3
Hull C	(3) 4	Macclesfield T	(0) 0
Northampton T	(1) 1	Bury	(0) 0
Oldham Ath	(2) 4	Leyton Orient	(0) 0
Peterborough U	(2) 2	Bath C	(0) 0
Rushden & D	(0) 2	Colchester U	(3) 5
Slough T	(1) 1	Yeading	(1) 3
Stevenage B	(0) 0	Rochdale	(0) 2
Stockport Co	(0) 0	Swansea C	(0) 0
Swindon T	(1) 1	Notts Co	(0) 1
Wycombe W	(0) 0	Luton T	(1) 3
Hinckley U	(0) 0	Brentford	(0) 0

SECOND ROUND REPLAYS

Brentford	(0) 2	Hinckley U	(0) 1
Swansea C	(0) 2	Stockport Co	(0) 1
Notts Co	(1) 2	Swindon T	(0) 0

THIRD ROUND

Birmingham C	(2) 3	Leeds U	(0) 0
Bournemouth	(1) 2	Chester C	(0) 1
Burnley	(0) 1	Liverpool	(0) 0
Cardiff C	(1) 1	Blackburn R	(1) 1
Charlton Ath	(2) 4	Rochdale	(0) 1
Chelsea	(1) 3	Scunthorpe U	(1) 1
Coventry C	(2) 3	Crewe Alex	(0) 0
Derby Co	(0) 2	Wigan Ath	(1) 1
Hartlepool U	(0) 0	Boston U	(0) 0
Hull C	(0) 0	Colchester U	(2) 2
Ipswich T	(0) 1	Bolton W	(0) 3
Leicester C	(1) 2	Blackpool	(1) 2
Luton T	(0) 0	Brentford	(0) 2
Manchester U	(0) 0	Exeter C	(0) 0
Milton Keynes D	(0) 0	Peterborough U	(1) 2
Northampton T	(1) 1	Southampton	(2) 3
Notts Co	(1) 1	Middlesbrough	(0) 2
Oldham Ath	(1) 1	Manchester C	(0) 0
Plymouth Arg	(1) 1	Everton	(2) 3
Portsmouth	(0) 1	Gillingham	(0) 0
Preston NE	(0) 0	WBA	(0) 2
QPR	(0) 0	Nottingham F	(2) 3
Reading	(0) 1	Swansea C	(1) 1
Rotherham U	(0) 0	Yeovil T	(0) 3
Sheffield U	(0) 3	Aston Villa	(0) 1
Sunderland	(1) 2	Crystal Palace	(1) 1
Tottenham H	(1) 2	Brighton & HA	(0) 1
Watford	(1) 1	Fulham	(1) 1
West Ham U	(0) 1	Norwich C	(0) 0
Wolverhampton W	(2) 2	Millwall	(0) 0
Arsenal	(0) 2	Stoke C	(1) 1
Yeading	(0) 0	Newcastle U	(0) 2

(at Loftus Road.)

THIRD ROUND REPLAYS

Blackpool	(0) 0	Leicester C	(1) 1
Blackburn R	(2) 3	Cardiff C	(1) 2
Boston U	(0) 0	Hartlepool U	(0) 1
Exeter C	(0) 0	Manchester U	(1) 2
Fulham	(1) 2	Watford	(0) 0
Swansea C	(0) 0	Reading	(0) 1
(aet.)			

FOURTH ROUND

Arsenal	(0) 2	Wolverhampton W	(0) 0
Blackburn R	(2) 3	Colchester U	(0) 0
Brentford	(0) 0	Hartlepool U	(0) 0
Burnley	(1) 2	Bournemouth	(0) 0
Charlton Ath	(1) 3	Yeovil T	(1) 2
Derby Co	(0) 1	Fulham	(0) 1
Everton	(2) 3	Sunderland	(0) 0
Manchester U	(1) 3	Middlesbrough	(0) 0
Newcastle U	(2) 3	Coventry C	(1) 1
Nottingham F	(1) 1	Peterborough U	(0) 0
Reading	(1) 1	Leicester C	(1) 2
Southampton	(0) 2	Portsmouth	(0) 1
WBA	(1) 1	Tottenham H	(1) 1
West Ham U	(1) 1	Sheffield U	(0) 1
Chelsea	(1) 2	Birmingham C	(0) 0
Oldham Ath	(0) 0	Bolton W	(1) 1

FOURTH ROUND REPLAYS

Fulham	(1) 4	Derby Co	(1) 2
(aet.)			
Hartlepool U	(0) 0	Brentford	(0) 1
Tottenham H	(1) 3	WBA	(1) 1
Sheffield U	(1) 1	West Ham U	(0) 1
(aet; Sheffield U won 3-1 on penalties.)			

FIFTH ROUND

Arsenal	(0) 1	Sheffield U	(0) 1
Bolton W	(1) 1	Fulham	(0) 0
Charlton Ath	(1) 1	Leicester C	(1) 2
Everton	(0) 0	Manchester U	(1) 2
Southampton	(2) 2	Brentford	(1) 2
Burnley	(0) 0	Blackburn R	(0) 0
Newcastle U	(1) 1	Chelsea	(0) 0
Tottenham H	(1) 1	Nottingham F	(0) 1

FIFTH ROUND REPLAYS

Blackburn R	(1) 2	Burnley	(1) 1
Brentford	(1) 1	Southampton	(1) 3
Sheffield U	(0) 0	Arsenal	(0) 0
(aet; Arsenal won 4-2 on penalties.)			
Nottingham F	(0) 0	Tottenham H	(0) 3

SIXTH ROUND

Bolton W	(0) 0	Arsenal	(1) 1
Southampton	(0) 0	Manchester U	(2) 4
Blackburn R	(0) 1	Leicester C	(0) 0
Newcastle U	(1) 1	Tottenham H	(0) 0

SEMI-FINALS

Arsenal	(1) 3	Blackburn R	(0) 0
Newcastle U	(0) 1	Manchester U	(2) 4

THE FA CUP FINAL

Saturday, 21 May 2005

(at Millennium Stadium, Cardiff, attendance 71,876)

Arsenal (0) 0 Manchester U (0) 0

Arsenal: Lehmann; Lauren, Cole, Vieira, Toure, Senderos, Fabregas (Van Persie), Silva, Reyes■, Bergkamp (Ljungberg), Pires (Edu).

Manchester U: Carroll; Brown, O'Shea (Fortune), Ferdinand, Keane, Silvestre, Fletcher (Giggs), Scholes, Van Nistelrooy, Rooney, Ronaldo.

aet; Arsenal won 5-4 on penalties: Van Nistelrooy scored; Lauren scored; Scholes saved; Ljungberg scored; Ronaldo scored; Van Persie scored; Rooney scored; Cole scored; Keane scored; Vieira scored.

Referee: R. Styles (Waterlooville).

■*Denotes player sent off.*

PAST FA CUP FINALS

Details of one goalscorer is not available in 1878.

1872	The Wanderers ....1 *Betts*	Royal Engineers 0
1873	The Wanderers ....2 *Kinnaird, Wollaston*	Oxford University 0
1874	Oxford University..................2 *Mackarness, Patton*	Royal Engineers 0
1875	Royal Engineers ....1 *Renny-Tailyour*	Old Etonians.......................................1* *Bonsor*
Replay	Royal Engineers ....2 *Renny-Tailyour, Stafford*	Old Etonians.......................................0
1876	The Wanderers ....1 *Edwards*	Old Etonians.......................................1* *Bonsor*
Replay	The Wanderers ....3 *Wollaston, Hughes 2*	Old Etonians.......................................0
1877	The Wanderers ....2 *Lindsay, Kenrick*	Oxford University ....1* *Kinnaird (og)*
1878	The Wanderers ....3 *Kenrick 2, Kinnaird*	Royal Engineers ....1 *Unknown*
1879	Old Etonians ....1 *Clerke*	Clapham Rovers..................................0
1880	Clapham Rovers ....1 *Lloyd-Jones*	Oxford University 0
1881	Old Carthusians.....................3 *Wyngard, Parry, Todd*	Old Etonians.......................................0
1882	Old Etonians ....1 *Anderson*	Blackburn Rovers................................0

1883	Blackburn Olympic	2	Old Etonians	1*
	Costley, Matthews		*Goodhart*	
1884	Blackburn Rovers	2	Queen's Park, Glasgow	1
	Sowerbutts, Forrest		*Christie*	
1885	Blackburn Rovers	2	Queen's Park, Glasgow	0
	Forrest, Brown			
1886	Blackburn Rovers	0	West Bromwich Albion	0
Replay	Blackburn Rovers	2	West Bromwich Albion	0
	Brown, Sowerbutts			
1887	Aston Villa	2	West Bromwich Albion	0
	Hunter, Hodgetts			
1888	West Bromwich Albion	2	Preston NE	1
	Woodhall, Bayliss		*Dewhurst*	
1889	Preston NE	3	Wolverhampton W	0
	Dewhurst, J. Ross, Thompson			
1890	Blackburn Rovers	6	Sheffield W	1
	Walton, John Southworth, Lofthouse, Townley 3		*Bennett*	
1891	Blackburn Rovers	3	Notts Co	1
	Dewar, John Southworth, Townley		*Oswald*	
1892	West Bromwich Albion	3	Aston Villa	0
	Geddes, Nicholls, Reynolds			
1893	Wolverhampton W	1	Everton	0
	Allen			
1894	Notts Co	4	Bolton W	1
	Watson, Logan 3		*Cassidy*	
1895	Aston Villa	1	West Bromwich Albion	0
	J. Devey			
1896	Sheffield W	2	Wolverhampton W	1
	Spiksley 2		*Black*	
1897	Aston Villa	3	Everton	2
	Campbell, Wheldon, Crabtree		*Boyle, Bell*	
1898	Nottingham F	3	Derby Co	1
	Cape 2, McPherson		*Bloomer*	
1899	Sheffield U	4	Derby Co	1
	Bennett, Beers, Almond, Priest		*Boag*	
1900	Bury	4	Southampton	0
	McLuckie 2, Wood, Plant			
1901	Tottenham H	2	Sheffield U	2
	Brown 2		*Bennett, Priest*	
Replay	Tottenham H	3	Sheffield U	1
	Cameron, Smith, Brown		*Priest*	
1902	Sheffield U	1	Southampton	1
	Common		*Wood*	
Replay	Sheffield U	2	Southampton	1
	Hedley, Barnes		*Brown*	
1903	Bury	6	Derby Co	0
	Ross, Sagar, Leeming 2, Wood, Plant			
1904	Manchester C	1	Bolton W	0
	Meredith			

Year	Winner		Runner-up	
1905	Aston Villa	2	Newcastle U	0
	Hampton 2			
1906	Everton	1	Newcastle U	0
	Young			
1907	Sheffield W	2	Everton	1
	Stewart, Simpson		*Sharp*	
1908	Wolverhampton W	3	Newcastle U	1
	Hunt, Hedley, Harrison		*Howey*	
1909	Manchester U	1	Bristol C	0
	A. Turnbull			
1910	Newcastle U	1	Barnsley	1
	Rutherford		*Tufnell*	
Replay	Newcastle U	2	Barnsley	0
	Shepherd 2 (1 pen)			
1911	Bradford C	0	Newcastle U	0
Replay	Bradford C	1	Newcastle U	0
	Speirs			
1912	Barnsley	0	West Bromwich Albion	0
Replay	Barnsley	1	West Bromwich Albion	0*
	Tufnell			
1913	Aston Villa	1	Sunderland	0
	Barber			
1914	Burnley	1	Liverpool	0
	Freeman			
1915	Sheffield U	3	Chelsea	0
	Simmons, Masterman, Kitchen			
1920	Aston Villa	1	Huddersfield T	0*
	Kirton			
1921	Tottenham H	1	Wolverhampton W	0
	Dimmock			
1922	Huddersfield T	1	Preston NE	0
	Smith (pen)			
1923	Bolton W	2	West Ham U	0
	Jack, J.R. Smith			
1924	Newcastle U	2	Aston Villa	0
	Harris, Seymour			
1925	Sheffield U	1	Cardiff C	0
	Tunstall			
1926	Bolton W	1	Manchester C	0
	Jack			
1927	Cardiff C	1	Arsenal	0
	Ferguson			
1928	Blackburn Rovers	3	Huddersfield T	1
	Roscamp 2, McLean		*A. Jackson*	
1929	Bolton W	2	Portsmouth	0
	Butler, Blackmore			
1930	Arsenal	2	Huddersfield T	0
	James, Lambert			
1931	West Bromwich Albion	2	Birmingham	1
	W.G. Richardson 2		*Bradford*	
1932	Newcastle U	2	Arsenal	1
	Allen 2		*John*	
1933	Everton	3	Manchester C	0
	Stein, Dean, Dunn			

1934	Manchester C ....2 *Tilson 2*	Portsmouth ....1 *Rutherford*
1935	Sheffield W ....4 *Rimmer 2, Palethorpe, Hooper*	West Bromwich Albion ....2 *Boyes, Sandford*
1936	Arsenal...................................1 *Drake*	Sheffield U..0
1937	Sunderland ....3 *Gurney, Carter, Burbanks*	Preston NE..1 *F. O'Donnell*
1938	Preston NE ....1 *Mutch (pen)*	Huddersfield T....................................0*
1939	Portsmouth ....4 *Parker 2, Barlow, Anderson*	Wolverhampton W..............................1 *Dorsett*
1946	Derby Co ....4 *H. Turner (og), Doherty, Stamps 2*	Charlton Ath.......................................1* *H. Turner*
1947	Charlton Ath ....1 *Duffy*	Burnley 0*
1948	Manchester U........................4 *Rowley 2, Pearson, Anderson*	Blackpool ....2 *Shimwell (pen), Mortensen*
1949	Wolverhampton W ....3 *Pye 2, Smyth,*	Leicester C ....1 *Griffiths*
1950	Arsenal..................................2 *Lewis 2*	Liverpool 0
1951	Newcastle U ....2 *Milburn 2*	Blackpool 0
1952	Newcastle U ....1 *G. Robledo*	Arsenal 0
1953	Blackpool..............................4 *Mortensen 3, Perry*	Bolton W ....3 *Lofthouse, Moir, Bell*
1954	West Bromwich Albion ....3 *Allen 2 (1 pen), Griffin*	Preston NE..2 *Morrison, Wayman*
1955	Newcastle U ....3 *Milburn, Mitchell, Hannah*	Manchester C.....................................1 *Johnstone*
1956	Manchester C ....3 *Hayes, Dyson, Johnstone*	Birmingham C.....................................1 *Kinsey*
1957	Aston Villa ....2 *McParland 2*	Manchester U ....1 *T. Taylor*
1958	Bolton W ....2 *Lofthouse 2*	Manchester U 0
1959	Nottingham F ....2 *Dwight, Wilson*	Luton T..1 *Pacey*
1960	Wolverhampton W ....3 *McGrath (og), Deeley 2*	Blackburn Rovers...............................0
1961	Tottenham H.........................2 *Smith, Dyson*	Leicester C 0
1962	Tottenham H.........................3 *Greaves, Smith, Blanchflower (pen)*	Burnley ....1 *Robson*
1963	Manchester U........................3 *Herd 2, Law*	Leicester C ....1 *Keyworth*

1964	West Ham U	3	Preston NE	2
	Sissons, Hurst, Boyce		*Holden, Dawson*	
1965	Liverpool	2	Leeds U	1*
	Hunt, St John		*Bremner*	
1966	Everton	3	Sheffield W	2
	Trebilcock 2, Temple		*McCalliog, Ford*	
1967	Tottenham H	2	Chelsea	1
	Robertson, Saul		*Tambling*	
1968	West Browmwich Albion	1	Everton	0*
	Astle			
1969	Manchester C	1	Leicester C	0
	Young			
1970	Chelsea	2	Leeds U	2*
	Houseman, Hutchinson		*Charlton, Jones*	
Replay	Chelsea	2	Leeds U	1*
	Osgood, Webb		*Jones*	
1971	Arsenal	2	Liverpool	1*
	Kelly, George		*Heighway*	
1972	Leeds U	1	Arsenal	0
	Clarke			
1973	Sunderland	1	Leeds U	0
	Porterfield			
1974	Liverpool	3	Newcastle	0
	Keegan 2, Heighway			
1975	West Ham U	2	Fulham	0
	A. Taylor 2			
1976	Southampton	1	Manchester U	0
	Stokes			
1977	Manchester U	2	Liverpool	1
	Pearson, J. Greenhoff		*Case*	
1978	Ipswich T	1	Arsenal	0
	Osborne			
1979	Arsenal	3	Manchester U	2
	Talbot, Stapleton, Sunderland		*McQueen, McIlroy*	
1980	West Ham U	1	Arsenal	0
	Brooking			
1981	Tottenham H	1	Manchester C	1*
	Hutchison (og)		*Hutchison*	
Replay	Totteham H	3	Manchester C	2
	Villa 2, Crooks		*MacKenzie, Reeves (pen)*	
1982	Tottenham H	1	QPR	1*
	Hoddle		*Fenwick*	
Replay	Tottenham H	1	QPR	0
	Hoddle (pen)			
1983	Manchester U	2	Brighton & HA	2*
	Stapleton, Wilkins		*Smith, Stevens*	
Replay	Manchester U	4	Brighton & HA	0
	Robson 2, Whiteside, Muhren (pen)			
1984	Everton	2	Watford	0
	Sharp, Gray			
1985	Manchester U	1	Everton	0*
	Whiteside			
1986	Liverpool	3	Everton	1
	Rush 2, Johnston		*Lineker*	

	Winner	Runner-up
1987	Coventry C ....3 *Bennett, Houchen, Mabbutt (og)*	Tottenham H......................................2* *C. Allen, Kilcline (og)*
1988	Wimbledon ....1 *Sanchez*	Liverpool 0
1989	Liverpool ....3 *Aldridge, Rush 2*	Everton ....2* *McCall 2*
1990	Manchester U........................3 *Robson, Hughes 2*	Crystal Palace ....3* *O'Reilly, Wright 2*
Replay	Manchester U........................1 *Martin*	Crystal Palace 0
1991	Tottenham H.........................2 *Stewart, Walker (og)*	Nottingham F.......................................1* *Pearce*
1992	Liverpool ....2 *Thomas, Rush*	Sunderland 0
1993	Arsenal..................................1 *Wright*	Sheffield W...1* *Hirst*
Replay	Arsenal..................................2 *Wright, Linighan*	Sheffield W...1* *Waddle*
1994	Manchester U........................4 *Cantona 2 (2 pens), Hughes, McClair*	Chelsea 0
1995	Everton ....1 *Rideout*	Manchester U 0
1996	Manchester U........................1 *Cantona*	Liverpool 0
1997	Chelsea..................................2 *Di Matteo, Newton*	Middlesbrough......................................0
1998	Arsenal..................................2 *Overmars, Anelka*	Newcastle U 0
1999	Manchester U........................2 *Sheringham, Scholes*	Newcastle U 0
2000	Chelsea..................................1 *Di Matteo*	Aston Villa..0
2001	Liverpool ....2 *Owen 2*	Arsenal ....1 *Ljungberg*
2002	Arsenal..................................2 *Parlour, Ljungberg*	Chelsea 0
2003	Arsenal..................................1 *Pires*	Southampton...0
2004	Manchester U........................3 *Ronaldo, Van Nistelrooy 2 (1 pen)*	Millwall 0
2005	Arsenal..................................0 *Arsenal won 5-4 on penalties*	Manchester U 0*

**After extra time*

SUMMARY OF FA CUP WINNERS SINCE 1872

Club	Wins
Manchester United	11
Arsenal	10
Tottenham Hotspur	8
Aston Villa	7
Blackburn Rovers	6
Liverpool	6
Newcastle United	6
Everton	5
The Wanderers	5
West Bromwich Albion	5
Bolton Wanderers	4
Manchester City	4
Sheffield United	4
Wolverhampton Wanderers	4
Chelsea	3
Sheffield Wednesday	3
West Ham United	3
Bury	2
Nottingham Forest	2
Old Etonians	2
Preston North End	2
Sunderland	2
Barnsley	1
Blackburn Olympic	1
Blackpool	1
Bradford City	1
Burnley	1
Cardiff City	1
Charlton Athletic	1
Clapham Rovers	1
Coventry City	1
Derby County	1
Huddersfield Town	1
Ipswich Town	1
Leeds United	1
Notts County	1
Old Carthusians	1
Oxford University	1
Portsmouth	1
Royal Engineers	1
Southampton	1
Wimbledon	1

APPEARANCES IN FA CUP FINAL

Club	Appearances
Arsenal	17
Manchester United	17
Newcastle United	13
Everton	12
Liverpool	12
Aston Villa	10
West Bromwich Albion	10
Tottenham Hotspur	9
Blackburn Rovers	8
Manchester City	8
Wolverhampton Wanderers	8
Bolton Wanderers	7
Chelsea	7
Preston North End	7
Old Etonians	6
Sheffield United	6
Sheffield Wednesday	6
Huddersfield Town	5
The Wanderers	5
Derby County	4
Leeds United	4
Leicester City	4
Oxford University	4
Royal Engineers	4
Southampton	4
Sunderland	4
West Ham United	4
Blackpool	3
Burnley	3
Nottingham Forest	3
Portsmouth	3
Barnsley	2
Birmingham City	2
Bury	2
Cardiff City	2
Charlton Athletic	2
Clapham Rovers	2
Notts County	2
Queen's Park (Glasgow)	2
Blackburn Olympic	1
Bradford City	1
Brighton & Hove Albion	1
Bristol City	1
Coventry City	1
Crystal Palace	1
Fulham	1
Ipswich Town	1
Luton Town	1
Middlesbrough	1
Millwall	1
Old Carthusians	1
Queen's Park Rangers	1
Watford	1
Wimbledon	1

CARLING CUP REVIEW 2004–2005

For his first trophy in England Jose Mourinho was able to take the Carling Cup with Chelsea, but Liverpool pushed them all the way from the early moments when the Blues found themselves a goal down to a blistering finish by John Arne Riise.

Moreover it took an own goal from Steven Gerrard of all people to put Chelsea level in the 79th minute and the need for extra time to settle matters. Two in five minutes from Didier Drogba and Mateja Kezman edged Chelsea into a 3-1 lead only for Antonio Nunez to reply it seemed seconds later for Liverpool and ensure a tense finale.

Such is the shortness of the League Cup season from late August to late February with no replays of course there is a fleeting nature about the competition. But one highlight of the first round was the splendid 30,115 attendance for the Yorkshire derby in which Leeds United beat Huddersfield Town 1-0. Boston United pulled off a smart 4-3 win over Luton Town in a delayed tie. Disappointingly there were only three other crowds of a five figure nature in the opening round.

With the non-European involved Premier League teams entering in the second round there were the usual gathering of giant-killers preying on the unsuspecting. Colchester United beat West Bromwich Albion 2-1 in extra time, Bournemouth knocked out Blackburn Rovers at Ewood Park on penalties after a thrilling 3-3 draw and Everton needed a shoot-out of their own to account for Bristol City.

However, Manchester City whacked Barnsley 7-1 and Tottenham Hotspur won 6-0 at Oldham Athletic to balance it somewhat.

The chief surprise in the third round saw Burnley beat Aston Villa 3-1, but the doubling up of Premier teams whittled the elite down further. Meanwhile Liverpool won 3-0 at Millwall and a Kezman goal was enough for Chelsea against West Ham United. And brought down to earth quickly enough were Bournemouth on the wrong end of a penalty shoot-out at Cardiff.

Thus into the bag for the fourth round went just a dozen Premiership teams and the draw either ensured another reduction in their numbers or a certainty that half of them would survive into the next stage. Arsenal were at home to Everton, Liverpool to Middlesbrough, Manchester United to Crystal Palace and Newcastle United to Crystal Palace.

Of the other ties Burnley were to entertain Tottenham, Cardiff City expected Portsmouth, Nottingham Forest were at home to Fulham and Southampton made the trip to Watford. An unfamiliar looking Arsenal defeated Everton 3-1, free-scoring Spurs were 3-0 winners at Burnley and Pompey had a couple of goals against Cardiff.

Liverpool were similar 2-0 winners against Boro as were United over Palace and Chelsea at Newcastle. Fulham won 4-2 at Forest which left the big shock at Vicarage Road where Watford destroyed the Saints 5-2 and started the visitors on the slide from which they did not recover.

So after all only Watford from the Football League had survived and found themselves paired with Portsmouth. Proving they were no one match wonders they completed a neat south coast double by beating Pompey just as convincingly 3-0.

Neighbours also had a chance of meeting when Fulham met Chelsea at Craven Cottage. A late Frank Lampard goal edged the Blues to a 2-1 victory. Despite both teams fielding elevens who would not be first choice in the Premiership, the meeting of Manchester United and Arsenal at Old Trafford drew a competition best of the season 67,103 with a David Bellion goal in under a minute settling the issue. For Spurs and Liverpool there was no score during full time and during the extra period a Jermain Defoe goal for Spurs was cancelled out when Florent Sinama-Pongolle levelled the score from the penalty spot. Liverpool won 4-3 in the shoot-out.

Watford's reward was to be linked with Liverpool, while Chelsea and Manchester United provided the other semi-final. Liverpool took a Gerrard lead while Chelsea had to be content with being held goalless at Stamford Bridge by Manchester United.

It was Gerrard again who divided the teams at Watford who had carried the banner for the Football League with credit, while a Damien Duff goal with five minutes remaining gave Chelsea a 2-1 win at Old Trafford with both teams listing players with a far more representative standard of their respective strengths.

CARLING CUP 2004–2005

FIRST ROUND

Rochdale	(2) 2	Wolverhampton W	(1) 4
Brighton & HA	(1) 1	Bristol R	(2) 2
Bury	(2) 2	Burnley	(2) 3
Colchester U	(1) 2	Cheltenham T	(0) 1
Crewe Alex	(4) 4	Blackpool	(0) 1
Darlington	(0) 0	Barnsley	(1) 2
Doncaster R	(1) 3	Port Vale	(1) 1
Gillingham	(0) 1	Northampton T	(2) 2
Grimsby T	(1) 1	Wigan Ath	(0) 0
Hartlepool U	(0) 2	Macclesfield T	(0) 1
Hull C	(1) 2	Wrexham	(2) 2
(aet; Wrexham won 3-1 on penalties.)			
Ipswich T	(0) 2	Brentford	(0) 0
Kidderminster H	(1) 1	Cardiff C	(1) 1
(aet; Cardiff C won 5-4 on penalties.)			
Leeds U	(1) 1	Huddersfield T	(0) 0
Leyton Orient	(1) 1	Bournemouth	(1) 3
Lincoln C	(0) 3	Derby Co	(1) 1
Oldham Ath	(0) 2	Stoke C	(1) 1
Peterborough U	(0) 0	Milton Keynes D	(0) 3
QPR	(1) 3	Swansea C	(0) 0
Rotherham U	(1) 2	Chesterfield	(1) 1
Rushden & D	(0) 0	Swindon T	(0) 1
Sheffield U	(1) 4	Stockport Co	(1) 1
(aet.)			
Sunderland	(1) 3	Chester C	(0) 0
Tranmere R	(0) 2	Shrewsbury T	(0) 1
Watford	(0) 1	Cambridge U	(0) 0
West Ham U	(1) 2	Southend U	(0) 0
Wycombe W	(0) 0	Bristol C	(0) 1
Yeovil T	(1) 3	Plymouth Arg	(2) 2
(aet.)			
Bradford C	(1) 1	Notts Co	(0) 2
(aet.)			
Coventry C	(0) 4	Torquay U	(0) 1
Nottingham F	(1) 2	Scunthorpe U	(0) 0
Oxford U	(0) 0	Reading	(0) 2
Sheffield W	(1) 1	Walsall	(0) 0
Boston U	(1) 4	Luton T	(0) 3
(aet.)			
Mansfield T	(0) 0	Preston NE	(3) 4

SECOND ROUND

Birmingham C	(0) 3	Lincoln C	(0) 1
Burnley	(0) 1	Wolverhampton W	(1) 1
(aet; Burnley won 4-2 on penalties.)			
Colchester U	(1) 2	WBA	(0) 1
(aet.)			
Crewe Alex	(1) 3	Sunderland	(1) 3
(aet; Crewe Alex won 4-2 on penalties.)			
Crystal Palace	(0) 2	Hartlepool U	(0) 1
(aet.)			
Doncaster R	(1) 2	Ipswich T	(0) 0
Grimsby T	(0) 0	Charlton Ath	(1) 2
Leeds U	(1) 1	Swindon T	(0) 0

Manchester C	(5) 7	Barnsley	(0) 1
Milton Keynes D	(0) 1	Cardiff C	(3) 4
Norwich C	(1) 1	Bristol R	(0) 0
Reading	(0) 0	Watford	(1) 3
Tranmere R	(0) 0	Portsmouth	(0) 1
West Ham U	(1) 3	Notts Co	(1) 2
Wrexham	(2) 2	Sheffield U	(1) 3
Yeovil T	(0) 0	Bolton W	(0) 2
Aston Villa	(2) 3	QPR	(0) 1
Blackburn R	(1) 3	Bournemouth	(1) 3
(aet; Bournemouth won 7-6 on penalties.)			
Boston U	(0) 1	Fulham	(3) 4
Bristol C	(0) 2	Everton	(2) 2
(aet; Everton won 4-3 on penalties.)			
Coventry C	(1) 1	Sheffield W	(0) 0
Northampton T	(0) 0	Southampton	(2) 3
Nottingham F	(1) 2	Rotherham U	(1) 1
(aet.)			
Oldham Ath	(0) 0	Tottenham H	(1) 6
Leicester C	(0) 2	Preston NE	(1) 3
(aet.)			

THIRD ROUND

Bournemouth	(1) 3	Cardiff C	(1) 3
(aet; Cardiff C won 5-4 on penalties.)			
Burnley	(1) 3	Aston Villa	(0) 1
Crewe Alex	(0) 0	Manchester U	(1) 3
Doncaster R	(0) 0	Nottingham F	(1) 2
Millwall	(0) 0	Liverpool	(1) 3
Portsmouth	(2) 2	Leeds U	(1) 1
Sheffield U	(0) 0	Watford	(0) 0
(aet; Watford won 4-2 on penalties.)			
Birmingham C	(0) 0	Fulham	(0) 1
Bolton W	(1) 3	Tottenham H	(1) 4
(aet.)			
Charlton Ath	(1) 1	Crystal Palace	(1) 2
Chelsea	(0) 1	West Ham U	(0) 0
Everton	(0) 2	Preston NE	(0) 0
Manchester C	(0) 1	Arsenal	(0) 2
Middlesbrough	(2) 3	Coventry C	(0) 0
Newcastle U	(2) 2	Norwich C	(0) 1
Southampton	(0) 3	Colchester U	(1) 2

FOURTH ROUND

Arsenal	(1) 3	Everton	(1) 1
Burnley	(0) 0	Tottenham H	(1) 3
Cardiff C	(0) 0	Portsmouth	(0) 2
Watford	(1) 5	Southampton	(0) 2
Liverpool	(0) 2	Middlesbrough	(0) 0
Manchester U	(2) 2	Crystal Palace	(0) 0
Newcastle U	(0) 0	Chelsea	(0) 2
(aet.)			
Nottingham F	(0) 2	Fulham	(0) 4
(aet.)			

FIFTH ROUND

Fulham	(0) 1	Chelsea	(0) 2
Watford	(1) 3	Portsmouth	(0) 0

Manchester United	(1) 1	Arsenal	(0) 0
Tottenham H	(0) 1	Liverpool	(0) 1

(aet; Liverpool won 4-3 on penalties.)

SEMI-FINAL FIRST LEG

Liverpool	(0) 1	Watford	(0) 0
Chelsea	(0) 0	Manchester U	(0) 0

SEMI-FINAL SECOND LEG

Watford	(0) 0	Liverpool	(0) 1
Manchester U	(0) 1	Chelsea	(1) 2

CARLING CUP FINAL

Sunday, 27 February 2005

(at Millennium Stadium, Cardiff, attendance 78,000)

Liverpool (1) 2 Chelsea (0) 3

Liverpool: Dudek; Finnan, Traore (Biscan), Hamann, Carragher, Hyypia, Kewell (Nunez), Gerrard, Luis Garcia, Morientes (Baros), Riise.
Scorers: (Riise 1, Nunez 113)

Chelsea: Cech; Paulo Ferreira, Gallas (Kezman), Makelele, Terry, Ricardo Carvalho, Jarosik (Gudjohnsen), Lampard, Drogba, Cole (Johnson), Duff.
Scorers: (Gerrard 79 (og), Drogba 107, Kezman 112)

aet.

Referee: S. Bennett (Orpington).

PAST LEAGUE CUP FINALS

Played as two legs up to 1966

1961	Rotherham U	2	Aston Villa	0
	Webster, Kirkman			
	Aston Villa	3	Rotherham U	0*
	O'Neill, Burrows, McParland			
1962	Rochdale	0	Norwich C	3
	Lythgoe 2, Punton			
	Norwich C	1	Rochdale	0
	Hill			
1963	Birmingham C	3	Aston Villa	1
	Leek 2, Bloomfield		*Thomson*	
	Aston Villa	0	Birmingham C	0
1964	Stoke C	1	Leicester C	1
	Bebbington		*Gibson*	
	Leicester C	3	Stoke C	2
	Stringfellow, Gibson, Riley		*Viollet, Kinnell*	
1965	Chelsea	3	Leicester C	2
	Tambling, Venables (pen), McCreadie		*Appleton, Goodfellow*	
	Leicester C	0	Chelsea	0
1966	West Ham U	2	WBA	1
	Moore, Byrne		*Astle*	
	WBA	4	West Ham U	1
	Kaye, Brown, Clark, Williams		*Peters*	
1967	QPR	3	WBA	2
	Morgan R, Marsh, Lazarus		*Clark C 2*	
1968	Leeds U	1	Arsenal	0
	Cooper			
1969	Swindon T	3	Arsenal	1*
	Smart, Rogers 2		*Gould*	
1970	Manchester C	2	WBA	1*
	Doyle, Pardoe		*Astle*	
1971	Tottenham H	2	Aston Villa	0
	Chivers 2			
1972	Chelsea	1	Stoke C	2
	Osgood		*Conroy, Eastham*	
1973	Tottenham H	1	Norwich C	0
	Coates			
1974	Wolverhampton W	2	Manchester C	1
	Hibbitt, Richards		*Bell*	
1975	Aston Villa	1	Norwich C	0
	Graydon			
1976	Manchester C	2	Newcastle U	1
	Barnes, Tueart		*Gowling*	
1977	Aston Villa	0	Everton	0
Replay	Aston Villa	1	Everton	1*
	Kenyon (og)		*Latchford*	
Replay	Aston Villa	3	Everton	2*
	Little 2, Nicholl		*Latchford, Lyons*	
1978	Nottingham F	0	Liverpool	0*
Replay	Nottingham F	1	Liverpool	0
	Robertson (pen)			
1979	Nottingham F	3	Southampton	2
	Birtles 2, Woodcock		*Peach, Holmes*	
1980	Wolverhampton W	1	Nottingham F	0
	Gray			

Year	Winner		Runner-up	
1981	Liverpool	1	West Ham U	1*
	Kennedy A		*Stewart (pen)*	
Replay	Liverpool	2	West Ham U	1
	Dalglish, Hansen		*Goddard*	
1982	Liverpool	3	Tottenham H	1*
	Whelan 2, Rush		*Archibald*	
1983	Liverpool	2	Manchester U	1*
	Kennedy A, Whelan		*Whiteside*	
1984	Liverpool	0	Everton	0*
Replay	Liverpool	1	Everton	0
	Souness			
1985	Norwich C	1	Sunderland	0
	Chisholm (og)			
1986	Oxford U	3	QPR	0
	Hebberd, Houghton, Charles			
1987	Arsenal	2	Liverpool	1
	Nicholas 2		*Rush*	
1988	Luton T	3	Arsenal	2
	Stein B 2, Wilson		*Hayes, Smith*	
1989	Nottingham F	3	Luton T	1
	Clough 2, Webb		*Harford*	
1990	Nottingham F	1	Oldham Ath	0
	Jemson			
1991	Sheffield W	1	Manchester U	0
	Sheridan			
1992	Manchester U	1	Nottingham F	0
	McClair			
1993	Arsenal	2	Sheffield W	1
	Merson, Morrow		*Harkes*	
1994	Aston Villa	3	Manchester U	1
	Atkinson, Saunders 2 (1 pen)		*Hughes*	
1995	Liverpool	2	Bolton W	1
	McManaman 2		*Thompson*	
1996	Aston Villa	3	Leeds U	0
	Milosevic, Taylor, Yorke			
1997	Leicester C	1	Middlesbrough	1*
	Heskey		*Ravanelli*	
Replay	Leicester C	1	Middlesbrough	0*
	Claridge			
1998	Chelsea	2	Middlesbrough	0*
	Sinclair, Di Matteo			
1999	Tottenham H	1	Leicester C	0
	Nielsen			
2000	Leicester C	2	Tranmere R	1
	Elliott 2		*Kelly*	
2001	Liverpool	1	Birmingham C	1
	Fowler		*Purse (pen)*	
Liverpool won 5-4 on penalties.				
2002	Blackburn	2	Tottenham H	1
	Jansen, Cole		*Ziege*	
2003	Liverpool	2	Manchester U	0
	Gerrard, Owen			
2004	Middlesbrough	2	Bolton W	1
	Job, Zenden (pen)		*Davies*	
2005	Chelsea	3	Liverpool	2*
	Gerrard (og), Drogba, Kezman		*Riise, Nunez*	

**After extra time*

LDV VANS TROPHY 2004–2005

NORTHERN SECTION FIRST ROUND

Carlisle U	(1) 2	Grimsby T	(1) 1
Hartlepool U	(0) 3	Hull C	(1) 3
(aet; Hartlepool U won 4-1 on penalties.)			
Hereford U	(1) 1	Scunthorpe U	(0) 1
(aet; Hereford U won 4-3 on penalties.)			
Huddersfield T	(0) 3	Morecambe	(0) 0
Lincoln C	(0) 0	Doncaster R	(0) 1
Macclesfield T	(1) 2	Chesterfield	(0) 1
Mansfield T	(0) 0	Darlington	(0) 0
(aet; Mansfield T won 4-3 on penalties.)			
Notts Co	(1) 2	Wrexham	(1) 3
Port Vale	(1) 1	Barnsley	(0) 0
Rochdale	(1) 4	Scarborough	(1) 1
Stockport Co	(1) 3	Bury	(1) 1
(aet.)			
Bradford C	(1) 1	Accrington S	(1) 2
Sheffield W	(1) 1	Chester C	(0) 2
York C	(0) 0	Blackpool	(1) 2

SOUTHERN SECTION FIRST ROUND

Aldershot T	(0) 0	Wycombe W	(0) 1
Barnet	(0) 3	Stevenage B	(0) 1
Brentford	(0) 0	Milton Keynes D	(3) 3
Bristol R	(0) 1	Kidderminster H	(0) 0
Cheltenham T	(1) 5	Dagenham & R	(0) 1
Shrewsbury T	(1) 3	Bournemouth	(0) 2
Swansea C	(0) 2	Luton T	(0) 0
Torquay U	(1) 4	Yeovil T	(1) 3
(aet.)			
Walsall	(0) 1	Rushden & D	(0) 0
Woking	(0) 0	Leyton Orient	(1) 3
Boston U	(0) 0	Cambridge U	(0) 1
Bristol C	(1) 1	Peterborough U	(0) 0
Colchester U	(0) 1	Southend U	(1) 1
(aet; Southend U won 5-3 on penalties.)			
Oxford U	(1) 2	Exeter C	(1) 2
(aet; Exeter C won 3-1 on penalties.)			

NORTHERN SECTION SECOND ROUND

Blackpool	(1) 6	Huddersfield T	(0) 3
(aet.)			
Carlisle U	(0) 0	Hartlepool U	(0) 1
Chester C	(0) 1	Rochdale	(0) 0
Hereford U	(0) 1	Doncaster R	(0) 1
(aet; Hereford U won 3-1 on penalties.)			
Macclesfield T	(3) 4	Mansfield T	(0) 0
Oldham Ath	(1) 3	Accrington S	(1) 2
Tranmere R	(2) 2	Port Vale	(0) 1
Wrexham	(1) 2	Stockport Co	(0) 0

SOUTHERN SECTION SECOND ROUND

Bristol C	(1) 2	Milton Keynes D	(0) 1
Cambridge U	(0) 0	Leyton Orient	(0) 2
Cheltenham T	(1) 2	Walsall	(0) 2
(aet; Walsall won 4-3 on penalties.)			

Exeter C	(0) 1	Swindon T	(1) 2
Southend U	(3) 4	Shrewsbury T	(1) 1
Torquay U	(0) 1	Northampton T	(1) 3
Wycombe W	(1) 1	Swansea C	(0) 0
Bristol R	(1) 2	Barnet	(0) 0

NORTHERN QUARTER-FINALS

Chester C	(0) 0	Wrexham	(1) 1
Hereford U	(1) 2	Blackpool	(0) 1
Macclesfield T	(0) 0	Tranmere R	(1) 1
Oldham Ath	(2) 3	Hartlepool U	(1) 1

SOUTHERN QUARTER-FINALS

Bristol R	(0) 1	Wycombe W	(0) 0
Leyton Orient	(0) 1	Walsall	(0) 0
Northampton T	(0) 0	Southend U	(2) 2
Swindon T	(0) 1	Bristol C	(0) 0

NORTHERN SEMI-FINALS

Hereford U	(1) 1	Wrexham	(1) 2
Oldham Ath	(1) 1	Tranmere R	(1) 1

(aet; Oldham Ath won 5-4 on penalties.)

SOUTHERN SEMI-FINALS

Leyton Orient	(1) 1	Bristol R	(0) 2
Southend U	(1) 2	Swindon T	(0) 0

NORTHERN FINAL FIRST LEG

Oldham Ath	(1) 3	Wrexham	(2) 5

SOUTHERN FINAL FIRST LEG

Bristol R	(0) 1	Southend U	(1) 2

NORTHERN FINAL SECOND LEG

Wrexham	(0) 1	Oldham Ath	(0) 0

SOUTHERN FINAL SECOND LEG

Southend U	(1) 2	Bristol R	(1) 2

FINAL

Southend U	(0) 0	Wrexham	(0) 2

(aet.)

LDV VANS TROPHY FINAL

Sunday, 10 April 2005

(at Millennium Stadium, Cardiff, attendance 36,216)

Southend U (0) 0 **Wrexham (0) 2** *(Ugarte 99, Ferguson 118)*

Southend U: Flahavan; Jupp, Wilson, Maher, Barrett, Prior, Pettefer (Guttridge), Bentley, Gray, Eastwood (Dudfield), Gower (McCormack).

Wrexham: Foster; Edwards, Holt, Lawrence, Roberts (Pejic), Morgan, Crowell (Bennett), Ferguson, Ugarte, Llewellyn, Mark Jones (Williams).
aet.

Referee: B. Carson (Leicestershire).

FA CHARITY SHIELD WINNERS 1908–2004

1908 Manchester U v QPR 4-0 after 1-1 draw
1909 Newcastle U v Northampton T 2-0
1910 Brighton v Aston Villa 1-0
1911 Manchester U v Swindon T 8-4
1912 Blackburn R v QPR 2-1
1913 Professionals v Amateurs 7-2
1920 Tottenham H v Burnley 2-0
1921 Huddersfield T v Liverpool 1-0
1922 Not played
1923 Professionals v Amateurs 2-0
1924 Professionals v Amateurs 3-1
1925 Amateurs v Professionals 6-1
1926 Amateurs v Professionals 6-3
1927 Cardiff C v Corinthians 2-1
1928 Everton v Blackburn R 2-1
1929 Professionals v Amateurs 3-0
1930 Arsenal v Sheffield W 2-1
1931 Arsenal v WBA 1-0
1932 Everton v Newcastle U 5-3
1933 Arsenal v Everton 3-0
1934 Arsenal v Manchester C 4-0
1935 Sheffield W v Arsenal 1-0
1936 Sunderland v Arsenal 2-1
1937 Manchester C v Sunderland 2-0
1938 Arsenal v Preston NE 2-1
1948 Arsenal v Manchester U 4-3
1949 Portsmouth v Wolverhampton W 1-1*
1950 World Cup Team v Canadian Touring Team 4-2
1951 Tottenham H v Newcastle U 2-1
1952 Manchester U v Newcastle U 4-2
1953 Arsenal v Blackpool 3-1
1954 Wolverhampton W v WBA 4-4*
1955 Chelsea v Newcastle U 3-0
1956 Manchester U v Manchester C 1-0
1957 Manchester U v Aston Villa 4-0
1958 Bolton W v Wolverhampton W 4-1
1959 Wolverhampton W v Nottingham F 3-1
1960 Burnley v Wolverhampton W 2-2*
1961 Tottenham H v FA XI 3-2
1962 Tottenham H v Ipswich T 5-1
1963 Everton v Manchester U 4-0
1964 Liverpool v West Ham U 2-2*
1965 Manchester U v Liverpool 2-2*
1966 Liverpool v Everton 1-0
1967 Manchester U v Tottenham H 3-3*
1968 Manchester C v WBA 6-1
1969 Leeds U v Manchester C 2-1
1970 Everton v Chelsea 2-1
1971 Leicester C v Liverpool 1-0
1972 Manchester C v Aston Villa 1-0
1973 Burnley v Manchester C 1-0
1974 Liverpool† v Leeds U 1-1
1975 Derby Co v West Ham U 2-0
1976 Liverpool v Southampton 1-0
1977 Liverpool v Manchester U 0-0*
1978 Nottingham F v Ipswich T 5-0
1979 Liverpool v Arsenal 3-1
1980 Liverpool v West Ham U 1-0
1981 Aston Villa v Tottenham H 2-2*
1982 Liverpool v Tottenham H 1-0
1983 Manchester U v Liverpool 2-0
1984 Everton v Liverpool 1-0
1985 Everton v Manchester U 2-0
1986 Everton v Liverpool 1-1*
1987 Everton v Coventry C 1-0
1988 Liverpool v Wimbledon 2-1
1989 Liverpool v Arsenal 1-0
1990 Liverpool v Manchester U 1-1*
1991 Arsenal v Tottenham H 0-0*
1992 Leeds U v Liverpool 4-3
1993 Manchester U† v Arsenal 1-1
1994 Manchester U v Blackburn R 2-0
1995 Everton v Blackburn R 1-0
1996 Manchester U v Newcastle U 4-0
1997 Manchester U† v Chelsea 1-1
1998 Arsenal v Manchester U 3-0
1999 Arsenal v Manchester U 2-1
2000 Chelsea v Manchester U 2-0
2001 Liverpool v Manchester U 2-1
2002 Arsenal v Liverpool 1-0
2003 Manchester U† v Arsenal 1-1
2004 Arsenal v Manchester U 3-1

*Each club retained shield for six months. †Won on penalties.

THE FA COMMUNITY SHIELD 2004

Sunday, 8 August 2004

(at Millennium Stadium, Cardiff, attendance 63,317)

Arsenal (0) 3 Manchester U (0) 1

Arsenal: Lehmann; Lauren, Cole, Silva, Toure, Cygan, Pennant, Fabregas (Svard), Henry (Van Persie), Bergkamp (Aliadiere) (Clichy), Reyes (Hoyte).
Scorers: Silva 49, Reyes 59, Silvestre 79 (og).
Manchester U: Howard; Neville G, Fortune (Neville P), O'Shea (Spector), Keane (Fletcher), Silvestre, Bellion, Djemba-Djemba, Smith (Eagles), Scholes (Richardson), Giggs (Forlan).
Scorer: Smith 55.
Referee: M. Dean (Wirral).

SCOTTISH LEAGUE REVIEW 2004–2005

For ten seasons in either the First Division of the Scottish League or more recently the Scottish Premier League, the title has been between Rangers and Celtic. But few if any of the previous struggles between the two have culminated in such a dramatic climax as 2004–05.

On the last day of the season Celtic were two points ahead of their rivals with an inferior goal difference of four. A Celtic win would guarantee the title. They took an early lead at Motherwell. Rangers were still being held at Hibs and it took them just under the hour before they opened the scoring, but if scores remained thus, Celtic would be champions.

Incredibly in the last two minutes Celtic conceded two goals, lost the game and the title!

Celtic had probably been slight favourites over the season itself and the first Auld Firm affair went Celtic's way late in August with a 1-0 win at Parkhead. This was Rangers' only defeat in the League up to the next meeting at Ibrox in November and with a 2-0 win over Celtic they had closed the gap to one point.

The following week when Celtic were held 2-2 at Dundee, Rangers moved a point ahead. But the positions were reversed again a week from then when Rangers could only draw with Inverness Caley. On 20 February at Parkhead, Rangers beat Celtic 2-0 again. They were three points ahead but Celtic had a game in hand. However by the time of the split in the middle of April, Rangers were two points behind again.

On 24 April Celtic turned the tables on Rangers 2-1 at Ibrox for a five point lead which as explained was eroded in the final few games and ultimately at the death.

Overall there was a small percentage increase in attendances over the previous season with an average of 15,658. Third place, and with it a place in Europe, just went to Hibs but only by a goal difference of two because on the last day Aberdeen had beaten Hearts 2-0.

While Inverness had started sharing with the Dons they eventually staged games on their own ground and to finish fifth from the bottom was something of a success when they were expected to go down. Relegated were Dundee when at one stage it seemed Dundee United were to be the unlucky ones. A Tennent's Cup run to the final gave them confidence while both Livingston and Dunfermline narrowly survived. Dundee had needed a last match victory at Livingston but could only draw.

The expected avalanche of Tennent's Cup final goals did not materialise as Celtic were confined to a 1-0 win over Dundee United. Other cup honours went to Falkirk, runaway winners of the Scottish League First Division and promoted with ground approval. They beat Ross County 2-1 in the Bell's League Cup Final, while in the CIS Insurance Cup Rangers had a 5-1 romp with Motherwell.

There was no joy in Europe. Rangers were second from bottom in their UEFA Cup group, Hearts at the foot of their section, while Dunfermline failed at the first hurdle. Celtic were in a tough Champions League group which included AC Milan and Barcelona and won only one match, but produced their best in the last two games, drawing in Spain and holding the Italians at Parkhead.

Manager Martin O'Neill resigned as Celtic boss largely as a consequence of his wife's illness and he was replaced by Gordon Strachan.

As mentioned Falkirk finally streaked away in the First Division 15 points ahead of St Mirren who had caught Clyde for runners-up spot. Relegated were two famous clubs of a previous era Partick Thistle and Raith Rovers, who won only three matches.

Brechin City had nine points to spare over Stranraer who lost their way in the second half of the season but held off Morton to gain promotion from the Second Division. Down went Arbroath and Berwick Rangers.

Yet the story of the Scottish League was arguably the feat of Gretna in the Third Division. With a hundred per cent home record and losing only two and drawing two of their away programme they were 20 points to the good in front of the other promoted side Peterhead. Gretna scored goals for fun it seemed, 130 in total.

To emphasise the oddity of the entire division, Peterhead were 27 points ahead of third placed Cowdenbeath and only Queens Park had a positive goal difference and then only by one!

For once East Stirling though at the bottom of the table could at least point to winning five League matches, one more than Raith two divisions above them.

SCOTTISH LEAGUE TABLES 2004–2005

		Home					Away					Total						
Premier League	*P*	*W*	*D*	*L*	*F*	*A*	*W*	*D*	*L*	*F*	*A*	*W*	*D*	*L*	*F*	*A*	*Gd*	*Pts*
1 Rangers	38	15	2	2	48	12	14	4	1	30	10	29	6	3	78	22	56	93
2 Celtic	38	15	0	4	41	15	15	2	2	44	20	30	2	6	85	35	50	92
3 Hibernian	38	9	4	6	32	26	9	3	7	32	31	18	7	13	64	57	7	61
4 Aberdeen	38	8	4	6	22	17	10	3	7	22	22	18	7	13	44	39	5	61
5 Hearts	38	9	4	6	25	15	4	7	8	18	26	13	11	14	43	41	2	50
6 Kilmarnock	38	10	2	7	32	20	5	2	12	17	35	15	4	19	49	55	–6	49
7 Motherwell	38	8	4	7	29	22	5	5	9	17	27	13	9	16	46	49	–3	48
8 Inverness CT	38	7	4	9	23	24	4	7	7	18	23	11	11	16	41	47	–6	44
9 Dundee U	38	4	7	8	22	28	4	5	10	19	31	8	12	18	41	59	–18	36
10 Livingston	38	5	4	10	22	34	4	4	11	12	27	9	8	21	34	61	–27	35
11 Dunfermline	38	5	9	5	23	19	3	1	15	11	41	8	10	20	34	60	–26	34
12 Dundee	38	7	4	8	21	24	1	5	13	16	47	8	9	21	37	71	–34	33

		Home					Away					Total						
First Division	*P*	*W*	*D*	*L*	*F*	*A*	*W*	*D*	*L*	*F*	*A*	*W*	*D*	*L*	*F*	*A*	*Gd*	*Pts*
1 Falkirk	36	10	6	2	35	15	12	3	3	31	15	22	9	5	66	30	36	75
2 St Mirren	36	10	6	2	24	11	5	9	4	17	12	15	15	6	41	23	18	60
3 Clyde	36	9	4	5	17	13	7	8	3	18	16	16	12	8	35	29	6	60
4 Queen of the S	36	7	5	6	17	14	7	4	7	19	24	14	9	13	36	38	–2	51
5 Airdrie U	36	8	3	7	25	25	6	5	7	19	23	14	8	14	44	48	–4	50
6 Ross Co	36	6	5	7	20	16	7	3	8	20	21	13	8	15	40	37	3	47
7 Hamilton A	36	5	5	8	13	18	7	6	5	22	18	12	11	13	35	36	–1	47
8 St Johnstone	36	6	6	6	18	18	6	4	8	20	21	12	10	14	38	39	–1	46
9 Partick Th	36	7	5	6	23	25	3	4	11	15	27	10	9	17	38	52	–14	39
10 Raith R	36	3	4	11	19	33	0	3	15	7	34	3	7	26	26	67	–41	16

		Home					Away					Total						
Second Division	*P*	*W*	*D*	*L*	*F*	*A*	*W*	*D*	*L*	*F*	*A*	*W*	*D*	*L*	*F*	*A*	*Gd*	*Pts*
1 Brechin C	36	12	1	5	47	25	10	5	3	34	18	22	6	8	81	43	38	72
2 Stranraer	36	9	5	4	24	19	9	4	5	24	22	18	9	9	48	41	7	63
3 Morton	36	13	2	3	35	14	5	6	7	25	23	18	8	10	60	37	23	62
4 Stirling Alb	36	8	5	5	29	26	6	4	8	27	29	14	9	13	56	55	1	51
5 Forfar Ath	36	7	4	7	29	20	6	4	8	22	25	13	8	15	51	45	6	47
6 Alloa Ath	36	6	7	5	39	35	6	3	9	27	33	12	10	14	66	68	–2	46
7 Dumbarton	36	5	7	6	22	23	6	2	10	21	30	11	9	16	43	53	–10	42
8 Ayr U	36	6	6	6	22	23	5	3	10	17	31	11	9	16	39	54	–15	42
9 Arbroath	36	6	3	9	18	30	4	5	9	31	43	10	8	18	49	73	–24	38
10 Berwick R	36	5	3	10	20	33	3	7	8	20	31	8	10	18	40	64	–24	34

		Home					Away					Total						
Third Division	*P*	*W*	*D*	*L*	*F*	*A*	*W*	*D*	*L*	*F*	*A*	*W*	*D*	*L*	*F*	*A*	*Gd*	*Pts*
1 Gretna	36	18	0	0	70	10	14	2	2	60	19	32	2	2	130	29	101	98
2 Peterhead	36	11	6	1	46	17	12	3	3	35	21	23	9	4	81	38	43	78
3 Cowdenbeath	36	8	4	6	24	32	6	5	7	30	29	14	9	13	54	61	–7	51
4 Queen's Park	36	7	5	6	24	24	6	4	8	27	26	13	9	14	51	50	1	48
5 Montrose	36	7	2	9	27	29	6	5	7	20	24	13	7	16	47	53	–6	46
6 Elgin C	36	7	5	6	24	31	5	2	11	15	30	12	7	17	39	61	–22	43
7 Stenhousemuir	36	5	7	6	31	25	5	5	8	27	33	10	12	14	58	58	0	42
8 East Fife	36	7	4	7	17	19	3	4	11	23	37	10	8	18	40	56	–16	38
9 Albion R	36	3	4	11	20	46	5	6	7	20	32	8	10	18	40	78	–38	34
10 East Stirlingshire	36	4	3	11	17	39	1	4	13	15	49	5	7	24	32	88	–56	22

BANK OF SCOTLAND SCOTTISH LEAGUE—PREMIER LEAGUE RESULTS 2004–2005

	Aberdeen	Celtic	Dundee	Dundee U	Dunfermline Ath	Hearts	Hibernian	Inverness CT	Kilmarnock	Livingston	Motherwell	Rangers
Aberdeen	—	0-1	1-1	1-0	2-1	0-1 *2-0*	0-1	0-0	3-2	2-0	2-1	0-0 *1-3*
	—		1-1				3-0			2-0	1-3	1-2
Celtic	2-3 *2-0*	—	3-0	1-0	3-0	3-0	2-1 *1-3*	3-0	2-1	2-1	2-0	1-0
	3-2	—	3-0		6-0	0-2					2-0	0-2
Dundee	1-0	2-2	—	1-0 *1-2*	1-2	0-1	1-4	3-1 *1-1*	3-1	0-0	1-2	0-2
			—		2-1	1-1			1-0	0-1	2-1	0-2
Dundee U	1-1	0-3	1-2	—	1-2 *0-1*	1-1	1-4	2-1	3-0 *1-1*	1-0 *1-1*	0-1	1-1
	1-2	2-3	2-2	—		2-1		1-1				
Dunfermline Ath	0-1	0-2	3-1 *5-0*	1-1	—	1-0	1-1	1-1 *0-0*	4-1	0-0	1-1	1-2
	2-1			1-1	—	1-1	1-4				0-0	0-1
Hearts	0-0	0-2 *1-2*	3-0	3-2	3-0	—	2-1	1-0	3-0	0-0	0-1 *0-0*	0-0
	1-0					—	1-2	0-2	3-0	3-1		1-2
Hibernian	2-1 *1-2*	2-2	4-4	2-0	2-1	1-1 *2-2*	—	2-1	0-1	2-1	1-0	0-1 *0-1*
		1-3	4-0	3-2			—		3-0	0-3		
Inverness CT	1-3	1-3	2-1	1-1 *0-1*	2-0	1-1	1-2	—	0-2 *1-2*	2-0 *0-1*	1-1	1-1
	0-1	0-2	3-2		2-0		3-0	—			1-0	
Kilmarnock	0-1	2-4	3-1 *1-0*	5-2	1-0 *4-0*	1-1	3-1	2-2	—	1-3 *2-0*	2-0	0-1
	0-1	0-1		3-0	2-1			0-1	—			
Livingston	0-2	2-4	1-0 *1-1*	1-1	2-0 *2-0*	1-2	0-2	3-0	0-2	—	2-3	1-4
		0-4		0-2	1-1			1-4	3-1	—	1-1	
Motherwell	0-0 *0-1*	2-3 *2-1*	3-0	4-2	2-1	2-0	1-2 *2-2*	1-2	0-1	2-0	—	0-2
				2-0		2-0	1-1		1-1		—	2-3
Rangers	5-0	2-0 *1-2*	3-0	1-1	3-0	3-2 *2-1*	4-1	1-0	2-0	4-0	4-1 *4-1*	—
				0-1			3-0	1-1	2-1	3-0		—

BELL'S SCOTTISH LEAGUE—DIVISION ONE RESULTS 2004–2005

	Airdrie U	Clyde	Falkirk	Hamilton A	Partick Th	Queen of the S	Raith R	Ross Co	St Johnstone	St Mirren
Airdrie U	—	3-1	1-3	0-2	4-2	0-1	1-1	1-2	1-0	3-2
	—	2-4	2-2	1-0	0-1	2-0	2-1	2-1	0-0	0-2
Clyde	1-2	—	0-2	2-1	2-1	2-0	2-0	1-0	1-0	0-0
	1-0	—	0-1	1-3	1-1	0-1	1-0	1-0	1-1	0-0
Falkirk	5-0	1-1	—	1-1	3-0	4-2	4-2	2-2	3-1	0-0
	1-0	0-0	—	1-1	2-1	1-2	2-0	1-0	3-0	1-2
Hamilton A	1-3	0-1	0-1	—	0-1	1-0	2-0	1-2	1-1	2-2
	1-1	0-1	1-0	—	1-0	1-1	1-0	0-1	0-3	0-0
Partick Th	3-2	0-0	1-4	0-1	—	1-2	2-0	4-0	0-4	0-3
	1-1	1-0	2-1	1-1	—	3-1	4-1	0-0	0-4	0-0
Queen of the S	1-0	0-1	1-3	1-1	1-0	—	2-0	0-1	0-1	2-1
	0-0	0-1	1-1	1-2	3-1	—	1-1	1-0	2-0	0-0
Raith R	0-2	2-3	0-2	2-2	0-0	1-2	—	1-2	1-0	0-3
	0-1	3-3	3-3	0-2	2-1	0-1	—	1-4	1-2	2-0
Ross Co	1-2	0-1	0-1	1-1	0-1	1-0	1-1	—	0-1	1-1
	3-1	1-1	0-1	2-1	2-1	1-1	2-0	—	4-0	0-1
St Johnstone	1-1	3-0	1-2	3-0	2-1	1-3	1-0	1-1	—	1-0
	1-2	0-0	0-3	0-2	1-1	0-0	2-0	0-2	—	0-0
St Mirren	1-1	0-0	2-0	1-0	2-1	2-2	1-0	3-2	2-1	—
	1-0	0-0	0-1	0-1	1-1	3-0	3-0	1-0	1-1	—

BELL'S SCOTTISH LEAGUE—DIVISION TWO RESULTS 2004–2005

	Alloa Ath	Arbroath	Ayr U	Berwick R	Brechin C	Dumbarton	Forfar Ath	Morton	Stirling A	Stranraer
Alloa Ath	—	4-2	1-3	2-2	2-2	3-2	2-3	1-6	1-1	1-2
	—	2-2	5-1	2-2	1-1	4-2	0-2	2-2	3-0	3-0
Arbroath	0-3	—	0-0	1-1	2-2	0-2	0-2	0-3	2-1	0-1
	2-1	—	2-0	2-0	1-4	2-1	1-2	0-1	3-2	0-4
Ayr U	4-3	1-1	—	2-1	0-1	0-1	3-3	2-0	3-2	0-1
	1-1	2-2	—	0-1	0-1	1-1	1-0	2-1	0-3	0-0
Berwick R	2-3	0-3	0-1	—	0-2	0-4	1-0	2-1	0-1	1-2
	2-1	2-3	2-1	—	2-1	0-3	1-1	2-2	2-2	1-2
Brechin C	4-0	4-1	5-0	4-1	—	4-0	2-0	2-1	0-3	4-1
	1-3	4-3	3-0	1-1	—	0-2	0-3	1-2	5-3	2-1
Dumbarton	0-1	1-3	1-0	3-1	1-1	—	0-1	0-3	1-1	1-3
	3-2	3-0	1-1	1-1	1-1	—	1-1	3-0	0-2	1-1
Forfar Ath	3-1	5-0	2-3	1-1	1-0	0-2	—	2-0	0-2	0-1
	1-1	1-1	1-0	0-2	1-3	6-0	—	0-0	4-1	1-2
Morton	2-2	2-1	0-1	2-0	0-3	3-0	2-1	—	3-0	3-1
	2-0	2-0	2-1	4-2	0-2	0-0	4-0	—	2-0	2-0
Stirling A	2-0	5-2	1-1	3-1	1-5	1-0	3-1	1-1	—	1-1
	0-4	0-3	2-0	0-1	1-2	3-0	3-2	1-1	—	1-1
Stranraer	3-0	2-1	2-1	2-2	4-2	1-0	1-0	1-0	0-0	—
	0-1	3-3	1-3	1-0	0-1	2-1	0-0	1-1	0-3	—

BELL'S SCOTTISH LEAGUE—DIVISION THREE RESULTS 2004–2005

	Albion R	Cowdenbeath	East Fife	East Stirling	Elgin C	Gretna	Montrose	Peterhead	Queen's Park	Stenhousemuir
Albion R	—	2-3	2-0	3-3	2-2	2-6	1-2	0-1	0-4	1-0
	—	1-4	0-6	1-1	2-0	0-5	1-2	0-4	1-2	1-1
Cowdenbeath	2-0	—	1-1	2-1	3-1	0-8	0-0	0-4	2-1	0-6
	1-2	—	4-2	3-2	1-1	0-1	0-0	4-0	1-0	0-2
East Fife	1-0	1-1	—	1-0	2-0	1-3	1-0	0-2	1-4	0-0
	1-1	1-1	—	2-0	1-2	0-2	1-0	1-2	0-1	2-0
East Stirling	1-1	0-2	1-1	—	0-1	1-2	1-1	1-2	0-5	3-2
	0-2	2-1	1-0	—	0-3	0-4	1-2	1-5	3-1	1-4
Elgin C	1-0	0-4	2-1	1-3	—	1-3	1-3	2-2	1-0	1-1
	1-1	2-0	2-1	0-0	—	2-6	2-2	0-2	1-0	4-2
Gretna	6-0	2-1	5-1	8-1	3-0	—	1-0	2-1	4-1	3-0
	6-2	2-0	4-0	1-0	2-1	—	4-1	6-1	4-0	7-0
Montrose	1-1	3-1	2-1	4-1	2-0	2-3	—	0-1	2-4	0-2
	0-1	1-2	2-2	4-1	2-0	0-4	—	0-2	2-0	0-3
Peterhead	4-1	3-1	2-0	5-0	2-1	1-1	3-2	—	2-2	5-0
	2-3	1-1	0-0	3-0	3-0	4-2	4-1	—	1-1	1-1
Queen's Park	1-1	3-2	1-2	0-0	0-1	3-2	1-2	1-2	—	4-3
	0-3	2-3	2-1	2-0	1-0	1-1	1-0	1-1	—	0-0
Stenhousemuir	3-0	2-2	5-2	6-0	0-2	0-3	1-1	1-2	1-1	—
	1-1	1-1	1-2	3-2	4-0	1-4	0-1	1-1	0-0	—

ABERDEEN — PREMIER LEAGUE

Ground: Pittodrie Stadium, Aberdeen AB24 5QH (01224) 650400
Ground capacity: 21,467. **Colours:** All red with white trim.
Manager: Jim Calderwood.
League Appearances: Adams D 16(4); Anderson R 31; Blaha L 2(6); Byrne R 11(2); Clark C 30(1); Considine A 1; Craig S 6(7); Dempsey G (4); Diamond A 29; Esson R 21(2); Foster R 11(14); Hart M 28(4); Heikkinen M 29(1); Kristjansson T 1(2); Mackie D 33(1); McGuire P 22(8); McNaughton K 35; Morrison S 6(5); Muirhead S 6(8); Pasquinelli F 5(5); Preece D 17; Severin S 31; Stewart J 6(18); Tosh S 14(3); Whelan N 18(2); Winter J 9(3).
Goals – League (44): Mackie 12 (2 pens), Adams 4 (1 pen), Whelan 4, Diamond 3, Pasquinelli 3, Clarke 2, Craig 2 (1 pen), Foster 2, Heikkinen 2, McNaughton 2, Stewart 2, Anderson 1, Byrne 1, Severin 1, Tosh 1, own goals 2.
Scottish Cup (5): Mackie 3, Byrne 1, Heikkinen 1.
CIS Cup (3): Adams 1, Craig 1, Diamond 1.
Honours – Division 1: Champions – 1954-55, **Premier Division:** Champions – 1979-80, 1983-84, 1984-85. **Scottish Cup winners** 1947, 1970, 1982, 1983, 1984, 1986, 1990. **League Cup winners** 1956, 1977, 1986, 1990, 1996. **European Cup-Winners' Cup winners** 1983.

AIRDRIE UNITED — DIV. 1

Ground: Shyberry Excelsior Stadium, Airdrie ML6 8QZ (01236) 622000
Ground capacity: 10,000 (all seated). **Colours:** White shirts with red diamond, white shorts.
Manager: Sandy Stewart.
League Appearances: Barkey K 10(8); Christie K 17(1); Coyle O 33; Docherty S 24(4); Dunn D 12(12); Gow A 23(3); Hardie M 23(2); Hoey T (2); Hollis L 6; Lovering P 29; McDougall S 1; McGeown M 30; McGowan N 30(2); McGroarty C 2; McKenna S 8; McKeown S 18(4); McLaren W 22(5); McManus A 27(3); Roberts M 20(11); Stewart A 2; Vareille J 12(16); Wilson M 36; Wilson S 1(1); Wilson W 10(9).
Goals – League (44): Coyle 14, Gow 9 (2 pens), Hardie 4, McKeown 4 (1 pen), McLaren 3, Roberts 3, Wilson M 2, Barkey 1,Christie 1, Lovering 1, McManus 1, Vareille 1.
Scottish Cup (1): Hardie 1.
CIS Cup (3): Coyle 1, Roberts 1, Vareille 1.
Challenge Cup (0).
Honours – Second Division: Champions – 2003–04; **Division II:** Champions – 1902-03, 1954-55, 1973-74. **Scottish Cup winners** 1924. **B&Q Cup winners** 1995. **Bell's League Challenge winners** 2000-01, 2001-02.

ALBION ROVERS — DIV. 3

Ground: Cliftonhill Stadium, Main Street, Coatbridge ML5 3RB (01236) 606334
Ground capacity: 2496. **Colours:** Scarlet and yellow shirts, scarlet shorts.
Manager: Jim Chapman.
League Appearances: Black D 30; Boyle J 5(5); Bradford J 20(6); Connolly C 7(3); Crabbe S 7(3); Douglas I 2(2); Fahey C 28; Fleming G 4(6); Friel S 16; Gordon W 10(5); McCaul G 8(5); McGowan J 8; McInulty S 11(1); McKenzie M 28(5); McLaren G 17; McLaughlin P 3(1); McManus P 15(2); Mercer J 25; Paterson A 12(2); Patrick R 19(7); Peat M 8(1); Potter K 16(1); Preston F (1); Richardson G (5); Selkirk A 6(6); Silvestro C 27; Smith J 2; Stirling J 35; Thomson D 3; Wallace N 5(1); Wilson L 11(1); Yardley M 8(2).

Goals – League (40): Bradford 7 (2 pens), McManus 6 (1 pen), Wilson 6 (1 pen), Mercer 5, Stirling 4, Gordon 2, Connolly 1, Crabbe 1, Douglas 1, Fleming 1, McCaul 1, McKenzie 1, McLaughlin 1, Patrick 1, Potter 1, own goal 1.
Scottish Cup (0).
CIS Cup (4): Bradford 1, McKenzie 1, McLaren 1, Mercer 1.
Challenge Cup (3): Bradford 2, McCaul 1.
Honours – Division II: Champions – 1933-34. **Second Division:** Champions 1988-89.

ALLOA ATHLETIC — DIV. 2

Ground: Recreation Park, Alloa FK10 1RY (01259) 722695
Ground capacity: 3100. **Colours:** Gold shirts with black trim, black shorts with gold stripe.
Manager: Tom Hendrie.
League Appearances: Bolochoweckyj M 34; Brown A 25(1); Brown G 8(2); Calderon J 1(3); Callaghan S 16; Daly M 16(10); Ebanda H (1); Evans J 20(1); Ferguson B 26(3); Hamilton R 25(3); Hill D 13(2); Learmonth S (1); Mackie S (1); McDermott M 1(4); McGlynn G 16; McLaughlin P 4(5); McLeod R 1(3); McMillan A 2(9); Mortimer P 13(6); Nicholas S 5(2); Nicolson I 26(3); Ovenstone J 26; Quitongo J 16(1); Ross I 9(1); Stevenson J 24(7); Thomson D 3; Townsley C 34(1); Walker R 32(1).
Goals – League (66): Brown A 8, Bolochoweckyj 7, Ferguson 6 (2 pens), Nicolson 6, Callaghan 5, Hamilton 5, Quitongo 5, Ross 5, Ovenstone 3, Stevenson 3, Townsley 3, Brown G 2, Daly 2, Hill 2, Calderon 1, McMillan 1, Walker R 1, own goal 1.
Scottish Cup (4): Brown A 1, Ferguson 1 (pen), Ovenstone 1, Webster 1.
CIS Cup (3): Callaghan 1, Ferguson 1, Hamilton 1.
Challenge Cup (3): Callaghan 1, Ferguson 1, Hamilton 1.
Honours – Division II: Champions – 1921-22. **Third Division:** Champions – 1997-98. **Bell's League Challenge winners** 1999-2000.

ARBROATH — DIV. 3

Ground: Gayfield Park, Arbroath DD11 1QB (01241) 872157
Ground capacity: 4020. **Colours:** Maroon shirts with white trim, white shorts.
Manager: Steve Kirk.
League Appearances: Beith G 4(2); Bishop J 25(6); Brazil A 28(3); Collier J (5); Cook S 1(11); Coyle C 5; Cusick J 18(8); Diack I 11(2); Donaldson E 24(3); Farquharson P 5(8); Fraser S 2; Henslee G 34(1); Inglis N 27(1); MacDonald S 21(6); McAulay J (3); McCulloch M 11(1); McGlashan J 11; McLean D 9(6); McLeod C 34; McMullan K 29(5); Millar M 8(1); Miller G 21(3); Rennie S 28; Renwick M 1; Swankie G 34; Watson P 1; Woodcock T 4.
Goals – League (49): Henslee 11 (1 pen), Brazil 7, McLean 5, McMullan 5, McLeod 4, Swankie 4, Bishop 3, Diack 3, McGlashan 2, Cook 1, Cusick 1, Farquharson 1, Miller G 1, Rennie 1.
Scottish Cup (1): Brazil 1.
CIS Cup (1): Cusick 1.
Challenge Cup (2): Cusick 1, McLean 1.
Honours – Nil.

AYR UNITED — DIV. 2

Ground: Somerset Park, Ayr KA8 9NB (01292) 263435
Ground capacity: 10,243 (1549 seated). **Colours:** White shirts with black trim, black shorts.

Manager: Robert Connor.
League Appearances: Boyd S 10; Brown G 5(6); Buckley R 9(2); Burgess R 1(3); Cargill A (2); Chaplain S 16(7); Cherrie P 5(1); Connolly P 27(7); Conway C 22(1); Craig D 1; Crawford S (1); Doyle J 7(4); Dunlop M 24(4); Dunning A 3(1); Ferguson A 10(16); Ferguson S 2(5); Gilmour N 3(1); Henderson D 29; Hillcoat J 9(2); Johnston D (1); Kean S 14; Lyle W 29(4); McCulloch S 10(1); McGrady S 19(7); McKay G (1); McLaughlin B 34; Nesovic A 1; O'Neill M (2); Ramsay D 14(5); Reid A 3(5); Roy L 22; Smyth M 33; Tait T 22(3); Templeton P 1; Wardlaw G 11(4).
Goals – League (39): Kean 10 (1 pen), Connolly 7, Conway 3, Ferguson A 3, Smyth 3, Wardlaw 3, Chaplain 2, McCulloch 2, Boyd 1, Burgess 1, Henderson 1, Lyle 1 (pen), McGrady 1, own goal 1.
Scottish Cup (6): Ferguson A 2, Henderson 2, Conway 1, Lyle 1.
CIS Cup (1): Ferguson A 1.
Challenge Cup (0).
Honours – Division II: Champions – 1911-12, 1912-13, 1927-28, 1936-37, 1958-59, 1965-66. **Second Division:** Champions – 1987-88, 1996-97.

BERWICK RANGERS DIV. 3

Ground: Shielfield Park, Berwick-on-Tweed TD15 2EF (01289) 307424
Ground capacity: 4131. **Colours:** Black with broad gold stripe, black shorts with white trim.
Manager: John Couglin.
League Appearances: Brittain G (1); Clarke P 10; Connell G 31; Connelly G 20(5); Cowan M 33; Forrest G 9(3); Gordon K 25(5); Greenhill G 4(5); Hampshire P 13(6); Horn R 16(1); Hutchison G 21(9); Little I 24(7); MacSween I 1(6); McCann G 1; McGarty M 14(3); McKeown C 4; McLeish K 16; McNicoll G 17(3); Murie D 34; Neil M 9(1); O'Connor G 35; Seaton A 30(1); Smith D 26(5); Smith E 3(3).
Goals – League (40): Hutchison 8, Smith D 8, Gordon 6, Connelly 4, Little 4, McGarty 3 (1 pen), Seaton 3 (1 pen), Clarke 1, Forrest 1, McKeown 1, Mcleish 1.
Scottish Cup (4): Clarke 1, Connelly 1, Hutchison 1, McNicoll 1.
CIS Cup (3): Hampshire 1, McNicoll 1, Smith D 1.
Challenge Cup (4): Forrest 1, Gordon 1, Neil 1, Seaton 1 (pen).
Honours – Second Division: Champions – 1978-79.

BRECHIN CITY DIV. 1

Ground: Glebe Park, Brechin DD9 6BJ (01356) 622856
Ground capacity: 3980. **Colours:** Red with white trim.
Manager: Ian Campbell.
League Appearances: Black R 1(6); Byers K 17(8); Callaghan S 11(2); Deas P 33; Dennis S 4(1); Ferguson S 11; Gibson G 28(8); Hamilton S 22(2); Hampshire S 32(2); Hay D 2; Jackson C 3(7); Johnson G 10(14); King C 24(9); MacNicol S 1(2); McCulloch S 1(1); McLeish K 7(4); Mitchell A 8(11); Nelson C 34; Panther E 3(5); Ritchie P 29(6); Sharp J 13; Smith J 7(4); Templeman C 11(5); Walker S 33(2); White D 27(3); Winter C 24(3).
Goals – League (81): Hampshire 17 (1 pen), Ritchie 14 (2 pens), Templeman 14, Gibson 11 (1 pen), King 6, White 6, Walker 4, Callaghan 3, Winter 2, Byers 1, McLeish 1, Panther 1, Sharp 1.
Scottish Cup (7): Hampshire 3, Templeman 2, Ritchie 1, Winter 1.
CIS Cup (6): Gibson 2, Ritchie 2, Templeman 2.
Challenge Cup (0).
Honours – Second Division: Champions – 1982-83, 1989-90, 2004-05. **Third Division:** Champions – 2001-02. **C Division:** Champions – 1953-54.

CELTIC — PREMIER LEAGUE

Ground: Celtic Park, Glasgow G40 3RE (0141) 556 2611
Ground capacity: 60,355 (all seated). **Colours:** Green and white hooped shirts, white shorts.
Manager: Gordon Strachan.
League Appearances: Agathe D 14(2); Balde D 34; Beattie C (11); Bellamy C 12; Camara H 12(6); Douglas R 14; Fernandez D (1); Hartson J 38; Hedman M 6; Henchoz S 2(4); Juninho 9(5); Lambert P (4); Laursen U 12(5); Lennon N 38; Maloney S 1(1); Marshall D 18; McGeady A 20(7); McManus S 2; McNamara J 34; Pearson S 1(7); Petrov S 37; Sutton C 25(2); Sylla M 1(5); Thompson A 32; Valgaeren J 18(1); Varga S 34; Wallace R 4(12).
Goals – League (85): Hartson 23, Sutton 13 (3 pens), Petrov 12, Camara 8, Bellamy 7, Thompson 7 (2 pens), Beattie 4, McGeady 4 (1 pen), Varga 3, Balde 2, Juninho 1, McNamara 1.
Scottish Cup (13): Hartson 3, Sutton 3, Bellamy 2, Thompson 2, Varga 2, Petrov 1.
CIS Cup (9): Wallace 3, Balde 1, Hartson 1, Lambert 1, McGeady 1, McManus 1, Sylla 1.
Honours – Division I: Champions – 1892-93, 1893-94, 1895-96, 1897-98, 1904-05, 1905-06, 1906-07, 1907-08, 1908-09, 1909-10, 1913-14, 1914-15, 1915-16, 1916-17, 1918-19, 1921-22, 1925-26, 1935-36, 1937-38, 1953-54, 1965-66, 1966-67, 1967-68, 1968-69, 1969-70, 1970-71, 1971-72, 1972-73, 1973-74. **Premier Division:** Champions – 1976-77, 1978-79, 1980-81, 1981-82, 1985-86, 1987-88, 1997-98. **Premier League:** 2000-01, 2001-02, 2003–04. **Scottish Cup winners** 1892, 1899, 1900, 1904, 1907, 1908, 1911, 1912, 1914, 1923, 1925, 1927, 1931, 1933, 1937, 1951, 1954, 1965, 1967, 1969, 1971, 1972, 1974, 1975, 1977, 1980, 1985, 1988, 1989, 1995, 2001, 2004, 2005. **League Cup winners** 1957, 1958, 1966, 1967, 1968, 1969, 1970, 1975, 1983, 1998, 2000, 2001, 2004. **European Cup winners** 1967.

CLYDE — DIV. 1

Ground: Broadwood Stadium, Cumbernauld G68 9NE (01236) 451511
Ground capacity: 8200. **Colours:** White shirts with red and black trim, black shorts.
Manager: Graham Roberts.
League Appearances: Arbuckle G 12(14); Balmer S 12(1); Bollan G 25; Bradley K 2(12); Bryson C 23(5); Burns A 15; Conway A 5(6); Doyle P (1); Espinola M 6; Fotheringham K 3; Gardiner C 2(5); Gibson J 29; Gilhaney M 18(16); Greenhill D 2(3); Halliwell B 36; Harris R 1; Harty I 33; Jones G 11(2); Kerkar K 2; Malone E 27(1); Marsigua M 1; McKeever J (3); Mensing S 30; Morrison A (1); Potter J 36; Sheridan D 28(1); Walker A 8(6); Wilford A 12(6); Wilson S 17(2).
Goals – League (35): Harty 15 (4 pens), Bryson 3, Bollan 2, Jones 2, Potter 2, Sheridan 2, Wilford 2, Arbuckle 1, Burns 1, Conway 1, Gibson 1, Gilhaney 1, Wilson 1, Walker 1.
Scottish Cup (5): Harty 2, Arbuckle 1, Bollan 1, Bryson 1.
CIS Cup (1): Wilford 1.
Challenge Cup (2): Harty 1, Valois 1.
Honours – Division II: Champions – 1904-05, 1951-52, 1956-57, 1961-62, 1972-73. **Second Division:** Champions – 1977-78, 1981-82, 1992-93, 1999-2000. **Scottish Cup winners** 1939, 1955, 1958.

COWDENBEATH — DIV. 3

Ground: Central Park, Cowdenbeath KY4 9EY (01383) 610166
Ground capacity: 5268. **Colours:** Royal blue with white cuffs and collar, white shorts.
Manager: David Baikie.

League Appearances: Bain J 9(2); Baird S 2(1); Bathgate S (4); Buchanan L 18(13); Burns J 2; Campbell A 21; Cargill A 2(1); Carlin A 29; Carruth J 1; Findlay S 1; Fleming A 5(3); Fraser S 1; Fusco G 33(1); Gibson N (2); Gilfillan B 1; Gollasch S 1; Gray C 2(2); Gribben D 26(5); Howitt K (1); Kelly JP 5(19); Kelly P 2; Mallan S 1; Mauchlen I 19(7); McCallum R 13(7); McEwen M (1); McGregor D 13(3); McHale P 28(1); McKeown J 33(1); Millar M 10; Miller D 3(5); Mowat D 12(1); Newall C 7; Ritchie I 30; Scott C 1(2); Shand C 25(1); Shields D 18; Williams D 22(5).
Goals – League (54): Gribben 12, Shields 8, Buchanan 7, McHale 5, Fusco 4, Williams 4, McCallum 2, McKeown 2, Ritchie 2, Gilfillan 1, Kelly JP 1, McGregor 1, Mauchlen 1, Millar 1, Mowat 1, own goals 2.
Scottish Cup (2): Buchanan 1, Gribben 1.
CIS Cup (2): Gilfillan 1, Mauchlen 1.
Challenge Cup (0).
Honours – Division II: Champions – 1913-14, 1914-15, 1938-39.

DUMBARTON DIV. 2

Ground: Strathclyde Homes Stadium, Dumbarton G82 1JJ (01389) 762569/767864.
Ground capacity: 2050. **Colours:** Yellow shirts with black facing, shorts yellow with black stripe.
Manager: Paul Martin.
League Appearances: Allan D 5(2); Allan J 9(1); Anderson K 1; Annand E 22(6); Bonar S 15(2); Borris R 7(9); Boyle C 18(4); Bradley M 3(11); Brittain C 32(1); Dempsie M 14; Dillon J 26(5); Dobbins I 24(2); Donald B 19(4); Dunn R 8(6); Gemmell J 8(8); Grindlay S 30; Herd G 2(1); Holmes G 8(4); McEwan C 31; McGroarty C 4(2); McKinstry J 28(4); Rodgers A 17(14); Ronald P 18(5); Russell I 25(7); Walker R 16; Wight J 6.
Goals – League (43): Russell 11, Annand 7, Rodger 6, Dillon 4, McEwan 4 (3 pens), Boyle 2, Dunn 2, Gemmell 2, McKinstry 2, Donald 1, Holmes 1, Ronald 1.
Scottish Cup (5): Annand 1, Dillon 1, Dunn 1, McEwan 1 (pen), Russell 1.
CIS Cup (1): Russell 1.
Challenge Cup (1): Bonar 1.
Honours – Division I: Champions – 1890-91 (Shared), 1891-92. **Division II:** Champions – 1910-11, 1971-72. **Second Division:** Champions – 1991-92. **Scottish Cup winners** 1883.

DUNDEE DIV. 1

Ground: Dens Park, Dundee DD3 7JY (01382) 889966
Ground capacity: 11,760 (all seated). **Colours:** Navy shirts with white and red shoulder and sleeve flashes, white shorts with navy and red piping, navy stockings with two white hoops.
Manager: Jim Duffy.
League Appearances: Anderson I 18(2); Barrett N 25(5); Brady G 20(6); Caballero F 19(9); Cerdeira A 1(5); Conway A (2); Fotheringham M 20(7); Hernandez J 13(1); Hutchinson T 3(1); Jablonski N 2(4); Jack K 2; Kitamarike J 7; Larsen G 2(14); Lovell S 33; MacDonald C 32; Mann R 28(2); McManus T 14; McNally S 17(4); Reilly A (2); Robb S 32(1); Robertson S 1(8); Sancho B 24(3); Smith B 37; Soutar D 36(1); Sutton J 20(12); Wilkie L 12.
Goals – League (37): Lovell 10 (2 pens), Sutton 10 (1 pen), McManus 4, Anderson 2, Barrett 2, Robb 2, Sancho 2, Brady 1, Caballero 1, Hernandez 1, Larsen 1, MacDonald 1.
Scottish Cup (0).
CIS Cup (2): Lovell 1, Anderson 1.

Honours – Division I: Champions – 1961-62. **First Division:** Champions – 1978-79, 1991-92, 1997-98. **Division II:** Champions – 1946-47. **Scottish Cup winners** 1910. **League Cup winners** 1952, 1953, 1974. **B&Q (Centenary) Cup winners** 1991.

DUNDEE UNITED — PREMIER LEAGUE

Ground: Tannadice Park, Dundee DD3 7JW (01382) 833166
Ground capacity: 14,223. **Colours:** Tangerine shirts, tangerine shorts.
Manager: Gordon Chisholm.
League Appearances: Archibald A 38; Brebner G 31(3); Bullock A 26; Callaghan B (1); Cameron G (2); Colgan N 1; Crawford S 15(2); Dodds W 11(10); Duff S 21(4); Grady J 19(10); Hirschfeld L 1; Innes C 16; Jarvie P 10; Kenneth G 10(1); Kerkar K 4(6); Kerr M 28(2); Mair L 3(1); McCracken D 19(5); McInnes D 21(6); McIntyre J 32(3); McLaren A 1(5); Ritchie P 24; Robertson D (1); Robson B 34(2); Samuel C 5(13); Scotland J 11(18); Wilson M 37.
Goals – League (41): McIntyre 11, Robson 6, Wilson 4 (2 pens), Archibald 3, Crawford 3, Scotland 3, Dodds 2 (1 pen), Duff 2, Grady 2, McCracken 2, Brebner 1, Innes 1, own goal 1.
Scottish Cup (13): Crawford 2, Grady 2, McIntyre 2, Wilson 2, Archibald 1, Duff 1, Kerr 1, Robson 1, Scotland 1.
CIS Cup (10): McIntyre 3, Brebner 1, Grady 1, Innes 1, Kerr 1, Robson 1, Scotland 1, Wilson 1.
Honours – Premier Division: Champions – 1982-83. **Division II:** Champions – 1924-25, 1928-29. **Scottish Cup winners** 1994. **League Cup winners** 1980, 1981.

DUNFERMLINE ATHLETIC — PREMIER LEAGUE

Ground: East End Park, Dunfermline KY12 7RB (01383) 724295
Ground capacity: 12,500. **Colours:** Black and white striped shirts, white shorts.
Manager: Jim Leishman.
League Appearances: Bradley S 1(1); Brewster C 13(1); Butler T 6(6); Byrne R 5(1); Campbell I 11(2); Christiansen J 10(3); Dempsey G 16(1); Donnelly S 18(8); Hristov G 4(4); Hunt N 13(10); Labonte A 9(6); Makel L 11; Mason G 34(1); McGlinchey S (1); McKeown C (1); Mehmet W 16(15); Nicholson B 26(1); Ross G 11(3); Scullion P (1); Shields G 13; Skerla A 30; Stillie D 38; Thomson S 35; Tod A 24(7); Wilson C 4; Wilson S 31; Young Darren 29(6); Young Derek 10(7).
Goals – League (34): Tod 6, Derek Young 4, Brewster 3, Donnelly 3, Nicholson 3, Darren Young 3, Christiansen 2, Mehmet 2, Wilson S 2, Hunt 1, Skerla 1, Thomson 1, own goals 3.
Scottish Cup (3): Dempsey 1, Hunt 1, Tod 1.
CIS Cup (4): Brewster 1, Hunt 1, Mehmet 1, Thomson 1.
Honours – First Division: Champions – 1988-89, 1995-96. **Division II:** Champions – 1925-26. **Second Division:** Champions – 1985-86. **Scottish Cup winners** 1961, 1968.

EAST FIFE — DIV. 3

Ground: Bayview Park, Methil, Fife KY8 3RW (01333) 426323
Ground capacity: 2000 (all seated). **Colours:** Gold and black shirts, white shorts.
Manager: James Moffat.
League Appearances: Bain K 16(2); Beith G 10(2); Boyle J 6(4); Brash K 25(5); Byle L 18(4); Colquhoun D 7(1); Crawford R (2); Dodds J 8; Duncan F 10(1); Fairbairn B 25(3); Ferguson J 1(3); Gaughan P 4; Hall M 5; Herkes J 14(1); Kelly G 34; Linton S 2; Lumsden C 32; Mathie G 17(1); McCafferty J 5(1); McDonald G 22(3); McDonald I 3; Mitchell J 20(7); Morrison S 23; Nicholas S 25; Paliczka S 14(8); Renwick M 32; Steele K 9(5); Tarditi S 9(9).

Goals – League (40): Nicholas 9 (2 pens), Fairbairn 6 (1 pen), McDonald G 5, Mitchell 5, Paliczka 4, Colquhoun 3, Lumsden 2, Tarditi 2, Beith 1, Byle 1, Duncan 1, Herkes 1.
Scottish Cup (7): McDonald G 2, Mitchell 2, Byle 1, Lumsden 1, Nicholas 1.
CIS Cup (0).
Challenge Cup (0).
Honours – Division II: Champions – 1947-48. **Scottish Cup winners** 1938. **League Cup winners** 1948, 1950, 1954.

EAST STIRLINGSHIRE — DIV. 3

Ground: Firs Park, Falkirk FK2 7AY (01324) 623583
Ground capacity: 1880. **Colours:** Black shirts with white hoops, black shorts with white and red stripes.
Head Coach: Dennis Newall.
League Appearances: Baldwin C 7(2); Denham G 16; Diack I 5; Donaldson R 29; Dunbar J 11(4); Findlay G 3(8); Gerrard D 1; Gilpin R 9; Harvey D 29; Jackson D 15; Leishman J (3); Livingstone S 30; Mackay J 16(5); McAuley S 5(6); McGhee G 27(3); McGroarty C 16; Miller C 2; Mitchell A 12(1); Moffat A 4(2); Newall C 8(1); Oates S 20; Parks G (9); Peutherer S (3); Rae D 2(6); Robertson J 15(1); Ross P 21(10); Stuart W (1); Thywissen C 19(2); Tyrrell M 13; Tyrrell P 15; Ure D 26(8); Walker J 19(2); Walker N 1.
Goals – League (32): Robertson 7 (2 pens), McGroarty 5, Ure 5, Donaldson 3, Oates 3, Thywissen 3, Diack 1 (pen), Livingstone 1, Mackay 1, Miller 1, Ross 1, Tyrell M 1.
Scottish Cup (1): Livingstone 1.
CIS Cup (2): Parks 1, Ure 1.
Challenge Cup (1): Donaldson 1.
Honours – Division II: Champions – 1931-32. **C Division:** Champions – 1947-48.

ELGIN CITY — DIV. 3

Ground: Borough Briggs, Elgin IV30 1AP (01343) 551114
Ground capacity: 5000 (478 seated). **Colours:** Black and white vertical striped shirts, black shorts.
Manager: David Robertson.
League Appearances: Allison J 3(3); Black S 4; Bone A 4; Bremner F 23(3); Cumming S 33; Dempsie A 24; Dickson H 30(1); Donnachie S 10(1); Harty M 31(1); Higgins C 18; Huckins M (1); Kaczan P 25(1); Lennox A (2); Martin W 33; McDonald J (3); McKendrick K 2(1); McKenzie J 28; Melrose G (5); Napier P 4(22); Nelson A 34; Reid P 13(10); Renton K 36; Roddie A 24(2); Thomson D 3; Vigurs I 8(5); Vigurs P 4(7); Wood G 2(9).
Goals – League (39): Martin 9, Harty 4, Dickson 4, Bone 3 (1 pen), Donnachie 3, Kaczan 3, McKenzie J 3 (1 pen), Roddie 3, Cumming 1, Dempsie 1, Higgins 1, Napier 1, Nelson 1, Reid 1, own goal 1.
Scottish Cup (0).
CIS Cup (2): Bone 1, Martin 1.
Challenge Cup (0).
Honours – Nil.

FALKIRK — PREMIER LEAGUE

Ground: Brockville Park, Falkirk FK1 5AX (01324) 624121
Ground capacity: 6123. **Colours:** Navy blue shirts with white seams, navy shorts.
Head Coach: John Hughes.

League Appearances: Barr D (2); Campbell M 25(6); Duffy D 35; Ferguson A 26; Henry J (1); Hill D 10; Hughes J 17(2); James K 29; Kernaghan A 9; Latapy R 31(1); Lawrie A 27(4); Mackenzie S 34; Marshall C (12); McAnespie K (8); McBreen D 21(2); McPherson C 33; McStay R 10(5); Moutinho P 12(7); Nicholls D 12(6); O'Neil J 30(2); Rahim B (3); Ramsay M (1); Scally N 19(14); Scobbie T (1); Sharp J 3(1); Thomson A 13(11).
Goals – League (66): Duffy 17, McBreen 13, Thomson 9, Latapy 7 (1 pen), Lawrie 4, Moutinho 4, Nicholls 3, Hughes 2, Campbell 1, James 1 (pen), McAnespie 1, Mackenzie 1, McStay 1, O'Neil 1, Scally 1.
Scottish Cup (0).
CIS Cup (11): Duffy 4, Thomson 4, Latapy 1, Mackenzie 1, O'Neil 1.
Challenge Cup (15): Duffy 6, Latapy 3, Lawrie 2, Nicholls 1, O'Neil 1, Scally 1, Thomson 1.
Honours – Division II: Champions – 1935-36, 1969-70, 1974-75. **First Division:** Champions – 1990-91, 1993-94, 2002-03, 2004-05. **Second Division:** Champions – 1979-80. **Scottish Cup winners** 1913, 1957. **League Challenge Cup winners** 1998, 2005.

FORFAR ATHLETIC DIV. 2

Ground: Station Park, Forfar, Angus (01307) 463576
Ground capacity: 4640. **Colours:** Navy shirts with sky blue side panels, sky blue shorts with navy side panels.
Manager: Brian Fairley.
League Appearances: Bonar S 14; Booth M 11(7); Brown M 27; Cameron D 1(4); Clark N (5); Creer A 5; Davidson H 11(7); Dunn D 17(1); Ferrie N 4; Florence S 7(5); Forrest E 34; King D 16; King M 9(17); Lowing D 31; Lunan P 33(3); Maher M (11); McAlpine J 1(1); McClune D 34(1); McKenzie D 1(1); Rattray A 17; Sellars B 25; Shields P 33(3); Stein J 23(8); Tosh P 28(2); Waddell R 14(1).
Goals – League (51): Shields 20 (1 pen), Tosh 13 (1 pen), McClune 5, Stein 4, King M 3, Sellars 3, King D 1. Rattray 1, Waddell 1.
Scottish Cup (1): Tosh 1.
CIS Cup (4): Tosh 2, McClune 1, Sellars 1, own goal 1.
Challenge Cup (9): Shields 4, Tosh 3, Booth 1, McClune 1.
Honours – Second Division: Champions – 1983-84. **Third Division:** Champions – 1994-95.

GRETNA DIV. 2

Ground: Raydale Park, Gretna DG16 5AP (01461) 337602
Ground capacity: 2200. **Colours:** Black shirt with white hoops, black shorts with white trim.
Manager: Rowan Alexander.
League Appearances: Aitken A 34; Baldacchino R 29; Bingham D 36; Birch M 29(1); Boyd M 1(1); Collins D 7; Cosgrove S (6); Deuchar K 30(6); Galloway M 4(2); Gilfillan B 21(5); Gordon W 1; Graham D (11); Grainger D 2(1); Holdsworth D 4(1); Innes C 11; Irons D 19(1); Lennon D 2(1); Main A 4; Mathieson D 32; McGuffie R 30(6); McQuilken J 29(3); Nicholls D 3(9); Prokas R 5(1); Shields D (3); Skelton G 35; Smith A 6(6); Tosh S 13; Townsley D 9(11); Wake B (6).
Goals – League (130): Deuchar 38, Bingham 27, Skelton 12, Baldacchino 9, McGuffie 8, Birch 7 (3 pens), Gilfillan 6, Townsley 5, Smith 3, Wake 3, Aitken 2, Innes 2, McQuilken 2, Nicholls 2, Cosgrve 1, Galloway 1, Tosh 1, own goal 1.
Scottish Cup (6): Deuchar 3, Birch 1 (pen), Skelton 1, own goal 1.
CIS Cup (0).
Challenge Cup (4): Smith 2, Baldacchino 1, Bingham 1.
Honours – Third Division: Champions – 2004–05.

HAMILTON ACADEMICAL — DIV. 1

Ground: New Douglas Park, Cadzow Avenue, Hamilton ML3 0FT (01698) 368650
Ground capacity: 5396. **Colours:** Red and white hooped shirts, white shorts.
Manager: Allan Maitland.
League Appearances: Aitken C 9(8); Arbuckle A 3(5); Blackadder R 7(4); Carney D 6(2); Carrigan B 16(11); Convery S 4(8); Corcoran M 30(4); Cramb C 7(3); Ferguson D 16(1); Fyfe I 13(5); Halliday R 1; Hamilton D 15(10); Hardy L 12(1); Hodge A 30(2); Irons S (2); Javary J 11(2); Jellema R 1; Keogh P 23(3); Lumsden T 11(3); MahouvÇ M 12; McArthur J 5(1); McEwan D 35; McGlinchey K (1); McLaughlin M 29; McLeod P (2); McPhee B 18(10); Ortiz F 12; Thomson S 30(1); Tunbridge S 18(2); Waddell R 16(3); Walker R 6(1).
Goals – League (35): Tunbridge 5, Callaghan 4, Keogh 4, Corcoran 3, Hardy 3 (1 pen), McPhee 3, Convery 2, Cramb 2 (1 pen), McLaughlin 2, Hamilton 1, Javary 1, Lumsden 1, McLeod 1, Thomson 1, own goals 2.
Scottish Cup (0).
CIS Cup (4): Convery 3, Thomson 1.
Challenge Cup (0).
Honours – First Division: Champions – 1985-86, 1987-88. **Divison II:** Champions – 1903-04. **Division III:** Champions – 2000-01. **B&Q Cup winners** 1992, 1993.

HEART OF MIDLOTHIAN — PREMIER LEAGUE

Ground: Tynecastle Park, Gorgie Road, Edinburgh EH11 2NL (0131) 200 7200
Ground capacity: 17,412. **Colours:** Maroon shirts, white shorts.
Manager: George Burley.
League Appearances: Berra C 7(5); Burchill M 5(7); Cesnauskis D 7(1); De Vries M 7(2); Elliot C (4); Gordon C 38; Hamill J 25(7); Hartley P 32(1); Janczyk N 2(4); Kisnorbo P 17; Kizys M 2(5); MacFarlane N 16(4); Maybury A 16(1); McAllister J 23(7); McGeown D (2); McKenna K 7(6); Mikoliunus S 10(1); Miller L 17(1); Neilson R 35; Pereira R 12(4); Pressley S 32; Simmons S 5(6); Sives C 2; Sloan R (2); Stamp P 15(1); Stewart M 5(12); Thomson J 3; Thorradisson H (4); Tierney G (1); Wallace L 13; Webster A 35; Weir G 11(9); Wyness D 19(10).
Goals – League (43): Hartley 11 (5 pens), Miller 8, Wyness 4 (1 pen), Burchill 3, Pereira 3, Hamill 2, McKenna 2, Pressley 2 (2 pens), De Vries 1, Kisnorbo 1, Mikoliunas 1, Neilson 1, Webster 1, Weir 1, own goals 2.
Scottish Cup (10): Miller 3, Cesnauskis 2, Wyness 2, McAllister 1, MacFarlane 1, Wallace 1.
CIS Cup (7): Hartley 3, Burchill 1, Hamill 1, Thosarinsson 1, Webster 1.
Honours – Division I: Champions – 1894-95, 1896-97, 1957-58, 1959-60. **First Division:** Champions – 1979-80. **Scottish Cup winners** 1891, 1896, 1901, 1906, 1956, 1998. **League Cup winners** 1955, 1959, 1960, 1963.

HIBERNIAN — PREMIER LEAGUE

Ground: Easter Road Stadium, Edinburgh EH7 5QG (0131) 661 2159
Ground capacity: 17,400. **Colours:** Green shirts with white sleeves and collar, white shorts with green stripe.
Manager: Tony Mowbray.
League Appearances: Baillie J (1); Beuzelin G 21(5); Brebner G 2; Brown A (1); Scott Brown 18(2); Simon Brown 38; Caldwell G 37; Dobbie S (7); Fletcher S 11(9); Glass S 34(2); Konte A 3(9); McCluskey J (10); McDonald K (3); McManus T 2; Morrow S 5(17); Murdock C 5; Murphy D 27; Murray A 10(2); Murray I 29; Nicol K (1); O'Connor G 34(2); Orman A 10(2); Riordan D 36(1); Rocastle C 11(2); Shields J (6); Shiels D 28(9); Smith G 19(1); Sproule I 1(6); Thomson K (3); Whittaker S 37.

Goals – League (64): Riordan 20, O'Connor 14, Fletcher 5, Shiels 5, Beuzelin 4, Caldwell 3, Glass 2, Orman 2, Scott Brown 1, Konte 1, Morrow 1, Murphy 1, Murray I 1, Smith 1, Sproule 1, Whittaker 1, own goal 1.
Scottish Cup (9): O'Connor 3, Morrow 2, Scott Brown 1, Caldwell 1, Riordan 1 (pen), Whittaker 1.
CIS Cup (8): Riordan 2, Dobbie 1, Glass 1, Murdock 1, O'Connor 1, Orman 1, Shiels 1.
Honours – Division I: Champions – 1902-03, 1947-48, 1950-51, 1951-52. **First Division:** Champions – 1980-81, 1998-99. **Division II:** Champions – 1893-94, 1894-95, 1932-33. **Scottish Cup winners** 1887, 1902. **League Cup winners** 1973, 1992.

INVERNESS CALEDONIAN THISTLE PREMIER LEAGUE

Ground: Tulloch Caledonian Stadium, East Longman, Inverness IV1 1FF (01463) 715816
Ground capacity: 7400. **Colours:** Royal blue shirts with red stripes, royal blue shorts.
Manager: Craig Brewster.
League Appearances: Bayne G 32(6); Black I 7(6); Brewster C 11(2); Brown M 38; Dods D 28; Duncan R 27(2); Fetai B (8); Fox L 1(8); Fraser M (1); Golabek S 37; Hart R 34(3); Hastings R 5(6); Hislop S 2(5); Juanjo 26(3); Keogh L 16(5); McAllister R (4); McBain R 31(3); McCaffrey S 14(2); Munro G 36; Proctor D 1(3); Prunty B 8(19); Thomson D (1); Tokely R 34; Wilson B 30(6).
Goals – League (41): Wilson 11 (4 pens), Bayne 6, Juanjo 6 (1 pen), Brewster 4, Hart 3, Fox 2, McBain 2, Tokely 2, Dods 1, Duncan 1, Golabek 1, McCaffrey 1, Prunty 1.
Scottish Cup (2): Brewster 1, Golabek 1.
CIS Cup (2): Tokely 2.
Honours – First Division: Champions – 2003–04. **Third Division:** Champions – 1996-97. **Bell's League Challenge winners** 2004.

KILMARNOCK PREMIER LEAGUE

Ground: Rugby Park, Kilmarnock KA1 2DP (01563) 525184
Ground capacity: 18,128. **Colours:** Blue and white striped shirts, blue shorts.
Manager: Jim Jefferies.
League Appearances: Boyd K 29(1); Combe A 32; Dargo C 10(10); Dillon S 4(2); Dindeleux F 27(2); Dodds R 4(4); Fontaine L 3; Ford S 17(1); Fowler J 24(5); Greer G 19(3); Hay G 22(3); Invincibile D 28(3); Johnston A 19(10); Joly E (6); Leven P 29(3); Lilley D 33; Locke G 22(3); McDonald G 38; Murray S 8(13); Naismith S 16(8); Nish C 16(10); Smith G 6; Wales G 12(12).
Goals – League (49): Boyd 17 (2 pens), Invincibile 7, Leven 4 (1 pen), Nish 4, Johnston A 3, McDonald 3, Dargo 2, Wales 2, Dodds 1, Ford 1, Greer 1, Lilley 1, Locke 1, Murray 1, Maismith 1.
Scottish Cup (5): Boyd 2, McDonald 1, Naismith 1, Nish 1.
CIS Cup (4): Invincibile 2, Leven 1, McDonald 1.
Honours – Division I: Champions – 1964-65. **Division II:** Champions – 1897-98, 1898-99. **Scottish Cup winners** 1920, 1929, 1997.

LIVINGSTON PREMIER LEAGUE

Ground: Almondvale Stadium, Alderton Road, Livingston EH54 7DN (01506) 417 000
Ground capacity: 10,024. **Colours:** Gold shirts, black shorts, white stockings.
Team Manager: Paul Lambert.
League Appearances: Adam S 4(3); Bahoken S 17(1); Boyack S 4(2); Brittain R 8(5); Dair J 22(2); Deloumeaux E 13; Dorado E 30(1); Dorrans G (1); Easton C 24(7); Hamilton C 17(4); Hand J 5(2); Harding G 3; Horvath F 6(2); Kashloul H 7(1); Kernaghan A 4; Kriston A 3(2); Libbra M 2(9); Lilley D 23(8); Lovell S 19(1);

McKenzie R 33; McLaughlin S 7(3); McMenamin C 13(9); McNamee D 29; McPake J 7(8); Meldrum C 5; Nouma P (2); O'Brien B 38; Rubio O 24(3); Snodgrass R 8(9); Snowdon W 1(2); Stanic G 18(2); Strong G 6(3); Vincze G 14; Wilson M 4(1).
Goals – League (34): O'Brien 8, Hamilton 4, Easton 3, Lilley 3, Dair 2, Horvath 2, Kashloul 2, McMenamin 2, McPake 2, Snodgrass 2, Deloumeaux 1, Lovell 1, McNamee 1, own goal 1.
Scottish Cup (4): Easton 1, McMenamin 1, Rubio 1, Snodgrass 1.
CIS Cup (4): Easton 3 (1 pen), Hamilton 1.
Honours – First Division: Champions – 2000-01. **Second Division:** Champions – 1986-87, 1998-99. **Third Division:** Champions – 1995-96. **League Cup winners** 2004.

MONTROSE DIV. 3

Ground: Links Park, Montrose DD10 8QD (01674) 673200
Ground capacity: 3292. **Colours:** Royal blue shirts and shorts.
Manager: Henry Hall.
League Appearances: Bremner K (3); Budd A 6(2); Butter J 24; Dodds K 19(7); Donachie B 33(1); Doyle P 28; Ferguson s 25(1); Fraser S 7(1); Graham R (7); Greenhill D 8(4); Hall E 19(6); Hankinson M 12; Jones D (2); Kerrigan S 21; McLean D 8(2); Morrice K (1); O'Reilly C 4(6); Sharp G 27(6); Slater M 4(4); Smart C 31(1); Smith D 1(10); Smith E 11; Smith G 1; Spink D 7(9); Stephen N 33(1); Watson C 10(16); Webster K 28(3); Wood M 29(1).
Goals – League (47): Smart 14 (5 pens), Sharp 7, Webster 6, Wood 5, McLean 4, Doyle 2, Stephen 2, Watson 2, Ferguson 1, Greenhill 1, Hall 1, Kerrigan 1, own goal 1.
Scottish Cup (7): Sharp 2, Smart 2, Dodds 1, Webster 1, Wood 1.
CIS Cup (1): Jones 1.
Challenge Cup (0).
Honours – Second Division: Champions – 1984-85.

MORTON DIV. 2

Ground: Cappielow Park, Greenock (01475) 723571
Ground capacity: 11,612. **Colours:** Royal blue and white hooped shirts, white shorts with royal blue panel down side.
Manager: Jim McInally.
League Appearances: Adam J 6(9); Bannerman S 6(10); Collins D 21; Coyle C 14; Diack I 1(3); Dillon S 17; Greacen S 32; Harding R 9; Hawke W 4(2); Keenan D 15(5); Mahood A 8(3); Maisano J 19(11); Maisano M 9(1); McAlister J 35(1); McCluskey S 22; McCulloch M 8(3); McGurn D 22(1); McLaren A 12; McLaughlin S 14(1); McLean K 1; Millar C 34; Templeman C 18(1); Walker J 11(16); Walker P 20(11); Weatherson P 26(6); Williams A 12(5).
Goals – League (60): Millar 11, Weatherson 11 (2 pens), Maisano J 6 (1 pen), Templeman 6, Walker J 6, Walker P 5, McLaren 3, Greacen 2, McAlister 2, Dillon 1, Harding 1, Maisano M 1, McCluskey 1, Williams 1 (pen), own goals 3.
Scottish Cup (11): Millar 3, Weatherson 3, Walker J 2, Adam 1, Hawke 1, Williams 1.
CIS Cup (1): Walker P 1.
Challenge Cup (1): Walker J 1.
Honours – First Division: Champions – 1977-78, 1983-84, 1986-87. **Division II:** Champions – 1949-50, 1963-64, 1966-67. **Second Division:** Champions – 1994-95. **Third Division:** Champions 2002-03. **Scottish Cup winners** 1922.

MOTHERWELL PREMIER LEAGUE

Ground: Fir Park, Motherwell ML1 2QN (01698) 333333
Ground capacity: 13,742. **Colours:** Amber shirts with claret hoop and trim, amber shorts, amber stockings with claret trim.
First Team Coach: Terry Butcher.

League Appearances: Britton G (3); Burns A 4(7); Clarkson D 25(10); Corr B 5(1); Corrigan M 31; Craigan S 37; Fagan S 11(12); Fitzpatrick M 14(11); Foran R 25(10); Hamilton J 13(1); Hammell S 32; Keogh D (3); Kerr B 6(2); Kinniburgh W 10(3); Leitch S 28(1); Marshall G 33; McBride K 24(1); McDonald S 26(1); O'Donnell P 18; Partridge D 29; Paterson J 27(8); Quinn P 20(3); Smith D (1); Wright K (6).
Goals – League (46): McDonald 15, Foran 5 (2 pens), McBride 5 (3 pens), Clarkson 3, Craigan 3, O'Donnell 3, Paterson 3, Corrigan 2, Burns 1, Fitzpatrick 1, Hamilton 1, Partridge 1, own goals 3.
Scottish Cup (0).
CIS Cup (15): Foran 4, McBride 2, O'Donnell 2, Partridge 2, Craigan 1, Clarkson 1, Fitzpatrick 1, Paterson 1, Wright 1.
Honours – Division I: Champions – 1931-32. **First Division:** Champions – 1981-82, 1984-85. **Division II:** Champions – 1953-54, 1968-69. **Scottish Cup winners** 1952, 1991. **League Cup winners** 1951.

PARTICK THISTLE — DIV. 2

Ground: Firhill Stadium, Glasgow G20 7AL (0141) 579 1971
Ground capacity: 13,141. **Colours:** Red and yellow striped shirts, red shorts.
Manager: Dick Campbell.
League Appearances: Anis J 14(2); Arthur K 35; Bennett N 1; Brady D 10(1); Britton G (1); Cameron I (2); Dowie A 26(1); Escalas J 27(3); Fleming D 32(3); Fulton S 16(3); Gibson A 11(2); Gibson W 22(6); Hinds L 24(11); Howie W 4(3); Madaschi A 26(1); McConalogue S 8(4); McLaren A 5(4); Milne K 26(4); Mitchell J 17(4); Murray G 31(1); Oné A 15(12); Panther E 6(8); Paterson S 1; Ross A 11(3); Ross I 6(1); Snowdon W 7(1); Stewart M (2); Strachan A 6(7); Wilkinson A 9(2).
Goals – League (38): Escalas 10, Oné 6, Hinds 4, McConalogue 4, Fleming 2, Madaschi 2, Panther 2, Milne 1, Mitchell 1, Murray 1 (pen), Ross A 1, Wilkinson 1, own goals 3.
Scottish Cup (1): Oné 1.
CIS Cup (6): Hinds 2, Dowie 1, Escalas 1, Fleming 1, Gibson W 1.
Challenge Cup (6): Gibson W 2, Panther 2, Escalas 1, Hinds 1.
Honours – First Division: Champions – 1975-76, 2001-02. **Division II:** Champions – 1896-97, 1899-1900, 1970-71. **Second Division:** Champions 2000-01. **Scottish Cup winners** 1921. **League Cup winners** 1972.

PETERHEAD — DIV. 2

Ground: Balmoor Stadium, Peterhead AB42 1EU (01779) 478256
Ground capacity: 3250 (1000 seated). **Colours:** Royal blue with white shirts, royal blue shorts.
Manager: Iain Stewart.
League Appearances: Bavidge M 31(5); Buchan J 35(1); Cameron D 13(3); Campbell C 12(11); Duncan R (1); Gibson K 27(5); Good I 31(1); Hagen D 25(1); Hegarty C 4(1); Johnston M (5); Linn R 14(13); Mathers P 33; McSkimming S (3); Michie S 30(6); Milne D (1); Perry M 34; Raeside R 32(1); Robertson C 1; Robertson S 10(3); Shand R (1); Stewart G 13(8); Stewart I (2); Thompson B 3; Tindal K (2); Tully C 34; Youngson A 14(17).
Goals – League (81): Michie 21 (4 pens), Bavidge 13 (2 pens), Buchan 8, Tully 7, Linn 6, Stewart G 6, Cameron 4, Raeside 4, Hagen 3 (1 pen), Youngson 2, Campbell 1, Hegarty 1, Johnston 1, Robertson 1, Stewart I 1, own goals 2.
Scottish Cup (1): Bavidge 1.
CIS Cup (4): Bavidge 2, Michie 2 (1 pen).
Challenge Cup (5): Bavidge 3, Buchan 1, Gibson 1.
Honours – Nil.

QUEEN OF THE SOUTH DIV. 1

Ground: Palmerston Park, Dumfries DG2 9BA (01387) 254853
Ground capacity: 8352. **Colours:** Royal blue shirts with white sleeves, white shorts with blue piping.
Manager: Iain Scott.
League Appearances: Armstrong C 2(5); Bagan D 17(4); Bell S 1(1); Bernard R 13; Bowey S 34; Burns P 18(5); Carr C 2(1); Craig D 18; English T 29(1); George L (2); Gibson W 13(8); Jaconelli E 3(12); Lovell S 12; Lyle D 22(1); McColligan B 27(5); McLaughlin B 25(5); McNiven D 22(8); Paton E 28(2); Payne S 10(7); Reid B 21; Scott Christopher 1; Scott Colin 23(1); Thomson J 34; Williams A 1(4); Wood G 20(8).
Goals – League (36): McNiven 12, Lyle 7, Paton 4, Bowey 3, Wood 3, McLaughlin 2, Burns 1, Craig 1, English 1, Payne 1, own goal 1.
Scottish Cup (2): Gibson 1, Lyle 1.
CIS Cup (1): McNiven 1.
Challenge Cup (2): English 1, Wood 1.
Honours – Division II: Champions – 1950-51. **Second Division:** Champions – 2001-02. **Challenge Cup winners** 2003

QUEEN'S PARK DIV. 3

Ground: Hampden Park, Glasgow G42 9BA (0141) 632 1275
Ground capacity: 52,000. **Colours:** Black and white hooped shirts, white shorts.
Coach: Billy Stark.
League Appearances: Agostini D 10(3); Blair B 16(3); Bonnar M (3); Bowers R 4; Canning S (2); Carroll F 33; Clark R 33; Clarke D 2; Crawford D 34; Felvus B 4(16); Ferry D 17(1); Ferry M 26(3); Graham A 20(7); Harvey P 27(3); Kettlewell S 23(4); Livingston A (7); McCallum D 7; McCue B 1; McGinty A 4(2); McGovern S 1; Molloy S 26(2); Quin A 10; Reilly S 13(1); Rushford G 24(3); Sinclair R 24(1); Sloan T (1); Trouten A 31(2); Weatherston D 2(5); Weir J 1; Whelan J 3(5).
Goals – League (51): Carroll 14, Ferry M 7, Clark R 6 (2 pens), Graham 5, Trouten 3, Bowers 2, Felvus 2, Harvey 2, Kettlewell 2, McCallum 1, Quinn 1, Reilly 1 (pen), own goals 5.
Scottish Cup (0).
CIS Cup (2): Carroll 1, Clark R 1.
Challenge Cup (3): Carroll 1, Graham 1, Reilly 1.
Honours – Division II: Champions – 1922-23. **B Division:** Champions – 1955-56. **Second Division:** Champions – 1980-81. **Third Division:** Champions – 1999-2000. **Scottish Cup winners** 1874, 1875, 1876, 1880, 1881, 1882, 1884, 1886, 1890, 1893.

RAITH ROVERS DIV. 2

Ground: Stark's Park, Pratt Street, Kirkcaldy KY1 1SA (01592) 263514
Ground capacity: 10,104 (all seated). **Colours:** Navy blue shirts with white sleeves, white shorts with navy blue and red edges.
Manager: Gordon Dalziel.
League Appearances: Bartholome A 26; Berthelot D 26; Boyle J (5); Brady D 19; Clarke P 10(1); Crabbe S 12; Daly W 9(1); Davidson I 25(1); Dennis S 12; Ebanda H 13(4); Fullerton E 4(7); Gilfillan J (1); Hagan P 1; Hajovsky T 6; Hall S 1; Jablowski N 12; Leiper C 5(1); Lusamba N 1; Malcolm C 1(10); Martin J 19(14); Maxwell D 2(2); McAlpine J 6(5); McGowan M (1); McMullan P 10; Mendy M 8(1); Millar P 19(1); Murtagh C 10(1); O'Reilly C 5(4); Ouattara M 29(1); Perry J 6; Pounoussamy R 9(2); Raffell B 8(3); Rivas Ortiz F 14; Sacko H 19(3); Smart J 29(1); Tagro B 4(1); Tulloch S 10(3); Young L 6(9).

Goals – League (26): Clarke 4, Martin 4, Sacko 4, Ebanda 2, Jablowski 2, Tulloch 2, Brady 1, Daly 1, McMillan 1, Malcolm 1, Murtagh 1, Ouattara 1, Young 1, own goal 1.
Scottish Cup (0).
CIS Cup (1): Ortiz 1.
Challenge Cup (0).
Honours – First Division: Champions – 1992-93, 1994-95. **Second Division:** Champions – 2002-03. **Division II:** Champions – 1907-08, 1909-10 (Shared), 1937-38, 1948-49. **League Cup winners** 1995.

RANGERS — PREMIER LEAGUE

Ground: Ibrox Stadium, Glasgow G51 2XD (0870) 600 1972
Ground capacity: 50,444. **Colours:** Royal blue shirts with red and white trim, white shorts with blue and red trim.
Manager: Alex McLeish.
League Appearances: Adam C (1); Andrews M 30; Arveladze S 11(13); Ball M 12(2); Boumsong J 18; Buffel T 13(2); Burke C 7(5); Davidson R (1); Djordjic B 4; Ferguson B 13; Hughes S 6(5); Hutton A 8(2); Khizanishvili Z 14(2); Kirgiakos S 15; Klos S 23; Lovenkrands P 12(5); Malcolm R 19(3); McCormack R (1); McGregor A 2; Mladenovic D 6(1); Moore C 3; Namouchi H 13(7); Novo I 34(1); Prso D 33(1); Rae A 17(8); Ricksen F 38; Ross M 13; Smith S 2(2); Thompson S 7(17); Vanoli P 3(2); Vignal G 29(1); Waterreus R 13.
Goals – League (78): Novo 19 (3 pens), Prso 18 (1 pen), Arveladze 6, Ricksen 5, Thompson 5, Andrews 4, Buffel 4, Lovenjrands 3, Vignal 3, Boumsong 2, Ferguson 2, Hughes 2, Namouchi 2, Malcolm 1, Rae A 1, own goal 1.
Scottish Cup (1): Ricksen 1.
CIS Cup (16): Novo 3, Ricksen 3, Thompson 3, Kyrgiakos 2, Prso 2, Arveladze 1, Buffel 1, Ross 1.
Honours – Division I: Champions – 1890-91 (Shared), 1898-99, 1899-1900, 1900-01, 1901-02, 1910-11, 1911-12, 1912-13, 1917-18, 1919-20, 1920-21, 1922-23, 1923-24, 1924-25, 1926-27, 1927-28, 1928-29, 1929-30, 1930-31, 1932-33, 1933-34, 1934-35, 1936-37, 1938-39, 1946-47, 1948-49, 1949-50, 1952-53, 1955-56, 1956-57, 1958-59, 1960-61, 1962-63, 1963-64, 1974-75. **Premier Division:** Champions – 1975-76, 1977-78, 1986-87, 1988-89, 1989-90, 1990-91, 1991-92, 1992-93, 1993-94, 1994-95, 1995-96, 1996-97. **Premier League:** Champions – 1998-99, 1999-2000, 2002-03, 2004-05. **Scottish Cup winners** 1894, 1897, 1898, 1903, 1928, 1930, 1932, 1934, 1935, 1936, 1948, 1949, 1950, 1953, 1960, 1962, 1963, 1964, 1966, 1973, 1976, 1978, 1979, 1981, 1992, 1993, 1996, 1999, 2000, 2002, 2003. **League Cup winners** 1947, 1949, 1961, 1962, 1964, 1965, 1971, 1976, 1978, 1979, 1982, 1984, 1985, 1987, 1988, 1989, 1991, 1993, 1994, 1997, 1999, 2002, 2003, 2005. **European Cup-Winners' Cup winners** 1972.

ROSS COUNTY — DIV. 1

Ground: Victoria Park, Dingwall IV15 9QW (01349) 860860
Ground capacity: 6700. **Colours:** Navy blue with white and red pin stripe on collar and sleeves, white shorts with navy and red side stripe, navy stockings.
Manager: John Robertson.
League Appearances: Adam C 8(2); Burke A 28(4); Canning M 33; Cowie D 33(1); Garden S 15(1); Gunn C (1); Higgins S 13(13); Kerr S (3); Kilgannon S 20(9); Lauchlan J 28; Macdonald N 2(6); Mackay S 3(9); Mahood A (1); Malcolm S 10(3); McCulloch M 36; McCunnie J 24(3); McGarry S 19(14); McKinlay K 1(3); McSwegan G 10(7); Moffat A (2); Rankin J 28(2); Robertson J 25(1); Stewart C 21; Taylor S 5; Tiernan F 16; Winters D 18(14).
Goals – League (40): Burke 6, Winters 6, Cowie 5, Higgins 5, Canning 4, Lauchlan 4, McGarry 4, Adam 2, Kilgannon 1, Malcolm 1, own goals 2.
Scottish Cup (5): Winters 2, Burke 1 (pen), Rankin 1, own goal 1.

CIS Cup (3): Burke 3.
Challenge Cup (11): Winters 5, Burke 4, Canning 1, Cowie 1.
Honours – Third Division: Champions – 1998-99.

ST JOHNSTONE DIV. 1

Ground: McDiarmid Park, Crieff Road, Perth PH1 2SJ (01738) 459090
Ground capacity: 10,673. **Colours:** Royal blue shirts with white trim, white shorts.
Manager: Owen Coyle.
League Appearances: Anderson S 19(1); Bagan D 4(2); Baxter M 12(3); Bernard P 1(1); Cowan D 10; Cuthbert K 5; Dobbie S 5(3); Dyer W 7; Forsyth R 15(1); Fotheringham K 8; Fotheringham M (5); Fraser S 1(1); Hannah D 28(1); Hardy L 11(2); Hay C 13(16); Jackson A (6); Linn R (1); Macdonald P 26(1); Mahood A 4(3); Malone E 3; Marshall C 1(1); Maxwell I 33; McAnespie K 13(4); McCann R 24(2); McConalogue S 4(5); McGregor A 20; McManus S 4(3); Moore M 19(5); Rutkiewicz K 16(4); Samson C 11(1); Sheerin P 34; Sloan R 8; Stevenson R 7(3); Tait J 13(1); Webb S 15(4); Weir J 2.
Goals – League (38): MacDonald 11, Hay 4, Moore 4, McCann 3, Anderson 2, Baxter 2, Dobbie 2, Hannah 2 (pens), Sheerin 2, Fotheringham K 1, Fotheringham M 1, McAnespie 1, McManus 1, Maxwell 1, own goal 1.
Scottish Cup (0).
CIS Cup (2): Hannah 1, Hay 1.
Challenge Cup (7): Moore 2, Rutkiewicz 2, Fotheringham K 1, Hannah 1, Maxwell 1.
Honours – First Division: Champions – 1982-83, 1989-90, 1996-97. **Division II:** Champions – 1923-24, 1959-60, 1962-63.

ST MIRREN DIV. 1

Ground: St Mirren Park, Paisley PA3 2EJ (0141) 889 2558, 840 1337
Ground capacity: 10,866 (all seated). **Colours:** Black and white striped shirts, white shorts with black trim.
Manager: Gus MacPherson.
League Appearances: Annand E 1; Baird J 3(18); Broadfoot K 36; Crilly M 4(5); Dempsie M 1; Ellis L 14(8); Gillies R 11(13); Hinchcliffe C 34; Kean S 14(1); Lappin S 29(5); McCay R 6(5); McGinty B 24(8); McGowne K 31; McKenna D (3); Millen A 36; Molloy C 1; Murray H 30(2); O'Neil J 19(11); Paatelainen M 12(4); Reid A 8; Reilly M 35; Russell A 12(13); Smith C 2; Van Zanten D 33; Woods S (1).
Goals – League (41): O'Neil 7 (1 pen), Broadfoot 5, Kean 5, Russell 5, McGinty 4 (3 pens), Paatelainen 4, Baird 3, Ellis 2, Gillies 1, Lappin 1, Murray 1, Reilly 1, Van Zanten 1, own goal 1.
Scottish Cup (5): Kean 3, Murray 1, Russell 1.
CIS Cup (2): O'Neil 1, Paatelainen 1.
Challenge Cup (1): Gillies 1.
Honours – First Division: Champions – 1976-77, 1999-2000. **Division II:** Champions – 1967-68. **Scottish Cup winners** 1926, 1959, 1987.

STENHOUSEMUIR DIV. 3

Ground: Ochilview Park, Stenhousemuir FK5 5QL (01324) 562992
Ground capacity: 2374. **Colours:** Maroon shirts, white shorts.
Manager: Des McKeown.
League Appearances: Collins L 22; Davidson R 8(6); Easton S 14(2); Fallon S 23(1); Gardiner M (3); Henderson R 25(1); Kerrigan S 10; Kirkham J 1(1); Knox K 19(3); Lauchlan M 23(3); McBride J 32(1); McCulloch G 11(1); McCulloch W 34; McGregor S 16(3); McGrillen P 32(2); McInally D 27(3); Menzies C 3(4); Miles C

(1); Morrison D 7(4); Morrison M 1; Murphy P 29(3); Ogunmade D (1); Orr D 1(1); Savage J 24(6); Sinclair T 12(9); Smith A 16(4); Struthers K 4(3).
Goals – League (58): McGrillen 18 (3 pens), Savage 9, Davidson 5, McBride 5, Collins 4, Lauchlan 4, McInally 4, Murphy 2, Sinclair 2, Knox 1, McGregor 1, Morrison D 1, own goals 2.
Scottish Cup (1): Savage 1.
CIS Cup (4): Collins 1, McBride 1, McGrillen 1, Savage 1.
Challenge Cup (1): McGrillen 1.
Honours – League Challenge Cup: Winners – 1996.

STIRLING ALBION — DIV. 2

Ground: Forthbank Stadium, Springkerse Industrial Estate, Stirling FK7 7UJ (01786) 450399
Ground capacity: 3808. **Colours:** Red and white halved shirts, red shorts with white piping.
Player Coach: Allan Moore.
League Appearances: Aitken C 8(5); Allan J 3(6); Canning M 12(5); Christie S 1; Cummings D 1(5); Devine S 26(2); Di Giacomo P 16; Dunn R 16; Ferguson C 17(7); Ferguson W (2); Forbes D 2; Galloway M 8(1); Gethins C 3(9); Gibson A 5(2); Glancy M 18(10); Hay P 33(1); Hogarth M 35; Hutchison S 4(12); MacDonald K 27(4); McLean S 18; McNally M 21; Neville B 5(2); Nugent P 35; O'Brien D 33(1); Prentice M (1); Rowe G 14; Roycroft S 3; Scotland C 21(4); Taggart N (1); Wilson D 11(12).
Goals – League (56): McLean S 9 (3 pens), Dunn 7 (2 pens), Glancy 7, Di Giacomo 6, O'Brien 6, Devine 5, Hay 4, Aitken 3, Wilson 3, Gethins 2 (1 pen), Nugent 2, McDonald 1, Rowe 1.
Scottish Cup (0).
CIS Cup (3): McLean S 2, Glancy 1.
Challenge Cup (5): Mclean S 2, Cummings 1, Gethins 1, Rowe 1.
Honours – Division II: Champions – 1952-53, 1957-58, 1960-61, 1964-65. **Second Division:** Champions – 1976-77, 1990-91, 1995-96.

STRANRAER — DIV. 1

Ground: Stair Park, Stranraer DG9 8BS (01776) 703271
Ground capacity: 5600. **Colours:** Blue shirts with white side panels, blue shorts with white side panels.
Manager: Neil Watt.
League Appearances: Aitken S 12(3); Crawford B 3(8); Cruickshank C 2(2); Donnachie S (2); Finlayson K 36; Fox D 10(1); Fraser J 15(5); Gaughan K 23(6); Gaughan P (1); Graham D 20; Guy G 10(8); Henderson M 36; Jenkins A 35; McCaulay M (1); McCondichie A 14; McCutcheon G 4(13); McGovern M 19; McManus P 15(1); McPhee G 16(9); Meechan K 3; Moore M 7; Sharp L 23(7); Swift S 31; Turnbull D 4(7); Wingate D 23(2); Wright F 35.
Goals – League (48): Graham 14, Finlayson 5, Jenkins 5, Gaughan K 4, Henderson 4, McManus 3, Guy 2 (2 pens), Moore 2, Sharp 2, Swift 2, Wright 2, Fox 1, Fraser 1, own goal 1.
Scottish Cup (4): Gaughan K 1, McCutcheon 1, Swift 1, Wingate 1.
CIS Cup (3): Henderson 1, Sharp 1, Turnbull 1.
Challenge Cup (0).
Honours – Second Division: Champions – 1993-94, 1997-98. **Third Division:** Champions – 2003–04. **League Challenge Cup winners** 1997.

SCOTTISH LEAGUE HONOURS

*On goal average (ratio)/difference. †Held jointly after indecisive play-off. ‡Won on deciding match. ††Held jointly. ¶Two points deducted for fielding ineligible player. Competition suspended 1940–45 during war; Regional Leagues operating. ‡‡Two points deducted for registration irregularities.

PREMIER LEAGUE

	First	Pts	Second	Pts	Third	Pts
			Maximum points: 108			
1998–99	Rangers	77	Celtic	71	St Johnstone	57
1999–00	Rangers	90	Celtic	69	Hearts	54
			Maximum points: 114			
2000–01	Celtic	97	Rangers	82	Hibernian	66
2001–02	Celtic	103	Rangers	85	Livingston	58
2002–03	Rangers*	97	Celtic	97	Hearts	63
2003–04	Celtic	98	Rangers	81	Hearts	68
2004–05	Rangers	93	Celtic	92	Hibernian*	61

PREMIER DIVISION

	First	Pts	Second	Pts	Third	Pts
			Maximum points: 72			
1975–76	Rangers	54	Celtic	48	Hibernian	43
1976–77	Celtic	55	Rangers	46	Aberdeen	43
1977–78	Rangers	55	Aberdeen	53	Dundee U	40
1978–79	Celtic	48	Rangers	45	Dundee U	44
1979–80	Aberdeen	48	Celtic	47	St Mirren	42
1980–81	Celtic	56	Aberdeen	49	Rangers*	44
1981–82	Celtic	55	Aberdeen	53	Rangers	43
1982–83	Dundee U	56	Celtic*	55	Aberdeen	55
1983–84	Aberdeen	57	Celtic	50	Dundee U	47
1984–85	Aberdeen	59	Celtic	52	Dundee U	47
1985–86	Celtic*	50	Hearts	50	Dundee U	47
			Maximum points: 88			
1986–87	Rangers	69	Celtic	63	Dundee U	60
1987–88	Celtic	72	Hearts	62	Rangers	60
			Maximum points: 72			
1988–89	Rangers	56	Aberdeen	50	Celtic	46
1989–90	Rangers	51	Aberdeen*	44	Hearts	44
1990–91	Rangers	55	Aberdeen	53	Celtic*	41
			Maximum points: 88			
1991–92	Rangers	72	Hearts	63	Celtic	62
1992–93	Rangers	73	Aberdeen	64	Celtic	60
1993–94	Rangers	58	Aberdeen	55	Motherwell	54
			Maximum points: 108			
1994–95	Rangers	69	Motherwell	54	Hibernian	53
1995–96	Rangers	87	Celtic	83	Aberdeen*	55
1996–97	Rangers	80	Celtic	75	Dundee U	60
1997–98	Celtic	74	Rangers	72	Hearts	67

DIVISION 1

	First	Pts	Second	Pts	Third	Pts
			Maximum points: 52			
1975–76	Partick Th	41	Kilmarnock	35	Montrose	30
			Maximum points: 78			
1976–77	St Mirren	62	Clydebank	58	Dundee	51
1977–78	Morton*	58	Hearts	58	Dundee	57
1978–79	Dundee	55	Kilmarnock*	54	Clydebank	54
1979–80	Hearts	53	Airdrieonians	51	Ayr U*	44
1980–81	Hibernian	57	Dundee	52	St Johnstone	51

1981–82	Motherwell	61	Kilmarnock	51	Hearts	50
1982–83	St Johnstone	55	Hearts	54	Clydebank	50
1983–84	Morton	54	Dumbarton	51	Partick Th	46
1984–85	Motherwell	50	Clydebank	48	Falkirk	45
1985–86	Hamilton A	56	Falkirk	45	Kilmarnock	44
			Maximum points: 88			
1986–87	Morton	57	Dunfermline Ath	56	Dumbarton	53
1987–88	Hamilton A	56	Meadowbank Th	52	Clydebank	49
			Maximum points: 78			
1988–89	Dunfermline Ath	54	Falkirk	52	Clydebank	48
1989–90	St Johnstone	58	Airdrieonians	54	Clydebank	44
1990–91	Falkirk	54	Airdrieonians	53	Dundee	52
			Maximum points: 88			
1991–92	Dundee	58	Partick Th*	57	Hamilton A	57
1992–93	Raith R	65	Kilmarnock	54	Dunfermline Ath	52
1993–94	Falkirk	66	Dunfermline Ath	65	Airdrieonians	54
			Maximum points: 108			
1994–95	Raith R	69	Dunfermline Ath*	68	Dundee	68
1995–96	Dunfermline Ath	71	Dundee U*	67	Morton	67
1996–97	St Johnstone	80	Airdrieonians	60	Dundee*	58
1997–98	Dundee	70	Falkirk	65	Raith R*	60
1998–99	Hibernian	89	Falkirk	66	Ayr U	62
1999–00	St Mirren	76	Dunfermline Ath	71	Falkirk	68
2000–01	Livingston	76	Ayr U	69	Falkirk	56
2001–02	Partick Th	66	Airdrieonians	56	Ayr U	52
2002–03	Falkirk	81	Clyde	72	St Johnstone	67
2003–04	Inverness CT	70	Clyde	69	St Johnstone	57
2004–05	Falkirk	75	St Mirren*	60	Clyde	60

DIVISION 2

			Maximum points: 52			
1975–76	Clydebank*	40	Raith R	40	Alloa	35
			Maximum points: 78			
1976–77	Stirling A	55	Alloa	51	Dunfermline Ath	50
1977–78	Clyde*	53	Raith R	53	Dunfermline Ath	48
1978–79	Berwick R	54	Dunfermline Ath	52	Falkirk	50
1979–80	Falkirk	50	East Stirling	49	Forfar Ath	46
1980–81	Queen's Park	50	Queen of the S	46	Cowdenbeath	45
1981–82	Clyde	59	Alloa*	50	Arbroath	50
1982–83	Brechin C	55	Meadowbank Th	54	Arbroath	49
1983–84	Forfar Ath	63	East Fife	47	Berwick R	43
1984–85	Montrose	53	Alloa	50	Dunfermline Ath	49
1985–86	Dunfermline Ath	57	Queen of the S	55	Meadowbank Th	49
1986–87	Meadowbank Th	55	Raith R*	52	Stirling A*	52
1987–88	Ayr U	61	St Johnstone	59	Queen's Park	51
1988–89	Albion R	50	Alloa	45	Brechin C	43
1989–90	Brechin C	49	Kilmarnock	48	Stirling A	47
1990–91	Stirling A	54	Montrose	46	Cowdenbeath	45
1991–92	Dumbarton	52	Cowdenbeath	51	Alloa	50
1992–93	Clyde	54	Brechin C*	53	Stranraer	53
1993–94	Stranraer	56	Berwick R	48	Stenhousemuir*	47
			Maximum points: 108			
1994–95	Morton	64	Dumbarton	60	Stirling A	58
1995–96	Stirling A	81	East Fife	67	Berwick R	60
1996–97	Ayr U	77	Hamilton A	74	Livingston	64
1997–98	Stranraer	61	Clydebank	60	Livingston	59
1998–99	Livingston	77	Inverness CT	72	Clyde	53

1999–00	Clyde	65	Alloa	64	Ross County	62
2000–01	Partick Th	75	Arbroath	58	Berwick R*	54
2001–02	Queen of the S	67	Alloa	59	Forfar Ath	53
2002–03	Raith R	59	Brechin C	55	Airdrie U	54
2003–04	Airdrie U	70	Hamilton A	62	Dumbarton	60
2004–05	Brechin C	72	Stranraer	63	Morton	62

DIVISION 3

Maximum points: 108

1994–95	Forfar Ath	80	Montrose	67	Ross Co	60
1995–96	Livingston	72	Brechin C	63	Caledonian T	57
1996–97	Inverness CT	76	Forfar Ath*	67	Ross Co	67
1997–98	Alloa	76	Arbroath	68	Ross Co*	67
1998–99	Ross Co	77	Stenhousemuir	64	Brechin C	59
1999–00	Queen's Park	69	Berwick R	66	Forfar Ath	61
2000–01	Hamilton A*	76	Cowdenbeath	76	Brechin C	72
2001–02	Brechin C	73	Dumbarton	61	Albion R	59
2002–03	Morton	72	East Fife	71	Albion R	70
2003–04	Stranraer	79	Stirling A	77	Gretna	68
2004–05	Gretna	98	Peterhead	78	Cowdenbeath	51

DIVISION 1 to 1974–75

Maximum points: a 36; b 44; c 40; d 52; e 60; f 68; g 76; h 84.

	First	*Pts*	*Second*	*Pts*	*Third*	*Pts*
1890–91*a*	Dumbarton††	29	Rangers††	29	Celtic	21
1891–92*b*	Dumbarton	37	Celtic	35	Hearts	34
1892–93*a*	Celtic	29	Rangers	28	St Mirren	20
1893–94*a*	Celtic	29	Hearts	26	St Bernard's	23
1894–95*a*	Hearts	31	Celtic	26	Rangers	22
1895–96*a*	Celtic	30	Rangers	26	Hibernian	24
1896–97*a*	Hearts	28	Hibernian	26	Rangers	25
1897–98*a*	Celtic	33	Rangers	29	Hibernian	22
1898–99*a*	Rangers	36	Hearts	26	Celtic	24
1899–1900*a*	Rangers	32	Celtic	25	Hibernian	24
1900–01*c*	Rangers	35	Celtic	29	Hibernian	25
1901–02*a*	Rangers	28	Celtic	26	Hearts	22
1902–03*b*	Hibernian	37	Dundee	31	Rangers	29
1903–04*d*	Third Lanark	43	Hearts	39	Celtic*	38
1904–05*d*	Celtic‡	41	Rangers	41	Third Lanark	35
1905–06*e*	Celtic	49	Hearts	43	Airdrieonians	38
1906–07*f*	Celtic	55	Dundee	48	Rangers	45
1907–08*f*	Celtic	55	Falkirk	51	Rangers	50
1908–09*f*	Celtic	51	Dundee	50	Clyde	48
1909–10*f*	Celtic	54	Falkirk	52	Rangers	46
1910–11*f*	Rangers	52	Aberdeen	48	Falkirk	44
1911–12*f*	Rangers	51	Celtic	45	Clyde	42
1912–13*f*	Rangers	53	Celtic	49	Hearts*	41
1913–14*g*	Celtic	65	Rangers	59	Hearts*	54
1914–15*g*	Celtic	65	Hearts	61	Rangers	50
1915–16*g*	Celtic	67	Rangers	56	Morton	51
1916–17*g*	Celtic	64	Morton	54	Rangers	53
1917–18*f*	Rangers	56	Celtic	55	Kilmarnock*	43
1918–19*f*	Celtic	58	Rangers	57	Morton	47
1919–20*h*	Rangers	71	Celtic	68	Motherwell	57
1920–21*h*	Rangers	76	Celtic	66	Hearts	50
1921–22*h*	Celtic	67	Rangers	66	Raith R	51
1922–23*g*	Rangers	55	Airdrieonians	50	Celtic	46
1923–24*g*	Rangers	59	Airdrieonians	50	Celtic	46
1924–25*g*	Rangers	60	Airdrieonians	57	Hibernian	52
1925–26*g*	Celtic	58	Airdrieonians*	50	Hearts	50

1926–27*g*	Rangers	56	Motherwell	51	Celtic	49
1927–28*g*	Rangers	60	Celtic*	55	Motherwell	55
1928–29*g*	Rangers	67	Celtic	51	Motherwell	50
1929–30*g*	Rangers	60	Motherwell	55	Aberdeen	53
1930–31*g*	Rangers	60	Celtic	58	Motherwell	56
1931–32*g*	Motherwell	66	Rangers	61	Celtic	48
1932–33*g*	Rangers	62	Motherwell	59	Hearts	50
1933–34*g*	Rangers	66	Motherwell	62	Celtic	47
1934–35*g*	Rangers	55	Celtic	52	Hearts	50
1935–36*g*	Celtic	66	Rangers*	61	Aberdeen	61
1936–37*g*	Rangers	61	Aberdeen	54	Celtic	52
1937–38*g*	Celtic	61	Hearts	58	Rangers	49
1938–39*g*	Rangers	59	Celtic	48	Aberdeen	46
1946–47*e*	Rangers	46	Hibernian	44	Aberdeen	39
1947–48*e*	Hibernian	48	Rangers	46	Partick Th	36
1948–49*e*	Rangers	46	Dundee	45	Hibernian	39
1949–50*e*	Rangers	50	Hibernian	49	Hearts	43
1950–51*e*	Hibernian	48	Rangers*	38	Dundee	38
1951–52*e*	Hibernian	45	Rangers	41	East Fife	37
1952–53*e*	Rangers*	43	Hibernian	43	East Fife	39
1953–54*e*	Celtic	43	Hearts	38	Partick Th	35
1954–55*e*	Aberdeen	49	Celtic	46	Rangers	41
1955–56*f*	Rangers	52	Aberdeen	46	Hearts*	45
1956–57*f*	Rangers	55	Hearts	53	Kilmarnock	42
1957–58*f*	Hearts	62	Rangers	49	Celtic	46
1958–59*f*	Rangers	50	Hearts	48	Motherwell	44
1959–60*f*	Hearts	54	Kilmarnock	50	Rangers*	42
1960–61*f*	Rangers	51	Kilmarnock	50	Third Lanark	42
1961–62*f*	Dundee	54	Rangers	51	Celtic	46
1962–63*f*	Rangers	57	Kilmarnock	48	Partick Th	46
1963–64*f*	Rangers	55	Kilmarnock	49	Celtic*	47
1964–65*f*	Kilmarnock*	50	Hearts	50	Dunfermline Ath	49
1965–66*f*	Celtic	57	Rangers	55	Kilmarnock	45
1966–67*f*	Celtic	58	Rangers	55	Clyde	46
1967–68*f*	Celtic	63	Rangers	61	Hibernian	45
1968–69*f*	Celtic	54	Rangers	49	DunfermlineAth	45
1969–70*f*	Celtic	57	Rangers	45	Hibernian	44
1970–71*f*	Celtic	56	Aberdeen	54	St Johnstone	44
1971–72*f*	Celtic	60	Aberdeen	50	Rangers	44
1972–73*f*	Celtic	57	Rangers	56	Hibernian	45
1973–74*f*	Celtic	53	Hibernian	49	Rangers	48
1974–75*f*	Rangers	56	Hibernian	49	Celtic	45

DIVISION 2 to 1974–75

Maximum points: a 76; *b* 72; *c* 68; *d* 52; *e* 60; *f* 36; *g* 44.

1893–94*f*	Hibernian	29	Cowlairs	27	Clyde	24
1894–95*f*	Hibernian	30	Motherwell	22	Port Glasgow	20
1895–96*f*	Abercorn	27	Leith Ath	23	Renton	21
1896–97*f*	Partick Th	31	Leith Ath	27	Kilmarnock*	21
1897–98*f*	Kilmarnock	29	Port Glasgow	25	Morton	22
1898–99*f*	Kilmarnock	32	Leith Ath	27	Port Glasgow	25
1899–1900*f*	Partick Th	29	Morton	28	Port Glasgow	20
1900–01*f*	St Bernard's	25	Airdrieonians	23	Abercorn	21
1901–02*g*	Port Glasgow	32	Partick Th	31	Motherwell	26
1902–03*g*	Airdrieonians	35	Motherwell	28	Ayr U*	27
1903–04*g*	Hamilton A	37	Clyde	29	Ayr U	28
1904–05*g*	Clyde	32	Falkirk	28	Hamilton A	27
1905–06*g*	Leith Ath	34	Clyde	31	Albion R	27
1906–07*g*	St Bernard's	32	Vale of Leven*	27	Arthurlie	27

1907–08*g*	Raith R	30	Dumbarton‡‡	27	Ayr U	27
1908–09*g*	Abercorn	31	Raith R*	28	Vale of Leven	28
1909–10*g*	Leith Ath‡	33	Raith R	33	St Bernard's	27
1910–11*g*	Dumbarton	31	Ayr U	27	Albion R	25
1911–12*g*	Ayr U	35	Abercorn	30	Dumbarton	27
1912–13*d*	Ayr U	34	Dunfermline Ath	33	East Stirling	32
1913–14*g*	Cowdenbeath	31	Albion R	27	Dunfermline Ath*	26
1914–15*d*	Cowdenbeath*	37	St Bernard's*	37	Leith Ath	37
1921–22*a*	Alloa	60	Cowdenbeath	47	Armadale	45
1922–23*a*	Queen's Park	57	Clydebank ¶	50	St Johnstone ¶	45
1923–24*a*	St Johnstone	56	Cowdenbeath	55	Bathgate	44
1924–25*a*	Dundee U	50	Clydebank	48	Clyde	47
1925–26*a*	Dunfermline Ath	59	Clyde	53	Ayr U	52
1926–27*a*	Bo'ness	56	Raith R	49	Clydebank	45
1927–28*a*	Ayr U	54	Third Lanark	45	King's Park	44
1928–29*b*	Dundee U	51	Morton	50	Arbroath	47
1929–30*a*	Leith Ath*	57	East Fife	57	Albion R	54
1930–31*a*	Third Lanark	61	Dundee U	50	Dunfermline Ath	47
1931–32*a*	East Stirling*	55	St Johnstone	55	Raith R*	46
1932–33*c*	Hibernian	54	Queen of the S	49	Dunfermline Ath	47
1933–34*c*	Albion R	45	Dunfermline Ath*	44	Arbroath	44
1934–35*c*	Third Lanark	52	Arbroath	50	St Bernard's	47
1935–36*c*	Falkirk	59	St Mirren	52	Morton	48
1936–37*c*	Ayr U	54	Morton	51	St Bernard's	48
1937–38*c*	Raith R	59	Albion R	48	Airdrieonians	47
1938–39*c*	Cowdenbeath	60	Alloa*	48	East Fife	48
1946–47*d*	Dundee	45	Airdrieonians	42	East Fife	31
1947–48*e*	East Fife	53	Albion R	42	Hamilton A	40
1948–49*e*	Raith R*	42	Stirling A	42	Airdrieonians*	41
1949–50*e*	Morton	47	Airdrieonians	44	Dunfermline Ath*	36
1950–51*e*	Queen of the S*	45	Stirling A	45	Ayr U*	36
1951–52*e*	Clyde	44	Falkirk	43	Ayr U	39
1952–53*e*	Stirling A	44	Hamilton A	43	Queen's Park	37
1953–54*e*	Motherwell	45	Kilmarnock	42	Third Lanark*	36
1954–55*e*	Airdrieonians	46	Dunfermline Ath	42	Hamilton A	39
1955–56*b*	Queen's Park	54	Ayr U	51	St Johnstone	49
1956–57*b*	Clyde	64	Third Lanark	51	Cowdenbeath	45
1957–58*b*	Stirling A	55	Dunfermline Ath	53	Arbroath	47
1958–59*b*	Ayr U	60	Arbroath	51	Stenhousemuir	46
1959–60*b*	St Johnstone	53	Dundee U	50	Queen of the S	49
1960–61*b*	Stirling A	55	Falkirk	54	Stenhousemuir	50
1961–62*b*	Clyde	54	Queen of the S	53	Morton	44
1962–63*b*	St Johnstone	55	East Stirling	49	Morton	48
1963–64*b*	Morton	67	Clyde	53	Arbroath	46
1964–65*b*	Stirling A	59	Hamilton A	50	Queen of the S	45
1965–66*b*	Ayr U	53	Airdrieonians	50	Queen of the S	47
1966–67*a*	Morton	69	Raith R	58	Arbroath	57
1967–68*b*	St Mirren	62	Arbroath	53	East Fife	49
1968–69*b*	Motherwell	64	Ayr U	53	East Fife*	48
1969–70*b*	Falkirk	56	Cowdenbeath	55	Queen of the S	50
1970–71*b*	Partick Th	56	East Fife	51	Arbroath	46
1971–72*b*	Dumbarton*	52	Arbroath	52	Stirling A	50
1972–73*b*	Clyde	56	Dumfermline Ath	52	Raith R*	47
1973–74*b*	Airdrieonians	60	Kilmarnock	58	Hamilton A	55
1974–75*a*	Falkirk	54	Queen of the S*	53	Montrose	53

Elected to Division 1: 1894 Clyde; 1895 Hibernian; 1896 Abercorn; 1897 Partick Th; 1899 Kilmarnock; 1900 Morton and Partick Th; 1902 Port Glasgow and Partick Th; 1903 Airdrieonians and Motherwell; 1905 Falkirk and Aberdeen; 1906 Clyde and Hamilton A; 1910 Raith R, 1913 Ayr U and Dumbarton.

RELEGATED CLUBS

From Premier League

1998–99 Dunfermline Ath
1999–00 *No relegated team*
2000–01 St Mirren
2001–02 St Johnstone
2002–03 *No relegated team*
2003–04 Partick Th
2004–05 Dundee

From Premier Division

1974–75 *No relegation due to League reorganisation*
1975–76 Dundee, St Johnstone
1976–77 Hearts, Kilmarnock
1977–78 Ayr U, Clydebank
1978–79 Hearts, Motherwell
1979–80 Dundee, Hibernian
1980–81 Kilmarnock, Hearts
1981–82 Partick Th, Airdrieonians
1982–83 Morton, Kilmarnock
1983–84 St Johnstone, Motherwell
1984–85 Dumbarton, Morton
1985–86 *No relegation due to League reorganisation*
1986–87 Clydebank, Hamilton A
1987–88 Falkirk, Dunfermline Ath, Morton
1988–89 Hamilton A
1989–90 Dundee
1990–91 None
1991–92 St Mirren, Dunfermline Ath
1992–93 Falkirk, Airdrieonians
1993–94 *See footnote*
1994–95 Dundee U
1995–96 Partick Th, Falkirk
1996–97 Raith R
1997–98 Hibernian

From Division 1

1974–75 *No relegation due to League reorganisation*
1975–76 Dunfermline Ath, Clyde
1976–77 Raith R, Falkirk
1977–78 Alloa Ath, East Fife
1978–79 Montrose, Queen of the S
1979–80 Arbroath, Clyde
1980–81 Stirling A, Berwick R
1981–82 East Stirling, Queen of the S
1982–83 Dunfermline Ath, Queen's Park
1983–84 Raith R, Alloa
1984–85 Meadowbank Th, St Johnstone
1985–86 Ayr U, Alloa
1986–87 Brechin C, Montrose
1987–88 East Fife, Dumbarton
1988–89 Kilmarnock, Queen of the S
1989–90 Albion R, Alloa
1990–91 Clyde, Brechin C
1991–92 Montrose, Forfar Ath
1992–93 Meadowbank Th, Cowdenbeath
1993–94 *See footnote*
1994–95 Ayr U, Stranraer
1995–96 Hamilton A, Dumbarton
1996–97 Clydebank, East Fife
1997–98 Partick Th, Stirling A
1998–99 Hamilton A, Stranraer
1999–00 Clydebank
2000–01 Morton, Alloa
2001–02 Raith R
2002–03 Alloa, Arbroath
2003–04 Ayr U, Brechin C
2004–05 Partick Th, Raith R

From Division 2

1994–95 Meadowbank Th, Brechin C
1995–96 Forfar Ath, Montrose
1996–97 Dumbarton, Berwick R
1997–98 Stenhousemuir, Brechin C
1998–99 East Fife, Forfar Ath
1999–00 Hamilton A**
2000–01 Queen's Park, Stirling A
2001–02 Morton
2002–03 Stranraer, Cowdenbeath
2003–04 East Fife, Stenhousemuir
2004–05 Arbroath, Berwick R

From Division 1 1973–74

1921–22 *Queen's Park, Dumbarton, Clydebank
1922–23 Albion R, Alloa Ath
1923–24 Clyde, Clydebank
1924–25 Third Lanark, Ayr U
1925–26 Raith R, Clydebank
1926–27 Morton, Dundee U
1927–28 Dunfermline Ath, Bo'ness
1928–29 Third Lanark, Raith R
1929–30 St Johnstone, Dundee U
1930–31 Hibernian, East Fife
1931–32 Dundee U, Leith Ath
1932–33 Morton, East Stirling
1933–34 Third Lanark, Cowdenbeath
1934–35 St Mirren, Falkirk
1935–36 Airdrieonians, Ayr U
1936–37 Dunfermline Ath, Albion R
1937–38 Dundee, Morton
1938–39 Queen's Park, Raith R
1946–47 Kilmarnock, Hamilton A
1947–48 Airdrieonians, Queen's Park
1948–49 Morton, Albion R
1949–50 Queen of the S, Stirling A
1950–51 Clyde, Falkirk
1951–52 Morton, Stirling A
1952–53 Motherwell, Third Lanark
1953–54 Airdrieonians, Hamilton A
1954–55 *No clubs relegated*
1955–56 Stirling A, Clyde
1956–57 Dunfermline Ath, Ayr U
1957–58 East Fife, Queen's Park
1958–59 Queen of the S, Falkirk
1959–60 Arbroath, Stirling A
1960–61 Ayr U, Clyde
1961–62 St Johnstone, Stirling A
1962–63 Clyde, Raith R
1963–64 Queen of the S, East Stirling
1964–65 Airdrieonians, Third Lanark
1965–66 Morton, Hamilton A
1966–67 St Mirren, Ayr U
1967–68 Motherwell, Stirling A
1968–69 Falkirk, Arbroath
1969–70 Raith R, Partick Th
1970–71 St Mirren, Cowdenbeath
1971–72 Clyde, Dunfermline Ath
1972–73 Kilmarnock, Airdrieonians
1973–74 East Fife, Falkirk

*Season 1921–22 – only 1 club promoted, 3 clubs relegated.
***15 pts deducted for failing to field a team.*

Scottish League championship wins: Rangers 51, Celtic 38, Aberdeen 4, Hearts 4, Hibernian 4, Dumbarton 2, Dundee 1, Dundee U 1, Kilmarnock 1, Motherwell 1, Third Lanark 1.

The Scottish Football League was reconstructed into three divisions at the end of the 1974–75 season, so the usual relegation statistics do not apply. Further reorganization took place at the end of the 1985–86 season. From 1986–87, the Premier and First Division had 12 teams each. The Second Division remained at 14. From 1988–89, the Premier Division reverted to 10 teams, and the First Division to 14 teams but in 1991–92 the Premier and First Division reverted to 12. At the end of the 1997–98 season, the top nine clubs in Premier Division broke away from the Scottish League to form a new competition, the Scottish Premier League, with the club promoted from Division One. At the end of the 1999–2000 season two teams were added to the Scottish League. There was no relegation from the Premier League but two promoted from the First Division and three from each of the Second and Third Divisions. One team was relegated from the First Division and one from the Second Division, leaving 12 teams in each division. In season 2002–03, Falkirk were not promoted to the Premier League due to the failure of their ground to meet League standards. Inverness CT were promoted after a previous refusal in 2003–04 because of ground sharing.

PAST SCOTTISH LEAGUE CUP FINALS

Season	Winner	Score	Runner-up	Score
1946–47	Rangers	4	Aberdeen	0
1947–48	East Fife	0 4	Falkirk	0* 1
1948–49	Rangers	2	Raith Rovers	0
1949–50	East Fife	3	Dunfermline	0
1950–51	Motherwell	3	Hibernian	0
1951–52	Dundee	3	Rangers	2
1952–53	Dundee	2	Kilmarnock	0
1953–54	East Fife	3	Partick Th	2
1954–55	Hearts	4	Motherwell	2
1955–56	Aberdeen	2	St Mirren	1
1956–57	Celtic	0 3	Partick Th	0 0
1957–58	Celtic	7	Rangers	1
1958–59	Hearts	5	Partick Th	1
1959–60	Hearts	2	Third Lanark	1
1960–61	Rangers	2	Kilmarnock	0
1961–62	Rangers	1 3	Hearts	1 1
1962–63	Hearts	1	Kilmarnock	0
1963–64	Rangers	5	Morton	0
1964–65	Rangers	2	Celtic	1
1965–66	Celtic	2	Rangers	1
1966–67	Celtic	1	Rangers	0
1967–68	Celtic	5	Dundee	3
1968–69	Celtic	6	Hibernian	2
1969–70	Celtic	1	St Johnstone	0
1970–71	Rangers	1	Celtic	0
1971–72	Partick Th	4	Celtic	1
1972–73	Hibernian	2	Celtic	1
1973–74	Dundee	1	Celtic	0
1974–75	Celtic	6	Hibernian	3
1975–76	Rangers	1	Celtic	0
1976–77	Aberdeen	2	Celtic	1
1977–78	Rangers	2	Celtic	1*
1978–79	Rangers	2	Aberdeen	1
1979–80	Aberdeen	0 0	Dundee U	0* 3
1980–81	Dundee	0	Dundee U	3
1981–82	Rangers	2	Dundee U	1
1982–83	Celtic	2	Rangers	1
1983–84	Rangers	3	Celtic	2
1984–85	Rangers	1	Dundee U	0
1985–86	Aberdeen	3	Hibernian	0
1986–87	Rangers	2	Celtic	1
1987–88	Rangers†	3	Aberdeen	3*
1988–89	Aberdeen	2	Rangers	3*
1989–90	Aberdeen	2	Rangers	1
1990–91	Rangers	2	Celtic	1
1991–92	Hibernian	2	Dunfermline Ath	0
1992–93	Rangers	2	Aberdeen	1*
1993–94	Rangers	2	Hibernian	1
1994–95	Raith R†	2	Celtic	2*
1995–96	Aberdeen	2	Dundee	0
1996–97	Rangers	4	Hearts	3
1997–98	Celtic	3	Dundee U	0
1998–99	Rangers	2	St Johnstone	1
1999–2000	Celtic	2	Aberdeen	0
2000–01	Celtic	3	Kilmarnock	0
2001–02	Rangers	4	Ayr U	0
2002–03	Rangers	2	Celtic	1
2003–04	Livingston	2	Hibernian	0
2004–05	Rangers	5	Motherwell	1

†*Won on penalties* **After extra time*

CIS SCOTTISH LEAGUE CUP 2004–2005

FIRST ROUND

Airdrie U	(2) 3	East Fife	(0) 0
Berwick R	(0) 3	Elgin C	(1) 2
Brechin C	(1) 5	Cowdenbeath	(1) 2
(aet.)			
Dumbarton	(1) 1	Ross Co	(2) 3
Falkirk	(2) 4	Montrose	(0) 1
Peterhead	(1) 3	East Stirling	(0) 2
St Johnstone	(0) 2	Alloa Ath	(1) 3
St Mirren	(1) 2	Forfar Ath	(2) 5
Stenhousemuir	(0) 2	Arbroath	(1) 1
Stranraer	(0) 2	Raith R	(0) 1
Stirling Albion	(2) 3	Queen's Park	(0) 2
Hamilton A	(2) 4	Ayr U	(0) 1
Morton	(0) 1	Gretna	(0) 0
Queen of the S	(1) 1	Albion R	(0) 2

SECOND ROUND

Aberdeen	(2) 3	Berwick R	(0) 0
Airdrie U	(0) 0	Clyde	(0) 1
Albion R	(0) 1	Brechin C	(0) 1
(aet; Albion R won 4-3 on penalties.)			
Dundee	(0) 4	Forfar A	(0) 0
Hibernian	(1) 4	Alloa Ath	(0) 0
Kilmarnock	(0) 3	Hamilton A	(0) 0
Morton	(0) 0	Motherwell	(1) 3
Peterhead	(1) 1	Falkirk	(2) 6
Ross Co	(0) 0	Inverness CT	(0) 1
Stenhousemuir	(0) 2	Partick Th	(3) 5
Dundee U	(1) 3	Stranraer	(1) 1
Stirling Albion	(0) 0	Livingston	(1) 2

THIRD ROUND

Celtic	(4) 8	Falkirk	(0) 1
Dundee U	(2) 4	Clyde	(0) 0
Livingston	(0) 2	Dundee	(0) 1
(aet.)			
Aberdeen	(0) 0	Rangers	(1) 2
Albion R	(1) 1	Hibernian	(2) 3
Dunfermline Ath	(1) 3	Partick Th	(1) 1
Hearts	(1) 2	Kilmarnock	(0) 1
Inverness CT	(0) 1	Motherwell	(0) 3

QUARTER-FINALS

Dundee U	(0) 2	Hibernian	(1) 1
(aet)			
Livingston	(0) 0	Motherwell	(2) 5
Dunfermline Ath	(0) 1	Hearts	(1) 3
Rangers	(0) 2	Celtic	(0) 1
(aet.)			

SEMI-FINALS

Motherwell	(1) 3	Hearts	(0) 2
(aet.)			
Rangers	(2) 7	Dundee U	(0) 1

FINAL

Motherwell	(1) 1	Rangers	(3) 5

BELL'S LEAGUE CHALLENGE 2004–2005

FIRST ROUND

Airdrie U	(0) 0	Queen of the S	(0) 2
Alloa Ath	(2) 2	Elgin C	(0) 0
Arbroath	(1) 2	Peterhead	(1) 4
Ayr U	(0) 0	Falkirk	(0) 3
Dumbarton	(1) 1	Stirling Albion	(0) 2
East Fife	(0) 0	Cowdenbeath	(0) 0
(aet; Cowdenbeath won 4-3 on penalties.)			
East Stirling	(0) 1	Berwick R	(1) 2
Forfar Ath	(1) 3	Morton	(1) 1
Gretna	(2) 3	Montrose	(0) 0
Partick Th	(2) 3	Brechin C	(0) 0
Queen's Park	(0) 1	Stenhousemuir	(0) 1
(aet; Queen's Park won 4-2 on penalties.)			
Raith R	(0) 0	Albion R	(0) 2
Ross Co	(0) 2	St Mirren	(0) 1
St Johnstone	(1) 2	Hamilton A	(0) 0

SECOND ROUND

Albion R	(0) 1	Partick Th	(2) 2
Alloa Ath	(1) 1	Berwick R	(1) 2
Clyde	(0) 1	Stranraer	(0) 0
Falkirk	(2) 5	Stirling Albion	(1) 3
Forfar Ath	(1) 2	Queen's Park	(1) 2
(aet; Forfar Ath won 4-3 on penalties.)			
Gretna	(1) 1	Cowdenbeath	(0) 0
Peterhead	(0) 1	Ross Co	(2) 2
St Johnstone	(2) 3	Queen of the S	(0) 0

QUARTER-FINALS

Berwick R	(0) 0	St Johnstone	(1) 1
Falkirk	(1) 3	Gretna	(0) 0
Clyde	(1) 1	Forfar Ath	(1) 2
Ross Co	(0) 1	Partick Th	(0) 1
(aet; Ross Co won 4-3 on penalties.)			

SEMI-FINALS

Falkirk	(1) 2	St Johnstone	(1) 1
Ross Co	(2) 5	Forfar Ath	(2) 2

FINAL

Falkirk	(0) 2	Ross Co	(0) 1

TENNENT'S SCOTTISH CUP 2004–2005

FIRST ROUND

East Fife	(1) 3	Whitehill Welfare	(0) 0
Inverurie Locos	(1) 1	Keith	(1) 2
Glasgow University	(0) 0	Brechin C	(2) 3
Morton	(3) 3	East Stirling	(1) 1
Cove R	(3) 4	Dalbeattie	(0) 1
Cowdenbeath	(1) 2	Dumbarton	(1) 3
Forfar Ath	(0) 1	Montrose	(2) 5
Huntly	(2) 3	Peterhead	(0) 1

SECOND ROUND

Albion R	(0) 0	Arbroath	(1) 1
Alloa Ath	(1) 2	Stenhousemuir	(0) 1
Ayr U	(1) 3	Edinburgh C	(0) 0
Brechin C	(1) 1	Stirling Albion	(0) 0
Cove R	(1) 1	Morton	(3) 7
Dumbarton	(1) 1	Berwick R	(1) 1
Gretna	(0) 3	Elgin C	(0) 0
Huntly	(0) 0	East Fife	(0) 0
Keith	(0) 0	Montrose	(1) 1
Stranraer	(0) 1	Queen's Park	(0) 0

SECOND ROUND REPLAYS

Berwick R	(1) 3	Dumbarton	(1) 1
East Fife	(1) 3	Huntly	(2) 3

(aet; East Fife won 4-3 on penalties.)

THIRD ROUND

Arbroath	(0) 0	Aberdeen	(1) 2
Ayr U	(2) 3	Stranraer	(2) 3
Berwick R	(0) 0	Brechin C	(0) 3
Clyde	(1) 3	Falkirk	(0) 0
East Fife	(0) 0	Dunfermline Ath	(0) 0
Hibernian	(0) 2	Dundee	(0) 0
Kilmarnock	(2) 2	Motherwell	(0) 0
Montrose	(1) 1	Queen of the S	(1) 2
Partick Th	(0) 0	Hearts	(0) 0
Raith R	(0) 0	Alloa Ath	(1) 2
St Mirren	(1) 3	Hamilton A	(0) 0
Celtic	(1) 2	Rangers	(0) 1
Inverness CT	(0) 1	St Johnstone	(0) 0
Livingston	(1) 2	Morton	(1) 1
Gretna	(1) 3	Dundee U	(3) 4
Ross Co	(2) 4	Airdrie U	(1) 1

THIRD ROUND REPLAYS

Dunfermline Ath	(1) 3	East Fife	(0) 1
Hearts	(1) 2	Partick Th	(1) 1
Stranraer	(0) 0	Ayr U	(2) 2

FOURTH ROUND

Aberdeen	(2) 2	Inverness CT	(1) 1
Alloa Ath	(0) 0	Livingston	(0) 1
Ayr U	(0) 0	St Mirren	(1) 2

Hearts	(2) 2	Kilmarnock	(1) 2
Hibernian	(2) 4	Brechin C	(0) 0
Queen of the S	(0) 0	Dundee U	(3) 3
Ross Co	(0) 0	Clyde	(0) 0
Dunfermline Ath	(0) 0	Celtic	(3) 3

FOURTH ROUND REPLAYS

Clyde	(1) 2	Ross Co	(1) 1
(aet.)			
Kilmarnock	(0) 1	Hearts	(2) 3

QUARTER-FINALS

Hibernian	(1) 2	St Mirren	(0) 0
Clyde	(0) 0	Celtic	(1) 5
Dundee U	(3) 4	Aberdeen	(1) 1
Hearts	(2) 2	Livingston	(0) 1

SEMI-FINALS

Dundee U	(0) 2	Hibernian	(0) 1
Hearts	(0) 1	Celtic	(1) 2

FINAL

Celtic	(1) 1	Dundee U	(0) 0

PAST LEAGUE CHALLENGE FINALS

1991	Dundee	3	Ayr U	2
1992	Hamilton A	1	Ayr U	0
1993	Hamilton A	3	Morton	2
1994	St Mirren	9	Falkirk	3
1995	Airdrieonians	3	Dundee	2
1996	Stenhousemuir	0	Dundee U	0
	(Stenhousemuir won 5-4 on penalties)			
1997	Stranraer	1	St Johnstone	0
1998	Falkirk	1	Qeeen of the South	0
1999	no competition			
2000	Alloa	4	Inverness CT	4
	(Alloa won 5-4 on penalties)			
2001	Airdrieonians	2	Livingston	2
	(Airdrieonians won 3-2 on penalties)			
2002	Airdrieonians	2	Alloa	1
2003	Queen of the S	2	Brechin C	0
2004	Inverness CT	2	Airdrie U	0
2005	Falkirk	2	Ross Co	1

PAST SCOTTISH CUP FINALS

1874	Queen's Park	2	Clydesdale	0
1875	Queen's Park	3	Renton	0
1876	Queen's Park	1 2	Third Lanark	1 0
1877	Vale of Leven	0 1 3	Rangers	0 1 2
1878	Vale of Leven	1	Third Lanark	0
1879	Vale of Leven	1	Rangers	1
	Vale of Leven awarded cup, Rangers did not appear for replay			
1880	Queen's Park	3	Thornlibank	0
1881	Queen's Park	2 3	Dumbarton	1 1
	Replayed because of protest			
1882	Queen's Park	2 4	Dumbarton	2 1
1883	Dumbarton	2 2	Vale of Leven	2 1
1884	*Queen's Park awarded cup when Vale of Leven did not appear for the final*			
1885	Renton	0 3	Vale of Leven	0 1
1886	Queen's Park	3	Renton	1
1887	Hibernian	2	Dumbarton	1
1888	Renton	6	Cambuslang	1
1889	Third Lanark	3 2	Celtic	0 1
	Replayed because of protest			
1890	Queen's Park	1 2	Vale of Leven	1 1
1891	Hearts	1	Dumbarton	0
1892	Celtic	1 5	Queen's Park	0 1
	Replayed because of protest			
1893	Queen's Park	2	Celtic	1
1894	Rangers	3	Celtic	1
1895	St Bernards	3	Renton	1
1896	Hearts	3	Hibernian	1
1897	Rangers	5	Dumbarton	1
1898	Rangers	2	Kilmarnock	0
1899	Celtic	2	Rangers	0
1900	Celtic	4	Queen's Park	3
1901	Hearts	4	Celtic	3
1902	Hibernian	1	Celtic	0
1903	Rangers	1 0 2	Hearts	1 0 0
1904	Celtic	3	Rangers	2
1905	Third Lanark	0 3	Rangers	0 1
1906	Hearts	1	Third Lanark	0
1907	Celtic	3	Hearts	0
1908	Celtic	5	St Mirren	1
1909	*After two drawn games between Celtic and Rangers, 2.2, 1.1, there was a riot and the cup was withheld*			
1910	Dundee	2 0 2	Clyde	2 0 1
1911	Celtic	0 2	Hamilton Acad	0 0
1912	Celtic	2	Clyde	0
1913	Falkirk	2	Raith R	0
1914	Celtic	0 4	Hibernian	0 1
1920	Kilmarnock	3	Albion R	2
1921	Partick Th	1	Rangers	0
1922	Morton	1	Rangers	0
1923	Celtic	1	Hibernian	0
1924	Airdrieonians	2	Hibernian	0
1925	Celtic	2	Dundee	1
1926	St Mirren	2	Celtic	0

1927	Celtic	3	East Fife	1
1928	Rangers	4	Celtic	0
1929	Kilmarnock	2	Rangers	0
1930	Rangers	0 2	Partick Th	0 1
1931	Celtic	2 4	Motherwell	2 2
1932	Rangers	1 3	Kilmarnock	1 0
1933	Celtic	1	Motherwell	0
1934	Rangers	5	St Mirren	0
1935	Rangers	2	Hamilton Acad	1
1936	Rangers	1	Third Lanark	0
1937	Celtic	2	Aberdeen	1
1938	East Fife	1 4	Kilmarnock	1 2
1939	Clyde	4	Motherwell	0
1947	Aberdeen	2	Hibernian	1
1948	Rangers	1 1	Morton	1 0
1949	Rangers	4	Clyde	1
1950	Rangers	3	East Fife	0
1951	Celtic	1	Motherwell	0
1952	Motherwell	4	Dundee	0
1953	Rangers	1 1	Aberdeen	1 0
1954	Celtic	2	Aberdeen	1
1955	Clyde	1 1	Celtic	1 0
1956	Hearts	3	Celtic	1
1957	Falkirk	1 2	Kilmarnock	1 1
1958	Clyde	1	Hibernian	0
1959	St Mirren	3	Aberdeen	1
1960	Rangers	2	Kilmarnock	0
1961	Dunfermline Ath	0 2	Celtic	0 0
1962	Rangers	2	St Mirren	0
1963	Rangers	1 3	Celtic	1 0
1964	Rangers	3	Dundee	1
1965	Celtic	3	Dunfermline Ath	2
1966	Rangers	0 1	Celtic	0 0
1967	Celtic	2	Aberdeen	0
1968	Dunfermline Ath	3	Hearts	1
1969	Celtic	4	Rangers	0
1970	Aberdeen	3	Celtic	1
1971	Celtic	1 2	Rangers	1 1
1972	Celtic	6	Hibernian	1
1973	Rangers	3	Celtic	2
1974	Celtic	3	Dundee U	0
1975	Celtic	3	Airdrieonians	1
1976	Rangers	3	Hearts	1
1977	Celtic	1	Rangers	0
1978	Rangers	2	Aberdeen	1
1979	Rangers	0 0 3	Hibernian	0 0 2
1980	Celtic	1	Rangers	0
1981	Rangers	0 4	Dundee U	0 1
1982	Aberdeen	4	Rangers	1 (aet)
1983	Aberdeen	1	Rangers	0 (aet)
1984.	Aberdeen	2	Celtic	1 (aet)
1985	Celtic	2	Dundee U	1
1986	Aberdeen	3	Hearts	0
1987	St Mirren	1	Dundee U	0 (aet)
1988	Celtic	2	Dundee U	1

1989	Celtic	1	Rangers	0
1990	Aberdeen†	0	Celtic	0
1991	Motherwell	4	Dundee U	3 (aet)
1992	Rangers	2	Airdrieonians	1
1993	Rangers	2	Aberdeen	1
1994	Dundee U	1	Rangers	0
1995	Celtic	1	Airdrieonians	0
1996	Rangers	5	Hearts	1
1997	Kilmarnock	1	Falkirk	0
1998	Hearts	2	Rangers	1
1999	Rangers	1	Celtic	0
2000	Rangers	4	Aberdeen	0
2001	Celtic	3	Hibernian	0
2002	Rangers	3	Celtic	2
2003	Rangers	1	Dundee	0
2004	Celtic	3	Dunfermline Ath	1
2005	Celtic	1	Dundee U	0

†*won on penalties*

WELSH LEAGUE 2004–2005

VAUXHALL MASTERFIT RETAILERS WELSH PREMIER LEAGUE

			Home					*Away*						
		P	*W*	*D*	*L*	*F*	*A*	*W*	*D*	*L*	*F*	*A*	*GD*	*Pts*
1	Total Network Solutions	34	13	4	0	39	11	10	5	2	44	14	58	78
2	Rhyl	34	12	3	2	38	15	11	2	4	32	16	39	74
3	Bangor City	34	12	1	4	36	17	8	6	3	37	27	29	67
4	Haverfordwest County	34	9	8	0	29	9	8	4	5	21	19	22	63
5	Caersws	34	10	3	4	40	19	9	2	6	27	20	28	62
6	Carmarthen Town	34	7	7	3	34	21	10	3	4	26	13	26	61
7	Cwmbran Town	34	6	3	8	26	32	9	5	3	26	15	5	53
8	Aberystwyth Town	34	7	7	3	21	9	8	1	8	24	31	5	53
9	Welshpool Town	34	8	4	5	29	21	6	5	6	26	25	9	51
10	Newtown	34	6	3	8	23	30	7	4	6	26	25	–6	46
11	CPD Porthmadog	34	6	6	5	20	18	5	6	6	18	21	–1	45
12	Connah's Quay Nomads	34	4	3	10	25	37	5	6	6	23	21	–10	36
13	Port Talbot Town	34	3	7	7	20	22	3	4	10	16	27	–13	29
14	Llanelli	34	4	3	10	24	41	4	2	11	18	44	–43	29
15	Caernarfon Town	34	4	3	10	16	38	3	4	10	13	34	–43	28
16	Airbus UK	34	2	4	11	14	34	3	5	9	22	42	–40	24
17	Newi Cefn Druids	34	3	1	13	13	38	2	6	9	17	34	–42	22
18	Afan Lido*	34	4	3	10	13	20	2	3	12	16	32	23	21

** Deducted three points for fielding an ineligible player.*

NORTHERN IRELAND LEAGUE 2004–2005

DAILY MIRROR IRISH LEAGUE PREMIER DIVISION

	P	*W*	*D*	*L*	*F*	*A*	*GD*	*Pts*
Glentoran	30	24	2	4	73	22	51	74
Linfield	30	22	6	2	78	23	55	72
Portadown	30	18	4	8	64	29	35	58
Dungannon Swifts	30	15	5	10	57	40	17	50
Limavady United	30	13	9	8	52	36	16	48
Coleraine	30	14	5	11	62	47	15	47
Lisburn Distillery	30	13	8	9	49	42	7	47
Ballymena United	30	11	12	7	40	37	3	45
Institute	30	11	3	16	36	50	–14	36
Newry City	30	10	5	15	38	63	–25	35
Cliftonville	30	9	7	14	29	44	–15	34
Loughgall	30	8	6	16	34	53	–19	30
Larne	30	7	7	16	31	60	–29	28
Ards	30	6	8	16	33	54	–21	26
Crusaders+	30	5	9	16	27	48	–21	24
Omagh Town*	30	5	2	23	33	85	–55	17

PROMOTION/RELEGATION PLAY-OFF

First Leg
Glenavon 1, Crusaders 1 (*at Mourneview Park, Lurgan*)

Second Leg
Crusaders 1, Glenavon 2 (*at Seaview, Belfast*)

REPUBLIC OF IRELAND LEAGUE

	P	W	D	L	F	A	GD	Pts
Shelbourne	36	19	11	6	57	37	20	68
Cork City	36	18	11	7	52	32	20	65
Bohemians	36	15	15	6	51	30	19	60
Drogheda United	36	15	7	14	45	43	2	52
Waterford United	36	14	8	14	44	49	–5	50
Longford Town	36	11	13	12	32	34	–2	46
Derry City	36	11	11	14	23	32	–9	44
St Patrick's Ath	36	11	9	16	38	49	–11	42
Shamrock Rovers	36	10	8	18	41	47	–6	38
Dublin City*	36	6	7	23	39	69	–30	25

HIGHLAND LEAGUE

		Home					Away						
	P	W	D	L	F	A	W	D	L	F	A	GD	Pts
Huntly	28	11	2	2	43	16	9	3	1	36	16	47	65
Inverurie Locos	28	10	3	1	52	14	10	0	4	29	11	56	63
Fraserburgh	28	11	1	2	44	12	8	1	5	31	23	40	59
Deveronvale	28	11	1	2	39	17	8	1	5	36	23	35	59
Buckie Thistle	28	8	1	5	24	12	8	3	3	27	14	25	52
Cove Rangers	28	8	2	4	30	20	8	2	4	29	24	15	52
Clachnacuddin	28	8	2	4	33	17	6	1	7	27	20	23	45
Keith	28	8	1	5	32	26	6	2	6	24	19	11	45
Forres Mechanics	28	4	6	4	21	16	6	3	5	28	28	5	39
Nairn County	28	8	0	6	35	26	3	3	8	19	32	–4	36
Lossiemouth	28	6	0	7	29	34	4	1	10	20	46	–31	31
Wick Academy	28	4	0	10	19	31	2	1	11	11	40	–41	19
Fort William	28	3	0	11	13	40	2	1	11	13	49	–63	16
Rothes	28	2	2	10	14	32	2	0	12	16	46	–48	14
Brora	28	0	3	11	12	47	2	2	10	14	49	–70	11

EUROPEAN REVIEW 2004–2005

Whatever had gone on before the Champions League final in 2005 it was erased from the memory by the event in Istanbul on 25 May. No team in the last stage of the European Cup has had to retrieve a three-goal deficit, level the scores and go on to win the match on penalty kicks. Liverpool achieved this feat against AC Milan.

A goal down in the first minute to Paolo Maldini, two more in a five minute spell just before the interval from Hernan Crespo the Chelsea loanee, talk of damage limitation was a serious half-time consideration for the Anfield contingent.

But in the 54th minute Steven Gerrard reduced the arrears and sparked an incredible five minute revival which produced goals from Vladimir Smicer and Xabi Alonso and turned the game on its head. This combined with a subsequent double reflex save from Jerzy Dudek in the Liverpool goal from Andriy Shevchenko the European Footballer of the Year ensured a penalty shoot-out after extra time.

Here the hyped up Dudek stole the show, more of a whirling Dervish than a dancing Pole but presenting a frightening sight to Milan penalty takers. The ploy succeeded and he was not censured for coming off his line. Who is?

Liverpool undoubtedly reserved their best performances of the season for the Champions League. They had also held favourites Chelsea at Stamford Bridge in the semi-final and completed the task with a Luis Garcia goal early in the return at Anfield. AC Milan meanwhile had had a tougher time with PSV Eindhoven.

Having taken what appeared to be a commanding 2-0 lead from the home leg, the Italian side were being well beaten 3-0 when they scrambled an injury time goal to win the tie on away goals.

With the streamlining of the Champions League and dispensing of a second group stage in favour of a knock-out system, both Arsenal and Manchester United succeeded in reaching it. But United lost both legs 1-0 to AC Milan and being beaten 3-1 in Munich by Bayern was too big a hurdle for Arsenal and a Thierry Henry goal insufficent.

For the UEFA Cup there were English hopes, too. With more changes in the structure of this competition and the introduction of a group stage of their own, both Middlesbrough and Newcastle United flew the flag for the Premier League and the north-east into the knock-out stages.

In the third knock-out round Middlesbrough set themselves a difficult task when losing 3-2 at home to Sporting Lisbon. Newcastle for their part won 3-1 in Greece against Olympiakos. While Newcastle had little trouble in the return leg winning 4-0, Boro lost 1-0 and 4-2 on aggregate though they put up a fine performance.

Thus in the quarter-finals the draw gave United the opportunity to avenge their rivals' defeat as they were paired with Sporting. At home an Alan Shearer goal gave the Magpies a slender lead and all seemed to be going well in Lisbon when they took a 20th minute lead there through Kieron Dyer.

Even though the Portuguese equalised before the break there appeared to be no danger to United until the defence collapsed and conceded three goals, mirroring the problems the club was having on and off the field.

The UEFA Cup also saw a first time in Europe entry for Millwall as runners-up in the FA Cup. They managed to hold Ferencvaros to a 1-1 draw at the New Den but lost the return leg in Hungary 3-1.

Other survivors from the quarter-finals were AZ from Holland, CSKA Moscow and Parma. The last two named finished goalless in the first leg semi-final in Italy, while Sporting took a 2-1 lead over AZ in Lisbon.

The Dutch took an early lead at home, the Portuguese levelling before half-time. AZ went ahead again to force extra time over the two legs and though they added to make it 3-1 on the night, Sporting pulled the crucial goal back at the death to go through on away goals.

However the Russians had far less trouble with Parma and came through 3-0 to set up an interesting final in Sporting's own capital Lisbon. Scoring first and taking the lead into the second half it seemed smooth sailing for the home team before CSKA scored three times afterwards for a comfortable 3-1. Clearly the three goal second half was a European final tradition in 2005!

UEFA CHAMPIONS LEAGUE 2004–2005

FIRST QUALIFYING ROUND FIRST LEG

Pobeda	(0) 1	Pyunik	(3) 3
Siroki	(0) 2	Neftchi	(0) 1
Sliema Wanderers	(0) 0	Kaunas	(0) 2
Flora Tallinn	(0) 2	Gorica	(1) 4
Gomel	(0) 0	SK Tirana	(0) 2
KR Reykjavik	(0) 2	Shelbourne	(0) 2
Linfield	(0) 0	HJK Helsinki	(0) 1
Serif	(1) 2	Jeunesse Esch	(0) 0
Skonto Riga	(1) 4	Rhyl	(0) 0
WIT	(3) 5	HB Torshavn	(0) 0

FIRST QUALIFYING ROUND SECOND LEG

Gorica	(1) 3	Flora Tallinn	(0) 1
HB Torshavn	(0) 3	WIT	(0) 0
HJK Helsinki	(1) 1	Linfield	(0) 0
Jeunesse Esch	(0) 1	Serif	(0) 0
Kaunas	(2) 4	Sliema Wanderers	(0) 1
Neftchi	(0) 1	Siroki	(0) 0
Pyunik	(0) 1	Pobeda	(1) 1
Rhyl	(0) 1	Skonto Riga	(1) 3
SK Tirana	(0) 0	Gomel	(1) 1
Shelbourne	(0) 0	KR Reykjavik	(0) 0

SECOND QUALIFYING ROUND FIRST LEG

Gorica	(0) 1	FC Copenhagen	(1) 2
HJK Helsinki	(0) 0	Maccabi Tel Aviv	(0) 0
Neftchi	(0) 0	CSKA Moscow	(0) 0
Pyunik	(0) 1	Shakhtjor Donetsk	(1) 3
SK Tirana	(0) 2	Ferencvaros	(1) 3
WIT	(1) 2	Wisla	(4) 8
Apoel	(1) 2	Sparta Prague	(0) 2
Djurgaarden	(0) 0	Kaunas	(0) 0
FC Brugge	(0) 2	Lokomotiv Plovdiv	(0) 0
Hajduk Split	(1) 3	Shelbourne	(1) 2
Rosenborg	(1) 2	Serif	(1) 1
Skonto Riga	(0) 1	Trabzonspor	(0) 1
Young Boys	(1) 2	Red Star Belgrade	(0) 2
Zilina	(0) 0	Dinamo Bucharest	(0) 1

SECOND QUALIFYING ROUND SECOND LEG

CSKA Moscow	(0) 2	Neftchi	(0) 0
Dinamo Bucharest	(1) 1	Zilina	(0) 0
FC Copenhagen	(0) 0	Gorica	(3) 5
Ferencvaros	(0) 0	SK Tirana	(1) 1
Kaunas	(0) 0	Djurgaarden	(1) 2
Lokomotiv Plovdiv	(0) 0	FC Brugge	(2) 4
Maccabi Tel Aviv	(0) 1	HJK Helsinki	(0) 0
Red Star Belgrade	(1) 3	Young Boys	(0) 0
Serif	(0) 0	Rosenborg	(2) 2
Shakhtjor Donetsk	(1) 1	Pyunik	(0) 0
Shelbourne	(0) 2	Hajduk Split	(0) 0
Sparta Prague	(1) 2	Apoel	(0) 1
Trabzonspor	(0) 3	Skonto Riga	(0) 0
Wisla	(2) 3	WIT	(0) 0

THIRD QUALIFYING ROUND FIRST LEG

Benfica	(1) 1	Anderlecht	(0) 0
CSKA Moscow	(1) 2	Rangers	(1) 1
Dynamo Kiev	(1) 1	Trabzonspor	(1) 2
Graz	(0) 0	Liverpool	(1) 2

Juventus	(0) 2	Djurgaarden	(1) 2
PAOK Salonika	(0) 1	Maccabi Tel Aviv	(2) 2

(Result changed to 0-3 by UEFA.)

Basle	(1) 1	Internazionale	(1) 1
Dinamo Bucharest	(1) 1	Manchester United	(1) 2
Ferencvaros	(1) 1	Sparta Prague	(0) 0
Gorica	(0) 0	Monaco	(0) 3
Leverkusen	(1) 5	Banik Ostrava	(0) 0
Red Star Belgrade	(2) 3	PSV Eindhoven	(1) 2
Rosenborg	(2) 2	Maccabi Haifa	(1) 1
Shakhtjor Donetsk	(1) 4	FC Brugge	(0) 1
Shelbourne	(0) 0	La Coruna	(0) 0
Wisla	(0) 0	Real Madrid	(0) 2

THIRD QUALIFYING ROUND SECOND LEG

Anderlecht	(1) 3	Benfica	(0) 0
Internazionale	(2) 4	Basle	(0) 1
La Coruna	(0) 3	Shelbourne	(0) 0
Liverpool	(0) 0	Graz	(0) 1
Maccabi Haifa	(2) 2	Rosenborg	(0) 3

(aet.)

Monaco	(3) 6	Gorica	(0) 0
Banik Ostrava	(1) 2	Leverkusen	(0) 1
Djurgaarden	(1) 1	Juventus	(2) 4
FC Brugge	(2) 2	Shakhtjor Donetsk	(1) 2
Maccabi Tel Aviv	(1) 1	PAOK Salonika	(0) 0
Manchester United	(0) 3	Dinamo Bucharest	(0) 0
PSV Eindhoven	(2) 5	Red Star Belgrade	(0) 0
Rangers	(0) 1	CSKA Moscow	(0) 1
Real Madrid	(2) 3	Wisla	(0) 1
Sparta Prague	(1) 2	Ferencvaros	(0) 0

(aet.)

Trabzonspor	(0) 0	Dynamo Kiev	(2) 2

GROUP A

La Coruna	(0) 0	Olympiakos	(0) 0
Liverpool	(1) 2	Monaco	(0) 0
Monaco	(2) 2	La Coruna	(0) 0
Olympiakos	(1) 1	Liverpool	(0) 0
Liverpool	(0) 0	La Coruna	(0) 0
Monaco	(2) 2	Olympiakos	(0) 1
La Coruna	(0) 0	Liverpool	(1) 1
Olympiakos	(0) 1	Monaco	(0) 0
Monaco	(0) 1	Liverpool	(0) 0
Olympiakos	(0) 1	La Coruna	(0) 0
La Coruna	(0) 0	Monaco	(3) 5
Liverpool	(0) 3	Olympiakos	(1) 1

Group A Final Table	*P*	*W*	*D*	*L*	*F*	*A*	*Pts*
Monaco	6	4	0	2	10	4	12
Liverpool	6	3	1	2	6	3	10
Olympiakos	6	3	1	2	5	5	10
La Coruna	6	0	2	4	0	9	2

GROUP B

Leverkusen	(1) 3	Real Madrid	(0) 0
Roma	(0) 0	Dynamo Kiev	(0) 1

(abandoned at half-time; injury to referee Frisk.)

Dynamo Kiev	(1) 4	Leverkusen	(0) 2
Real Madrid	(1) 4	Roma	(2) 2
Leverkusen	(0) 3	Roma	(1) 1
Real Madrid	(0) 1	Dynamo Kiev	(0) 0
Dynamo Kiev	(2) 2	Real Madrid	(2) 2
Roma	(0) 1	Leverkusen	(0) 1

(behind closed doors.)

Dynamo Kiev	(0) 2	Roma	(0) 0
Real Madrid	(0) 1	Leverkusen	(1) 1
Leverkusen	(0) 3	Dynamo Kiev	(0) 0
Roma	(0) 0	Real Madrid	(1) 3

(behind closed doors.)

Group B Final Table	*P*	*W*	*D*	*L*	*F*	*A*	*Pts*
Leverkusen	6	3	2	1	13	7	11
Real Madrid	6	3	2	1	11	8	11
Dynamo Kiev	6	3	1	2	11	8	10
Roma	6	0	1	5	4	16	1

GROUP C

Ajax	(0) 0	Juventus	(1) 1
Maccabi Tel Aviv	(0) 0	Bayern Munich	(0) 1
Bayern Munich	(2) 4	Ajax	(0) 0
Juventus	(1) 1	Maccabi Tel Aviv	(0) 0
Ajax	(3) 3	Maccabi Tel Aviv	(0) 0
Juventus	(0) 1	Bayern Munich	(0) 0
Bayern Munich	(0) 0	Juventus	(0) 1
Maccabi Tel Aviv	(0) 2	Ajax	(0) 1
Bayern Munich	(3) 5	Maccabi Tel Aviv	(0) 1
Juventus	(1) 1	Ajax	(0) 0
Ajax	(1) 2	Bayern Munich	(1) 2
Maccabi Tel Aviv	(1) 1	Juventus	(0) 1

Group C Final Table	*P*	*W*	*D*	*L*	*F*	*A*	*Pts*
Juventus	6	5	1	0	6	1	16
Bayern Munich	6	3	1	2	12	5	10
Ajax	6	1	1	4	6	10	4
Maccabi Tel Aviv	6	1	1	4	4	12	4

GROUP D

Fenerbahce	(1) 1	Sparta Prague	(0) 0
Lyon	(2) 2	Manchester United	(0) 2
Manchester United	(3) 6	Fenerbahce	(0) 2
Sparta Prague	(1) 1	Lyon	(1) 2
Fenerbahce	(0) 1	Lyon	(0) 3
Sparta Prague	(0) 0	Manchester United	(0) 0
Lyon	(1) 4	Fenerbahce	(1) 2
Manchester United	(2) 4	Sparta Prague	(0) 1
Manchester United	(1) 2	Lyon	(1) 1
Sparta Prague	(0) 0	Fenerbahce	(1) 1
Fenerbahce	(0) 3	Manchester United	(0) 0
Lyon	(2) 5	Sparta Prague	(0) 0

Group D Final Table	*P*	*W*	*D*	*L*	*F*	*A*	*Pts*
Lyon	6	4	1	1	17	8	13
Manchester United	6	3	2	1	14	9	11
Fenerbahce	6	3	0	3	10	13	9
Sparta Prague	6	0	1	5	2	13	1

GROUP E

Arsenal	(1) 1	PSV Eindhoven	(0) 0
Panathinaikos	(1) 2	Rosenborg	(0) 1
PSV Eindhoven	(0) 1	Panathinaikos	(0) 0
Rosenborg	(0) 1	Arsenal	(1) 1
Panathinaikos	(0) 2	Arsenal	(1) 2
Rosenborg	(1) 1	PSV Eindhoven	(1) 2
Arsenal	(1) 1	Panathinaikos	(0) 1
PSV Eindhoven	(1) 1	Rosenborg	(0) 0
PSV Eindhoven	(1) 1	Arsenal	(1) 1
Rosenborg	(0) 2	Panathinaikos	(1) 2
Arsenal	(4) 5	Rosenborg	(1) 1
Panathinaikos	(2) 4	PSV Eindhoven	(1) 1

Group E Final Table	P	W	D	L	F	A	Pts
Arsenal	6	2	4	0	11	6	10
PSV Eindhoven	6	3	1	2	6	7	10
Panathinaikos	6	2	3	1	11	8	9
Rosenborg	6	0	2	4	6	13	2

GROUP F

Celtic	(0) 1	Barcelona	(1) 3
Shakhtjor Donetsk	(0) 0	AC Milan	(0) 1
AC Milan	(1) 3	Celtic	(0) 1
Barcelona	(1) 3	Shakhtjor Donetsk	(0) 0
AC Milan	(1) 1	Barcelona	(0) 0
Shakhtjor Donetsk	(0) 3	Celtic	(0) 0
Barcelona	(1) 2	AC Milan	(1) 1
Celtic	(1) 1	Shakhtjor Donetsk	(0) 0
AC Milan	(0) 4	Shakhtjor Donetsk	(0) 0
Barcelona	(1) 1	Celtic	(1) 1
Celtic	(0) 0	AC Milan	(0) 0
Shakhtjor Donetsk	(2) 2	Barcelona	(0) 0

Group F Final Table	P	W	D	L	F	A	Pts
AC Milan	6	4	1	1	10	3	13
Barcelona	6	3	1	2	9	6	10
Shakhtjor Donetsk	6	2	0	4	5	9	6
Celtic	6	1	2	3	4	10	5

GROUP G

Internazionale	(1) 2	Werder Bremen	(0) 0
Valencia	(2) 2	Anderlecht	(0) 0
Anderlecht	(0) 1	Internazionale	(1) 3
Werder Bremen	(0) 2	Valencia	(1) 1
Anderlecht	(1) 1	Werder Bremen	(1) 2
Valencia	(0) 1	Internazionale	(0) 5
Internazionale	(0) 0	Valencia	(0) 0
Werder Bremen	(3) 5	Anderlecht	(1) 1
Anderlecht	(1) 1	Valencia	(1) 2
Werder Bremen	(0) 1	Internazionale	(0) 1
Internazionale	(1) 3	Anderlecht	(0) 0
Valencia	(0) 0	Werder Bremen	(0) 2

Group G Final Table	P	W	D	L	F	A	Pts
Internazionale	6	4	2	0	14	3	14
Werder Bremen	6	4	1	1	12	6	13
Valencia	6	2	1	3	6	10	7
Anderlecht	6	0	0	6	4	17	0

GROUP H

Paris St Germain	(0) 0	Chelsea	(2) 3
Porto	(0) 0	CSKA Moscow	(0) 0
CSKA Moscow	(0) 2	Paris St Germain	(0) 0
Chelsea	(1) 3	Porto	(0) 1
Chelsea	(2) 2	CSKA Moscow	(0) 0
Paris St Germain	(2) 2	Porto	(0) 0
CSKA Moscow	(0) 0	Chelsea	(1) 1
Porto	(0) 0	Paris St Germain	(0) 0
CSKA Moscow	(0) 0	Porto	(1) 1
Chelsea	(0) 0	Paris St Germain	(0) 0
Paris St Germain	(1) 1	CSKA Moscow	(1) 3
Porto	(0) 2	Chelsea	(1) 1

Group H Final Table	P	W	D	L	F	A	Pts
Chelsea	6	4	1	1	10	3	13
Porto	6	2	2	2	4	6	8
CSKA Moscow	6	2	1	3	5	5	7
Paris St Germain	6	1	2	3	3	8	5

KNOCK-OUT ROUND FIRST LEG

Bayern Munich	(1) 3	Arsenal	(0) 1
Liverpool	(2) 3	Leverkusen	(0) 1
PSV Eindhoven	(1) 1	Monaco	(0) 0
Real Madrid	(1) 1	Juventus	(0) 0
Barcelona	(0) 2	Chelsea	(1) 1
Manchester United	(0) 0	AC Milan	(0) 1
Porto	(0) 1	Internazionale	(1) 1
Werder Bremen	(0) 0	Lyon	(1) 3

KNOCK-OUT ROUND SECOND LEG

AC Milan	(0) 1	Manchester United	(0) 0
Chelsea	(3) 4	Barcelona	(2) 2
Lyon	(3) 7	Werder Bremen	(1) 2
Arsenal	(0) 1	Bayern Munich	(0) 0
Juventus	(0) 2	Real Madrid	(0) 0
(aet.)			
Leverkusen	(0) 1	Liverpool	(2) 3
Monaco	(0) 0	PSV Eindhoven	(1) 2
Internazionale	(1) 3	Porto	(0) 1

QUARTER-FINALS FIRST LEG

Liverpool	(2) 2	Juventus	(0) 1
Lyon	(1) 1	PSV Eindhoven	(0) 1
AC Milan	(1) 2	Internazionale	(0) 0
Chelsea	(1) 4	Bayern Munich	(0) 2

QUARTER-FINALS SECOND LEG

Bayern Munich	(0) 3	Chelsea	(1) 2
Internazionale	(0) 0	AC Milan	(0) 1
(abandoned 71 minutes; crowd trouble.)			
Juventus	(0) 0	Liverpool	(0) 0
PSV Eindhoven	(0) 1	Lyon	(1) 1
(aet; PSV Eindhoven won 4-2 on penalties.)			

SEMI-FINAL FIRST LEG

AC Milan	(1) 2	PSV Eindhoven	(0) 0
Chelsea	(0) 0	Liverpool	(0) 0

SEMI-FINAL SECOND LEG

Liverpool	(1) 1	Chelsea	(0) 0
PSV Eindhoven	(1) 3	AC Milan	(0) 1

UEFA CHAMPIONS LEAGUE FINAL 2005

Wednesday, 25 May 2005

Liverpool (0) 3 *(Gerrard 54, Smicer 56, Xabi Alonso 59)*
AC Milan (3) 3 *(Maldini 1, Crespo 39, 44)*

(at Atatürk Olimpiyat, Istanbul, Turkey, 65,000)

Liverpool: Dudek; Finnan (Hamann 46), Traore, Xabi Alonso, Carragher, Hyypia, Luis Garcia, Gerrard, Baros (Cisse 85), Kewell (Smicer 23), Riise.

AC Milan: Dida; Cafu, Maldini, Pirlo, Nesta, Stam, Gattuso (Rui Costa 111), Kaka, Crespo (Tomasson 85), Shevchenko, Seedorf (Serginho 85).

aet; Liverpool won 3-2 on penalties: Serginho missed, Hamann scored, Pirlo saved, Cisse scored, Tomasson scored, Riise saved, Kaka scored, Smicer scored, Shevchenko saved.

Referee: M. González (Spain)

UEFA CHAMPIONS LEAGUE 2005–2006

PARTICIPATING CLUBS

Liverpool FC; FC Barcelona; Real Madrid CF; Villarreal CF; Real Betis Balompié; Chelsea FC; Arsenal FC; Manchester United FC; Everton FC; Juventus FC; AC Milan; FC Internazionale Milano; Udinese Calcio; FC Bayern München; FC Schalke 04; Werder Bremen; Olympique Lyonnais; LOSC Lille Métropole; AS Monaco FC; SL Benfica; FC Porto; Sporting Clube de Portugal; Olympiacos CFP; Panathinaikos FC; PSV Eindhoven; AFC Ajax; AC Sparta Praha; SK Slavia Praha; Fenerbahçe SK; Trabzonspor; Rangers FC; Celtic FC; Club Brugge KV; RSC Anderlecht; FC Basel 1893; FC Thun; FC Shakhtar Donetsk; FC Dynamo Kyiv ; Rosenborg BK; Vålerenga IF; Wisla Kraków; Maccabi Haifa FC; SK Rapid Wien; FK Partizan; PFC CSKA Sofia; FC Lokomotiv Moskva; Brøndby IF; HNK Hajduk Split; Malmö FF ; Debreceni VSC; FC Steaua Bucuresti; FC Artmedia Bratislava; NK Gorica; Anorthosis Famagusta FC; FC Sheriff; Skonto FC; FC Haka; NK Zrinjski; FC Dinamo Tbilisi; FK Rabotnicki; FBK Kaunas; FC Dinamo Minsk; FH Hafnarfjördur ; Sliema Wanderers FC; Shelbourne FC; FC Pyunik; Total Network Solutions FC; KF Tirana; Glentoran FC; FC Levadia Tallinn; F91 Dudelange; PFC Neftchi; HB Tórshavn ; FC Kairat Almaty

INTERTOTO CUP 2004

1st leg home team v 1st leg away team, first leg score, second leg score, aggregate score

FIRST ROUND

Hibernians v Slaven, 2-1, 0-3, 2-4
Aberystwyth v Dinaburg, 0-0, 0-4, 0-4
EfB v NSI, 3-1, 4-0, 7-1
Achnas v Vardar, 1-5, 1-5, 2-10
Sopron v Teplice, 1-0, 1-3, 2-3
Spartak Trnava v Debrecen, 3-0, 1-4, 4-4
Spartak Trnava won on away goals.
Publikum v Sloboda, 2-1, 0-1, 2-2
Sloboda won on away goals.
Cork v Malmö, 3-1, 1-0, 4-1
Vetra v Trans, 3-0, 1-0, 4-0
OB v Ballymena, 0-0, 7-0, 7-0
Vllaznia v H. Beer-Sheva, 1-2, 3-0*, 4-2
**H. Beer-Sheva forfeited match.*
Sant Julià v Sartid, 0-8, 0-3, 0-11
Bregenz v Khazar, 0-3*, 1-2, 1-5
**Bregenz Sheva forfeited match.*
AA Gent v Fylkir, 2-1, 1-0, 3-1
Odra v Dinamo Minsk, 1-0, 0-2, 1-2
Teuta v Dubnica, 0-0, 0-4, 0-4
MyPa v Zlín, 1-1, 2-3, 3-4
Marek v Dila, 0-0, 2-0, 2-0
Spartak Moskva v Atlantas, 2-0, 0-1, 2-1
Thun v Gloria, 2-0, 0-0, 2-0
Grevenmacher v Tampere, 1-1, 0-0, 1-1
Tampere won on away goals.

SECOND ROUND

OB v Villarreal, 0-3, 0-2, 0-5
Teplice v Shinnik, 1-2, 0-2, 1-4
Dubnica v Liberec, 1-2, 0-5, 1-7
Westerlo v Zlín, 0-0, 0-3, 0-3
Hibernian v Vetra, 1-1, 0-1, 1-2
Spartak Moskva v Kamen Ingrad, 4-1, 1-0, 5-1
Spartak Trnava v Sloboda, 2-1, 1-0, 3-1
Vardar v AA Gent, 1-0, 0-1, 1-1
Vardar won 4-3 on penalties.
Slaven v Vllaznia, 2-0, 0-1, 2-1
NEC v Cork, 0-0, 0-1, 0-1
EfB v Nice, 1-0, 1-1, 2-1
Wolfsburg v Thun, 2-3, 1-4, 3-7
OFK v Dinaburg, 3-1, 2-0, 5-1
Genk v Marek, 2-1, 0-0, 2-1
Tampere v Khazar, 3-0, 0-1, 3-1
Dinamo Minsk v Sartid, 1-2, 3-1, 4-3
Dinamo Minsk won on Silver Goal.

THIRD ROUND

Genk v Borussia Dortmund, 0-1, 2-1, 2-2
Lille v Dinamo Minsk, 2-1, 2-2, 4-3
Nantes v Cork City, 3-1, 1-1, 4-2
Schalke v Vardar, 5-0, 2-1, 7-1
Shinnik v Uniao Leiria, 1-4, 1-2, 2-6
Slaven v Spartak Trnava, 0-0, 2-2, 2-2
Slovan Liberec v Roda JC, 1-0, 1-1, 2-1
Tampere v OFK Belgrade, 0-0, 0-1, 0-1
Thun v Hamburg, 2-2, 1-3, 3-5
Vetra v Esbjerg, 1-1, 0-4, 1-5
Villarreal v Spartak Moscow, 1-0, 2-2, 3-2
Zlin v Atletico Madrid, 2-4, 2-0, 4-4

SEMI-FINALS

Esbjerg v Schalke, 1-3, 0-3, 1-6
Genk v Uniao Leiria, 0-0, 0-2, 0-2
Lille v Slaven, 3-0, 1-1, 4-1
OFK Belgrade v Atletico Madrid, 1-3, 0-2, 1-5
Slovan Liberec v Nantes, 1-0, 1-2, 2-2
Villarreal v Hamburg, 1-0, 1-0, 2-0

FINALS

Lille v Uniao Leiria, 0-0, 2-0, 2-0
Schalke v Slovan Liberec, 2-1, 1-0, 3-1
Villarreal v Atletico Madrid, 2-0, 0-2, 2-2
Villarreal won 3-1 on penalties.

Lille, Schalke and Villarreal qualified for the UEFA Cup.

UEFA CUP 2004–2005

First Qualifying Round, First Leg

B36	(1) 1	Metalurgs	(2) 3
B68	(0) 0	Ventspils	(2) 3
BATE	(2) 2	Dynamo Tbilisi	(1) 3
Bystrica	(0) 3	Karabakh	(0) 0
Ekranas	(1) 1	Dudelange	(0) 0
Haka	(2) 2	Etzella	(1) 1
IA Akranes	(2) 4	VMK	(0) 2
Mariupol	(0) 2	Banants	(0) 0
Marsaxlokk	(0) 0	Primorje	(1) 1
Mika	(0) 0	Kispest Honved	(0) 1
Omonia	(1) 4	Sloga	(0) 0
Otaci	(0) 1	Shakhtjor Donetsk	(0) 1
Otelul	(4) 4	Dinamo Tirana	(0) 0
Partizani	(2) 4	Birkirkara	(1) 2
Pennarossa	(0) 1	Zeljeznicar	(4) 5
Santa Coloma	(0) 0	Modrica	(0) 1
Shirak	(0) 1	Tiraspol	(2) 2
Sileks	(0) 0	Maribor	(1) 1
Tbilisi	(1) 1	Shamkir	(0) 0
Glentoran	(1) 2	Allianssi	(0) 2
Haverfordwest	(0) 0	Hafnarfjordur	(0) 1
Levadia	(0) 0	Bohemians	(0) 0
Oster	(0) 2	TNS	(0) 0
Portadown	(2) 2	Zalgiris	(0) 2
Vaduz	(0) 1	Longford Town	(0) 0

First Qualifying Round, Second Leg

Banants	(0) 0	Mariupol	(1) 2
Birkirkara	(0) 2	Partizani	(1) 1
Dinamo Tirana	(1) 1	Otelul	(2) 4
Dudelange	(0) 1	Ekranas	(1) 2
Dynamo Tbilisi	(0) 1	BATE	(0) 0
Etzella	(1) 1	Haka	(1) 3
Karabakh	(0) 0	Bystrica	(0) 1
Kispest Honved	(0) 1	Mika	(1) 1
Maribor	(1) 1	Sileks	(0) 1
Metalurgs	(6) 8	B36	(0) 1
Modrica	(1) 3	Santa Coloma	(0) 0
Primorje	(2) 2	Marsaxlokk	(0) 0
Shakhtjor Donetsk	(1) 1	Otaci	(1) 2
Shamkir	(0) 1	Tbilisi	(2) 4
Sloga	(0) 1	Omonia	(1) 4
Tiraspol	(1) 2	Shirak	(0) 0
Ventspils	(3) 8	B68	(0) 0
VMK	(0) 1	IA Akranes	(1) 2
Zeljeznicar	(2) 4	Pennarossa	(0) 0
Bohemians	(0) 1	Levadia	(1) 3
Allianssi	(1) 1	Glentoran	(0) 2
Hafnarfjordur	(1) 3	Haverfordwest	(1) 1
Longford Town	(0) 2	Vaduz	(1) 3
TNS	(0) 1	Oster	(1) 2
Zalgiris	(2) 2	Portadown	(0) 0

Second Qualifying Round, First Leg

AEK Larnaca	(3) 3	Maccabi Petah Tikva	(0) 0
Amica	(1) 1	Kispest Honved	(0) 0
Beveren	(2) 3	Vaduz	(0) 1
Bodo Glimt	(1) 2	Levadia	(1) 1
Buducnost	(1) 1	Maribor	(1) 2
Bystrica	(0) 3	Wil	(0) 1
Dynamo Zagreb	(3) 4	Primorje	(0) 0

Genclerbirligi	(1) 1	Rijeka	(0) 0
Hammarby	(1) 2	IA Akranes	(0) 0
Hapoel Bnei	(2) 3	Partizani	(0) 0
Levski	(2) 5	Modrica	(0) 0
Mariupol	(0) 0	FK Austria	(0) 0
Metalurg Donetsk	(1) 3	Tiraspol	(0) 0
Odd	(0) 3	Ekranas	(1) 1
Omonia	(0) 1	CSKA Sofia	(0) 1
Oster	(1) 2	Metalurgs	(1) 2
Otaci	(0) 1	Sigma Olomouc	(0) 2
Otelul	(0) 0	Partizan Belgrade	(0) 0
Pasching	(2) 3	Zenit	(1) 1
Petrzalka	(0) 0	Dnepr	(0) 3
Rapid Vienna	(0) 0	Rubin	(0) 2
Slavia Prague	(0) 3	Dynamo Tbilisi	(1) 1
Stabaek	(0) 3	Haka	(0) 1
Tbilisi	(0) 0	Legia	(0) 1
Terek	(0) 1	Lech	(0) 0
Ujpest	(1) 3	Servette	(0) 1
Ventspils	(0) 0	Brondby	(0) 0
Zalgiris	(1) 1	Aalborg	(0) 3
Zeleznik	(0) 2	Steaua	(3) 4
Zeljeznicar	(0) 1	Litets	(0) 2
Glentoran	(0) 0	Elfsborg	(0) 1
Hafnarfjordur	(2) 2	Dunfermline Athletic	(0) 2

Second Qualifying Round, Second Leg

Aalborg	(0) 0	Zalgiris	(0) 0
Brondby	(1) 1	Ventspils	(1) 1
CSKA Sofia	(0) 3	Omonia	(0) 1
Dynamo Tbilisi	(1) 2	Slavia Prague	(0) 0
Dnepr	(1) 1	Petrzalka	(1) 1
Ekranas	(2) 2	Odd	(0) 1
FK Austria	(1) 3	Mariupol	(0) 0
Haka	(1) 1	Stabaek	(2) 3
IA Akranes	(1) 1	Hammarby	(2) 2
Kispest Honved	(0) 1	Amica	(0) 0
(aet; Amica won 5-4 on penalties.)			
Lech	(0) 0	Terek	(0) 1
Legia	(3) 6	Tbilisi	(0) 0
Levadia	(2) 2	Bodo Glimt	(0) 1
(aet; Bodo Glimt won 8-7 on penalties.)			
Litets	(5) 7	Zeljeznicar	(0) 0
Maccabi Petah Tikva	(4) 4	AEK Larnaca	(0) 0
Maribor	(0) 0	Buducnost	(0) 1
Metalurgs	(0) 1	Oster	(1) 1
Modrica	(0) 0	Levski	(1) 3
Partizan Belgrade	(1) 1	Otelul	(0) 0
Partizani	(0) 1	Hapoel Bnei	(2) 3
Primorje	(0) 2	Dynamo Zagreb	(0) 0
Rijeka	(1) 2	Genclerbirligi	(0) 1
Rubin	(0) 0	Rapid Vienna	(2) 3
Servette	(0) 0	Ujpest	(0) 2
Sigma Olomouc	(2) 4	Otaci	(0) 0
Steaua	(0) 1	Zeleznik	(1) 2
Tiraspol	(1) 1	Metalurg Donetsk	(0) 2
Vaduz	(0) 1	Beveren	(1) 2
Wil	(0) 1	Bystrica	(0) 1
Zenit	(2) 2	Pasching	(0) 0
Elfsborg	(1) 2	Glentoran	(1) 1
Dunfermline Athletic	(0) 1	Hafnarfjordur	(0) 2

First Round, First Leg

Aalborg	(1) 1	Auxerre	(1) 1
Aigaleo	(1) 1	Genclerbirligi	(0) 0

FK Austria	(0) 1	Legia	(0) 0
Bodo Glimt	(1) 1	Besiktas	(0) 1
FC Brugge	(2) 4	Chateauroux	(0) 0
Bystrica	(0) 0	Benfica	(1) 3
Dynamo Zagreb	(1) 2	Elfsborg	(0) 0
Gorica	(1) 1	AEK Athens	(1) 1
Graz	(3) 5	Litets	(0) 0
Hafnarfjordur	(0) 1	Aachen	(3) 5
Hammarby	(1) 1	Villarreal	(2) 2
Levski	(0) 1	Beveren	(0) 1
Maccabi Haifa	(1) 1	Dnepr	(0) 0
Metalurg Donetsk	(0) 0	Lazio	(0) 3
Odd	(0) 0	Feyenoord	(0) 1
PAOK Salonika	(2) 2	AZ	(2) 3
Panionios	(2) 3	Udinese	(1) 1
Parma	(2) 3	Maribor	(1) 2
Partizan Belgrade	(0) 3	Dynamo Bucharest	(1) 1
Schalke	(1) 5	Metalurgs	(1) 1
Sevilla	(1) 2	Nacional	(0) 0
Sochaux	(1) 4	Stabaek	(0) 0
Sporting lisbon	(0) 2	Rapid Vienna	(0) 0
Standard Liege	(0) 0	Bochum	(0) 0
Steaua	(1) 2	CSKA Sofia	(1) 1
Terek	(1) 1	Basle	(0) 1
Trabzonspor	(2) 3	Athletic Bilbao	(0) 2
Ujpest	(0) 1	Stuttgart	(2) 3
Utrecht	(2) 4	Djurgaarden	(0) 0
Ventspils	(0) 1	Amica	(1) 1
Wisla	(0) 4	Dinamo Tbilisi	(2) 3
Zaragoza	(0) 1	Sigma Olomouc	(0) 0
Zenit	(3) 4	Red Star Belgrade	(0) 0
Hearts	(0) 3	Braga	(0) 1
Maritimo	(1) 1	Rangers	(0) 0
Middlesbrough	(0) 3	Banik Ostrava	(0) 0
Millwall	(0) 1	Ferencvaros	(0) 1
Newcastle United	(2) 2	Hapoel Bnei	(0) 0
Shelbourne	(0) 2	Lille	(2) 2

First Round, Second Leg

Aachen	(0) 0	Hafnarfjordur	(0) 0
AEK Athens	(0) 1	Gorica	(0) 0
Amica	(1) 1	Ventspils	(0) 0
Athletic Bilbao	(1) 2	Trabzonspor	(0) 0
Auxerre	(1) 2	Aalborg	(0) 0
AZ	(1) 2	PAOK Salonika	(1) 1
Basle	(1) 2	Terek	(0) 0
Benfica	(2) 2	Bystrica	(0) 0
Besiktas	(1) 1	Bodo Glimt	(0) 0
Beveren	(1) 1	Levski	(0) 0
Bochum	(1) 1	Standard Liege	(1) 1
Chateauroux	(1) 1	FC Brugge	(2) 2
CSKA Sofia	(1) 2	Steaua	(2) 2
Dinamo Bucharest	(0) 0	Partizan Belgrade	(0) 0
Dynamo Tbilisi	(0) 2	Wisla	(0) 1
Djurgaarden	(2) 3	Utrecht	(0) 0
Dnepr	(1) 2	Maccabi Haifa	(0) 0
Elfsborg	(0) 0	Dynamo Zagreb	(0) 0
Feyenoord	(2) 4	Odd	(0) 1
Genclerbirligi	(0) 1	Aigaleo	(1) 1
Heerenveen	(2) 5	Maccabi Petah Tikva	(0) 0
(tie decided on Second Leg only; First Leg cancelled.)			
Lazio	(3) 3	Metalurg Donetsk	(0) 0
Legia	(0) 1	FK Austria	(2) 3
Litets	(0) 1	Graz	(0) 0
Maribor	(0) 0	Parma	(0) 0

Metalurgs	(0) 0	Schalke	(1) 4
Nacional	(0) 1	Sevilla	(1) 2
Rapid Vienna	(0) 0	Sporting Lisbon	(0) 0
Red Star Belgrade	(1) 1	Zenit	(0) 2
Sigma Olomouc	(1) 2	Zaragoza	(0) 3
Stabaek	(0) 0	Sochaux	(2) 5
Stuttgart	(4) 4	Ujpest	(0) 0
Udinese	(0) 1	Panionios	(0) 0
Villarreal	(1) 3	Hammarby	(0) 0
Banik Ostrava	(1) 1	Middlesbrough	(0) 1
Braga	(1) 2	Hearts	(1) 2
Ferencvaros	(3) 3	Millwall	(1) 1
Hapoel Bnei	(1) 1	Newcastle United	(3) 5
Lille	(2) 2	Shelbourne	(0) 0
Rangers	(0) 1	Maritimo	(0) 0

(aet; Rangers won 4-2 on penalties.)

GROUP A

Feyenoord	(1) 3	Hearts	(0) 0
Schalke	(1) 1	Basle	(0) 1
Ferencvaros	(1) 1	Feyenoord	(0) 1
Hearts	(0) 0	Schalke	(0) 1
Basle	(0) 1	Hearts	(1) 2
Schalke	(2) 2	Ferencvaros	(0) 0
Ferencvaros	(1) 1	Basle	(0) 2
Feyenoord	(2) 2	Schalke	(1) 1
Basle	(0) 1	Feyenoord	(0) 0
Hearts	(0) 0	Ferencvaros	(1) 1

Group A Final Table	*P*	*W*	*D*	*L*	*F*	*A*	*Pts*
Feyenoord	4	2	1	1	6	3	7
Schalke	4	2	1	1	5	3	7
Basle	4	2	1	1	5	4	7
Ferencvaros	4	1	1	2	3	5	4
Hearts	4	1	0	3	2	6	3

GROUP B

Athletic Bilbao	(1) 2	Parma	(0) 0
Steaua	(0) 2	Standard Liege	(0) 0
Besiktas	(1) 3	Athletic Bilbao	(0) 1
Parma	(0) 1	Steaua	(0) 0
Standard Liege	(0) 2	Parma	(1) 1
Steaua	(2) 2	Besiktas	(0) 1
Athletic Bilbao	(1) 1	Steaua	(0) 0
Besiktas	(1) 1	Standard Liege	(0) 1
Parma	(2) 3	Besiktas	(1) 2
Standard Liege	(1) 1	Athletic Bilbao	(3) 7

Group B Final Table	*P*	*W*	*D*	*L*	*F*	*A*	*Pts*
Athletic Bilbao	4	3	0	1	11	4	9
Steaua	4	2	0	2	4	3	6
Parma	4	2	0	2	5	6	6
Besiktas	4	1	1	2	7	7	4
Standard Liege	4	1	1	2	4	11	4

GROUP C

Dnepr	(0) 3	FC Brugge	(0) 2
Zaragoza	(0) 2	Utrecht	(0) 0
FK Austria	(0) 1	Zaragoza	(0) 0
Utrecht	(0) 1	Dnepr	(1) 2
Dnepr	(1) 1	FK Austria	(0) 0
FC Brugge	(0) 1	Utrecht	(0) 0
FK Austria	(0) 1	FC Brugge	(0) 1
Zaragoza	(1) 2	Dnepr	(1) 1
FC Brugge	(0) 1	Zaragoza	(1) 1
Utrecht	(0) 1	FK Austria	(1) 2

Group C Final Table	P	W	D	L	F	A	Pts
Dnepr	4	3	0	1	7	5	9
Zaragoza	4	2	1	1	5	3	7
FK Austria	4	2	1	1	4	3	7
FC Brugge	4	1	2	1	5	5	5
Utrecht	4	0	0	4	2	7	0

GROUP D

Dynamo Tbilisi	(0) 0	Sochaux	(2) 2
Panionios	(0) 0	Newcastle United	(0) 1
Newcastle United	(1) 2	Dynamo Tbilisi	(0) 0
Sporting Lisbon	(2) 4	Panionios	(1) 1
Dynamo Tbilisi	(0) 0	Sporting Lisbon	(2) 4
Sochaux	(0) 0	Newcastle United	(1) 4
Panionios	(0) 5	Dynamo Tbilisi	(1) 2
Sporting Lisbon	(0) 0	Sochaux	(1) 1
Newcastle United	(1) 1	Sporting Lisbon	(1) 1
Sochaux	(0) 1	Panionios	(0) 0

Group D Final Table	P	W	D	L	F	A	Pts
Newcastle United	4	3	1	0	8	1	10
Sochaux	4	3	0	1	4	4	9
Sporting Lisbon	4	2	1	1	9	3	7
Panionios	4	1	0	3	6	8	3
Dinamo Tbilisi	4	0	0	4	2	13	0

GROUP E

Aigaleo	(0) 0	Middlesbrough	(0) 1
Lazio	(0) 1	Villarreal	(1) 1
Middlesbrough	(1) 2	Lazio	(0) 0
Partizan Belgrade	(1) 4	Aigaleo	(0) 0
Lazio	(0) 2	Partizan Belgrade	(2) 2
Villarreal	(1) 2	Middlesbrough	(0) 0
Aigaleo	(1) 2	Lazio	(2) 2
Partizan Belgrade	(0) 1	Villarreal	(1) 1
Middlesbrough	(2) 3	Partizan Belgrade	(0) 0
Villarreal	(2) 4	Aigaleo	(0) 0

Group E Final Table	P	W	D	L	F	A	Pts
Middlesbrough	4	3	0	1	6	2	9
Villarreal	4	2	2	0	8	2	8
Partizan Belgrade	4	1	2	1	7	6	5
Lazio	4	0	3	1	5	7	3
Aigaleo	4	0	1	3	2	11	1

GROUP F

Amica	(0) 0	Rangers	(1) 5
Auxerre	(0) 0	Graz	(0) 0
AZ	(2) 2	Auxerre	(0) 0
Graz	(1) 3	Amica	(1) 1
Amica	(0) 1	AZ	(3) 3
Rangers	(0) 3	Graz	(0) 0
AZ	(1) 1	Rangers	(0) 0
Auxerre	(4) 5	Amica	(1) 1
Graz	(1) 2	AZ	(0) 0
Rangers	(0) 0	Auxerre	(1) 2

Group F Final Table	P	W	D	L	F	A	Pts
AZ	4	3	0	1	6	3	9
Auxerre	4	2	1	1	7	3	7
Graz	4	2	1	1	5	4	7
Rangers	4	2	0	2	8	3	6
Amica	4	0	0	4	3	16	0

GROUP G

Benfica	(2) 4	Heerenveen	(0) 2
Beveren	(0) 1	Stuttgart	(2) 5
Dynamo Zagreb	(4) 6	Beveren	(0) 1
Stuttgart	(1) 3	Benfica	(0) 0
Benfica	(2) 2	Dynamo Zagreb	(0) 0
Heerenveen	(0) 1	Stuttgart	(0) 0
Beveren	(0) 0	Benfica	(2) 3
Dynamo Zagreb	(1) 2	Heerenveen	(0) 2
Heerenveen	(1) 1	Beveren	(0) 0
Stuttgart	(1) 2	Dynamo Zagreb	(0) 1

Group G Final Table	*P*	*W*	*D*	*L*	*F*	*A*	*Pts*
Stuttgart	4	3	0	1	10	3	9
Benfica	4	3	0	1	9	5	9
Heerenveen	4	2	1	1	6	6	7
Dynamo Zagreb	4	1	1	2	9	7	4
Beveren	4	0	0	4	2	15	0

GROUP H

Aachen	(0) 1	Lille	(0) 0
(in Cologne.)			
Zenit	(1) 5	AEK Athens	(1) 1
Lille	(2) 2	Zenit	(1) 1
Sevilla	(1) 2	Aachen	(0) 0
AEK Athens	(0) 1	Lille	(1) 2
Zenit	(1) 1	Sevilla	(0) 1
Aachen	(1) 2	Zenit	(1) 2
Sevilla	(2) 3	AEK Athens	(1) 2
AEK Athens	(0) 0	Aachen	(0) 2
Lille	(0) 1	Sevilla	(0) 0

Group H Final Table	*P*	*W*	*D*	*L*	*F*	*A*	*Pts*
Lille	4	3	0	1	5	3	9
Sevilla	4	2	1	1	6	4	7
Aachen	4	2	1	1	5	4	7
Zenit	4	1	2	1	9	6	5
AEK Athens	4	0	0	4	4	12	0

THIRD ROUND FIRST LEG

Ajax	(1) 1	Auxerre	(0) 0
Panathinaikos	(0) 1	Sevilla	(0) 0
Parma	(0) 0	Stuttgart	(0) 0
Partizan Belgrade	(2) 2	Dnepr	(1) 2
Shakhtjor Donetsk	(0) 1	Schalke	(1) 1
Sporting Lisbon	(2) 2	Feyenoord	(1) 1
Valencia	(1) 2	Steaua	(0) 0
Aachen	(0) 0	AZ	(0) 0
Basle	(0) 0	Lille	(0) 0
CSKA Moscow	(1) 2	Benfica	(0) 0
Dynamo Kiev	(0) 0	Villarreal	(0) 0
Fenerbahce	(0) 0	Zaragoza	(0) 1
Graz	(0) 2	Middlesbrough	(0) 2
Heerenveen	(1) 1	Newcastle U	(1) 2
Olympiakos	(1) 1	Sochaux	(0) 0
FK Austria	(0) 0	Athletic Bilbao	(0) 0

THIRD ROUND SECOND LEG

AZ	(0) 2	Aachen	(1) 1
Auxerre	(1) 3	Ajax	(1) 1
Benfica	(0) 1	CSKA Moscow	(0) 1
Dnepr	(0) 0	Partizan Belgrade	(0) 1
Feyenoord	(0) 1	Sporting Lisbon	(0) 2
Lille	(1) 2	Basle	(0) 0
Middlesbrough	(1) 2	Graz	(1) 1
Newcastle United	(2) 2	Heerenveen	(0) 1

Schalke	(0) 0	Shakhtjor Donetsk	(1) 1
Sevilla	(0) 2	Panathinaikos	(0) 0
Sochaux	(0) 0	Olympiakos	(0) 1
Steaua	(0) 2	Valencia	(0) 0
(aet; Steaua won 4-3 on penalties.)			
Stuttgart	(0) 0	Parma	(0) 2
(aet.)			
Villarreal	(2) 2	Dynamo Kiev	(0) 0
Zaragoza	(1) 2	Fenerbahce	(0) 1
Athletic Bilbao	(1) 1	FK Austria	(1) 2

FOURTH ROUND FIRST LEG

FK Austria	(1) 1	Zaragoza	(0) 1
Lille	(0) 0	Auxerre	(1) 1
Middlesbrough	(0) 2	Sporting Lisbon	(0) 3
Olympiakos	(1) 1	Newcastle United	(2) 3
Partizan Belgrade	(0) 1	CSKA Moscow	(1) 1
Sevilla	(0) 0	Parma	(0) 0
Shakhtjor Donetsk	(1) 1	AZ	(1) 3
Steaua	(0) 0	Villarreal	(0) 0

FOURTH ROUND SECOND LEG

AZ	(1) 2	Shakhtjor Donetsk	(0) 1
Newcastle United	(2) 4	Olympiakos	(0) 0
Auxerre	(0) 0	Lille	(0) 0
CSKA Moscow	(0) 2	Partizan Belgrade	(0) 0
Parma	(1) 1	Sevilla	(0) 0
Sporting Lisbon	(0) 1	Middlesbrough	(0) 0
Zaragoza	(0) 2	FK Austria	(2) 2
Villarreal	(1) 2	Steaua	(0) 0

QUARTER-FINALS FIRST LEG

CSKA Moscow	(1) 4	Auxerre	(0) 0
FK Austria	(0) 1	Parma	(1) 1
Newcastle United	(1) 1	Sporting Lisbon	(0) 0
Villarreal	(1) 1	AZ	(1) 2

QUARTER-FINALS SECOND LEG

AZ	(1) 1	Villarreal	(0) 1
Auxerre	(1) 2	CSKA Moscow	(0) 0
Parma	(0) 0	FK Austria	(0) 0
Sporting Lisbon	(1) 4	Newcastle United	(1) 1

SEMI-FINALS FIRST LEG

Parma	(0) 0	CSKA Moscow	(0) 0
Sporting Lisbon	(1) 2	AZ	(1) 1

SEMI-FINALS SECOND LEG

AZ	(1) 3	Sporting Lisbon	(1) 2
(aet.)			
CSKA Moscow	(1) 3	Parma	(0) 0

UEFA CUP FINAL 2005

Wednesday, 18 May 2005

(in Lisbon, 48,000)

Sporting Lisbon (1) 1 *(Rogerio 28)*

CSKA Moscow (0) 3 *(Berezutski A 57, Zhirkov 66, Vagner Love 75)*

Sporting Lisbon: Ricardo; Miguel Garcia, Beto, Enakahire, Tello, Rogerio (Douala 79), Rochemback, Joao Moutinho (Viana 87), Pedro Barbosa, Leidson, Sa Pinto (Niculae 72).

CSKA Moscow: Akinfeev; Berezutski A, Ignashevich, Zhirkov, Odiah, Aldonin (Gusev 86), Berezutski V, Daniel Carvalho (Semberas 82), Rahimic, Olic (Krasic 67), Vagner Love.

Referee: G. Poll (England).

PAST EUROPEAN CUP FINALS

Year	Winner	Score	Runner-up	Score
1956	Real Madrid	4	Stade de Rheims	3
1957	Real Madrid	2	Fiorentina	0
1958	Real Madrid	3	AC Milan	2*
1959	Real Madrid	2	Stade de Rheims	0
1960	Real Madrid	7	Eintracht Frankfurt	3
1961	Benfica	3	Barcelona	2
1962	Benfica	5	Real Madrid	3
1963	AC Milan	2	Benfica	1
1964	Internazionale	3	Real Madrid	1
1965	Internazionale	1	SL Benfica	0
1966	Real Madrid	2	Partizan Belgrade	1
1967	Celtic	2	Internazionale	1
1968	Manchester U	4	Benfica	1*
1969	AC Milan	4	Ajax	1
1970	Feyenoord	2	Celtic	1*
1971	Ajax	2	Panathinaikos	0
1972	Ajax	2	Internazionale	0
1973	Ajax	1	Juventus	0
1974	Bayern Munich	1 4	Atletico Madrid	1 0
1975	Bayern Munich	2	Leeds U	0
1976	Bayern Munich	1	St Etienne	0
1977	Liverpool	3	Borussia Moenchengladbach	1
1978	Liverpool	1	FC Brugge	0
1979	Nottingham F	1	Malmö	0
1980	Nottingham F	1	Hamburg	0
1981	Liverpool	1	Real Madrid	0
1982	Aston Villa	1	Bayern Munich	0
1983	Hamburg	1	Juventus	0
1984	Liverpool†	1	Roma	1
1985	Juventus	1	Liverpool	0
1986	Steaua Bucharest†	0	Barcelona	0
1987	Porto	2	Bayern Munich	1
1988	PSV Eindhoven†	0	Benfica	0
1989	AC Milan	4	Steaua Bucharest	0
1990	AC Milan	1	Benfica	0
1991	Red Star Belgrade†	0	Marseille	0
1992	Barcelona	1	Sampdoria	0

PAST UEFA CHAMPIONS LEAGUE FINALS

Year	Winner	Score	Runner-up	Score
1993	Marseille	1	AC Milan	0
	(Marseille subsequently stripped of title)			
1994	AC Milan	4	Barcelona	0
1995	Ajax	1	AC Milan	0
1996	Juventus†	1	Ajax	1
1997	Borussia Dortmund	3	Juventus	1
1998	Real Madrid	1	Juventus	0
1999	Manchester U	2	Bayern Munich	1
2000	Real Madrid	3	Valencia	0
2001	Bayern Munich†	1	Valencia	1
2002	Real Madrid	2	Leverkusen	1
2003	AC Milan†	0	Juventus	0
2004	Porto	3	Monaco	0
2005	Liverpool†	3	AC Milan	3

† *aet; won on penalties.*
* *aet.*

PAST EUROPEAN CUP-WINNERS FINALS

Year	Winner	Score	Runner-up	Score
1961	Fiorentina	4	Rangers	1‡
1962	Atletico Madrid	1 3	Fiorentina	1 0
1963	Tottenham H	5	Atletico Madrid	1
1964	Sporting Lisbon	3 1	MTK Budapest	3* 0
1965	West Ham U	2	Munich 1860	0
1966	Borussia Dortmund	2	Liverpool	1*
1967	Bayern Munich	1	Rangers	0*
1968	AC Milan	2	Hamburg	0
1969	Slovan Bratislava	3	Barcelona	2
1970	Manchester C	2	Gornik Zabrze	1
1971	Chelsea	1 2	Real Madrid	1* 1*
1972	Rangers	3	Dynamo Moscow	2
1973	AC Milan	1	Leeds U	0
1974	Magdeburg	2	AC Milan	0
1975	Dynamo Kiev	3	Ferencvaros	0
1976	Anderlecht	4	West Ham U	2
1977	Hamburg	2	Anderlecht	0
1978	Anderlecht	4	Austria Vienna	0
1979	Barcelona	4	Fortuna Dusseldorf	3*
1980	Valencia†	0	Arsenal	0
1981	Dynamo Tbilisi	2	Carl Zeiss Jena	1
1982	Barcelona	2	Standard Liege	1
1983	Aberdeen	2	Real Madrid	1*
1984	Juventus	2	Porto	1
1985	Everton	3	Rapid Vienna	1
1986	Dynamo Kiev	3	Atletico Madrid	0
1987	Ajax	1	Lokomotiv Leipzig	0
1988	Mechelen	1	Ajax	0
1989	Barcelona	2	Sampdoria	0
1990	Sampdoria	2	Anderlecht	0
1991	Manchester U	2	Barcelona	1
1992	Werder Bremen	2	Monaco	0
1993	Parma	3	Antwerp	1
1994	Arsenal	1	Parma	0
1995	Real Zaragoza	2	Arsenal	1*
1996	Paris St Germain	1	Rapid Vienna	0
1997	Barcelona	1	Paris St Germain	0
1998	Chelsea	1	Stuttgart	0
1999	Lazio	2	Mallorca	1

PAST FAIRS CUP FINALS

Year	Winner	Score	Runner-up	Score
1958	Barcelona	8	London	2‡
1960	Barcelona	4	Birmingham C	1‡
1961	Roma	4	Birmingham C	2‡
1962	Valencia	7	Barcelona	3‡
1963	Valencia	4	Dynamo Zagreb	1‡
1964	Real Zaragoza	2	Valencia	1
1965	Ferencvaros	1	Juventus	0
1966	Barcelona	4	Real Zaragoza	3‡
1967	Dynamo Zagreb	2	Leeds U	0‡
1968	Leeds U	1	Ferencvaros	0‡
1969	Newcastle U	6	Ujpest Dozsa	2‡
1970	Arsenal	4	Anderlecht	3‡
1971	Leeds U**	3	Juventus	3‡

**After extra time　**Won on away goals　†Won on penalties　‡Aggregate score*

PAST UEFA CUP FINALS

Year	Winners	Score	Runners-up	Score
1972	Tottenham H	2 1	Wolverhampton W	1 1
1973	Liverpool	3 0	Borussia Moenchengladbach	0 2
1974	Feyenoord	2 2	Tottenham H	2 0
1975	Borussia Moenchengladbach	0 5	Twente Enschede	0 1
1976	Liverpool	3 1	FC Brugge	2 1
1977	Juventus**	1 1	Athletic Bilbao	0 2
1978	PSV Eindhoven	0 3	SEC Bastia	0 0
1979	Borussia Moenchengladbach	1 1	Red Star Belgrade	1 0
1980	Borussia Moenchengladbach	3 0	Eintracht Frankfurt**	2 1
1981	Ipswich T	3 2	AZ 67 Alkmaar	0 4
1982	IFK Gothenburg	1 3	SV Hamburg	0 0
1983	Anderlecht	1 1	Benfica	0 1
1984	Tottenham H†	1 1	RSC Anderlecht	1 1
1985	Real Madrid	3 0	Videoton	0 1
1986	Real Madrid	5 0	Cologne	1 2
1987	IFK Gothenburg	1 1	Dundee U	0 1
1988	Bayer Leverkusen†	0 3	Espanol	0 3
1989	Napoli	2 3	Stuttgart	1 3
1990	Juventus	3 0	Fiorentina	1 0
1991	Internazionale	2 0	AS Roma	0 1
1992	Ajax**	0 2	Torino	0 2
1993	Juventus	3 3	Borussia Dortmund	1 0
1994	Internazionale	1 1	Salzburg	0 0
1995	Parma	1 1	Juventus	0 1
1996	Bayern Munich	2 3	Bordeaux	0 1
1997	Schalke*†	1 0	Internazionale	0 1
1998	Internazionale	3	Lazio	0
1999	Parma	3	Marseille	0
2000	Galatasaray†	0	Arsenal	0
2001	Liverpool§	5	Alaves	4
2002	Feyenoord	3	Borussia Dortmund	2
2003	Porto*	3	Celtic	2
2004	Valencia	2	Marseille	0
2005	CSKA Moscow	3	Sporting Lisbon	1

**After extra time* ***Won on away goals* †*Won on penalties*
§*Won on sudden death.*

PAST EUROPEAN CHAMPIONSHIP FINALS

Year	*Winners*		*Runners-up*		*Venue*	*Attendance*
1960	USSR	2	Yugoslavia	1	Paris	17,966
1964	Spain	2	USSR	1	Madrid	120,000
1968	Italy	2	Yugoslavia	0	Rome	60,000
	(After 1-1 draw)					75,000
1972	West Germany	3	USSR	0	Brussels	43,437
1976	Czechoslovakia	2	West Germany	2	Belgrade	45,000
	(Czechoslovakia won on penalties)					
1980	West Germany	2	Belgium	1	Rome	47,864
1984	France	2	Spain	0	Paris	48,000
1988	Holland	2	USSR	0	Munich	72,308
1992	Denmark	2	Germany	0	Gothenburg	37,800
1996	Germany	2	Czech Republic	1	Wembley	73,611
	(Germany won on sudden death)					
2000	France	2	Italy	1	Rotterdam	50,000
	(France won on sudden death)					
2004	Greece	1	Portugal	0	Lisbon	62,865

UEFA CUP 2005–2006

PARTICIPATING CLUBS

PFC CSKA Moskva; RCD Espanyol; Sevilla FC; CA Osasuna; Bolton Wanderers FC; Middlesbrough FC; UC Sampdoria; US Città di Palermo; AS Roma; Hertha BSC Berlin; VfB Stuttgart; Bayer 04 Leverkusen; AJ Auxerre; Stade Rennais FC; RC Strasbourg; Vitória FC; SC Braga; Vitória SC; AEK Athens FC; Xanthi FC; PAOK FC; Aris Thessaloniki FC; AZ Alkmaar; Feyenoord; SC Heerenveen; Willem II; FC Baník Ostrava; Galatasaray SK; Hibernian FC; KFC Germinal Beerschot Antwerpen FC; FK Teplice; Besiktas JK; Dundee United FC; KRC Genk; FC Zürich; Grasshopper-Club; FC Metalurh Donetsk; FC Dnipro Dnipropetrovsk; SK Brann; Tromsø IL; Groclin Grodzisk Wielkopolski; Legia Warszawa; Wisla Plock; Maccabi Tel-Aviv FC; Maccabi Petach-Tikva FC; FC Ashdod; FK Austria Wien; Grazer AK; SV Pasching; FK Crvena Zvezda; FK Zeta; OFK Beograd; PFC Levski Sofia; PFC Lokomotiv Plovdiv; PFC Litex Lovech; FC Krylya Sovetov Samara; FC Zenit St. Petersburg; FC København; FC Midtjylland; HNK Rijeka; NK Inter Zapres˘ic; Djurgårdens IF ; Halmstads BK; Matáv Football Club Sopron; FC Dinamo Bucuresti; FK Dukla Banská Bystrica; NK Publikum; Viking FK; 1. FSV Mainz 05; Esbjerg fB; Ferencvárosi TC ; AFC Rapid Bucuresti; MS˘K Z˘ilina ; NK Domzale; AC Omonia; APOEL FC; FC Nistru Otaci; FC Dacia Chisinau ; FK Ventspils; FHK Liepajas Metalurgs; Myllykosken Pallo-47; AC Allianssi; NK S˘iroki Brijeg; NK Zepce; FC Lokomotiv Tbilisi; FC Torpedo Kutaisi; FK Baskimi; FK Vardar; FK Ekranas; FK Atlantas; FC MTZ-RIPO Minsk; FC BATE Borisov; Keflavík; ÍBV Vestmannaeyjar; Birkirkara FC; Hibernians FC; Longford Town FC; Cork City FC; FC MIKA; FC Banants; Rhyl FC; Carmarthen Town AFC; FC Vaduz; KS Teuta; KS Elbasani; Portadown FC; Linfield FC; FC TVMK Tallinn; FC Flora; CS Pétange; FC Etzella Ettelbrück; FK Baku; FK Khazar Lenkoran ; B36 Tórshavn; NSÍ Runavík; UE Sant Julià; SP Domagnano

PAST WORLD CUP FINALS

Year	Winners		Runners-up		Venue	Att.	Referee
1930	Uruguay	4	Argentina	2	Montevideo	90,000	Langenus (B)
1934	Italy *(after extra time)*	2	Czechoslovakia	1	Rome	50,000	Eklind (Se)
1938	Italy	4	Hungary	2	Paris	45,000	Capdeville (F)
1950	Uruguay	2	Brazil	1	Rio de Janeiro	199,854	Reader (E)
1954	West Germany	3	Hungary	2	Berne	60,000	Ling (E)
1958	Brazil	5	Sweden	2	Stockholm	49,737	Guigue (F)
1962	Brazil	3	Czechoslovakia	1	Santiago	68,679	Latychev (USSR)
1966	England *(after extra time)*	4	West Germany	2	Wembley	93,802	Dienst (Sw)
1970	Brazil	4	Italy	1	Mexico City	107,412	Glockner (EG)
1974	West Germany	2	Holland	1	Munich	77,833	Taylor (E)
1978	Argentina *(after extra time)*	3	Holland	1	Buenos Aires	77,000	Gonella (I)
1982	Italy	3	West Germany	1	Madrid	90,080	Coelho (Br)
1986	Argentina	3	West Germany	2	Mexico City	114,580	Filho (Br)
1990	West Germany	1	Argentina	0	Rome	73,603	Mendez (Mex)
1994	Brazil *(Brazil won 3-2 on penalties aet)*	0	Italy	0	Los Angeles	94,194	Puhl (H)
1998	France	3	Brazil	0	St-Denis	75,000	Belqola (Mor)
2002	Brazil	2	Germany	0	Yokohama	69,029	Collina (I)

WORLD CUP 2006 QUALIFYING RESULTS

EUROPE

■ *Denotes player sent off.*

GROUP 1

Skopje, 18 August 2004, 10,000

Macedonia (2) 3 *(Pandev 5, Sakiri 38, Sumolikoski 90)*

Armenia (0) 0

Macedonia: Milosevski; Stavrevski, Krstev M, Mitreski I, Mitreski A, Trajanov V (Vasoski 67), Sumulikoski, Pandev, Sakiri (Toleski G 85), Dimitrovski, Sedloski.
Armenia: Ambartsumian; Melikian, Hovsepian, Vardanian■, Dokhoyan, Khachatrian (Aleksanian K 46), Petrossian, Nazarian, Sargsian A, Art Karamian, Movsesian.
Referee: Genov (Bulgaria).

Bucharest, 18 August 2004, 15,000

Romania (0) 2 *(Mutu 50, Petre 89)*

Finland (0) 1 *(Eremenko Jr 90 (pen))*

Romania: Lobont; Stoican (Iencsi 84), Rat, Barcauan■, Ghioane, Radoi, Dica (Soava 75), Petre, Caramarin (Cernat 46), Mutu, Danciulescu.
Finland: Niemi; Pasanen (Koppinen 60), Saarinen, Hyypia, Vayrynen■, Nurmela (Kopteff 84), Litmanen (Eremenko Jr 57), Kolkka, Quivasto, Riihilahti, Johansson.
Referee: Gilewski (Poland).

Tampere, 4 September 2004, 7437

Finland (1) 3 *(Eremenko Jr 41, 63, Riihilahti 57)*

Andorra (0) 0

Finland: Niemi; Pasanen, Hyypia, Nurmela, Litmanen (Johansson 70), Kolkka (Heikkinen 81), Quivasto, Pohja (Kopteff 58), Riihilahti, Forssell, Eremenko Jr.
Andorra: Koldo; Ayala, Txema, Juli, Lima A, Sonejee, Pujol, Juli Sanchez (Silva 74), Sivera, Moreno, Ruiz (Jimenez 70).
Referee: Siric (Croatia).

Craiova, 4 September 2004, 26,000

Romania (1) 2 *(Pancu 15, Mutu 87)*

Macedonia (0) 1 *(Vasovski 75)*

Romania: Lobont; Stoican, Rat, Iencsi, Moldovan, Soava, Dica (Neaga 80), Petre, Pancu (Marica 62), Mutu, Danciulescu (Cernat 46).
Macedonia: Milosevski; Jancevski (Trajanov V 88), Krstev M (Bozinovski 46), Stojanovski, Mitreski I, Mitreski A, Vasoski, Sumulikoski■, Popov, Sakiri (Toleski G 83), Pandev.
Referee: Plautz (Austria).

La Valle, 8 September 2004, 900

Andorra (1) 1 *(Pujol 30 (pen))*

Romania (3) 5 *(Cernat 2, Pancu 5, 85, Niculae 16, 72)*

Andorra: Koldo; Txema, Lima I■, Fernandez (Sonejee 73), Lima A, Sivera, Ruiz, Bernaus, Juli Sanchez (Jimenez 13), Ayala, Pujol.
Romania: Lobont; Cernat, Pancu, Niculae (Dica 85), Barcauan, Rat, Stoican, Iencsi, Soava, Caramarin (Paraschiv 75), Neaga (Marica 60).
Referee: Kircher (Germany).

Erevan, 8 September 2004, 10,000

Armenia (0) 0

Finland (1) 2 *(Forssell 24, Eremenko Jr 67)*

Armenia: Berezovski; Melikian, Dokhoyan, Hovsepian, Mkrtchian, Khachatrian, Art Petrossian, Nazarian (Aleksanian K 73), Sarkissian (Manucharian 54), Arman Karamian (Gregorian 79), Movsesian.
Finland: Niemi; Nurmela, Quivasto, Hyypia, Pasanen, Riihilahti, Litmanen (Lagerblom 46), Eremenko Jr (Kopteff 73), Vayrynen, Kolkka (Pohja 85), Forssell.
Referee: Malzinskas (Lithuania).

Amsterdam, 8 September 2004, 48,000

Holland (1) 2 *(Van Hooijdonk 33, 84)*

Czech Republic (0) 0

Holland: Van der Sar; De Jong, Heitinga, Ooijer, Sneijder, Van der Vaart (Boulahrouz 64), Van Bommel, Davids, Castelen (Makaay 74), Van Hooijdonk (Van Bronckhorst 86), Kuijt.
Czech Republic: Cech; Ujfalusi, Bolf, Jiranek (Grygera 58), Jankulovski, Rosicky, Hubschman (Vachousek 62), Tyce (Lokvenc 76), Heinz, Baros, Koller.
Referee: Merk (Germany).

Prague, 9 October 2004, 16,028

Czech Republic (1) 1 *(Koller 36 (pen))*

Romania (0) 0

Czech Republic: Cech; Ujfalusi, Jankulovski, Galasek, Bolf, Jiranek, Rosicky (Kovak 90), Vachousek, Baros (Jarosik 84), Koller, Heinz (Sionko 69).
Romania: Lobont; Stoican, Rat, Petre (Sernat 58), Iencsi, Barcauan (Moldovan 46), Soava, Codrea, Marica, Mutu, Pancu (Dica 75).
Referee: Rosetti (Italy).

Tampere, 9 October 2004, 16,000

Finland (2) 3 *(Kuqi 8, 87, Eremenko Jr 28)*

Armenia (1) 1 *(Shahgeldian 32)*

Finland: Niemi; Nurmela, Pasanen, Saarinen (Kallio 68), Kuivasto (Tainio 46), Hyypia, Riihilahti, Eremenko Jr, Kolkka (Johansson 83), Kuqi, Vayrynen.
Armenia: Ambartsumian; Dokhoyan, Hovsepian, Vardanian, Khachatrian (Aleksanian K 37), Nazarian, Mkhitarian, Shahgeldian, Movsesian, Gregorian (Manucharian 61), Tadevosian.
Referee: Fandel (Germany).

Skopje, 9 October 2004, 20,000

Macedonia (1) 2 *(Pandev 45, Stoikov 70)*

Holland (1) 2 *(Bouma 43, Kuijt 65)*

Macedonia: Nikoloski; Bozinovski, Sedloski, Mitreski I, Vasoski, Krstev M, Mitreski A, Jancevski (Trajanov V 71), Sakiri, Pandev (Grozdanovski 87), Stoikov (Bajevski 75).
Holland: Van der Sar; Boulahrouz, De Jong, Cocu (Van der Vaart 60), Bouma (Landzaat 81), Van Bommel, Sneijder, Davids, Van Hooijdonk (Makaay 60), Kuijt, Castelen.
Referee: Frojdpeldt (Sweden).

La Valle, 13 October 2004, 200

Andorra (0) 1 *(Bernaus 60)*

Macedonia (0) 0

Andorra: Koldo; Escura, Lima A, Fernandez, Txema, Sonejee, Pujol (Garcia 78), Silva (Sanchez 85), Bernaus, Ruiz (Jonas 90), Sivera.
Macedonia: Nikoloski; Mitreski I, Mitreski A (Bozinovski 78), Stavrevski, Trajanov V (Bajevski 46), Jancevski, Grozdanovski, Stojanovski, Sakiri, Pandev, Stoikov.
Referee: Podeschi (San Marino).

Erevan, 13 October 2004, 8000

Armenia (0) 0

Czech Republic (2) 3 *(Koller 3, 78, Rosicky 30)*

Armenia: Bete; Dokhoyan (Mkrtchian 46), Hovsepian, Vardanian, Melikian, Nazarian, Mkhitarian, Shahgeldian (Movsesian 83), Aleksanian K (Sarkissian 73), Petrossian, Manucharian.
Czech Republic: Cech; Grygera, Bolf, Ujfalusi, Jankulovski, Galasek (Kovac 60), Sionko, Rosicky, Vachousek, Koller (Lokvenc 82), Heinz.
Referee: Granat (Poland).

Amsterdam, 13 October 2004, 49,000

Holland (2) 3 *(Sneijder 39, Van Nistelrooy 41, 63)*

Finland (1) 1 *(Tainio 14)*

Holland: Van der Sar; De Jong, Landzaat, Van der Vaart (Van Bronkhorst 72), Heitinga, Cocu, Sneijder (Van Bommel 83), Castelen (Makaay 77), Van Nistelrooy, Kuijt, Davids.
Finland: Niemi; Pasanen, Nurmela, Riihilahti (Johansson 60), Quivasto, Hyypia, Vayrynen (Pohja 85), Tainio, Kolkka, Kuqi, Eremenko Jr (Saarinen 72).
Referee: Bennett (England).

Barcelona, 17 November 2004, 2000

Andorra (0) 0

Holland (2) 3 *(Cocu 21, Robben 31, Sneijder 78)*

Andorra: Koldo; Escura, Fernandez, Lima A, Lima I, Sivera (Garcia 86), Txema, Jimenez (Ayala 78), Ruiz, Sonejee, Silva (Juli Sanchez 71).
Holland: Van der Sar; Ooijer, Van Bronckhorst, Cocu (Mathijsen 82), Melchiot, Sneijder, Van Galen (Van Hooijdonk 67), Landzaat, Kuijt, Van Nistelrooy (Makaay 35), Robben.
Referee: Yefet (Israel).

Erevan, 17 November 2004, 2500

Armenia (0) 1 *(Dokhoyan 62)*

Romania (1) 1 *(Marica 29)*

Armenia: Bete; Dokhoyan, Tadevosian, Hovsepian, Vardanian, Nazarian, Shahgeldian (Aleksanian K 87), Mikitarian, Gregorian (Mkrtchian A 73), Manucharian, Voskanian (Arman Karamian 74).
Romania: Lobont; Stoican, Barcauan, Moldovan, Dancia, Paraschiv (Bratu 74), Caramarian (Dica 46), Tararache, Cernat, Marica, Neaga.
Referee: De Bleeckere (Belgium).

Skopje, 17 November 2004, 12,000

Macedonia (0) 0

Czech Republic (0) 2 *(Lokvenc 88, Koller 90)*

Macedonia: Milosevski; Noveski, Sedloski, Mitreski I, Mitreski A, Krstev M (Jancevski 46), Pandev, Sakiri (Ignatov 77), Cadikovski (Stoikov 64), Bozinovski, Vasoski.

Czech Republic: Cech; Grygera (Lokvenc 77), Galasek, Bolf, Jankulovski, Poborsky, Koller, Rosicky, Vachousek (Jun 59), Baros (Heinz 17), Ujfalusi.
Referee: Meier (Switzerland).

Skopje, 9 February 2005, 1000

Macedonia (0) 0

Andorra (0) 0

Macedonia: Milosevski; Sedloski, Novevski, Mitreski A, Vasoski (Stavrevski 46), Krstev, Stoikov (Rajevski 68), Bozinovski (Popov G 75), Pandev, Sakiri, Cadikovski.
Andorra: Koldo; Txema, Escura, Lima A, Lima I, Pujol (Jonas 90), Sonejee, Silva (Juli Sanchez 62), Ruiz (Garcia 85), Sivera, Bernaus.
Referee: Verlist (Belgium).

Erevan, 26 March 2005, 9566

Armenia (1) 2 *(Hakobian 32, Khachatrian 73)*

Andorra (0) 1 *(Silva 57)*

Armenia: Berezovski; Aleksanian K, Arzumanian, Dokhoyan, Melikian, Khachatrian, Hakobian (Voskanian 90), Art Karamian (Mkrtchian 72), Nazarian (Jenebian 73), Shahgeldian, Michitarian.
Andorra: Koldo; Ayala, Escura, Fernandez, Txema, Sonejee, Pujol, Sivera (Juli Sanchez 89), Silva (Javi Sanchez 90), Jimenez (Genis Garcia 79), Ruiz.
Referee: Attard (Malta).

Teplice, 26 March 2005, 16,200

Czech Republic (2) 4 *(Baros 8, Rosicky 34, Polak 58, Lokvenc 87)*

Finland (0) 3 *(Litmanen 46, Riihilahti 73, Johansson 79)*

Czech Republic: Cech; Jirasek, Bolf, Ujfalusi, Jankulovski, Poborsky, Rosicky, Polak (Jun 82), Sionko (Jarosik 72), Lokvenc, Baros (Plasil 53).
Finland: Jaaskelainen; Pasanen, Kopteff, Nurmela, Tihinen, Hyypia, Litmanen (Johansson 78), Riihilahti, Kolkka (Eremenko Jr 60), Ilola, Kuqi.
Referee: Bo Larsen (Denmark).

Bucharest, 26 March 2005, 19,000

Romania (0) 0

Holland (1) 2 *(Cocu 1, Babel 85)*

Romania: Lobont; Ogararu, Radoi, Chiu, Marin, Petre, Ghioane (Plesan 46), Pancu, Munteanu, Moldovan (Cristea 69), Ilie (Bucur 86).
Holland: Van der Sar; Kromkamp, Boulahrouz, Mathijsen, Van Bronckhorst, Van Bommel (Maduro 73), Landzaat, Cocu, Kuijt (Kastelen 90), Van Nistelrooy, Robben (Babel 24).
Referee: Cantalejo (Spain).

La Valle, 30 March 2005, 1000

Andorra (0) 0

Czech Republic (2) 4 *(Jankulovski 31 (pen), Baros 40, Lokvenc 53, Rosicky 90 (pen))*

Andorra: Koldo; Escura, Txema (Ayala 59), Lima I, Sonejee, Pujol, Sivera, Silva (Juli Sanchez 65), Bernaus, Lima A, Ruiz (Fernandez 67).
Czech Republic: Cech; Jiranek (Plasil 75), Rozehnal, Ujfalusi, Jankulovski, Poborsky, Tyce (Polak 46), Rosicky, Vachousek, Lokvenc, Baros (Jun 60).
Referee: Messner (Austria).

Eindhoven, 30 March 2005, 34,000

Holland (2) 2 *(Castelen 3, Van Nistelrooy 34)*

Armenia (0) 0

Holland: Van der Sar; Kromkamp, Van Bronckhorst, Mathijsen, Bouma, Van Bommel, Landzaat (Van der Vaart 50), Cocu, Castelen (Babel 50), Van Nistelrooy, Kujit (Vennegoor of Hesselink 80).
Armenia: Berezovski; Hovsepian, Dokhoyan, Arzumanian (Tadevosian 85), Melikan, Mkhitarian, Shahgeldian, Khachatrian, Gregorian (Art Karamian 60), Voskanian, Hakobian (Nazarian 46).
Referee: Trefoloni (Italy).

Skopje, 30 March 2005, 12,000

Macedonia (1) 1 *(Maznov 31)*

Romania (1) 2 *(Mitea 18, 58)*

Macedonia: Milosevski; Popov R, Petrov (Bozinovski 46), Sedloski, Vasoski, Grozdanovski, Mitreski A, Krstev M, Sumulikoski (Ignatov 72), Jancevski (Bajevski 81), Maznov.
Romania: Lobont; Contra, Radoi, Chivu (Ghionea 46), Rat, Petre, Dica, Pancu, Munteanu, Moldovan (Cristea 78), Mitea (Ghioane 70).
Referee: Ovrebo (Norway).

Erevan, 4 June 2005, 8000

Armenia (0) 1 *(Manucharyan 55)*

Macedonia (1) 2 *(Pandev 29 (pen), 46)*

Armenia: Berezovski; Hovsepian, Dokhoyan, Tadevosian, Khachatrian, Sarkissian, Mkrtchian, Mkhitarian (Manucharyan 52), Aleksanian K (Dzenebian 78), Voskanian (Hakobian 67), Shahgeldian.
Macedonia: Madzovski; Petrov, Popov G (Krstev M 57), Sedloski, Vasoski, Grozdanovski, Mitreski A, Sumulikoski (Kralevski 83), Lazarevski, Pandev, Maznov (Ismaili 66).
Referee: Mikulski (Poland).

Liberec, 4 June 2005, 9520

Czech Republic (3) 8 *(Lokvenc 13, 90, Koller 29, Smicer 38, Galasek 52 (pen), Baros 80, Rosicky 85 (pen), Polak 87)*

Andorra (1) 1 *(Riera 35)*

Czech Republic: Cech; Ujfalusi, Grygera, Rozehnal (Polak 46), Galasek, Poborsky, Rosicky, Smicer (Plasil 46), Lokvenc, Koller (Jun 64), Baros.
Andorra: Koldo; Txema, Fernandez, Sonejee, Lima A, Escura, Ayala, Ruiz■, Jimenez (Moreno 88), Riera (Andorra 70), Sivera (Garcia 80).
Referee: Selcuk (Turkey).

Rotterdam, 4 June 2005, 50,000

Holland (1) 2 *(Robben 26, Kuijt 46)*

Romania (0) 0

Holland: Van der Sar; Lucius, Heitinga, Opdam, Van Bronkhorst, Landzaat, Van Bommel (De Jong 49), Van der Vaart (Maduro 80), Kuijt, Van Nistelrooy (Van Persie 62), Robben.
Romania: Lobont; Contra, Tamas, Chivu, Stoica, Petre, Munteanu, Mitea (Niculae 65), Mutu (Coman 83), Niculesci, Pancu.
Referee: De Santis (Italy).

Teplice, 8 June 2005, 14,150

Czech Republic (2) 6 *(Koller 42, 45, 49, 53, Rosicky 74 (pen), Baros 88)*

Macedonia (1) 1 *(Pandev 14)*

Czech Republic: Cech; Grygera, Hubschman, Ujfalusi, Poborsky (Zelenka 78), Galasek, Rosicky, Smicer (Plasil 61), Baros, Koller, Lokvenc (Polak 46).
Macedonia: Madzovski; Lazarevski, Petrov, Popov G, Sedloski, Vasoski, Krstev M (Banduliev 74), Mitreski A, Sumulikoski (Kralevski 70), Maznov, Pandev (Grozdanovski 67).
Referee: Ibanez (Spain).

Helsinki, 8 June 2005, 37,000

Finland (0) 0

Holland (2) 4 *(Van Nistelrooy 36, Kuijt 77, Cocu 84, Van Persie 87)*

Finland: Jaaskelainen; Nurmela, Tihinen, Hyypia, Saarinen, Tainio (Forssell 74), Riihilahti, Vayrynen, Litmanen (Johansson 29), Eremenko Jr (Kopteff 81), Kuqi.
Holland: Van der Sar; Lucius (Melchiot 27), Heitinga, Opdam, Van Bronckhorst, De Jong (Maduro 67), Landzaat, Cocu, Kuijt, Van Nistelrooy (Van Persie 74), Robben.
Referee: Hamer (Luxembourg).

Constanta, 8 June 2005, 15,000

Romania (2) 3 *(Petre 29, Bucur 40, 80)*

Armenia (0) 0

Romania: Lobont; Contra (Stoican 68), Tamas, Chivu, Rat, Petre, Piesan, Munteanu (Mazilu 87), Coman (Mitea 79), Niculae, Bucur.
Armenia: Berezovski; Melikian, Dokhoyan, Hovsepian, Khachatrian, Mkhitarian (Grigorian 82), Hakobian, Voskanian (Arzumanian 46), Tadevosian, Manucharian (Arman Karamian 50), Shahgeldian.
Referee: Briakos (Greece).

Group 1 Table

	P	*W*	*D*	*L*	*F*	*A*	*Pts*
Holland	8	7	1	0	20	3	22
Czech Republic	8	7	0	1	28	7	21
Romania	9	5	1	3	15	10	16
Finland	7	3	0	4	13	14	9
Macedonia	9	2	2	5	10	16	8
Armenia	9	1	1	7	5	20	4
Andorra	8	1	1	6	4	25	4

GROUP 2

Tirana, 4 September 2004, 19,000

Albania (2) 2 *(Murati 2, Aliaj 11)*

Greece (1) 1 *(Giannakopoulos 38)*

Albania: Strakosha; Beqiri E, Hasi, Aliaj, Cana, Lala, Skela, Duro (Beqiri A 86), Murati, Myrtaj (Dragusha 76), Tare.
Greece: Nikopolidis; Seitaridis, Fyssas (Tsartas 32), Dabizas (Giannakopoulos 27), Kapsis, Basinas, Zagorakis, Katsouranis, Charisteas, Karagounis, Vryzas (Papadopoulos 66).
Referee: Gonzalez (Spain).

Copenhagen, 4 September 2004, 36,335

Denmark (1) 1 *(Jorgensen 9)*

Ukraine (0) 1 *(Gusin 56)*

Denmark: Sorensen; Bogelund (Priske 43), Poulsen (Jensen C 65), Kroldrup, Jensen N, Helveg, Gravesen, Gronkjaer, Tomasson, Jorgensen, Madsen (Pedersen 79).
Ukraine: Shovkovskyi; Nesmachni, Rusol, Tymoschuk, Yezerski, Shelayev, Shevchenko, Gusin (Matykhin 67), Gusev (Zakarliuka 75), Starostiak, Vorobei (Radchenko 83).
Referee: Meier (Switzerland).

Trabzon, 4 September 2004, 15,000

Turkey (0) 1 *(Fatih 49)*

Georgia (0) 1 *(Astiani M 85)*

Turkey: Rustu; Serkan, Umit O, Deniz, Ibrahim, Okan B, Emre B, Tuncay (Huseyin 72), Hasan Sas■, Hakan Sukur (Nihat 79), Fatih (Gokdeniz 72).
Georgia: Devadze; Mzhavanadze, Khizanishvili, Khizaneishvili, Kaladze, Tskitshvili, Kvirkevlia, Rekhviashvili (Asatiani M 80), Jamarauli, Arveladze, S Demetradze (Jakobia 75).
Referee: Medina (Spain).

Tbilisi, 8 September 2004, 22,000

Georgia (1) 2 *(Iashvili 15, Demetradze 90)*

Albania (0) 0

Georgia: Devadze; Mzhavanadze, Kaladze, Khizanieshvili, Salukvadze, Tskitishvili, Jamarauli (Kvirkvelia 78), Asatiani M (Kankava 60), Kobiashvili, Iashvili, Arveladze S (Demetradze 89).
Albania: Strakosha; Beqiri A■, Cana, Aliaj, Hasi, Duro (Dragusha 59), Lala, Skela, Murati (Shkembi 81), Tare, Myrtaj (Bushi 63).
Referee: Courtney (Northern Ireland).

Piraeus, 8 September 2004, 33,000

Greece (0) 0

Turkey (0) 0

Greece: Nikopolidis; Seitaridis, Katsouranis, Kapsis, Fyssas (Papadopoulos 80), Karagounis, Giannakopoulos (Tsartas 80), Zagorakis, Basinas, Vryzas, Charisteas.
Turkey: Rustu; Serkan, Deniz, Servet, Umit O, Ibrahim, Okan B (Huseyin 73), Emre B, Gokdeniz, Fatih (Hamit 89), Nihat (Serhat 90).
Referee: Frisk (Sweden).

Almaty, 8 September 2004, 24,500

Kazakhstan (1) 1 *(Karpovich 35)*

Ukraine (1) 2 *(Bielik 15, Rotan 90)*

Kazakhstan: Novikov; Familtsev, Avdeyev, Irismetov, Dubinsky, Smakov (Musin 72), Baltiev, Chichulin (Urazbakhtin 53), Nizovtsev, Tieshev (Radionov 63), Karpovich.
Ukraine: Shovkovskyi; Rusol, Yezersky, Tymoschuk, Nesmachni, Gusin (Rotan 67), Bielik (Chelayev 90), Gusev, Zakarliouka, Starostiak (Voronin 51), Vorobei.
Referee: Garcia (Portugal).

Tirana, 9 October 2004, 20,000

Albania (0) 0

Denmark (0) 2 *(Jorgensen 52, Tomasson 72)*

Albania: Strakosha; Beqiri A, Murati, Haxhi, Cana, Hasi, Skela, Lala, Muka (Bushaj 78), Duro, Tare.

Denmark: Skov-Jensen; Priske, Helveg, Kroldrup, Jensen N, Poulsen, Gravesen, Tomasson, Gronkjaer (Kahlenberg 77), Jorgensen (Kristiansen 82), Pedersen (Rommedahl 46).
Referee: Baskalov (Russia).

Istanbul, 9 October 2004, 45,000

Turkey (1) 4 *(Gokdeniz 17, Nihat 50, Fatih 89, 90)*

Kazakhstan (0) 0

Turkey: Rustu; Umit O, Tolga, Servet, Deniz, Huseyin, Serkan (Hasan Sas 64), Gokdeniz (Tuncay 69), Necati, Nihat (Altintop 84), Fatih.
Kazakhstan: Novikov (Morev 52); Avdeyev, Chichulin (Baltiev 33), Dubinski, Lyapkin, Smakov (Kozulin 59), Irismetov, Karpovich, Nizovtsev, Buleshev, Familtsev.
Referee: Hrinak (Slovakia).

Kiev, 9 October 2004, 62,000

Ukraine (0) 1 *(Shevchenko 48)*

Greece (0) 1 *(Tsartas 81)*

Ukraine: Shovkovskyi; Nesmachni, Fedorov, Tymoschuk, Yezerski, Rusol, Shevchenko, Shelayev (Zakarliuka 85), Gusev, Voronin (Belik 90), Vorobei (Gusin 65).
Greece: Nikopolidis; Dellas, Seitaridis, Kapsis, Fyssas, Basinas (Georgiadis 78), Karagounis, Zagorakis, Giannakopoulos (Charisteas 61), Katsouranis, Vryzas (Tsartas 69).
Referee: Gonzalez (Spain).

Copenhagen, 13 October 2004, 41,331

Denmark (1) 1 *(Tomasson 27 (pen))*

Turkey (0) 1 *(Nihat 70)*

Denmark: Skov-Jensen; Priske, Jensen N, Gravesen, Poulsen, Kroldrup, Helveg, Tomasson, Perez (Rommedahl 62), Jorgensen (Kristiansen 77), Gronkjaer■.
Turkey: Rustu; Umit O, Ibrahim (Tuncay 46), Okan B, Tolga, Servet (Necati 67), Huseyin, Gokdeniz (Serkan 83), Fatih, Nihat, Emre B.
Referee: De Santis (Italy).

Almaty, 13 October 2004, 26,000

Kazakhstan (0) 0

Albania (0) 1 *(Bushaj 60)*

Kazakhstan: Morev; Lyapkin, Avdeyev, Smakov (Kamelov 53), Dubinski, Familtsev, Baltiev, Karpovitch (Shevchenko 62), Irismetov, Nizovtsev, Ourazbakhtin (Boulechev 56).
Albania: Strakosha; Beqiri A, Dragusha (Shkembi 90), Cana, Hasi, Lala, Skela, Bushaj (Rraklli 85), Haxhi, Luka (Lici 53), Tare.
Referee: Stuchlik (Austria).

Lvov, 13 October 2004, 28,000

Ukraine (1) 2 *(Bielik 9, Shevchenko 80)*

Georgia (0) 0

Ukraine: Shovkovskyi; Yezerski (Checher 46), Fedorov, Rusol, Nesmachni, Gusev, Tymoshchuk, Gusin, Bielik, Shevchenko, Vorinin (Shelayev 39) (Zakarliouka 64).
Georgia: Devadze; Saluquaze, Khizaneishvili, Khizanishvili, Mjavanadze (Burduli 46), Asatiani M, Jamarauli (Demetradze 85), Tskitishvili, Kobiashvili, Arveladze S, Iashvili.
Referee: Stark (Germany).

Tbilisi, 17 November 2004, 30,000

Georgia (1) 2 *(Demetradze 33, Asatiani 74)*

Denmark (1) 2 *(Tomasson 9, 64)*

Georgia: Devadze; Khizaneishvili, Khizanishvili, Kaladze, Mzhavanadze, Kobiashvili, Tskitishvili, Jikia (Kvirkvelia 72), Asatiani M, Iashvili (Arveladze S 73), Demetradze.
Denmark: Sorensen; Poulsen, Priske, Kroldrup, Jensen N, Lustu, Gravesen, Jensen D (Skoubo 84), Tomasson, Jorgensen (Lovenkrands 84), Perez (Rommedahl 46).
Referee: Ceferin (Slovenia).

Athens, 17 November 2004, 35,000

Greece (2) 3 *(Charisteas 24, 45, Katsouranis 86)*

Kazakhstan (0) 1 *(Baltiev 88 (pen))*

Greece: Nikopolidis; Dellas, Fyssas, Kapsis (Katsouranis 60), Zagorakis (Kaves 71), Seitaridis, Basinas, Karagounis, Tsartas (Georgiadis 72), Charisteas, Vryzas.
Kazakhstan: Novikov; Chichulin, Dubinsky, Lyapkin, Smakov, Irismetov, Karpovich, Urazbakhtin (Rodionov 53), Baltiev, Buleshev (Shevchenko 66), Zhalmagambetov (Kamelov 68).
Referee: Kostadinov (Bulgaria).

Istanbul, 17 November 2004, 52,000

Turkey (0) 0

Ukraine (2) 3 *(Gusev 9, Shevchenko 17, 90)*

Turkey: Rustu; Deniz, Servet (Tuncay 28), Umit O, Seyhan, Okan B, Huseyin (Necati 66), Emre B, Gokdeniz (Basturk 54), Nihat, Fatih.
Ukraine: Shovkovskyi; Gusev, Fedorov, Nesmachni, Rusol, Yezerski, Gusin, Shelayev, Vorobei (Dmitrulin 75), Shevchenko (Nazarenko 90), Voronin (Rykun 61).
Referee: Baptista (Portugal).

Tirana, 9 February 2005, 14,000

Albania (0) 0

Ukraine (1) 2 *(Rusol 39, Gusin 59)*

Albania: Strakosha; Duro, Cana, Haxhi, Cipi (Osmani 58), Lala, Aliaj, Skela, Tare (Bogdani 65), Bushi (Myrtaj 76), Dullku.
Ukraine: Shovkovskyi; Tymoschuk, Nesmachni, Yerzersky, Rusol, Shelayev, Gusev, Shevchenko, Voronin (Rykun 80), Rotan (Vorobei 66), Gusin.
Referee: Bennett (England).

Piraeus, 9 February 2005, 32,430

Greece (2) 2 *(Zakorakis 25, Basinas 31 (pen))*

Denmark (1) 1 *(Rommedahl 45)*

Greece: Nikopolidis; Seitaridis, Fyssas, Katsouranis, Dellas, Zakorakis (Kyrgiakos 46), Basinas, Giannakopoulos, Karagounis (Kafes 61), Charisteas, Vryzas (Amantidis 83).
Denmark: Sorensen; Poulsen, Kroldrup, Lustu (Nielsen P 64), Jensen N (Madsen 64), Priske, Gravesen, Rommedahl, Tomasson, Jensen D, Perez (Jorgensen 46).
Referee: Collina (Italy).

Copenhagen, 26 March 2005, 20,980

Denmark (2) 3 *(Moller 10, 48, Poulsen 33)*

Kazakhstan (0) 0

Denmark: Sorensen; Priske, Laursen, Helveg, Jensen N, Poulsen, Tomasson (Perez 46), Jensen D (Jensen C 46), Gronkjaer (Silberbauer 74), Moller, Jorgensen.

Kazakhstan: Novikov; Familtsev, Avdejev, Smakov, Lyapin, Chichulin (Larim 46), Travin (Baizhanov 56), Baltev, Karpovich, Utabajev (Baizjanov 78), Rodionov.
Referee: Gilewski (Poland).

Tbilisi, 26 March 2005, 25,000

Georgia (1) 1 *(Asatiani 23)*

Greece (2) 3 *(Kapsis 44, Vryzas 45, Giannakopoulos 54)*

Georgia: Lomaia; Mzhavanadze, Khizanishvili, Khizaneishvili, Kaladze, Kvirkvelia, Gogua (Tskitishvili 46), Asatiani M, Kobiashvili, Demetradze, Arveladze S (Iashvili 62).
Greece: Nikopolidis; Seitaridis, Goumas, Kapsis, Katsouranis, Zagorakis, Basinas, Karagounis, Giannakopoulos, Charisteas, Vryzas.
Referee: Rosetti (Italy).

Istanbul, 26 March 2005, 30,000

Turkey (2) 2 *(Necati 3 (pen), Beqiri E 5 (og))*

Albania (0) 0

Turkey: Rustu; Avci, Seyhan, Balci, Umit O, Ibrahim, Emre B (Bulent K 84), Basturk, Altintop (Gokdeniz 76), Necati, Fatih (Ayhan 63).
Albania: Lika; Beqiri E, Dalku, Haxhi, Lala, Duro (Bushi 79), Cana, Bogdani, Aliaj, Skela, Tare.
Referee: Plautz (Austria).

Tbilisi, 30 March 2005, 20,000

Georgia (2) 2 *(Amisulashvili 13, Iashvili 41)*

Turkey (3) 5 *(Seyhan 12, Fatih 19, 35, Koray 74, Tuncay 85)*

Georgia: Asatiani M; Mzhavanadze, Khizaneishvili (Salukvadze 17), Kaladze, Devadze (Lomaia 20), Gogua■, Tskitishvili (Burduli 71), Iashvili, Kobiashvili, Amisulashvili, Ashvetia.
Turkey: Rustu; Seyhan, Ibrahim, Umit O, Koray, Basturk (Huseyin 46), Emre B, Gokdeniz, Altintop, Fatih, Necati (Tuncay 64).
Referee: Hauge (Norway).

Athens, 30 March 2005, 38,000

Greece (1) 2 *(Charisteas 35, Karagounis 85)*

Albania (0) 0

Greece: Nikopolidis; Seitaridis, Goumas, Kyrgiakos, Katsouranis, Zagorakis, Basinas, Karagounis, Giannakopoulos (Amanatidis 87), Charisteas, Vryzas (Gekas 89).
Albania: Lika; Beqiri E, Haxhi, Lici, Lala, Duro (Dalku 84), Cana, Osmani, Mukaj (Rraklli 46), Skela, Bogdani (Tare 65).
Referee: Layec (France).

Kiev, 30 March 2005, 55,000

Ukraine (0) 1 *(Voronin 67)*

Denmark (0) 0

Ukraine: Shovkoskyi; Sviderski, Yezersky, Rusol, Nesmachni, Gusev, Tymoschuk, Vorobei, Gusin, Voronin (Matyshin 90), Kosyrin (Bielik 59) (Radchenko 80).
Denmark: Sorensen; Priske, Helveg, Kroldrup, Jensen N (Moller 70), Gravesen, Jorgensen (Jensen C 84), Poulsen, Rommedahl (Silberbauer 75), Tomasson, Gronkjaer.
Referee: Michel (Slovakia).

Tirana, 4 June 2005

Albania (2) 3 *(Tare 6, 55, Skela 33)*

Georgia (0) 2 *(Burduli 85, Kobiashvili 90)*

Albania: Lika; Hasi, Beqiri E, Osmani (Cipi 27), Aliaj, Haxhi, Duro, Skela (Shkembi 85), Jupi, Tare, Bogdani (Myrtaj 64).
Georgia: Sturua; Khizanishvili, Kaladze, Salukvadze, Rekhviashvili, Kobiashvili, Asatiani M (Daraselia 58), Kvirkvelia, Magradze (Burduli 64), Demetradze (Bobokhidze 76), Jakobia.
Behind closed doors.
Referee: Tudor (Romania).

Istanbul, 4 June 2005, 32,000

Turkey (0) 0

Greece (0) 0

Turkey: Rustu; Tolga, Ibrahim, Umit O, Mustafa (Tuncay 46), Altintop, Emre B (Serkan 78), Basturk■, Huseyin, Gokdeniz (Necati 60), Fatih.
Greece: Nikopolidis; Seitaridis, Goumas, Kapsis, Fyssas, Karagounis, Basinas, Katsouranis, Giannakopoulos (Lakis 66), Charisteas, Vryzas.
Referee: Merk (Germany).

Kiev, 4 June 2005, 40,000

Ukraine (1) 2 *(Shevchenko 18, Avdeyev 83 (og))*

Kazakhstan (0) 0

Ukraine: Shovkovskyi; Yezersky, Nesmachni, Rusol, Radchenko (Fedorov 86), Tymoschuk, Rotan, Gusev (Gusin 46), Shevchenko, Vorobei, Voronin (Bielik 69).
Kazakhstan: Novikov; Lyapkin, Familtsev (Travin 78), Avdeyev, Dubinsky, Smakov (Nizovtsev 55), Karpovich, Baizhanov, Rodionov (Chichulin 30), Baltiev, Krokhmal.
Referee: Lehner (Austria).

Copenhagen, 8 June 2005, 26,366

Denmark (1) 3 *(Larsen S 4, 46, Jorgensen 54)*

Albania (0) 1 *(Bogdani 72)*

Denmark: Sorensen; Helveg, Nielsen P, Kroldrup, Jensen N, Poulsen, Gravesen (Jensen D 60), Tomasson (Perez 87), Rommedahl (Silberbauer 71), Larsen S, Jorgensen.
Albania: Lika; Beqiri E, Osmani, Hasi, Allaj, Cana, Lala, Jupi (Sina 90), Skela (Duro 67), Tare (Myrtaj 81), Bogdani.
Referee: Frojdfeldt (Sweden).

Piraeus, 8 June 2005, 33,000

Greece (0) 0

Ukraine (0) 1 *(Gusin 82)*

Greece: Nikopolidis; Seitaridis, Kapsis (Vyntra 58), Goumas (Papadopoulos 86), Fyssas, Basinas, Zagorakis, Karagounis (Tsartas 35), Giannakopoulos, Charisteas, Vryzas.
Ukraine: Shovkovskyi; Fedorov, Rusol, Yezersky, Nesmachni, Gusev, Gusin, Tymoshchuk, Vorobei (Rotan 55), Shevchenko (Bielik 80), Voronin (Shelayev 90).
Referee: Temmink (Holland).

Almaty, 8 June 2005, 20,000

Kazakhstan (0) 0

Turkey (3) 6 *(Fatih 13, 80, Ibrahim 15, Tuncay 38, 90, Hamit Altintop 88)*

Kazakhstan: Novikov; Lyapkin, Avdejev, Baizhanov (Chichulin 46), Baltiev, Karpovich, Familtsev (Smakov 62), Nizovtsev, Rodionov (Larin 73), Krokhmal, Dubinsky.
Turkey: Omer; Hamit Altintop, Tolga, Ibrahim, Umit O, Gokdeniz (Serhat 68), Huseyin, Emre B (Serkan 66), Necati (Halil Altintop 46), Tuncay, Fatih.
Referee: Kassai (Hungary).

Group 2 Table

	P	*W*	*D*	*L*	*F*	*A*	*Pts*
Ukraine	9	7	2	0	15	3	23
Turkey	9	4	4	1	19	7	16
Greece	9	4	3	2	12	7	15
Denmark	8	3	3	2	13	8	12
Albania	9	3	0	6	7	16	9
Georgia	7	1	2	4	10	16	5
Kazakhstan	7	0	0	7	2	21	0

GROUP 3

Vaduz, 18 August 2004, 1000

Liechtenstein (0) 1 *(D'Elia 48)*

Estonia (1) 2 *(Viikmae 31, Lindpere 80)*

Liechtenstein: Heeb; Hasler D, Ritter■, Michael Stocklasa, Telser, Gerster■, Martin Stocklasa, Beck R (Rohrer 65), Beck T (Vogt 80), Frick M, D'Elia.
Estonia: Kojenko; Allas, Jaager, Piiroja, Rooba U, Rahn, Smirnov (Haavistu 66), Reim, Viikmae, Zahhovaiko, Terehhov (Lindpere 60).
Referee: Bozinovski (Macedonia).

Bratislava, 18 August 2004, 4500

Slovakia (1) 3 *(Vittek 26, Gresko 48, Demo 89)*

Luxembourg (1) 1 *(Strasser 2)*

Slovakia: Konig; Kratochvil, Varga, Zabavnik, Gresko, Janocko (Demo 68), Karhan, Michalik (Sech 46), Mintal, Nemeth (Sestak 84), Vittek.
Luxembourg: Besic; Braun G (Molitor 61), Cardoni, Hoffmann, Huss (Leweck C 73), Leweck A (Mannon 61), Peters, Reiter, Remy, Schauls, Strasser.
Referee: Kassai (Hungary).

Tallinn, 4 September 2004, 4200

Estonia (2) 4 *(Teever 7, Schauls 41 (og), Oper 61, Viikmae 67)*

Luxembourg (0) 0

Estonia: Poom; Allas, Jaager, Piiroja, Rooba U, Rahn, Teever, Reim (Leetmae 75), Viikmae, Zahhovaiko (Oper 46), Lindpere (Klavan 64).
Luxembourg: Besic; Peters, Reiter (Hellenbrand 88), Hoffmann, Strasser, Remy, Schauls, Cardoni (Di Domenico 81), Huss■, Leweck A, Braun G (Leweck C 68).
Referee: Kelly (Republic of Ireland).

Riga, 4 September 2004, 9500

Latvia (0) 0

Portugal (0) 2 *(Ronaldo 58, Pauleta 59)*

Latvia: Kolinko; Isakov, Zemlinsky, Stepanovs, Laizans, Bleidelis, Lobanov, Astafjevs, Rubins, Prohorenkovs (Rimkus 77), Verpakovskis.
Portugal: Ricardo; Paulo Ferreira, Ricardo Carvalho, Jorge Andrade, Nuno Valente (Caneira 74), Costinha, Maniche, Simao Sabrosa (Boa Morte 68), Deco, Ronaldo (Petit 82), Pauleta.
Referee: Poll (England).

Moscow, 4 September 2004, 14,000

Russia (1) 1 *(Bulykin 14)*

Slovakia (0) 1 *(Vittek 87)*

Russia: Malafeev; Aniukov, Sharonov, Kolodin, Evseev (Sennikov 46), Smertin, Alenichev, Khokhlov (Boyarintsev 66), Bulykin, Karayaka, Kerzahkov.
Slovakia: Contofalsky; Zabavnik, Kratochvil, Varga, Gresko, Karhan, Hanek (Reiter 84), Mintal, Vittek, Michalik (Cech 76), Nemeth (Breska 76).
Referee: Mejuto (Spain).

Luxembourg, 8 September 2004, 2000

Luxembourg (1) 3 *(Braun G 11, Leweck A 55, Cardoni 62)*

Latvia (2) 4 *(Verpakovskis 4, Zemlinsky 40 (pen), Hoffmann 65 (og), Prohorenkovs 67)*

Luxembourg: Besic; Peters (Di Domenico 90), Hellenbrand, Hoffmann, Strasser, Remy, Schauls, Leweck A (Colette 87), Braun G (Leweck C 77), Cardoni, Molitor.
Latvia: Kolinko; Stepanovs, Astafjevs, Zemlinsky, Laizans, Lobanov, Isakov, Bleidelis (Prohorenkovs 32), Verpakovskis, Rubins, Rimkus (Semyonovs 64).
Referee: Kasnaferis (Greece).

Leiria, 8 September 2004, 27,214

Portugal (0) 4 *(Ronaldo 75, Helder Postiga 84, 90, Pauleta 87)*

Estonia (0) 0

Portugal: Ricardo; Paulo Ferreira, Ricardo Carvalho, Jorge Andrade, Rui Jorge (Miguel 56), Costinha, Maniche (Helder Postiga 46), Simao Sabrosa (Boa Morte 70), Deco, Ronaldo, Pauleta.
Estonia: Poom; Allas, Piroja, Rooba U (Klavan 46), Jaager, Leetma, Reim, Teever (Viikmae 62), Lindpere, Oper, Terehhov (Zahovaiko 70).
Referee: Demirlek (Turkey).

Bratislava, 8 September 2004, 5620

Slovakia (2) 7 *(Vitek 15, 59, 81 (pen), Karhan 41, Nemeth 84, Mintal 85, Zabavnik 90)*

Liechtenstein (0) 0

Slovakia: Contofalsky; Zabavnik, Kratochvil (Petrus 46), Gresko (Breska 67), Karhan, Demo (Janocko 46), Mintal, Vitek, Nemeth, Hanek, Cech.
Liechtenstein: Heeb; Telser, Vogt, D'Elia, Martin Stocklasa, Rohrer (Frick C 70), Buchel R (Alabor 76), Burgmeier, Frick M, Beck R, Beck T.
Referee: Delevic (Serbia-Montenegro).

Vaduz, 9 October 2004, 3518

Liechtenstein (0) 2 *(Burgmeier 48, Beck T 76)*

Portugal (2) 2 *(Pauleta 23, Hasler 39 (og))*

Liechtenstein: Jehle; Telser, Michael Stocklasa, Martin Stocklasa, Hasler D, Ritter, Rohrer (Beck R 46), Frick M (Frick D 90), Gerster, Burgmeier, Beck T (Buchel R 89).

Portugal: Ricardo; Paulo Ferreira, Jorge Ribeiro, Maniche, Ricardo Carvalho, Jorge Andrade, Costinha (Tiago 46), Simao Sabrosa (Petit 57), Pauleta, Deco, Ronaldo (Helder Postiga 61).
Referee: Panic (Bosnia).

Luxembourg, 9 October 2004, 4000

Luxembourg (0) 0

Russia (0) 4 *(Sychev 56, 69, 86, Arshavin 62)*

Luxembourg: Besic; Federspiel, Hoffmann, Schauls (Schnell 58), Strasser, Cardoni (Leweck C 77), Leweck A, Molitor (Mannon 77), Peters, Remy, Braun G.
Russia: Malafeev; Aniukov, Bugaev, Evseev, Ignachevitch, Gusev (Aldonin 75), Kantonistov (Boyarintsev 46), Smertin, Arshavin, Bulykin (Kirichenko 67), Sychev.
Referee: Braamhaar (Holland).

Bratislava, 9 October 2004, 13,025

Slovakia (0) 4 *(Nemeth 47, Reiter 50, Karhan 55, 87)*

Latvia (1) 1 *(Verpakovskis 3)*

Slovakia: Contofalsky; Zabavnik, Gresko, Hanek, Kratochvl (Reiter 46), Varga, Karhan, Mintal (Janocko 46), Michalik (Cech 75), Vittek, Nemeth.
Latvia: Kolinko; Isakov, Koravlovs, Smirnovs, Zirnis, Astafjevs (Kolesnicenko 90), Bleidelis (Semyonovs 87), Lobanov, Laizans, Rimkus (Mikholap 76), Verpakovskis.
Referee: Farina (Italy).

Riga, 13 October 2004, 8200

Latvia (0) 2 *(Astafjevs 65, Laizans 82)*

Estonia (0) 2 *(Oper 72, Teever 79)*

Latvia: Kolinko; Isakov, Zemlinksy, Zirinis, Laizans, Bleidelis (Rimkus 81), Lobanov, Astafjevs, Stepanovs (Rubins 46), Verpakovskis, Prohorenkovs.
Estonia: Poom; Allas, Jaager, Piroja, Rooba U, Rhan, Teever (Leetma 85), Oper, Lindpere, Viikmae, Terehhov (Kruglov 85).
Referee: Meier (Germany).

Luxembourg, 13 October 2004, 3500

Luxembourg (0) 0

Liechtenstein (2) 4 *(Martin Stocklasa 41, Burgmeier 44, 85, Frick M 57 (pen))*

Luxembourg: Besic; Federspiel, Hoffmann, Strasser, Hellenbrand, Leweck C, Molitor (Colette 46), Cardoni, Remy, Braun G, Leweck A (Di Domenico 74).
Liechtenstein: Jehle; Telser, Hasler D, Ritter, Michael Stocklasa, Beck R (D'Elia 57), Martin Stocklasa, Frick M (Rohrer 81), Gerster, Burgmeier, Beck T (Buchel 87).
Referee: Jara (Czech Republic).

Lisbon, 13 October 2004, 27,578

Portugal (3) 7 *(Ronaldo 39, 69, Pauleta 26, Deco 45, Simao Sabrosa 82, Petit 89, 90)*

Russia (0) 1 *(Arshavin 79)*

Portugal: Ricardo; Miguel, Paulo Ferreira, Maniche (Petit 73), Ricardo Carvalho, Jorge Andrade, Costinha, Simao Sabrosa, Pauleta (Nuno Gomes 67), Deco, Ronaldo (Boa Morte 84).
Russia: Malafeev; Aniukov, Bougayev, Ignachevitch, Sennikov (Gusev 46), Arshavin, Smertin, Aldonin (Boyarintsev 71), Evseev, Bulykin, Sychev (Kiritchenko 46).
Referee: Vassaras (Greece).

Vaduz, 17 November 2004, 1500

Liechtenstein (1) 1 *(Frick M 31)*

Latvia (1) 3 *(Verpakovsky 7, Zemlinsky 57 (pen), Prohorenkovs 89)*

Liechtenstein: Jehle; Hasler D, Ritter, Michael Stocklasa, Vogt (Buchel R 88), Burgmeier, Gerster (Frick D 82), Martin Stocklasa, Beck R (Rohrer 65), Beck T, Frick M.
Latvia: Kolinko; Isakovs, Stepanovs, Zemlinsky, Zirnis, Astafjevs, Bleidelis, Laizans (Lobanov 90), Rubins (Zakresevski 90), Rimkus (Prohorenkovs 59), Verpakovskis.
Referee: Szabo (Hungary).

Luxembourg, 17 November 2004, 8300

Luxembourg (0) 0

Portugal (2) 5 *(Federspiel 11 (og), Ronaldo 28, Maniche 51, Pauleta 67, 83 (pen))*

Luxembourg: Besic; Federspiel, Hoffmann, Peters, Reiter, Schauls, Leweck A, Mannon (Di Domenico 78), Remy, Huss (Colette 78), Leweck C.
Portugal: Ricardo; Jorge Andrade, Ribeiro, Paulo Ferreira, Ricardo Carvalho, Costinha (Petit 59), Deco (Tiago 73), Maniche, Boa Morte (Quaresma 46), Ronaldo, Pauleta.
Referee: Godulyan (Ukraine).

Krasnodar, 17 November 2004, 28,000

Russia (3) 4 *(Karayaka 25, Izmailov 27, Sychev 34, Lozkov 69 (pen))*

Estonia (0) 0

Russia: Malafeev; Evseev, Bugaev, Smertin, Berezutski A, Izmailov, Khokhlov (Gusev 87), Lozkov (Shemshov 82), Karayaka, Kerzhakov, Sychev.
Estonia: Kaalma; Allas, Jaager, Piroja, Rooba U, Rahn, Teever (Kruglov 90), Lindpere, Viikmae, Oper, Terehhov (Klavan 82).
Referee: Busacca (Switzerland).

Tallinn, 26 March 2005, 4000

Estonia (0) 1 *(Oper 58)*

Slovakia (0) 2 *(Mintal 59, Reiter 66)*

Estonia: Kotenka; Allas, Stepanov, Jaager, Rooba U (Klavan 79), Reim, Lindpere (Zahovaiko 86), Oper, Terehhov (Teever 79), Viikmae, Kruglov.
Slovakia: Contofalsky; Zabavnik, Valachovic, Varga, Petras, Kisel (Jakubko 54), Hlinka, Karhan, Mintal, Michalik (Reiter 46), Nemeth (Cech 90).
Referee: Frojdfeldt (Sweden).

Vaduz, 26 March 2005, 2500

Liechtenstein (1) 1 *(Beck T 40)*

Russia (2) 2 *(Kerzhakov 23, Karayaka 37)*

Liechtenstein: Jehle; Telser, Ritter, Hasler D, Michael Stocklasa, Beck R (Vogt 60), D'Elia (Buchel R 53), Gerster, Burgmeier, Frick M, Beck T.
Russia: Malafeev; Berezutski A, Berezutski V, Evseev, Ignachevitch, Arshavin (Sychev 55), Bystrov (Izmailov 67), Karayaka, Khokhlov (Aldonin 78), Lozkov, Kerzhakov.
Referee: Berntsen (Norway).

Tallinn, 30 March 2005, 9300

Estonia (0) 1 *(Terehhov 63)*

Russia (1) 1 *(Arshavin 18)*

Estonia: Kotenko; Allas, Stepanov, Jaager, Kruglov, Rahn, Reim, Oper, Terehhov (Smirnov 83), Lindpere (Klavan 24), Viikmae (Teever 90).

Russia: Akinfeev; Smertin, Ignachevitch, Berezutski V, Berezutski A, Bystrov, Khokhlov (Kolodin 63), Loskov, Zhirkov (Kariaka 72), Arshavin (Sychev 67), Kerzhakov.
Referee: Paparesta (Italy).

Riga, 30 March 2005, 3000

Latvia (2) 4 *(Bleidelis 33, Laizans 38 (pen), Verpakovskis 73, 90)*

Luxembourg (0) 0

Latvia: Kolinko; Zirnis, Smirnovs, Stepanovs, Bleidelis (Miholaps 68), Astafjevs, Laizans, Rubins (Zavoronkovs 39), Morozs, Verpakovskis, Prohorekovs (Rimkus 82).
Luxembourg: Oberweis; Schauls (Lang 82), Hoffmann, Strasser, Heinz, Capela, Pace (Mannon 89), Remy, Peters (Leweck C 50), Durrer, Collette.
Referee: Kovacic (Croatia).

Bratislava, 30 March 2005, 30,000

Slovakia (1) 1 *(Karhan 7 (pen))*

Portugal (0) 1 *(Helder Postiga 62)*

Slovakia: Contofalsky; Zabavnik, Varga, Hanek (Kisel 80), Petras, Hlinka, Karhan, Mintel, Michalik (Had 35), Jakubko (Reiter 64), Nemeth.
Portugal: Ricardo; Paulo Ferreira (Miguel 63), Ricardo Carvalho, Jorge Andrade, Nuno Valente, Costinha, Maniche, Ronaldo, Deco, Pauleta (Helder Postiga 56), Simao Sabrosa (Viana 90).
Referee: Sars (France).

Tallinn, 4 June 2005, 5000

Estonia (1) 2 *(Stepanov 27, Oper 57)*

Liechtenstein (0) 0

Estonia: Kotenko; Allas, Stepanov, Jaager, Kruglov, Reim, Lindpere, Oper, Terehhov (Smirnov 89), Viikmae (Teever 71), Klavan (Saharov 87).
Liechtenstein: Jehle; Telser, D'Elia (Alabor 84), Hasler D, Ritter, Martin Stocklasa, Beck R (Buchel R 56), Gerster, Beck T, Frick M, Burgmeier.
Referee: Whitby (Wales).

Lisbon, 4 June 2005, 60,000

Portugal (2) 2 *(Fernando Meira 21, Ronaldo 41)*

Slovakia (0) 0

Portugal: Ricardo; Alex, Fernando Meira, Jorge Andrade, Caneira, Petit, Maniche, Figo, Deco (Tiago 88), Ronaldo (Ricardo Quaresma 76), Pauleta (Helder Postiga 78).
Slovakia: Contofalsky; Zabavnik, Varga, Petras, Had, Hanek (Kisel 64), Karhan, Hlinka, Mintal, Jakubko (Vittek 59), Nemeth (Slovak 59).
Referee: Collina (Italy).

St Petersburg, 4 June 2005, 8400

Russia (0) 2 *(Arshavin 57, Loskov 78 (pen))*

Latvia (0) 0

Russia: Akinfeev; Berezutski A, Smertin, Berezutski V, Aldonin (Bistrov 56), Semchov (Sennikov 67), Anukov, Arshavin (Izmailov 82), Loskov, Jirkov, Kerzhakov.
Latvia: Piedels; Stepanovs, Astafjevs, Smirnovs, Laizans, Zirnis, Isakovs (Zavoronkovs 84), Bleidelis, Rubins, Prohorenkovs (Rimkus 78), Verpakovskis.
Referee: Poulat (France).

Tallinn, 8 June 2005, 7000

Estonia (0) 0

Portugal (1) 1 *(Ronaldo 33)*

Estonia: Kotenko; Allas, Stepanov, Jaager, Rooba U, Terehhov (Saharov 79), Reim, Rahn, Kruglov (Klavan 80), Oper, Viikmae (Zahovaiko 55).
Portugal: Ricardo; Alex, Fernando Meira, Jorge Andrade, Caneira, Costinha, Deco, Maniche (Petit 73), Figo, Pauleta (Helder Postiga 66), Ronaldo (Tiago 90).
Referee: Riley (England).

Riga, 8 June 2005, 8000

Latvia (1) 1 *(Bleidelis 16)*

Liechtenstein (0) 0

Latvia: Piedels; Astafjevs, Stepanovs, Laizans, Smirnovs, Bleidelis, Korablovs, Zavoronkovs, Rubins, Verpakovskis, Prohorenkovs (Rimkus 60).
Liechtenstein: Jehle; Telser, Hasler D, Ritter, D'Elia (Vogt 56), Beck R (Rohrer 77), Buchel R (Buchel M 90), Martin Stocklasa, Burgmeier, Frick M, Beck T.
Referee: Eriksson (Sweden).

Luxembourg, 8 June 2005, 4000

Luxembourg (0) 0

Slovakia (2) 4 *(Nemeth 5, Mintal 15, Kisel 54, Reiter 60)*

Luxembourg: Oberweis; Federspiel (Sabotic 62), Heinz, Hoffmann, Reiter, Lang (Durrer 90), Strasser, Leweck A, Collette, Leweck C, Remy.
Slovakia: Contofalsky; Had (Slovak 46), Varga, Petras (Reiter 59), Kisel, Hanek, Karhan, Hlinka (Sninsky 46), Nemeth, Mintal, Vittek.
Referee: Styles (England).

Group 3 Table

	P	*W*	*D*	*L*	*F*	*A*	*Pts*
Portugal	8	6	2	0	24	4	20
Slovakia	8	5	2	1	22	7	17
Russia	7	4	2	1	15	10	14
Latvia	8	4	1	3	15	14	13
Estonia	9	3	2	4	12	15	11
Liechtenstein	8	1	1	6	9	19	4
Luxembourg	8	0	0	8	4	32	0

GROUP 4

Saint-Denis, 4 September 2004, 43,526

France (0) 0

Israel (0) 0

France: Coupet; Gallas, Squillaci, Givet, Mendy (Giuly 57), Makelele, Vieira, Rothen (Pires 66), Evra, Henry, Saha.
Israel: Davidovitch; Ben-Haim, Saban, Antebi (Keisi 12), Benado, Afek (Gazal 71), Badir, Katan, Benayoun (Nimni 80), Goian, Tal.
Referee: Temmink (Holland).

Dublin, 4 September 2004, 35,900

Republic of Ireland (2) 3 *(Morrison 33, Reid A 38, Robbie Keane 55 (pen))*

Cyprus (0) 0

Republic of Ireland: Given; Carr (Finnan 70), O'Shea (Maybury 83), Kavanagh, O'Brien, Cunningham, Reid A, Kilbane, Robbie Keane, Morrison (Lee 81), Duff.

Cyprus: Panayiotou N; Theodotou, Kakoyiannis, Okkarides, Lambrou, Charalambous (Ilia 65), Makirdis, Satsias, Okkas (Krassas 77), Charalambides (Michael 70), Konstantinou.
Referee: Paniashvili (Georgia).

Basle, 4 September 2004, 13,013

Switzerland (4) 6 *(Vonlanthen 10, 14, 57, Rey 29, 44, 55)*

Faeroes (0) 0

Switzerland: Zuberbuhler; Haas, Yakin M, Muller, Spycher (Magnin 46), Cabanas (Huggel 63), Vogel, Wicky, Yakin H, Rey (Haberli 75), Vonlanthen.
Faeroes: Knudsen; Thorsteinsson, Johannesen O, Jacobsen JR, Olsen, Borg (Danielsen 64), Johnsson J, Benjaminsen, Jorgensen (Hansen 70), Frederiksberg, Petersen J (Jacobsen R 57).
Referee: Tudor (Romania).

Torshavn, 8 September 2004, 6000

Faeroes (0) 0

France (1) 2 *(Giuly 37, Cisse 73)*

Faeroes: Mikkelsen; Thorsteinsson, Olsen, Johannesen O, Jacobsen JR, Jacobsen R (Flotum 75), Borg, Benjaminsen, Johnsson J, Jorgensen (Danielsen A 83), Frederiksberg (Petersen J 68).
France: Coupet; Gallas, Evra, Vieira■, Squillaci, Givet, Giuly, Pedretti, Saha (Cisse 9), Henry (Dhorasoo 64), Pires.
Referee: Thompson (Scotland).

Tel Aviv, 8 September 2004, 17,000

Israel (0) 2 *(Benayoun 64, Badir 74)*

Cyprus (0) 1 *(Konstantinou 58)*

Israel: Davidovich; Saban, Ben-Haim, Benado, Keissi, Nimny (Balili 57), Badir, Benayoun, Tal (Afek 71), Katan (Gazal 84), Goian.
Cyprus: Panayiotou N; Okkarides, Kakoyiannis, Nikolaou, Theodotou (Georgiou 30), Makirdis, Satsias, Ilia, Charalambides (Michail 72), Okkas (Yiasoumi 79), Konstantinou.
Referee: Shmolik (Belarus).

Basle, 8 September 2004, 28,000

Switzerland (1) 1 *(Yakin H 17)*

Republic of Ireland (1) 1 *(Morrison 8)*

Switzerland: Zuberbuhler; Vogel, Barnetta, Yakin M, Muller, Magnin, Haas, Cabanas, Yakin H, Vonlanthen (Lonfat 73), Rey.
Republic of Ireland: Given; Carr, Finnan, Roy Keane, O'Brien, Cunningham, Reid A (Kavanagh 73), Kilbane, Robbie Keane, Morrison (Doherty 84), Duff
Referee: Vassaras (Greece).

Nicosia, 9 October 2004, 3000

Cyprus (1) 2 *(Konstantinou 14 (pen), Okkas 82)*

Faeroes (2) 2 *(Jorgensen 22, Jacobsen R 43)*

Cyprus: Panayiotou N; Nikolaou, Okkarides (Kaiafas 51), Makridis, Okkas (Kakoyiannis 69), Charalambides, Konstantinou, Charalambous, Georgiou, Elia, Krassias (Satsias 46).
Faeroes: Mikkelsen; Thorsteinsson, Johannesen O Jacobsen JR (Petersen J 76), Olsen, Johnsson J, Benjaminsen, Borg, Jorgensen (Danielsen A 46), Jacobsen R, Frederiksberg (Flotum 69).
Referee: Gadiev (Azerbaijan).

Saint-Denis, 9 October 2004, 78,863

France (0) 0

Republic of Ireland (0) 0

France: Barthez; Gallas, Silvestre, Mavuba, Squillaci, Givet, Wiltord, Dacourt (Diarra 64), Cisse (Gouvou 83), Henry, Pires.
Republic of Ireland: Given; Carr, O'Shea, Roy Keane, O'Brien, Cunningham, Finnan, Kilbane, Robbie Keane, Morrison (Reid A 41), Duff.
Referee: Ibanez (Spain).

Tel Aviv, 9 October 2004, 37,981

Israel (1) 2 *(Benayoun 9, 48)*

Switzerland (2) 2 *(Frei 26, Vonlanthen 34)*

Israel: Davidovich; Benado, Ben-Haim, Gershon (Saban 78), Gazal (Nimny 46), Badir, Tal, Keissi, Afek, Benayoun, Balili (Golan 58).
Switzerland: Zuberbuhler; Haas, Magnin, Vogel, Yakin M (Henchoz 63), Muller, Cabanas, Barnetta (Gygax 33), Frei, Vonlanthen, Yakin H (Lonfat 80).
Referee: Shield (Australia).

Nicosia, 13 October 2004, 4000

Cyprus (0) 0

France (1) 2 *(Wiltord 38, Henry 72)*

Cyprus: Panayiotou N; Ilia, Charalambous, Okkarides, Nikolaou (Lambrou 77), Kakoyiannis, Georgiou (Yiasoumi 83), Satsias, Charalambides (Makridis 56), Okkas, Konstantinou.
France: Barthez; Gallas, Silvestre, Vieira, Squillaci, Givet, Wiltord, Dacourt (Diarra 90), Luyindula (Evra 66), Henry, Pires (Moreira 46).
Referee: Larsen (Denmark).

Dublin, 13 October 2004, 36,000

Republic of Ireland (2) 2 *(Robbie Keane 14 (pen), 32)*

Faeroes (0) 0

Republic of Ireland: Given; Carr, O'Shea (Miller 57), Roy Keane, O'Brien, Cunningham, Finnan, Kilbane, Robbie Keane, Duff, Reid A.
Faeroes: Mikkelsen; Thorsteinsson, Olsen, Johnsson J, Johannesen O, Jacobsen JR, Borg (Danielsen 85), Benjaminsen, Petersen J, Frederiksberg (Flotum 82), Jacobsen R (Lakjuni 58).
Referee: Lajuks (Latvia).

Nicosia, 17 November 2004, 3500

Cyprus (1) 1 *(Okkas 45)*

Israel (1) 2 *(Keissi 17, Nimny 86)*

Cyprus: Panayiotou N; Kaiafas, Kakoyannis, Okkarides, Makrides, Okkas (Yiasoumi 55), Charalambides (Nikolaou 85), Konstantinou, Charalambous, Georgiou (Goumenos 70), Ilia.
Israel: Davidovich; Benado, Ben-Haim, Keissi, Balili (Goian 53), Nimny, Badir, Benayoun, Afek (Revivo 79), Kafan, Saban.
Referee: Kaldma (Estonia).

Paris, 26 March 2005, 79,373

France (0) 0

Switzerland (0) 0

France: Barthez; Sagnol, Boumsong, Givet, Gallas, Giuly, Pedretti, Vieira, Dhorasoo (Meriem 59), Trezeguet, Wiltord (Govou 82).

Switzerland: Zuberbuhler; Degen P, Senderos, Muller, Spycher, Gygax (Henchoz 90), Lonfat (Huggel 29), Cabanas, Vogel, Ziegler (Magnin 69), Frei.
Referee: De Santis (Italy).

Tel Aviv, 26 March 2005, 44,000

Israel (0) 1 *(Swan 90)*

Republic of Ireland (1) 1 *(Morrison 4)*

Israel: Awat; Afek (Nimny 65), Ben-Haim, Gershon, Benado, Keissi, Badir, Benayoun, Tal (Balili 65), Katan, Golan (Swan 73).
Republic of Ireland: Given; Carr, O'Shea, Finnan, O'Brien, Cunningham, Duff, Roy Keane, Robbie Keane, Morrison (Holland 85), Kilbane.
Referee: Ivanov (Russia).

Tel Aviv, 30 March 2005, 43,000

Israel (0) 1 *(Badir 83)*

France (0) 1 *(Trezeguet 50)*

Israel: Awat; Sabas, Gershon, Ben-Haim, Keissi, Badir, Nimny, Tal (Afek 67), Katan, Benayoun, Balili.
France: Barthez; Sagnol, Boumsong, Givet, Gallas, Vieira, Pedreti, Diarra, Wiltord (Dhorasoo 90), Trezeguet■, Malouda.
Referee: Merk (Germany).

Zurich, 30 March 2005, 16,066

Switzerland (0) 1 *(Frei 88)*

Cyprus (0) 0

Switzerland: Zuberbuhler; Degen P, Muller, Senderos, Spycher (Magnin 82), Gygax, Lonfat (Yakin H 62), Vogel, Cabanas, Ziegler (Vonlanthen 41), Frei.
Cyprus: Panayiotou■; Elia, Louka, Lambrou, Garpozis (Aloneftis 90), Charalambides, Makridis (Michael 65), Satsias, Krassas (Yiasoumi 80), Okkas, Konstantinou.
Referee: Dougal (Scotland).

Toftir, 4 June 2005, 2043

Faeroes (0) 1 *(Jacobsen R 70)*

Switzerland (1) 3 *(Wicky 25, Frei 73, 86)*

Faeroes: Mikkelsen; Hansen, Johannesen O, Jacobsen JR, Olsen, Danielsen A, Borg (Frederiksberg 66), Benjaminsen, Jacobsen R, Jorgensen (Lakjuni 75), Flotum (Jacobsen C 63).
Switzerland: Zuberbuhler; Degen P, Muller, Rochat, Magnin, Gygas, Vogel, Wicky (Lonfat 90), Barnetta (Margairaz 68), Frei, Vonlanthen (Ziegler 77).
Referee: Gumienny (Belgium).

Dublin, 4 June 2005, 36,000

Republic of Ireland (2) 2 *(Harte 6, Robbie Keane 11)*

Israel (2) 2 *(Yehiel 39, Nimni 45 (pen))*

Republic of Ireland: Given; O'Shea, O'Brien■, Cunningham, Harte, Holland, Kilbane, Duff, Robbie Keane (Kavanagh 27), Morrison, Reid A (Doherty 64).
Israel: Awat; Yehiel, Gershon, Benado, Saban, Suan, Tal, Nimni (Goian 79), Keissi, Benayoun, Katan (Balili 66).
Referee: Vassaras (Greece).

Torshavn, 8 June 2005, 10,000

Faeroes (0) 0

Republic of Ireland (0) 2 *(Harte 51 (pen), Kilbane 58)*

Faeroes: Mikkelsen; Hansen, Johannesen O, Danielsen A, Olsen, Johnsson J, Benjaminsen (Borg 79), Jorgensen (Akselsen 79), Jacobsen R, Lakjuni, Flotum (Jacobsen C 59).
Republic of Ireland: Given; Carr, Harte, Roy Keane, O'Shea, Cunningham, Reid, Kilbane, Morrison (Doherty 79), Elliott, Duff.
Referee: Genov (Bulgaria).

Group 4 Table

	P	*W*	*D*	*L*	*F*	*A*	*Pts*
Republic of Ireland	7	3	4	0	11	4	13
Switzerland	6	3	3	0	13	4	12
Israel	7	2	5	0	10	8	11
France	6	2	4	0	5	1	10
Cyprus	6	0	1	5	4	12	1
Faeroes	6	0	1	5	3	17	1

GROUP 5

Palermo, 4 September 2004, 21,463

Italy (1) 2 *(De Rossi 4, Toni 79)*

Norway (1) 1 *(Carew 1)*

Italy: Buffon; Bonera, Nesta, Materazzi, Favalli (Diana 67), Fiore, Gattuso, De Rossi, Zambrotta, Gilardino (Corradi 59), Miccoli (Toni 68).
Norway: Johnsen E; Basma, Riseth, Lundekvam, Riise, Hoseth (Solli 90), Andresen, Sorensen (Pedersen M 85), Johnsen F, Rudi, Carew (Rushfeldt 72).
Referee: Sars (France).

Celje, 4 September 2004, 4000

Slovenia (2) 3 *(Acimovic 6, 28, 49)*

Moldova (0) 0

Slovenia: Mavric B; Karic, Pokore (Sukalo 81), Mavric M, Knavs, Seslar, Komac (Tanjic 74), Ceh (Koren 89), Acimovic, Dedic, Siljak.
Moldova: Hmaruc; Covalenco (Ivanov 71), Lascencov, Olexici (Lungu 46), Catinsus, Priganiuc, Covalciuc, Savinov, Rogaciov (Dadu 82), Cebotari, Miterev.
Referee: Hyytia (Finland).

Chisinau, 8 September 2004, 8500

Moldova (0) 0

Italy (1) 1 *(Del Piero 33)*

Moldova: Hmaruc; Lungu, Olexici, Catinsus, Lascencov, Priganiuc, Covalciuc, Ivanov, Rogaciov (Cebotari 81), Bursuc, Mitere (Dadu 62).
Italy: Buffon; Bonera (Blasi 84), Nesta, Materazzi, Zambrotta, Gattuso, Pirlo, Ambrosini (Oddo 74), Diana, Del Piero, Gilardino (Toni 80).
Referee: Benes (Czech Republic).

Oslo, 8 September 2004, 25,272

Norway (1) 1 *(Riseth 39)*

Belarus (0) 1 *(Kutuzov 77)*

Norway: Myhre; Hoiland, Riseth, Lundekvam, Riise, Andresen, Hoseth, Johnsen F, Rudi (Sorensen 46), Pedersen M, Rushfeldt (Carew 81).

Belarus: Khomutovski; Kulchi, Omelyunchuk, Shtanyuk, Yaskovich, Lavrik, Gurenko, Bulyga (Sashcheka 63), Romashchenko, Hleb V (Blizuk 44) (Suchkov 90), Kutuzov.
Referee: Costa (Portugal).

Glasgow, 8 September 2004, 38,278

Scotland (0) 0

Slovenia (0) 0

Scotland: Gordon; Caldwell G, Naysmith (Holt 59), Ferguson B, Webster, Mackay, McNamara, Fletcher, Dickov (Crawford 79), Quashie, McFadden.
Slovenia: Mavric B; Pokorn, Mavric M, Knavs, Karic, Ceh, Seslar, Komac, Acimovic, Siljak (Lavric 64), Dedic (Sukalo 79).
Referee: Larsen (Denmark).

Minsk, 9 October 2004, 20,000

Belarus (1) 4 *(Omelianchuk 44, Kutuzov 65, Bulyga 76, Romashchenko 90)*

Moldova (0) 0

Belarus: Khomutovski; Kulchi (Kovba 79), Yaskovich, Omelianchuk, Shtanyuk, Gurenko, Lavrik, Belkevich (Koval 83), Romashchenko, Korytko, Kutuzov (Bulyga 66).
Moldova: Hmaruc; Savinov, Lascencov, Olexici, Catinsus, Barisev (Pobreban 79), Covalciuc (Epureanu 84), Ivanov, Rogaciov, Bursuc, Miterev (Golban 77).
Referee: Selcuk (Turkey).

Glasgow, 9 October 2004, 48,882

Scotland (0) 0

Norway (0) 1 *(Iversen 55 (pen))*

Scotland: Gordon; Caldwell G, Naysmith, Ferguson B, Anderson, Webster, Fletcher, Holt (Thompson 80), Dickov (Miller 75), McFadden■, Hughes (Pearson 63).
Norway: Myhre; Bergdolmo, Hagen, Lundekvam, Riise, Sorensen (Andresen 74), Solli, Hoseth (Pedersen M 58), Carew, Iversen (Johnsen F 89), Larsen.
Referee: Allaerts (Belgium).

Celje, 9 October 2004, 9000

Slovenia (0) 1 *(Cesar 82)*

Italy (0) 0

Slovenia: Mavric B; Pokorn, Mavric M, Mitrakovic (Cesar 76), Karic (Dedic 65), Sukalo, Komac, Ceh (Lazic 88), Acimovic, Siljak, Seslar.
Italy: Buffon; Bonera, Zambrotta, De Rossi, Cannavaro, Nesta, Gattuso, Camoranesi (Di Vaio 83), Gilardino (Toni 69), Totti, Esposito (Fiore 69).
Referee: De Bleeckere (Belgium).

Parma, 13 October 2004, 16,510

Italy (2) 4 *(Totti 26 (pen), 73, De Rossi 33, Gilardino 86)*

Belarus (0) 3 *(Romashchenko 52, 90, Bulyga 77)*

Italy: Buffon; Oddo (Cannavaro 68), Pancaro, De Rossi (Blasi 75), Nesta, Materazzi, Diana (Perrotta 65), Gattuso, Gilardino, Totti, Zambrotta.
Belarus: Khomutovski; Kulchi (Koval 84), Shtanyuk, Yaskovich■, Gurenko, Lavrik (Kovba 76), Tarlovski, Korytko (Bulyga 3), Belkevich, Kutuzov, Romashchenko.
Referee: Davila (Spain).

Chisinau, 13 October 2004, 4500

Moldova (1) 1 *(Dadu 27)*

Scotland (1) 1 *(Thompson 30)*

Moldova: Hmaruc; Lascencov, Savinov, Ivanov, Catinsus, Priganiuc, Olexici (Cebotari 38), Bursuc, Dadu, Rogaciov, Covalciuc.
Scotland: Gordon; Caldwell G, Naysmith (Murray 46), Ferguson B, Caldwell S, Webster, Fletcher (Miller 66), Holt, Crawford, Thompson (McCulloch 86), Cameron.
Referee: Jacobsson (Iceland).

Oslo, 13 October 2004, 24,907

Norway (1) 3 *(Carew 7, Pedersen 60, Odegaard 90)*

Slovenia (0) 0

Norway: Myhre; Bergdolmo, Riise, Andresen, Hagen, Lundekvam, Solli, Larsen, Carew (Rushfeldt 77), Iversen (Johnsen F 88), Pedersen M (Odegaard 80).
Slovenia: Mavric B; Pokorn, Mitrakovic, Seslar (Komac 66), Mavric M, Cesar, Sukalo, Ceh, Lavric (Dedic 78), Siljak, Acimovic.
Referee: Ivanov (Russia).

Milan, 26 March 2005, 40,745

Italy (1) 2 *(Pirlo 35, 85)*

Scotland (0) 0

Italy: Buffon; Bonera, Cannavaro, Materazzi, Chiellini, Camoranesi, Pirlo, Totti (De Rossi 72), Gattuso, Gilardino, Cassano (Toni 83).
Scotland: Douglas (Gordon 38); McNamara, Naysmith, Caldwell G, Weir, Pressley, Hartley (Crawford 76), Ferguson, Miller (O'Connor 86), McCulloch, Quashie.
Referee: Vassaras (Greece).

Chisinau, 30 March 2005, 6000

Moldova (0) 0

Norway (0) 0

Moldova: Hmaruc; Savinov, Lascencov (Bursuc 85), Olexici, Epureanu (Barisev 80), Catinsus, Priganiuc, Boret, Ivanov, Dadu, Rogaciov (Frunza 89).
Norway: Myhre; Bergdolmo, Riise, Larsen F, Hagen, Lundekvam, Solli, Hoset (Carew 59), Pedersen M, Iversen, Rushfeldt (Karadas 81).
Referee: Meyer (Germany).

Celje, 30 March 2005, 6000

Slovenia (1) 1 *(Rodic 44)*

Belarus (0) 1 *(Kulchi 49)*

Slovenia: Handanovic; Ilic, Mavric M (Rodic 29), Knavs, Filekovic (Siljak 54), Komac, Cipot (Koren 71), Ceh, Seslar, Acimovic, Lazic.
Belarus: Zhevnov; Belkevich, Gurenko, Hleb, Katskevich (Ostrovski 85), Kovba, Kulchi, Kutuzov (Bulyga 64), Omelyunchuk, Romashchenko (Kalatzov 76), Lavrik.
Referee: Al Ghamdi (Saudi Arabia).

Minsk, 4 June 2005, 20,000

Belarus (1) 1 *(Belkevich 19)*

Slovenia (1) 1 *(Ceh 16)*

Belarus: Zhevnov; Gurenko, Yaskovich (Lavrik 76), Omelyunchuk (Tarlovsky 85), Shtanyuk, Kulchi, Kovba, Belkevich, Hleb A, Bulyga, Kutuzov (Kornilenko 72).
Slovenia: Handanovic; Cipot, Mavric M, Cesar, Ilic (Sukalo 68), Filekovic, Pokorn, Komac (Zlogar 90), Ceh, Lavrik K, Rodic Cimirotic 58).
Referee: Hansson (Sweden).

Oslo, 4 June 2005, 24,829

Norway (0) 0

Italy (0) 0

Norway: Myhre; Bergdolmo, Hagen, Lundekvam, Riise, Solli (Karadas 71), Andresen, Hestad, Pedersen M, Iversen (Johnsen F 84), Carew.
Italy: Buffon; Bonera (Diana 81), Cannavaro, Materazzi, Grosso, Camoranesi, Pirlo, De Rossi, Zambrotta, Vieri (Toni 57), Cassano (Iaquinta 68).
Referee: Gonzalez (Spain).

Glasgow, 4 June 2005, 45,317

Scotland (0) 2 *(Dailly 53, McFadden 89)*

Moldova (0) 0

Scotland: Gordon; Pressley, Webster (Dailly 26), Ferguson B, Weir, Alexander, McNamara, Hartley, Fletcher, Miller, McCulloch (McFadden 74).
Moldova: Hmaruc; Olexici, Priganiuc, Lascencov (Covalenko 46), Catinsus, Epureanu, Boret, Ivanov, Dadu, Savinov (Covalciuc 60), Rogaciov (Frunza 82).
Referee: Braamhaar (Holland).

Minsk, 8 June 2005, 20,000

Belarus (0) 0

Scotland (0) 0

Belarus: Zhevnov; Omelyunchuk, Kalachev (Hleb V 61), Gurenko, Shtanyuk, Jaskovic, Kovba, Hleb A, Bulyga (Kulchi 86), Belkevich, Kornichenko.
Scotland: Gordon; Weir, Webster, Caldwell G, Pressley, Dailly, Fletcher, Ferguson B, Miller (McFadden 76), Alexander, McCulloch.
Referee: Benquerenca (Portugal).

Group 5 Table	*P*	*W*	*D*	*L*	*F*	*A*	*Pts*
Italy	6	4	1	1	9	5	13
Norway	6	2	3	1	6	3	9
Slovenia	6	2	3	1	6	5	9
Belarus	6	1	4	1	10	7	7
Scotland	6	1	3	2	3	4	6
Moldova	6	0	2	4	1	11	2

GROUP 6

Vienna, 4 September 2004, 48,500

Austria (0) 2 *(Kollmann 71, Ivanschitz 73)*

England (1) 2 *(Lampard 24, Gerrard 64)*

Austria: Manninger; Standfest, Stranzl, Martin Hiden, Pogatetz, Sick, Kuhbauer, Aufhauser (Kiesenebner 74), Ivanschitz, Glieder (Kollmann 68), Haas (Hleblinger 89).
England: James; Neville G, Cole A, Gerrard (Carragher 82), Terry, King, Beckham, Lampard, Smith (Defoe 74), Owen, Bridge (Cole J 84).
Referee: Michel (Slovakia).

Baku, 4 September 2004, 15,000

Azerbaijan (0) 1 *(Sadykhov 56)*

Wales (0) 1 *(Speed 48)*

Azerbaijan: Kramarenko; Shukurov, Hajiev, Agayev, Sadykhov, Kurbanov M, Huseynov (Mamedov A 73), Ponomarev (Kurbanov I 84), Kurbanov G, Aliyev (Noybiyev 71), Kerimov.
Wales: Jones P; Delaney, Gabbidon, Savage, Melville, Page, Koumas (Earnshaw 87), Speed, Hartson, Bellamy, Pembridge (Oster 46).
Referee: Trivkovic (Croatia).

Belfast, 4 September 2004, 14,000

Northern Ireland (0) 0

Poland (2) 3 *(Zurawski 4, Wlodarczyk 37, Krzynowek 57)*

Northern Ireland: Taylor; Hughes A, Capaldi, Whitley, Williams, Craigan, Johnson, Hughes M (Jones S 53), Quinn (Smith 73), Healy, Elliott (McVeigh 62).
Poland: Dudek; Michal Zewlakow, Bak, Glowacki, Rzasa, Krzynowek (Gorawski 67), Lewandowski M, Mila (Radomski 75), Zienczuk, Wlodarczyk▪, Zurawski (Kryszalowicz 84).
Referee: Wegereef (Holland).

Vienna, 8 September 2004, 26,400

Austria (2) 2 *(Stranzl 23, Kollmann 44)*

Azerbaijan (0) 0

Austria: Manninger; Standfest, Stranzl, Martin Hiden, Pogatetz, Schopp (Dollinger 57), Kuhbauer, Aufhauser, Ivanschitz, Haas (Glieder 72), Kollmann (Linz 79).
Azerbaijan: Kramarenko; Agayev, Hajiev, Sadykhov, Shukurov, Guseynov, Kurbanov M (Mamedov I 46), Kerimov, Ponomarev (Nabiyev 46), Kurbanov G, Aliyev (Kurbanov I 46).
Referee: Sammut (Malta).

Chorzow, 8 September 2004, 38,000

Poland (0) 1 *(Zurawski 48)*

England (1) 2 *(Defoe 37, Glowacki 58 (og))*

Poland: Dudek; Michal Zewlakow, Bak, Glowacki, Krzynowek, Rzasa, Lewandowski M, Mila (Kukielka 63), Kosowski (Gorawski 80), Zurawski, Rasiak (Niedzielan 69).
England: Robinson; Neville G (Carragher 32), Cole A, Gerrard, Terry, King, Beckham (Hargreaves 90), Lampard, Defoe (Dyer 87), Owen, Bridge.
Referee: Farina (Italy).

Cardiff, 8 September 2004, 63,500

Wales (1) 2 *(Hartson 32, Earnshaw 75)*

Northern Ireland (2) 2 *(Whitley 11, Healy 21)*

Wales: Jones P; Delaney (Earnshaw 28), Thatcher (Parry 63), Savage▪, Collins, Gabbidon, Oster, Speed, Hartson, Bellamy, Koumas.
Northern Ireland: Taylor; Clyde, Capaldi (McCartney 90), Murdock, Hughes A, Williams, Johnson, Whitley, Quinn (Smith 58) (McVeigh 89), Healy▪, Hughes M▪.
Referee: Messina (Italy).

Vienna, 9 October 2004, 46,100

Austria (1) 1 *(Schopp 30)*

Poland (1) 3 *(Kaluzny 9, Krzynowek 79, Frankowski 90)*

Austria: Manninger; Standfest, Pogatetz, Schopp, Stranzl, Martin Hiden, Kuhbauer, Aufhauser (Kiesenebner 46), Ivanschitz, Haas (Kollmann 38), Vastic (Mayrleb 80).
Poland: Dudek; Baszczynski, Rzasa, Hajto, Bak, Mila, Krzynowek, Zajac (Kosowski 46), Kaluzny (Radomski▪ 72), Zurawski, Rasiak (Frankowski 67).
Referee: Batista (Portugal).

Baku, 9 October 2004, 20,000

Azerbaijan (0) 0

Northern Ireland (0) 0

Azerbaijan: Hasanzade; Amirbekov, Hajiev, Kuliyev E, Kuliyev K, Kurbanov M (Ponomarev 58), Nabiyev, Sadykhov, Mamedov I (Kurbanov I 55), Aliyev (Kurbanov G), Shukurov.

Northern Ireland: Taylor; Clyde, Hughes A, Doherty, Williams, Murdock, Johnson, Whitley, Quinn (Smith 76), Elliott, Baird (Gillespie 9).
Referee: Hanaczek (Hungary).

Old Trafford, 9 October 2004, 65,224

England (1) 2 *(Lampard 4, Beckham 76)*

Wales (0) 0

England: Robinson; Neville G, Cole A, Butt, Campbell, Ferdinand, Beckham (Hargreaves 85), Rooney (King 86), Owen, Defoe (Smith 70), Lampard.
Wales: Jones P; Delaney, Thatcher, Pembridge (Robinson 59), Gabbidon, Speed, Koumas (Earnshaw 73), Bellamy, Hartson, Giggs, Davies.
Referee: Haughe (Norway).

Baku, 13 October 2004, 20,000

Azerbaijan (0) 0

England (1) 1 *(Owen 22)*

Azerbaijan: Hasanzade; Hajiev, Shukurov, Kuliyev E (Kurbanov I 75), Sadykhov, Amirbekov, Kerimov, Ponomarev, Kuliyev K, Nabiyev (Abdullayev 79), Aliyev (Kurbanov G 59).
England: Robinson; Neville G, Cole A, Butt, Campbell, Ferdinand, Jenas (Wright-Phillips 72), Rooney (Cole J 85), Owen, Defoe (Smith 55), Lampard.
Referee: Hamer (Luxembourg).

Belfast, 13 October 2004, 11,830

Northern Ireland (1) 3 *(Healy 36, Murdock 60, Elliott 90)*

Austria (1) 3 *(Schopp 14, 72, Mayrleb 61)*

Northern Ireland: Carroll; Hughes A, McCarthy, Doherty (Jones S 86), Williams, Murdock (Elliott 78), Gillespie, Whitley (McVeigh 89), Quinn, Healy, Johnson.
Austria: Manninger; Ibertsberger, Pogatetz, Kuhbauer, Martin Hiden, Feldhofer, Schopp (Sick 81), Kiesenebner, Kirchler (Ivanschitz 64), Vastic, Mayrleb (Kollmann 81).
Referee: Shield (Australia).

Cardiff, 13 October 2004, 74,000

Wales (0) 2 *(Earnshaw 56, Hartson 90)*

Poland (0) 3 *(Frankowski 72, Zurawski 81, Krzynowek 85)*

Wales: Jones P; Delaney, Thatcher, Savage, Gabbidon, Collins, Davies, Speed (Hartson 79), Earnshaw, Bellamy, Koumas (Parry 86).
Poland: Dudek; Baszczynski, Krzynowek, Szymkowiak, Hajto, Bak (Klos 46), Kosowski, Kaluzny (Mila 71), Zurawski, Wlodarczyk (Frankowski 60), Rzasa.
Referee: Sars (France).

Old Trafford, 26 March 2005, 65,239

England (0) 4 *(Cole J 47, Owen 52, Baird 54 (og), Lampard 67)*

Northern Ireland (0) 0

England: Robinson; Neville G, Cole A, Gerrard (Hargreaves 72), Ferdinand, Terry, Beckham (Dyer 72), Lampard, Owen, Rooney (Defoe 80), Cole J.
Northern Ireland: Taylor; Baird, Capaldi, Doherty (Davis 59), Hughes A, Murdock, Gillespie, Johnson, Healy (Kirk 88), Elliott, Whitley (Jones S 80).
Referee: Stark (Germany).

Warsaw, 26 March 2005, 12,500

Poland (3) 8 *(Frankowski 12, 62, 65, Hajiev 16 (og), Kosowski 40, Krzynowek 71, Saganowski 83, 90)*

Azerbaijan (0) 0

Poland: Dudek; Baszczynski, Bak, Klos, Rzasa, Kosowski (Smolarek 46), Szymkowiak, Sobolewski, Krzynowek, Frankowski (Niedzielan 66), Zurawski (Saganowski 73).
Azerbaijan: Kramarenko; Hajiev, Sadykhov, Amirbekov, Kuliyev E (Malikov 20), Sjoeboerov, Kerimov (Actianov 46), Kuliyev V, Nadyov (Kurbanov I 46), Kurbanov G, Nabiev.
Referee: Vollquartz (Denmark).

Cardiff, 26 March 2005, 47,760

Wales (0) 0

Austria (0) 2 *(Vastic 82, Stranzl 86)*

Wales: Coyne; Delaney, Ricketts, Robinson, Gabbidon, Page, Davies (Earnshaw 75), Fletcher, Hartson, Bellamy, Giggs.
Austria: Payer; Dospel, Pogatetz, Ehmann, Katzer, Kirchler, Stranzl, Aufhauser, Ivanschitz (Hleblinger 90), Mayrleb (Mair 87), Haas (Vastic 78).
Referee: Allaerts (Belgium).

Vienna, 30 March 2005, 29,500

Austria (0) 1 *(Aufhauser 87)*

Wales (0) 0

Austria: Payer; Stranzl, Dospel (Kiesenebner 84), Ehmann, Katzer, Kirchler (Mair 77), Kuhbauer, Aufhauser, Ivanschitz, Mayrleb, Haas (Vastic 55).
Wales: Coyne; Delaney, Ricketts, Robinson, Gabbidon, Collins (Page 58), Partridge, Fletcher, Davies, Bellamy, Giggs.
Referee: Gonzalez (Spain).

Newcastle, 30 March 2005, 49,046

England (0) 2 *(Gerrard 51, Beckham 62)*

Azerbaijan (0) 0

England: Robinson; Neville G, Cole A, Ferdinand (King 77), Terry, Gerrard, Beckham (Defoe 84), Lampard, Owen, Rooney (Dyer 77), Cole J.
Azerbaijan: Kramarenko; Abdurahmanov, Amirbekov (Kuliyev V 46), Sadykhov, Hajiev, Hashimov, Bakhshiev, Malikov, Kerimov, Kurbanov G (Actiamov 74), Nabiev (Ponomarev 74).
Referee: Gomes Costa (Portugal).

Warsaw, 30 March 2005, 25,000

Poland (0) 1 *(Zurawski 86)*

Northern Ireland (0) 0

Poland: Dudek; Baszczynski, Bak, Klos, Rzasa (Kielbowicz 46), Karwan (Rasiak 74), Kaluzny (Mila 67), Symkowiak, Krzynowek, Frankowski, Zurawski.
Northern Ireland: Taylor; Baird, Capaldi, Williams (Elliott 88), Hughes A, Murdock, Gillespie, Davis, Quinn (Feeney 35), Healy (Smith 81), Whitley.
Referee: Frojdfeldt (Sweden).

Baku, 4 June 2005, 8000

Azerbaijan (0) 0

Poland (1) 3 *(Frankowski 27, Klos 56, Zurawski 77)*

Azerbaijan: Gasanzade; Kuliyev K, Sadykhov, Hajiev (Ismailov 75), Chukurov, Abdurahmanov (Kurbanov I 75), Kuliyev E, Abdullayev, Malikov (Ramazanov 59), Karimov, Kurbanov G.

Poland: Dudek; Baszczynski, Bak, Klos, Rzasa, Kosowski, Sobolewski, Szymkowiak (Radomski 89), Mila (Zienczuk 84), Frankowski (Niedzielan 55), Zurawski.
Referee: Mallenco (Spain).

Group 6 Table	*P*	*W*	*D*	*L*	*F*	*A*	*Pts*
Poland	7	6	0	1	22	5	18
England	6	5	1	0	13	3	16
Austria	6	3	2	1	11	8	11
Northern Ireland	6	0	3	3	5	13	3
Wales	6	0	2	4	5	11	2
Azerbaijan	7	0	2	5	1	17	2

GROUP 7

Charleroi, 4 September 2004, 20,000

Belgium (0) 1 *(Sonck 61)*

Lithuania (0) 1 *(Jankauskas 72)*

Belgium: Peersman; Deflandre (Kompany 46), Dheedene, Simons, Van Buyten, Clement, Goor, Mpenza M (Dufer 22), Vernant (Pieroni 73), Buffel, Sonck.
Lithuania: Karcemarskas; Dziaukstas, Skarbalius (Morinas 8), Skerla, Stankevicius, Barasa, Cesnauskis, Vencevicius (Razanauskas 57), Danilevicius (Mikoliunas 66), Jankauskas, Poskus.
Referee: Loizou (Cyprus).

Serravalle, 4 September 2004, 500

San Marino (0) 0

Serbia-Montenegro (2) 3 *(Vukic 5, Jestrovic 15, 82)*

San Marino: Gasperoni F; Valentini C, Morani, Bacciocchi, Della Valle, Crescentini (Moretti M 46), Domenicioni, Gasperoni A (Maiani 85), Ciacci, Vannucci, Ugolini (Montagna 23).
Serbia-Montenegro: Jevric; Dragutinovic, Mladenovic (Duljaj 82), Vidic, Gavrancic, Koroman, Milosevic (Kezman 68), Stankovic, Jestrovic, Vukic (Brnovic 86), Krstajic.
Referee: Kholmatov (Kazakhstan).

Zenica, 8 September 2004, 15,000

Bosnia (0) 1 *(Bolic 74)*

Spain (0) 1 *(Vicente 66)*

Bosnia: Hasagic; Salihamidzic, Bajic, Spahic, Music, Grujic, Barbarez, Beslija, Baljic (Blatnjak 63), Misimovic, Bolic (Hililovic 83).
Spain: Casillas, Michel Salgado, Romero, Albelda (Xabi Alonso 71), Puyol, Helguera, Victor (Morientes 50), Baraja (Valeron 58), Reyes, Raul, Vicente.
Referee: De Santis (Italy).

Kaunas, 8 September 2004, 5000

Lithuania (1) 4 *(Jankauskas 18, 50, Danilevicius 65, Gedgaudas 90)*

San Marino (0) 0

Lithuania: Karcemarskas; Stankevicius, Dziaukstas, Skerla, Barasa, Vencevicius, Mikoliunas (Gedgaudas 74), Cesnauskis (Morinas 46), Danilevicius, Poskus, Jankauskas (Radzinevicius 68).
San Marino: Gasperoni F; Valentini C, Bacciocchi, Della Valle, Marani, Albani (Maiani 87), Domeniconi, Gasperoni A, Giacci, Vannucci (Nanni 82), Montagna (Moretti M 65).
Referee: Jareci (Albania).

Sarajevo, 9 October 2004, 32,000

Bosnia (0) 0

Serbia-Montenegro (0) 0

Bosnia: Tolja; Blatnjak, Spahic, Bajic (Hrgovic 62), Papac (Crnogorac 79), Grlic, Misimovic, Bolic, Barbarez, Baljic (Baiano 80), Beslija.
Serbia-Montenegro: Jevric; Gavrancic, Krstajic, Djordjevic (Markovic 57), Duljaj, Dragutinovic, Stankovic, Koroman (Brnovic 90), Vukic, Milosevic (Pantelic 77), Ljuboja.
Referee: Veissiere (France).

Santander, 9 October 2004, 20,000

Spain (0) 2 *(Luque 59, Raul 63)*

Belgium (0) 0

Spain: Casillas; Michel Salgado, Del Horno, Albelda (Xabi Alonso 58), Marchena, Puyol, Joachim, Xavi (Baraja 73), Raul, Fernando Torres (Luque 53), Reyes.
Belgium: Peersman; Deflandre■, Deschacht, Clement, Kompany, Van Buyten, Buffel (Dufer 79), Bisconti (Doll 60), Mpenza M (Huysegems 73), Sonck, Goor■.
Referee: Nielsen (Denmark).

Vilnius, 13 October 2004, 6000

Lithuania (0) 0

Spain (0) 0

Lithuania: Karcemarskas; Stankevicius, Dziaukstas, Skerla, Skarbalius, Gedgaudas (Mikoliunas 75), Vencevcius, Barasa, Cesnauskas, Jankauskas, Danilevicius (Radzinevicius 82).
Spain: Casillas; Michel Salgado, Capdevila (Torres 79), Albelda, Puyol, Marchena, Victor (Tamudo 53), Baraja (Reyes 65), Xavi, Raul, Luque.
Referee: Poulat (France).

Belgrade, 13 October 2004, 3000

Serbia-Montenegro (2) 5 *(Milosevic 35, Stankovic 45, 50, Koroman 52, Vukic 69)*

San Marino (0) 0

Serbia-Montenegro: Jevric; Markovic, Gavrancic, Dragutinovic (Vitakic 62), Koroman, Krstajic, Duljaj, Vukic, Stankovic, Milosevic, Ljuboja (Pantelic 70).
San Marino: Gasperoni F; Valentini C, Marani, Bacciocchi, Della Valle, Albani, Domeniconi (Moretti L 90), Vannucci, Ciacci (De Luigi 77), Gasperoni A, Moretti M (Gasperoni B 65).
Referee: Isaksen (Faeroes).

Brussels, 17 November 2004, 32,000

Belgium (0) 0

Serbia-Montenegro (1) 2 *(Vukic 7, Kezman 59)*

Belgium: Proto; De Cock, Kompany, Simons, Deschacht (Daerden 27), Van der Heyden, Bisconti (Pieroni 58), Baseggio, Clement, Buffel, Sonck (Huysegems 65).
Serbia-Montenegro: Jevric; Markovic, Mladenovic (Djordjevic N 77), Gavrancic, Dragutinovic, Stankovic, Djordjevic P, Koroman (Duljaj 55), Vukic, Milosevic (Kezman 29), Vidic.
Referee: Frojdfeldt (Sweden).

Serravalle, 17 November 2004, 1457

San Marino (0) 0

Lithuania (1) 1 *(Cesnauskis D 41)*

San Marino: Gasperoni F; Valentini C, Marani, Bacciocchi, Della Valle, Albani, Muccioli (Domeniconi 67), Gasperoni A, De Luigi (Bonifazi 82), Selva A, Vannucci.

Lithuania: Karcemarkas; Semberas, Dziaukstas, Stankevicius, Gedgaudas (Vencevicius 85), Zvirgzdauskas, Skarbalius, Cesnauskis E, Danilevicius, Cesnauskis D (Mikoliunas 76), Radzinevicius (Morinas 46).
Referee: Nalbandyan (Armenia).

Almeria, 9 February 2005, 15,000

Spain (3) 5 *(Joaquin 14, Torres 32, Raul 42, Guti 65, Del Horno 79)*

San Marino (0) 0

Spain: Casillas; Marchena, Puyol, Michel Salgado, De la Pena (Guayre 76), Del Horno, Joaquin, Xavi, Luque (Guti 46), Raul (Villa 46), Torres.
San Marino: Gasperoni F; Albani, Andreini (Gasperoni B 58), Bacciocchi, Domeniconi (Moretti 75), Vannucci, Della Valle, Gasperoni A, Marani, Valentini C, Selva A.
Referee: Clark (Scotland).

Brussels, 26 March 2005, 35,000

Belgium (2) 4 *(Mpenza E 15, 54, Daerden 44, Buffel 76)*

Bosnia (1) 1 *(Bajramovic 1)*

Belgium: Proto; Doll, Kompany, Van Buyten, Vanderheyden, Buffel (Bisconti 90), Vanderheyghe, Simons, Daerden, Mpenza E (Clement 90), Pieroni (Vandenbergh 86).
Bosnia: Hasagic; Spahic, Bajic, Milenkovic, Papac (Misimovic 58), Beslija, Grlic (Grujic 72), Barbarez, Bolic, Baljic (Halimovic 58), Bajramovic.
Referee: Hrinak (Slovakia).

Sarajevo, 30 March 2005, 15,000

Bosnia (1) 1 *(Bolic 21)*

Lithuania (0) 1 *(Stankevicius 64)*

Bosnia: Hasagic; Spahic, Bajic (Halilovic 73), Milenkovic, Vidic, Bajramovic, Grlic, Beslija (Baljic 46), Misimovic (Grujic 64), Barbarez, Bolic.
Lithuania: Karcemarskas; Stankevicius■, Skerla, Zutartas, Dziaukstas, Cesnauskis D (Barasa 54), Semberas, Cesnauskis E, Poskus, Danilevicius (Vencevicius 90), Jankauskas.
Referee: Baskakov (Russia).

Serravalle, 30 March 2005, 3000

San Marino (1) 1 *(Selva A 40)*

Belgium (1) 2 *(Simons 19 (pen), Van Buyten 65)*

San Marino: Gasperoni F; Albani, Della Valle, Bacciocchi, Marani, Valentini C, Vannucci, Domeniconi (Montagna 89), Gasperoni A, Ciacci (Gasperoni B 61), Selva A.
Belgium: Proto; Doll (Vandenbergh 58), Kompany, Van Buyten, Van der Heyden, Buffel (Chatelle 38), Simons, Vanderhaeghe, Daerden, Pieroni (Bisconti 83), Mpenza E.
Referee: Kasnaferis (Greece).

Belgrade, 30 March 2005, 56,000

Serbia-Montenegro (0) 0

Spain (0) 0

Serbia-Montenegro: Jevric; Vidic, Gavrancic, Krstajic, Dragutinovic, Koroman (Basta 77), Duljaj, Stankovic, Djordjevic, Kezman (Jestrovic 80), Milosevic (Ilic 65).
Spain: Casillas; Sergio Ramos, Pablo, Puyol (Juanito 46), Del Horno, Xavi, Albelda, De La Pena (Raul 46), Joaquin, Fernando Torres, Reyes (Antonio Lopez 62).
Referee: Busacca (Switzerland).

Serravalle, 4 June 2005, 747

San Marino (1) 1 *(Selva A 40)*

Bosnia (2) 3 *(Salihamidzic 17, 39, Barbarez 75)*

San Marino: Ceccoli; Valentini C (Gasperoni B 65), Crescentini, Della Valle, Bacciocchi, Marani, Gasperoni D, Domeniconi, Vannucci, De Luigi (Andreini 72), Selva A (Montagna 85).
Bosnia: Tolja; Berberovic, Vidic, Papac, Milenkovic, Beslija (Bartolovic 56), Grlic, Bajramovic (Kerkez 82), Misimovic (Halilovic 59), Barbarez, Salihamidzic.
Referee: Demirlek (Turkey).

Belgrade, 4 June 2005, 45,000

Serbia-Montenegro (0) 0

Belgium (0) 0

Serbia-Montenegro: Jevric; Dragutinovic, Krstajic, Gavrancic, Vidic, Vukic, Duljaj, Koroman (Vukcevic 81), Stankovic (Mladenovic 82), Ljuboja, Jestrovic (Vucinic 53).
Belgium: Proto; Clement, Van Buyten, Deschacht, Borre, Vanderhaeghe, Bisconti, Daerden (Leonard 79), Buffel (Pieroni 88), Mpenza E, Mpenza M (Vandenbergh 83).
Referee: Ivanov (Russia).

Valencia, 4 June 2005, 25,000

Spain (0) 1 *(Luque 68)*

Lithuania (0) 0

Spain: Casillas; Michel Salgado, Marchena, Puyol, Del Horno (Luis Garcia 61), Joaquim, Xavi, Albelda, Vicente, Fernando Torres (Luque 59), Raul (Sergio 79).
Lithuania: Karcemarskas; Skerla, Dziaukstas, Zvirgzdauskas, Paulauskas, Barasa, Kucys (Preksaitis 46), Cesnauskis D (Mikoliunas 73), Danilevicius, Poskus, Morinas (Cesnauskis E 77).
Referee: Farina (Italy).

Valencia, 8 June 2005, 36,400

Spain (0) 1 *(Marchena 90)*

Bosnia (1) 1 *(Misimovic 38)*

Spain: Casillas; Michel Salgado, Marchena, Puyol (Juanito 8), Antonio Lopez (Xabi Alonso 62), Joaquin, Xavi, Albelda, Vicente, Raul, Fernando Torres (Luque 35).
Bosnia: Tolja; Spahic, Bajic, Vidic (Milenkovic 76), Music, Grlic, Bajramovic, Grujic (Damjanovic 74), Barbarez, Misimovic (Halilovic■ 65), Beslija■.
Referee: Bennett (England).

Group 7 Table	*P*	*W*	*D*	*L*	*F*	*A*	*Pts*
Spain	7	3	4	0	10	2	13
Serbia-Montenegro	6	3	3	0	10	0	12
Lithuania	6	2	3	1	7	3	9
Belgium	6	2	2	2	7	7	8
Bosnia	6	1	4	1	7	8	7
San Marino	7	0	0	7	2	23	0

GROUP 8

Zagreb, 4 September 2004, 25,000

Croatia (1) 3 *(Prso 32, Klasnic 57, Gyepes 80 (og))*

Hungary (0) 0

Croatia: Butina; Srna (Mornar 84), Simunic, Kovac R, Tudor, Vranjes, Kranjcar (Leko I 77), Babic, Prso (Olic 75), Kovac N, Klasnic.

Hungary: Kiraly; Bodnar, Huszti■, Stark (Gyepes 59), Toth A (Kovacs 81), Molnar, Rosa, Szabics, Gera, Simek (Low 18), Juhasz.
Referee: Riley (England).

Reykjavik, 4 September 2004, 5000

Iceland (0) 1 *(Gudjohnsen E 51 (pen))*

Bulgaria (1) 3 *(Berbatov 35, 49, Yanev 62)*

Iceland: Arason; Bjarnason, Sigurdsson K, Gunnarsson B■, Sigurdsson I (Helgason 65), Gretarsson (Gudjonsson J 57), Hreidarsson, Einarsson, Gudjohnsen E, Gudjonsson T, Helguson (Sigurdsson H 70).
Bulgaria: Ivankov; Kishishev, Kirilov, Petkov I, Yankov (Kamburov 80), Berbatov, Lazarov (Yanev 42), Hristov, Petrov S, Bojinov (Bukarev 72), Stoyanov.
Referee: Hamer (Luxembourg).

Ta'Qali, 4 September 2004, 4000

Malta (0) 0

Sweden (3) 7 *(Ibrahimovic 4, 11, 14, 71, Ljungberg 46, 74, Larsson 76)*

Malta: Muscat; Briffa, Pullicino, Said, Azzopardi, Dimech, Giglio, Woods (Mallia 79), Zahra (Agius G 57), Michael Mifsud, Galea.
Sweden: Isaksson; Lucic, Mellberg (Nilsson 61), Hansson (Ostlund 49), Edman, Linderoth, Wilhelmsson (Jonson 76), Anders Svensson, Ljungberg, Ibrahimovic, Larsson.
Referee: Jakov (Israel).

Budapest, 8 September 2004, 8000

Hungary (0) 3 *(Gera 62, Torghelle 76, Szabics 80)*

Iceland (1) 2 *(Gudjohnsen E 40, Sigurdsson I 78)*

Hungary: Kiraly; Juhasz, Gyepes, Toth A, Szelesi (Szabics 46), Molnar, Rosa, Bodnar, Simek (Low 18), Gera, Kovacs (Torghelle 66).
Iceland: Arason; Sigurdsson K, Bjarnason, Hreidarsson, Gudjonsson T (Einarsson 75), Gretarsson (Gunnarsson V 85), Vidarsson, Gudjonsson J, Sigurdsson I, Helguson, Gudjohnsen E (Sigurdsson H 86).
Referee: Ovrebo (Norway).

Gothenburg, 8 September 2004, 40,023

Sweden (0) 0

Croatia (0) 1 *(Srna 64)*

Sweden: Isaksson; Ostlund, Mellberg, Lucic (Allback 80), Edman, Linderoth, Wilhelmsson, Anders Svensson (Jonson 73), Ljungberg, Larsson, Ibrahimovic.
Croatia: Butina; Kovac R, Tudor, Simunic, Srna, Kovac N, Kranjcar (Leko J 63), Vranjes, Babic, Prso (Tokic 90), Klasnic (Olic 46).
Referee: Ibanez (Spain).

Zagreb, 9 October 2004, 30,000

Croatia (2) 2 *(Srna 15, 32 (pen))*

Bulgaria (0) 2 *(Petrov M 77, Berbatov 86)*

Croatia: Butina; Srna, Simunic, Kovac N, Kovac R (Banovic 77), Tokic, Babic, Vranjes, Kranjcar (Balaban 69), Prso, Klasnic (Leko J 57).
Bulgaria: Ivankov; Kishishev (Manchev 55), Markov, Petkov I, Stoyanov, Petrov S, Yankov, Berbatov, Bojinov (Yanev 55), Petrov M, Georgiev (Paskov 90).
Referee: Collina (Italy).

Valletta, 9 October 2004, 6000

Malta (0) 0

Iceland (0) 0

Malta: Haber; Azzopardi, Briffa, Ciantar, Dimech, Said, Agius G (Mallia 65), Giglio, Mattocks, Woods (Galea 78), Michael Mifsud.
Iceland: Arason; Bjarnason, Hreidarsson, Gunnarsson B (Gretarsson 78), Sigurdsson K, Einarsson, Gudjonsson T (Gunnarsson V 68), Sigurdsson I (Sigurdsson H 59), Helguson, Gudjohnsen E, Vidarsson.
Referee: Corpodean (Romania).

Stockholm, 9 October 2004, 32,228

Sweden (1) 3 *(Ljungberg 26, Larsson 50, Anders Svensson 67)*

Hungary (0) 0

Sweden: Isaksson; Ostlund, Lucic, Linderoth, Mellberg, Mjallby (Nilsson 46), Wilhelmsson (Alexandersson N 74), Ljungberg, Allback, Larsson, Anders Svensson (Kallstrom 80).
Hungary: Kiraly; Gyepes, Bodnar (Feher C 80), Dardai, Stark, Toth A, Molnar (Hajnal 55), Gera, Szabics, Torghelle (Kovacs 70), Bodor.
Referee: Dougal (Scotland).

Sofia, 13 October 2004, 17,700

Bulgaria (1) 4 *(Berbatov 43, 66, Yanev 47, Yankov 87)*

Malta (1) 1 *(Michael Mifsud 12)*

Bulgaria: Ivankov; Stoyanov, Petkov I, Georgiev, Petrov S, Yankov, Yanev (Kirilov 71), Bojinov (Sakaliev 67), Manchev (Gargorov 64), Berbatov, Petrov M.
Malta: Haber; Briffa (Zahra 46), Said, Azzopardi, Ciantar, Dimech, Woods (Pulicino 75), Giglio, Agius G, Mattocks, Michael Mifsud.
Referee: Richards (Wales).

Reykjavik, 13 October 2004, 7035

Iceland (0) 1 *(Gudjohnsen E 66)*

Sweden (4) 4 *(Larsson 24, 39, Allback 27, Wilhelmsson 44)*

Iceland: Arason; Bjarnason (Gudjonsson T 57), Sigurdsson L (Jonsson 25), Gunnarsson B, Sigurdsson K, Einarsson, Marteinsson, Hreidarsson, Helguson (Sigurdsson H 81), Gudjohnsen E, Gudjonsson J.
Sweden: Isaksson (Hedman 31); Ostlund, Lucic, Linderoth, Mellberg, Nilsson, Wilhelmsson, Ljungberg (Alexandersson N 57), Allback, Larsson (Ibrahimovic 53), Anders Svensson.
Referee: Busacca (Switzerland).

Ta'Qali, 17 November 2004, 2000

Malta (0) 0

Hungary (1) 2 *(Gera 39, Kovacs 90)*

Malta: Haber; Ciantar, Azzopardi, Briffa, Said, Dimech, Agius G (Barbara 86), Giglio, Michael Mifsud, Woods (Cohen 73), Mattocks (Galea 60).
Hungary: Kiraly; Rosa (Gyepes 90), Huszti, Juhasz, Stark, Hajnal, Feher C, Dardai, Torghelle (Kovacs 66), Gera, Wallner (Lipcsei 79).
Referee: Asumaa (Finland).

Sofia, 26 March 2005, 42,563

Bulgaria (0) 0

Sweden (1) 3 *(Ljungberg 17, 90, Edman 74)*

Bulgaria: Ivankov; Markov■, Stoyanov, Petkov I, Kishishev (Kirilov 74), Borimirov (Janev 76), Yankov, Georgiev, Berbatov, Ivanov G, Lazarov (Topuzakov 60).

Sweden: Isaksson; Ostlund, Mellberg, Lucic, Edman, Alexandersson N (Wilhelmsson 61), Linderoth, Anders Svensson, Ljungberg, Ibrahimovic, Jonson (Allback 80).
Referee: Fandel (Germany).

Zagreb, 26 March 2005, 25,000

Croatia (1) 4 *(Kovac N 39, 76, Simunic 71, Prso 90)*

Iceland (0) 0

Croatia: Butina; Tomas, Tudor, Simunic, Seric (Bosnjak 86), Srna, Kovac N, Leko I (Leko J 79), Kranjcar, Klasnic (Olic 73), Prso.
Iceland: Arason; Bjarnason, Sigurdsson K, Gunnarsson B, Sigurdsson I, Sigurdsson H (Steinsson 50), Vidarsson, Helguson (Gislason 73), Einarsson, Gudjonsson I (Gudjonsson B 60), Marteinsson.
Referee: Damon (South Africa).

Zagreb, 30 March 2005, 10,000

Croatia (2) 3 *(Prso 24, 35, Tudor 80)*

Malta (0) 0

Croatia: Butina; Tomas, Kovac R (Olic 46), Tudor, Bosnjak (Tokic 68), Kovac N (Vranjes 77), Leko I, Kranjcar, Babic, Prso, Klasnic.
Malta: Haber; Pollicino, Said (Mallia 59), Dimech, Azzopardi, Agius G, Sammut, Grima (Woods 46), Giglio, Mattocks, Michael Mifsud (Barbara 68).
Referee: Kapitanis (Cyprus).

Budapest, 30 March 2005, 12,000

Hungary (0) 1 *(Rajczi 90)*

Bulgaria (0) 1 *(Petrov S 52)*

Hungary: Kiraly; Juhasz, Stark, Komlosi, Bodnar, Boor, Vincze (Rajczi 79), Korsos G (Kerekes 74), Huszti, Szabics, Torghelle.
Bulgaria: Ivankov; Kirilov, Stojanov, Petkov I, Georgiev, Lazarov (Borimirov 75), Petrov S, Yankov (Manchev 64), Petrov M (Ivanov 79), Berbatov, Topuzakov.
Referee: Wegereef (Holland).

Sofia, 4 June 2005, 30,738

Bulgaria (0) 1 *(Petrov M 73)*

Croatia (1) 3 *(Babic 18, Tudor 58, Kranjcar 80)*

Bulgaria: Ivankov; Kirilov, Stoyanov, Iliev, Kishishev (Lazarov 54), Yankov, Petrov S, Georgiev, Berbatov, Ivanov G (Bojinov 46), Petrov M.
Croatia: Butina; Tomas, Kovac R, Tudor, Simunic, Srna, Kovac N, Babic, Kranjcar (Leko J 82), Olic (Balaban 90), Prso.
Referee: Nielsen (Denmark).

Reykjavik, 4 June 2005, 4613

Iceland (1) 2 *(Gudjohnsen E 18, Sigurdsson K 69)*

Hungary (1) 3 *(Gera 45 (pen), 56 (pen), Huszti 73)*

Iceland: Arason; Sigurdsson K, Bjarnasson■, Gislason, Sigurdsson I, Gunnarsson B, Marteinsson (Gudmundsson H 25), Steinsson (Arnason 46), Einarsson (Thorvaldsson 57), Vidarsson, Gujohnsen E.
Hungary: Kiraly; Bodnar, Stark, Huszti, Vanczak (Balog Z 14), Takacs, Hajnal, Baranyos (Szabics 75), Toth N (Rajczi 90), Gera, Kerekes.
Referee: Batista (Portugal).

Gothenburg, 4 June 2005, 40,000

Sweden (4) 6 *(Jonson 6, Anders Svensson 18, Wilhelmsson 30, Ibrahimovic 40, Ljungberg 57, Elmander 81)*

Malta (0) 0

Sweden: Isaksson; Alexandersson N (Elmander 77), Mellberg, Lucic, Edman, Linderoth, Wilhelmsson, Anders Svensson (Kallstrom 62), Ljungberg, Ibrahimovic, Jonson (Allback 62).
Malta: Haber; Pullicino, Dimech, Said, Pulis, Sammut, Giglio, Agius (Mallia 73), Pace (Briffa 46), Woods, Michael Mifsud.
Referee: Ivanov (Russia).

Reykjavik, 8 June 2005, 4884

Iceland (2) 4 *(Thorvaldsson 28, Gudjohnsen E 34, Gudmundsson T 75, Gunnarsson V 86)*

Malta (0) 1 *(Said 59)*

Iceland: Arason; Vidarsson, Helgason, Gunnarsson B, Steinsson, Gislason, Gunnarsson V, Arnason (Hardarson 63), Thorvaldsson (Sigurdsson H 84), Gudmundsson T, Gudjohnsen E (Danielsson 81).
Malta: Gauci; Said, Dimech, Briffa, Pulis, Agius G, Sammut, Pullicino, Mattocks (Cohen 59), Mallia, Michael Mifsud.
Referee: Skomina (Slovenia).

Group 8 Table	*P*	*W*	*D*	*L*	*F*	*A*	*Pts*
Croatia	6	5	1	0	16	3	16
Sweden	6	5	0	1	23	2	15
Hungray	6	3	1	2	9	11	10
Bulgaria	6	2	2	2	11	11	8
Iceland	7	1	1	5	10	18	4
Malta	7	0	1	6	2	26	1

SOUTH AMERICA

Argentina	(2) 2	Chile	(0) 2
Ecuador	(1) 2	Venezuela	(0) 0
Peru	(2) 4	Paraguay	(1) 1
Colombia	(1) 1	Brazil	(1) 2
Uruguay	(2) 5	Bolivia	(0) 0
Chile	(1) 2	Peru	(0) 1
Venezuela	(0) 0	Argentina	(3) 3
Bolivia	(2) 4	Colombia	(0) 0
Brazil	(1) 1	Ecuador	(0) 0
Paraguay	(1) 4	Uruguay	(1) 1
Argentina	(0) 3	Bolivia	(0) 0
Colombia	(0) 0	Venezuela	(1) 1
Paraguay	(1) 2	Ecuador	(0) 1
Uruguay	(1) 2	Chile	(1) 1
Peru	(0) 1	Brazil	(1) 1
Chile	(0) 0	Paraguay	(1) 1
Venezuela	(0) 2	Bolivia	(0) 1
Colombia	(0) 1	Argentina	(1) 1
Ecuador	(0) 0	Peru	(0) 0
Brazil	(2) 3	Uruguay	(0) 3
Argentina	(0) 1	Ecuador	(0) 0
Bolivia	(0) 0	Chile	(1) 2
Paraguay	(0) 0	Brazil	(0) 0
Peru	(0) 0	Colombia	(2) 2
Uruguay	(0) 0	Venezuela	(1) 3
Bolivia	(1) 2	Paraguay	(1) 1
Uruguay	(0) 1	Peru	(2) 3

Venezuela	(0) 0	Chile	(0) 1
Brazil	(1) 3	Argentina	(0) 1
Ecuador	(1) 2	Colombia	(0) 1
Ecuador	(3) 3	Bolivia	(0) 2
Argentina	(0) 0	Paraguay	(0) 0
Chile	(0) 1	Brazil	(1) 1
Colombia	(3) 5	Uruguay	(0) 0
Peru	(0) 0	Venezuela	(0) 0
Peru	(0) 1	Argentina	(1) 3
Brazil	(3) 3	Bolivia	(0) 1
Chile	(0) 0	Colombia	(0) 0
Paraguay	(0) 1	Venezuela	(0) 0
Uruguay	(0) 1	Ecuador	(0) 0
Argentina	(3) 4	Uruguay	(0) 2
Bolivia	(0) 1	Peru	(0) 0
Colombia	(1) 1	Paraguay	(0) 1
Venezuela	(0) 2	Brazil	(2) 5
Ecuador	(0) 2	Chile	(0) 0
Bolivia	(0) 0	Uruguay	(0) 0
Brazil	(0) 0	Colombia	(0) 0
Chile	(0) 0	Argentina	(0) 0
Paraguay	(1) 1	Peru	(0) 1
Venezuela	(1) 3	Ecuador	(1) 1
Argentina	(2) 3	Venezuela	(1) 2
Colombia	(1) 1	Bolivia	(0) 0
Ecuador	(0) 1	Brazil	(0) 0
Peru	(0) 2	Chile	(0) 1
Uruguay	(0) 1	Paraguay	(0) 0
Bolivia	(0) 1	Argentina	(0) 2
Chile	(0) 1	Uruguay	(1) 1
Venezuela	(0) 0	Colombia	(0) 0
Brazil	(0) 1	Peru	(0) 0
Ecuador	(2) 5	Paraguay	(2) 2
Bolivia	(2) 3	Venezuela	(0) 1
Argentina	(0) 1	Colombia	(0) 0
Paraguay	(1) 2	Chile	(0) 1
Peru	(1) 2	Ecuador	(2) 2
Uruguay	(0) 1	Brazil	(0) 1
Chile	(2) 3	Bolivia	(0) 1
Colombia	(1) 5	Peru	(0) 0
Ecuador	(0) 2	Argentina	(0) 0
Venezuela	(0) 1	Uruguay	(1) 1
Brazil	(2) 4	Paraguay	(0) 1
Peru	(0) 0	Uruguay	(0) 0
Argentina	(3) 3	Brazil	(0) 1
Chile	(1) 2	Venezuela	(0) 1
Colombia	(2) 3	Ecuador	(0) 0
Paraguay	(2) 4	Bolivia	(1) 1

OCEANIA

Second Stage

Six qualifiers in final group; winners and runners-up advance to third stage.
Vanuatu 0, Soloman Islands 1; Tahiti 0, Fiji 0; Australia 1, New Zealand 0; New Zealand 3, Soloman Islands 0; Australia 9, Tahiti 0; Fiji 1, Vanuatu 0; Australia 6, Fiji 1; Tahiti 0, Soloman Islands 4; New Zealand 2, Vanuatu 4; New Zealand 10, Tahiti 0; Fiji 1, Soloman Islands 2; Vanuatu 0, Australia 3, Tahiti 2, Vanuatu 1; Fiji 0, New Zealand 2; Soloman Islands 2, Australia 2.

Third Stage

Two qualifiers Australia and Soloman Islands play-off, the winners meet fifth placed South American team for place in finals.

ASIA

Second Stage

Group A: South Korea 2, Kuwait 0; Uzbekistan 1, Saudi Arabia 1, Kuwait 2, Uzbekistan 1; Saudi Arabia 2, South Korea 0; Kuwait 0, Saudi Arabia 0; South Korea 2, Uzbekistan 1; Saudi Arabia 3, Kuwait 0; Uzbekistan 1, South Korea 1; Kuwait 0, South Korea 4; Saudi Arabia 3, Uzbekistan 0.

Group B: Bahrain 0, Iran 0; Japan 2, North Korea 1; Iran 2, Japan 1; North Korea 1, Bahrain 2; Japan 1, Bahrain 0; North Korea 0, Iran 2; Iran 1, North Korea 0; Bahrain 0, Japan 1; Iran 1, Bahrain 0; North Korea 0, Japan 2.

CONCACAF

Third Stage

Costa Rica 1, Mexico 2; Panama 0, Guatemala 0; Trinidad & Tobago 1, United States 2; Costa Rica 2, Panama 1; Guatemala 5, Trinidad & Tobago 1; Mexico 2, United States 1; Panama 1, Mexico 1; Trinidad & Tobago 0, Costa Rica 0; United States 2, Guatemala 0; Guatemala 0, Mexico 2; Trinidad & Tobago 2, Panama 0; United States 3, Costa Rica 0; Costa Rica 3, Guatemala 2; Mexico 2, Trinidad & Tobago 0; Panama 0, United States 3.

AFRICA

Group 1: Senegal 2, Congo 0; Zambia 1, Togo 0; Liberia 1, Mali 0; Mali 1, Zambia 1; Congo 3, Liberia 0; Togo 3, Senegal 1; Senegal 1, Zambia 0; Congo 1, Mali 0; Liberia 0, Togo 0; Zambia 1, Liberia 0; Mali 2, Senegal 2; Togo 2, Congo 0; Congo 2, Zambia 3; Togo 1, Mali 0; Liberia 0, Senegal 3; Senegal 6, Liberia 1; Zambia 2, Congo 0; Mali 1, Togo 2; Congo 0, Senegal 0; Mali 4, Liberia 1; Togo 4, Zambia 1; Senegal 2, Togo 2; Zambia 2, Mali 1; Liberia 0, Congo 2.

Group 2: Burkina Faso 1, Ghana 0; South Africa 2, Cape Verde Islands 1; Uganda 1, DR Congo 0; Ghana 3, South Africa 0; DR Congo 3, Burkina Faso 2; Cape Verde Islands 1, DR Congo 1; South Africa 2, Burkina Faso 0; Uganda 1, Ghana 1; Burkina Faso 2, Uganda 0; DR Congo 1, South Africa 0; Ghana 2, Cape Verde Islands 0; Cape Verde Islands 1, Burkina Faso 0; Uganda 0, South Africa 1; Ghana 0, DR Congo 0; Burkina Faso 1, Cape Verde Islands 2; South Africa 2, Uganda 1; DR Congo 1, Ghana 1; Cape Verde Islands 1, South Africa 2; DR Congo 4, Uganda 0; Ghana 2, Burkina Faso 1; Burkina Faso 2, DR Congo 0; South Africa 0, Ghana 2; Uganda 1, Cape Verde Islands 0.

Group 3: Cameroon 2, Benin 1; Ivory Coast 2, Libya 0; Sudan 0, Egypt 3; Liberia 0, Cameroon 0; Benin 1, Sudan 1; Egypt 1, Ivory Coast 2; Sudan 0, Libya 1; Benin 3, Egypt 3; Cameroon 2, Ivory Coast 0; Libya 4, Benin 1; Egypt 3, Cameroon 2; Ivory Coast 5, Sudan 0; Libya 2, Egypt 1; Sudan 1, Cameroon 1; Benin 0, Ivory Coast 1; Cameroon 2, Sudan 1; Egypt 4, Libya 1; Ivory Coast 3, Benin 0; Libya 0, Ivory Coast 0; Benin 1, Cameroon 4; Egypt 6, Sudan 1; Cameroon 1, Libya 0; Ivory Coast 2, Egypt 0.

Group 4: Algeria 0, Angola 0; Gabon 1, Zimbabwe 1; Nigeria 2, Rwanda 0; Rwanda 3, Gabon 1; Angola 1, Nigeria 0; Zimbabwe 1, Algeria 1; Gabon 2, Angola 2; Nigeria 1, Algeria 0; Rwanda 0, Zimbabwe 2; Zimbabwe 0, Nigeria 3; Algeria 0, Gabon 3; Angola 1, Rwanda 0; Gabon 1, Nigeria 1; Rwanda 1, Algeria 1; Angola 1, Zimbabwe 0; Nigeria 2, Gabon 0; Algeria 1, Rwanda 0; Zimbabwe 2, Angola 0; Angola 2, Algeria 1; Rwanda 1, Nigeria 1; Zimbabwe 1, Gabon 0; Gabon 3, Rwanda 0; Nigeria 1, Angola 1; Algeria 2, Zimbabwe 2.

Group 5: Malawi 1, Morocco 1; Tunisia 4, Botswana 1; Botswana 2, Malawi 0; Guinea 2, Tunisia 1; Botswana 0, Morocco 1; Malawi 1, Guinea 1; Kenya 3, Malawi 2; Morocco 1, Tunisia 1; Guinea 4, Botswana 0; Malawi 2, Tunisia 2; Botswana 2, Kenya 1; Guinea 1, Morocco 1; Kenya 2, Guinea 1; Morocco 5, Kenya 1; Kenya 1, Botswana 0; Morocco 1, Guinea 0; Tunisia 7, Malawi 0; Botswana 1, Tunisia 3; Morocco 4, Malawi 1; Guinea 1, Kenya 0; Tunisia 2, Guinea 0; Kenya 0, Morocco 0; Malawi 1, Botswana 3.

Group winners qualify for finals.

WORLD CUP 2006 REMAINING FIXTURES

EUROPE

Group winners and two best runners-up qualify for finals. Remaining six runners-up paired in two leg play-off matches, the winners of which also qualify for finals. Group runners-up ranked according to results against teams finishing in order in their respective groups.

GROUP 1

03.09.05 – Andorra v Finland; Armenia v Holland; Romania v Czech Republic

07.09.05 – Czech Republic v Armenia; Finland v Macedonia; Holland v Andorra

08.10.05 – Czech Republic v Holland; Finland v Romania

12.10.05 – Andorra v Armenia; Finland v Czech Republic; Holland v Macedonia

GROUP 2

03.09.05 – Albania v Kazakhstan; Georgia v Ukraine; Turkey v Denmark

07.09.05 – Denmark v Georgia; Kazakhstan v Greece; Ukraine v Turkey

08.10.05 – Denmark v Greece; Georgia v Kazakhstan; Ukraine v Albania

12.10.05 – Albania v Turkey; Greece v Georgia; Kazakhstan v Denmark

GROUP 3

17.08.05 – Latvia v Russia; Liechtenstein v Slovakia

03.09.05 – Estonia v Latvia; Portugal v Luxembourg; Russia v Liechtenstein

07.09.05 – Latvia v Slovakia; Liechtenstein v Luxembourg; Russia v Portugal

08.10.05 – Portugal v Liechtenstein; Russia v Luxembourg; Slovakia v Estonia

12.10.05 – Luxembourg v Estonia; Portugal v Latvia; Slovakia v Russia

GROUP 4

17.08.05 – Faeroes v Cyprus

03.09.05 – France v Faeroes; Switzerland v Israel

07.09.05 – Cyprus v Switzerland; Faeroes v Israel; Republic of Ireland v France

08.10.05 – Cyprus v Republic of Ireland; Switzerland v France

08.10.05 – Israel v Faeroes

12.10.05 – France v Cyprus; Republic of Ireland v Switzerland

GROUP 5

03.09.05 – Moldova v Belarus; Scotland v Italy; Slovenia v Norway

07.09.05 – Belarus v Italy; Moldova v Slovenia; Norway v Scotland

08.10.05 – Italy v Slovenia; Norway v Moldova; Scotland v Belarus

12.10.05 – Belarus v Norway; Italy v Moldova; Slovenia v Scotland

GROUP 6

03.09.05 – Northern Ireland v Azerbaijan; Poland v Austria; Wales v England

07.09.05 – Azerbaijan v Austria; Northern Ireland v England; Poland v Wales

08.10.05 – England v Austria; Northern Ireland v Wales

12.10.05 – Austria v Northern Ireland; England v Poland; Wales v Azerbaijan

GROUP 7

03.09.05 – Bosnia v Belgium; Serbia & M v Lithuania

07.09.05 – Belgium v San Marino; Lithuania v Bosnia; Spain v Serbia & M

08.10.05 – Belgium v Spain; Bosnia v San Marino; Lithuania v Serbia & M

12.10.05 – Lithuania v Belgium; San Marino v Spain; Serbia & M v Bosnia

GROUP 8

03.09.05 – Hungary v Malta; Iceland v Croatia; Sweden v Bulgaria

07.09.05 – Bulgaria v Iceland; Hungary v Sweden; Malta v Croatia

08.10.05 – Bulgaria v Hungary; Croatia v Sweden

12.10.05 – Hungary v Croatia; Malta v Bulgaria; Sweden v Iceland

SOUTH AMERICA

Top four qualify for finals; fifth placed team enters play-off against Oceania winners for a place in finals.

03/04.09.05 – Bolivia v Ecuador; Brazil v Chile; Paraguay v Argentina; Uruguay v Colombia; Venezuela v Peru

08/09.10.05 – Argentina v Peru; Bolivia v Brazil; Colombia v Chile; Ecuador v Uruguay; Venezuela v Paraguay

11/12.10.05 – Brazil v Venezuela; Chile v Ecuador; Paraguay v Colombia; Peru v Bolivia; Uruguay v Argentina

WORLD CLUB CHAMPIONSHIP

Played annually up to 1974 and intermittently since then between the winners of the European Cup and the winners of the South American Champions Cup — known as the Copa Libertadores. In 1980 the winners were decided by one match arranged in Tokyo in February 1981 and the venue has been the same since. AC Milan replaced Marseille who had been stripped of their European Cup title in 1993.

1960 Real Madrid beat Penarol 0-0, 5-1
1961 Penarol beat Benfica 0-1, 5-0, 2-1
1962 Santos beat Benfica 3-2, 5-2
1963 Santos beat AC Milan 2-4, 4-2, 1-0
1964 Inter-Milan beat Independiente 0-1, 2-0, 1-0
1965 Inter-Milan beat Independiente 3-0, 0-0
1966 Penarol beat Real Madrid 2-0, 2-0
1967 Racing Club beat Celtic 0-1, 2-1, 1-0
1968 Estudiantes beat Manchester United 1-0, 1-1
1969 AC Milan beat Estudiantes 3-0, 1-2
1970 Feyenoord beat Estudiantes 2-2, 1-0
1971 Nacional beat Panathinaikos* 1-1, 2-1
1972 Ajax beat Independiente 1-1, 3-0
1973 Independiente beat Juventus* 1-0
1974 Atlético Madrid* beat Independiente 0-1, 2-0
1975 Independiente and Bayern Munich could not agree dates; no matches.
1976 Bayern Munich beat Cruzeiro 2-0, 0-0
1977 Boca Juniors beat Borussia Moenchengladbach* 2-2, 3-0
1978 Not contested
1979 Olimpia beat Malmö* 1-0, 2-1
1980 Nacional beat Nottingham Forest 1-0
1981 Flamengo beat Liverpool 3-0
1982 Penarol beat Aston Villa 2-0
1983 Gremio Porto Alegre beat SV Hamburg 2-1
1984 Independiente beat Liverpool 1-0
1985 Juventus beat Argentinos Juniors 4-2 on penalties after a 2-2 draw
1986 River Plate beat Steaua Bucharest 1-0
1987 FC Porto beat Penarol 2-1 after extra time
1988 Nacional (Uru) beat PSV Eindhoven 7-6 on penalties after 1-1 draw
1989 AC Milan beat Atletico Nacional (Col) 1-0 after extra time
1990 AC Milan beat Olimpia 3-0
1991 Red Star Belgrade beat Colo Colo 3-0
1992 Sao Paulo beat Barcelona 2-1
1993 Sao Paulo beat AC Milan 3-2
1994 Velez Sarsfield beat AC Milan 2-0
1995 Ajax beat Gremio Porto Alegre 4-3 on penalties after 0-0 draw
1996 Juventus beat River Plate 1-0
1997 Borussia Dortmund beat Cruzeiro 2-0
1998 Real Madrid beat Vasco da Gama 2-1
1999 Manchester U beat Palmeiras 1-0
2000 Boca Juniors beat Real Madrid 2-1
2001 Bayern Munich beat Boca Juniors 1-0 after extra time
2002 Real Madrid beat Olimpia 2-0
2003 Boca Juniors beat AC Milan 3-1 on penalties after 1-1 draw
2004 Porto beat Once Caldas 8-7 on penalties afer 0-0 draw

**European Cup runners-up; winners declined to take part.*

2004

12 December 2004, in Yokohama

Porto (0) 0 Once Caldas (0) 0 45,748

aet; Porto won 8-7 on penalties: Venegas scored for Once Caldas; Diego scored for Porto and was sent off; Alcazar scored for Once Caldas; Carlos Alberto scored for Porto; Rojas scored for Once Caldas; Ricardo Quaresma scored for Porto; De Nigris scored for Once Caldas; Maniche hit the bar for Porto; Fabbro hit a post for Once Caldas; McCarthy scored for Porto.

sudden death: Velasquez scored for Once Caldas; Costinha scored for Porto; Diaz scored for Once Caldas; Jorge Costa scored for Porto; Catano scored for Once Caldas; Ricardo Costa scored for Porto; Garcia shot over for Once Caldas and Pedro Emanuel scored for Porto.

Porto: Vitor Baia (Nuno 105); Seitaridis, Jorge Costa, Pedro Emanuel, Ricardo Costa, Costinha, Maniche, Diego, Derlei (Carlos Alberto 78), McCarthy, Luis Fabbiano (Ricardo Quaresma 88).

Once Caldas: Henao; Rojas, Venegas, Cambindo (Catano 46), Garcia, Viafara, Velasquez, Arango (Diaz 61), Fabbro, Soto (Alcazar 97), De Nigris.

Referee: Larrionda (Uruguay).

EUROPEAN SUPER CUP

Played annually between the winners of the European Champions' Cup and the European Cup-Winners' Cup (UEFA Cup from 2000). AC Milan replaced Marseille in 1993–94.

Previous Matches

1972 Ajax beat Rangers 3-1, 3-2
1973 Ajax beat AC Milan 0-1, 6-0
1974 Not contested
1975 Dynamo Kiev beat Bayern Munich 1-0, 2-0
1976 Anderlecht beat Bayern Munich 4-1, 1-2
1977 Liverpool beat Hamburg 1-1, 6-0
1978 Anderlecht beat Liverpool 3-1, 1-2
1979 Nottingham F beat Barcelona 1-0, 1-1
1980 Valencia beat Nottingham F 1-0, 1-2
1981 Not contested
1982 Aston Villa beat Barcelona 0-1, 3-0
1983 Aberdeen beat Hamburg 0-0, 2-0
1984 Juventus beat Liverpool 2-0
1985 Juventus v Everton not contested due to UEFA ban on English clubs
1986 Steaua Bucharest beat Dynamo Kiev 1-0
1987 FC Porto beat Ajax 1-0, 1-0
1988 KV Mechelen beat PSV Eindhoven 3-0, 0-1
1989 AC Milan beat Barcelona 1-1, 1-0
1990 AC Milan beat Sampdoria 1-1, 2-0
1991 Manchester U beat Red Star Belgrade 1-0
1992 Barcelona beat Werder Bremen 1-1, 2-1
1993 Parma beat AC Milan 0-1, 2-0
1994 AC Milan beat Arsenal 0-0, 2-0
1995 Ajax beat Zaragoza 1-1, 4-0
1996 Juventus beat Paris St Germain 6-1, 3-1
1997 Barcelona beat Borussia Dortmund 2-0, 1-1
1998 Chelsea beat Real Madrid 1-0
1999 Lazio beat Manchester U 1-0
2000 Galatasaray beat Real Madrid 2-1 *(aet; Galatasaray won on sudden death.)*
2001 Liverpool beat Bayern Munich 3-2
2002 Real Madrid beat Feyenoord 3-1
2003 AC Milan beat Porto 1-0
2004 Valencia beat Porto 2-1

2004–05

27 August 2004, in Monaco

Porto (0) 1 *(Ricardo Quaresma 78)* **Valencia (1) 2** *(Baraja 33, Di Vaio 67)* 18,500

Porto: Vitor Baia; Seitaridis, Jorge Costa, Pepe, Nuno Valente, Hugo Leal (Ricardo Quaresma 61), Costinha, Maniche, Carlos Alberto, Helder Postiga, McCarthy (Cesar Peixanto 72).

Valencia: Canizares; Curro Torres, Navarro, Marchena, Carboni, Vicente, Baraja, Albelda, Rufete, Corradi (Aimar 67), Di Vaio (Mista 77).

Referee: Hauge (Norway).

OLYMPICS 2004

▪ *Denotes player sent off.*

GROUP A

Greece 2, South Korea 2
Mali 0, Mexico 0
South Korea 1, Mexico 0
Greece 0, Mali 2
South Korea 3, Mali 3
Greece 2, Mexico 3

	P	*W*	*D*	*L*	*F*	*A*	*Pts*
Mali	3	1	2	0	5	3	5
South Korea	3	1	2	0	6	5	5
Mexico	3	1	1	1	3	3	4
Greece	3	0	1	2	4	7	1

GROUP B

Paraguay 4, Japan 3
Ghana 2, Italy 2
Paraguay 1, Ghana 2
Japan 2, Italy 3
Paraguay 1, Italy 0
Japan 1, Ghana 0

	P	*W*	*D*	*L*	*F*	*A*	*Pts*
Paraguay	3	2	0	1	6	5	6
Italy	3	1	1	1	5	5	4
Ghana	3	1	1	1	4	4	4
Japan	3	1	0	2	6	7	3

GROUP C

Tunisia 1, Australia 1
Argentina 6, Serbia & Montenegro 0
Serbia & Montenegro 1, Australia 5
Argentina 2, Tunisia 0
Argentina 1, Australia 0
Serbia & Montenegro 2, Tunisia 3

	P	*W*	*D*	*L*	*F*	*A*	*Pts*
Argentina	3	3	0	0	9	0	9
Australia	3	1	1	1	6	3	4
Tunisia	3	1	1	1	4	5	4
Serbia & Montenegro	3	0	0	3	3	14	0

WOMEN'S OLYMPIC FINAL

USA 2, Brazil 1

GROUP D

Costa Rica 0, Morocco 0
Iraq 4, Portugal 2
Costa Rica 0, Iraq 2
Morocco 1, Portugal 2
Costa Rica 4, Portugal 2
Morocco 2, Iraq 1

	P	*W*	*D*	*L*	*F*	*A*	*Pts*
Iraq	3	2	0	1	7	4	6
Costa Rica	3	1	1	1	4	4	4
Morocco	3	1	1	1	3	3	4
Portugal	3	1	0	2	6	9	3

QUARTER-FINALS

Mali 0, Italy 1
Iraq 1, Australia 0
Argentina 4, Costa Rica 0
Paraguay 3, South Korea 2

SEMI-FINALS

Italy 0, Argentina 3
Iraq 1, Paraguay 3

MATCH FOR THIRD PLACE

Italy 1, Iraq 0

FINAL (in Athens)

28 August 2004

Argentina (1) 1 Paraguay (0) 0

Argentina: Lux; Ayala, Mascherano, Rosales, Heinze, Coloccini, Tevez, D'Alessandro, Delgado (Rodriguez 76), Kily Gonzalez, Gonzalez L.
Scorer: Tevez 18.
Paraguay: Barreto; Martinez▪, Esquivel (Gonzalez 76), Gimenez, Manzur, Gamarra, Barreto E (Cristaldo 72), Figueredo▪, Torres, Enciso (Diaz 63), Bareiro.
Attendance: 41,116
Referee: K. Vassaras (Greece).

OTHER BRITISH AND IRISH INTERNATIONAL MATCHES 2004–2005

St James' Park, 18 August 2004, 35,387

England (1) 3 *(Beckham 27, Owen 50, Wright-Phillips 72)*

Ukraine (0) 0

England: James; Neville G (Johnson G 46), Cole A (Carragher 60), Gerrard (Dyer 46), Terry, King, Beckham, Butt (Wright-Phillips 52), Smith (Defoe 46), Owen, Lampard (Jenas 75).
Ukraine: Shovkovskyi; Rusol, Fedorov, Yezersky, Vorobei, Tymoschuk, Shelayev, Nesmachni (Radchenko 61), Gusev (Korniytsev 61), Rotan (Zakaryluka 64), Shevchenko (Voronin 52).
Referee: M. McCurry (Scotland).

Madrid, 17 November 2004, 48,000

Spain (1) 1 *(Del Horno 10)*

England (0) 0

Spain: Casillas; Michel Salgado, Del Horno, Xavi, Juanito, Marchena (Pablo 46), Joaquin (Romero 80), Xabi Alonso (Orbaiz 69, Fernando Torres (Luque 46), Raul (Guti 46), Reyes (Angulo 53).
England: Robinson; Neville G, Cole A (Defoe 76), Butt, Terry (Upson 65), Ferdinand (Carragher 62), Beckham (Wright-Phillips 60), Lampard (Jenas 60), Rooney (Smith 42), Owen, Bridge.
Referee: G. Kasnaferis (Greece).

Villa Park, 9 February 2005, 40,705

England (0) 0

Holland (0) 0

England: Robinson; Neville G, Cole A, Gerrard (Jenas 80), Carragher, Brown, Beckham (Dyer 80), Lampard (Hargreaves 46), Rooney (Johnson A 61), Owen, Wright-Phillips (Downing 61).
Holland: Van der Sar; Kromkamp, Van Bronckhorst, Landzaat, Boulahrouz, Mathijsen, Heitinga (Van Bommel 61), Van der Vaart, Makaay, Kuijt, Castelen (Yildirim 62).
Referee: P. Frojdfeldt (Sweden).

Chicago, 28 May 2005, 45,000

USA (0) 1 *(Dempsey 79)*

England (2) 2 *(Richardson 4, 44)*

USA: Keller; Cherundolo, Vanney, Zavagnin, Pope (Bocanegra 73), Gibbs, Ralston (Convey 73), Donovan, McBride (Casey 81), Wolff, Dempsey (Simms 90).
England: James; Johnson G, Cole A (Defoe 63), Jenas, Campbell (Knight 46), Brown, Cole J, Carrick, Smith, Johnson A (Young 76), Richardson (Neville P 59).
Referee: B. Archundia (Mexico).

New Jersey, 31 May 2005, 58,000

Colombia (1) 2 *(Yepes 45, Ramirez 78)*

England (2) 3 *(Owen 36, 42, 58)*

Colombia: Mondragon; Palacio (Ramirez 72), Benitez, Viafara (Anchico 60), Perea, Yepes (Mendoza 81), Hurtado (Vargas 46), Restrepo (Diaz 72), Angel (Perea E 60), Rey, Soto.

England: James (Green 46); Neville P, Cole A (Young 85), Jenas, Johnson G, Knight, Beckham (Richardson 72), Carrick, Crouch (Smith 72), Owen (Defoe 72), Cole J.
Referee: B. Hall (USA).

Hampden Park, 18 August 2004, 15,933

Scotland (0) 0

Hungary (1) 3 *(Huszti 45 (pen), 53, Marshall 73 (og))*

Scotland: Marshall; Holt, Naysmith, Caldwell G (Thompson 46), Pressley, Webster, Fletcher (Pearson 74), Ferguson B (Severin 70), Miller (Crawford 57), McFadden, Quashie.
Hungary: Kiraly; Juhasz, Bodnar, Huszti (Bodor 87), Stark, Toth, Feher (Rosa 63), Gera (Leandro 76), Torghelle (Kovacs 25), Simek, Molnar.
Referee: L. Duhamel (France).

Valencia, 3 September 2004, 15,000

Spain (0) 1 *(Raul 57 (pen))*

Scotland (1) 1 *(Baraja 18 (og))*

Spain: Casillas; Lopez Rekarte, Del Horno, Baraja (Valeron 46), Puyol, Marchena (Helguera 57), Joaquin, Xabi Alonso, Fernando Torres (Raul 46), Tamudo (Vicente 46), Reyes.
Scotland: Gordon; Caldwell G, Naysmith, McNamara, Mackay, Webster, Quashie, Ferguson B, Crawford (Cameron 57), McFadden (Pearson 46), Fletcher (Miller 57).
Referee: S. Bre (France).
Match abandoned 60 minutes; floodlight failure.

Edinburgh, 17 November 2004, 15,071

Scotland (0) 1 *(McFadden 78 (pen))*

Sweden (1) 4 *(Allback 27, 49, Elmander 72, Berglund 73)*

Scotland: Marshall; McNaughton, Murray, Nicholson, Anderson, Webster (Hammell 53), McNamara (Severin 64), Quashie (Hughes 82), Miller (Crawford 71), Pearson.
Sweden: Hedman; Nilsson (Ostlund 62), Dorsin, Andersson, Mellberg, Lucic, Alexandersson N, Kallstrom, Allback, Berglund, Wilhelmsson (Touma 78).
Referee: J. Jara (Czech Republic).

Riga, 18 August 2004, 10,000

Latvia (0) 0

Wales (0) 2 *(Hartson 80, Bellamy 89)*

Latvia: Kolinko; Isakovs, Blagonadezhdin (Korablovs 74), Miholaps (Semyonov 61), Zemlinskis, Stepanovs, Laizans, Labanovs, Prohorenkovs (Rimkus 66), Verpakovskis, Rubins.
Wales: Jones (Crossley 46); Delaney, Thatcher, Savage (Johnson 46), Page, Melville (Collins J 24), Koumas (Robinson 89), Speed, Hartson (Taylor 84), Bellamy, Pembridge (Roberts G 69).
Referee: V. Ivanov (Russia).

Cardiff, 9 February 2005, 16,672

Wales (0) 2 *(Bellamy 63, 80)*

Hungary (0) 0

Wales: Coyne; Edwards (Weston 50), Ricketts, Fletcher, Page, Gabbidon, Partridge (Collins D 65), Davies, Earnshaw (Roberts G 75), Bellamy, Robinson (Roberts S 90).
Hungary: Kiraly; Juhasz, Hajnal (Leandro 58), Bodnar, Gyepes (Vincze 80), Dragoner, Huszti, Korsos G (Rosa 65), Gera, Torghelle, Lipcsei (Kovacs 68).
Referee: C. Richmond (Scotland).

Zurich, 18 August 2004, 4000

Switzerland (0) 0

Northern Ireland (0) 0

Switzerland: Zuberbuhler; Haas, Spycher, Vogel (Lonfat 77), Yakin M (Henchoz 46), Muller, Huggel (Magnin 46), Wicky, Yakin H, Vonlanthen (Muff 60), Cabanas (Frei 82).
Northern Ireland: Carroll; Hughes A, Capaldi, Johnson, Williams (Murdock 67), Craigan (Duff 78), Gillespie (McVeigh 51), Sonner, Healy (Hamilton 70), Smith, Elliott (Brunt 81).
Referee: N. Vollquartz (Denmark).

Windsor Park, 9 February 2005, 11,156

Northern Ireland (0) 0

Canada (1) 1 *(Occean 32)*

Northern Ireland: Taylor (Carroll 46); Baird, McCartney, Doherty (Mulryne 46), Hughes A, Murdock (Kirk 46), Gillespie (Jones S 75), Whitley, Healy, Davis, Capaldi (Craigan 79).
Canada: Sutton; Reda, Simpson, Serioux (Peters 86), McKenna (Klokowski 47), Gervais, Bernier, Imhof, De Rosario, Occean, Brennan (Hume 83).
Referee: J. Attard (Malta).

Windsor Park, 4 June 2005, 14,000

Northern Ireland (1) 1 *(Healy 15 (pen))*

Germany (1) 4 *(Asamoah 17, Ballack 62, 66 (pen), Podolski 81)*

Northern Ireland: Taylor (Ingham 77); Gillespie (McAuley 77), Craigan (Smith 77), Clyde, Baird, McCartney, Johnson, Davis, Healy (Brunt 77), Jones S (Feeney 67), Elliott (Kirk 67).
Germany: Lehmann; Owormeyela, Hitzlsperger, Ernst, Huth, Mertesacker, Schneider (Diesler 46), Ballack (Borowski 73), Asamoah (Schweinsteiger 46), Kuranyi (Podolski 46), Frings.
Referee: C. Richmond (Scotland).

Dublin, 18 August 2004, 31,887

Republic of Ireland (1) 1 *(Reid A 15)*

Bulgaria (0) 1 *(Bozhinov 70)*

Republic of Ireland: Given (Kenny 71); Finnan (Quinn 71), O'Shea, Roy Keane (Kavanagh 64), Cunningham, Doherty (Breen 46), Miller (Carr 52), Kilbane, Morrison (Macken 64), Duff, Reid A.
Bulgaria: Zdravkov; Kishishev, Stoyanov (Topuzakov 64), Yakov (Kamburov 77), Kirilov, Markov, Petrov S, Hristov (Yanev 46), Bozhinov, Berbatov (Gargorov 46), Lazarov (Manchev 56).
Referee: I. Brines (Scotland).

Dublin, 16 November 2004, 30,000

Republic of Ireland (1) 1 *(Robbie Keane 24)*

Croatia (0) 0

Republic of Ireland: Kenny (Given 80); Finnan, O'Shea, Kavanagh, Breen (Cunningham 62), Dunne, Miller, Kilbane (Quinn 80), Elliott (Barrett 84), Robbie Keane (McGeady 90), Duff.
Croatia: Butina; Tomas (Tokic 65), Simunic (Neretijak 74), Tudor (Balaban 46), Kovac R, Vranjes (Leko I 65), Srna, Kranjcar, Babic (Pranjic 59), Kovac N, Klasnic (Da Silva 59).
Referee: G. Orrason (Iceland).

Dublin, 9 February 2005, 44,100

Republic of Ireland (1) 1 *(O'Brien 21)*

Portugal (0) 0

Republic of Ireland: Given; Finnan, O'Shea, Holland, Cunningham (Dunne 60), O'Brien, Reid A, Kilbane (Kavanagh 46), Morrison, Robbie Keane (McGeady 84), Duff (Miller 69).
Portugal: Ricardo; Paulo Ferreira (Hugo Viana 46), Matias, Simao Sabrosa (Boa Morte 61), Caneira, Jorge Andrade, Tiago (Fernando Meira 46), Petit, Pauleta (Nuno Gomes 46), Deco (Ricardo Costa 46), Cristiano Ronaldo (Manuel Fernandes 70).
Referee: M. Messias (England).

Dublin, 29 March 2005, 35,222

Republic of Ireland (0) 1 *(Morrison 82)*

China (0) 0

Republic of Ireland: Kenny; Maybury, O'Shea, Kavanagh, Cunningham (O'Brien 46), Dunne, Reid A, Kilbane (Roy Keane 65), Robbie Keane (Morrison 62), Elliott (Doherty 74), Duff (Miller 46).
China: Li Leilei; Wei (Wang 46), Zhang Yongha (Zhang Yaokun 75), Li Weifeng, Ji, Sun, Hu (Zheng 86), Chen (Li Yan 38), Zhano, Shao (Du 64), Li Yi (Shi 46).
Referee: A. Casha (Malta).

ENGLAND UNDER-21 TEAMS 2004–2005

■*Denotes player sent off.*

Middlesbrough, 17 August 2004, 5658

England (2) 3 *(Cole C 13, 42, Bent 90)*

Ukraine (0) 1 *(Alyev 88)*

England: Carson; Hunt (Hoyte 46), Kilgallon, Ferdinand, Richards (Harding 46), Pennant, Milner (Bent 60), O'Neil, Downing (Reo-Coker 76), Cole C (Ashton 46), Stead (Whittingham 46).

Krems, 3 September 2004, 4500

Austria (0) 0

England (1) 2 *(Cole C 32, Bent 89)*

England: Carson; Hunt, Davenport, Ferdinand, Pennant (Hoyte 90), O'Neil, Reo-Coker, Downing (Milner 74), Stead (Bent 66), Cole C.

Rybnik, 7 September 2004, 2500

Poland (1) 1 *(Burkhardt 5)*

England (1) 3 *(Cole C 45, Bent 72 (pen), 83)*

England: Carson; Johnson G, Ferdinand (Kilgallon 38), Davenport, Baines (Hoyte 83), Pennant, O'Neil, Bentley (Bent 64), Milner, Reo-Coker, Cole C.

Blackburn, 8 October 2004, 17,500

England (0) 2 *(Milner 46, Bent 73)*

Wales (0) 0

England: Carson; Johnson G (Taylor S 84), Hunt, Davenport, Harding, Pennant (Whittingham 75), O'Neil, Milner, Downing, Cole C (Bent 19), Stead.
Wales: Price; Anthony, Duffy, Parslow, Gilbert, Fowler (Crowell 69), Pipe, Tolley, Vaughan, Birchall (Carpenter 76), Calliste.

Baku, 12 October 2004, 1500

Azerbaijan (0) 0

England (0) 0

England: Carson; Johnson G, Hunt, Davenport (Kilgallon 70), Harding, O'Neil (Downing 46), Reo-Coker■, Whittingham, Pennant, Stead, Milner.

Alcala, 16 November 2004, 3000

Spain (0) 1 *(Fabregas 63)*

England (0) 0

England: Carson (Camp 46); Johnson G■, Dawson (Davenport 79), Hunt (Ridgewell 79), Harding (Watson 46), Ambrose (Routledge 60), Hoyte, Whittingham, Milner (Downing 60), Cole C, Bent.

Derby, 8 February 2005, 33,184

England (0) 1 *(Lita 90)*

Holland (2) 2 *(John 19, Jager 37)*

England: Carson (Camp 46); Hoyte (Lita 64), Taylor S, Ridgewell, Baines (Welsh 46), Huddlestone, Routledge (Marney 69), Whittingham, Milner, Cole C (Stead 40), Ashton (Richardson 46).

Hull, 25 March 2005, 21,746

England (0) 2 *(Bent 50, Ashton 52)*

Germany (0) 2 *(Klessling 49, Hilbert 89)*

England: Carson; Johnson G, Hunt, Davenport, Ridgewell (Welsh 46), Milner, O'Neil (Taylor S 90), Huddlestone, Richardson (Rosenior 80), Ashton, Bent.

Middlesbrough, 29 March 2005, 19,095

England (2) 2 *(Welsh 27, Ashton 42)*

Azerbaijan (0) 0

England: Carson; Rosenior, Taylor S, Davenport, Huddlestone, Whittingham, Milner, Welsh, Richardson (Routledge 56), Ashton (Stead 67), Bent (Ambrose 81).

POST-WAR INTERNATIONAL APPEARANCES

As at July 2005 *(Season of first cap given)*

ENGLAND

A'Court, A. (5) 1957/8 Liverpool
Adams, T. A. (66) 1986/7 Arsenal
Allen, C. (5) 1983/4 QPR, Tottenham H
Allen, R. (5) 1951/2 WBA
Allen, T. (3) 1959/60 Stoke C
Anderson, S. (2) 1961/2 Sunderland
Anderson, V. (30) 1978/9 Nottingham F, Arsenal, Manchester U
Anderton, D. R. (30) 1993/4 Tottenham H
Angus, J. (1) 1960/1 Burnley
Armfield, J. (43) 1958/9 Blackpool
Armstrong, D. (3) 1979/80 Middlesbrough, Southampton
Armstrong, K. (1) 1954/5 Chelsea
Astall, G. (2) 1955/6 Birmingham C
Astle, J. (5) 1968/9 WBA
Aston, J. (17) 1948/9 Manchester U
Atyeo, J. (6) 1955/6 Bristol C

Bailey, G. R. (2) 1984/5 Manchester U
Bailey, M. (2) 1963/4 Charlton
Baily, E. (9) 1949/50 Tottenham H
Baker, J. (8) 1959/60 Hibernian, Arsenal
Ball, A. (72) 1964/5 Blackpool, Everton, Arsenal
Ball, M. J. (1) 2000/01 Everton
Banks, G. (73) 1962/3 Leicester C, Stoke C
Banks, T. (6) 1957/8 Bolton W
Bardsley, D. (2) 1992/3 QPR
Barham, M. (2) 1982/3 Norwich C
Barlow, R. (1) 1954/5 WBA
Barmby, N. J. (23) 1994/5 Tottenham H, Middlesbrough, Everton, Liverpool
Barnes, J. (79) 1982/3 Watford, Liverpool
Barnes, P. (22) 1977/8 Manchester C, WBA, Leeds U
Barrass, M. (3) 1951/2 Bolton W
Barrett, E. D. (3) 1990/1 Oldham Ath, Aston Villa
Barry, G. (8) 1999/00 Aston Villa
Barton, W. D. (3) 1994/5 Wimbledon, Newcastle U
Batty, D. (42) 1990/1 Leeds U, Blackburn R, Newcastle U, Leeds U
Baynham, R. (3) 1955/6 Luton T
Beardsley, P. A. (59) 1985/6 Newcastle U, Liverpool, Newcastle U
Beasant, D. J. (2) 1989/90 Chelsea
Beattie, J. S. (5) 2002/03 Southampton
Beattie, T. K. (9) 1974/5 Ipswich T
Beckham, D. R. J. (81) 1996/7 Manchester U, Real Madrid
Bell, C. (48) 1967/8 Manchester C
Bentley, R. (12) 1948/9 Chelsea
Berry, J. (4) 1952/3 Manchester U
Birtles, G. (3) 1979/80 Nottingham F
Blissett, L. (14) 1982/3 Watford, AC Milan
Blockley, J. (1) 1972/3 Arsenal
Blunstone, F. (5) 1954/5 Chelsea
Bonetti, P. (7) 1965/6 Chelsea
Bould, S. A. (2) 1993/4 Arsenal
Bowles, S. (5) 1973/4 QPR
Bowyer, L. D. (1) 2002/03 Leeds U
Boyer, P. (1) 1975/6 Norwich C
Brabrook, P. (3) 1957/8 Chelsea
Bracewell, P. W. (3) 1984/5 Everton
Bradford, G. (1) 1955/6 Bristol R
Bradley, W. (3) 1958/9 Manchester U
Bridge, W. M. (20) 2001/02 Southampton, Chelsea
Bridges, B. (4) 1964/5 Chelsea
Broadbent, P. (7) 1957/8 Wolverhampton W
Broadis, I. (14) 1951/2 Manchester C, Newcastle U
Brooking, T. (47) 1973/4 West Ham U
Brooks, J. (3) 1956/7 Tottenham H
Brown, A. (1) 1970/1 WBA
Brown, K. (1) 1959/60 West Ham U
Brown, W. M. (9) 1998/9 Manchester U
Bull, S. G. (13) 1988/9 Wolverhampton W
Butcher, T. (77) 1979/80 Ipswich T, Rangers
Butt, N. (39) 1996/7 Manchester U, Newcastle U
Byrne, G. (2) 1962/3 Liverpool
Byrne, J. (11) 1961/2 Crystal P, West Ham U
Byrne, R. (33) 1953/4 Manchester U

Callaghan, I. (4) 1965/6 Liverpool
Campbell, S. (65) 1995/6 Tottenham H, Arsenal
Carragher, J. L. (17) 1998/9 Liverpool
Carrick, M. (4) 2000/01 West Ham U, Tottenham H
Carter, H. (7) 1946/7 Derby Co
Chamberlain, M. (8) 1982/3 Stoke C

Channon, M. (46) 1972/3 Southampton, Manchester C
Charles, G. A. (2) 1990/1 Nottingham F
Charlton, J. (35) 1964/5 Leeds U
Charlton, R. (106) 1957/8 Manchester U
Charnley, R. (1) 1962/3 Blackpool
Cherry, T. (27) 1975/6 Leeds U
Chilton, A. (2) 1950/1 Manchester U
Chivers, M. (24) 1970/1 Tottenham H
Clamp, E. (4) 1957/8 Wolverhampton W
Clapton, D. (1) 1958/9 Arsenal
Clarke, A. (19) 1969/70 Leeds U
Clarke, H. (1) 1953/4 Tottenham H
Clayton, R. (35) 1955/6 Blackburn R
Clemence, R (61) 1972/3 Liverpool, Tottenham H
Clement, D. (5) 1975/6 QPR
Clough, B. (2) 1959/60 Middlesbrough
Clough, N. H. (14) 1988/9 Nottingham F
Coates, R. (4) 1969/70 Burnley, Tottenham H
Cockburn, H. (13) 1946/7 Manchester U
Cohen, G. (37) 1963/4 Fulham
Cole, Andy (15) 1994/5 Manchester U
Cole, Ashley (41) 2000/01 Arsenal
Cole, J. J. (23) 2000/01 West Ham U, Chelsea
Collymore, S. V. (3) 1994/5 Nottingham F, Aston Villa
Compton, L. (2) 1950/1 Arsenal
Connelly, J. (20) 1959/60 Burnley, Manchester U
Cooper, C. T. (2) 1994/5 Nottingham F
Cooper, T. (20) 1968/9 Leeds U
Coppell, S. (42) 1977/8 Manchester U
Corrigan, J. (9) 1975/6 Manchester C
Cottee, A. R. (7) 1986/7 West Ham U, Everton
Cowans, G. (10) 1982/3 Aston Villa, Bari, Aston Villa
Crawford, R. (2) 1961/2 Ipswich T
Crouch, P. J. (1) 2004/05 Southampton
Crowe, C. (1) 1962/3 Wolverhampton W
Cunningham, L. (6) 1978/9 WBA, Real Madrid
Curle, K. (3) 1991/2 Manchester C
Currie, A. (17) 1971/2 Sheffield U, Leeds U

Daley, A. M. (7) 1991/2 Aston Villa
Davenport, P. (1) 1984/5 Nottingham F
Deane, B. C. (3) 1990/1 Sheffield U
Deeley, N. (2) 1958/9 Wolverhampton W
Defoe, J. C. (12) 2003/04 Tottenham H
Devonshire, A. (8) 1979/80 West Ham U
Dickinson, J. (48) 1948/9 Portsmouth
Ditchburn, E. (6) 1948/9 Tottenham H
Dixon, K. M. (8) 1984/5 Chelsea
Dixon, L. M. (22) 1989/90 Arsenal
Dobson, M. (5) 1973/4 Burnley, Everton
Dorigo, A. R. (15) 1989/90 Chelsea, Leeds U
Douglas, B. (36) 1957/8 Blackburn R
Downing S. (1) 2004/05 Middlesbrough
Doyle, M. (5) 1975/6 Manchester C
Dublin, D. (4) 1997/8 Coventry C, Aston Villa
Dunn, D. J. I. (1) 2002/03 Blackburn R
Duxbury, M. (10) 1983/4 Manchester U
Dyer, K. C. (28) 1999/00 Newcastle U

Eastham, G. (19) 1962/3 Arsenal
Eckersley, W. (17) 1949/50 Blackburn R
Edwards, D. (18) 1954/5 Manchester U
Ehiogu, U. (4) 1995/6 Aston Villa, Middlesbrough
Ellerington, W. (2) 1948/9 Southampton
Elliott, W. H. (5) 1951/2 Burnley

Fantham, J. (1) 1961/2 Sheffield W
Fashanu, J. (2) 1988/9 Wimbledon
Fenwick, T. (20) 1983/4 QPR, Tottenham H
Ferdinand, L. (17) 1992/3 QPR, Newcastle U, Tottenham H
Ferdinand, R. G. (38) 1997/8 West Ham U, Leeds U, Manchester U
Finney, T. (76) 1946/7 Preston NE
Flowers, R. (49) 1954/5 Wolverhampton W
Flowers, T. (11) 1992/3 Southampton, Blackburn R
Foster, S. (3) 1981/2 Brighton
Foulkes, W. (1) 1954/5 Manchester U
Fowler, R. B. (26) 1995/6 Liverpool, Leeds U
Francis, G. (12) 1974/5 QPR
Francis, T. (52) 1976/7 Birmingham C, Nottingham F, Manchester C, Sampdoria
Franklin, N. (27) 1946/7 Stoke C
Froggatt, J. (13) 1949/50 Portsmouth
Froggatt, R. (4) 1952/3 Sheffield W

Gardner, A. (1) 2003/04 Tottenham H
Garrett, T. (3) 1951/2 Blackpool

Gascoigne, P. J. (57) 1988/9 Tottenham H, Lazio, Rangers, Middlesbrough
Gates, E. (2) 1980/1 Ipswich T
George, F. C. (1) 1976/7 Derby Co
Gerrard, S. G. (34) 1999/00 Liverpool
Gidman, J. (1) 1976/7 Aston Villa
Gillard, I. (3) 1974/5 QPR
Goddard, P. (1) 1981/2 West Ham U
Grainger, C. (7) 1955/6 Sheffield U, Sunderland
Gray, A. A. (1) 1991/2 Crystal P
Gray, M. (3) 1998/9 Sunderland
Greaves, J. (57) 1958/9 Chelsea, Tottenham H
Green, R. P. (1) 2004/05 Norwich C
Greenhoff, B. (18) 1975/6 Manchester U, Leeds U
Gregory, J. (6) 1982/3 QPR
Guppy, S. (1) 1999/00 Leicester C

Hagan, J. (1) 1948/9 Sheffield U
Haines, J. (1) 1948/9 WBA
Hall, J. (17) 1955/6 Birmingham C
Hancocks, J. (3) 1948/9 Wolverhampton W
Hardwick, G. (13) 1946/7 Middlesbrough
Harford, M. G. (2) 1987/8 Luton T
Hargreaves, O. (26) 2001/02 Bayern Munich
Harris, G. (1) 1965/6 Burnley
Harris, P. (2) 1949/50 Portsmouth
Harvey, C. (1) 1970/1 Everton
Hassall, H. (5) 1950/1 Huddersfield T, Bolton W
Hateley, M. (32) 1983/4 Portsmouth, AC Milan, Monaco, Rangers
Haynes, J. (56) 1954/5 Fulham
Hector, K. (2) 1973/4 Derby Co
Hellawell, M. (2) 1962/3 Birmingham C
Hendrie, L. A. (1) 1998/9 Aston Villa
Henry, R. (1) 1962/3 Tottenham H
Heskey, E. W. (43) 1998/9 Leicester C, Liverpool, Birmingham C
Hill, F. (2) 1962/3 Bolton W
Hill, G. (6) 1975/6 Manchester U
Hill, R. (3) 1982/3 Luton T
Hinchcliffe, A. G. (7) 1996/7 Everton, Sheffield W
Hinton, A. (3) 1962/3 Wolverhampton W, Nottingham F
Hirst, D. E. (3) 1990/1 Sheffield W
Hitchens, G. (7) 1960/1 Aston Villa, Internazionale
Hoddle, G. (53) 1979/80 Tottenham H, Monaco
Hodge, S. B. (24) 1985/6 Aston Villa, Tottenham H, Nottingham F
Hodgkinson, A. (5) 1956/7 Sheffield U
Holden, D. (5) 1958/9 Bolton W
Holliday, E. (3) 1959/60 Middlesbrough
Hollins, J. (1) 1966/7 Chelsea
Hopkinson, E. (14) 1957/8 Bolton W
Howe, D. (23) 1957/8 WBA
Howe, J. (3) 1947/8 Derby Co
Howey, S. N. (4) 1994/5 Newcastle U
Hudson, A. (2) 1974/5 Stoke C
Hughes, E. (62) 1969/70 Liverpool, Wolverhampton W
Hughes, L. (3) 1949/50 Liverpool
Hunt, R. (34) 1961/2 Liverpool
Hunt, S. (2) 1983/4 WBA
Hunter, N. (28) 1965/6 Leeds U
Hurst, G. (49) 1965/6 West Ham U

Ince, P. (53) 1992/3 Manchester U, Internazionale, Liverpool, Middlesbrough

James, D. B. (32) 1996/7 Liverpool, Aston Villa, West Ham U, Manchester C
Jeffers, F. (1) 2002/03 Arsenal
Jenas, J. A. (12) 2002/03 Newcastle U
Jezzard, B. (2) 1953/4 Fulham
Johnson, A. (2) 2004/05 Crystal P
Johnson, D. (8) 1974/5 Ipswich T, Liverpool
Johnson, G. M. C. (4) 2003/04 Chelsea
Johnson, S. A. M. (1) 2000/01 Derby Co
Johnston, H. (10) 1946/7 Blackpool
Jones, M. (3) 1964/5 Sheffield U, Leeds U
Jones, R. (8) 1991/2 Liverpool
Jones, W. H. (2) 1949/50 Liverpool

Kay, A. (1) 1962/3 Everton
Keegan, K. (63) 1972/3 Liverpool, SV Hamburg, Southampton
Kennedy, A. (2) 1983/4 Liverpool
Kennedy, R. (17) 1975/6 Liverpool
Keown, M. R. (43) 1991/2 Everton, Arsenal
Kevan, D. (14) 1956/7 WBA
Kidd, B. (2) 1969/70 Manchester U
King, L. B. (12) 2001/02 Tottenham H
Knight, Z. (2) 2004/05 Fulham
Knowles, C. (4) 1967/8 Tottenham H
Konchesky, P. M. (1) 2002/03 Charlton Ath

Labone, B. (26) 1962/3 Everton
Lampard, F. J. (32) 1999/00 West Ham U, Chelsea
Lampard, F. R. G. (2) 1972/3 West Ham U

Langley, J. (3) 1957/8 Fulham
Langton, R. (11) 1946/7 Blackburn R, Preston NE, Bolton W
Latchford, R. (12) 1977/8 Everton
Lawler, C. (4) 1970/1 Liverpool
Lawton, T. (15) 1946/7 Chelsea, Notts Co
Lee, F. (27) 1968/9 Manchester C
Lee, J. (1) 1950/1 Derby C
Lee, R. M. (21) 1994/5 Newcastle U
Lee, S. (14) 1982/3 Liverpool
Le Saux, G. P. (36) 1993/4 Blackburn R, Chelsea
Le Tissier, M. P. (8) 1993/4 Southampton
Lindsay, A. (4) 1973/4 Liverpool
Lineker, G. (80) 1983/4 Leicester C, Everton, Barcelona, Tottenham H
Little, B. (1) 1974/5 Aston Villa
Lloyd, L. (4) 1970/1 Liverpool, Nottingham F
Lofthouse, N. (33) 1950/1 Bolton W
Lowe, E. (3) 1946/7 Aston Villa

Mabbutt, G. (16) 1982/3 Tottenham H
Macdonald, M. (14) 1971/2 Newcastle U
Madeley, P. (24) 1970/1 Leeds U
Mannion, W. (26) 1946/7 Middlesbrough
Mariner, P. (35) 1976/7 Ipswich T, Arsenal
Marsh, R. (9) 1971/2 QPR, Manchester C
Martin, A. (17) 1980/1 West Ham U
Martyn, A. N. (23) 1991/2 Crystal P, Leeds U
Marwood, B. (1) 1988/9 Arsenal
Matthews, R. (5) 1955/6 Coventry C
Matthews, S. (37) 1946/7 Stoke C, Blackpool
McCann, G. P. (1) 2000/01 Sunderland
McDermott, T. (25) 1977/8 Liverpool
McDonald, C. (8) 1957/8 Burnley
McFarland, R. (28) 1970/1 Derby C
McGarry, W. (4) 1953/4 Huddersfield T
McGuinness, W. (2) 1958/9 Manchester U
McMahon, S. (17) 1987/8 Liverpool
McManaman, S. (37) 1994/5 Liverpool, Real Madrid
McNab, R. (4) 1968/9 Arsenal
McNeil, M. (9) 1960/1 Middlesbrough
Meadows, J. (1) 1954/5 Manchester C
Medley, L. (6) 1950/1 Tottenham H
Melia, J. (2) 1962/3 Liverpool
Merrick, G. (23) 1951/2 Birmingham C
Merson, P. C. (21) 1991/2 Arsenal, Middlesbrough, Aston Villa
Metcalfe, V. (2) 1950/1 Huddersfield T
Milburn, J. (13) 1948/9 Newcastle U
Miller, B. (1) 1960/1 Burnley
Mills, D. J. (19) 2000/01 Leeds U
Mills, M. (42) 1972/3 Ipswich T
Milne, G. (14) 1962/3 Liverpool
Milton, C. A. (1) 1951/2 Arsenal
Moore, R. (108) 1961/2 West Ham U
Morley, A. (6) 1981/2 Aston Villa
Morris, J. (3) 1948/9 Derby Co
Mortensen, S. (25) 1946/7 Blackpool
Mozley, B. (3) 1949/50 Derby Co
Mullen, J. (12) 1946/7 Wolverhampton W
Mullery, A. (35) 1964/5 Tottenham H
Murphy, D. B. (9) 2001/02 Liverpool

Neal, P. (50) 1975/6 Liverpool
Neville, G. A. (76) 1994/5 Manchester U
Neville, P. J. (52) 1995/6 Manchester U
Newton, K. (27) 1965/6 Blackburn R, Everton
Nicholls, J. (2) 1953/4 WBA
Nicholson, W. (1) 1950/1 Tottenham H
Nish, D. (5) 1972/3 Derby Co
Norman, M. (23) 1961/2 Tottenham H

O'Grady, M. (2) 1962/3 Huddersfield T, Leeds U
Osgood, P. (4) 1969/70 Chelsea
Osman, R. (11) 1979/80 Ipswich T
Owen, M. J. (70) 1997/8 Liverpool, Real Madrid
Owen, S. (3) 1953/4 Luton T

Paine, T. (19) 1962/3 Southampton
Pallister, G. (22) 1987/8 Middlesbrough, Manchester U
Palmer, C. L. (18) 1991/2 Sheffield W
Parker, P. A. (19) 1988/9 QPR, Manchester U
Parker, S. M. (2) 2003/04 Charlton Ath, Chelsea
Parkes, P. (1) 1973/4 QPR
Parlour, R. (10) 1998/9 Arsenal
Parry, R. (2) 1959/60 Bolton W
Peacock, A. (6) 1961/2 Middlesbrough, Leeds U
Pearce, S. (78) 1986/7 Nottingham F, West Ham U
Pearson, Stan (8) 1947/8 Manchester U
Pearson, Stuart (15) 1975/6 Manchester U
Pegg, D. (1) 1956/7 Manchester U
Pejic, M. (4) 1973/4 Stoke C
Perry, W. (3) 1955/6 Blackpool
Perryman, S. (1) 1981/2 Tottenham H

Peters, M. (67) 1965/6 West Ham U, Tottenham H
Phelan, M. C. (1) 1989/90 Manchester U
Phillips, K. (8) 1998/9 Sunderland
Phillips, L. (3) 1951/2 Portsmouth
Pickering, F. (3) 1963/4 Everton
Pickering, N. (1) 1982/3 Sunderland
Pilkington, B. (1) 1954/5 Burnley
Platt, D. (62) 1989/90 Aston Villa, Bari, Juventus, Sampdoria, Arsenal
Pointer, R. (3) 1961/2 Burnley
Powell, C. G. (5) 2000/01 Charlton Ath
Pye, J. (1) 1949/50 Wolverhampton W

Quixall, A. (5) 1953/4 Sheffield W

Radford, J. (2) 1968/9 Arsenal
Ramsey, A. (32) 1948/9 Southampton, Tottenham H
Reaney, P. (3) 1968/9 Leeds U
Redknapp, J. F. (17) 1995/6 Liverpool
Reeves, K. (2) 1979/80 Norwich C, Manchester C
Regis, C. (5) 1981/2 WBA, Coventry C
Reid, P. (13) 1984/5 Everton
Revie, D. (6) 1954/5 Manchester C
Richards, J. (1) 1972/3 Wolverhampton W
Richardson, K. (1) 1993/4 Aston Villa
Richardon, K. E. (2) 2004/05 Manchester U
Rickaby, S. (1) 1953/4 WBA
Ricketts, M. B. (1) 2001/02 Bolton W
Rimmer, J. (1) 1975/6 Arsenal
Ripley, S. E. (2) 1993/4 Blackburn R
Rix, G. (17) 1980/1 Arsenal
Robb, G. (1) 1953/4 Tottenham H
Roberts, G. (6) 1982/3 Tottenham H
Robinson, P. W. (12) 2002/03 Leeds U, Tottenham H
Robson, B. (90) 1979/80 WBA, Manchester U
Robson, R. (20) 1957/8 WBA
Rocastle, D. (14) 1988/9 Arsenal
Rooney, W. (23) 2002/03 Everton. Manchester U
Rowley, J. (6) 1948/9 Manchester U
Royle, J. (6) 1970/1 Everton, Manchester C
Ruddock, N. (1) 1994/5 Liverpool

Sadler, D. (4) 1967/8 Manchester U
Salako, J. A. (5) 1990/1 Crystal P
Sansom, K. (86) 1978/9 Crystal P, Arsenal
Scales, J. R. (3) 1994/5 Liverpool
Scholes, P. (66) 1996/7 Manchester U
Scott, L. (17) 1946/7 Arsenal
Seaman, D. A. (75) 1988/9 QPR, Arsenal
Sewell, J. (6) 1951/2 Sheffield W
Shackleton, L. (5) 1948/9 Sunderland
Sharpe, L. S. (8) 1990/1 Manchester U
Shaw, G. (5) 1958/9 Sheffield U
Shearer, A. (63) 1991/2 Southampton, Blackburn R, Newcastle U
Shellito, K. (1) 1962/3 Chelsea
Sheringham, E. (51) 1992/3 Tottenham H, Manchester U, Tottenham H
Sherwood, T. A. (3) 1998/9 Tottenham H
Shilton, P. (125) 1970/1 Leicester C, Stoke C, Nottingham F, Southampton, Derby Co
Shimwell, E. (1) 1948/9 Blackpool
Sillett, P. (3) 1954/5 Chelsea
Sinclair, T. (12) 2001/02 West Ham U, Manchester C
Sinton, A. (12) 1991/2 QPR, Sheffield W
Slater, W. (12) 1954/5 Wolverhampton W
Smith, A. (15) 2000/01 Leeds U, Mancheser U
Smith, A. M. (13) 1988/9 Arsenal
Smith, L. (6) 1950/1 Arsenal
Smith, R. (15) 1960/1 Tottenham H
Smith, Tom (1) 1970/1 Liverpool
Smith, Trevor (2) 1959/60 Birmingham C
Southgate, G. (57) 1995/6 Aston Villa, Middlesbrough
Spink, N. (1) 1982/3 Aston Villa
Springett, R. (33) 1959/60 Sheffield W
Staniforth, R. (8) 1953/4 Huddersfield T
Statham, D. (3) 1982/3 WBA
Stein, B. (1) 1983/4 Luton T
Stepney, A. (1) 1967/8 Manchester U
Sterland, M. (1) 1988/9 Sheffield W
Steven, T. M. (36) 1984/5 Everton, Rangers, Marseille
Stevens, G. A. (7) 1984/5 Tottenham H
Stevens, M. G. (46) 1984/5 Everton, Rangers
Stewart, P. A. (3) 1991/2 Tottenham H
Stiles, N. (28) 1964/5 Manchester U
Stone, S. B. (9) 1995/6 Nottingham F
Storey-Moore, I. (1) 1969/70 Nottingham F
Storey, P. (19) 1970/1 Arsenal
Streten, B. (1) 1949/50 Luton T
Summerbee, M. (8) 1967/8 Manchester C
Sunderland, A. (1) 1979/80 Arsenal
Sutton, C. R. (1) 1997/8 Blackburn R
Swan, P. (19) 1959/60 Sheffield W
Swift, F. (19) 1946/7 Manchester C

Talbot, B. (6) 1976/7 Ipswich T, Arsenal
Tambling, R. (3) 1962/3 Chelsea
Taylor, E. (1) 1953/4 Blackpool

Taylor, J. (2) 1950/1 Fulham
Taylor, P. H. (3) 1947/8 Liverpool
Taylor, P. J. (4) 1975/6 Crystal P
Taylor, T. (19) 1952/3 Manchester U
Temple, D. (1) 1964/5 Everton
Terry, J. G. (17) 2002/03 Chelsea
Thomas, Danny (2) 1982/3 Coventry C
Thomas, Dave (8) 1974/5 QPR
Thomas, G. R. (9) 1990/1 Crystal P
Thomas, M. L. (2) 1988/9 Arsenal
Thompson, A. (1) 2003/04 Celtic
Thompson, P. (16) 1963/4 Liverpool
Thompson, P. B. (42) 1975/6 Liverpool
Thompson, T. (2) 1951/2 Aston Villa, Preston NE
Thomson, R. (8) 1963/4 Wolverhampton W
Todd, C. (27) 1971/2 Derby Co
Towers, T. (3) 1975/6 Sunderland
Tueart, D. (6) 1974/5 Manchester C

Ufton, D. (1) 1953/4 Charlton Ath
Unsworth, D. G. (1) 1994/5 Everton
Upson, M. J. (7) 2002/03 Birmingham C

Vassell, D. (22) 2001/02 Aston Villa
Venables, T. (2) 1964/5 Chelsea
Venison, B. (2) 1994/5 Newcastle U
Viljoen, C. (2) 1974/5 Ipswich T
Viollet, D. (2) 1959/60 Manchester U

Waddle, C. R. (62) 1984/5 Newcastle U, Tottenham H, Marseille
Waiters, A. (5) 1963/4 Blackpool
Walker, D. S. (59) 1988/9 Nottingham F, Sampdoria, Sheffield W
Walker, I. M. (4) 1995/6 Tottenham H, Leicester C
Wallace, D. L. (1) 1985/6 Southampton
Walsh, P. (5) 1982/3 Luton T
Walters, K. M. (1) 1990/1 Rangers
Ward, P. (1) 1979/80 Brighton
Ward, T. (2) 1947/8 Derby C
Watson, D. (12) 1983/4 Norwich C, Everton
Watson, D. V. (65) 1973/4 Sunderland, Manchester C, Werder Bremen, Southampton, Stoke C
Watson, W. (4) 1949/50 Sunderland
Webb, N. (26) 1987/8 Nottingham F, Manchester U
Weller, K. (4) 1973/4 Leicester C
West, G. (3) 1968/9 Everton
Wheeler, J. (1) 1954/5 Bolton W
White, D. (1) 1992/3 Manchester C
Whitworth, S. (7) 1974/5 Leicester C
Whymark, T. (1) 1977/8 Ipswich T
Wignall, F. (2) 1964/5 Nottingham F
Wilcox, J. M. (3) 1995/6 Blackburn R, Leeds U
Wilkins, R. (84) 1975/6 Chelsea, Manchester U, AC Milan
Williams, B. (24) 1948/9 Wolverhampton W
Williams, S. (6) 1982/3 Southampton
Willis, A. (1) 1951/2 Tottenham H
Wilshaw, D. (12) 1953/4 Wolverhampton W
Wilson, R. (63) 1959/60 Huddersfield T, Everton
Winterburn, N. (2) 1989/90 Arsenal
Wise, D. F. (21) 1990/1 Chelsea
Withe, P. (11) 1980/1 Aston Villa
Wood, R. (3) 1954/5 Manchester U
Woodcock, A. (42) 1977/8 Nottingham F, FC Cologne, Arsenal
Woodgate, J. S. (5) 1998/9 Leeds U, Newcastle U
Woods, C. C. E. (43) 1984/5 Norwich C, Rangers, Sheffield W
Worthington, F. (8) 1973/4 Leicester C
Wright, I. E. (33) 1990/1 Crystal P, Arsenal, West Ham U
Wright, M. (45) 1983/4 Southampton, Derby C, Liverpool
Wright, R. I. (2) 1999/00 Ipswich T, Arsenal
Wright, T. (11) 1967/8 Everton
Wright, W. (105) 1946/7 Wolverhampton W
Wright-Phillips, S. C. (4) 2004/05 Manchester C
Young, G. (1) 1964/5 Sheffield W
Young, L. P. (2) 2004/05 Charlton Ath

NORTHERN IRELAND

Aherne, T. (4) 1946/7 Belfast Celtic, Luton T
Anderson, T. (22) 1972/3 Manchester U, Swindon T, Peterborough U
Armstrong, G. (63) 1976/7 Tottenham H, Watford, Real Mallorca, WBA, Chesterfield

Baird, C. P. (16) 2002/03 Southampton
Barr, H. (3) 1961/2 Linfield, Coventry C
Best, G. (37) 1963/4 Manchester U, Fulham
Bingham, W. (56) 1950/1 Sunderland, Luton T, Everton, Port Vale
Black, K. (30) 1987/8 Luton T, Nottingham F
Blair, R. (5) 1974/5 Oldham Ath

Blanchflower, D. (54) 1949/50 Barnsley, Aston Villa, Tottenham H
Blanchflower, J. (12) 1953/4 Manchester U
Bowler, G. (3) 1949/50 Hull C
Braithwaite, R. (10) 1961/2 Linfield, Middlesbrough
Brennan, R. (5) 1948/9 Luton T, Birmingham C, Fulham
Briggs, R. (2) 1961/2 Manchester U, Swansea
Brotherston, N. (27) 1979/80 Blackburn R
Bruce, W. (2) 1960/1 Glentoran
Brunt, C. (2) 2004/05 Sheffield W

Campbell, A. (2) 1962/3 Crusaders
Campbell, D. A. (10) 1985/6 Nottingham F, Charlton Ath
Campbell, J. (2) 1950/1 Fulham
Campbell, R. M. (2) 1981/2 Bradford C
Campbell, W. (6) 1967/8 Dundee
Capaldi, A. C. (11) 2003/04 Plymouth Arg
Carey, J. (7) 1946/7 Manchester U
Carroll, R. E. (17) 1996/7 Wigan Ath, Manchester U
Casey, T. (12) 1954/5 Newcastle U, Portsmouth
Caskey, A. (8) 1978/9 Derby C, Tulsa Roughnecks
Cassidy, T. (24) 1970/1 Newcastle U, Burnley
Caughey, M. (2) 1985/6 Linfield
Clarke, C. J. (38) 1985/6 Bournemouth, Southampton, Portsmouth
Cleary, J. (5) 1981/2 Glentoran
Clements, D. (48) 1964/5 Coventry C, Sheffield W, Everton, New York Cosmos
Clyde, M.G. (3) 2004/05 Wolverhampon W
Cochrane, D. (10) 1946/7 Leeds U
Cochrane, T. (26) 1975/6 Coleraine, Burnley, Middlesbrough, Gillingham
Connell, T. E. (1) 1977/8 Coleraine
Coote, A. (6) 1998/9 Norwich C
Cowan, J. (1) 1969/70 Newcastle U
Coyle, F. (4) 1955/6 Coleraine, Nottingham F
Coyle, L. (1) 1988/9 Derry C
Coyle, R. (5) 1972/3 Sheffield W
Craig, D. (25) 1966/7 Newcastle U
Craigan, S. (12) 2002/03 Partick T, Motherwell
Crossan, E. (3) 1949/50 Blackburn R
Crossan, J. (24) 1959/60 Sparta Rotterdam, Sunderland, Manchester C, Middlesbrough
Cunningham, W. (30) 1950/1 St Mirren, Leicester C, Dunfermline Ath
Cush, W. (26) 1950/1 Glentoran, Leeds U, Portadown

D'Arcy, S. (5) 1951/2 Chelsea, Brentford
Davis, S. (4) 2004/05 Aston Villa
Davison, A. J. (3) 1995/6 Bolton W, Bradford C, Grimsby T
Dennison, R. (18) 1987/8 Wolverhampton W
Devine, J. (1) 1989/90 Glentoran
Dickson, D. (4) 1969/70 Coleraine
Dickson, T. (1) 1956/7 Linfield
Dickson, W. (12) 1950/1 Chelsea, Arsenal
Doherty, L. (2) 1984/5 Linfield
Doherty, P. (6) 1946/7 Derby Co, Huddersfield T, Doncaster R
Doherty, T. E. (9) 2002/03 Bristol C
Donaghy, M. (91) 1979/80 Luton T, Manchester U, Chelsea
Dougan, D. (43) 1957/8 Portsmouth, Blackburn R, Aston Villa, Leicester C, Wolverhampton W
Douglas, J. P. (1) 1946/7 Belfast Celtic
Dowd, H. (3) 1973/4 Glenavon, Sheffield W
Dowie, I. (59) 1989/90 Luton T, West Ham U, Southampton, Crystal P, West Ham U, QPR
Duff, M. J. (4) 2001/02 Cheltenham T, Burnley
Dunlop, G. (4) 1984/5 Linfield

Eglington, T. (6) 1946/7 Everton
Elder, A. (40) 1959/60 Burnley, Stoke C
Elliott, S. (27) 2000/01 Motherwell, Hull C

Farrell, P. (7) 1946/7 Everton
Feeney, J. (2) 1946/7 Linfield, Swansea T
Feeney, W. (1) 1975/6 Glentoran
Feeney, W. J. (5) 2001/02 Bournemouth, Luton T
Ferguson, G. (5) 1998/9 Linfield
Ferguson, W. (2) 1965/6 Linfield
Ferris, R. (3) 1949/50 Birmingham C
Fettis, A. (25) 1991/2 Hull C, Nottingham F, Blackburn R
Finney, T. (14) 1974/5 Sunderland, Cambridge U
Fleming, J. G. (31) 1986/7 Nottingham F, Manchester C, Barnsley
Forde, T. (4) 1958/9 Ards

Gallogly, C. (2) 1950/1 Huddersfield T
Garton, R. (1) 1968/9 Oxford U
Gillespie, K. R. (62) 1994/5 Manchester U, Newcastle U, Blackburn R, Leicester C
Gorman, W. (4) 1946/7 Brentford
Graham, W. (14) 1950/1 Doncaster R
Gray, P. (26) 1992/3 Luton T, Sunderland, Nancy, Luton T, Burnley, Oxford U
Gregg, H. (25) 1953/4 Doncaster R, Manchester U
Griffin, D. J. (29) 1995/6 St Johnstone, Dundee U, Stockport Co

Hamill, R. (1) 1998/9 Glentoran
Hamilton, B. (50) 1968/9 Linfield, Ipswich T, Everton, Millwall, Swindon T
Hamilton, G. (5) 2002/03 Portadown
Hamilton, W. (41) 1977/8 QPR, Burnley, Oxford U
Harkin, T. (5) 1967/8 Southport, Shrewsbury T
Harvey, M. (34) 1960/1 Sunderland
Hatton, S. (2) 1962/3 Linfield
Healy, D. J. (43) 1999/00 Manchester U, Preston NE, Leeds U
Healy, P. J. (4) 1981/2 Coleraine, Glentoran
Hegan, D. (7) 1969/70 WBA, Wolverhampton W
Hill, C. F. (27) 1989/90 Sheffield U, Leicester C, Trelleborg, Northampton T
Hill, J. (7) 1958/9 Norwich C, Everton
Hinton, E. (7) 1946/7 Fulham, Millwall
Holmes, S. P. (1) 2001/02 Wrexham
Horlock, K. (32) 1994/5 Swindon T, Manchester C
Hughes, A. W. (43) 1997/8 Newcastle U
Hughes, M. E. (71) 1991/2 Manchester C, Strasbourg, West Ham U, Wimbledon, Crystal P
Hughes, P. (3) 1986/7 Bury
Hughes, W. (1) 1950/1 Bolton W
Humphries, W. (14) 1961/2 Ards, Coventry C, Swansea T
Hunter, A. (53) 1969/70 Blackburn R, Ipswich T
Hunter, B. V. (15) 1994/5 Wrexham, Reading
Hunter, V. (2) 1961/2 Coleraine

Ingham, M.G. (1) 2004/05 Sunderland
Irvine, R. (8) 1961/2 Linfield, Stoke C
Irvine, W. (23) 1962/3 Burnley, Preston NE, Brighton & HA

Jackson, T. (35) 1968/9 Everton, Nottingham F, Manchester U
Jamison, A. (1) 1975/6 Glentoran
Jenkins, I. (6) 1996/7 Chester C, Dundee U
Jennings, P. (119) 1963/4 Watford, Tottenham H, Arsenal, Tottenham H, Everton, Tottenham H
Johnson, D. M. (37) 1998/9 Blackburn R, Birmingham C
Johnston, W. (2) 1961/2 Glenavon, Oldham Ath
Jones, J. (3) 1955/6 Glenavon
Jones, S. G. (16) 2002/03 Crewe Alex

Keane, T. (1) 1948/9 Swansea T
Kee, P. V. (9) 1989/90 Oxford U, Ards
Keith, R. (23) 1957/8 Newcastle U
Kelly, H. (4) 1949/50 Fulham, Southampton
Kelly, P. (1) 1949/50 Barnsley
Kennedy, P. H. (20) 1998/9 Watford, Wigan Ath
Kirk, A. R. (8) 1999/00 Heart of Midlothian, Boston U, Northampton T

Lawther, I. (4) 1959/60 Sunderland, Blackburn R
Lennon, N. F. (40) 1993/4 Crewe Alex, Leicester C, Celtic
Lockhart, N. (8) 1946/7 Linfield, Coventry C, Aston Villa
Lomas, S. M. (45) 1993/4 Manchester C, West Ham U
Lutton, B. (6) 1969/70 Wolverhampton W, West Ham U

Magill, E. (26) 1961/2 Arsenal, Brighton & HA
Magilton, J. (52) 1990/1 Oxford U, Southampton, Sheffield W, Ipswich T
Mannus, A. (1) 2003/04 Linfield
Martin, C. (6) 1946/7 Glentoran, Leeds U, Aston Villa
McAdams, W. (15) 1953/4 Manchester C, Bolton W, Leeds U
McAlinden, J. (2) 1946/7 Portsmouth, Southend U
McAuley, G. (1) 2004/05 Lincoln C
McBride, S. (4) 1990/1 Glenavon
McCabe, J. (6) 1948/9 Leeds U
McCann, G. S. (9) 2001/02 West Ham U, Cheltenham T
McCarthy, J. D. (18) 1995/6 Port Vale, Birmingham C
McCartney, G. (20) 2001/02 Sunderland
McCavana, T. (3) 1954/5 Coleraine

McCleary, J. W. (1) 1954/5 Cliftonville
McClelland, J. (6) 1960/1 Arsenal, Fulham
McClelland, J. (53) 1979/80 Mansfield T, Rangers, Watford, Leeds U
McCourt, F. (6) 1951/2 Manchester C
McCourt, P. J. (1) 2001/02 Rochdale
McCoy, R. (1) 1986/7 Coleraine
McCreery, D. (67) 1975/6 Manchester U, QPR, Tulsa Roughnecks, Newcastle U, Heart of Midlothian
McCrory, S. (1) 1957/8 Southend U
McCullough, W. (10) 1960/1 Arsenal, Millwall
McCurdy, C. (1) 1979/80 Linfield
McDonald, A. (52) 1985/6 QPR
McElhinney, G. (6) 1983/4 Bolton W
McEvilly, L. R. (1) 2001/02 Rochdale
McFaul, I. (6) 1966/7 Linfield, Newcastle U
McGarry, J. K. (3) 1950/1 Cliftonville
McGaughey, M. (1) 1984/5 Linfield
McGibbon, P. C. G. (7) 1994/5 Manchester U, Wigan Ath
McGrath, R. (21) 1973/4 Tottenham H, Manchester U
McIlroy, J. (55) 1951/2 Burnley, Stoke C
McIlroy, S. B. (88) 1971/2 Manchester U, Stoke C, Manchester C
McKeag, W. (2) 1967/8 Glentoran
McKenna, J. (7) 1949/50 Huddersfield T
McKenzie, R. (1) 1966/7 Airdrieonians
McKinney, W. (1) 1965/6 Falkirk
McKnight, A. (10) 1987/8 Celtic, West Ham U
McLaughlin, J. (12) 1961/2 Shrewsbury T, Swansea T
McMahon, G. J. (17) 1994/5 Tottenham H, Stoke C
McMichael, A. (39) 1949/50 Newcastle U
McMillan, S. (2) 1962/3 Manchester U
McMordie, E. (21) 1968/9 Middlesbrough
McMorran, E. (15) 1946/7 Belfast Celtic, Barnsley, Doncaster R
McNally, B. A. (5) 1985/6 Shrewsbury T
McParland, P. (34) 1953/4 Aston Villa, Wolverhampton W
McVeigh, P. (20) 1998/9 Tottenham H, Norwich C
Montgomery, F. J. (1) 1954/5 Coleraine
Moore, C. (1) 1948/9 Glentoran
Moreland, V. (6) 1978/9 Derby Co
Morgan, S. (18) 1971/2 Port Vale, Aston Villa, Brighton & HA, Sparta Rotterdam
Morrow, S. J. (39) 1989/90 Arsenal, QPR
Mullan, G. (4) 1982/3 Glentoran
Mulryne, P. P. (26) 1996/7 Manchester U, Norwich C
Murdock, C. J. (28) 1999/00 Preston NE, Hibernian, Crewe Alex

Napier, R. (1) 1965/6 Bolton W
Neill, T. (59) 1960/1 Arsenal, Hull C
Nelson, S. (51) 1969/70 Arsenal, Brighton & HA
Nicholl, C. (51) 1974/5 Aston Villa, Southampton, Grimsby T
Nicholl, J. M. (73) 1975/6 Manchester U, Toronto Blizzard, Sunderland, Rangers, WBA
Nicholson, J. (41) 1960/1 Manchester U, Huddersfield T
Nolan, I. R. (18) 1996/7 Sheffield W, Bradford C, Wigan Ath

O'Boyle, G. (13) 1993/4 Dunfermline Ath, St Johnstone
O'Doherty, A. (2) 1969/70 Coleraine
O'Driscoll, J. (3) 1948/9 Swansea T
O'Kane, L. (20) 1969/70 Nottingham F
O'Neill, C. (3) 1988/9 Motherwell
O'Neill, H. M. (64) 1971/2 Distillery, Nottingham F, Norwich C, Manchester C, Norwich C, Notts Co
O'Neill, J. (1) 1961/2 Sunderland
O'Neill, J. P. (39) 1979/80 Leicester C
O'Neill, M. A. (31) 1987/8 Newcastle U, Dundee U, Hibernian, Coventry C

Parke, J. (13) 1963/4 Linfield, Hibernian, Sunderland
Patterson, D. J. (17) 1993/4 Crystal P, Luton T, Dundee U
Peacock, R. (31) 1951/2 Celtic, Coleraine
Penney, S. (17) 1984/5 Brighton & HA
Platt, J. A. (23) 1975/6 Middlesbrough, Ballymena U, Coleraine

Quinn, J. M. (46) 1984/5 Blackburn R, Swindon T, Leicester, Bradford C, West Ham U, Bournemouth, Reading
Quinn, S. J. (37) 1995/6 Blackpool, WBA, Willem II, Sheffield W

Rafferty, P. (1) 1979/80 Linfield
Ramsey, P. (14) 1983/4 Leicester C
Rice, P. (49) 1968/9 Arsenal
Robinson, S. (5) 1996/7 Bournemouth
Rogan, A. (18) 1987/8 Celtic, Sunderland, Millwall
Ross, E. (1) 1968/9 Newcastle U

Rowland, K. (19) 1994/5 West Ham U, QPR
Russell, A. (1) 1946/7 Linfield
Ryan, R. (1) 1949/50 WBA

Sanchez, L. P. (3) 1986/7 Wimbledon
Scott, J. (2) 1957/8 Grimsby T
Scott, P. (10) 1974/5 Everton, York C, Aldershot
Sharkey, P. (1) 1975/6 Ipswich T
Shields, J. (1) 1956/7 Southampton
Simpson, W. (12) 1950/1 Rangers
Sloan, D. (2) 1968/9 Oxford
Sloan, T. (3) 1978/9 Manchester U
Sloan, W. (1) 1946/7 Arsenal
Smith, A. W. (18) 2002/03 Glentoran, Preston NE
Smyth, S. (9) 1947/8 Wolverhampton W, Stoke C
Smyth, W. (4) 1948/9 Distillery
Sonner, D. J. (13) 1997/8 Ipswich T, Sheffield W, Birmingham C, Nottingham F, Peterborough U
Spence, D. (29) 1974/5 Bury, Blackpool, Southend U
Stevenson, A. (3) 1946/7 Everton
Stewart, A. (7) 1966/7 Glentoran, Derby
Stewart, D. (1) 1977/8 Hull C
Stewart, I. (31) 1981/2 QPR, Newcastle U
Stewart, T. (1) 1960/1 Linfield

Taggart, G. P. (51) 1989/90 Barnsley, Bolton W, Leicester C
Taylor, M. S. (45) 1998/9 Fulham, Birmingham C
Todd, S. (11) 1965/6 Burnley, Sheffield W
Toner, C. (2) 2002/03 Leyton Orient
Trainor, D. (1) 1966/7 Crusaders
Tully, C. (10) 1948/9 Celtic

Uprichard, N. (18) 1951/2 Swindon T, Portsmouth

Vernon, J. (17) 1946/7 Belfast Celtic, WBA

Walker, J. (1) 1954/5 Doncaster R
Walsh, D. (9) 1946/7 WBA
Walsh, W. (5) 1947/8 Manchester C
Watson, P. (1) 1970/1 Distillery
Welsh, S. (4) 1965/6 Carlisle U
Whiteside, N. (38) 1981/2 Manchester U, Everton
Whitley, Jeff (19) 1996/7 Manchester C, Sunderland
Whitley, Jim (3) 1997/8 Manchester C
Williams, M. S. (36) 1998/9 Chesterfield, Watford, Wimbledon, Stoke C, Wimbledon, Milton Keynes D
Williams, P. (1) 1990/1 WBA
Wilson, D. J. (24) 1986/7 Brighton & HA, Luton, Sheffield W
Wilson, K. J. (42) 1986/7 Ipswich T, Chelsea, Notts C, Walsall
Wilson, S. (12) 1961/2 Glenavon, Falkirk, Dundee
Wood, T. J. (1) 1995/6 Walsall
Worthington, N. (66) 1983/4 Sheffield W, Leeds U, Stoke C
Wright, T. J. (31) 1988/9 Newcastle U, Nottingham F, Manchester C

SCOTLAND

Aird, J. (4) 1953/4 Burnley
Aitken, G. G. (8) 1948/9 East Fife, Sunderland
Aitken, R. (57) 1979/80 Celtic, Newcastle U, St Mirren
Albiston, A. (14) 1981/2 Manchester U
Alexander, G. (16) 2001/02 Preston NE
Allan, T. (2) 1973/4 Dundee
Anderson, J. (1) 1953/4 Leicester C
Anderson, R. (6) 2002/03 Aberdeen
Archibald, S. (27) 1979/80 Aberdeen, Tottenham H, Barcelona
Auld, B. (3) 1958/9 Celtic

Baird, H. (1) 1955/6 Airdrieonians
Baird, S. (7) 1956/7 Rangers
Bannon, E. (11) 1979/80 Dundee U
Bauld, W. (3) 1949/50 Heart of Midlothian
Baxter, J. (34) 1960/1 Rangers, Sunderland
Bell, W. (2) 1965/6 Leeds U
Bernard, P. R. (2) 1994/5 Oldham Ath
Bett, J. (25) 1981/2 Rangers, Lokeren, Aberdeen
Black, E. (2) 1987/8 Metz
Black, I. (1) 1947/8 Southampton
Blacklaw, A. (3) 1962/3 Burnley
Blackley, J. (7) 1973/4 Hibernian
Blair, J. (1) 1946/7 Blackpool
Blyth, J. (2) 1977/8 Coventry C
Bone, J. (2) 1971/2 Norwich C
Booth, S. (21) 1992/3 Aberdeen, Borussia Dortmund, Twente

Bowman, D. (6) 1991/2 Dundee U
Boyd, T. (72) 1990/1 Motherwell, Chelsea, Celtic
Brand, R. (8) 1960/1 Rangers
Brazil, A. (13) 1979/80 Ipswich T, Tottenham H
Bremner, D. (1) 1975/6 Hibernian
Bremner, W. (54) 1964/5 Leeds U
Brennan, F. (7) 1946/7 Newcastle U
Brogan, J. (4) 1970/1 Celtic
Brown, A. (14) 1949/50 East Fife, Blackpool
Brown, H. (3) 1946/7 Partick Thistle
Brown, J. (1) 1974/5 Sheffield U
Brown, R. (3) 1946/7 Rangers
Brown, W. (28) 1957/8 Dundee, Tottenham H
Brownlie, J. (7) 1970/1 Hibernian
Buchan, M. (34) 1971/2 Aberdeen, Manchester U
Buckley, P. (3) 1953/4 Aberdeen
Burchill, M. J. (6) 1999/00 Celtic
Burley, C. W. (46) 1994/5 Chelsea, Celtic, Derby Co
Burley, G. (11) 1978/9 Ipswich T
Burns, F. (1) 1969/70 Manchester U
Burns, K. (20) 1973/4 Birmingham C, Nottingham F
Burns, T. (8) 1980/1 Celtic

Calderwood, C. (36) 1994/5 Tottenham H, Aston Villa
Caldow, E. (40) 1956/7 Rangers
Caldwell, G. (14) 2001/02 Newcastle U, Hibernian
Caldwell, S. (6) 2000/01 Newcastle U, Sunderland
Callaghan, W. (2) 1969/70 Dunfermline
Cameron, C. (28) 1998/9 Heart of Midlothian, Wolverhampton W
Campbell, R. (5) 1946/7 Falkirk, Chelsea
Campbell, W. (5) 1946/7 Morton
Canero, P. (1) 2003/04 Leicester C
Carr, W. (6) 1969/70 Coventry C
Chalmers, S. (5) 1964/5 Celtic
Clark, J. (4) 1965/6 Celtic
Clark, R. (17) 1967/8 Aberdeen
Clarke, S. (6) 1987/8 Chelsea
Collins, J. (58) 1987/8 Hibernian, Celtic, Monaco, Everton
Collins, R. (31) 1950/1 Celtic, Everton, Leeds U
Colquhoun, E. (9) 1971/2 Sheffield U
Colquhoun, J. (2) 1987/8 Heart of Midlothian
Combe, R. (3) 1947/8 Hibernian
Conn, A. (1) 1955/6 Heart of Midlothian
Conn, A. (2) 1974/5 Tottenham H
Connachan, E. (2) 1961/2 Dunfermline Ath
Connelly, G. (2) 1973/4 Celtic
Connolly, J. (1) 1972/3 Everton
Connor, R. (4) 1985/6 Dundee, Aberdeen
Cooke, C. (16) 1965/6 Dundee, Chelsea
Cooper, D. (22) 1979/80 Rangers, Motherwell
Cormack, P. (9) 1965/6 Hibernian, Nottingham F
Cowan, J. (25) 1947/8 Morton
Cowie, D. (20) 1952/3 Dundee
Cox, C. (1) 1947/8 Heart of Midlothian
Cox, S. (24) 1947/8 Rangers
Craig, J. (1) 1976/7 Celtic
Craig, J. P. (1) 1967/8 Celtic
Craig, T. (1) 1975/6 Newcastle U
Crainey, S. (6) 2001/02 Celtic, Southampton
Crawford, S. (25) 1994/5 Raith R, Dunfermline Ath, Plymouth Arg
Crerand, P. (16) 1960/1 Celtic, Manchester U
Cropley, A. (2) 1971/2 Hibernian
Cruickshank, J. (6) 1963/4 Heart of Midlothian
Cullen, M. (1) 1955/6 Luton T
Cumming, J. (9) 1954/5 Heart of Midlothian
Cummings. W. (1) 2001/02 Chelsea
Cunningham, W. (8) 1953/4 Preston NE
Curran, H. (5) 1969/70 Wolverhampton W

Dailly, C. (55) 1996/7 Derby Co, Blackburn R, West Ham U
Dalglish, K. (102) 1971/2 Celtic, Liverpool
Davidson, C. I. (17) 1998/9 Blackburn R, Leicester C
Davidson, J. (8) 1953/4 Partick Thistle
Dawson, A. (5) 1979/80 Rangers
Deans, D. (2) 1974/5 Celtic
Delaney, J. (4) 1946/7 Manchester U
Devlin, P. J. (10) 2002/03 Birmingham C
Dick, J. (1) 1958/9 West Ham U
Dickov, P. (10) 2000/01 Mancheser C, Leicester C, Blackburn R
Dickson, W. (5) 1969/70 Kilmarnock
Dobie, R. S. (6) 2001/02 WBA
Docherty, T. (25) 1951/2 Preston NE, Arsenal
Dodds, D. (2) 1983/4 Dundee U
Dodds, W. (26) 1996/7 Aberdeen, Dundee U, Rangers

Donachie, W. (35) 1971/2 Manchester C
Donnelly, S. (10) 1996/7 Celtic
Dougall, C. (1) 1946/7 Birmingham C
Dougan, R. (1) 1949/50 Heart of Midlothian
Douglas, R. (18) 2001/02 Celtic
Doyle, J. (1) 1975/6 Ayr U
Duncan, A. (6) 1974/5 Hibernian
Duncan, D. (3) 1947/8 East Fife
Duncanson, J. (1) 1946/7 Rangers
Durie, G. S. (43) 1987/8 Chelsea, Tottenham H, Rangers
Durrant, I. (20) 1987/8 Rangers, Kilmarnock

Elliott, M. S. (18) 1997/8 Leicester C
Evans, A. (4) 1981/2 Aston Villa
Evans, R. (48) 1948/9 Celtic, Chelsea
Ewing, T. (2) 1957/8 Partick Thistle

Farm, G. (10) 1952/3 Blackpool
Ferguson, B. (29) 1998/9 Rangers, Blackburn R, Rangers
Ferguson, Derek (2) 1987/8 Rangers
Ferguson, Duncan (7) 1991/2 Dundee U, Everton
Ferguson, I. (9) 1988/9 Rangers
Ferguson, R. (7) 1965/6 Kilmarnock
Fernie, W. (12) 1953/4 Celtic
Flavell, R. (2) 1946/7 Airdrieonians
Fleck, R. (4) 1989/90 Norwich C
Fleming, C. (1) 1953/4 East Fife
Fletcher, D. B. (15) 2003/04 Manchester U
Forbes, A. (14) 1946/7 Sheffield U, Arsenal
Ford, D. (3) 1973/4 Heart of Midlothian
Forrest, J. (1) 1957/8 Motherwell
Forrest, J. (5) 1965/6 Rangers, Aberdeen
Forsyth, A. (10) 1971/2 Partick Thistle, Manchester U
Forsyth, C. (4) 1963/4 Kilmarnock
Forsyth, T. (22) 1970/1 Motherwell, Rangers
Fraser, D. (2) 1967/8 WBA
Fraser, W. (2) 1954/5 Sunderland
Freedman, D. A. (2) 2001/02 Crystal P

Gabriel, J. (2) 1960/1 Everton
Gallacher, K. W. (53) 1987/8 Dundee U, Coventry C, Blackburn R, Newcastle U
Gallacher, P. (8) 2001/02 Dundee U
Gallagher, P. (1) 2003/04 Blackburn R
Galloway, M. (1) 1991/2 Celtic
Gardiner, W. (1) 1957/8 Motherwell
Gemmell, T. (2) 1954/5 St Mirren
Gemmell, T. (18) 1965/6 Celtic
Gemmill, A. (43) 1970/1 Derby Co, Nottingham F, Birmingham C
Gemmill, S. (26) 1994/5 Nottingham F, Everton
Gibson, D. (7) 1962/3 Leicester C
Gillespie, G. T. (13) 1987/8 Liverpool
Gilzean, A. (22) 1963/4 Dundee, Tottenham H
Glass, S. (1) 1998/9 Newcastle U
Glavin, R. (1) 1976/7 Celtic
Glen, A. (2) 1955/6 Aberdeen
Goram, A. L. (43) 1985/6 Oldham Ath, Hibernian, Rangers
Gordon, C. S. (8) 2003/04 Heart of Midlothian
Gough, C. R. (61) 1982/3 Dundee U, Tottenham H, Rangers
Gould, J. (2) 1999/00 Celtic
Govan, J. (6) 1947/8 Hibernian
Graham, A. (10) 1977/8 Leeds U
Graham, G. (12) 1971/2 Arsenal, Manchester U
Grant, J. (2) 1958/9 Hibernian
Grant, P. (2) 1988/9 Celtic
Gray, A. (20) 1975/6 Aston Villa, Wolverhampton W, Everton
Gray, A. D. (2) 2002/03 Bradford C
Gray, E. (12) 1968/9 Leeds U
Gray F. (32) 1975/6 Leeds U, Nottingham F, Leeds U
Green, A. (6) 1970/1 Blackpool, Newcastle U
Greig, J. (44) 1963/4 Rangers
Gunn, B. (6) 1989/90 Norwich C

Haddock, H. (6) 1954/5 Clyde
Haffey, F. (2) 1959/60 Celtic
Hamilton, A. (24) 1961/2 Dundee
Hamilton, G. (5) 1946/7 Aberdeen
Hamilton, W. (1) 1964/5 Hibernian
Hammell, S. (1) 2004/05 Motherwell
Hansen, A. (26) 1978/9 Liverpool
Hansen, J. (2) 1971/2 Partick Thistle
Harper, J. (4) 1972/3 Aberdeen, Hibernian, Aberdeen
Hartford, A. (50) 1971/2 WBA, Manchester C, Everton, Manchester C
Hartley, P.J. (2) 2004/05 Heart of Midlothian
Harvey, D. (16) 1972/3 Leeds U
Haughney, M. (1) 1953/4 Celtic
Hay, D. (27) 1969/70 Celtic
Hegarty, P. (8) 1978/9 Dundee U
Henderson, J. (7) 1952/3 Portsmouth, Arsenal
Henderson, W. (29) 1962/3 Rangers
Hendry, E. C. J. (51) 1992/3 Blackburn R, Rangers, Coventry C, Bolton W

Herd, D. (5) 1958/9 Arsenal
Herd, G. (5) 1957/8 Clyde
Herriot, J. (8) 1968/9 Birmingham C
Hewie, J. (19) 1955/6 Charlton Ath
Holt, D. D. (5) 1962/3 Heart of Midlothian
Holt, G. J. (10) 2000/01 Kilmarnock, Norwich C
Holton, J. (15) 1972/3 Manchester U
Hope, R. (2) 1967/8 WBA
Hopkin, D. (7) 1996/7 Crystal P, Leeds U
Houliston, W. (3) 1948/9 Queen of the South
Houston, S. (1) 1975/6 Manchester U
Howie, H. (1) 1948/9 Hibernian
Hughes, J. (8) 1964/5 Celtic
Hughes, R. D. (4) 2003/04 Portsmouth
Hughes, W. (1) 1974/5 Sunderland
Humphries, W. (1) 1951/2 Motherwell
Hunter, A. (4) 1971/2 Kilmarnock, Celtic
Hunter, W. (3) 1959/60 Motherwell
Husband, J. (1) 1946/7 Partick Thistle
Hutchison, D. (26) 1998/9 Everton, Sunderland, West Ham U
Hutchison, T. (17) 1973/4 Coventry C

Imlach, S. (4) 1957/8 Nottingham F
Irvine, B. (9) 1990/1 Aberdeen

Jackson, C. (8) 1974/5 Rangers
Jackson, D. (28) 1994/5 Hibernian, Celtic
Jardine, A. (38) 1970/1 Rangers
Jarvie, A. (3) 1970/1 Airdrieonians
Jess, E. (18) 1992/3 Aberdeen, Coventry C, Aberdeen
Johnston, A. (18) 1998/9 Sunderland, Rangers, Middlesbrough
Johnston, M. (38) 1983/4 Watford, Celtic, Nantes, Rangers
Johnston, L. (2) 1947/8 Clyde
Johnston, W. (22) 1965/6 Rangers, WBA
Johnstone, D. (14) 1972/3 Rangers
Johnstone, J. (23) 1964/5 Celtic
Johnstone, R. (17) 1950/1 Hibernian, Manchester C
Jordan, J. (52) 1972/3 Leeds U, Manchester U, AC Milan

Kelly, H. (1) 1951/2 Blackpool
Kelly, J. (2) 1948/9 Barnsley
Kennedy, Jim (6) 1963/4 Celtic
Kennedy, John (1) 2003/04 Celtic
Kennedy, S. (5) 1974/5 Rangers
Kennedy, S. (8) 1977/8 Aberdeen
Kerr, A. (2) 1954/5 Partick Thistle
Kerr, B. (3) 2002/03 Newcastle U
Kyle, K. (9) 2001/02 Sunderland

Lambert, P. (40) 1994/5 Motherwell, Borussia Dortmund, Celtic
Law, D. (55) 1958/9 Huddersfield T, Manchester C, Torino, Manchester U, Manchester C
Lawrence, T. (3) 1962/3 Liverpool
Leggat, G. (18) 1955/6 Aberdeen, Fulham
Leighton, J. (91) 1982/3 Aberdeen, Manchester U, Hibernian, Aberdeen
Lennox, R. (10) 1966/7 Celtic
Leslie, L. (5) 1960/1 Airdrieonians
Levein, C. (16) 1989/90 Heart of Midlothian
Liddell, W. (28) 1946/7 Liverpool
Linwood, A. (1) 1949/50 Clyde
Little, R. J. (1) 1952/3 Rangers
Logie, J. (1) 1952/3 Arsenal
Long, H. (1) 1946/7 Clyde
Lorimer, P. (21) 1969/70 Leeds U

Macari, L. (24) 1971/2 Celtic, Manchester U
Macaulay, A. (7) 1946/7 Brentford, Arsenal
MacDougall, E. (7) 1974/5 Norwich C
Mackay, D. (22) 1956/7 Heart of Midlothian, Tottenham H
Mackay, G. (4) 1987/8 Heart of Midlothian
Mackay, M. (5) 2003/04 Norwich C
Malpas, M. (55) 1983/4 Dundee U
Marshall, D. J. (2) 2004/05 Celtic
Marshall, G. (1) 1991/2 Celtic
Martin, B. (2) 1994/5 Motherwell
Martin, F. (6) 1953/4 Aberdeen
Martin, N. (3) 1964/5 Hibernian, Sunderland
Martis, J. (1) 1960/1 Motherwell
Mason, J. (7) 1948/9 Third Lanark
Masson, D. (17) 1975/6 QPR, Derby C
Mathers, D. (1) 1953/4 Partick Thistle
Matteo, D. (6) 2000/01 Leeds U
McAllister, B. (3) 1996/7 Wimbledon
McAllister, G. (57) 1989/90 Leicester C, Leeds U, Coventry C
McAllister, J. R. (1) 2003/04 Livingston
McAvennie, F. (5) 1985/6 West Ham U, Celtic
McBride, J. (2) 1966/7 Celtic
McCall, S. M. (40) 1989/90 Everton, Rangers
McCalliog, J. (5) 1966/7 Sheffield W, Wolverhampton W
McCann, N. D. (23) 1998/9 Heart of Midlothian, Rangers, Southampton
McCann, R. (5) 1958/9 Motherwell

McClair, B. (30) 1986/7 Celtic, Manchester U
McCloy, P. (4) 1972/3 Rangers
McCoist, A. (61) 1985/6 Rangers, Kilmarnock
McColl, I. (14) 1949/50 Rangers
McCreadie, E. (23) 1964/5 Chelsea
McCulloch, L. (4) 2004/05 Wigan Ath
MacDonald, A. (1) 1975/6 Rangers
McDonald, J. (2) 1955/6 Sunderland
McFadden, J. (21) 2001/02 Motherwell, Everton
McFarlane, W. (1) 1946/7 Heart of Midlothian
McGarr, E. (2) 1969/70 Aberdeen
McGarvey, F. (7) 1978/9 Liverpool, Celtic
McGhee, M. (4) 1982/3 Aberdeen
McGinlay, J. (13) 1993/4 Bolton W
McGrain, D. (62) 1972/3 Celtic
McGrory, J. (3) 1964/5 Kilmarnock
McInally, A. (8) 1988/9 Aston Villa, Bayern Munich
McInally, J. (10) 1986/7 Dundee U
McInnes, D. (2) 2002/03 WBA
MacKay, D. (14) 1958/9 Celtic
McKean, R. (1) 1975/6 Rangers
MacKenzie, J. (9) 1953/4 Partick Thistle
McKimmie, S. (40) 1988/9 Aberdeen
McKinlay, T. (22) 1995/6 Celtic
McKinlay, W. (29) 1993/4 Dundee U, Blackburn R
McKinnon, Rob (3) 1993/4 Motherwell
McKinnon, Ronnie (28) 1965/6 Rangers
McLaren, Alan (24) 1991/2 Heart of Midlothian, Rangers
McLaren, Andy (4) 1946/7 Preston NE
McLaren, Andy (1) 2000/01 Kilmarnock
McLean, G. (1) 1967/8 Dundee
McLean, T. (6) 1968/9 Kilmarnock
McLeish, A. (77) 1979/80 Aberdeen
McLeod, J. (4) 1960/1 Hibernian
MacLeod, M. (20) 1984/5 Celtic, Borussia Dortmund, Hibernian
McLintock, F. (9) 1962/3 Leicester C, Arsenal
McMillan, I. (6) 1951/2 Airdrieonians, Rangers
McNamara, J. (30) 1996/7 Celtic
McNamee, D. (2) 2003/04 Livingston
McNaught, W. (5) 1950/1 Raith R
McNaughton, K. (3) 2001/02 Aberdeen
McNeill, W. (29) 1960/1 Celtic
McPhail, J. (5) 1949/50 Celtic
McPherson, D. (27) 1988/9 Heart of Midlothian, Rangers
McQueen, G. (30) 1973/4 Leeds U, Manchester U
McStay, P. (76) 1983/4 Celtic
McSwegan, G. (2) 1999/00 Heart of Midlothian
Millar, J. (2) 1962/3 Rangers
Miller, C. (1) 2000/01 Dundee U
Miller, K. (20) 2000/01 Rangers, Wolverhampton W
Miller, W. (6) 1946/7 Celtic
Miller, W. (65) 1974/5 Aberdeen
Mitchell, R. (2) 1950/1 Newcastle U
Mochan, N. (3) 1953/4 Celtic
Moir, W. (1) 1949/50 Bolton W
Moncur, R. (16) 1967/8 Newcastle U
Morgan, W. (21) 1967/8 Burnley, Manchester U
Morris, H. (1) 1949/50 East Fife
Mudie, J. (17) 1956/7 Blackpool
Mulhall, G. (3) 1959/60 Aberdeen, Sunderland
Munro, F. (9) 1970/1 Wolverhampton W
Munro, I. (7) 1978/9 St Mirren
Murdoch, R. (12) 1965/6 Celtic
Murray, I. (3) 2002/03 Hibernian
Murray, J. (5) 1957/8 Heart of Midlothian
Murray, S. (1) 1971/2 Aberdeen
Murty, G. S. (1) 2003/04 Reading

Narey, D. (35) 1976/7 Dundee U
Naysmith, G. A. (28) 1999/00 Heart of Midlothian, Everton
Nevin, P. K. F. (28) 1985/6 Chelsea, Everton, Tranmere R
Nicholas, C. (20) 1982/3 Celtic, Arsenal, Aberdeen
Nicholson, B. (3) 2000/01 Dunfermline Ath
Nicol, S. (27) 1984/5 Liverpool

O'Connor, G. (4) 2001/02 Hibernian
O'Donnell, P. (1) 1993/4 Motherwell
O'Hare, J. (13) 1969/70 Derby Co
O'Neil, B. (6) 1995/6 Celtic, Wolfsburg, Derby Co
O'Neil, J. (1) 2000/01 Hibernian
Ormond, W. (6) 1953/4 Hibernian
Orr, T. (2) 1951/2 Morton

Parker, A. (15) 1954/5 Falkirk, Everton
Parlane, D. (12) 1972/3 Rangers
Paton, A. (2) 1951/2 Motherwell
Pearson, S. P. (6) 2003/04 Motherwell, Celtic
Pearson, T. (2) 1946/7 Newcastle U
Penman, A. (1) 1965/6 Dundee
Pettigrew, W. (5) 1975/6 Motherwell
Plenderleith, J. (1) 1960/1 Manchester C

Pressley, S. J. (23) 1999/00 Heart of Midlothian
Provan, David (10) 1979/80 Celtic
Provan, Davie (5) 1963/4 Rangers

Quashie, N. F. (7) 2003/04 Portsmouth, Southampton
Quinn, P. (4) 1960/1 Motherwell

Rae, G. (9) 2000/01 Dundee, Rangers
Redpath, W. (9) 1948/9 Motherwell
Reilly, L. (38) 1948/9 Hibernian
Ring, T. (12) 1952/3 Clyde
Rioch, B. (24) 1974/5 Derby Co, Everton, Derby Co
Ritchie, P. S. (7) 1998/9 Heart of Midlothian, Bolton W, Walsall
Ritchie, W. (1) 1961/2 Rangers
Robb, D. (5) 1970/1 Aberdeen
Robertson, A. (5) 1954/5 Clyde
Robertson, D. (3) 1991/2 Rangers
Robertson, H. (1) 1961/2 Dundee
Robertson, J. (16) 1990/1 Heart of Midlothian
Robertson, J. G. (1) 1964/5 Tottenham H
Robertson, J. N. (28) 1977/8 Nottingham F, Derby Co
Robinson, B. (4) 1973/4 Dundee
Ross, M. (13) 2001/02 Rangers
Rough, A. (53) 1975/6 Partick Thistle, Hibernian
Rougvie, D. (1) 1983/4 Aberdeen
Rutherford, E. (1) 1947/8 Rangers

St John, I. (21) 1958/9 Motherwell, Liverpool
Schaedler, E. (1) 1973/4 Hibernian
Scott, A. (16) 1956/7 Rangers, Everton
Scott, Jimmy (1) 1965/6 Hibernian
Scott, Jocky (2) 1970/1 Dundee
Scoular, J. (9) 1950/1 Portsmouth
Severin, S. D. (10) 2001/02 Heart of Midlothian, Aberdeen
Sharp, G. M. (12) 1984/5 Everton
Shaw, D. (8) 1946/7 Hibernian
Shaw, J. (4) 1946/7 Rangers
Shearer, D. (7) 1993/4 Aberdeen
Shearer, R. (4) 1960/1 Rangers
Simpson, N. (4) 1982/3 Aberdeen
Simpson, R. (5) 1966/7 Celtic
Sinclair, J. (1) 1965/6 Leicester C
Smith, D. (2) 1965/6 Aberdeen, Rangers
Smith, E. (2) 1958/9 Celtic
Smith, G. (18) 1946/7 Hibernian
Smith, H. G. (3) 1987/8 Heart of Midlothian
Smith, J. (4) 1967/8 Aberdeen, Newcastle U
Smith, J. (2) 2002/03 Celtic
Souness, G. (54) 1974/5 Middlesbrough, Liverpool, Sampdoria
Speedie, D. R. (10) 1984/5 Chelsea, Coventry C
Spencer, J. (14) 1994/5 Chelsea, QPR
Stanton, P. (16) 1965/6 Hibernian
Steel, W. (30) 1946/7 Morton, Derby C, Dundee
Stein, C. (21) 1968/9 Rangers, Coventry C
Stephen, J. (2) 1946/7 Bradford PA
Stewart, D. (1) 1977/8 Leeds U
Stewart, J. (2) 1976/7 Kilmarnock, Middlesbrough
Stewart, M. J. (3) 2001/02 Manchester U
Stewart, R. (10) 1980/1 West Ham U
Stockdale, R. K. (5) 2001/02 Middlesbrough
Strachan, G. (50) 1979/80 Aberdeen, Manchester U, Leeds U
Sturrock, P. (20) 1980/1 Dundee U
Sullivan, N. (28) 1996/7 Wimbledon, Tottenham H

Telfer, P. N. (1) 1999/00 Coventry C
Telfer, W. (1) 1953/4 St Mirren
Thompson, S. (16) 2001/02 Dundee U, Rangers
Thomson, W. (7) 1979/80 St Mirren
Thornton, W. (7) 1946/7 Rangers
Toner, W. (2) 1958/9 Kilmarnock
Turnbull, E. (8) 1947/8 Hibernian

Ure, I. (11) 1961/2 Dundee, Arsenal

Waddell, W. (17) 1946/7 Rangers
Walker, A. (3) 1987/8 Celtic
Walker, J. N. (2) 1992/3 Heart of Midlothian, Partick Thistle
Wallace, I. A. (3) 1977/8 Coventry C
Wallace, W. S. B. (7) 1964/5 Heart of Midlothian, Celtic
Wardhaugh, J. (2) 1954/5 Heart of Midlothian
Wark, J. (29) 1978/9 Ipswich T, Liverpool
Watson, J. (2) 1947/8 Motherwell, Huddersfield T
Watson, R. (1) 1970/1 Motherwell
Webster, A. (16) 2002/03 Heart of Midlothian
Weir, A. (6) 1958/9 Motherwell
Weir, D. G. (40) 1996/7 Heart of Midlothian, Everton
Weir, P. (6) 1979/80 St Mirren, Aberdeen
White, J. (22) 1958/9 Falkirk, Tottenham H
Whyte, D. (12) 1987/8 Celtic, Middlesbrough, Aberdeen

Wilkie, L. (11) 2001/02 Dundee
Williams, G. (5) 2001/02 Nottingham F
Wilson, A. (1) 1953/4 Portsmouth
Wilson, D. (22) 1960/1 Rangers
Wilson, I. A. (5) 1986/7 Leicester C, Everton
Wilson, P. (1) 1974/5 Celtic
Wilson, R. (2) 1971/2 Arsenal
Winters, R. (1) 1998/9 Aberdeen
Wood, G. (4) 1978/9 Everton, Arsenal
Woodburn, W. (24) 1946/7 Rangers
Wright, K. (1) 1991/2 Hibernian
Wright, S. (2) 1992/3 Aberdeen
Wright, T. (3) 1952/3 Sunderland

Yeats, R. (2) 1964/5 Liverpool
Yorston, H. (1) 1954/5 Aberdeen
Young, A. (8) 1959/60 Heart of Midlothian, Everton
Young, G. (53) 1946/7 Rangers
Younger, T. (24) 1954/5 Hibernian, Liverpool

WALES

Aizlewood, M. (39) 1985/6 Charlton Ath, Leeds U, Bradford C, Bristol C, Cardiff C
Allchurch, I. (68) 1950/1 Swansea T, Newcastle U, Cardiff C, Swansea T
Allchurch, L. (11) 1954/5 Swansea T, Sheffield U
Allen, B. (2) 1950/1 Coventry C
Allen, M. (14) 1985/6 Watford, Norwich C, Millwall, Newcastle U

Baker, C. (7) 1957/8 Cardiff C
Baker, W. (1) 1947/8 Cardiff C
Barnard, D. S. (22) 1997/8 Barnsley, Grimsby T
Barnes, W. (22) 1947/8 Arsenal
Bellamy, C. D. (33) 1997/8 Norwich C, Coventry C, Newcastle U
Berry, G. (5) 1978/9 Wolverhampton W, Stoke C
Blackmore, C. G. (39) 1984/5 Manchester U, Middlesbrough
Blake, N. (29) 1993/4 Sheffield U, Bolton W, Blackburn R, Wolverhampton W
Bodin, P. J. (23) 1989/90 Swindon T, Crystal P, Swindon T
Bowen, D. (19) 1954/5 Arsenal
Bowen, J. P. (2) 1993/4 Swansea C, Birmingham C
Bowen, M. R. (41) 1985/6 Tottenham H, Norwich C, West Ham U
Boyle, T. (2) 1980/1 Crystal P
Browning, M. T. (5) 1995/6 Bristol R, Huddersfield T
Burgess, R. (32) 1946/7 Tottenham H
Burton, O. (9) 1962/3 Norwich C, Newcastle U

Cartwright, L. (7) 1973/4 Coventry C, Wrexham
Charles, J. (38) 1949/50 Leeds U, Juventus, Leeds U, Cardiff C
Charles, J. M. (19) 1980/1 Swansea C, QPR, Oxford U
Charles, M. (31) 1954/5 Swansea T, Arsenal, Cardiff C
Clarke, R. (22) 1948/9 Manchester C
Coleman, C. (32) 1991/2 Crystal P, Blackburn R, Fulham
Collins, D.L. (1) 2004/05 Sunderland
Collins, J. M. (6) 2003/04 Cardiff C
Cornforth, J. M. (2) 1994/5 Swansea C
Coyne, D. (8) 1995/6 Tranmere R, Grimsby T, Leicester C
Crossley, M. G. (8) 1996/7 Nottingham F, Middlesbrough, Fulham
Crowe, V. (16) 1958/9 Aston Villa
Curtis, A. (35) 1975/6 Swansea C, Leeds U, Swansea C, Southampton, Cardiff C

Daniel, R. (21) 1950/1 Arsenal, Sunderland
Davies, A. (13) 1982/3 Manchester U, Newcastle U, Swansea C, Bradford C
Davies, C. (1) 1971/2 Charlton Ath
Davies, D. (52) 1974/5 Everton, Wrexham, Swansea C
Davies, G. (16) 1979/80 Fulham, Manchester C
Davies, R. Wyn (34) 1963/4 Bolton W, Newcastle U, Manchester C, Manchester U, Blackpool
Davies, Reg (6) 1952/3 Newcastle U
Davies, Ron (29) 1963/4 Norwich C, Southampton, Portsmouth
Davies, S. (24) 2000/01 Tottenham H
Davies, S. I. (1) 1995/6 Manchester U
Davis, G. (3) 1977/8 Wrexham
Deacy, N. (12) 1976/7 PSV Eindhoven, Beringen
Delaney, M. A. (33) 1999/00 Aston Villa
Derrett, S. (4) 1968/9 Cardiff C
Dibble, A. (3) 1985/6 Luton T, Manchester C
Durban, A. (27) 1965/6 Derby C
Dwyer, P. (10) 1977/8 Cardiff C

Earnshaw, R. (19) 2001/02 Cardiff C, WBA
Edwards, C. N. H. (1) 1995/6 Swansea C
Edwards, G. (12) 1946/7 Birmingham C, Cardiff C
Edwards, I. (4) 1977/8 Chester, Wrexham
Edwards, R. O. (7) 2002/03 Aston Villa, Wolverhampton W
Edwards, R. W. (4) 1997/8 Bristol C
Edwards, T. (2) 1956/7 Charlton Ath
Emanuel, J. (2) 1972/3 Bristol C
England, M. (44) 1961/2 Blackburn R, Tottenham H
Evans, B. (7) 1971/2 Swansea C, Hereford U
Evans, I. (13) 1975/6 Crystal P
Evans, P. S. (2) 2001/02 Brentford, Bradford C
Evans, R. (1) 1963/4 Swansea T

Felgate, D. (1) 1983/4 Lincoln C
Fletcher, C. N. (7) 2003/04 Bournemouth, West Ham U
Flynn, B. (66) 1974/5 Burnley, Leeds U, Burnley
Ford, T. (38) 1946/7 Swansea T, Aston Villa, Sunderland, Cardiff C
Foulkes, W. (11) 1951/2 Newcastle U
Freestone, R. (1) 1999/00 Swansea C

Gabbidon, D. L. (19) 2001/02 Cardiff C
Giggs, R. J. (51) 1991/2 Manchester U
Giles, D. (12) 1979/80 Swansea C, Crystal P
Godfrey, B. (3) 1963/4 Preston NE
Goss, J. (9) 1990/1 Norwich C
Green, C. (15) 1964/5 Birmingham C
Green, R. M. (2) 1997/8 Wolverhampton W
Griffiths, A. (17) 1970/1 Wrexham
Griffiths, H. (1) 1952/3 Swansea T
Griffiths, M. (11) 1946/7 Leicester C

Hall, G. D. (9) 1987/8 Chelsea
Harrington, A. (11) 1955/6 Cardiff C
Harris, C. (24) 1975/6 Leeds U
Harris, W. (6) 1953/4 Middlesbrough
Hartson, J. (46) 1994/5 Arsenal, West Ham U, Wimbledon, Coventry C, Celtic
Haworth, S. O. (5) 1996/7 Cardiff C, Coventry C
Hennessey, T. (39) 1961/2 Birmingham C, Nottingham F, Derby Co
Hewitt, R. (5) 1957/8 Cardiff C
Hill, M. (2) 1971/2 Ipswich T
Hockey, T. (9) 1971/2 Sheffield U, Norwich C, Aston Villa
Hodges, G. (18) 1983/4 Wimbledon, Newcastle U, Watford, Sheffield U
Holden, A. (1) 1983/4 Chester C
Hole, B. (30) 1962/3 Cardiff C, Blackburn R, Aston Villa, Swansea C
Hollins, D. (11) 1961/2 Newcastle U
Hopkins, J. (16) 1982/3 Fulham, Crystal P
Hopkins, M. (34) 1955/6 Tottenham H
Horne, B. (59) 1987/8 Portsmouth, Southampton, Everton, Birmingham C
Howells, R. (2) 1953/4 Cardiff C
Hughes, C. M. (8) 1991/2 Luton T, Wimbledon
Hughes, I. (4) 1950/1 Luton T
Hughes, L. M. (72) 1983/4 Manchester U, Barcelona, Manchester U, Chelsea, Southampton
Hughes, W. (3) 1946/7 Birmingham C
Hughes, W. A. (5) 1948/9 Blackburn R
Humphreys, J. (1) 1946/7 Everton

Jackett, K. (31) 1982/3 Watford
James, G. (9) 1965/6 Blackpool
James, L. (54) 1971/2 Burnley, Derby C, QPR, Burnley, Swansea C, Sunderland
James, R. M. (47) 1978/9 Swansea C, Stoke C, QPR, Leicester C, Swansea C
Jarvis, A. (3) 1966/7 Hull C
Jenkins, S. R. (16) 1995/6 Swansea C, Huddersfield T
Johnson, A. J. (15) 1998/9 Nottingham F, WBA
Johnson, M. (1) 1963/4 Swansea T
Jones, A. (6) 1986/7 Port Vale, Charlton Ath
Jones, Barrie (15) 1962/3 Swansea T, Plymouth Argyle, Cardiff C
Jones, Bryn (4) 1946/7 Arsenal
Jones, C. (59) 1953/4 Swansea T, Tottenham H, Fulham
Jones, D. (8) 1975/6 Norwich C
Jones, E. (4) 1947/8 Swansea T, Tottenham H
Jones, J. (72) 1975/6 Liverpool, Wrexham, Chelsea, Huddersfield T
Jones, K. (1) 1949/50 Aston Villa
Jones, M. G. (13) 1999/00 Leeds U, Leicester C
Jones, P. L. (2) 1996/7 Liverpool, Tranmere R
Jones, P. S. (43) 1996/7 Stockport Co, Southampton, Wolverhampton W
Jones, R. (1) 1993/4 Sheffield W
Jones, T. G. (13) 1946/7 Everton

Jones, V. P. (9) 1994/5 Wimbledon
Jones, W. (1) 1970/1 Bristol R

Kelsey, J. (41) 1953/4 Arsenal
King, J. (1) 1954/5 Swansea T
Kinsey, N. (7) 1950/1 Norwich C, Birmingham C
Knill, A. R. (1) 1988/9 Swansea C
Koumas, J. (14) 2000/01 Tranmere R, WBA
Krzywicki, R. (8) 1969/70 WBA, Huddersfield T

Lambert, R. (5) 1946/7 Liverpool
Law, B. J. (1) 1989/90 QPR
Lea, C. (2) 1964/5 Ipswich T
Leek, K. (13) 1960/1 Leicester C, Newcastle U, Birmingham C, Northampton T
Legg, A. (6) 1995/6 Birmingham C, Cardiff C
Lever, A. (1) 1952/3 Leicester C
Lewis, D. (1) 1982/3 Swansea C
Llewellyn, C. M. (4) 1997/8 Norwich C, Wrexham
Lloyd, B. (3) 1975/6 Wrexham
Lovell, S. (6) 1981/2 Crystal P, Millwall
Lowndes, S. (10) 1982/3 Newport Co, Millwall, Barnsley
Lowrie, G. (4) 1947/8 Coventry C, Newcastle U
Lucas, M. (4) 1961/2 Leyton Orient
Lucas, W. (7) 1948/9 Swansea T

Maguire, G. T. (7) 1989/90 Portsmouth
Mahoney, J. (51) 1967/8 Stoke C, Middlesbrough, Swansea C
Mardon, P. J. (1) 1995/6 WBA
Margetson, M. W. (1) 2003/04 Cardiff C
Marriott, A. (5) 1995/6 Wrexham
Marustik, C. (6) 1981/2 Swansea C
Medwin, T. (30) 1952/3 Swansea T, Tottenham H
Melville, A. K. (65) 1989/90 Swansea C, Oxford U, Sunderland, Fulham, West Ham U
Mielczarek, R. (1) 1970/1 Rotherham U
Millington, A. (21) 1962/3 WBA, Crystal P, Peterborough U, Swansea C
Moore, G. (21) 1959/60 Cardiff C, Chelsea, Manchester U, Northampton T, Charlton Ath
Morris, W. (5) 1946/7 Burnley

Nardiello, D. (2) 1977/8 Coventry C
Neilson, A. B. (5) 1991/2 Newcastle U, Southampton
Nicholas, P. (73) 1978/9 Crystal P, Arsenal, Crystal P, Luton T, Aberdeen, Chelsea, Watford
Niedzwiecki, E. A. (2) 1984/5 Chelsea
Nogan, L. M. (2) 1991/2 Watford, Reading
Norman, A. J. (5) 1985/6 Hull C
Nurse, M. T. G. (12) 1959/60 Swansea T, Middlesbrough

O'Sullivan, P. (3) 1972/3 Brighton & HA
Oster, J. M. (13) 1997/8 Everton, Sunderland

Page, M. (28) 1970/1 Birmingham C
Page, R. J. (38) 1996/7 Watford, Sheffield U, Cardiff C
Palmer, D. (3) 1956/7 Swansea T
Parry, J. (1) 1950/1 Swansea T
Parry, P. I. (5) 2003/04 Cardiff C
Partridge, D. W. (2) 2004/05 Motherwell
Pascoe, C. (10) 1983/4 Swansea C, Sunderland
Paul, R. (33) 1948/9 Swansea T, Manchester C
Pembridge, M. A. (54) 1991/2 Luton T, Derby C, Sheffield W, Benfica, Everton, Fulham
Perry, J. (1) 1993/4 Cardiff C
Phillips, D. (62) 1983/4 Plymouth Argyle, Manchester C, Coventry C, Norwich C, Nottingham F
Phillips, J. (4) 1972/3 Chelsea
Phillips, L. (58) 1970/1 Cardff C, Aston Villa, Swansea C, Charlton Ath
Pipe, D. R. (1) 2002/03 Coventry C
Pontin, K. (2) 1979/80 Cardiff C
Powell, A. (8) 1946/7 Leeds U, Everton, Birmingham C
Powell, D. (11) 1967/8 Wrexham, Sheffield U
Powell, I. (8) 1946/7 QPR, Aston Villa
Price, P. (25) 1979/80 Luton T, Tottenham H
Pring, K. (3) 1965/6 Rotherham U
Pritchard, H. K. (1) 1984/5 Bristol C

Rankmore, F. (l) 1965/6 Peterborough U
Ratcliffe, K. (59) 1980/1 Everton, Cardiff C
Ready, K. (5) 1996/7 QPR
Reece, G. (29) 1965/6 Sheffield U, Cardiff C
Reed, W. (2) 1954/5 Ipswich T
Rees, A. (1) 1983/4 Birmingham C
Rees, J. M. (1) 1991/2 Luton T

Rees, R. (39) 1964/5 Coventry C, WBA, Nottingham F
Rees, W. (4) 1948/9 Cardiff C, Tottenham H
Richards, S. (1) 1946/7 Cardiff C
Ricketts, S. (3) 2004/05 Swansea C
Roberts, A. M. (2) 1992/3 QPR
Roberts, D. (17) 1972/3 Oxford U, Hull C
Roberts, G. W. (8) 1999/00 Tranmere R
Roberts, I. W. (15) 1989/90 Watford, Huddersfield T, Leicester C, Norwich C
Roberts, J. G. (22) 1970/1 Arsenal, Birmingham C
Roberts, J. H. (1) 1948/9 Bolton W
Roberts, N. W. (4) 1999/00 Wrexham, Wigan Ath
Roberts, P. (4) 1973/4 Portsmouth
Roberts, S. W. (1) 2004/05 Wrexham
Robinson, C. P. (22) 1999/00 Wolverhampton W, Portsmouth, Sunderland
Robinson, J. R. C. (30) 1995/6 Charlton Ath
Rodrigues, P. (40) 1964/5 Cardiff C, Leicester C, Sheffield W
Rouse, V. (1) 1958/9 Crystal P
Rowley, T. (1) 1958/9 Tranmere R
Rush, I. (73) 1979/80 Liverpool, Juventus, Liverpool

Saunders, D. (75) 1985/6 Brighton & HA, Oxford U, Derby C, Liverpool, Aston Villa, Galatasaray, Nottingham F, Sheffield U, Benfica, Bradford C
Savage, R. W. (39) 1995/6 Crewe Alexandra, Leicester C, Birmingham C
Sayer, P. (7) 1976/7 Cardiff C
Scrine, F. (2) 1949/50 Swansea T
Sear, C. (1) 1962/3 Manchester C
Sherwood, A. (41) 1946/7 Cardiff C, Newport C
Shortt, W. (12) 1946/7 Plymouth Argyle
Showers, D. (2) 1974/5 Cardiff C
Sidlow, C. (7) 1946/7 Liverpool
Slatter, N. (22) 1982/3 Bristol R, Oxford U
Smallman, D. (7) 1973/4 Wrexham, Everton
Southall, N. (92) 1981/2 Everton
Speed, G. A. (85) 1989/90 Leeds U, Everton, Newcastle U, Bolton W
Sprake, G. (37) 1963/4 Leeds U, Birmingham C
Stansfield, F. (1) 1948/9 Cardiff C
Stevenson, B. (15) 1977/8 Leeds U, Birmingham C
Stevenson, N. (4) 1981/2 Swansea C
Stitfall, R. (2) 1952/3 Cardiff C
Sullivan, D. (17) 1952/3 Cardiff C
Symons, C. J. (37) 1991/2 Portsmouth, Manchester C, Fulham, Crystal P

Tapscott, D. (14) 1953/4 Arsenal, Cardiff C
Taylor, G. K. (15) 1995/6 Crystal P, Sheffield U, Burnley, Nottingham F
Thatcher, B. D. (7) 2003/04 Leicester C, Manchester C
Thomas, D. (2) 1956/7 Swansea T
Thomas, M. (51) 1976/7 Wrexham, Manchester U, Everton, Brighton & HA, Stoke C, Chelsea, WBA
Thomas, M. R. (1) 1986/7 Newcastle U
Thomas, R. (50) 1966/7 Swindon T, Derby C, Cardiff C
Thomas, S. (4) 1947/8 Fulham
Toshack, J. (40) 1968/9 Cardiff C, Liverpool, Swansea C
Trollope, P. J. (9) 1996/7 Derby Co, Fulham, Coventry C, Northampton T

Van Den Hauwe, P. W. R. (13) 1984/5 Everton
Vaughan, D. O. (2) 2002/03 Crewe Alex
Vaughan, N. (10) 1982/3 Newport Co, Cardiff C
Vearncombe, G. (2) 1957/8 Cardiff C
Vernon, R. (32) 1956/7 Blackburn R, Everton, Stoke C.
Villars, A. (3) 1973/4 Cardiff C

Walley, T. (1) 1970/1 Watford
Walsh, I. (18) 1979/80 Crystal P, Swansea C
Ward, D. (2) 1958/9 Bristol R, Cardiff C
Ward, D. (5) 1999/00 Notts Co, Nottingham F
Webster, C. (4) 1956/7 Manchester U
Weston, R. D. (7) 1999/00 Arsenal, Cardiff C
Williams, A. (13) 1993/4 Reading, Wolverhampton W, Reading
Williams, A. P. (2) 1997/8 Southampton
Williams, D. G. 1987/8 13, Derby Co, Ipswich T
Williams, D. M. (5) 1985/6 Norwich C
Williams, G. (1) 1950/1 Cardiff C
Williams, G. E. (26) 1959/60 WBA
Williams, G. G. (5) 1960/1 Swansea T

Williams, H. (4) 1948/9 Newport Co, Leeds U
Williams, Herbert (3) 1964/5 Swansea T
Williams, S. (43) 1953/4 WBA, Southampton
Witcomb, D. (3) 1946/7 WBA, Sheffield W
Woosnam, P. (17) 1958/9 Leyton Orient, West Ham U, Aston Villa
Yorath, T. (59) 1969/70 Leeds U, Coventry C, Tottenham H, Vancouver Whitecaps
Young, E. (21) 1989/90 Wimbledon, Crystal P, Wolverhampton W

EIRE

Aherne, T. (16) 1945/6 Belfast Celtic, Luton T
Aldridge, J. W. (69) 1985/6 Oxford U, Liverpool, Real Sociedad, Tranmere R
Ambrose, P. (5) 1954/5 Shamrock R
Anderson, J. (16) 1979/80 Preston NE, Newcastle U

Babb, P. (35) 1993/4 Coventry C, Liverpool, Sunderland
Bailham, E. (1) 1963/4 Shamrock R
Barber, E. (2) 1965/6 Shelbourne, Birmingham C
Barrett, G. (6) 2002/03 Arsenal, Coventry C
Beglin, J. (15) 1983/4 Liverpool
Bonner, P. (80) 1980/1 Celtic
Braddish, S. (1) 1977/8 Dundalk
Brady, T. R. (6) 1963/4 QPR
Brady, W. L. (72) 1974/5 Arsenal, Juventus, Sampdoria, Internazionale, Ascoli, West Ham U
Branagan, K. G. (1) 1996/7 Bolton W
Breen, G. (62) 1995/6 Birmingham C, Coventry C, West Ham U, Sunderland
Breen, T. (3) 1946/7 Shamrock R
Brennan, F. (1) 1964/5 Drumcondra
Brennan, S. A. (19) 1964/5 Manchester U, Waterford
Browne, W. (3) 1963/4 Bohemians
Buckley, L. (2) 1983/4 Shamrock R, Waregem
Burke, F. (1) 1951/2 Cork Ath
Butler, P. J. (1) 1999/00 Sunderland
Butler, T. (2) 2002/03 Sunderland
Byrne, A. B. (14) 1969/70 Southampton
Byrne, J. (23) 1984/5 QPR, Le Havre, Brighton & HA, Sunderland, Millwall
Byrne, J. (1) 2003/04 Shelbourne
Byrne, P. (8) 1983/4 Shamrock R

Campbell, A. (3) 1984/5 Santander
Campbell, N. (11) 1970/1 St Patrick's Ath, Fortuna Cologne
Cantwell, N. (36) 1953/4 West Ham U, Manchester U
Carey, B. P. (3) 1991/2 Manchester U, Leicester C
Carey, J. J. (21) 1945/6 Manchester U
Carolan, J. (2) 1959/60 Manchester U
Carr, S. (37) 1998/9 Tottenham H, Newcastle U
Carroll, B. (2) 1948/9 Shelbourne
Carroll, T. R. (17) 1967/8 Ipswich T, Birmingham C
Carsley, L. K. (29) 1997/8 Derby Co, Blackburn R, Coventry C, Everton
Cascarino, A. G. (88) 1985/6 Gillingham, Millwall, Aston Villa, Celtic, Chelsea, Marseille, Nancy
Chandler, J. (2) 1979/80 Leeds U
Clarke, C. R. (2) 2003/04 Stoke C
Clarke, J. (1) 1977/8 Drogheda U
Clarke, K. (2) 1947/8 Drumcondra
Clarke, M. (1) 1949/50 Shamrock R
Clinton, T. J. (3) 1950/1 Everton
Coad, P. (11) 1946/7 Shamrock R
Coffey, T. (1) 1949/50 Drumcondra
Colfer, M. D. (2) 1949/50 Shelbourne
Colgan, N, (8) 2001/02 Hibernian
Conmy, O. M. (5) 1964/5 Peterborough U
Connolly, D. J. (40) 1995/6 Watford, Feyenoord, Wolverhampton W, Excelsior, Wimbledon, West Ham U
Conroy, G. A. (27) 1969/70 Stoke C
Conway, J. P. (20) 1966/7 Fulham, Manchester C
Corr, P. J. (4) 1948/9 Everton
Courtney, E. (1) 1945/6 Cork U
Coyle, O. (1) 1993/4 Bolton W
Coyne, T. (22) 1991/2 Celtic, Tranmere R, Motherwell
Crowe, G. (2) 2002/03 Bohemians
Cummins, G. P. (19) 1953/4 Luton T
Cuneen, T. (1) 1950/1 Limerick
Cunningham, K. (68) 1995/6 Wimbledon, Birmingham C
Curtis, D. P. (17) 1956/7 Shelbourne, Bristol C, Ipswich T, Exeter C
Cusack, S. (1) 1952/3 Limerick

Daish, L. S. (5) 1991/2 Cambridge U, Coventry C
Daly, G. A. (48) 1972/3 Manchester U, Derby C, Coventry C, Birmingham C, Shrewsbury T
Daly, M. (2) 1977/8 Wolverhampton W
Daly, P. (1) 1949/50 Shamrock R
Deacy, E. (4) 1981/2 Aston Villa
Delap, R. J. (11) 1997/8 Derby Co, Southampton
De Mange, K. J. P. P. (2) 1986/7 Liverpool, Hull C
Dempsey, J. T. (19) 1966/7 Fulham, Chelsea
Dennehy, J. (11) 1971/2 Cork Hibernian, Nottingham F, Walsall
Desmond, P. (4) 1949/50 Middlesbrough
Devine, J. (13) 1979/80 Arsenal, Norwich C
Doherty, G. M. T. (31) 1999/00 Luton T, Tottenham H, Norwich C
Donovan, D. C. (5) 1954/5 Everton
Donovan, T. (1) 1979/80 Aston Villa
Douglas, J. (2) 2003/04 Blackburn R
Doyle, C. (1) 1958/9 Shelbourne
Doyle, M. P. (1) 2003/04 Coventry C
Duff, D. A. (54) 1997/8 Blackburn R, Chelsea
Duffy, B. (1) 1949/50 Shamrock R
Dunne, A. P. (33) 1961/2 Manchester U, Bolton W
Dunne, J. C. (1) 1970/1 Fulham
Dunne, P. A. J. (5) 1964/5 Manchester U
Dunne, R. P. (23) 1999/00 Everton, Manchester C
Dunne, S. (15) 1952/3 Luton T
Dunne, T. (3) 1955/6 St Patrick's Ath
Dunning, P. (2) 1970/1 Shelbourne
Dunphy, E. M. (23) 1965/6 York C, Millwall
Dwyer, N. M. (14) 1959/60 West Ham U, Swansea T

Eccles, P. (1) 1985/6 Shamrock R
Eglington, T. J. (24) 1945/6 Shamrock R, Everton
Elliott, S. W. (3) 2004/05 Sunderland
Evans, M. J. (1) 1997/8 Southampton

Fagan, E. (1) 1972/3 Shamrock R
Fagan, F. (8) 1954/5 Manchester C, Derby C
Fairclough, M. (2) 1981/2 Dundalk
Fallon, S. (8) 1950/1 Celtic
Farrell, P. D. (28) 1945/6 Shamrock R, Everton
Farrelly, G. (6) 1995/6 Aston Villa, Everton, Bolton W
Finnan, S. (36) 1999/00 Fulham, Liverpool
Finucane, A. (11) 1966/7 Limerick
Fitzgerald, F. J. (2) 1954/5 Waterford
Fitzgerald, P. J. (5) 1960/1 Leeds U, Chester
Fitzpatrick, K. (1) 1969/70 Limerick
Fitzsimons, A. G. (26) 1949/50 Middlesbrough, Lincoln C
Fleming, C. (10) 1995/6 Middlesbrough
Fogarty, A. (11) 1959/60 Sunderland, Hartlepool U
Foley, D. J. (6) 1999/00 Watford
Foley, T. C. (9) 1963/4 Northampton T
Fullam, J. 1960/1 Preston NE, Shamrock R

Gallagher, C. (2) 1966/7 Celtic
Gallagher, M. (1) 1953/4 Hibernian
Galvin, A. (29) 1982/3 Tottenham H, Sheffield W, Swindon T
Gannon, E. (14) 1948/9 Notts Co, Sheffield W, Shelbourne K
Gannon, M. (1) 1971/2 Shelbourne
Gavin, J. T. (7) 1949/50 Norwich C, Tottenham H, Norwich C
Gibbons, A. (4) 1951/2 St Patrick's Ath
Gilbert, R. (1) 1965/6 Shamrock R
Giles, C. (1) 1950/1 Doncaster R
Giles, M. J. (59) 1959/60 Manchester U, Leeds U, WBA, Shamrock R
Given, S. J. J. (70) 1995/6 Blackburn R, Newcastle U
Givens, D. J. (56) 1968/9 Manchester U, Luton T, QPR, Birmingham C, Neuchatel Xamax
Glynn, D. (2) 1951/2 Drumcondra
Godwin, T. F. (13) 1948/9 Shamrock R, Leicester C, Bournemouth
Goodman, J. (4) 1996/7 Wimbledon
Goodwin, J. (1) 2002/03 Stockport Co
Gorman, W. C. (2) 1946/7 Brentford
Grealish, A. (45) 1975/6 Orient, Luton T, Brighton & HA, WBA
Gregg, E. (8) 1977/8 Bohemians
Grimes, A. A. (18) 1977/8 Manchester U, Coventry C, Luton T

Hale, A. (13) 1961/2 Aston Villa, Doncaster R, Waterford
Hamilton, T. (2) 1958/9 Shamrock R
Hand, E. K. (20) 1968/9 Portsmouth
Harte, I. P. (58) 1995/6 Leeds U, Levante
Hartnett, J. B. (2) 1948/9 Middlesbrough
Haverty, J. (32) 1955/6 Arsenal, Blackburn R, Millwall, Celtic, Bristol R, Shelbourne

Hayes, A. W. P. (1) 1978/9 Southampton
Hayes, W. E. (2) 1946/7 Huddersfield T
Hayes, W. J. (1) 1948/9 Limerick
Healey, R. (2) 1976/7 Cardiff C
Healy, C. (13) 2001/02 Celtic, Sunderland
Heighway, S. D. (34) 1970/1 Liverpool, Minnesota Kicks
Henderson, B. (2) 1947/8 Drumcondra
Hennessy, J. (5) 1964/5 Shelbourne, St Patrick's Ath
Herrick, J. (3) 1971/2 Cork Hibernians, Shamrock R
Higgins, J. (1) 1950/1 Birmingham C
Holland, M. R. (46) 1999/00 Ipswich T, Charlton Ath
Holmes, J. (30) 1970/1 Coventry C, Tottenham H, Vancouver Whitecaps
Houghton, R. J. (73) 1985/6 Oxford U, Liverpool, Aston Villa, Crystal P, Reading
Howlett, G. (1) 1983/4 Brighton & HA
Hughton, C. (53) 1979/80 Tottenham H, West Ham U
Hurley, C. J. (40) 1956/7 Millwall, Sunderland, Bolton W

Irwin, D. J. (56) 1990/1 Manchester U

Kavanagh, G. A. (12) 1997/8 Stoke C, Cardiff C, Wigan Ath
Keane, R. D. (61) 1997/8 Wolverhampton W, Coventry C, Internazionale, Leeds U, Tottenham H
Keane, R. M. (66) 1990/1 Nottingham F, Manchester U
Keane, T. R. (4) 1948/9 Swansea T
Kearin, M. (1) 1971/2 Shamrock R
Kearns, F. T. (1) 1953/4 West Ham U
Kearns, M. (18) 1969/70 Oxford U, Walsall, Wolverhampton W
Kelly, A. T. (34) 1992/3 Sheffield U, Blackburn R
Kelly, D. T. (26) 1987/8 Walsall, West Ham U, Leicester C, Newcastle U, Wolverhampton W, Sunderland, Tranmere R
Kelly, G. (52) 1993/4 Leeds U
Kelly, J. A. (48) 1956/7 Drumcondra, Preston NE
Kelly, J. P. V. (5) 1960/1 Wolverhampton W
Kelly, M. J. (4) 1987/8 Portsmouth
Kelly, N. (1) 1953/4 Nottingham F
Kenna, J. J. (27) 1994/5 Blackburn R
Kennedy, M. (34) 1995/6 Liverpool, Wimbledon, Manchester C, Wolverhampton W
Kennedy, M. F. (2) 1985/6 Portsmouth
Kenny, P. (5) 2003/04 Sheffield U
Keogh, J. (1) 1965/6 Shamrock R
Keogh, S. (1) 1958/9 Shamrock R
Kernaghan, A. N. (22) 1992/3 Middlesbrough, Manchester C
Kiely, D. L. (8) 1999/00 Charlton Ath
Kiernan, F. W. (5) 1950/1 Shamrock R, Southampton
Kilbane, K. D. (64) 1997/8 WBA, Sunderland, Everton
Kinnear, J. P. (26) 1966/7 Tottenham H, Brighton & HA
Kinsella, M. A. (48) 1997/8 Charlton Ath, Aston Villa, WBA

Langan, D. (26) 1977/8 Derby Co, Birmingham C, Oxford U
Lawler, J. F. (8) 1952/3 Fulham
Lawlor, J. C. (3) 1948/9 Drumcondra, Doncaster R
Lawlor, M. (5) 1970/1 Shamrock R
Lawrenson, M. (38) 1976/7 Preston NE, Brighton & HA, Liverpool
Lee, A. L. (8) 2002/03 Rotherham U, Cardiff C
Leech, M. (8) 1968/9 Shamrock R
Lowry, D. (1) 1961/2 St Patrick's Ath

McAlinden, J. (2) 1945/6 Portsmouth
McAteer, J. W. (52) 1993/4 Bolton W, Liverpool, Blackburn R, Sunderland
McCann, J. (1) 1956/7 Shamrock R
McCarthy, M. (57) 1983/4 Manchester C, Celtic, Lyon, Millwall
McConville, T. (6) 1971/2 Dundalk, Waterford
McDonagh, Jim (25) 1980/1 Everton, Bolton W, Notts C
McDonagh, Jacko (3) 1983/4 Shamrock R
McEvoy, M. A. (17) 1960/1 Blackburn R
McGeady, A. (3) 2003/04 Celtic
McGee, P. (15) 1977/8 QPR, Preston NE
McGoldrick, E. J. (15) 1991/2 Crystal P, Arsenal
McGowan, D. (3) 1948/9 West Ham U
McGowan, J. (1) 1946/7 Cork U
McGrath, M. (22) 1957/8 Blackburn R, Bradford Park Avenue
McGrath, P. (83) 1984/5 Manchester U, Aston Villa, Derby C
McLoughlin, A. F. (42) 1989/90 Swindon T, Southampton, Portsmouth
McMillan, W. (2) 1945/6 Belfast Celtic
McNally, J. B. (3) 1958/9 Luton T
McPhail, S. (10) 1999/00 Leeds U

Macken, A. (1) 1976/7 Derby Co
Macken, J.P. (1) 2004/05 Manchester C
Mackey, G. (3) 1956/7 Shamrock R
Mahon, A. J. (2) 1999/00 Tranmere R
Malone, G. (1) 1948/9 Shelbourne
Mancini, T. J. (5) 1973/4 QPR, Arsenal
Martin, C. J. (30) 1945/6 Glentoran, Leeds U, Aston Villa
Martin, M. P. (52) 1971/2 Bohemians, Manchester U, WBA, Newcastle U
Maybury, A. (10) 1997/8 Leeds U, Heart of Midlothian, Leicester C
Meagan, M. K. (17) 1960/1 Everton, Huddersfield T, Drogheda
Miller, L. W. P. (9) 2003/04 Celtic, Manchester U
Milligan, M. J. (1) 1991/2 Oldham Ath
Mooney, J. (2) 1964/5 Shamrock R
Moore, A. (8) 1995/6 Middlesbrough
Moran, K. (71) 1979/80 Manchester U, Sporting Gijon, Blackburn R
Moroney, T. (12) 1947/8 West Ham U, Evergreen U
Morris, C. B. (35) 1987/8 Celtic, Middlesbrough
Morrison, C. H. (30) 2001/02 Crystal P, Birmingham C
Moulson, G. B. (3) 1947/8 Lincoln C
Mucklan, C. (1) 1977/8 Drogheda
Mulligan, P. M. (50) 1968/9 Shamrock R, Chelsea, Crystal P, WBA, Shamrock R
Munroe, L. (1) 1953/4 Shamrock R
Murphy, A. (1) 1955/6 Clyde
Murphy, B. (1) 1985/6 Bohemians
Murphy, Jerry (1) 1979/80 Crystal P
Murphy, Joe (1) 2003/04 WBA
Murray, T. (1) 1949/50 Dundalk

Newman, W. (1) 1968/9 Shelbourne
Nolan, R. (10) 1956/7 Shamrock R

O'Brien, A. J. (21) 2000/01 Newcastle U
O'Brien, F. (3) 1979/80 Philadelphia Fury
O'Brien, L. (16) 1985/6 Shamrock R, Manchester U, Newcastle U, Tranmere R
O'Brien, R. (5) 1975/6 Notts Co
O'Byrne, L. B. (1) 1948/9 Shamrock R
O'Callaghan, B. R. (6) 1978/9 Stoke C
O'Callaghan, K. (21) 1980/1 Ipswich T, Portsmouth
O'Connell, A. (2) 1966/7 Dundalk, Bohemians
O'Connor, T. (4) 1949/50 Shamrock R
O'Connor, T. (7) 1967/8 Fulham, Dundalk, Bohemians
O'Driscoll, J. F. (3) 1948/9 Swansea T
O'Driscoll, S. (3) 1981/2 Fulham
O'Farrell, F. (9) 1951/2 West Ham U, Preston NE
O'Flanagan, K. P. (3) 1946/7 Arsenal
O'Flanagan, M. (1) 1946/7 Bohemians
O'Hanlon, K. G. (1) 1987/8 Rotherham U
O'Keefe, E. (5) 1980/1 Everton, Port Vale
O'Leary, D. (68) 1976/7 Arsenal
O'Leary, P. (7) 1979/80 Shamrock R
O'Neill, F. S. (20) 1961/2 Shamrock R
O'Neill, J. (17) 1951/2 Everton
O'Neill, J. (1) 1960/1 Preston NE
O'Neill, K. P. (13) 1995/6 Norwich C, Middlesbrough
O'Regan, K. (4) 1983/4 Brighton & HA
O'Reilly, J. (2) 1945/6 Cork U
O'Shea, J. F. (24) 2001/02 Manchester U

Peyton, G. (33) 1976/7 Fulham, Bournemouth, Everton
Peyton, N. (6) 1956/7 Shamrock R, Leeds U
Phelan, T. (42) 1991/2 Wimbledon, Manchester C, Chelsea, Everton, Fulham

Quinn, A. (6) 2002/03 Sheffield W, Sheffield U
Quinn, B. S. (4) 1999/00 Coventry C
Quinn, N. J. (91) 1985/6 Arsenal, Manchester C, Sunderland

Reid, A. M. (16) 2003/04 Nottingham F, Tottenham H
Reid, S. J. (13) 2001/02 Millwall, Blackburn R
Richardson, D. J. (3) 1971/2 Shamrock R, Gillingham
Ringstead, A. (20) 1950/1 Sheffield U
Robinson, M. (24) 1980/1 Brighton & HA, Liverpool, QPR
Roche, P. J. (8) 1971/2 Shelbourne, Manchester U
Rogers, E. (19) 1967/8 Blackburn R, Charlton Ath
Rowlands, M. C. (3) 2003/04 QPR
Ryan, G. (18) 1977/8 Derby Co, Brighton & HA
Ryan, R. A. (16) 1949/50 WBA, Derby C

Sadlier, R. T. (1) 2001/02 Millwall
Savage, D. P. T. (5) 1995/6 Millwall
Saward, P. (18) 1953/4 Millwall, Aston Villa, Huddersfield T

Scannell, T. (1) 1953/4 Southend U
Scully, P. J. (1) 1988/9 Arsenal
Sheedy, K. (45) 1983/4 Everton, Newcastle U
Sheridan, J. J. (34) 1987/8 Leeds U, Sheffield W
Slaven, B. (7) 1989/90 Middlesbrough
Sloan, J. W. (2) 1945/6 Arsenal
Smyth, M. (1) 1968/9 Shamrock R
Stapleton, F. (71) 1976/7 Arsenal, Manchester U, Ajax, Le Havre, Blackburn R
Staunton, S. (102) 1988/9 Liverpool, Aston Villa, Liverpool, Aston Villa
Stevenson, A. E. (6) 1946/7 Everton
Strahan, F. (5) 1963/4 Shelbourne
Swan, M. M. G. (1) 1959/60 Drumcondra
Synott, N. (3) 1977/8 Shamrock R

Taylor T. (1) 1958/9 Waterford
Thomas, P. (2) 1973/4 Waterford
Thompson, J. (1) 2003/04 Nottingham F
Townsend, A. D. (70) 1988/9 Norwich C, Chelsea, Aston Villa, Middlesbrough
Traynor, T. J. (8) 1953/4 Southampton
Treacy, R. C. P. (42) 1965/6 WBA, Charlton Ath, Swindon T, Preston NE, WBA, Shamrock R
Tuohy, L. (8) 1955/6 Shamrock R, Newcastle U, Shamrock R
Turner, P. (2) 1962/3 Celtic

Vernon, J. (2) 1945/6 Belfast Celtic

Waddock, G. (21) 1979/80 QPR, Millwall
Walsh, D. J. (20) 1945/6 Linfield, WBA, Aston Villa
Walsh, J. (1) 1981/2 Limerick
Walsh, M. (21) 1975/6 Blackpool, Everton, QPR, Porto
Walsh, M. (4) 1981/2 Everton
Walsh, W. (9) 1946/7 Manchester C
Waters, J. (2) 1976/7 Grimsby T
Whelan, R. (2) 1963/4 St Patrick's Ath
Whelan, R. (53) 1980/1 Liverpool, Southend U
Whelan, W. (4) 1955/6 Manchester U
Whittaker, R. (1) 1958/9 Chelsea

BRITISH ISLES INTERNATIONAL GOALSCORERS SINCE 1946

ENGLAND

Player	Goals
A'Court, A.	1
Adams, T.A.	5
Allen, R.	2
Anderson, V.	2
Anderton, D.R.	7
Astall, G.	1
Atyeo, P.J.W.	5
Baily, E.F.	5
Baker, J.H.	3
Ball, A.J.	8
Barnes, J.	11
Barnes, P.S.	4
Barmby, N.J.	4
Beardsley, P.A.	9
Beattie, J.K.	1
Beckham, D.R.J.	16
Bell, C.	9
Bentley, R.T.F.	9
Blissett, L.	3
Bowles, S.	1
Bradford, G.R.W.	1
Bradley, W.	2
Bridge, W. M.	1
Bridges, B.J.	1
Broadbent, P.F.	2
Broadis, I.A.	8
Brooking, T.D.	5
Brooks, J.	2
Bull, S.G.	4
Butcher, T.	3
Byrne, J.J.	8
Campbell, S. J.	1
Carter, H.S.	5
Chamberlain, M.	1
Channon, M.R.	21
Charlton, J.	6
Charlton, R.	49
Chivers, M.	13
Clarke, A.J.	10
Cole, A.	1
Cole, J.J.	3
Connelly, J.M.	7
Coppell, S.J.	7
Cowans, G.	2
Crawford, R.	1
Currie, A.W.	3
Defoe, J. C.	1
Dixon, L.M.	1
Dixon, K.M.	4
Douglas, B.	11
Eastham, G.	2
Edwards, D.	5
Ehiogu, U.	1
Elliott, W.H.	3
Ferdinand, L.	5
Ferdinand, R.G.	1
Finney, T.	30
Flowers, R.	10
Fowler, R.B.	7
Francis, G.C.J.	3
Francis, T.	12
Froggatt, J.	2
Froggatt, R.	2
Gascoigne, P.J.	10
Gerrard, S.G.	6
Goddard, P.	1
Grainger, C.	3
Greaves, J.	44
Haines, J.T.W.	2
Hancocks, J.	2
Hassall, H.W.	4
Hateley, M.	9
Haynes, J.N.	18
Heskey, E.W.	5
Hirst, D.E.	1
Hitchens, G.A.	5
Hoddle, G.	8
Hughes, E.W.	1
Hunt, R.	18
Hunter, N.	2
Hurst, G.C.	24
Ince P.E.C.	2
Jeffers, F.	1
Johnson, D.E.	6
Kay, A.H.	1
Keegan, J.K.	21
Kennedy, R.	3
Keown, M.R.	2
Kevan, D.T.	8
Kidd, B.	1
King, L.B.	1
Lampard, F.J.	8
Langton, R.	1
Latchford, R.D.	5
Lawler, C.	1
Lawton, T.	16
Lee, F.	10
Lee, J.	1
Lee, R.M.	2
Lee, S.	2
Le Saux, G.P.	1
Lineker, G.	48
Lofthouse, N.	30
Mabbutt, G.	1
McDermott, T.	3
Macdonald, M.	6
McManaman, S.	3
Mannion, W.J.	11
Mariner, P.	13
Marsh, R.W.	1
Matthews, S.	3
Medley, L.D.	1
Melia, J.	1
Merson, P.C.	3
Milburn, J.E.T.	10
Moore, R.F.	2
Morris, J.	3
Mortensen, S.H.	23
Mullen, J.	6
Mullery, A.P.	1
Murphy, D. B.	1
Neal, P.G.	5
Nicholls, J.	1
Nicholson, W.E.	1
O'Grady, M.	3
Owen, M.J.	32
Own goals	19
Paine, T.L.	7
Palmer, C.L.	1
Parry, R.A.	1
Peacock, A.	3
Pearce, S.	5
Pearson, J.S.	5
Pearson, S.C.	5
Perry, W.	2
Peters, M.	20
Pickering, F.	5
Platt, D.	27
Pointer, R.	2
Ramsay, A.E.	3
Redknapp, J.F.	1

Revie, D.G. 4
Richardson, K.E. 2
Robson, B. 26
Robson, R. 4
Rooney, W. 9
Rowley, J.F. 6
Royle, J. 2

Sansom, K. 1
Scholes, P. 14
Sewell, J. 3
Shackleton, L.F. 1
Shearer, A. 30
Sheringham, E.P. 11
Smith, A. 1
Smith, A.M. 2
Smith, R. 13
Southgate, G. 2
Steven, T.M. 4
Stiles, N.P. 1
Stone, S.B. 2
Summerbee, M.G. 1

Tambling, R.V. 1
Taylor, P.J. 2
Taylor, T. 16
Thompson, P.B. 1
Tueart, D. 2

Vassell, D. 6
Viollet, D.S. 1

Waddle, C.R. 6
Wallace, D.L. 1
Walsh, P. 1
Watson, D.V. 4
Webb, N. 4
Weller, K. 1
Wignall, F. 2
Wilkins, R.G. 3
Wilshaw, D.J. 10
Wise, D.F. 1
Withe, P. 1
Woodcock, T. 16
Worthington, F.S. 2
Wright, I.E. 9
Wright, M. 1
Wright, W.A. 3
Wright-Phillips, S.C. 1

SCOTLAND

Aitken, R. 1
Archibald, S. 4

Baird, S. 2
Bannon, E. 1
Bauld, W. 2
Baxter, J.C. 3
Bett, J. 1
Bone, J. 1
Booth, S. 6
Boyd, T. 1
Brand, R. 8
Brazil, A. 1
Bremner, W.J. 3
Brown, A.D. 6
Buckley, P. 1
Burley, C.W. 3
Burns, K. 1

Caldwell, G. 1
Calderwood, C. 1
Caldow, E. 4
Cameron, C. 2
Campbell, R. 1
Chalmers, S. 3
Collins, J. 12
Collins, R.V. 10
Combe, J.R. 1
Conn, A. 1
Cooper, D. 6
Craig, J. 1
Crawford, S. 4
Curran, H.P. 1

Dailly, C. 5
Dalglish, K. 30
Davidson, J.A. 1
Dickov, P. 1
Dobie, R. S. 1
Docherty, T.H. 1
Dodds, D. 1
Dodds, W. 7
Duncan, D.M. 1
Durie, G.S. 7

Elliott, M.S. 1

Ferguson, B. 2
Fernie, W. 1
Flavell, R. 2
Fleming, C. 2
Fletcher, D. 2
Freedman, D.A. 1

Gallacher, K.W. 9
Gemmell, T.K *(St Mirren)* 1
Gemmell, T.K *(Celtic)* 1
Gemmill, A. 8
Gemmill, S. 1
Gibson, D.W. 3
Gilzean, A.J. 12
Gough, C.R. 6
Graham, A. 2
Graham, G. 3
Gray, A. 5
Gray, E. 3
Gray, F. 1
Greig, J. 3

Hamilton, G. 4
Harper, J.M. 2
Hartford, R.A. 4
Henderson, J.G. 1
Henderson, W. 5
Hendry, E.C.J. 3
Herd, D.G. 3
Herd, G. 1
Hewie, J.D. 2
Holt, G.J. 1
Holton, J.A. 2
Hopkin, D. 2
Houliston, W. 2
Howie, H. 1
Hughes, J. 1
Hunter, W. 1
Hutchison, D. 6
Hutchison, T. 1

Jackson, C. 1
Jackson, D. 4
Jardine, A. 1
Jess, E. 2
Johnston, A. 2
Johnston, L.H. 1
Johnston, M. 14
Johnstone, D. 2
Johnstone, J. 4
Johnstone, R. 9
Jordan, J. 11

Kyle, K. 1

Lambert, P. 1
Law, D. 30
Leggat, G. 8
Lennox, R. 3
Liddell, W. 6
Linwood, A.B. 1
Lorimer, P. 4

Macari, L. 5
McAllister, G. 5
MacDougall, E.J. 3
MacKay, D.C. 4
Mackay, G. 1
MacKenzie, J.A. 1
MacLeod, M 1

McAvennie, F. 1
McCall, S.M. 1
McCalliog, J. 1
McCann, N. 3
McClair, B. 2
McCoist, A. 19
McFadden, J. 6
McGhee, M. 2
McGinlay, J. 3
McInally, A. 3
McKimmie, S.I. 1
McKinlay, W. 4
McKinnon, R. 1
McLaren, A. 4
McLean, T. 1
McLintock, F. 1
McMillan, I.L. 2
McNeill, W. 3
McPhail, J. 3
McQueen, G. 5
McStay, P. 9
McSwegan, G.J. 1
Mason, J. 4
Masson, D.S. 5
Miller, K. 2
Miller, W. 1
Mitchell, R.C. 1
Morgan, W. 1
Morris, H. 3
Mudie, J.K. 9
Mulhall, G. 1
Murdoch, R. 5
Murray, J. 1

Narey, D. 1
Naysmith, G.A. 1
Nevin, P.K.F. 5
Nicholas, C. 5

O'Hare, J. 5
Ormond, W.E. 1
Orr, T. 1
Own goals 10

Parlane, D. 1
Pettigrew, W. 2
Provan, D. 1

Quashie, N.F. 1
Quinn, J. 7
Quinn, P. 1

Reilly, L. 22
Ring, T. 2
Rioch, B.D. 6
Ritchie, P.S. 1
Robertson, A. 2
Robertson, J. 2
Robertson, J.N. 9

St John, I. 9
Scott, A.S. 5
Sharp, G. 1
Shearer, D. 2
Smith, G. 4
Souness, G.J. 4
Steel, W. 12
Stein, C. 10
Stewart, R. 1
Strachan, G. 5
Sturrock, P. 3

Thompson, S. 3
Thornton, W. 1

Waddell, W. 6
Wallace, I.A. 1
Wark, J. 7
Weir, A. 1
Weir, D. 1
White, J.A. 3
Wilkie, L. 1
Wilson, D. 9

Young, A. 2

WALES

Allchurch, I.J. 23
Allen, M. 3

Barnes, W. 1
Bellamy, C.D. 9
Blackmore, C.G. 1
Blake, N.A. 4
Bodin, P.J. 3
Bowen, D.I. 3
Bowen, M. 2
Boyle, T. 1
Burgess, W.A.R. 1

Charles, J. 1
Charles, M. 6
Charles, W.J. 15
Clarke, R.J. 5
Coleman, C. 4
Curtis, A. 6

Davies, G. 2
Davies, R.T. 9
Davies, R.W. 6
Davies, Simon 4
Deacy, N. 4
Durban, A. 2
Dwyer, P. 2

Earnshaw, R. 9
Edwards, G. 2
Edwards, R.I. 4
England, H.M. 4
Evans, I. 1

Flynn, B. 7
Ford, T. 23
Foulkes, W.J. 1

Giggs, R.J. 8
Giles, D. 2
Godfrey, B.C. 2
Griffiths, A.T. 6
Griffiths, M.W. 2

Harris, C.S. 1
Hartson, J. 14
Hewitt, R. 1
Hockey, T. 1
Hodges, G. 2
Horne, B. 2
Hughes, L.M. 16

James, L. 10
James, R. 7
Jones, A. 1
Jones, B.S. 2
Jones, Cliff 16
Jones, D.E. 1
Jones, J.P. 1

Koumas, J. 1
Kryzwicki, R.I. 1

Leek, K. 5
Lovell, S. 1
Lowrie, G. 2

Mahoney, J.F. 1
Medwin, T.C. 6
Melville, A.K. 3
Moore, G. 1

Nicholas, P. 2

O'Sullivan, P.A. 1
Own goals 5

Palmer, D. 1
Parry, P.I. 1
Paul, R. 1
Pembridge, M.A. 6
Phillips, D. 2
Powell, A. 1
Powell, D. 1
Price, P. 1

Reece, G.I. 2
Rees, R.R. 3
Roberts, P.S. 1
Robinson, J.R.C. 3
Rush, I. 28

Saunders, D. 22
Savage R.W. 2
Slatter, N. 2
Smallman, D.P. 1
Speed, G.A. 7
Symons, C.J. 2

Tapscott, D.R. 4
Taylor, G.J. 1
Thomas, M. 4
Toshack, J.B. 12

Vernon, T.R. 8

Walsh, I. 7
Williams, A. 1
Williams, G.E. 1
Williams, G.G. 1
Woosnam, A.P. 3

Yorath, T.C. 2
Young, E. 1

NORTHERN IRELAND

Anderson, T. 4
Armstrong, G. 12

Barr, H.H. 1
Best, G. 9
Bingham, W.L. 10
Black, K. 1
Blanchflower, D. 2
Blanchflower, J. 1
Brennan, R.A. 1
Brotherston, N. 3

Campbell, W.G. 1
Casey, T. 2
Caskey, W. 1
Cassidy, T. 1
Clarke, C.J. 13
Clements, D. 2
Cochrane, T. 1
Crossan, E. 1
Crossan, J.A. 10
Cush, W.W. 5

D'Arcy, S.D. 1
Doherty, I. 1
Doherty, P.D. 2
Dougan, A.D. 8
Dowie, I. 12

Elder, A.R. 1
Elliott, S. 3

Ferguson, W. 1
Ferris, R.O. 1
Finney, T. 2

Gillespie, K.R. 1
Gray, P. 6
Griffin, D.J. 1

Hamilton, B. 4
Hamilton, W. 5
Harkin, J.T. 2
Harvey, M. 3
Healy, D.J. 17
Hill, C.F. 1
Humphries, W. 1
Hughes, M.E. 5
Hunter, A. 1
Hunter, B.V. 1

Irvine, W.J. 8

Johnston, W.C. 1
Jones, J. 1
Jones, S. 1

Lennon, N.F. 2
Lockhart, N. 3
Lomas, S.M. 3

Magilton, J. 5
McAdams, W.J. 7
McCartney, G. 1
McClelland, J. 1
McCrory, S. 1
McCurdy, C. 1
McDonald, A. 3
McGarry, J.K. 1
McGrath, R.C. 4
McIlroy, J. 10
McIlroy, S.B. 5
McLaughlin, J.C. 6
McMahon, G.J. 2
McMordie, A.S. 3
McMorran, E.J. 4
McParland, P.J. 10
Moreland, V. 1
Morgan, S. 3
Morrow, S.J. 1
Mulryne, P.P. 3
Murdoch, C.J. 1

Neill, W.J.T. 2
Nelson, S. 1
Nicholl, C.J. 3
Nicholl, J.M. 1
Nicholson, J.J. 6

O'Boyle, G. 1
O'Kane, W.J. 1
O'Neill, J. 2
O'Neill, M.A. 4
O'Neill, M.H. 8
Own goals 3

Patterson, D.J. 1
Peacock, R. 2
Penney, S. 2

Quinn, J.M. 12
Quinn, S.J. 4

Rowland, K. 1

Simpson, W.J. 5
Smyth, S. 5
Spence, D.W. 3
Stewart, I. 2

Taggart, G.P. 7
Tully, C.P. 3

Walker, J. 1
Walsh, D.J. 5
Welsh, E. 1
Whiteside, N. 9
Whitley, Jeff 2
Williams, M.S. 1
Wilson, D.J. 1
Wilson, K.J. 6
Wilson, S.J. 7

EIRE

Aldridge, J. 19
Ambrose, P. 1
Anderson, J. 1

Barrett, G. 2
Brady, L. 9
Breen, G. 6
Byrne, J. *(QPR)* 4

Cantwell, J. 14
Carey, J. 3
Carroll, T. 1
Cascarino, A. 19
Coad, P. 3
Connolly, D.J. 9
Conroy, T. 2

Conway, J.	3
Coyne, T.	6
Cummings, G.	5
Curtis, D.	8
Daly, G.	13
Dempsey, J.	1
Dennehy, M.	2
Doherty, G.M.T.	4
Duff, D.A.	6
Duffy, B.	1
Dunne, R.P.	4
Eglinton, T.	2
Fagan, F.	5
Fallon, S.	2
Farrell, P.	3
Finnan, S.	1
Fitzgerald, J.	1
Fitzgerald, P.	2
Fitzsimons, A.	7
Fogarty, A.	3
Foley, D.	2
Fullam, J.	1
Galvin, A.	1
Gavin, J.	2
Giles, J.	5
Givens, D.	19
Glynn, D.	1
Grealish, T.	8
Grimes, A.A.	1
Hale, A.	2
Hand, E.	2
Harte, I.P.	11
Haverty, J.	3
Healy, C.	1
Holland, M.R.	5
Holmes, J.	1
Houghton, R.	6
Hughton, C.	1
Hurley, C.	2
Irwin, D.	4
Kavanagh, G.A.	1
Keane, R.D.	25
Keane, R.M.	9
Kelly, D.	9
Kelly, G.	2
Kennedy, M.	3
Kernaghan, A.	1
Kilbane, K.D.	5
Kinsella, M.A.	3
Lawrenson, M.	5
Leech, M.	2
McAteer, J.W.	3
McCann, J.	1
McCarthy, M.	2
McEvoy, A.	6
McGee, P.	4
McGrath, P.	8
McLoughlin, A.	2
McPhail, S.	1
Mancini, T.	1
Martin, C.	6
Martin, M.	4
Mooney, J.	1
Moran, K.	6
Moroney, T.	1
Morrison, C.H.	9
Mulligan, P.	1
O'Brien, A.J.	1
O'Callaghan, K.	1
O'Connor, T.	2
O'Farrell, F.	2
O'Keefe, E.	1
O'Leary, D.A.	1
O'Neill, F.	1
O'Neill, K.P.	4
O'Reilly, J.	1
O'Shea, J.F.	1
Own goals	10
Quinn, N.	21
Reid, A.M.	2
Reid, S.J.	2
Ringstead, A.	7
Robinson, M.	4
Rogers, E.	5
Ryan, G.	1
Ryan, R.	3
Sheedy, K.	9
Sheridan, J.	5
Slaven, B.	1
Sloan, W.	1
Stapleton, F.	20
Staunton, S.	7
Strahan, F.	1
Townsend, A.D.	7
Treacy, R.	5
Tuohy, L.	4
Waddock, G.	3
Walsh, D.	5
Walsh, M.	3
Waters, J.	1
Whelan, R.	3

UEFA UNDER-21 CHAMPIONSHIP 2004–06

GROUP 1

Romania 1, Finland 0
Macedonia 4, Armenia 0
Romania 5, Macedonia 1
Holland 0, Czech Republic 0
Armenia 0, Finland 1
Czech Republic 4, Romania 1
Finland 0, Armenia 1
Macedonia 0, Holland 2
Holland 4, Finland 1
Armenia 0, Czech Republic 4
Armenia 0, Romania 5
Macedonia 2, Czech Republic 2
Romania 2, Holland 0
Czech Republic 3, Finland 0
Holland 0, Armenia 0
Macedonia 1, Romania 0
Holland 2, Romania 0
Armenia 0, Macedonia 0
Czech Republic 2, Macedonia 0
Finland 1, Holland 2
Romania 2, Armenia 0

GROUP 2

Albania 1, Greece 1
Denmark 3, Ukraine 2
Turkey 0, Georgia 0
Kazakhstan 0, Ukraine 1
Georgia 2, Albania 1
Greece 2, Turkey 1
Albania 1, Denmark 2
Ukraine 1, Greece 0
Turkey 1, Kazakhstan 0
Kazakhstan 0, Albania 1
Ukraine 6, Georgia 0
Denmark 1, Turkey 1
Greece 5, Kazakhstan 0
Georgia 2, Denmark 4
Turkey 1, Ukraine 0
Albania 1, Ukraine 1
Greece 0, Denmark 1
Denmark 5, Kazakhstan 1
Georgia 1, Greece 1
Turkey 4, Albania 0
Georgia 0, Turkey 2
Greece 2, Albania 0
Ukraine 0, Denmark 1
Albania 0, Georgia 1
Ukraine 2, Kazakhstan 1
Turkey 0, Greece 2
Kazakhstan 2, Turkey 1
Denmark 7, Albania 0
Greece 0, Ukraine 1

GROUP 3

Slovakia 1, Luxembourg 0
Estonia 0, Luxembourg 0
Latvia 1, Portugal 2
Russia 4, Slovakia 0
Luxembourg 1, Latvia 2
Portugal 3, Estonia 0
Luxembourg 0, Russia 4
Slovakia 3, Latvia 1
Latvia 0, Estonia 0
Portugal 2, Russia 0
Russia 3, Estonia 0
Luxembourg 1, Portugal 6
Estonia 0, Slovakia 2
Latvia 2, Luxembourg 1
Slovakia 0, Portugal 1
Estonia 1, Russia 5
Portugal 2, Slovakia 1
Russia 1, Latvia 1
Luxembourg 0, Slovakia 2
Estonia 0, Portugal 5

GROUP 4

France 1, Israel 0
Republic of Ireland 3, Cyprus 0
Israel 1, Cyprus 0
Switzerland 4, Republic of Ireland 2
Israel 1, Switzerland 1
France 1, Republic of Ireland 0
Cyprus 0, France 1
Cyprus 0, Israel 1
Israel 3, Republic of Ireland 1
France 1, Switzerland 1
Israel 3, France 2
Switzerland 3, Cyprus 0
Republic of Ireland 2, Israel 2

GROUP 5

Italy 2, Norway 0
Slovenia 1, Moldova 0
Norway 2, Belarus 3
Scotland 1, Slovenia 1
Moldova 0, Italy 1
Belarus 2, Moldova 3
Scotland 0, Norway 2
Slovenia 0, Italy 3
Moldova 0, Scotland 0
Norway 0, Slovenia 0
Italy 2, Belarus 1
Italy 2, Scotland 0
Moldova 1, Norway 3
Slovenia 1, Belarus 4
Belarus 1, Slovenia 2
Scotland 0, Moldova 0
Norway 1, Italy 0
Belarus 3, Scotland 2

GROUP 6

Azerbaijan 0, Wales 1
Austria 0, England 2

Austria 3, Azerbaijan 0
Poland 1, England 3
Austria 0, Poland 3
England 2, Wales 0
Azerbaijan 0, Germany 2
Wales 2, Poland 2
Germany 2, Austria 0
Azerbaijan 0, England 0
Germany 1, Poland 1
Wales 0, Germany 4
Wales 1, Austria 0
Poland 3, Azerbaijan 0
England 2, Germany 2
Austria 2, Wales 0
England 2, Azerbaijan 0
Azerbaijan 1, Poland 1

GROUP 7
Belgium 3, Lithuania 0
San Marino 0, Serbia & Montenegro 5
Bosnia 0, Spain 2
Lithuania 2, San Marino 0
Bosnia 1, Serbia & Montenegro 3
Spain 2, Belgium 2
Serbia & Montenegro 9, San Marino 0
Lithuania 1, Spain 1
Belgium 4, Serbia & Montenegro 0
San Marino 1, Lithuania 2
Spain 14, San Marino 0
Belgium 2, Bosnia 1
Serbia & Montenegro 1, Spain 0
Bosnia 2, Lithuania 0
San Marino 0, Belgium 4
Serbia & Montenegro 1, Belgium 1
San Marino 1, Bosnia 4
Spain 2, Lithuania 0
Spain 4, Bosnia 2

GROUP 8
Iceland 3, Bulgaria 1
Croatia 1, Hungary 0
Malta 0, Sweden 1
Hungary 1, Iceland 0
Sweden 0, Croatia 2
Croatia 1, Bulgaria 0
Malta 1, Iceland 0
Sweden 2, Hungary 1
Iceland 3, Sweden 1
Bulgaria 2, Malta 1
Malta 0, Hungary 2
Bulgaria 1, Sweden 2
Croatia 2, Iceland 1
Hungary 1, Bulgaria 0
Croatia 1, Malta 0
Bulgaria 2, Croatia 1
Iceland 0, Hungary 1
Sweden 6, Malta 0
Iceland 0, Malta 0

Competition still being played.

UEFA UNDER-21 CHAMPIONSHIP PAST WINNERS
1978 Yugoslavia
1980 USSR
1982 England
1984 England
1986 Spain
1988 France
1990 USSR
1992 Italy
1994 Italy
1996 Italy
1998 Spain
2000 Italy
2002 Czech Republic
2004 Italy

CONFERENCE NATIONAL 2004–2005

			Home					*Away*					*Total*					
	P	*W*	*D*	*L*	*F*	*A*	*W*	*D*	*L*	*F*	*A*	*W*	*D*	*L*	*F*	*A*	*Gd*	*Pts*
1 Barnet	42	16	2	3	56	20	10	6	5	34	24	26	8	8	90	44	46	86
2 Hereford U	42	10	7	4	28	14	11	4	6	40	27	21	11	10	68	41	27	74
3 Carlisle U	42	12	5	4	39	18	8	8	5	35	19	20	13	9	74	37	37	73
4 Aldershot T	42	13	3	5	38	22	8	7	6	30	30	21	10	11	68	52	16	73
5 Stevenage B	42	13	2	6	35	21	9	4	8	30	31	22	6	14	65	52	13	72
6 Exeter C	42	11	5	5	39	22	9	6	6	32	28	20	11	11	71	50	21	71
7 Morecambe	42	12	5	4	38	23	7	9	5	31	27	19	14	9	69	50	19	71
8 Woking	42	11	6	4	29	19	7	8	6	29	26	18	14	10	58	45	13	68
9 Halifax T	42	13	4	4	45	24	6	5	10	29	32	19	9	14	73	56	18	66
10 Accrington S	42	11	6	4	43	26	7	5	9	29	32	18	11	13	72	58	14	65
11 Dagenham & R	42	12	4	5	39	27	7	4	10	29	33	19	8	15	68	60	8	65
12 Crawley T	42	13	4	4	35	18	3	5	13	15	32	16	9	17	50	50	0	57
13 Scarborough	42	9	12	0	42	17	5	2	14	18	29	14	14	14	60	46	14	56
14 Gravesend & N	42	7	7	7	34	31	6	4	11	24	33	13	11	18	58	64	–6	50
15 Tamworth*	42	10	3	8	22	22	4	8	9	31	41	14	11	17	53	63	–10	50
16 Burton Alb	42	6	7	8	25	29	7	4	10	25	37	13	11	18	50	66	–16	50
17 York C	42	7	6	8	22	23	4	4	13	17	43	11	10	21	39	65	–27	43
18 Canvey Is	42	6	10	5	34	31	3	5	13	19	34	9	15	18	53	65	–12	42
19 Northwich Vic†	42	9	5	7	37	29	5	5	11	21	43	14	10	18	58	72	–14	42
20 Forest Green R	42	2	9	10	19	40	4	6	11	22	41	6	15	21	41	81	–40	33
21 Farnborough T	42	4	5	12	20	40	2	6	13	15	49	6	11	25	35	89	–54	29
22 Leigh RMI	42	2	2	17	18	52	2	4	15	13	46	4	6	32	31	98	–67	18

**Tamworth deducted 3 points – breach of league rules.*

†Northwich Victoria deducted 10 points – entered administration.

Leading Goalscorers 2004–05

	League	*P-offs*	*FA Cup*	*LDV*	*Trophy*	*Total*
Guiliano Grazioli *(Barnet)*	29	0	0	0	0	29
Michael Twiss *(Morecambe)*	22	0	3	0	0	25
Paul Mullin *(Accrington S)*	20	0	0	0	0	20
Anthony Elding *(Stevenage B)*	19	0	1	1	0	21
Chris Moore *(Dagenham & R)*	19	0	1	1	0	21
Adam Stansfield *(Hereford U)*	19	0	1	0	1	20
Bob Taylor *(Tamworth)*	19	0	0	0	0	19
Charlie Griffin *(Forest Green R)*	17	0	1	0	0	18
Lee McEvilly *(Accrington S)*	15	0	0	2	0	17
John Allan *(Northwich Vic)*	15	0	0	0	1	16
Lee Boylan *(Canvey Island)*	14	0	0	0	3	17
Tim Sills *(Aldershot T)*	14	0	2	0	0	16
Justin Richards *(Woking)*	14	0	1	0	1	16
Neil Redfearn *(Scarborough)*	14	0	0	0	0	14
Karl Hawley *(Carlisle U)*	13	0	1	0	1	15
Paul Brayson *(Northwich Vic)*	13	0	0	0	0	13

CONFERENCE NATIONAL RESULTS 2004–2005

	Accrington S	Aldershot T	Barnet	Burton Alb	Canvey Is	Carlisle U	Crawley T	Dagenham & R	Exeter C	Farnborough T	Forest Green R	Gravesend & N	Halifax T	Hereford U	Leigh RMI	Morecambe	Northwich Vic	Scarborough	Stevenage B	Tamworth	Woking	York C
Accrington S	—	3-3	4-1	3-1	1-0	1-2	4-0	0-3	0-0	2-1	2-2	1-2	1-1	2-1	2-1	2-1	5-0	2-1	4-1	2-3	0-0	2-2
Aldershot T	0-0	—	2-3	3-0	2-0	0-5	1-0	4-0	2-1	3-1	1-2	1-0	0-0	0-2	2-0	3-3	2-1	2-0	0-1	4-3	4-0	2-0
Barnet	3-0	2-1	—	2-3	1-0	1-1	3-0	5-0	1-0	7-1	3-1	4-1	3-1	0-2	3-2	5-1	4-0	1-0	2-1	0-3	2-2	4-0
Burton Alb	2-2	1-3	1-1	—	1-1	0-1	1-0	1-3	1-0	0-0	4-1	3-2	2-2	3-0	0-0	1-3	1-0	2-3	0-3	1-1	0-1	0-2
Canvey Is	0-2	2-2	0-1	2-2	—	0-3	2-2	4-2	2-2	1-1	2-1	1-1	0-1	0-4	3-0	0-0	2-2	1-0	3-0	3-3	2-2	4-0
Carlisle U	2-0	1-1	1-3	0-0	0-0	—	1-0	1-0	0-2	7-0	0-1	2-2	1-0	3-1	3-0	3-3	1-0	2-1	1-2	2-1	2-1	6-0
Crawley T	2-0	1-0	1-3	4-0	2-1	1-0	—	2-0	0-1	2-0	4-2	1-1	1-2	1-1	2-2	2-1	0-0	2-1	1-2	3-0	2-1	1-0
Dagenham & R	0-5	3-0	2-0	3-1	3-1	1-0	1-0	—	2-3	0-0	2-2	5-0	4-2	3-1	2-0	2-1	2-3	0-3	3-1	0-0	1-1	0-3
Exeter C	1-2	3-1	0-3	3-1	0-1	0-0	3-2	1-1	—	2-1	2-0	3-0	2-1	4-0	5-1	1-1	2-3	3-1	2-0	2-2	0-0	0-1
Farnborough T	2-1	1-2	0-0	1-3	1-3	1-2	2-3	2-1	2-1	—	1-1	0-3	3-2	0-6	0-1	1-2	0-2	0-1	0-3	2-2	0-0	1-1
Forest Green R	1-0	0-0	0-2	3-2	2-2	0-3	1-1	1-4	2-3	1-1	—	1-5	0-0	1-3	1-1	0-3	1-3	0-1	1-1	1-1	1-3	1-1
Gravesend & N	2-2	1-3	1-3	0-2	3-2	1-3	0-0	2-1	1-1	2-2	0-0	—	0-3	1-2	4-1	1-2	2-2	4-0	2-1	2-0	1-1	4-0
Halifax T	1-2	2-0	2-3	2-0	4-1	2-2	1-0	2-2	2-1	2-0	4-0	1-0	—	0-1	5-1	1-3	2-2	2-1	2-1	3-3	3-1	2-0
Hereford U	0-0	2-0	1-1	0-0	1-0	0-0	0-0	0-1	1-2	3-1	2-1	1-0	2-3	—	3-0	1-1	4-0	1-0	0-1	2-1	2-2	2-0
Leigh RMI	0-6	3-3	0-3	1-4	2-1	1-6	1-2	0-1	0-1	1-2	2-0	0-1	0-3	3-4	—	0-2	0-1	1-1	1-2	2-3	0-3	0-3
Morecambe	1-2	0-0	1-1	3-0	4-0	1-1	1-2	1-0	2-2	1-1	3-1	1-3	2-1	2-1	2-1	—	3-1	2-1	1-3	3-0	2-1	2-1
Northwich Vic	3-3	1-2	2-0	4-0	3-1	2-2	1-0	2-2	1-2	2-0	2-1	1-2	1-2	1-4	2-0	2-2	—	1-0	1-1	1-2	1-3	3-0
Scarborough	4-0	2-2	1-1	1-1	1-1	1-1	2-2	2-0	1-1	4-0	0-0	1-0	3-1	0-0	3-0	1-1	3-0	—	3-3	2-2	2-0	5-1
Stevenage B	5-0	0-1	2-1	0-1	1-4	2-1	1-0	1-0	3-2	3-1	2-2	2-0	2-1	0-1	2-0	0-1	4-1	1-0	—	2-0	0-2	2-2
Tamworth	1-0	1-2	0-2	0-2	1-0	1-0	1-0	0-4	1-2	0-2	4-0	2-1	2-1	2-2	0-1	0-0	3-0	1-0	0-0	—	1-3	1-0
Woking	2-1	1-2	1-1	1-0	1-0	1-1	2-0	2-4	3-3	2-0	0-1	2-0	2-1	1-1	1-0	0-0	2-0	1-1	1-2	2-1	—	1-0
York C	0-1	0-2	2-1	1-2	0-0	2-1	3-1	0-0	1-2	4-0	1-3	0-0	1-1	0-3	1-1	1-0	0-0	0-2	3-1	2-0	0-2	—

APPEARANCES AND GOALSCORERS 2004–2005

ACCRINGTON STANLEY

Goals: *League (72):* Mullin 20, McEvilly 15, Craney 10, Brannan 6 (3 pens), Prendergast 5, Jagielka 3, Cavanagh 2, James 2 (1 pen), Roberts 2, Smith 2, Williams 2, Brown 1, Flitcroft 1, Howarth 1.

LDV Vans Trophy (4): McEvilly 2, Craney 1, Flynn 1.

League Appearances: Alcock, 5; Banim, 0+3; Bimson, 6; Brannan, 26+3; Brown, 9; Butler, 27; Cavanagh, 34; Cook, 4+21; Craney, 30+8; Crichton, 19; Flitcroft, 11+2; Flynn, 31; Gerrard, 5; Halford, 4; Howarth, 11+6; Howson, 5+3; Ikeme, 3; Jagielka, 35+4; James, 6+7; Kennedy, 15; McEvilly, 36+3; Mullin, 42; O'Neill, 2+2; Prendergast, 20+12; Proctor, 24+2; Roberts, 6+2; Smith, 8+17; Tuck, 0+1; Williams, 38.

ALDERSHOT TOWN

Goals: *League (68):* Sills 14, Challinor 9, Barnard D 7 (1 pen), Dixon 7 (1 pen), Crittenden N 6, Miller 4 (1 pen), Robinson 4, Watson 4, D'Sane 3 (1 pen), Johnson 2, McLean 2, Smith 2, Clarke 1, Giles 1, Lee 1 (pen), own goal 1.

FA Cup (7): Dixon 2, McLean 2, Sills 2, Crittenden N 1.

Play-offs (2): Crittenden N 1, Slabber 1.

League Appearances: Antwi, 23+9; Barnard, D. 35; Barnes-Homer, 0+2; Bull, 42; Caceres, 6; Challinor, 30+7; Clarke, 13+10; Crittenden, A. 0+2; Crittenden, N. 29+12; D'Sane, 7+3; Dixon, 10; Eribenne, 1+2; Giles, 28+5; Holloway, 9; Jinadu, 5+6; Johnson, 25+4; Lee, 10+1; McAuley, 24+2; McLean, 19+6; Miller, 15; Mustafa, 10+2; Reeves, 1; Rendell, 1+6; Robinson, 8; Sills, 30+8; Slabber, 1+1; Smith, 3+9; Viveash, 6; Warburton, 22+3; Warner, 18+1; Watson, 31.

BARNET

Goals: *League (90):* Grazioli 29, Sinclair 11, Hatch 10, Roache 6, Strevens 6, Bailey 5, Hendon 5 (4 pens), Graham 4, King 4, Lee 4, Yakubu 2, Batt 1, own goals 3.

FA Cup (3): Graham 1, Hatch 1, Yakubu 1.

LDV Vans Trophy (3): Bailey 2 (1 pen), Roache 1.

FA Trophy (2): Bailey 2.

League Appearances: Ada, 0+2; Bailey, 23+13; Batt, 8+7; Champion, 0+2; Charles, 8+1; Clist, 40; Dobson, 0+3; Elmes, 0+2; Gore, 7; Graham, 38+1; Grazioli, 37; Hatch, 32+4; Hendon, 37; King, 40; Lee, 35+2; Lopez, 2+11; McBean, 0+4; Millard, 8; Plummer, 3; Roache, 8+20; Sinclair, 39; Strevens, 35+4; Tynan, 27+1; Yakubu, 35.

BURTON ALBION

Goals: *League (50):* Shaw 11 (1 pen), Dudley 8 (3 pens), Ducros 5, Talbot 5, Anderson 4, Hall 4, Taylor K 3, Miller 2, Clough 1, Corbett 1, Robins 1, Shilton 1, Simpkins 1, Stride 1, Ward 1, Wilson 1.

FA Cup (1): Ayres 1.

FA Trophy (7): Anderson 1, Miller 1, Shaw 1, Stride 1, Talbot 1, Taylor 1, Webster 1 (pen).

League Appearances: Alexis, 1; Anderson, 14+15; Austin, 26+5; Ayers, 23+3; Briscoe, 10; Britton, 0+1; Clough, 21+4; Coates, 1+1; Corbett, 30+7; Crane, 36; Crosby, 0+1; Ducros, 32+5; Dudley, 33+2; Elam, 1; Garner, 0+1; Hall, 29+10; Henshaw, 3+2; Jones, 1; Kirkwood, 12+15; Midworth, 4+3; Miller, 17+2; Price, 3; Robins, 8+2; Shaw, 18+1; Shilton, 28+3; Simpkins, 14+6; Stride, 25; Talbot, 9+5; Taylor, K. 5; Taylor, M. 5; Ward, 3+1; Wassall, 0+1; Webster, 36+2; Wilson, 13+7; Wright, 1+1.

CANVEY ISLAND

Goals: *League (53):* Boylan 14 (1 pen), Berquez 9, McDougald 6 (1 pen), Duffy 4, Gregory 4 (2 pens), Midgley 4, Keeling 3, Braniff 1, Burton 1, McGhee 1, Minton 1, Noto 1, Pearson 1, Sedgemore 1, Theobald 1, own goal 1.

FA Cup (4): Berquez 1, Gregory 1 (pen), McDougald 1, Midgley 1.

FA Trophy (7): Boylan 3, Berquez 2, Minton 1, Sedgemore 1.

League Appearances: Berquez, 26+6; Boylan, 24+4; Braniff, 3+1; Burton, 5+3; Chenery, 14+1; Cowan, 8+3; Duffy, 36+3; Gooden, 2+2; Goodwin, 0+4; Gregory, 29+5; Hallett, 3+4; Harrison, 2+1; Joseph, 11+4; Keeling, 24+9; Kennedy, 21+4; Mapes, 1+1; McDougald, 10+24; McGhee, 22; Midgley, 20+6; Minton, 18+1; Noto, 5+4; Pearson, 5; Potter, 40; Sedgemore, 36+1; Smith, 16+7; Sterling, 34; Theobald, 15+2; Ward, 23; Williamson, 9+3.

CARLISLE UNITED

Goals: *League (74):* Hawley 13, Vieira 10, Lumsdon 9 (3 pens), Murphy 7, Preece 7 (1 pen), Holmes 5, McGill 4, Billy 2, Cowan 2, Farrell 2, Grand 2, Gray 2, Henderson 2, Livesey 2, Murray G 2, Beharall 1, Murray A 1, own goal 1.

FA Cup (6): Farrell 1, Gray 1, Hawley 1, McGill 1, Preece 1, Viera 1.

LDV Vans Trophy (2): Grand 1, Henderson 1.

FA Trophy (7): Farrell 2, Vieira 2, Hawley 1, Livesey 1, Preece 1.

Play-offs (3): Billy 1, Livesey 1, Murphy 1.

League Appearances: Andrews, 12+2; Arnison, 15+10; Beech, 2; Beharall, 13+1; Billy, 37+1; Cowan, 29; Farrell, 3+15; Glennon, 38; Grand, 23; Gray, 30; Hackney, 0+2; Hawley, 36+4; Henderson, 2+11; Holmes, 13; Livesey, 20; Lumsdon, 38; McGill, 26+2; Murphy, 38; Murray, A. 8; Murray, G. 5+15; Preece, 10+5; Roca, 4+7; Shelley, 20+1; Simpson, 0+2; Tierney, 10; Vieira, 26+10; Westwood, 4.

CRAWLEY TOWN
Goals: *League (50):* Tait 10, MacDonald 8 (3 pens), Marney 5, Jenkins 4, Armstrong 3, Davidson 3, Harkin 2 (1 pen), Robinson 2, Burton N 1, Burton S 1, Deane 1, Dolan 1, Hankin 1, Manuella 1, Mapes 1, Opinel 1, Palmer 1, Watkins 1, Wormull 1, own goals 2.
FA Cup (1): Tait 1.
FA Trophy (7): MacDonald 2, Davidson 1, Harkin 1 (pen), Opinel 1, Tait 1, Wormull 1 (pen).
League Appearances: Armstrong, 25+5; Burton, N. 7; Burton, S. 4; Davidson, 16+12; Day, 1; Deane, 6+5; Dolan, 12; Donovan, 6; El-Abd, 0+1; Gooding, 6+1; Hankin, 24+2; Harkin, 16+5; Healy, 1+3; Hemsley, 4+3; Jenkins, 40+1; Judge, 29+2; Keehan, 0+2; Kember, 22+4; Little, 7; MacDonald, 26+3; Manuella, 4+2; Mapes, 20+7; Marney, 17+12; Opinel, 7+1; Palmer, 19+4; Platel, 1+1; Rees, 4+1; Robinson, 8; Simpemba, 39; Smith, 35; Tait, 23+11; Traynor, 9+5; Watkins, 5; Wormull, 19+1.

DAGENHAM & REDBRIDGE
Goals: *League (68):* Moore 19 (3 pens), Mackail-Smith 12, Southam 10, Boot 6, Bruce 3, Leberl 3, Flynn 2 (1 pen), Janney 2, Uddin 2, Clark 1, Cole 1, Goodwin 1, Harrold 1, Midson 1, Taylor 1, Vickers 1, own goals 2.
FA Cup (3): Boot 1, Janney 1, Moore 1 (pen).
LDV Vans Trophy (1): Moore 1.
FA Trophy (1): Uddin 1.
League Appearances: Baimass, 0+1; Barton, 0+2; Baruwa, 0+1; Bastock, 1; Blackett, 12+13; Boot, 13+14; Brennan, 0+1; Bruce, 30+2; Clark, 11+1; Cole, 20; Douglas, 0+5; Flynn, 24+2; Foster, 19; Francis, 0+1; Goodwin, 32+1; Griffiths, 17+1; Harrold, 2+2; Hill, 1+5; Janney, 21+4; Leberl, 35+1; Lettejallon, 0+2; Mackail-Smith, 30+10; McGowen, 0+1; Midson, 2+8; Moore, 38; O'Reilly, 3; Roberts, 38; Southam, 41; Taylor, 4+1; Uddin, 41+1; Vaughan, 0+1; Vickers, 27+3.

EXETER CITY
Goals: *League (71):* Flack 12, Devine 11 (1 pen), Gaia 7, Edwards 6, Taylor 5, Phillips 4, Sheldon 4, McConnell 3 (2 pens), Moxey 3, Jeannin 2, Sawyer 2, Ampadu 1, Buckle 1, Hiley 1, Ibe 1, Martin 1, O'Sullivan 1, Todd 1, own goals 5.
FA Cup (3): Edwards 1, Devine 1, Gaia 1.
LDV Vans Trophy (3): Edwards 1, Gaia 1, Jeannin 1.
FA Trophy (9): Devine 3 (1 pen), Edwards 2, Ampadu 1, Clay 1, Sheldon 1, Taylor 1.
League Appearances: Afful, 33+6; Ampadu, 29+1; Bittner, 5; Buckle, 9+2; Canham, 1+1; Clay, 9+4; Cronin, 3+1; Devine, 25+12; Edwards, 22+12; Flack, 20+16; Gaia, 33; Hiley, 42; Ibe, 2+2; Jeannin, 33; Jones, 22+1; Martin, 9+12; McConnell, 5+5; Moxey, 22+8; O'Sullivan, 1+8; Phillips, 11+3; Rice, 15; Sawyer, 27+5; Sheldon, 18+10; Taylor, 39+2; Todd, 27; Tully, 0+2.

FARNBOROUGH TOWN
Goals: *League (35):* Taggart 6 (3 pens), Blackman 5, Harkness 4, Charles M 3, Hughes S 3, Gibbs 2, Holloway G 2, Johnson 2, Opinel 2, Allen-Page 1, Eribenne 1 (pen), Pacquette 1, Smith 1, Townsend 1, Traynor 1.
FA Cup (1): Hughes S 1.
League Appearances: Allen-Page, 27+2; Ashwood, 0+1; Belaid, 0+1; Bernard, 4; Blackman, 24+2; Braley, 4; Burton, 21+1; Canham, 7+2; Chabaan, 5+9; Charles, A. 15+2; Charles, M. 0+11; Cole, 1; Deane, 5+7; Eribenne, 4; Fenton, 8; Gibbs, 9; Hamilton, 3+4; Harkness, 15+4; Heeroo, 2+4; Hemsley, 2; Holloway, C. 30; Holloway, G. 28; Howe, 0+2; Hughes, R. 10+1; Hughes, S. 18+3; Johnson, 8+4; Kightly, 10+1; Miles, 22+7; Mulhern, 4+17; Opinel, 20+1; Osborn, 7; Pacquette, 2+3; Parker, 3; Petterson, 4; Riddell, 0+3; Rooney, 21+1; Smith, 26; Taggart, 38+3; Theo, 24+6; Townsend, 12+2; Traynor, 9+4; Turner, 9; Williams, 1.

FOREST GREEN ROVERS
Goals: *League (41):* Griffin 17 (4 pens), Beesley 9, Gadsby 3, Rogers 2, Searle 2, Warhurst 2, Alsop 1, Cleverley 1, Harris 1, Hodgson 1, Louis 1, Williams 1 (pen).
FA Cup (7): Beesley 2, Louis 2, Griffin 1, Lyttle 1, Richardson 1.
FA Trophy (1): own goal 1.
League Appearances: Alexis, 0+2; Alsop, 3; Appleby, 4+3; Beesley, 25+7; Beswetherick, 8+2; Betts, 3; Brown, Marvin, 0+4; Brown, Matt, 0+1; Burns, 2+1; Cleverley, 8+8; Cowe, 5+1; Danks, 3+15; Davies, 27+2; Davis, 0+4; Gadsby, 36+2; Garner, 24+2; Gill, 2+4; Gould, 4; Greaves, 2; Green, 7+6; Griffin, 33+6; Haldane, 6; Harkin, 5+1; Harris, 12; Hodgson, 5+2; Holloway, 9+1; Louis, 7+1; Loxton, 3; Lyttle, 36; McAuley, 8+2; Perrin, 19; Rapley, 5; Reed, 7; Richardson, 28+2; Roberts, 16+3; Rogers,

28+9; Rushbury, 2+1; Searle, 26; Sykes, 6; Turner, 1; Warhurst, 6; Watson, 4+3; Williams, 27.

GRAVESEND & NORTHFLEET

Goals: *League (58):* Essandoh 9, Saunders 7, Drury 6, Omoyinmi 6, Skinner 5 (5 pens), Protheroe 3, Jackson 2, Louis 2, Lovell 2, McAllister 2 (1 pen), McKimm 2, Moore 2, Pinnock 2, Sidibe 2, Bunce 1, McCarthy 1, Sigere 1, own goals 3.
FA Cup (2): Saunders 1, Skinner 1 (pen).
FA Trophy (9): Omoyinmi 4, Jackson 2, Saunders 2, McCarthy 1.
League Appearances: Anselin, 0+1; Bouadji, 2; Bunce, 10; Davis, 0+2; Deane, 3+2; Drury, 35+3; Essandoh, 31+5; Gledhill, 21+2; Groombridge, 0+1; Harrhy, 0+1; Jackson, 19+9; Louis, 3+2; Lovell, 15+8; McAllister, 5; McCarthy, 13; McKimm, 34+1; Mitten, 1; Moore, 19+4; Omoyinmi, 21+2; Peters, 0+1; Pinnock, 14+17; Popovic, 5; Porter, 20+1; Protheroe, 28+3; Pullen, 17; Rouse, 0; Saunders, 36; Shearer, 4+1; Sidibe, 10+16; Sigere, 11; Skinner, 33; Surey, 28+3; Wilkerson, 24.

HALIFAX TOWN

Goals: *League (74):* Killeen 12, Midgley 11 (5 pens), Sugden 11, Howell 6 (1 pen), Mansaram 6, Foster 4, Monington 4, Ross 4 (2 pens), Quinn 3, Bushell 2, Mallon 2, Young 2, Blunt 1, Chin 1, Grant 1, Ingram 1, Meechan 1, Stoneman 1, own goal 1.
FA Cup (7): Midgley 3 (1 pen), Ross 2, Foster 1, Bushell 1.
League Appearances: Blunt, 22+4; Bushell, 24; Chin, 2+7; Clarke, 3+1; Doughty, 28; Dunbavin, 39; Farrell, 0+1; Foster, 33+2; Grant, 6+2; Haslam, 32; Hockenhull, 5+2; Howell, 26+8; Ingram, 37; Killeen, 28+11; Mallon, 4+10; Mansaram, 12+6; McClare, 1; McStay, 7+1; Meechan, 4+5; Midgley, 30+9; Monington, 5+4; Munroe, 5+1; Naylor, 0+1; Parry, 1+1; Quinn, 37+2; Ross, 4+9; Salisbury, 2; Sanasy, 0+2; Senior, 3+1; Stoneman, 10+6; Sugden, 38+1; Toulson, 0+1; Willis, 2; Young, 12+1.

HEREFORD UNITED

Goals: *League (68):* Stansfield 19, Brown 8, Mills 8, Williams D 7, Carey-Bertram 6 (1 pen), Mkandawire 4, Stanley 3, Pitman 2, Purdie 2 (1 pen), Green 1, James 1 (pen), Travis 1, Tretton 1, Williams L 1, own goals 4.
FA Cup (7): Mills 2, Mkandawire 1, Purdie 1, Stanley 1, Stansfield 1, Travis 1.
LDV Vans Trophy (5): Carey-Bertram 1, Mills 1, Pitman 1, Stanley 1, Williams D 1.
FA Trophy (14): Carey-Bertram 4, James 2 (1 pen), Mkandawire 1, Purdie 1, Robinson 1, Smikie 1, Smith 1, Stanley 1, Stansfield 1, Williams D 1.
Play-offs (1): Carey-Bertram 1.
League Appearances: Anyinsah, 3; Brown, 23+6; Carey-Bertram, 12+9; Gould, 14; Green, 20+6; Hyde, 21+11; James, 29+1; Mawson, 27; Mills, 16+15; Mkandawire, 33+1; Pitman, 30+2; Purdie, 22+9; Robinson, 34+2; Scott, 1; Smikle, 3; Smith, 8+3; Stanley, 41; Stansfield, 30+9; Taylor, 5; Travis, 33+2; Tretton, 26+1; Williams, D. 30+6; Williams, L. 1+4.

LEIGH RMI

Goals: *League (31):* Stoker 5, Williams 5, Byrne 3, Mulvaney 2, Rose 2, Simms 2, Allen 1, Connell 1, Fitzpatrick 1, Gaunt 1, Jones 1, Lane 1, Meechan 1, Miller 1, Peers 1, Peyton 1, Smith S 1, Taylor 1.
FA Cup (3): Simms 2, Rose 1 (pen).
FA Trophy (1): Reed 1.
League Appearances: Adams, 3+2; Allen, 2+7; Ashmole, 3+8; Burton, 2; Byrne, 7; Clarke, C. 4; Clarke, R. 21+1; Connell, 3; Coyne, 6+3; Crichton, 4; Douglas-Pringle, 1; Drew, 10+8; Farrer, 0+1; Fitzpatrick, 6; Gaunt, 16; Gibson, 12; Hockless, 2; Holmes, 10+1; Houlickin, 2; Howarth, 1; Jones, 7+5; Lane, 39; Mann, 6; Marrison, 1+1; Martin, 17; McGuire, 0+1; Meechan, 12+2; Miller, 18; Mitchell, 5+7; Moran, 7; Mulvaney, 9; Murray, 6; Peers, 3+4; Peyton, 30+4; Reed, 2+1; Rezai, 1; Ridler, 6; Rioch, 2; Robertson, 5; Roscoe, 27+3; Rose, 20+1; Ryder, 3; Sanasy, 1; Shillito, 15+2; Shilton, 1+2; Simms, 15+10; Simpkins, 6; Smith, C. 6; Smith, N. 1+1; Smith, S. 8+13; Starbuck, 0+2; Stoker, 22; Taylor, 2+6; Tench, 1+3; Turner, 4+1; Warrick, 1; Walsh, 3; Warsnop, 15; Williams, 20+2.

MORECAMBE

Goals: *League (69):* Twiss 22 (4 pens), Carlton 12, Curtis 12, Thompson 5, Bentley 4, Walmsley 4, Elam 3, Hunter 3 (1 pen), Kempson 2, McFlynn 1, Stringfellow 1.
FA Cup (7): Twiss 3, Curtis 2, Bentley 1, Hunter 1.
FA Trophy (4): Carlton 1, Curtis 1, Hunter 1, McFlynn 1.
League Appearances: Bentley, 38; Blackburn, 39; Carlton, 21+17; Curtis, 36+4; Dodgson, 0+4; Edwards, 0+1; Elam, 18+6; Heard, 20+7; Howard, 30+2; Hunter, 28+7; Kelly, 6+1; Kempson, 19; McFlynn, 8+5; O'Connor, 2; Osborne, 1; Perkins, 35; Robinson, 15+1; Rogan, 1+8; Sollitt, 27; Stringfellow, 5+9; Swan, 30+4; Thompson, 15+20; Twiss, 40; Walmsley, 28+9.

NORTHWICH VICTORIA

Goals: *League (58):* Allan 15, Brayson 13 (5 pens), Quayle 9 (2 pens), Devlin 6, Carr 2, Garvey 2, Hughes 2, Band 1, Brisco 1, Foran 1, Mayman 1, Thompson 1, Young 1, own goals 3.

FA Cup (1): Quayle 1.
FA Trophy (1): Allan 1.
League Appearances: Allan, 36; Bailey, 2+3; Band, 17+2; Brayson, 26+4; Briggs, 0+1; Brisco, 10; Burke, 8; Byrne, 1+7; Came, 1+1; Carr, 16; Carratt, 0+4; Charnock, 39; Clegg, 1+1; Connett, 14+2; Devlin, 38+1; Fitzpatrick, 0+2; Foran, 10+1; Forsyth, 3; Gaghan, 1+6; Garner, 6+2; Garvey, 29+5; Hadland, 4+9; Handyside, 30; Harrison, 7; Hildred, 2+2; Hughes, 6+2; Hunter, 4+1; Kuduzovic, 1; Lancaster, 5; Mayman, 19+1; McCarthy, 34+1; McLachlan, 3; Munroe, 7+3; Norris, 1+4; O'Neill, 1; Pearce, 7+1; Quayle, 27+5; Ralph, 21; Roca, 3+1; Rogers, 7; Royle, 8+5; Thompson, 0+2; Tierney, 1+2; Young, 6.

SCARBOROUGH
Goals: *League (60):* Redfearn 14 (4 pens), Senior 12, Hackworth 8, Cryan 4, Reeves 4 (1 pen), Burton 2, Coulson 2, Gill 2, Hotte 2, Nicholson 2, Thompson 2, Bishop 1, Gilroy 1, Kerr 1, Lyth 1, Pounder 1, own goal 1.
FA Cup (1): Hotte 1.
LDV Vans Trophy (1): Gilroy 1.
FA Trophy (1): Senior 1.
League Appearances: Baker, 30; Beadle, 0+1; Bishop, 10; Burton, 5+10; Coulson, 0+11; Cryan, 42; Foot, 23+3; Foster, 4+3; Gill, 14+6; Gilroy, 19+4; Grant, 0+1; Hackworth, 28+9; Horrigan, 0+1; Hotte, 34+1; Jones, 0+2; Keen, 3; Kerr, 35+3; Lyth, 10+15; Nicholson, 42; Pounder, 8+10; Redfearn, 36+3; Reeves, 10; Senior, 24+18; Thompson, 42; Townson, 4; Walker, 39.

STEVENAGE BOROUGH
Goals: *League (65):* Elding 19, Maamria 10 (1 pen), Stamp 8, Goodliffe 5, Brady 4, Boyd 2, Bulman 2, Flack 2, Hanlon 2, Hunter 2, Quailey 2, Weatherstone 2, Brough 1, Hocking 1, Laker 1, Nurse 1, Quinn 1.
FA Cup (6): Boyd 1, Brough 1, Elding 1, Hanlon 1, McAlister 1, Quinn 1.
LDV Vans Trophy (1): Elding 1.
Play-offs (2): Maamria 2.
League Appearances: Boyd, 20+12; Brady, 23+11; Brough, 12+10; Bulman, 39+1; Burch, 3; Croudson, 1; Elding, 39+2; Farrow, 1+1; Flack, 1+17; Goodliffe, 37; Gregory, 36+1; Hanlon, 14+4; Henry, 6+5; Hocking, 34+3; Hunter, 2+5; Jarrett, 1+3; Julian, 14; Laker, 30+1; Lee, 0+1; Maamria, 23+6; Marshall, 2; McAllister, 2+4; Nurse, 8+9; Pacquette, 1; Quailey, 8+2; Quinn, 28+2; Rogers, 16; Schillaci, 0+1; Stamp, 15+1; Stewart, 0+1; Sullivan, 0+1; Warner, 12+2; Weatherstone, 13+8; Woodman, 21.

TAMWORTH
Goals: *League (53):* Taylor 19, Whitman 11, Ebdon 4 (2 pens), Harrad 3 (1 pen), Redmile 3, Ross 2, Smith A 2, Bampton 1, Brown A 1, Brown M 1, Colkin 1, Cooper 1, May 1, Rawle 1, Soares 1, Storer 1.
FA Cup (2): Cooper 2.
FA Trophy (5): Ebdon 3 (1 pen), Cooper 1, Smith 1.
League Appearances: Bampton, 17+5; Blunt, 7; Brown, A. 18+6; Brown, M. 5; Colkin, 17+2; Cooper, 22+3; Curtis, 3+3; Douglas, 0+1; Ebdon, 31; Francis, 0+11; Harrad, 6; Hawkins, 1+1; Johnson, 2+2; Marcelle, 6+4; May, 2+6; McIntyre, 2+1; Millard, 2; Morrison, 6; Neal, 5; Price, 35; Rawle, 3; Redmile, 38; Robinson, 20+1; Rose, 6; Ross, 7; Shaw, 1+5; Sheppard, 10+12; Simpson, 27+2; Smith, A. 34; Smith, N. 1+4; Soares, 6+1; Stamps, 29+1; Stirling, 5; Storer, 17+12; Sylla, 1; Taylor, 31+4; Turner, 12+1; Whitman, 27+7.

WOKING
Goals: *League (58):* Richards 14, Nade 9, Selley 7 (4 pens), Evans 5, Oliver 5, Murray 4, Louis 3, Canham 2, Ferguson 2, MacDonald 2, Sharpling 2, Boardman 1, Foyewa 1, own goal 1.
FA Cup (5): Murray 2, Richards 1, Selley 1, Tiesse 1.
FA Trophy (5): Louis 2, Evans 1, Murray 1, Richards 1.
League Appearances: Basso, 22; Boardman, 40; Canham, 11+4; Cockerill, 10+3; Cooney, 1; Evans, 28+1; Ferguson, 6+11; Foyewa, 11+24; Gosling, 2+6; Jackson, 20+5; Jalal, 20+1; Johnson, 9+6; Louis, 21+2; MacDonald, 33+1; Murray, 38+1; Nade, 33+7; Oliver, 38+1; Richards, 34+7; Selley, 39; Sharpling, 18+5; Smith, 27+5; Tiesse, 1+2.

YORK CITY
Goals: *League (39):* Bishop 11 (1 pen), Robinson P 4, Dunning 3 (1 pen), Groves 3, Maloney 4, Nogan 3, Donovan 2, Grant 2, Merris 2, Yalcin 2, Brass 1, Robinson P 1, Stewart 1, Webster 1.
FA Cup (1): Dunning 1.
League Appearances: Armstrong, 3+2; Arthur, 0+1; Ashcroft, 2; Bishop, 37+1; Brass, 20+2; Clarke, 5; Coad, 1+1; Constable, 2; Crichton, 4; Davies, 16; Davis, 14+1; Donovan, 30+1; Dunning, 37+1; Grant, 7+1; Groves, 38+4; Harrison, 0+3; Haw, 0+2; Jackson, 7+3; Law, 24+7; Maloney, 13; McGurk, 5+1; Merris, 38+2; Nogan, 18+4; Pearson, 12; Porter, 18; Robinson, P. 5+8; Robinson, PD. 22+11; Smith, 16+3; Staley, 10+2; Stewart, 15+3; Stockdale, 20+1; Webster, 13+2; Yalcin, 10+21.

CONFERENCE NATIONAL PLAY-OFFS 2004–2005

SEMI-FINALS FIRST LEG

Monday, 2 May 2005

Aldershot T (0) 1 *(Crittenden N 48)*

Carlisle U (0) 0 6617

Aldershot T: Bull; Mustafa, Barnard D, Lee, Antwi, Johnson, Crittenden N, Holloway (Challinor), Sills (Slabber), Watson, Clarke.
Carlisle U: Glennon; Arnison, Beharall, Billy, Gray, Cowan, Lumsdon, Murray A (McGill), Vieira (Hawley), Holmes (Murray G), Murphy.

Stevenage B (0) 1 *(Maamria 87)*

Hereford U (0) 1 *(Carey-Bertram 74)* 6520

Stevenage B: Julian; Warner, Gregory, Bulman, Henry, Goodliffe, Brady, Stamp, Maamria, Elding, Nurse (Boyd).
Hereford U: Mawson; Green, Robinson, Pitman, Mkandawire, Tretton, Stanley, Purdie, Stansfield (James), Mills (Carey-Bertram), Travis (Williams D).

SEMI-FINALS SECOND LEG

Friday, 6 May 2005

Carlisle U (2) 2 *(Livesey 13, Billy 35)*

Aldershot T (0) 1 *(Slabber 90)* 10,803

Carlisle U: Glennon; Beharall, Cowan, Billy, Gray, Livesey, McGill, Lumsdon, Murray G, Holmes (Vieira), Murphy.
Aldershot T: Bull; Mustafa, Barnard D (Giles), Lee, Antwi, Johnson, Crittenden N, Watson, Sills (Slabber), Holloway, Clarke (Challinor).
aet; Carlisle U won 5-4 on penalties: Antwi (scored), Lumsdon (scored), Lee (scored), McGill (saved), Slabber (scored), Murray G (saved), Giles (saved), Vieira (scored), Crittenden N (saved), Murphy (scored), Holloway (scored), Billy (scored), Challinor (saved), Levesey (scored).

Hereford U (0) 0

Stevenage B (0) 1 *(Maamria 69)* 6862

Hereford U: Mawson; Green, Robinson, Hyde (Travis), Mkandawire, Tretton, Stanley, Purdie, Stansfield, Carey-Bertram, Williams D (Williams L).
Stevenage B: Julian; Warner, Gregory, Bulman, Henry, Goodliffe, Brady, Stamp (Nurse), Maamria, Elding, Laker (Boyd).

FINAL (at Britannia Stadium)

Saturday, 14 May 2005

Stevenage B (0) 0

Carlisle U (1) 1 *(Murphy 23)* 13,422

Stevenage B: Julian; Warner, Gregory, Bulman, Henry, Goodliffe (Weatherstone), Brady, Stamp (Nurse), Maamria, Elding, Laker (Boyd).
Carlisle U: Glennon; Beharall, Cowan, Billy, Gray, Livesey, McGill, Lumsdon, Murray G (Vieira), Holmes (Hawley), Murphy.
Referee: J. Moss (West Yorkshire).

ATTENDANCES BY CLUB 2004–2005

	Aggregate 2004–05	*Average 2004–05*	*Highest Attendance 2004–05*
Carlisle United	115,772	5,513	9,215 v Barnet
Exeter City	71,166	3,389	4,529 v Scarborough
Hereford United	64,429	3,068	3,978 v Exeter City
Aldershot Town	63,904	3,043	4,458 v Woking
Barnet	52,753	2,512	3,924 v Halifax Town
York City	48,941	2,331	4,439 v Scarborough
Woking	47,940	2,283	3,718 v Aldershot Town
Stevenage Borough	43,985	2,095	4,307 v Barnet
Crawley Town	42,368	2,018	2,949 v Barnet
Scarborough	37,423	1,782	4,586 v York City
Morecambe	36,783	1,752	4,660 v Carlisle United
Halifax Town	36,099	1,719	2,696 v Carlisle United
Accrington Stanley	32,278	1,537	3,024 v Carlisle United
Dagenham & Redbridge	28,938	1,378	1,923 v Barnet
Burton Albion	28,738	1,368	1,914 v Carlisle United
Gravesend & Northfleet	28,061	1,336	2,030 v Carlisle United
Tamworth	27,219	1,296	2,443 v Burton Albion
Farnborough Town	19,029	906	2,369 v Aldershot Town
Northwich Victoria	18,134	864	1,803 v Carlisle United
Forest Green Rovers	17,956	855	2,142 v Hereford United
Canvey Island	16,879	804	1,309 v Dagenham & Redbridge
Leigh RMI	9,129	435	1,540 v Carlisle United

CONFERENCE SECOND DIVISION NORTH 2004–2005

FINAL LEAGUE TABLE

			Home					*Away*					*Total*						
		P	*W*	*D*	*L*	*F*	*A*	*W*	*D*	*L*	*F*	*A*	*W*	*D*	*L*	*F*	*A*	*Gd*	*Pts*
1	Southport	42	12	6	3	35	20	13	3	5	48	25	25	9	8	83	45	38	84
2	Nuneaton Borough	42	13	3	5	29	17	12	3	6	39	28	25	6	11	68	45	23	81
3	Droylsden	42	13	3	5	46	26	11	4	6	36	26	24	7	11	82	52	30	79
4	Kettering Town	42	10	4	7	22	21	11	3	7	34	29	21	7	14	56	50	6	70
5	Altrincham	42	12	6	3	45	21	7	6	8	21	25	19	12	11	66	46	20	69
6	Harrogate Town	42	13	5	3	40	22	6	6	9	22	27	19	11	12	62	49	13	68
7	Worcester City	42	10	5	6	32	25	6	7	8	27	28	16	12	14	59	53	6	60
8	Stafford Rangers	42	8	10	3	33	20	6	7	8	19	24	14	17	11	52	44	8	59
9	Redditch United*	42	11	3	7	36	32	7	5	9	29	27	18	8	16	65	59	6	59
10	Hucknall Town	42	7	8	6	31	32	8	6	7	28	25	15	14	13	59	57	2	59
11	Gainsborough Trinity	42	7	8	6	27	22	9	1	11	28	33	16	9	17	55	55	0	57
12	Hinckley United	42	8	5	8	29	31	7	6	8	26	31	15	11	16	55	62	–7	56
13	Lancaster City	42	9	4	8	23	22	5	8	8	28	37	14	12	16	51	59	–8	54
14	Alfreton Town	42	7	5	9	24	23	8	3	10	29	32	15	8	19	53	55	–2	53
15	Vauxhall Motors	42	7	7	7	20	22	7	4	10	28	35	14	11	17	48	57	–9	53
16	Barrow	42	8	5	8	32	39	6	5	10	18	25	14	10	18	50	64	–14	52
17	Worksop Town†	42	11	4	6	36	29	5	8	8	23	30	16	12	14	59	59	0	50
18	Moor Green	42	8	4	9	26	28	5	6	10	29	36	13	10	19	55	64	–9	49
19	Stalybridge Celtic	42	7	6	8	30	36	5	6	10	22	34	12	12	18	52	70	–18	48
20	Runcorn FC Halton	42	7	6	8	24	26	3	6	12	20	37	10	12	20	44	63	–19	42
21	Ashton United	42	6	2	13	27	39	2	7	12	19	40	8	9	25	46	79	–33	33
22	Bradford Park Av	42	3	5	13	20	37	2	4	15	17	33	5	9	28	37	70	–33	24

**Redditch United deducted 3 points.*

†*Worksop Town deducted 10 points.*

LEADING GOALSCORERS

Terry Fearns *(Southport)*	32
Colin Little *(Altrincham)*	24
Norman Sylla *(Redditch United)*	22
Adam Webster *(Worcester City)*	22
Peter Duffield *(Alfreton Town)*	20

CONFERENCE SECOND DIVISION NORTH PLAY-OFFS
SEMI-FINALS

Droylsden 1, Kettering Town 2
Nuneaton Borough 1, Altrincham 1
(Altrincham won 4-2 on penalties.)

FINAL

Kettering Town 2, Altrincham 3

CONFERENCE SECOND DIVISION NORTH/SOUTH PLAY-OFF

FINAL

Cambridge C 0, Eastbourne Borough 3

CONFERENCE SECOND DIVISION NORTH RESULTS 2004–2005

	Alfreton T	Altrincham	Ashton U	Barrow	Bradford PA	Droylsden	Gainsborough T	Harrogate T	Hinckley U	Hucknall T	Kettering T	Lancaster C	Moor Green	Nuneaton B	Redditch U	Runcorn	Southport	Stafford R	Stalybridge C	Vauxhall M	Worcester C	Worksop T
Alfreton T	—	0-2	1-1	1-1	2-1	0-1	0-1	2-0	0-2	0-2	1-2	2-3	2-2	2-0	1-2	4-0	2-1	0-1	1-0	3-1	0-0	0-0
Altrincham	1-2	—	1-2	2-0	0-0	2-2	4-1	3-0	4-1	1-1	3-3	4-0	0-2	1-0	0-0	3-3	2-1	1-0	4-1	3-1	2-0	4-1
Ashton U	3-1	0-1	—	1-2	0-0	1-0	1-3	3-2	0-2	0-0	0-2	2-0	1-3	2-3	2-3	5-4	0-3	1-2	2-3	0-2	1-0	2-3
Barrow	0-3	2-0	1-1	—	3-2	1-3	2-0	1-0	3-0	0-3	2-1	2-2	3-4	1-3	1-6	1-1	0-2	2-2	2-1	1-2	2-2	2-1
Bradford PA	0-4	1-2	3-3	0-1	—	2-0	0-3	1-2	1-1	2-4	1-2	1-0	1-1	2-2	0-3	0-1	3-1	3-1	0-1	0-1	0-1	1-1
Droylsden	3-2	2-0	4-0	2-0	3-3	—	2-1	2-1	1-0	3-1	2-3	3-4	2-2	1-0	1-0	3-0	1-3	4-0	0-0	4-0	2-3	1-3
Gainsborough T	1-2	0-1	1-0	1-0	2-0	1-1	—	0-0	1-1	0-1	1-1	4-2	1-1	1-2	2-1	2-3	1-0	1-1	2-2	1-2	3-0	1-1
Harrogate T	2-1	1-1	5-1	2-1	2-1	2-1	5-1	—	1-1	0-0	2-1	1-1	1-2	3-1	4-2	1-0	2-5	0-1	2-0	2-1	2-0	0-0
Hinckley U	1-0	2-1	3-1	1-0	4-0	3-3	3-1	0-1	—	0-3	0-1	2-2	2-1	2-3	1-2	0-0	0-0	0-2	1-1	1-4	0-4	3-1
Hucknall T	4-0	4-2	2-1	1-2	0-0	0-4	2-5	1-1	1-1	—	2-1	0-2	1-1	1-3	2-1	0-0	2-4	2-1	3-0	1-1	2-2	0-0
Kettering T	1-1	0-1	0-0	2-0	1-0	0-2	0-1	0-0	3-1	3-1	—	0-2	1-2	1-0	1-0	2-1	0-5	0-1	2-0	1-1	2-1	2-1
Lancaster C	0-1	1-1	2-0	2-1	0-1	0-1	2-0	0-3	2-3	2-2	1-0	—	3-1	0-2	0-0	2-1	1-1	1-0	0-1	3-1	0-2	1-0
Moor Green	0-1	2-2	2-0	1-1	1-0	1-2	2-1	2-1	2-1	1-1	1-2	0-2	—	1-3	1-0	2-1	2-3	0-1	2-2	0-2	1-2	2-0
Nuneaton B	1-1	0-0	1-0	1-1	2-1	3-2	1-0	2-0	0-1	1-3	2-0	2-0	1-0	—	0-1	3-0	0-1	4-3	1-0	2-1	2-0	0-2
Redditch U	1-3	0-1	3-2	2-0	3-1	1-1	0-1	2-1	3-0	1-1	2-3	0-0	3-1	1-5	—	1-0	3-2	1-0	2-3	4-1	0-4	3-2
Runcorn	1-0	2-1	2-0	1-0	2-1	1-3	0-1	0-0	1-2	1-2	2-0	2-2	2-1	0-0	0-1	—	0-2	3-3	1-1	1-1	2-2	0-1
Southport	3-1	2-1	1-2	0-0	1-0	3-0	2-1	2-3	3-2	1-0	1-3	0-0	2-1	3-0	1-1	3-1	—	0-0	2-0	2-1	2-2	1-1
Stafford R	3-1	0-1	1-1	2-2	1-0	2-0	2-0	1-1	1-1	1-2	3-0	2-2	2-1	2-3	1-1	0-0	1-1	—	3-2	1-1	0-0	4-0
Stalybridge C	2-3	1-1	2-1	1-2	1-4	1-3	2-2	1-3	0-2	2-0	1-2	2-2	2-2	1-1	1-0	1-0	3-5	1-0	—	2-1	1-0	2-2
Vauxhall M	2-0	2-0	0-0	0-2	1-0	1-2	1-0	1-1	0-2	1-0	0-2	3-1	1-0	1-1	1-1	1-2	0-3	0-0	1-2	—	2-2	1-1
Worcester C	0-0	2-1	2-2	0-1	2-1	3-1	1-2	1-2	1-1	3-0	2-2	3-1	4-1	0-2	2-1	2-1	1-3	0-0	2-1	1-0	—	0-2
Worksop T	3-2	1-1	3-1	2-1	2-1	0-2	1-3	2-0	3-1	2-1	0-3	2-0	1-0	2-3	5-3	1-1	1-2	0-0	1-1	2-3	2-0	—

CONFERENCE SECOND DIVISION SOUTH 2004–2005

FINAL LEAGUE TABLE

		Home					Away					Total						
	P	W	D	L	F	A	W	D	L	F	A	W	D	L	F	A	GD	Pts
1 Grays Athletic	42	15	4	2	60	13	15	4	2	58	18	30	8	4	118	31	87	98
2 Cambridge City	42	10	3	8	29	25	13	3	5	31	19	23	6	13	60	44	16	75
3 Thurrock	42	9	3	9	29	32	12	3	6	32	24	21	6	15	61	56	5	69
4 Lewes	42	11	6	4	42	29	7	5	9	31	35	18	11	13	73	64	9	65
5 Eastbourne Borough	42	10	5	6	38	26	8	5	8	27	21	18	10	14	65	47	18	64
6 Basingstoke Town	42	12	3	6	37	20	7	3	11	20	32	19	6	17	57	52	5	63
7 Weymouth	42	8	8	5	32	28	9	3	9	30	31	17	11	14	62	59	3	62
8 Dorchester Town	42	11	5	5	40	33	6	6	9	37	48	17	11	14	77	81	–4	62
9 Bognor Regis Town	42	11	4	6	46	31	6	5	10	24	34	17	9	16	70	65	5	60
10 Bishop's Stortford	42	13	3	5	39	25	4	5	12	31	41	17	8	17	70	66	4	59
11 Weston–super–Mare	42	12	5	4	33	23	3	8	10	22	37	15	13	14	55	60	–5	58
12 Hayes	42	9	4	8	29	30	6	7	8	26	27	15	11	16	55	57	–2	56
13 Havant and W	42	12	3	6	38	26	4	4	13	26	43	16	7	19	64	69	–5	55
14 St Albans City	42	8	3	10	34	37	8	3	10	30	39	16	6	20	64	76	–12	54
15 Sutton United	42	5	6	10	25	38	9	5	7	35	33	14	11	17	60	71	–11	53
16 Welling United	42	5	5	11	23	30	10	2	9	41	38	15	7	20	64	68	–4	52
17 Hornchurch†	42	11	5	5	44	24	6	5	10	27	39	17	10	15	71	63	8	51
18 Newport County	42	8	5	8	36	34	5	6	10	20	27	13	11	18	56	61	–5	50
19 Carshalton Athletic	42	7	3	11	19	31	6	6	9	25	41	13	9	20	44	72	–28	48
20 Maidenhead United	42	5	7	9	31	41	7	3	11	23	40	12	10	20	54	81	–27	46
21 Margate†	42	9	3	9	30	29	3	5	13	24	46	12	8	22	54	75	–21	34
22 Redbridge*	42	6	3	12	25	40	5	0	16	25	46	11	3	28	50	86	–36	33

**Redbridge deducted 3 points.*

†Hornchurch and Margate deducted 10 points.

LEADING GOALSCORERS

Luke Nightingale *(Bognor Regis Town)*	28
Lee Clarke *(St Albans City)*	25
Matt Groves *(Dorchester Town)*	24
Dean Holdsworth *(Havant & Waterlooville)*	23
Paul Booth *(Welling United)*	20

CONFERENCE SECOND DIVISION SOUTH PLAY-OFFS SEMI-FINALS

(Lewes declined place)
Thurrock 2, Eastbourne Borough 4

FINAL

Cambridge C 0, Eastbourne Borough 3

CONFERENCE SECOND DIVISION NORTH/SOUTH PLAY-OFF

FINAL

Cambridge C 0, Eastbourne Borough 3

CONFERENCE SECOND DIVISION SOUTH RESULTS 2004–2005

	Basingstoke T	Bishop's Stortford	Bognor Regis T	Cambridge C	Carshalton Ath	Dorchester T	Eastbourne B	Grays Ath	Havant & W	Hayes	Hornchurch	Lewes	Maidenhead U	Margate	Newport Co	Redbridge	St Albans C	Sutton U	Thurrock	Welling U	Weston-S-Mare	Weymouth
Basingstoke T	—	2-3	2-1	2-1	0-1	2-2	0-2	0-3	3-2	2-0	2-0	0-0	0-1	2-1	3-0	3-0	5-1	1-0	3-0	4-0	1-1	0-1
Bishop's Stortford	1-3	—	2-3	3-0	2-0	2-1	2-0	1-2	1-1	0-4	3-1	1-0	2-1	3-0	3-0	2-1	2-0	3-2	0-0	4-2	2-2	0-2
Bognor Regis T	2-1	3-1	—	1-2	1-0	7-2	1-0	0-0	1-1	1-2	3-1	1-3	1-2	2-2	0-2	4-1	4-1	0-1	3-2	6-5	3-0	2-2
Cambridge C	2-1	3-2	1-0	—	3-0	2-2	2-2	0-2	2-0	1-0	0-3	2-3	0-1	2-1	2-0	2-1	2-0	0-1	0-0	0-1	1-2	4-1
Carshalton Ath	2-0	0-3	0-0	0-2	—	4-3	1-4	0-2	2-1	3-2	0-2	1-0	1-1	0-1	1-0	1-0	1-3	1-2	0-2	0-1	1-1	0-1
Dorchester T	0-1	4-3	1-0	0-0	1-1	—	3-1	0-7	2-1	1-1	3-1	1-1	4-2	2-0	1-0	4-1	2-3	2-2	0-2	3-2	2-3	4-1
Eastbourne B	2-0	1-1	4-1	1-2	1-4	3-2	—	2-2	1-2	1-0	4-2	1-2	0-0	1-1	1-0	1-2	1-0	2-2	4-0	0-1	3-0	4-2
Grays Ath	0-1	3-0	6-0	1-2	4-0	2-2	1-1	—	3-0	1-0	5-1	4-0	4-0	5-0	0-0	4-1	2-0	5-1	2-1	4-2	2-0	2-0
Havant & W	5-1	0-4	0-0	0-2	4-1	4-0	2-1	1-2	—	0-0	4-1	2-1	2-1	3-1	1-0	1-0	1-1	2-3	0-2	2-3	3-2	1-0
Hayes	0-1	2-3	0-1	4-0	1-3	0-1	1-1	1-1	1-5	—	1-1	3-2	2-1	1-0	3-1	1-0	3-2	1-0	1-3	1-1	1-0	1-3
Hornchurch	6-0	3-1	1-1	0-1	2-2	2-3	2-0	1-2	4-0	1-1	—	3-2	6-0	1-0	1-1	2-0	1-1	3-0	0-1	0-5	3-2	2-1
Lewes	0-0	2-1	2-1	2-2	1-1	3-1	1-0	3-2	3-1	3-2	1-2	—	0-1	7-3	2-2	5-4	1-2	0-1	1-1	2-1	3-1	0-0
Maidenhead U	1-1	2-2	2-3	1-5	4-0	0-1	1-2	0-3	1-0	1-1	2-2	1-0	—	2-4	0-2	4-3	3-3	2-2	0-3	2-1	0-0	2-3
Margate	2-1	1-0	2-3	0-2	0-1	1-2	2-1	0-6	5-1	3-1	0-1	1-1	2-0	—	1-1	2-0	2-3	1-1	2-1	1-2	2-0	0-1
Newport Co	0-1	6-3	1-0	0-1	0-1	3-2	1-3	1-4	1-1	1-1	2-2	2-2	2-1	2-0	—	2-3	1-0	2-4	1-2	4-1	2-2	2-0
Redbridge	0-3	1-1	1-2	0-0	1-3	4-1	0-3	1-3	3-1	0-1	0-1	0-1	4-1	2-1	0-5	—	2-1	0-5	1-2	1-2	1-1	3-2
St Albans C	2-1	2-0	4-0	1-0	3-1	1-1	0-0	1-4	3-1	0-1	4-3	2-3	1-2	3-3	0-1	2-3	—	1-2	1-3	2-5	1-0	0-3
Sutton U	1-0	0-0	0-0	0-3	4-1	3-2	0-0	0-6	1-1	2-4	1-2	3-5	2-2	2-0	0-0	2-3	1-2	—	1-2	1-0	1-2	0-3
Thurrock	3-1	1-0	0-5	0-1	2-2	1-2	1-0	2-4	1-3	2-1	1-0	2-0	1-2	1-2	2-2	1-0	1-2	1-2	—	1-1	3-1	2-1
Welling U	0-1	0-0	1-1	0-2	4-0	1-4	0-3	1-2	0-1	1-1	1-1	1-0	1-2	1-0	3-1	1-2	2-3	3-2	1-2	—	1-1	0-1
Weston-S-Mare	2-1	2-1	2-1	2-1	1-1	2-2	0-2	2-0	2-1	0-1	0-0	1-2	2-1	2-2	3-1	1-0	3-0	2-1	2-1	0-2	—	2-2
Weymouth	1-1	3-2	2-1	1-2	2-2	1-1	0-1	1-1	3-2	3-1	2-0	3-3	3-1	2-2	0-1	1-0	1-0	1-1	1-2	0-3	1-1	—

CONFERENCE CUP 2004–2005

PRELIMINARY ROUND NORTH
Ashton United 6, Altrincham 2
Moor Green 1, Redditch United 2

PRELIMINARY ROUND SOUTH
Redbridge 0, Grays Athletic 3
Basingstoke Town 2, Lewes 1

FIRST ROUND NORTH
Droylsden 1, Ashton United 0
Worcester City 2, Stafford Rangers 1
Hucknall Town 1, Gainsborough Trinity 4
Nuneaton Borough 4, Redditch United 3
Vauxhall Motors 1, Runcorn FC Halton 2
Barrow 4, Southport 1
Kettering Town 4, Hinckley United 2
Alfreton Town 0, Worksop Town 1
Harrogate Town 0, Bradford Park Avenue 1
Stalybridge Celtic 4, Lancaster City 2

FIRST ROUND SOUTH
Bishops Stortford 5, Cambridge City 0
Bognor Regis Town 2, Eastbourne Borough 1
Hayes 1, Maidstone United 2
Hornchurch 1, Thurrock 2
St Albans City 2, Grays Athletic 6
Welling United 0, Margate 2
Dorchester Town 2, Weston-Super-Mare 1
Sutton United 3, Carshalton Athletic 2
Weymouth 0, Newport County 2
Havant & Waterlooville 2, Basingstoke Town 1

SECOND ROUND NORTH
Droylsden 1, Worcester City 2
Kettering Town 4, Nuneaton Borough 2
Barrow 0, Runcorn FC Halton 1
Worksop Town 4, Gainsborough Trinity 1
Stalybridge Celtic 1, Bradford Park Avenue 0

SECOND ROUND SOUTH
Thurrock 1, Margate 2
Dorchester Town 0, Newport County 1
Grays Athletic w.o. v Bishops Stortford withdrew
Maidstone United 2, Sutton United 4
Havant & Waterlooville 5, Bognor Regis Town 1
Third Round North
Burton Albion 2, Hereford United 4
Kettering Town 1, Worksop Town 2
Tamworth 3, Worcester City 1
Morecambe 2, Scarborough 1
Northwich Victoria 1, Leigh RMI 0
Runcorn FC Halton 2, Carlisle United 6
Accrington Stanley 2, York City 1
Stalybridge Celtic 7, Halifax Town 3

THIRD ROUND SOUTH
Barnet 0, Grays Athletic 3
Forest Green Rovers 4, Newport County 2
Margate 2, Dagenham & Redbridge 1
Gravesend & Northfleet 0, Stevenage Borough 1
Sutton United 0, Woking 3
Havant & Waterlooville 2, Farnborough Town 0
Aldershot Town 1, Exeter City 0
Canvey Island 0, Crawley Town 0
Crawley Town won 6-4 on penalties.

FOURTH ROUND NORTH
Accrington Stanley 6, Tamworth 0
Morecambe 1, Carlisle United 1
Morecambe won 3-1 on penalties.
Hereford United 0, Northwich Victoria 1
Worksop Town 0, Stalybridge Celtic 1

FOURTH ROUND SOUTH
Stevenage Borough 1, Grays Athletic 1
Stevenage Borough won 3-1 on penalties.
Forest Green Rovers 5, Aldershot Town 1
Woking 2, Havant & Waterlooville 2
Woking won 4-3 on penalties.
Crawley Town 2, Margate 1

FIFTH ROUND NORTH
Accrington Stanley 4, Northwich Victoria 3
Morecambe 1, Stalybridge Celtic 2

FIFTH ROUND SOUTH
Stevenage Borough 2, Crawley Town 1
Woking 3, Forest Green Rovers 1

SEMI-FINAL NORTH
Stalybridge Celtic 0, Accrington Stanley 0
Stalybridge Celtic won 5-4 on penalties.

SEMI-FINAL SOUTH
Woking 4, Stevenage Borough 2

FINAL
Stalybridge Celtic 0, Woking 1
Stalybridge Celtic had won the toss for choice of ground.

UNIBOND LEAGUE 2004–2005

Premier Division

		Home					*Away*					*Total*						
	P	*W*	*D*	*L*	*F*	*A*	*W*	*D*	*L*	*F*	*A*	*W*	*D*	*L*	*F*	*A*	*Gd*	*Pts*
1 Hyde U*	42	14	6	1	42	18	11	7	3	38	25	25	13	4	80	43	37	88
2 Workington	42	13	3	5	38	15	13	4	4	35	15	26	7	9	73	30	43	85
3 Farsley Celtic	42	11	5	5	37	17	14	3	4	44	24	25	8	9	81	41	40	83
4 Whitby T	42	14	3	4	37	24	9	8	4	28	25	23	11	8	65	49	16	80
5 Prescot Cables**	42	10	3	8	28	31	11	5	5	35	23	21	8	13	63	54	9	71
6 Burscough	42	11	3	7	57	40	10	4	7	36	34	21	7	14	93	74	19	70
7 Leek T**	42	8	9	4	32	22	8	6	7	31	30	16	15	11	63	52	11	63
8 Witton A	42	10	6	5	29	22	5	11	5	27	22	15	17	10	56	44	12	62
9 Radcliffe B*	42	5	10	6	27	30	11	4	6	33	31	16	14	12	60	61	–1	62
10 Guiseley	42	9	7	5	40	33	7	6	8	30	31	16	13	13	70	64	6	61
11 Matlock T	42	7	7	7	28	29	7	6	8	31	38	14	13	15	59	67	–8	55
12 Blyth Spartans	42	10	4	7	33	25	3	9	9	20	30	13	13	16	53	55	–2	52
13 Wakefield & Emley	42	9	6	6	33	24	5	4	12	27	43	14	10	18	60	67	–7	52
14 Lincoln U*	42	9	0	12	30	33	6	4	11	23	33	15	4	23	53	66	–13	49
15 Marine*	42	5	11	5	32	31	5	7	9	21	29	10	18	14	53	60	–7	48
16 Ossett T	42	10	4	7	33	26	1	9	11	20	36	11	13	18	53	62	–9	46
17 Gateshead	42	7	9	5	36	35	4	3	14	25	49	11	12	19	61	84	–23	45
18 Frickley Ath	42	7	6	8	25	29	3	8	10	19	28	10	14	18	44	57	–13	44
19 Bishop Auckland	42	8	3	10	34	33	3	4	14	17	41	11	7	24	51	74	–23	40
20 Bridlington T*	42	4	10	7	21	24	3	4	14	23	42	7	14	21	44	66	–22	35
21 Bamber Bridge	42	5	4	12	23	41	4	3	14	25	51	9	7	26	48	92	–44	34
22 Spennymoor U†	42	6	5	10	24	26	3	5	13	20	39	9	10	23	44	65	–21	13

**FA ruling on 4/5/05 – 3pts were awarded to Spennymoor United opponents for each unfulfilled fixture.*

†Spennymoor United deducted 24 pts.

SOUTHERN LEAGUE 2004–2005

Premier Division

		Home					*Away*					*Total*						
	P	*W*	*D*	*L*	*F*	*A*	*W*	*D*	*L*	*F*	*A*	*W*	*D*	*L*	*F*	*A*	*Gd*	*Pts*
1 Histon	42	13	3	5	45	26	11	3	7	48	31	24	6	12	93	57	36	78
2 Chippenham T	42	10	5	6	39	30	12	4	5	42	25	22	9	11	81	55	26	75
3 Merthyr Tydfil	42	8	9	4	29	23	11	5	5	33	24	19	14	9	62	47	15	71
4 Hednesford T	42	12	3	6	36	22	8	7	6	32	18	20	10	12	68	40	28	70
5 Bedford T	42	13	5	3	39	19	6	7	8	31	33	19	12	11	70	52	18	69
6 Bath C	42	9	6	6	27	23	10	6	5	30	20	19	12	11	57	43	14	69
7 Cirencester T	42	12	4	5	39	23	7	7	7	24	29	19	11	12	63	52	11	68
8 Tiverton T	42	13	4	4	48	30	5	9	7	22	25	18	13	11	70	55	15	67
9 Halesowen T	42	10	5	6	31	23	9	4	8	33	29	19	9	14	64	52	12	66
10 Aylesbury U	42	11	1	9	36	34	9	2	10	31	32	20	3	19	67	66	1	63
11 Kings Lynn	42	12	3	6	49	28	7	1	13	29	41	19	4	19	78	69	9	61
12 Chesham U	42	9	2	10	42	38	9	3	9	42	44	18	5	19	84	82	2	59
13 Grantham T	42	12	2	7	34	24	5	5	11	23	31	17	7	18	57	55	2	58
14 Team Bath	42	9	5	7	30	35	5	7	9	24	32	14	12	16	54	68	–14	54
15 Gloucester C	42	9	7	5	40	30	3	10	8	23	31	12	17	13	63	61	2	53
16 Rugby U	42	5	9	7	18	20	8	3	10	30	38	13	12	17	48	60	–12	51
17 Banbury U	42	7	7	7	31	32	6	2	13	24	35	13	9	20	56	69	–13	48
18 Hitchin T	42	6	5	10	24	35	7	4	10	31	42	13	9	20	55	77	–22	48
19 Hemel Hempstead T*	42	6	6	9	30	40	5	4	12	30	48	11	10	21	60	88	–28	42
20 Dunstable T	42	8	1	12	31	48	3	5	13	24	49	11	6	25	56	98	–42	39
21 Stamford	42	4	11	6	23	22	2	7	12	17	38	6	18	18	40	60	–20	36
22 Solihull Borough	42	5	3	13	22	39	5	1	15	23	46	10	4	28	45	85	–40	34

**1 point deducted for fielding an ineligible player.*

RYMAN LEAGUE 2004–2005

Premier Division		*Home*					*Away*					*Total*						
	P	*W*	*D*	*L*	*F*	*A*	*W*	*D*	*L*	*F*	*A*	*W*	*D*	*L*	*F*	*A*	*Gd*	*Pts*
1 Yeading	42	12	6	3	38	23	13	5	3	36	25	25	11	6	74	48	26	86
2 Billericay T	42	13	6	2	36	14	10	5	6	42	26	23	11	8	78	40	38	80
3 Eastleigh	42	12	7	2	44	19	10	6	5	40	30	22	13	7	84	49	35	79
4 Braintree T	42	11	8	2	35	12	8	9	4	32	21	19	17	6	67	33	34	74
5 Leyton	42	11	3	7	36	33	10	5	6	35	24	21	8	13	71	57	14	71
6 Hampton & Rich	42	15	4	2	37	21	6	4	11	27	32	21	8	13	64	53	11	71
7 Heybridge Swifts	42	10	4	7	43	29	8	5	8	33	36	18	9	15	76	65	11	63
8 Chelmsford C	42	11	3	7	39	32	6	8	7	24	26	17	11	14	63	58	5	62
9 Staines T	42	6	8	7	28	28	11	1	9	31	25	17	9	16	59	53	6	60
10 Worthing	42	10	6	5	32	21	6	5	10	18	24	16	11	15	50	45	5	59
11 Hendon	42	9	4	8	21	23	8	3	10	27	37	17	7	18	48	60	–12	58
12 Salisbury C	42	9	5	7	23	23	7	4	10	37	41	16	9	17	60	64	–4	57
13 Slough T	42	9	4	8	29	32	6	6	9	32	34	15	10	17	61	66	–5	55
14 Folkestone Invicta	42	11	4	6	33	25	3	6	12	18	28	14	10	18	51	53	–2	52
15 Windsor & Eton	42	7	8	6	24	28	5	6	10	24	34	12	14	16	48	62	–14	50
16 Harrow Borough	42	8	5	8	26	31	5	5	11	15	23	13	10	19	41	54	–13	49
17 Northwood	42	9	2	10	27	33	5	5	11	22	33	14	7	21	49	66	–17	49
18 Wealdstone	42	7	4	10	39	42	6	4	11	21	31	13	8	21	60	73	–13	47
19 Cheshunt	42	6	8	7	24	33	6	3	12	34	38	12	11	19	58	71	–13	47
20 Tonbridge Angels	42	8	3	10	30	42	3	7	11	17	31	11	10	21	47	73	–26	43
21 Dover Ath	42	7	4	10	28	32	3	5	13	22	34	10	9	23	50	66	–16	39
22 Kingstonian	42	2	3	16	13	41	5	2	14	30	52	7	5	30	43	93	–50	26

CUP FINALS 2004–2005

UNIBOND LEAGUE CHALLENGE CUP FINAL
Matlock Town 2, 3, Whitby Town 2, 1

PRESIDENT'S CUP FINAL
Witton Albion 1, 1, Bamber Bridge 1, 2

CHAIRMAN'S CUP FINAL
Woodley Sports 3, 3 Kidsgrove Athletic 3, 4

UNIBOND LEAGUE PLAY-OFF FINAL
AFC Telford United 2, Kendal Town 1

SOUTHERN LEAGUE CUP FINAL
First Leg
Bedford Town 2, King's Lynn 2

Second Leg
King's Lynn 1, Bedford Town 0

BRYCO CUP FINAL
Hampton & Richmond Borough 1, Slough Town 3

ASSOCIATE MEMBERS CUP FINAL
Ilford 2, Flackwell Heath 1

PONTIN'S HOLIDAYS LEAGUE 2004–2005

PREMIER DIVISION

	P	*W*	*D*	*L*	*F*	*A*	*GD*	*Pts*
Hull C	22	14	5	3	58	28	30	47
Barnsley	22	12	3	7	44	30	14	39
Sheffield W	22	11	4	7	36	28	8	37
Sheffield U	22	9	7	6	41	34	7	34
Stoke C	22	10	3	9	28	26	2	33
Hartlepool U	22	8	7	7	35	33	2	31
Tranmere R	22	9	4	9	25	26	–1	31
Preston NE	22	7	6	9	31	46	–15	27
Rotherham U	22	6	8	8	31	39	–8	26
Walsall	22	6	5	11	40	46	–6	23
Wigan Ath	22	5	6	11	21	32	–11	21
Bradford C	22	3	6	13	21	43	–22	15

DIVISION ONE WEST

	P	*W*	*D*	*L*	*F*	*A*	*GD*	*Pts*
Manchester U	22	14	5	3	49	28	21	47
Carlisle U	22	13	3	6	43	36	7	42
Blackpool	22	12	4	6	34	21	13	40
Oldham Ath	22	12	3	7	48	34	14	39
Bury	22	10	7	5	30	23	7	37
Macclesfield T	22	8	7	7	31	27	4	31
Burnley	22	5	11	6	24	21	3	26
Chester C	22	7	3	12	25	37	–12	24
Stockport Co	22	5	7	10	28	37	–9	22
Shrewsbury T	22	5	6	11	25	31	–6	21
Rochdale	22	4	6	12	23	38	–15	18
Wrexham	22	6	0	16	27	54	–27	18

DIVISION ONE EAST

	P	*W*	*D*	*L*	*F*	*A*	*GD*	*Pts*
Huddersfield T	18	4	0	4	41	16	25	42
Scunthorpe U	18	12	2	4	33	21	12	38
Doncaster R	18	11	4	3	42	26	16	37
Lincoln C	18	9	2	7	35	27	8	29
York C	18	6	5	7	21	27	–6	23
Grimsby T	18	7	1	10	33	37	–4	22
Boston U	17	6	3	8	27	27	0	21
Halifax T	17	4	3	10	18	33	–15	15
Notts Co	18	4	3	11	17	36	–19	15
Darlington	18	3	3	12	14	31	–17	12

PONTIN'S HOLIDAYS COMBINATION 2004–2005

CENTRAL AND EAST DIVISION

	P	*W*	*D*	*L*	*F*	*A*	*GD*	*Pts*
Luton T	15	11	3	1	34	10	24	36
Reading	15	9	3	3	41	16	25	30
Millwall	15	8	5	2	28	14	14	29
Brighton & HA	15	7	6	2	19	9	10	27
Northampton T	15	7	6	2	20	12	8	27
QPR	15	8	2	5	21	13	8	26
Peterborough U	15	6	4	5	27	24	3	22
Colchester U	15	5	4	6	35	23	12	19
MK Dons	15	6	1	8	26	26	0	19
Crawley T	15	4	5	6	27	42	–15	17
Southend U	15	4	4	7	25	27	–2	16
Gillingham	15	3	6	6	16	22	–6	15
Oxford U	15	3	6	6	16	29	–13	15
Aldershot T	15	4	1	10	12	34	–22	13
Woking	15	3	2	10	19	41	–22	11
Stevenage B	15	1	4	10	14	38	–24	7

WALES AND WEST DIVISION

	P	*W*	*D*	*L*	*F*	*A*	*GD*	*Pts*
Cardiff C	16	10	2	4	34	19	15	32
Plymouth Arg	16	9	2	5	31	24	7	29
Cheltenham T	16	7	6	3	25	19	6	27
Yeovil T	16	7	2	7	31	27	4	23
Bristol C	16	7	2	7	29	27	2	23
Bristol R	16	6	4	6	30	35	–5	22
Swindon T	16	5	2	9	29	28	1	17
Swansea C	16	5	2	9	25	45	–20	17
Bournemouth	16	3	4	9	18	28	–10	13

FA ACADEMY UNDER-18 LEAGUE 2004–05

GROUP A	P	W	D	L	F	A	GD	Pts
Southampton	28	23	2	3	62	25	37	71
Charlton Ath	28	14	6	8	35	28	7	48
Arsenal	28	13	3	12	45	39	6	42
Ipswich T	28	11	6	11	39	39	0	39
West Ham U	28	11	4	13	37	53	–16	37
Millwall	28	11	2	15	34	44	–10	35
Chelsea	28	8	5	15	24	33	–9	29
Crystal P	27	7	7	13	35	51	–16	28
Norwich C	28	6	7	15	26	38	–12	25
Fulham	27	4	5	18	23	54	–31	17

Crystal P v Fulham, fixture not completed.

GROUP B	P	W	D	L	F	A	GD	Pts
Coventry C	28	17	5	6	58	32	26	56
Reading	28	15	8	5	58	36	22	53
Aston Villa	28	16	4	8	55	42	13	52
Watford	28	15	6	7	46	27	19	51
Leicester C	28	13	0	15	59	52	7	39
Cardiff C	28	9	11	8	39	37	2	38
Birmingham C	28	10	6	12	44	45	–1	36
Tottenham H	28	8	11	9	41	47	–6	35
Bristol C	28	5	5	18	31	55	–24	20
Milton Keynes Dons	28	5	5	18	34	64	–30	20

GROUP C	P	W	D	L	F	A	GD	Pts
Blackburn R	28	19	4	5	57	24	33	61
Manchester U	28	17	6	5	61	41	20	57
Everton	28	14	9	5	46	34	12	51
Manchester C	28	13	10	5	66	37	29	49
Crewe Alex	28	13	6	9	53	44	9	45
Stoke C	28	10	9	9	39	46	–7	39
Wolverhampton W	28	8	13	7	38	39	–1	37
Bolton W	28	6	7	15	38	53	–15	25
Liverpool	28	5	7	16	24	52	–28	22

GROUP D	P	W	D	L	F	A	GD	Pts
Newcastle U	28	17	8	3	55	26	29	59
Sheffield W	28	15	6	7	51	33	18	51
Barnsley	28	11	8	9	41	43	–2	41
Leeds U	28	12	4	12	50	43	7	40
Sunderland	28	10	5	13	32	34	–2	35
Nottingham F	28	8	8	12	33	40	–7	32
Sheffield U	28	5	11	12	39	45	–6	26
Derby Co	28	5	9	14	28	56	–28	24
Huddersfield T	28	5	7	16	30	47	–17	22
Middlesbrough	28	4	9	15	31	58	–27	21

FA PREMIER RESERVE LEAGUES

NORTH SECTION

	P	W	D	L	F	A	GD	Pts
Manchester U	28	19	6	3	68	23	45	63
Aston Villa	28	16	6	6	62	38	24	54
Manchester C	28	16	6	6	55	32	23	54
Blackburn R	28	11	12	5	45	28	17	45
Birmingham C	28	12	7	9	37	36	1	43
Wolverhampton W	28	9	9	10	32	32	0	36
Middlesbrough	28	10	6	12	41	42	–1	36
Everton	28	8	11	9	23	34	–11	35
Sunderland	28	8	9	11	38	44	–6	33
Bolton W	28	8	9	11	32	41	–9	33
WBA	28	6	13	9	29	36	–7	31
Newcastle U	28	8	7	13	30	41	–11	31
Leeds U	28	7	7	14	31	52	–21	28
Liverpool	28	6	8	14	27	47	–20	26
Nottingham F	28	5	6	17	21	45	–24	21

Leading Goalscorers

Moore L (Aston Villa)	18
Wright-Phillips B (Manchester C)	17
Rossi G (Manchester U)	16
Graham D (Middlesbrough)	15
Clarke L (Wolverhampton W)	13
Vaz Te R (Bolton W)	11
Ebanks-Blake S (Manchester U)	11
Elvins R (WBA)	10
Negouai C (Manchester C)	9
Kyle K (Sunderland)	9
Miller I (Manchester C)	8
Vaughan J (Everton)	7
Mellor N (Liverpool)	7
Jones D (Manchester U)	7
Bridges M (Sunderland)	7
Agbonlahor G (Aston Villa)	6
Derbyshire M (Blackburn R)	6
Johnson J (Blackburn R)	6
Bermingham K (Manchester C)	6
Bellion D (Manchester U)	6
Poole D (Manchester U)	6
Craddock T (Middlesbrough)	6

Highest attendance
Birmingham City v Manchester United
7822 (*at St Andrews*)

SOUTH SECTION

	P	W	D	L	F	A	GD	Pts
Charlton Ath	28	18	7	3	46	21	25	61
Southampton	28	18	4	6	68	29	39	58
Arsenal	28	17	5	6	65	38	27	56
Crystal P	28	16	5	7	47	22	25	53
Tottenham H	28	13	8	7	47	35	12	47
Chelsea	28	10	8	10	28	28	0	38
Watford	28	9	9	10	32	33	–1	36
Norwich C	28	10	4	14	24	40	–16	34
Fulham	28	8	9	11	29	35	–6	33
Derby Co	28	9	6	13	29	48	–19	33
West Ham U	28	7	9	12	33	51	–18	30
Coventry C	28	7	8	13	29	50	–21	29
Ipswich T	28	6	6	16	24	35	–11	24
Leicester C	28	5	9	14	36	49	–13	24
Portsmouth	28	5	7	16	28	51	–23	22

Leading Goalscorers

Lupoli A (Arsenal)	19
Barnard L (Tottenham H)	17
Best L (Southampton)	13
Junior (Derby Co)	10
Keene J (Portsmouth)	9
Aliadiere J (Arsenal)	8
Stokes A (Arsenal)	8
Sam L (Charlton Ath)	8
Freedman D (Crystal P)	7
Crow D (Norwich C)	7
Blackstock D (Southampton)	7
Ashikodi M (West Ham U)	7
Rebrov S (West Ham U)	7
Stuart G (Charlton Ath)	6
Andrews W (Crystal P)	6
Counago P (Ipswich T)	6
Jarvis R (Norwich C)	6
Silva Sousa E (Tottenham H)	6
Norville J (Watford)	6

Highest attendance
Norwich City v Arsenal
6014 (*at Carrow Road*)

WOMEN'S FOOTBALL 2004–2005

NATIONAL DIVISION

	P	W	D	L	GD	Pts
1 Arsenal LFC	18	15	3	0	44	48
2 Charlton Ath WFC	18	13	2	3	26	41
3 Everton LFC	18	11	4	3	21	37
4 Birmingham C LFC	18	9	3	6	9	30
5 Bristol R WFC	18	9	1	8	7	28
6 Leeds U LFC	18	8	2	8	–3	26
7 Fulham LFC	18	3	5	10	–21	14
8 Doncaster R Belles LFC	18	3	3	12	–28	12
9 Liverpool LFC *	18	3	2	13	–28	10
10 Bristol C WFC	18	2	3	13	–27	9

**One point deducted*

NORTHERN DIVISION

	P	W	D	L	GD	Pts
1 Sunderland LFC Ladies	22	17	2	3	40	53
2 Wolverhampton W WFC	22	14	5	3	27	47
3 Blackburn R LFC	22	10	9	3	20	39
4 Stockport Co LFC	22	7	9	6	–2	30
5 Lincoln C LFC	22	8	5	9	–5	29
6 Aston Villa LFC	22	8	4	10	–7	28
7 Middlesbrough LFC	22	6	6	10	–7	24
8 Tranmere R LFC	22	7	3	12	–7	24
9 Oldham Curzon LFC	22	6	6	10	–8	24
10 Manchester C LFC	22	7	3	12	–16	24
11 Sheffield W LFC	22	5	8	9	–14	23
12 Coventry C LFC	22	4	6	12	–21	18

SOUTHERN DIVISION

	P	W	D	L	GD	Pts
1 Chelsea LFC	22	16	4	2	47	52
2 Portsmouth LFC	22	13	5	4	16	44
3 Brighton & HA WFC	22	11	3	8	16	36
4 Crystal Palace LFC	22	10	6	6	11	36
5 AFC Wimbledon LFC	22	11	2	9	19	35
6 Millwall Lionesses LFC	22	9	8	5	4	35
7 Cardiff C LFC	22	9	7	6	11	34
8 Southampton Saints WFC	22	7	6	9	–1	27
9 Watford LFC	22	7	6	9	–2	27
10 Langford LFC	22	6	5	11	–24	23
11 Enfield T LFC	22	1	6	15	–41	9
12 Ipswich T LFC	22	2	2	18	–56	8

THE FA WOMEN'S CUP FINAL 2004–2005

Monday, 2 May 2004
(at Upton Park)

Charlton Athletic (0) 1 *(Aluko 58)*

Everton (0) 0 8567

Charlton Athletic: Cope; Hills, Coss, Stoney, Sinclair-Chambers, Murphy, Smith, Williams, Broadhurst, Aluko, Heatherson (Clarke 69).
Everton: Hill; Eason, Britton, Johnson, Unitt, Williams, McDougall, Duffy (Evans 66), Handley, Parry, Kane (J. Jones 87)

WOMEN'S EUROPEAN CHAMPIONSHIP

GROUP A MATCHES

Sweden 1 Denmark 1
England 3 Finland 2
Denmark 2 England 1
Sweden 0 Finland 0
England 0 Sweden 1
Finland 2 Denmark 1

Table	*P*	*W*	*D*	*L*	*F*	*A*	*GD*	*Pts*
Sweden	3	1	2	0	2	1	1	5
Finland	3	1	1	1	4	4	0	4
Denmark	3	1	1	1	4	4	0	4
England	3	1	0	2	4	5	–1	3

GROUP B MATCHES

Germany 1 Norway 0
France 3 Italy 1
Italy 0 Germany 4
France 1 Norway 1
Germany 3 France 0
Norway 5 Italy 3

Table	*P*	*W*	*D*	*L*	*F*	*A*	*GD*	*Pts*
Sweden	3	1	2	0	2	1	1	5
Finland	3	1	1	1	4	4	0	4
Denmark	3	1	1	1	4	4	0	4
England	3	1	0	2	4	5	–1	3

SEMI-FINALS

Germany 4 Finland 1
Norway 3 Sweden 2 *(aet.)*

FINAL

Germany 3 Norway 1
(Blackburn Rovers FC)

THE CONFEDERATIONS CUP 2005

GROUP A

Argentina 2, Tunisia 1
Germany 4, Australia 3
Tunisia 0, Germany 3
Australia 2, Argentina 4
Australia 0, Tunisia 2
Argentina 2, Germany 2

	P	*W*	*D*	*L*	*F*	*A*	*Pts*
Germany	3	2	1	0	9	5	7
Argentina	3	2	1	0	8	5	7
Tunisia	3	1	0	2	3	5	3
Australia	3	0	0	3	5	10	0

GROUP B

Japan 1, Mexico 2
Brazil 3, Greece 0
Greece 0, Japan 1
Mexico 1, Brazil 0
Greece 0, Mexico 0
Japan 2, Brazil 2

	P	*W*	*D*	*L*	*F*	*A*	*Pts*
Mexico	3	2	1	0	3	1	7
Brazil	3	1	1	1	5	3	4
Japan	3	1	1	1	4	4	4
Greece	3	0	1	0	0	4	1

SEMI-FINALS

Germany 2, Brazil 3
Mexico 1, Argentina 1
Argentina won 6-5 on penalties.

MATCH FOR THIRD PLACE

Germany 4, Mexico 3 *(aet.)*

THE CONFEDERATIONS CUP FINAL 2005 (in Frankfurt)

29 June 2005

Brazil (2) 4, Argentina (0) 1

Brazil: Dida; Cicinho (Maicon 86), Ze Roberto, Emerson, Lucio, Roque Junior, Kaka (Renato 90), Robinho (Juninho Pernambucano 90), Adriano, Silva, Ronaldinho.
Scorers: Adriano 11, 63, Kaka 16, Ronaldinho 47.
Argentina: Lux; Zanetti, Sorin, Coloccini, Heinze, Placente, Bernardi, Figueroa (Tevez 72), Cambiasso (Aimar 56), Delgado (Galletti 81), Riquelme.
Scorer: Aimar 65.
Attendance: 45,591.
Referee: Michel (Slovakia).

THE FA TROPHY 2004–2005

FINAL (at Villa Park) – Sunday, 22 May 2005

Grays Athletic (0) 1 *(Martin 64)*

Hucknall Town (0) 1 *(Bacon 77)* 8116

Grays Athletic: Bayes; Brennan, Nutter, Thurgood, Matthews, Stuart, Hooper (Carthy), Martin, Oli (Powell), Battersby (West), Cole.
Hucknall Town: Smith G; Asher, Barrick (Plummer), Palmer (Heathcote), Cooke, Timons, Smith M (Ward), Hunter, Ricketts, Bacon, Todd.
aet; Grays Athletic won 6-5 on penalties.
Referee: P. Dowd (Stoke).

THE FA VASE 2004–2005

FINAL (at White Hart Lane) – Sunday, 14 May 2005

AFC Sudbury (0) 2 *(Wardley 65, Calver 90 (pen))*

Didcot Town (0) 3 *(Beavon 55, 89, Wardley 68 (og))* 8862

AFC Sudbury: Greygoose; Girling, Wardley, Bennett, Hyde (Hayes 78), Owen (Norfolk 64), Claydon (Banya 57), Head, Calver, Betson, Rayner.
Didcot Town: Webb; Goodall, Heapy, Campbell, Green, Parrott, Hannigan, Ward, Concannon (Jones 88), Beavon (Bianchini 90), Powell.
Referee: R. Beeby (Northamptonshire).

THE FA YOUTH CUP 2004–2005

FINAL (First Leg) – Monday, 18 April 2005

Southampton (1) 2 *(McGoldrick 45 (pen), Best 62)*

Ipswich Town (0) 2 *(Lordan 48, 58)* 9902

Souhampton: McNeil; Richards, Wallis-Taylor, McGoldrick, Rudd, Cranie, James, Sparv, Walcott, Best (Condesso 82), Dyer.
Ipswich Town: Supple; Synott (Haynes 63), Krause, Garvan, Casement, Collins, Moore, Lordan, Knights (Hammond 85), Trotter (Sheringham 90), Craig.
Referee: A. Marriner (West Midlands).

FINAL (Second Leg) – Thursday, 21 April 2005

Ipswich Town (0) 1 *(Upson 118)*

Southampton (0) 0 14,889

Ipswich Town: Supple; Synott, Krause, Haynes (Sheringham 71), Casement, Collins, Moore, Lordan (Hammond 82), Knights, Trotter (Upson 105), Craig.
Southampton: McNeil; Richards, Wallis-Taylor, McGoldrick (Condesso 86), Rudd, Cranie, James, Sparv (Lallana 106), Walcott, Best, Dyer.
aet.
Referee: A. Marriner (West Midlands).

THE FA SUNDAY CUP 2004–2005

FINAL (at Liverpool FC)
Albion Sports 2 *(Zoll 2)*
Gossoms End 3 *(Porter 2, Osborne)*

THE FA COUNTY YOUTH CUP 2004–2005

FINAL
Suffolk 2
Hampshire 1 991

SOUTH AMERICAN CHAMPIONSHIP

(Copa America)

1916 Uruguay
1917 Uruguay
1919 Brazil
1920 Uruguay
1921 Argentina
1922 Brazil
1923 Uruguay
1924 Uruguay
1925 Argentina
1926 Uruguay
1927 Argentina
1929 Argentina
1935 Uruguay
1937 Argentina
1939 Peru
1941 Argentina
1942 Uruguay
1945 Argentina
1946 Argentina
1947 Argentina
1949 Brazil
1953 Paraguay
1955 Argentina
1956 Uruguay
1957 Argentina
1959 Argentina
1959 Uruguay
1963 Bolivia
1967 Uruguay
1975 Peru
1979 Paraguay
1983 Uruguay
1987 Uruguay
1989 Brazil
1991 Argentina
1993 Argentina
1995 Uruguay
1997 Brazil
1999 Brazil
2001 Colombia
2004 Brazil

SOUTH AMERICAN CUP

(Copa Libertadores)

1960 Penarol (Uruguay)
1961 Penarol
1962 Santos (Brazil)
1963 Santos
1964 Independiente (Argentina)
1965 Independiente
1966 Penarol
1967 Racing Club (Argentina)
1968 Estudiantes (Argentina)
1969 Estudiantes
1970 Estudiantes
1971 Nacional (Uruguay)
1972 Independiente
1973 Independiente
1974 Independiente
1975 Independiente
1976 Cruzeiro (Brazil)
1977 Boca Juniors (Argentina)
1978 Boca Juniors
1979 Olimpia (Paraguay)
1980 Nacional
1981 Flamengo (Brazil)
1982 Penarol
1983 Gremio Porto Alegre (Brazil)
1984 Independiente
1985 Argentinos Juniors (Argentina)
1986 River Plate (Argentina)
1987 Penarol
1988 Nacional (Uruguay)
1989 Nacional (Colombia)
1990 Olimpia
1991 Colo Colo (Chile)
1992 São Paulo (Brazil)
1993 São Paulo
1994 Velez Sarsfield (Argentina)
1995 Gremio Porto Alegre
1996 River Plate
1997 Cruzeiro
1998 Vasco da Gama
1999 Palmeiras
2000 Boca Juniors
2001 Boca Juniors
2002 Olimpia
2003 Boca Juniors
2004 Once Caldas

NATIONAL LIST OF REFEREES FOR SEASON 2004–2005

No changes announced from last season at time of going to press.
**Indicates Select Group Referees.*

Armstrong, P (Paul) Berkshire
Atkinson, M (Martin) W. Yorkshire
Barry, NS (Neale) N. Lincolnshire*
Bates, A (Tony) Staffordshire
Beeby, RJ (Richard) Northamptonshire
Bennett, SG (Steve) Kent*
Booth, RJ (Russell) Nottinghamshire
Boyeson, C (Carl) E. Yorkshire
Cable, LE (Lee) Surrey
Clattenburg, M (Mark) Tyne & Wear*
Cowburn, MG (Mark) Lancashire
Crossley, PT (Phil) Kent
Curson, B (Brian) Leicestershire
Danson, PS (Paul) Leicestershire
Dean, ML (Mike) Wirral*
Dowd, P (Phil) Staffordshire*
Drysdale, D (Darren) Lincolnshire
Dunn, SW (Steve) Gloucestershire*
D'Urso, AP (Andy) Essex*
Evans, EM (Eddie) Greater Manchester
Fletcher, M (Mick) Worcestershire
Foy, CJ (Chris) Merseyside*
Friend, KA (Kevin) Leicestershire
Gallagher, DJ (Dermot) Oxfordshire*
Graham, F (Fred) Essex
Hall, AR (Andy) W. Midlands
Halsey, MR (Mark) Lancashire*
Hegley, GK (Grant) Hertfordshire
Hill, KD (Keith) Hertfordshire
Ilderton, EL (Eddie) Tyne & Wear
Jones, MJ (Michael) Cheshire
Joslin, PJ (Phil) Nottinghamshire
Kaye, A (Alan) W. Yorkshire
Kettle, TM (Trevor) Berkshire
Knight, B (Barry) Kent*
Laws, G (Graham) Tyne & Wear
Leake, AR (Tony) Lancashire
Lewis, GJ (Gary) Haddenham, Cambridgeshire
Marriner, AM (Andre) W. Midlands
Mason, LS (Lee) Lancashire
Mathieson, SW (Scott) Cheshire
Melin, PW (Paul) Surrey
Messias, MD (Matt) W. Yorkshire*
Miller, NS (Nigel) Co. Durham
Oliver, CW (Clive) Northumberland
Olivier, RJ (Ray) W. Midlands
Parkes, TA (Trevor) W. Midlands
Penn, AM (Andy) W. Midlands
Penton, C (Clive) Sussex
Pike, MS (Mike) Cumbria
Poll, G (Graham) Hertfordshire*
Probert, LW (Lee) Gloucestershire
Prosser, PJ (Phil) W. Yorkshire
Rennie, UD (Uriah) S. Yorkshire*
Riley, MA (Mike) W. Yorkshire*
Robinson, JP (Paul) E. Yorkshire
Ross, JJ (Joe) London
Russell, MP (Mike) Hertfordshire
Ryan, M (Michael) Lancashire
Salisbury, G (Graham) Lancashire
Singh, J (Jarnall) Middlesex
Stroud, KP (Keith) Dorset
Styles, R (Rob) Hampshire*
Tanner, SJ (Steve) Somerset
Taylor, P (Paul) Hertfordshire
Thorpe, M (Mike) Suffolk
Tomlin, SG (Steve) E. Sussex
Walton, P (Peter) Northamptonshire*
Warren, MR (Mark) W. Midlands
Webb, HM (Howard) S. Yorkshire*
Webster, CH (Colin) Tyne & Wear
Wiley, AG (Alan) Staffordshire*
Williamson, IG (Iain) Berkshire
Woolmer, KA (Andy) Northamptonshire
Wright, KK (Kevin) Cambridgeshire

USEFUL ADDRESSES

The Football Association: The Secretary, 25 Soho Square, London W1D 4FA. *0207 745 4545*

Scotland: D. Taylor, Hampden Park, Glasgow G42 9AY. *0141 616 6000*

Northern Ireland (Irish FA): Chief Executive: Howard J. C. Wells, 20 Windsor Avenue, Belfast BT9 6EG. *028 9066 9458*

Wales: D. Collins, 3 Westgate Street, Cardiff, South Glamorgan CF10 1DP. *029 2037 2325*

Republic of Ireland (FA of Ireland): B. Menton, 80 Merrion Square South, Dublin 2. *00353 16766864*

International Federation (FIFA): Secretary, PO Box 85 8030 Zurich, Switzerland. *00 411 384 9595. Fax: 00 411 384 9696*

Union of European Football Associations: Secretary, Route de Geneve 46, Case Postale, CH-1260 Nyon, Switzerland. *0041 22 994 4444. Fax: 0041 22 994 4488*

The Premier League: M. Foster, 11 Connaught Place, London W2 2ET. *0207 298 1600*

The Football League: Secretary, The Football League, Unit 5, Edward VII Quay, Navigation Way, Preston, Lancashire PR2 2YF. *01772 325800. Fax 01772 325801*

Scottish Premier League: R. Mitchell, Hampden Park, Somerville Drive, Glasgow G42 9BA. *0141 646 6962*

The Scottish League: The Secretary, Hampden Park, Glasgow G42 9AY. *0141 616 6000*

The Irish League: Secretary, 96 University Street, Belfast BT7 1HE. *028 9024 2888*

Football League of Ireland: D. Crowther, 80 Merrion Square, Dublin 2. *00353 167 65120*

Conference National: Riverside House, 14b High Street, Crayford DA1 4HG. *01322 411021*

Northern Premier: R. D. Bayley, 22 Woburn Drive, Hale, Altrincham, Cheshire WA15 8LZ. *0161 980 7007*

Isthmian League: Triumph House, Station Approach, Sanderstead Road, South Croydon, Surrey CR2 0PL. *020 8409 1978. Fax 020 7639 5726*

English Schools FA: J. Read, 1/2 Eastgate Street, Stafford ST16 2NG. *01785 251142*

Southern League: D. J. Strudwick, 8 College Yard, Worcester WR1 2LA. *01905 330444*

The Football Supporters Federation: Chairman: Ian D. Todd MBE, 8 Wyke Close, Wyke Gardens, Isleworth, Middlesex TW7 5PE. *020 8847 2905 (and fax). Mobile: 0961 558908.* National Secretary: Mark Agate, 'The Stadium', 14 Coombe Close, Lordswood, Chatham, Kent ME5 8NU. *01634 319461 (and fax)*

Professional Footballers' Association: G. Taylor, 2 Oxford Court, Bishopsgate, Off Lower Mosley Street, Manchester M2 3WQ. *0161 236 0575*

Referees' Association: A. Smith, 1 Westhill Road, Coundon, Coventry CV6 2AD. *024 7660 1701*

Women's Football Alliance: The Football Association, 25 Soho Square, London W1D 4FA. *0207 745 4545*

The Football Programme Directory: David Stacey, 'The Beeches', 66 Southend Road, Wickford, Essex SS11 8EN. *01268 732041 (and fax)*

England Football Supporters Association: Publicity Officer, David Stacey, 66 Southend Road, Wickford, Essex SS11 8EN. *01268 732041 (and fax)*

World Cup (1966) Association: Hon. Secretary: David Duncan, 96 Glenlea Road, Eltham, London SE9 1DZ.

The Football Foundation Ltd: 25 Soho Square, London W1D 4FF. *0207 534 4210. Fax 0207 287 0459*

ENGLISH LEAGUE FIXTURES 2005–2006

**Sky Sports; †PremPlus pay per view*

Saturday, 6 August 2005

Coca-Cola Football League Championship

Coventry C v Norwich C
Crewe Alex v Burnley
Crystal Palace v Luton T
Derby Co v Brighton & HA
Hull C v QPR
Ipswich T v Cardiff C
Reading v Plymouth Arg
Sheffield U v Leicester C* (12.45)
Southampton v Wolverhampton W* (5.15)
Stoke C v Sheffield W
Watford v Preston NE

Coca-Cola Football League One

Barnsley v Swindon T
Blackpool v Chesterfield
Brentford v Scunthorpe U
Bristol C v Doncaster R
Gillingham v Colchester U
Hartlepool U v Bradford C
Milton Keynes Dons v Bournemouth
Nottingham F v Huddersfield T
Oldham Ath v Yeovil T
Rotherham U v Walsall
Southend U v Port Vale
Swansea C v Tranmere R

Coca-Cola Football League Two

Barnet v Bristol R
Cheltenham T v Bury
Grimsby T v Oxford U
Leyton Orient v Macclesfield T
Lincoln C v Northampton T
Peterborough U v Chester C
Rushden & D'monds v Darlington
Shrewsbury T v Rochdale
Stockport Co v Mansfield T
Torquay U v Notts Co
Wrexham v Boston U
Wycombe W v Carlisle U

Sunday, 7 August 2005

FA Community Shield

Arsenal v Chelsea* (3.00)

Coca-Cola Football League Championship

Leeds U v Millwall* (12.15)

Monday, 8 August 2005

Coca-Cola Football League Championship

Preston NE v Derby Co* (7.45)

Tuesday, 9 August 2005

Coca-Cola Football League Championship

Brighton & HA v Reading
Burnley v Sheffield U
Cardiff C v Leeds U
Leicester C v Stoke C
Luton T v Southampton
Millwall v Coventry C
Norwich C v Crewe Alex
Plymouth Arg v Watford
QPR v Ipswich T
Sheffield W v Hull C
Wolverhampton W v Crystal Palace

Coca-Cola Football League One

Bournemouth v Hartlepool U
Bradford C v Southend U
Colchester U v Swansea C
Doncaster R v Milton Keynes Dons
Huddersfield T v Bristol C
Port Vale v Gillingham
Scunthorpe U v Barnsley
Swindon T v Oldham Ath
Tranmere R v Blackpool
Walsall v Nottingham F
Yeovil T v Rotherham U

Coca-Cola Football League Two

Bristol R v Grimsby T
Bury v Leyton Orient
Carlisle U v Peterborough U
Chester C v Lincoln C
Darlington v Stockport Co
Macclesfield T v Cheltenham T
Mansfield T v Rushden & D'monds
Northampton T v Barnet
Notts Co v Wrexham
Rochdale v Wycombe W

Wednesday, 10 August 2005
Coca-Cola Football League One
Chesterfield v Brentford

Coca-Cola Football League Two
Boston U v Shrewsbury T
Oxford U v Torquay U

Friday, 12 August 2005
Coca-Cola Football League Championship
Cardiff C v Watford* (7.45)

Saturday, 13 August 2005
Barclays Premiership
Aston Villa v Bolton W
Everton v Manchester U† (12.45)
Fulham v Birmingham C
Manchester C v WBA
Middlesbrough v Liverpool† (5.15)
Portsmouth v Tottenham H
Sunderland v Charlton Ath
West Ham U v Blackburn R

Coca-Cola Football League Championship
Brighton & HA v Crewe Alex
Burnley v Coventry C
Leicester C v Ipswich T
Luton T v Leeds U
Millwall v Stoke C
Norwich C v Crystal Palace
Plymouth Arg v Derby Co
Preston NE v Reading
QPR v Sheffield U
Sheffield W v Southampton
Wolverhampton W v Hull C

Coca-Cola Football League One
Bournemouth v Bristol C
Bradford C v Milton Keynes Dons
Chesterfield v Rotherham U
Colchester U v Barnsley
Doncaster R v Hartlepool U
Huddersfield T v Swansea C
Scunthorpe U v Gillingham
Swindon T v Nottingham F
Tranmere R v Oldham Ath
Walsall v Southend U
Yeovil T v Blackpool

Coca-Cola Football League Two
Boston U v Stockport Co
Bristol R v Peterborough U
Bury v Shrewsbury T
Carlisle U v Barnet
Chester C v Grimsby T
Darlington v Leyton Orient
Macclesfield T v Rushden & D'monds
Mansfield T v Torquay U
Northampton T v Wrexham
Notts Co v Lincoln C
Oxford U v Wycombe W
Rochdale v Cheltenham T

Sunday, 14 August 2005
Barclays Premiership
Arsenal v Newcastle U* (1.30)
Wigan Ath v Chelsea* (4.00)

Monday, 15 August 2005
Coca-Cola Football League One
Port Vale v Brentford* (7.45)

Saturday, 20 August 2005
Barclays Premiership
Birmingham C v Manchester C† (5.15)
Blackburn R v Fulham
Charlton Ath v Wigan Ath
Liverpool v Sunderland
Manchester U v Aston Villa† (12.45)
Newcastle U v West Ham U
Tottenham H v Middlesbrough
WBA v Portsmouth

Coca-Cola Football League Championship
Coventry C v QPR
Crewe Alex v Leicester C
Crystal Palace v Plymouth Arg
Derby Co v Cardiff C
Hull C v Brighton & HA
Ipswich T v Sheffield W
Leeds U v Wolverhampton W
Reading v Millwall
Sheffield U v Preston NE
Southampton v Norwich C
Stoke C v Luton T
Watford v Burnley

Coca-Cola Football League One
Barnsley v Yeovil T
Blackpool v Swindon T
Brentford v Tranmere R
Bristol C v Port Vale
Gillingham v Bournemouth
Hartlepool U v Walsall
Milton Keynes Dons v Colchester U
Nottingham F v Scunthorpe U
Oldham Ath v Chesterfield
Rotherham U v Bradford C
Southend U v Huddersfield T
Swansea C v Doncaster R

Coca-Cola Football League Two
Barnet v Macclesfield T
Cheltenham T v Boston U
Grimsby T v Darlington

Leyton Orient v Rochdale
Lincoln C v Oxford U
Peterborough U v Mansfield T
Rushden & D'monds v Chester C
Shrewsbury T v Northampton T
Stockport Co v Notts Co
Torquay U v Bristol R
Wrexham v Carlisle U
Wycombe W v Bury

Sunday, 21 August 2005
Barclays Premiership
Bolton W v Everton* (1.30)
Chelsea v Arsenal* (4.00)

Tuesday, 23 August 2005
Barclays Premiership
Arsenal v Fulham
Birmingham C v Middlesbrough
Bolton W v Newcastle U
Charlton Ath v Liverpool
Portsmouth v Aston Villa
Sunderland v Manchester C

Wednesday, 24 August 2005
Barclays Premiership
Blackburn R v Tottenham H
Chelsea v WBA
Everton v West Ham U
Manchester U v Wigan Ath

Friday, 26 August 2005
Coca-Cola Football League Championship
QPR v Sheffield W* (7.45)

Saturday, 27 August 2005
Barclays Premiership
Aston Villa v Blackburn R
Fulham v Everton
Liverpool v Arsenal
Manchester C v Portsmouth
Tottenham H v Chelsea
WBA v Birmingham C† (12.15)
West Ham U v Bolton W
Wigan Ath v Sunderland

Coca-Cola Football League Championship
Burnley v Derby Co
Cardiff C v Wolverhampton W
Crystal Palace v Stoke C
Leicester C v Luton T
Millwall v Ipswich T
Norwich C v Leeds U
Plymouth Arg v Hull C
Preston NE v Brighton & HA
Sheffield U v Coventry C
Southampton v Crewe Alex
Watford v Reading* (5.15)

Coca-Cola Football League One
Barnsley v Brentford
Bradford C v Bournemouth
Bristol C v Milton Keynes Dons
Chesterfield v Tranmere R
Colchester U v Oldham Ath
Gillingham v Nottingham F
Huddersfield T v Hartlepool U
Port Vale v Doncaster R
Rotherham U v Blackpool
Scunthorpe U v Southend U
Swindon T v Yeovil T
Walsall v Swansea C

Coca-Cola Football League Two
Barnet v Grimsby T
Boston U v Mansfield T
Bury v Wrexham
Carlisle U v Northampton T
Cheltenham T v Leyton Orient
Chester C v Darlington
Notts Co v Bristol R
Oxford U v Stockport Co
Peterborough U v Torquay U
Rochdale v Macclesfield T
Rushden & D'monds v Lincoln C
Shrewsbury T v Wycombe W

Sunday, 28 August 2005
Barclays Premiership
Middlesbrough v Charlton Ath* (1.30)
Newcastle U v Manchester U* (4.00)

Monday, 29 August 2005
Coca-Cola Football League Championship
Brighton & HA v Plymouth Arg
Coventry C v Southampton
Crewe Alex v Sheffield U
Derby Co v Watford
Hull C v Leicester C
Ipswich T v Preston NE
Luton T v Millwall
Reading v Burnley
Sheffield W v Cardiff C
Stoke C v Norwich C
Wolverhampton W v QPR

Coca-Cola Football League One
Blackpool v Bradford C
Bournemouth v Walsall
Brentford v Gillingham
Doncaster R v Huddersfield T
Hartlepool U v Scunthorpe U
Milton Keynes Dons v Port Vale
Nottingham F v Bristol C

Oldham Ath v Rotherham U
Southend U v Colchester U
Swansea C v Barnsley
Tranmere R v Swindon T
Yeovil T v Chesterfield

Coca-Cola Football League Two
Bristol R v Oxford U
Darlington v Rochdale
Grimsby T v Rushden & D'monds
Leyton Orient v Shrewsbury T
Lincoln C v Carlisle U
Macclesfield T v Bury
Mansfield T v Notts Co
Northampton T v Boston U
Stockport Co v Peterborough U
Torquay U v Chester C
Wrexham v Barnet
Wycombe W v Cheltenham T

Tuesday, 30 August 2005
Coca-Cola Football League Championship
Leeds U v Crystal Palace* (7.45)

Saturday, 3 September 2005
Coca-Cola Football League One
Bournemouth v Tranmere R
Bradford C v Chesterfield
Bristol C v Colchester U* (12.05)
Doncaster R v Blackpool
Gillingham v Barnsley
Hartlepool U v Yeovil T
Huddersfield T v Scunthorpe U
Milton Keynes Dons v Swansea C
Nottingham F v Brentford
Port Vale v Rotherham U
Southend U v Oldham Ath
Walsall v Swindon T

Coca-Cola Football League Two
Bury v Carlisle U
Cheltenham T v Barnet
Chester C v Mansfield T
Darlington v Notts Co
Grimsby T v Stockport Co
Leyton Orient v Bristol R
Lincoln C v Wrexham
Macclesfield T v Boston U
Rochdale v Torquay U
Rushden & D'monds v Peterborough U
Shrewsbury T v Oxford U
Wycombe W v Northampton T

Saturday, 10 September 2005
Barclays Premiership
Birmingham C v Charlton Ath
Chelsea v Sunderland
Everton v Portsmouth
Manchester U v Manchester C
Middlesbrough v Arsenal† (5.15)
Newcastle U v Fulham
Tottenham H v Liverpool
WBA v Wigan Ath

Coca-Cola Football League Championship
Burnley v Cardiff C
Coventry C v Reading
Crystal Palace v Hull C
Leeds U v Brighton & HA
Leicester C v Sheffield W
Luton T v Wolverhampton W
Millwall v Preston NE
Norwich C v Plymouth Arg* (12.45)
Sheffield U v Ipswich T
Southampton v QPR
Stoke C v Watford

Coca-Cola Football League One
Barnsley v Nottingham F
Blackpool v Hartlepool U
Brentford v Milton Keynes Dons
Chesterfield v Bournemouth
Colchester U v Doncaster R
Oldham Ath v Huddersfield T
Rotherham U v Gillingham
Scunthorpe U v Port Vale
Swansea C v Bristol C
Swindon T v Southend U
Tranmere R v Bradford C
Yeovil T v Walsall

Coca-Cola Football League Two
Barnet v Leyton Orient
Boston U v Rochdale
Bristol R v Lincoln C
Carlisle U v Macclesfield T
Mansfield T v Darlington
Northampton T v Bury
Notts Co v Chester C
Oxford U v Rushden & D'monds
Peterborough U v Grimsby T
Stockport Co v Wycombe W
Torquay U v Shrewsbury T
Wrexham v Cheltenham T

Sunday, 11 September 2005
Coca-Cola Football League Championship
Bolton W v Blackburn R* (4.00)
Crewe Alex v Derby Co* (1.30)

Monday, 12 September 2005
West Ham U v Aston Villa* (8.00)

Tuesday, 13 September 2005
Coca-Cola Football League Championship
Brighton & HA v Sheffield U
Cardiff C v Leicester C
Hull C v Stoke C
Ipswich T v Southampton
Plymouth Arg v Crewe Alex
Preston NE v Burnley
QPR v Luton T
Reading v Crystal Palace
Sheffield W v Leeds U
Watford v Norwich C
Wolverhampton W v Millwall

Wednesday, 14 September 2005
Coca-Cola Football League Championship
Derby Co v Coventry C

Friday, 16 September 2005
Preston NE v Stoke C* (7.45)

Saturday, 17 September 2005
Barclays Premiership
Aston Villa v Tottenham H† (5.15)
Charlton Ath v Chelsea
Fulham v West Ham U
Manchester C v Bolton W
Portsmouth v Birmingham C
Sunderland v WBA
Wigan Ath v Middlesbrough

Coca-Cola Football League Championship
Brighton & HA v Coventry C
Cardiff C v Crystal Palace
Hull C v Luton T* (12.45)
Ipswich T v Norwich C
Plymouth Arg v Burnley
QPR v Leeds U
Reading v Crewe Alex
Sheffield W v Millwall
Watford v Sheffield U
Wolverhampton W v Leicester C

Coca-Cola Football League One
Bournemouth v Swindon T
Bradford C v Yeovil T
Bristol C v Blackpool
Doncaster R v Scunthorpe U
Gillingham v Oldham Ath
Hartlepool U v Swansea C
Huddersfield T v Brentford
Milton Keynes Dons v Barnsley
Nottingham F v Rotherham U
Port Vale v Colchester U
Southend U v Tranmere R
Walsall v Chesterfield

Coca-Cola Football League Two
Bury v Boston U
Cheltenham T v Carlisle U
Chester C v Bristol R
Darlington v Oxford U
Grimsby T v Torquay U
Leyton Orient v Wrexham
Lincoln C v Peterborough U
Macclesfield T v Northampton T
Rochdale v Mansfield T
Rushden & D'monds v Stockport Co
Shrewsbury T v Notts Co
Wycombe W v Barnet

Sunday, 18 September 2005
Barclays Premiership
Blackburn R v Newcastle U† (2.00)
Liverpool v Manchester U* (12.00)

Coca-Cola Football League Championship
Derby Co v Southampton* (4.00)

Monday, 19 September 2005
Barclays Premiership
Arsenal v Everton* (8.00)

Friday, 23 September 2005
Coca-Cola Football League Championship
Luton T v Sheffield W* (7.45)

Saturday, 24 September 2005
Barclays Premiership
Birmingham C v Liverpool† (12.45)
Bolton W v Portsmouth† (5.15)
Chelsea v Aston Villa
Everton v Wigan Ath
Manchester U v Blackburn R
Newcastle U v Manchester C
WBA v Charlton Ath
West Ham U v Arsenal

Coca-Cola Football League Championship
Burnley v Brighton & HA
Coventry C v Hull C
Crewe Alex v Watford
Crystal Palace v Preston NE
Leeds U v Ipswich T
Leicester C v QPR
Millwall v Cardiff C
Norwich C v Reading
Sheffield U v Derby Co
Southampton v Plymouth Arg
Stoke C v Wolverhampton W

Coca-Cola Football League One
Barnsley v Doncaster R
Blackpool v Milton Keynes Dons

Brentford v Bristol C
Chesterfield v Hartlepool U
Colchester U v Huddersfield T
Oldham Ath v Bournemouth
Rotherham U v Southend U
Scunthorpe U v Walsall
Swansea C v Nottingham F
Swindon T v Bradford C
Tranmere R v Gillingham
Yeovil T v Port Vale

Coca-Cola Football League Two
Barnet v Rochdale
Boston U v Grimsby T
Bristol R v Darlington
Carlisle U v Leyton Orient
Mansfield T v Wycombe W
Northampton T v Cheltenham T
Notts Co v Rushden & D'monds
Oxford U v Bury
Peterborough U v Shrewsbury T
Stockport Co v Chester C
Torquay U v Lincoln C
Wrexham v Macclesfield T

Sunday, 25 September 2005
Barclays Premiership
Middlesbrough v Sunderland* (4.00)

Monday, 26 September 2005
Barclays Premiership
Tottenham H v Fulham* (8.00)

Tuesday, 27 September 2005
Coca-Cola Football League Championship
Burnley v Ipswich T
Crewe Alex v Wolverhampton W
Crystal Palace v Sheffield W
Leeds U v Derby Co
Leicester C v Brighton & HA
Luton T v Preston NE
Millwall v QPR
Norwich C v Hull C
Sheffield U v Plymouth Arg
Stoke C v Cardiff C

Coca-Cola Football League One
Bournemouth v Swansea C
Bradford C v Colchester U
Bristol C v Barnsley
Doncaster R v Swindon T
Gillingham v Chesterfield
Hartlepool U v Rotherham U
Huddersfield T v Tranmere R
Milton Keynes Dons v Scunthorpe U
Nottingham F v Blackpool
Port Vale v Oldham Ath
Southend U v Yeovil T
Walsall v Brentford

Coca-Cola Football League Two
Bury v Bristol R
Cheltenham T v Peterborough U
Chester C v Carlisle U
Darlington v Boston U
Grimsby T v Notts Co
Leyton Orient v Torquay U
Lincoln C v Stockport Co
Macclesfield T v Mansfield T
Rochdale v Oxford U
Rushden & D'monds v Northampton T
Shrewsbury T v Barnet
Wycombe W v Wrexham

Wednesday, 28 September 2005
Coca-Cola Football League Championship
Coventry C v Watford
Southampton v Reading

Friday, 30 September 2005
Coca-Cola Football League Championship
Wolverhampton W v Burnley* (7.45)

Saturday, 1 October 2005
Barclays Premiership
Aston Villa v Middlesbrough
Blackburn R v WBA
Charlton Ath v Tottenham H
Fulham v Manchester U
Manchester C v Everton† (12.45)
Portsmouth v Newcastle U
Sunderland v West Ham U† (5.15)
Wigan Ath v Bolton W

Coca-Cola Football League Championship
Brighton & HA v Norwich C
Cardiff C v Luton T
Derby Co v Leicester C
Hull C v Millwall
Ipswich T v Crewe Alex
Plymouth Arg v Stoke C
Preston NE v Southampton
Reading v Sheffield U
Sheffield W v Coventry C
Watford v Leeds U

Coca-Cola Football League One
Barnsley v Oldham Ath
Brentford v Rotherham U
Bristol C v Hartlepool U
Colchester U v Chesterfield
Doncaster R v Bradford C
Gillingham v Southend U

Huddersfield T v Bournemouth
Milton Keynes Dons v Swindon T
Nottingham F v Tranmere R
Port Vale v Walsall
Scunthorpe U v Yeovil T
Swansea C v Blackpool

Coca-Cola Football League Two
Barnet v Oxford U
Boston U v Peterborough U
Bury v Lincoln C
Carlisle U v Bristol R
Cheltenham T v Torquay U
Leyton Orient v Mansfield T
Macclesfield T v Notts Co
Northampton T v Darlington
Rochdale v Rushden & D'monds
Shrewsbury T v Grimsby T
Wrexham v Stockport Co
Wycombe W v Chester C

Sunday, 2 October 2005
Barclays Premiership
Arsenal v Birmingham C* (1.30)
Liverpool v Chelsea* (4.00)

Monday, 3 October 2005
Coca-Cola Football League Championship
QPR v Crystal Palace* (7.45)

Saturday, 8 October 2005
Coca-Cola Football League One
Blackpool v Colchester U
Bournemouth v Doncaster R
Chesterfield v Bristol C
Hartlepool U v Gillingham
Oldham Ath v Brentford
Rotherham U v Barnsley
Swindon T v Port Vale
Tranmere R v Scunthorpe U
Walsall v Milton Keynes Dons
Yeovil T v Swansea C

Coca-Cola Football League Two
Bristol R v Northampton T
Chester C v Rochdale
Darlington v Macclesfield T
Grimsby T v Wycombe W
Lincoln C v Cheltenham T
Mansfield T v Shrewsbury T
Notts Co v Boston U
Oxford U v Carlisle U
Peterborough U v Wrexham
Rushden & D'monds v Bury
Stockport Co v Leyton Orient
Torquay U v Barnet

Sunday, 9 October 2005
Coca-Cola Football League One
Southend U v Nottingham F* (4.00)

Monday, 10 October 2005
Coca-Cola Football League One
Bradford C v Huddersfield T* (7.45)

Saturday, 15 October 2005
Barclays Premiership
Birmingham C v Aston Villa
Chelsea v Bolton W
Liverpool v Blackburn R
Middlesbrough v Portsmouth* (5.15)
Sunderland v Manchester U
Tottenham H v Everton
WBA v Arsenal
Wigan Ath v Newcastle U† (12.45)

Coca-Cola Football League Championship
Brighton & HA v Cardiff C
Burnley v Leeds U
Coventry C v Crystal Palace
Crewe Alex v Luton T
Derby Co v Stoke C
Norwich C v Millwall
Plymouth Arg v Sheffield W
Preston NE v QPR
Sheffield U v Wolverhampton W
Southampton v Hull C
Watford v Leicester C

Coca-Cola Football League One
Barnsley v Blackpool
Brentford v Swindon T
Bristol C v Tranmere R
Colchester U v Bournemouth
Doncaster R v Southend U
Gillingham v Yeovil T
Huddersfield T v Walsall
Milton Keynes Dons v Chesterfield
Nottingham F v Hartlepool U
Port Vale v Bradford C
Scunthorpe U v Rotherham U
Swansea C v Oldham Ath

Coca-Cola Football League Two
Barnet v Chester C
Boston U v Bristol R
Bury v Darlington
Carlisle U v Mansfield T
Cheltenham T v Grimsby T
Leyton Orient v Lincoln C
Macclesfield T v Peterborough U
Northampton T v Oxford U
Rochdale v Notts Co
Shrewsbury T v Stockport Co
Wrexham v Torquay U
Wycombe W v Rushden & D'monds

Sunday, 16 October 2005

Barclays Premiership
Manchester C v West Ham U* (4.00)

Coca-Cola Football League Championship
Reading v Ipswich T* (1.30)

Monday, 17 October 2005

Barclays Premiership
Charlton Ath v Fulham* (8.00)

Tuesday, 18 October 2005

Coca-Cola Football League Championship
Cardiff C v Preston NE
Crystal Palace v Brighton & HA
Hull C v Reading
Ipswich T v Coventry C
Leeds U v Southampton
Leicester C v Burnley
Luton T v Norwich C
Millwall v Sheffield U
QPR v Plymouth Arg
Sheffield W v Watford
Stoke C v Crewe Alex
Wolverhampton W v Derby Co

Friday, 21 October 2005

Coca-Cola Football League Championship
Leeds U v Sheffield U* (7.45)

Saturday, 22 October 2005

Barclays Premiership
Arsenal v Manchester C
Aston Villa v Wigan Ath
Blackburn R v Birmingham C* (12.45)
Bolton W v WBA
Fulham v Liverpool
Manchester U v Tottenham H
Portsmouth v Charlton Ath† (5.15)
West Ham U v Middlesbrough

Coca-Cola Football League Championship
Cardiff C v Crewe Alex
Crystal Palace v Burnley
Hull C v Derby Co
Ipswich T v Watford
Leicester C v Coventry C
Luton T v Plymouth Arg
Millwall v Southampton
QPR v Norwich C
Sheffield W v Brighton & HA
Stoke C v Reading
Wolverhampton W v Preston NE

Coca-Cola Football League One
Blackpool v Brentford
Bournemouth v Port Vale
Bradford C v Gillingham
Chesterfield v Huddersfield T
Hartlepool U v Milton Keynes Dons
Oldham Ath v Bristol C
Rotherham U v Swansea C
Southend U v Barnsley
Swindon T v Scunthorpe U
Tranmere R v Colchester U
Walsall v Doncaster R
Yeovil T v Nottingham F

Coca-Cola Football League Two
Bristol R v Wrexham
Chester C v Bury
Darlington v Cheltenham T
Grimsby T v Leyton Orient
Lincoln C v Wycombe W
Mansfield T v Barnet
Notts Co v Carlisle U
Oxford U v Boston U
Peterborough U v Rochdale
Rushden & D'monds v Shrewsbury T
Stockport Co v Northampton T
Torquay U v Macclesfield T

Sunday, 23 October 2005

Barclays Premiership
Everton v Chelsea* (4.00)
Newcastle U v Sunderland† (1.30)

Friday, 28 October 2005

Coca-Cola Football League Championship
Burnley v Hull C* (7.45)

Saturday, 29 October 2005

Barclays Premiership
Birmingham C v Everton
Charlton Ath v Bolton W
Chelsea v Blackburn R
Liverpool v West Ham U
Middlesbrough v Manchester U† (5.15)
Sunderland v Portsmouth
Tottenham H v Arsenal
Wigan Ath v Fulham† (12.45)

Coca-Cola Football League Championship
Brighton & HA v Ipswich T
Coventry C v Luton T
Crewe Alex v Crystal Palace
Derby Co v QPR
Norwich C v Sheffield W
Preston NE v Leicester C
Reading v Leeds U
Sheffield U v Cardiff C

Southampton v Stoke C
Watford v Wolverhampton W

Coca-Cola Football League One
Barnsley v Walsall
Brentford v Bournemouth
Bristol C v Southend U
Colchester U v Yeovil T
Doncaster R v Tranmere R
Gillingham v Blackpool
Huddersfield T v Swindon T
Milton Keynes Dons v Rotherham U
Nottingham F v Bradford C
Port Vale v Hartlepool U
Scunthorpe U v Oldham Ath
Swansea C v Chesterfield

Coca-Cola Football League Two
Barnet v Rushden & D'monds
Boston U v Torquay U
Bury v Notts Co
Carlisle U v Stockport Co
Cheltenham T v Mansfield T
Leyton Orient v Oxford U
Macclesfield T v Bristol R
Northampton T v Grimsby T
Rochdale v Lincoln C
Shrewsbury T v Chester C
Wrexham v Darlington
Wycombe W v Peterborough U

Sunday, 30 October 2005
Barclays Premiership
WBA v Newcastle U* (4.00)

Coca-Cola Football League Championship
Plymouth Arg v Millwall* (1.30)

Monday, 31 October 2005
Barclays Premiership
Manchester C v Aston Villa* (8.00)

Tuesday, 1 November 2005
Coca-Cola Football League Championship
Brighton & HA v Wolverhampton W
Burnley v Millwall
Crewe Alex v Leeds U
Norwich C v Cardiff C
Plymouth Arg v Leicester C
Preston NE v Hull C
Reading v Sheffield W
Sheffield U v Luton T
Watford v QPR

Wednesday, 2 November 2005
Coca-Cola Football League Championship
Coventry C v Stoke C
Derby Co v Ipswich T
Southampton v Crystal Palace

Saturday, 5 November 2005
Barclays Premiership
Arsenal v Sunderland
Aston Villa v Liverpool† (12.45)
Blackburn R v Charlton Ath
Everton v Middlesbrough
Fulham v Manchester C
Newcastle U v Birmingham C
Portsmouth v Wigan Ath* (5.15)
West Ham U v WBA

Coca-Cola Football League Championship
Cardiff C v Coventry C
Crystal Palace v Sheffield U
Hull C v Watford
Ipswich T v Plymouth Arg
Leeds U v Preston NE
Leicester C v Southampton
Luton T v Burnley
Millwall v Crewe Alex
QPR v Reading
Sheffield W v Derby Co
Stoke C v Brighton & HA
Wolverhampton W v Norwich C

Sunday, 6 November 2005
Barclays Premiership
Manchester U v Chelsea* (4.00)

Monday, 7 November 2005
Barclays Premiership
Bolton W v Tottenham H* (8.00)

Friday, 11 November 2005
Coca-Cola Football League One
Swindon T v Bristol C* (7.45)

Saturday, 12 November 2005
Coca-Cola Football League One
Bournemouth v Nottingham F
Bradford C v Barnsley
Chesterfield v Port Vale
Hartlepool U v Brentford
Oldham Ath v Doncaster R
Rotherham U v Colchester U
Southend U v Swansea C
Tranmere R v Milton Keynes Dons
Walsall v Gillingham
Yeovil T v Huddersfield T

Coca-Cola Football League Two
Bristol R v Rochdale
Chester C v Northampton T
Darlington v Wycombe W
Grimsby T v Macclesfield T
Lincoln C v Shrewsbury T
Mansfield T v Bury
Notts Co v Cheltenham T
Oxford U v Wrexham
Peterborough U v Leyton Orient
Rushden & D'monds v Boston U
Torquay U v Carlisle U

Sunday, 13 November 2005
Coca-Cola Football League One
Blackpool v Scunthorpe U* (4.00)

Coca-Cola Football League Two
Stockport Co v Barnet* (1.30)

Friday, 18 November 2005
Coca-Cola Football League Championship
Derby Co v Wolverhampton W* (7.45)

Saturday, 19 November 2005
Barclays Premiership
Charlton Ath v Manchester U
Chelsea v Newcastle U
Liverpool v Portsmouth
Manchester C v Blackburn R
Sunderland v Aston Villa
Tottenham H v West Ham U
WBA v Everton† (5.15)
Wigan Ath v Arsenal* (12.45)

Coca-Cola Football League Championship
Burnley v Leicester C
Coventry C v Ipswich T
Crewe Alex v Stoke C
Norwich C v Luton T
Plymouth Arg v QPR
Preston NE v Cardiff C
Reading v Hull C
Sheffield U v Millwall
Southampton v Leeds U
Watford v Sheffield W

Coca-Cola Football League One
Barnsley v Rotherham U
Brentford v Oldham Ath
Bristol C v Chesterfield
Colchester U v Blackpool
Doncaster R v Bournemouth
Gillingham v Hartlepool U
Huddersfield T v Bradford C
Milton Keynes Dons v Walsall
Nottingham F v Southend U
Port Vale v Swindon T
Scunthorpe U v Tranmere R
Swansea C v Yeovil T

Coca-Cola Football League Two
Barnet v Torquay U
Boston U v Notts Co
Bury v Rushden & D'monds
Carlisle U v Oxford U
Cheltenham T v Lincoln C
Leyton Orient v Stockport Co
Macclesfield T v Darlington
Northampton T v Bristol R
Rochdale v Chester C
Shrewsbury T v Mansfield T
Wrexham v Peterborough U
Wycombe W v Grimsby T

Sunday, 20 November 2005
Barclays Premiership
Middlesbrough v Fulham* (4.00)

Coca-Cola Football League Championship
Brighton & HA v Crystal Palace* (1.30)

Monday, 21 November 2005
Barclays Premiership
Birmingham C v Bolton W* (8.00)

Tuesday, 22 November 2005
Coca-Cola Football League Championship
Cardiff C v Brighton & HA
Crystal Palace v Coventry C
Hull C v Southampton
Ipswich T v Reading
Leeds U v Burnley
Leicester C v Watford
Luton T v Crewe Alex
Millwall v Norwich C
QPR v Preston NE
Sheffield W v Plymouth Arg
Stoke C v Derby Co
Wolverhampton W v Sheffield U

Saturday, 26 November 2005
Barclays Premiership
Arsenal v Blackburn R
Aston Villa v Charlton Ath
Fulham v Bolton W
Manchester C v Liverpool
Middlesbrough v WBA
Portsmouth v Chelsea† (5.15)
Sunderland v Birmingham C
Wigan Ath v Tottenham H

Coca-Cola Football League Championship
Brighton & HA v Derby Co
Burnley v Crewe Alex
Cardiff C v Ipswich T
Leicester C v Sheffield U
Luton T v Crystal Palace
Millwall v Leeds U
Norwich C v Coventry C
Plymouth Arg v Reading
Preston NE v Watford
QPR v Hull C
Sheffield W v Stoke C
Wolverhampton W v Southampton

Coca-Cola Football League One
Bournemouth v Milton Keynes Dons
Bradford C v Hartlepool U
Chesterfield v Blackpool
Colchester U v Gillingham
Doncaster R v Bristol C
Huddersfield T v Nottingham F
Port Vale v Southend U
Scunthorpe U v Brentford
Swindon T v Barnsley
Tranmere R v Swansea C
Walsall v Rotherham U
Yeovil T v Oldham Ath

Coca-Cola Football League Two
Boston U v Wrexham
Bristol R v Barnet
Bury v Cheltenham T
Carlisle U v Wycombe W
Chester C v Peterborough U
Darlington v Rushden & D'monds
Macclesfield T v Leyton Orient
Mansfield T v Stockport Co
Northampton T v Lincoln C
Notts Co v Torquay U
Oxford U v Grimsby T
Rochdale v Shrewsbury T

Sunday, 27 November 2005
Barclays Premiership
Everton v Newcastle U* (1.30)
West Ham U v Manchester U* (4.00)

Saturday, 3 December 2005
Barclays Premiership
Blackburn R v Everton
Bolton W v Arsenal
Chelsea v Middlesbrough
Liverpool v Wigan Ath
Manchester U v Portsmouth† (5.15)
Newcastle U v Aston Villa
Tottenham H v Sunderland
WBA v Fulham

Coca-Cola Football League Championship
Coventry C v Plymouth Arg
Crewe Alex v Preston NE
Crystal Palace v Millwall
Derby Co v Norwich C
Hull C v Cardiff C
Ipswich T v Wolverhampton W
Leeds U v Leicester C
Reading v Luton T
Sheffield U v Sheffield W
Southampton v Burnley
Stoke C v QPR
Watford v Brighton & HA

Sunday, 4 December 2005
Barclays Premiership
Charlton Ath v Manchester C* (4.00)

Monday, 5 December 2005
Barclays Premiership
Birmingham C v West Ham U* (8.00)

Tuesday, 6 December 2005
Coca-Cola Football League One
Barnsley v Tranmere R
Blackpool v Bournemouth
Brentford v Yeovil T
Bristol C v Bradford C
Gillingham v Doncaster R
Hartlepool U v Colchester U
Milton Keynes Dons v Huddersfield T
Nottingham F v Port Vale
Oldham Ath v Walsall
Rotherham U v Swindon T
Southend U v Chesterfield
Swansea C v Scunthorpe U

Coca-Cola Football League Two
Barnet v Bury
Cheltenham T v Oxford U
Grimsby T v Rochdale
Leyton Orient v Chester C
Lincoln C v Macclesfield T
Peterborough U v Notts Co
Rushden & D'monds v Carlisle U
Shrewsbury T v Darlington
Stockport Co v Bristol R
Torquay U v Northampton T
Wrexham v Mansfield T
Wycombe W v Boston U

Saturday, 10 December 2005
Barclays Premiership
Birmingham C v Fulham
Blackburn R v West Ham U
Bolton W v Aston Villa
Charlton Ath v Sunderland
Chelsea v Wigan Ath

Liverpool v Middlesbrough* (12,45)
Newcastle U v Arsenal† (5.15)
WBA v Manchester C

Coca-Cola Football League Championship
Coventry C v Millwall
Crewe Alex v Norwich C
Crystal Palace v Wolverhampton W
Derby Co v Preston NE
Hull C v Sheffield W
Ipswich T v QPR
Leeds U v Cardiff C
Reading v Brighton & HA
Sheffield U v Burnley
Southampton v Luton T
Stoke C v Leicester C
Watford v Plymouth Arg

Coca-Cola Football League One
Barnsley v Scunthorpe U
Blackpool v Tranmere R
Brentford v Chesterfield
Bristol C v Huddersfield T
Gillingham v Port Vale
Hartlepool U v Bournemouth
Milton Keynes Dons v Doncaster R
Nottingham F v Walsall
Oldham Ath v Swindon T
Rotherham U v Yeovil T
Southend U v Bradford C
Swansea C v Colchester U

Coca-Cola Football League Two
Barnet v Northampton T
Cheltenham T v Macclesfield T
Grimsby T v Bristol R
Leyton Orient v Bury
Lincoln C v Chester C
Peterborough U v Carlisle U
Rushden & D'monds v Mansfield T
Shrewsbury T v Boston U
Stockport Co v Darlington
Torquay U v Oxford U
Wrexham v Notts Co
Wycombe W v Rochdale

Sunday, 11 December 2005
Barclays Premiership
Manchester U v Everton* (4.00)

Monday, 12 December 2005
Barclays Premiership
Tottenham H v Portsmouth* (8.00)

Saturday, 17 December 2005
Barclays Premiership
Aston Villa v Manchester U† (12.45)
Everton v Bolton W
Fulham v Blackburn R
Manchester C v Birmingham C
Portsmouth v WBA
Sunderland v Liverpool† (5.15)
West Ham U v Newcastle U
Wigan Ath v Charlton Ath

Coca-Cola Football League Championship
Brighton & HA v Hull C
Burnley v Watford
Cardiff C v Derby Co
Leicester C v Crewe Alex
Luton T v Stoke C
Millwall v Reading
Norwich C v Southampton
Plymouth Arg v Crystal Palace
Preston NE v Sheffield U
QPR v Coventry C
Sheffield W v Ipswich T
Wolverhampton W v Leeds U

Coca-Cola Football League One
Bournemouth v Gillingham
Bradford C v Rotherham U
Chesterfield v Oldham Ath
Colchester U v Milton Keynes Dons
Doncaster R v Swansea C
Huddersfield T v Southend U
Port Vale v Bristol C
Scunthorpe U v Nottingham F
Swindon T v Blackpool
Tranmere R v Brentford
Walsall v Hartlepool U
Yeovil T v Barnsley

Coca-Cola Football League Two
Boston U v Cheltenham T
Bristol R v Torquay U
Bury v Wycombe W
Carlisle U v Wrexham
Chester C v Rushden & D'monds
Darlington v Grimsby T
Macclesfield T v Barnet
Mansfield T v Peterborough U
Northampton T v Shrewsbury T
Notts Co v Stockport Co
Oxford U v Lincoln C
Rochdale v Leyton Orient

Sunday, 18 December 2005
Barclays Premiership
Arsenal v Chelsea* (4.00)
Middlesbrough v Tottenham H* (1.30)

Monday, 26 December 2005
Barclays Premiership
Aston Villa v Everton* (5.15)
Charlton Ath v Arsenal* (12.45)

Chelsea v Fulham
Liverpool v Newcastle U† (3.00)
Manchester U v WBA
Middlesbrough v Blackburn R
Portsmouth v West Ham U
Sunderland v Bolton W
Tottenham H v Birmingham C
Wigan Ath v Manchester C

Coca-Cola Football League Championship
Brighton & HA v QPR
Burnley v Stoke C
Cardiff C v Plymouth Arg
Crewe Alex v Hull C
Derby Co v Luton T
Ipswich T v Crystal Palace
Leeds U v Coventry C
Leicester C v Millwall
Preston NE v Sheffield W
Sheffield U v Norwich C
Watford v Southampton
Wolverhampton W v Reading

Coca-Cola Football League One
Barnsley v Hartlepool U
Brentford v Swansea C
Gillingham v Bristol C
Nottingham F v Doncaster R
Oldham Ath v Bradford C
Port Vale v Blackpool
Rotherham U v Huddersfield T
Scunthorpe U v Chesterfield
Southend U v Milton Keynes Dons
Swindon T v Colchester U
Walsall v Tranmere R
Yeovil T v Bournemouth

Coca-Cola Football League Two
Barnet v Peterborough U
Bristol R v Shrewsbury T
Bury v Grimsby T
Carlisle U v Darlington
Cheltenham T v Chester C
Leyton Orient v Rushden & D'monds
Lincoln C v Boston U
Macclesfield T v Stockport Co
Northampton T v Mansfield T
Oxford U v Notts Co
Torquay U v Wycombe W
Wrexham v Rochdale

Wednesday, 28 December 2005

Barclays Premiership
Arsenal v Portsmouth
Birmingham C v Manchester U
Blackburn R v Sunderland
Bolton W v Middlesbrough
Everton v Liverpool* (8.00)
Fulham v Aston Villa
Manchester C v Chelsea
Newcastle U v Charlton Ath
WBA v Tottenham H
West Ham U v Wigan Ath

Coca-Cola Football League Championship
Coventry C v Crewe Alex
Crystal Palace v Derby Co
Hull C v Ipswich T
Luton T v Brighton & HA
Millwall v Watford
Norwich C v Burnley
Plymouth Arg v Preston NE
QPR v Cardiff C
Reading v Leicester C
Sheffield W v Wolverhampton W
Southampton v Sheffield U
Stoke C v Leeds U

Coca-Cola Football League One
Blackpool v Oldham Ath
Bournemouth v Barnsley
Bradford C v Walsall
Bristol C v Rotherham U
Chesterfield v Swindon T
Colchester U v Scunthorpe U
Doncaster R v Brentford
Hartlepool U v Southend U
Huddersfield T v Port Vale
Milton Keynes Dons v Nottingham F
Swansea C v Gillingham
Tranmere R v Yeovil T

Coca-Cola Football League Two
Boston U v Carlisle U
Chester C v Wrexham
Darlington v Barnet
Grimsby T v Lincoln C
Mansfield T v Bristol R
Notts Co v Northampton T
Peterborough U v Oxford U
Rochdale v Bury
Rushden & D'monds v Cheltenham T
Shrewsbury T v Macclesfield T
Stockport Co v Torquay U
Wycombe W v Leyton Orient

Saturday, 31 December 2005

Barclays Premiership
Aston Villa v Arsenal* (12.45)
Charlton Ath v West Ham U
Chelsea v Birmingham C
Liverpool v WBA
Manchester U v Bolton W
Middlesbrough v Manchester C
Portsmouth v Fulham
Sunderland v Everton

Tottenham H v Newcastle U
Wigan Ath v Blackburn R

Coca-Cola Football League Championship
Brighton & HA v Millwall
Burnley v Sheffield W
Cardiff C v Southampton
Crewe Alex v QPR
Derby Co v Reading
Ipswich T v Luton T
Leeds U v Hull C
Leicester C v Norwich C
Preston NE v Coventry C
Sheffield U v Stoke C
Watford v Crystal Palace
Wolverhampton W v Plymouth Arg

Coca-Cola Football League One
Barnsley v Huddersfield T
Brentford v Colchester U
Gillingham v Milton Keynes Dons
Nottingham F v Chesterfield
Oldham Ath v Hartlepool U
Port Vale v Tranmere R
Rotherham U v Doncaster R
Scunthorpe U v Bradford C
Southend U v Bournemouth
Swindon T v Swansea C
Walsall v Blackpool
Yeovil T v Bristol C

Coca-Cola Football League Two
Barnet v Boston U
Bristol R v Wycombe W
Bury v Stockport Co
Carlisle U v Rochdale
Cheltenham T v Shrewsbury T
Leyton Orient v Notts Co
Lincoln C v Darlington
Macclesfield T v Chester C
Northampton T v Peterborough U
Oxford U v Mansfield T
Torquay U v Rushden & D'monds
Wrexham v Grimsby T

Monday, 2 January 2006
Barclays Premiership
Birmingham C v Wigan Ath
Blackburn R v Portsmouth
Bolton W v Liverpool
Everton v Charlton Ath
Fulham v Sunderland
Manchester C v Tottenham H
Newcastle U v Middlesbrough
WBA v Aston Villa
West Ham U v Chelsea† (12.45)

Coca-Cola Football League Championship
Coventry C v Wolverhampton W
Crystal Palace v Leicester C
Hull C v Sheffield U
Luton T v Watford
Millwall v Derby Co
Norwich C v Preston NE
Plymouth Arg v Leeds U
QPR v Burnley
Reading v Cardiff C
Sheffield W v Crewe Alex
Southampton v Brighton & HA
Stoke C v Ipswich T

Coca-Cola Football League One
Blackpool v Southend U
Bournemouth v Scunthorpe U
Bradford C v Brentford
Bristol C v Walsall
Chesterfield v Barnsley
Colchester U v Nottingham F
Doncaster R v Yeovil T
Hartlepool U v Swindon T
Huddersfield T v Gillingham
Milton Keynes Dons v Oldham Ath
Swansea C v Port Vale
Tranmere R v Rotherham U

Coca-Cola Football League Two
Boston U v Leyton Orient
Chester C v Oxford U
Darlington v Torquay U
Grimsby T v Carlisle U
Mansfield T v Lincoln C
Notts Co v Barnet
Peterborough U v Bury
Rochdale v Northampton T
Rushden & D'monds v Bristol R
Shrewsbury T v Wrexham
Stockport Co v Cheltenham T
Wycombe W v Macclesfield T

Tuesday, 3 January 2006
Barclays Premiership
Arsenal v Manchester U* (8.00)

Saturday, 7 January 2006
Coca-Cola Football League One
Barnsley v Gillingham
Blackpool v Doncaster R
Brentford v Nottingham F
Chesterfield v Bradford C
Colchester U v Bristol C
Oldham Ath v Southend U
Rotherham U v Port Vale
Scunthorpe U v Huddersfield T
Swansea C v Milton Keynes Dons
Swindon T v Walsall

Tranmere R v Bournemouth
Yeovil T v Hartlepool U

Coca-Cola Football League Two
Barnet v Cheltenham T
Boston U v Macclesfield T
Bristol R v Leyton Orient
Carlisle U v Bury
Mansfield T v Chester C
Northampton T v Wycombe W
Notts Co v Darlington
Oxford U v Shrewsbury T
Peterborough U v Rushden & D'monds
Stockport Co v Grimsby T
Torquay U v Rochdale
Wrexham v Lincoln C

Saturday, 14 January 2006
Barclays Premiership
Arsenal v Middlesbrough
Aston Villa v West Ham U
Blackburn R v Bolton W† (5.15)
Charlton Ath v Birmingham C
Fulham v Newcastle U
Liverpool v Tottenham H
Manchester C v Manchester U* (12.45)
Portsmouth v Everton

Coca-Cola Football League Championship
Brighton & HA v Leeds U
Cardiff C v Burnley
Derby Co v Crewe Alex
Hull C v Crystal Palace
Ipswich T v Sheffield U
Plymouth Arg v Norwich C
Preston NE v Millwall
QPR v Southampton
Reading v Coventry C
Sheffield W v Leicester C
Watford v Stoke C
Wolverhampton W v Luton T

Coca-Cola Football League One
Bournemouth v Rotherham U
Bradford C v Swansea C
Bristol C v Scunthorpe U
Doncaster R v Chesterfield
Gillingham v Swindon T
Hartlepool U v Tranmere R
Huddersfield T v Blackpool
Milton Keynes Dons v Yeovil T
Nottingham F v Oldham Ath
Port Vale v Barnsley
Southend U v Brentford
Walsall v Colchester U

Coca-Cola Football League Two
Bury v Torquay U
Cheltenham T v Bristol R
Chester C v Boston U
Darlington v Peterborough U
Grimsby T v Mansfield T
Leyton Orient v Northampton T
Lincoln C v Barnet
Macclesfield T v Oxford U
Rochdale v Stockport Co
Rushden & D'monds v Wrexham
Shrewsbury T v Carlisle U
Wycombe W v Notts Co

Sunday, 15 January 2006
Barclays Premiership
Sunderland v Chelsea* (4.00)
Wigan Ath v WBA* (1.30)

Saturday, 21 January 2006
Barclays Premiership
Birmingham C v Portsmouth
Bolton W v Manchester C
Chelsea v Charlton Ath
Everton v Arsenal
Manchester U v Liverpool
Middlesbrough v Wigan Ath
Newcastle U v Blackburn R
Tottenham H v Aston Villa
WBA v Sunderland
West Ham U v Fulham

Coca-Cola Football League Championship
Burnley v Preston NE
Coventry C v Derby Co
Crewe Alex v Plymouth Arg
Crystal Palace v Reading
Leeds U v Sheffield W
Leicester C v Cardiff C
Luton T v QPR
Millwall v Wolverhampton W
Norwich C v Watford
Sheffield U v Brighton & HA
Southampton v Ipswich T
Stoke C v Hull C

Coca-Cola Football League One
Barnsley v Milton Keynes Dons
Blackpool v Bristol C
Brentford v Huddersfield T
Chesterfield v Walsall
Colchester U v Port Vale
Oldham Ath v Gillingham
Rotherham U v Nottingham F
Scunthorpe U v Doncaster R
Swansea C v Hartlepool U
Swindon T v Bournemouth
Tranmere R v Southend U
Yeovil T v Bradford C

Coca-Cola Football League Two
Barnet v Wycombe W
Boston U v Bury
Bristol R v Chester C
Carlisle U v Cheltenham T
Mansfield T v Rochdale
Northampton T v Macclesfield T
Notts Co v Shrewsbury T
Oxford U v Darlington
Peterborough U v Lincoln C
Stockport Co v Rushden & D'monds
Torquay U v Grimsby T
Wrexham v Leyton Orient

Saturday, 28 January 2006
Coca-Cola Football League One
Bournemouth v Chesterfield
Bradford C v Tranmere R
Bristol C v Swansea C
Doncaster R v Colchester U
Gillingham v Rotherham U
Hartlepool U v Blackpool
Huddersfield T v Oldham Ath
Milton Keynes Dons v Brentford
Nottingham F v Barnsley
Port Vale v Scunthorpe U
Southend U v Swindon T
Walsall v Yeovil T

Coca-Cola Football League Two
Bury v Northampton T
Cheltenham T v Wrexham
Chester C v Notts Co
Darlington v Mansfield T
Grimsby T v Peterborough U
Leyton Orient v Barnet
Lincoln C v Bristol R
Macclesfield T v Carlisle U
Rochdale v Boston U
Rushden & D'monds v Oxford U
Shrewsbury T v Torquay U
Wycombe W v Stockport Co

Tuesday, 31 January 2006
Barclays Premiership
Arsenal v West Ham U
Charlton Ath v WBA
Liverpool v Birmingham C
Portsmouth v Bolton W
Sunderland v Middlesbrough
Wigan Ath v Everton

Coca-Cola Football League Championship
Brighton & HA v Burnley
Cardiff C v Millwall
Hull C v Coventry C
Ipswich T v Leeds U
Plymouth Arg v Southampton
Preston NE v Crystal Palace
QPR v Leicester C
Reading v Norwich C
Sheffield W v Luton T
Watford v Crewe Alex
Wolverhampton W v Stoke C

Wednesday, 1 February 2006
Barclays Premiership
Aston Villa v Chelsea
Blackburn R v Manchester U
Fulham v Tottenham H
Manchester C v Newcastle U

Coca-Cola Football League Championship
Derby Co v Sheffield U

Saturday, 4 February 2006
Barclays Premiership
Birmingham C v Arsenal
Bolton W v Wigan Ath
Chelsea v Liverpool
Everton v Manchester C
Manchester U v Fulham
Middlesbrough v Aston Villa
Newcastle U v Portsmouth
Tottenham H v Charlton Ath
WBA v Blackburn R
West Ham U v Sunderland

Coca-Cola Football League Championship
Burnley v Plymouth Arg
Coventry C v Brighton & HA
Crewe Alex v Reading
Crystal Palace v Cardiff C
Leeds U v QPR
Leicester C v Wolverhampton W
Luton T v Hull C
Millwall v Sheffield W
Norwich C v Ipswich T
Sheffield U v Watford
Southampton v Derby Co
Stoke C v Preston NE

Coca-Cola Football League One
Barnsley v Bristol C
Blackpool v Nottingham F
Brentford v Walsall
Chesterfield v Gillingham
Colchester U v Bradford C
Oldham Ath v Port Vale
Rotherham U v Hartlepool U
Scunthorpe U v Milton Keynes Dons
Swansea C v Bournemouth
Swindon T v Doncaster R
Tranmere R v Huddersfield T
Yeovil T v Southend U

Coca-Cola Football League Two
Barnet v Shrewsbury T
Boston U v Darlington
Bristol R v Bury
Carlisle U v Chester C
Mansfield T v Macclesfield T
Northampton T v Rushden & D'monds
Notts Co v Grimsby T
Oxford U v Rochdale
Peterborough U v Cheltenham T
Stockport Co v Lincoln C
Torquay U v Leyton Orient
Wrexham v Wycombe W

Saturday, 11 February 2006
Barclays Premiership
Arsenal v Bolton W
Aston Villa v Newcastle U
Everton v Blackburn R
Fulham v WBA
Manchester C v Charlton Ath
Middlesbrough v Chelsea
Portsmouth v Manchester U
Sunderland v Tottenham H
West Ham U v Birmingham C
Wigan Ath v Liverpool

Coca-Cola Football League Championship
Brighton & HA v Leicester C
Cardiff C v Stoke C
Derby Co v Leeds U
Hull C v Norwich C
Ipswich T v Burnley
Plymouth Arg v Sheffield U
Preston NE v Luton T
QPR v Millwall
Reading v Southampton
Sheffield W v Crystal Palace
Watford v Coventry C
Wolverhampton W v Crewe Alex

Coca-Cola Football League One
Bournemouth v Oldham Ath
Bradford C v Swindon T
Bristol C v Brentford
Doncaster R v Barnsley
Gillingham v Tranmere R
Hartlepool U v Chesterfield
Huddersfield T v Colchester U
Milton Keynes Dons v Blackpool
Nottingham F v Swansea C
Port Vale v Yeovil T
Southend U v Rotherham U
Walsall v Scunthorpe U

Coca-Cola Football League Two
Bury v Oxford U
Cheltenham T v Northampton T
Chester C v Stockport Co
Darlington v Bristol R
Grimsby T v Boston U
Leyton Orient v Carlisle U
Lincoln C v Torquay U
Macclesfield T v Wrexham
Rochdale v Barnet
Rushden & D'monds v Notts Co
Shrewsbury T v Peterborough U
Wycombe W v Mansfield T

Tuesday, 14 February 2006
Coca-Cola Football League Championship
Burnley v Wolverhampton W
Crewe Alex v Ipswich T
Crystal Palace v QPR
Leeds U v Watford
Leicester C v Derby Co
Luton T v Cardiff C
Millwall v Hull C
Norwich C v Brighton & HA
Sheffield U v Reading
Stoke C v Plymouth Arg

Coca-Cola Football League One
Barnsley v Port Vale
Blackpool v Huddersfield T
Brentford v Southend U
Colchester U v Walsall
Oldham Ath v Nottingham F
Rotherham U v Bournemouth
Scunthorpe U v Bristol C
Swansea C v Bradford C
Swindon T v Gillingham
Tranmere R v Hartlepool U
Yeovil T v Milton Keynes Dons

Coca-Cola Football League Two
Barnet v Lincoln C
Bristol R v Cheltenham T
Carlisle U v Shrewsbury T
Mansfield T v Grimsby T
Northampton T v Leyton Orient
Notts Co v Wycombe W
Peterborough U v Darlington
Stockport Co v Rochdale
Torquay U v Bury
Wrexham v Rushden & D'monds

Wednesday, 15 February 2006
Coca-Cola Football League Championship
Coventry C v Sheffield W
Southampton v Preston NE

Coca-Cola Football League One
Chesterfield v Doncaster R

Coca-Cola Football League Two
Boston U v Chester C
Oxford U v Macclesfield T

Saturday, 18 February 2006
Coca-Cola Football League Championship
Brighton & HA v Watford
Burnley v Southampton
Cardiff C v Hull C
Leicester C v Leeds U
Luton T v Reading
Millwall v Crystal Palace
Norwich C v Derby Co
Plymouth Arg v Coventry C
Preston NE v Crewe Alex
QPR v Stoke C
Sheffield W v Sheffield U
Wolverhampton W v Ipswich T

Coca-Cola Football League One
Bournemouth v Blackpool
Bradford C v Bristol C
Chesterfield v Southend U
Colchester U v Hartlepool U
Doncaster R v Gillingham
Huddersfield T v Milton Keynes Dons
Port Vale v Nottingham F
Scunthorpe U v Swansea C
Swindon T v Rotherham U
Tranmere R v Barnsley
Walsall v Oldham Ath
Yeovil T v Brentford

Coca-Cola Football League Two
Boston U v Wycombe W
Bristol R v Stockport Co
Bury v Barnet
Carlisle U v Rushden & D'monds
Chester C v Leyton Orient
Darlington v Shrewsbury T
Macclesfield T v Lincoln C
Mansfield T v Wrexham
Northampton T v Torquay U
Notts Co v Peterborough U
Oxford U v Cheltenham T
Rochdale v Grimsby T

Saturday, 25 February 2006
Barclays Premiership
Birmingham C v Sunderland
Blackburn R v Arsenal
Bolton W v Fulham
Charlton Ath v Aston Villa
Chelsea v Portsmouth
Liverpool v Manchester C
Manchester U v West Ham U
Newcastle U v Everton
Tottenham H v Wigan Ath
WBA v Middlesbrough

Coca-Cola Football League Championship
Coventry C v Burnley
Crewe Alex v Brighton & HA
Crystal Palace v Norwich C
Derby Co v Plymouth Arg
Hull C v Wolverhampton W
Ipswich T v Leicester C
Leeds U v Luton T
Reading v Preston NE
Sheffield U v QPR
Southampton v Sheffield W
Stoke C v Millwall
Watford v Cardiff C

Coca-Cola Football League One
Barnsley v Colchester U
Blackpool v Yeovil T
Brentford v Port Vale
Bristol C v Bournemouth
Gillingham v Scunthorpe U
Hartlepool U v Doncaster R
Milton Keynes Dons v Bradford C
Nottingham F v Swindon T
Oldham Ath v Tranmere R
Rotherham U v Chesterfield
Southend U v Walsall
Swansea C v Huddersfield T

Coca-Cola Football League Two
Barnet v Carlisle U
Cheltenham T v Rochdale
Grimsby T v Chester C
Leyton Orient v Darlington
Lincoln C v Notts Co
Peterborough U v Bristol R
Rushden & D'monds v Macclesfield T
Shrewsbury T v Bury
Stockport Co v Boston U
Torquay U v Mansfield T
Wrexham v Northampton T
Wycombe W v Oxford U

Saturday, 4 March 2006
Barclays Premiership
Aston Villa v Portsmouth
Fulham v Arsenal
Liverpool v Charlton Ath
Manchester C v Sunderland
Middlesbrough v Birmingham C
Newcastle U v Bolton W
Tottenham H v Blackburn R
WBA v Chelsea
West Ham U v Everton
Wigan Ath v Manchester U

Coca-Cola Football League Championship
Burnley v Reading

Cardiff C v Sheffield W
Crystal Palace v Leeds U
Leicester C v Hull C
Millwall v Luton T
Norwich C v Stoke C
Plymouth Arg v Brighton & HA
Preston NE v Ipswich T
QPR v Wolverhampton W
Sheffield U v Crewe Alex
Southampton v Coventry C
Watford v Derby Co

Coca-Cola Football League One
Barnsley v Swansea C
Bradford C v Blackpool
Bristol C v Nottingham F
Chesterfield v Yeovil T
Colchester U v Southend U
Gillingham v Brentford
Huddersfield T v Doncaster R
Port Vale v Milton Keynes Dons
Rotherham U v Oldham Ath
Scunthorpe U v Hartlepool U
Swindon T v Tranmere R
Walsall v Bournemouth

Coca-Cola Football League Two
Barnet v Wrexham
Boston U v Northampton T
Bury v Macclesfield T
Carlisle U v Lincoln C
Cheltenham T v Wycombe W
Chester C v Torquay U
Notts Co v Mansfield T
Oxford U v Bristol R
Peterborough U v Stockport Co
Rochdale v Darlington
Rushden & D'monds v Grimsby T
Shrewsbury T v Leyton Orient

Saturday, 11 March 2006
Barclays Premiership
Arsenal v Liverpool
Birmingham C v WBA
Blackburn R v Aston Villa
Bolton W v West Ham U
Charlton Ath v Middlesbrough
Chelsea v Tottenham H
Everton v Fulham
Manchester U v Newcastle U
Portsmouth v Manchester C
Sunderland v Wigan Ath

Coca-Cola Football League Championship
Brighton & HA v Preston NE
Coventry C v Sheffield U
Crewe Alex v Southampton
Derby Co v Burnley
Hull C v Plymouth Arg
Ipswich T v Millwall
Leeds U v Norwich C
Luton T v Leicester C
Reading v Watford
Sheffield W v QPR
Stoke C v Crystal Palace
Wolverhampton W v Cardiff C

Coca-Cola Football League One
Blackpool v Rotherham U
Bournemouth v Bradford C
Brentford v Barnsley
Doncaster R v Port Vale
Hartlepool U v Huddersfield T
Milton Keynes Dons v Bristol C
Nottingham F v Gillingham
Oldham Ath v Colchester U
Southend U v Scunthorpe U
Swansea C v Walsall
Tranmere R v Chesterfield
Yeovil T v Swindon T

Coca-Cola Football League Two
Bristol R v Notts Co
Darlington v Chester C
Grimsby T v Barnet
Leyton Orient v Cheltenham T
Lincoln C v Rushden & D'monds
Macclesfield T v Rochdale
Mansfield T v Boston U
Northampton T v Carlisle U
Stockport Co v Oxford U
Torquay U v Peterborough U
Wrexham v Bury
Wycombe W v Shrewsbury T

Saturday, 18 March 2006
Barclays Premiership
Arsenal v Charlton Ath
Birmingham C v Tottenham H
Blackburn R v Middlesbrough
Bolton W v Sunderland
Everton v Aston Villa
Fulham v Chelsea
Manchester C v Wigan Ath
Newcastle U v Liverpool
WBA v Manchester U
West Ham U v Portsmouth

Coca-Cola Football League Championship
Coventry C v Leeds U
Crystal Palace v Ipswich T
Hull C v Crewe Alex
Luton T v Derby Co
Millwall v Leicester C
Norwich C v Sheffield U
Plymouth Arg v Cardiff C

QPR v Brighton & HA
Reading v Wolverhampton W
Sheffield W v Preston NE
Southampton v Watford
Stoke C v Burnley

Coca-Cola Football League One
Blackpool v Port Vale
Bournemouth v Yeovil T
Bradford C v Oldham Ath
Bristol C v Gillingham
Chesterfield v Scunthorpe U
Colchester U v Swindon T
Doncaster R v Nottingham F
Hartlepool U v Barnsley
Huddersfield T v Rotherham U
Milton Keynes Dons v Southend U
Swansea C v Brentford
Tranmere R v Walsall

Coca-Cola Football League Two
Boston U v Lincoln C
Chester C v Cheltenham T
Darlington v Carlisle U
Grimsby T v Bury
Mansfield T v Northampton T
Notts Co v Oxford U
Peterborough U v Barnet
Rochdale v Wrexham
Rushden & D'monds v Leyton Orient
Shrewsbury T v Bristol R
Stockport Co v Macclesfield T
Wycombe W v Torquay U

Saturday, 25 March 2006
Barclays Premiership
Aston Villa v Fulham
Charlton Ath v Newcastle U
Chelsea v Manchester C
Liverpool v Everton
Manchester U v Birmingham C
Middlesbrough v Bolton W
Portsmouth v Arsenal
Sunderland v Blackburn R
Tottenham H v WBA
Wigan Ath v West Ham U

Coca-Cola Football League Championship
Brighton & HA v Luton T
Burnley v Norwich C
Cardiff C v QPR
Crewe Alex v Coventry C
Derby Co v Crystal Palace
Ipswich T v Hull C
Leeds U v Stoke C
Leicester C v Reading
Preston NE v Plymouth Arg
Sheffield U v Southampton
Watford v Millwall
Wolverhampton W v Sheffield W

Coca-Cola Football League One
Barnsley v Bournemouth
Brentford v Doncaster R
Gillingham v Swansea C
Nottingham F v Milton Keynes Dons
Oldham Ath v Blackpool
Port Vale v Huddersfield T
Rotherham U v Bristol C
Scunthorpe U v Colchester U
Southend U v Hartlepool U
Swindon T v Chesterfield
Walsall v Bradford C
Yeovil T v Tranmere R

Coca-Cola Football League Two
Barnet v Darlington
Bristol R v Mansfield T
Bury v Rochdale
Carlisle U v Boston U
Cheltenham T v Rushden & D'monds
Leyton Orient v Wycombe W
Lincoln C v Grimsby T
Macclesfield T v Shrewsbury T
Northampton T v Notts Co
Oxford U v Peterborough U
Torquay U v Stockport Co
Wrexham v Chester C

Saturday, 1 April 2006
Barclays Premiership
Arsenal v Aston Villa
Birmingham C v Chelsea
Blackburn R v Wigan Ath
Bolton W v Manchester U
Everton v Sunderland
Fulham v Portsmouth
Manchester C v Middlesbrough
Newcastle U v Tottenham H
WBA v Liverpool
West Ham U v Charlton Ath

Coca-Cola Football League Championship
Coventry C v Preston NE
Crystal Palace v Watford
Hull C v Leeds U
Luton T v Ipswich T
Millwall v Brighton & HA
Norwich C v Leicester C
Plymouth Arg v Wolverhampton W
QPR v Crewe Alex
Reading v Derby Co
Sheffield W v Burnley
Southampton v Cardiff C
Stoke C v Sheffield U

Coca-Cola Football League One
Blackpool v Walsall
Bournemouth v Southend U
Bradford C v Scunthorpe U
Bristol C v Yeovil T
Chesterfield v Nottingham F
Colchester U v Brentford
Doncaster R v Rotherham U
Hartlepool U v Oldham Ath
Huddersfield T v Barnsley
Milton Keynes Dons v Gillingham
Swansea C v Swindon T
Tranmere R v Port Vale

Coca-Cola Football League Two
Boston U v Barnet
Chester C v Macclesfield T
Darlington v Lincoln C
Grimsby T v Wrexham
Mansfield T v Oxford U
Notts Co v Leyton Orient
Peterborough U v Northampton T
Rochdale v Carlisle U
Rushden & D'monds v Torquay U
Shrewsbury T v Cheltenham T
Stockport Co v Bury
Wycombe W v Bristol R

Saturday, 8 April 2006
Barclays Premiership
Aston Villa v WBA
Charlton Ath v Everton
Chelsea v West Ham U
Liverpool v Bolton W
Manchester U v Arsenal
Middlesbrough v Newcastle U
Portsmouth v Blackburn R
Sunderland v Fulham
Tottenham H v Manchester C
Wigan Ath v Birmingham C

Coca-Cola Football League Championship
Brighton & HA v Southampton
Burnley v QPR
Cardiff C v Reading
Crewe Alex v Sheffield W
Derby Co v Millwall
Ipswich T v Stoke C
Leeds U v Plymouth Arg
Leicester C v Crystal Palace
Preston NE v Norwich C
Sheffield U v Hull C
Watford v Luton T
Wolverhampton W v Coventry C

Coca-Cola Football League One
Barnsley v Chesterfield
Brentford v Bradford C
Gillingham v Huddersfield T
Nottingham F v Colchester U
Oldham Ath v Milton Keynes Dons
Port Vale v Swansea C
Rotherham U v Tranmere R
Scunthorpe U v Bournemouth
Southend U v Blackpool
Swindon T v Hartlepool U
Walsall v Bristol C
Yeovil T v Doncaster R

Coca-Cola Football League Two
Barnet v Notts Co
Bristol R v Rushden & D'monds
Bury v Peterborough U
Carlisle U v Grimsby T
Cheltenham T v Stockport Co
Leyton Orient v Boston U
Lincoln C v Mansfield T
Macclesfield T v Wycombe W
Northampton T v Rochdale
Oxford U v Chester C
Torquay U v Darlington
Wrexham v Shrewsbury T

Saturday, 15 April 2006
Barclays Premiership
Arsenal v WBA
Aston Villa v Birmingham C
Blackburn R v Liverpool
Bolton W v Chelsea
Everton v Tottenham H
Fulham v Charlton Ath
Manchester U v Sunderland
Newcastle U v Wigan Ath
Portsmouth v Middlesbrough
West Ham U v Manchester C

Coca-Cola Football League Championship
Cardiff C v Sheffield U
Crystal Palace v Crewe Alex
Hull C v Burnley
Ipswich T v Brighton & HA
Leeds U v Reading
Leicester C v Preston NE
Luton T v Coventry C
Millwall v Plymouth Arg
QPR v Derby Co
Sheffield W v Norwich C
Stoke C v Southampton
Wolverhampton W v Watford

Coca-Cola Football League One
Blackpool v Swansea C
Bournemouth v Huddersfield T
Bradford C v Doncaster R
Chesterfield v Colchester U
Hartlepool U v Bristol C

Oldham Ath v Barnsley
Rotherham U v Brentford
Southend U v Gillingham
Swindon T v Milton Keynes Dons
Tranmere R v Nottingham F
Walsall v Port Vale
Yeovil T v Scunthorpe U

Coca-Cola Football League Two
Bristol R v Carlisle U
Chester C v Wycombe W
Darlington v Northampton T
Grimsby T v Shrewsbury T
Lincoln C v Bury
Mansfield T v Leyton Orient
Notts Co v Macclesfield T
Oxford U v Barnet
Peterborough U v Boston U
Rushden & D'monds v Rochdale
Stockport Co v Wrexham
Torquay U v Cheltenham T

Monday, 17 April 2006
Barclays Premiership
Birmingham C v Blackburn R
Charlton Ath v Portsmouth
Chelsea v Everton
Liverpool v Fulham
Manchester C v Arsenal
Middlesbrough v West Ham U
Sunderland v Newcastle U
Tottenham H v Manchester U
WBA v Bolton W
Wigan Ath v Aston Villa

Coca-Cola Football League Championship
Brighton & HA v Sheffield W
Burnley v Crystal Palace
Coventry C v Leicester C
Crewe Alex v Cardiff C
Derby Co v Hull C
Norwich C v QPR
Plymouth Arg v Luton T
Preston NE v Wolverhampton W
Reading v Stoke C
Sheffield U v Leeds U
Southampton v Millwall
Watford v Ipswich T

Coca-Cola Football League One
Barnsley v Southend U
Brentford v Blackpool
Bristol C v Oldham Ath
Colchester U v Tranmere R
Doncaster R v Walsall
Gillingham v Bradford C
Huddersfield T v Chesterfield
Milton Keynes Dons v Hartlepool U
Nottingham F v Yeovil T
Port Vale v Bournemouth
Scunthorpe U v Swindon T
Swansea C v Rotherham U

Coca-Cola Football League Two
Barnet v Mansfield T
Boston U v Oxford U
Bury v Chester C
Carlisle U v Notts Co
Cheltenham T v Darlington
Leyton Orient v Grimsby T
Macclesfield T v Torquay U
Northampton T v Stockport Co
Rochdale v Peterborough U
Shrewsbury T v Rushden & D'monds
Wrexham v Bristol R
Wycombe W v Lincoln C

Saturday, 22 April 2006
Barclays Premiership
Arsenal v Tottenham H
Aston Villa v Manchester C
Blackburn R v Chelsea
Bolton W v Charlton Ath
Everton v Birmingham C
Fulham v Wigan Ath
Manchester U v Middlesbrough
Newcastle U v WBA
Portsmouth v Sunderland
West Ham U v Liverpool

Coca-Cola Football League Championship
Cardiff C v Norwich C
Crystal Palace v Southampton
Hull C v Preston NE
Ipswich T v Derby Co
Leeds U v Crewe Alex
Leicester C v Plymouth Arg
Luton T v Sheffield U
Millwall v Burnley
QPR v Watford
Sheffield W v Reading
Stoke C v Coventry C
Wolverhampton W v Brighton & HA

Coca-Cola Football League One
Blackpool v Barnsley
Bournemouth v Colchester U
Bradford C v Port Vale
Chesterfield v Milton Keynes Dons
Hartlepool U v Nottingham F
Oldham Ath v Swansea C
Rotherham U v Scunthorpe U
Southend U v Doncaster R
Swindon T v Brentford
Tranmere R v Bristol C
Walsall v Huddersfield T
Yeovil T v Gillingham

Coca-Cola Football League Two
Bristol R v Boston U
Chester C v Barnet
Darlington v Bury
Grimsby T v Cheltenham T
Lincoln C v Leyton Orient
Mansfield T v Carlisle U
Notts Co v Rochdale
Oxford U v Northampton T
Peterborough U v Macclesfield T
Rushden & D'monds v Wycombe W
Stockport Co v Shrewsbury T
Torquay U v Wrexham

Saturday, 29 April 2006
Barclays Premiership
Birmingham C v Newcastle U
Charlton Ath v Blackburn R
Chelsea v Manchester U
Liverpool v Aston Villa
Manchester C v Fulham
Middlesbrough v Everton
Sunderland v Arsenal
Tottenham H v Bolton W
WBA v West Ham U
Wigan Ath v Portsmouth

Coca-Cola Football League One
Barnsley v Bradford C
Brentford v Hartlepool U
Bristol C v Swindon T
Colchester U v Rotherham U
Doncaster R v Oldham Ath
Gillingham v Walsall
Huddersfield T v Yeovil T
Milton Keynes Dons v Tranmere R
Nottingham F v Bournemouth
Port Vale v Chesterfield
Scunthorpe U v Blackpool
Swansea C v Southend U

Coca-Cola Football League Two
Barnet v Stockport Co
Boston U v Rushden & D'monds
Bury v Mansfield T
Carlisle U v Torquay U
Cheltenham T v Notts Co
Leyton Orient v Peterborough U
Macclesfield T v Grimsby T
Northampton T v Chester C
Rochdale v Bristol R
Shrewsbury T v Lincoln C
Wrexham v Oxford U
Wycombe W v Darlington

Sunday, 30 April 2006
Coca-Cola Football League Championship
Brighton & HA v Stoke C
Burnley v Luton T
Coventry C v Cardiff C
Crewe Alex v Millwall
Derby Co v Sheffield W
Norwich C v Wolverhampton W
Plymouth Arg v Ipswich T
Preston NE v Leeds U
Reading v QPR
Sheffield U v Crystal Palace
Southampton v Leicester C
Watford v Hull C

Saturday, 6 May 2006
Coca-Cola Football League One
Blackpool v Gillingham
Bournemouth v Brentford
Bradford C v Nottingham F
Chesterfield v Swansea C
Hartlepool U v Port Vale
Oldham Ath v Scunthorpe U
Rotherham U v Milton Keynes Dons
Southend U v Bristol C
Swindon T v Huddersfield T
Tranmere R v Doncaster R
Walsall v Barnsley
Yeovil T v Colchester U

Coca-Cola Football League Two
Bristol R v Macclesfield T
Chester C v Shrewsbury T
Darlington v Wrexham
Grimsby T v Northampton T
Lincoln C v Rochdale
Mansfield T v Cheltenham T
Notts Co v Bury
Oxford U v Leyton Orient
Peterborough U v Wycombe W
Rushden & D'monds v Barnet
Stockport Co v Carlisle U
Torquay U v Boston U

Sunday, 7 May 2006
Barclays Premiership
Arsenal v Wigan Ath
Aston Villa v Sunderland
Blackburn R v Manchester C
Bolton W v Birmingham C
Everton v WBA
Fulham v Middlesbrough
Manchester U v Charlton Ath
Newcastle U v Chelsea
Portsmouth v Liverpool
West Ham U v Tottenham H

CONFERENCE NATIONAL FIXTURES 2005-06

Saturday, 13 August 2005
Accrington Stanley v Canvey Island
Aldershot T v Tamworth
Burton Alb v Grays Ath
Dagenham & Red v Southport
Forest Green v Cambridge U
Gravesend & N v Exeter C
Hereford U v Scarborough
Kidderminster H v Woking
Morecambe v Halifax T
Stevenage B v Altrincham
York C v Crawley T

Tuesday, 16 August 2005
Altrincham v Accrington Stanley
Cambridge U v Hereford U
Canvey Island v Aldershot T
Crawley T v Dagenham & Red
Exeter C v Kidderminster H
Grays Ath v Gravesend & N
Halifax T v Burton Alb
Scarborough v Morecambe
Southport v York C
Tamworth v Forest Green
Woking v Stevenage B

Saturday, 20 August 2005
Altrincham v Forest Green
Cambridge U v Accrington Stanley
Canvey Island v Gravesend & N
Crawley T v Hereford U
Exeter C v Morecambe
Grays Ath v York C
Halifax T v Aldershot T
Scarborough v Kidderminster H
Southport v Stevenage B
Tamworth v Dagenham & Red
Woking v Burton Alb

Saturday, 27 August 2005
Accrington Stanley v Exeter C
Aldershot T v Altrincham
Burton Alb v Canvey Island
Dagenham & Red v Scarborough
Forest Green v Halifax T
Gravesend & N v Cambridge U
Hereford U v Grays Ath
Kidderminster H v Southport
Morecambe v Crawley T
Stevenage B v Tamworth
York C v Woking

Monday, 29 August 2005
Altrincham v Morecambe
Cambridge U v Kidderminster H
Canvey Island v Dagenham & Red
Crawley T v Stevenage B
Exeter C v Forest Green
Grays Ath v Aldershot T
Halifax T v York C
Scarborough v Accrington Stanley
Southport v Burton Alb
Tamworth v Hereford U
Woking v Gravesend & N

Saturday, 3 September 2005
Accrington Stanley v Woking
Aldershot T v Crawley T
Burton Alb v Scarborough
Dagenham & Red v Exeter C
Forest Green v Grays Ath
Gravesend & N v Southport
Hereford U v Altrincham
Kidderminster H v Canvey Island
Morecambe v Tamworth
Stevenage B v Halifax T
York C v Cambridge U

Saturday, 10 September 2005
Altrincham v Dagenham & Red
Burton Alb v Accrington Stanley
Crawley T v Canvey Island
Exeter C v Cambridge U
Forest Green v York C
Grays Ath v Kidderminster H
Halifax T v Tamworth
Morecambe v Aldershot T
Scarborough v Gravesend & N
Stevenage B v Hereford U
Woking v Southport

Saturday, 17 September 2005
Accrington Stanley v Crawley T
Aldershot T v Stevenage B
Cambridge U v Woking
Canvey Island v Scarborough
Dagenham & Red v Burton Alb
Gravesend & N v Halifax T
Hereford U v Morecambe
Kidderminster H v Forest Green
Southport v Exeter C
Tamworth v Grays Ath
York C v Altrincham

Tuesday, 20 September 2005
Accrington Stanley v Aldershot T
Altrincham v Scarborough
Burton Alb v Morecambe
Forest Green v Crawley T
Grays Ath v Cambridge U
Hereford U v Gravesend & N
Kidderminster H v Halifax T
Southport v Tamworth
Stevenage B v Exeter C
Woking v Canvey Island
York C v Dagenham & Red

Saturday, 24 September 2005
Aldershot T v York C
Cambridge U v Altrincham
Canvey Island v Southport
Crawley T v Grays Ath
Dagenham & Red v Accrington Stanley
Exeter C v Burton Alb
Gravesend & N v Kidderminster H
Halifax T v Hereford U
Morecambe v Stevenage B
Scarborough v Forest Green
Tamworth v Woking

Tuesday, 27 September 2005
Aldershot T v Hereford U
Cambridge U v Burton Alb
Canvey Island v Stevenage B
Crawley T v Kidderminster H
Dagenham & Red v Grays Ath
Exeter C v Woking
Gravesend & N v Forest Green
Halifax T v Altrincham
Morecambe v Accrington Stanley
Scarborough v Southport
Tamworth v York C

Saturday, 1 October 2005
Accrington Stanley v Gravesend & N
Altrincham v Crawley T
Burton Alb v Aldershot T
Forest Green v Morecambe
Grays Ath v Halifax T
Hereford U v Canvey Island
Kidderminster H v Tamworth
Southport v Cambridge U
Stevenage B v Dagenham & Red
Woking v Scarborough
York C v Exeter C

Saturday, 8 October 2005
Accrington Stanley v Hereford U
Burton Alb v Stevenage B
Cambridge U v Tamworth
Canvey Island v Altrincham
Dagenham & Red v Aldershot T
Exeter C v Halifax T
Gravesend & N v York C
Kidderminster H v Morecambe
Scarborough v Crawley T
Southport v Forest Green
Woking v Grays Ath

Saturday, 15 October 2005
Aldershot T v Kidderminster H
Altrincham v Southport
Crawley T v Exeter C
Forest Green v Woking
Grays Ath v Scarborough
Halifax T v Cambridge U
Hereford U v Burton Alb
Morecambe v Dagenham & Red
Stevenage B v Accrington Stanley
Tamworth v Gravesend & N
York C v Canvey Island

Saturday, 29 October 2005
Accrington Stanley v York C
Burton Alb v Altrincham
Cambridge U v Crawley T
Canvey Island v Morecambe
Dagenham & Red v Forest Green
Exeter C v Tamworth
Gravesend & N v Stevenage B
Kidderminster H v Hereford U
Scarborough v Aldershot T
Southport v Grays Ath
Woking v Halifax T

Saturday, 12 November 2005
Aldershot T v Gravesend & N
Altrincham v Exeter C
Crawley T v Southport
Forest Green v Canvey Island
Grays Ath v Accrington Stanley
Halifax T v Dagenham & Red
Hereford U v Woking
Morecambe v Cambridge U
Stevenage B v Kidderminster H
Tamworth v Scarborough
York C v Burton Alb

Saturday, 19 November 2005
Accrington Stanley v Forest Green
Burton Alb v Crawley T
Cambridge U v Aldershot T
Canvey Island v Tamworth
Dagenham & Red v Hereford U

Exeter C v Grays Ath
Gravesend & N v Altrincham
Kidderminster H v York C
Scarborough v Stevenage B
Southport v Halifax T
Woking v Morecambe

Saturday, 26 November 2005
Accrington Stanley v Southport
Aldershot T v Forest Green
Altrincham v Tamworth
Burton Alb v Kidderminster H
Canvey Island v Cambridge U
Crawley T v Gravesend & N
Dagenham & Red v Woking
Hereford U v Exeter C
Morecambe v York C
Scarborough v Halifax T
Stevenage B v Grays Ath

Saturday, 3 December 2005
Cambridge U v Scarborough
Exeter C v Canvey Island
Forest Green v Burton Alb
Gravesend & N v Morecambe
Grays Ath v Altrincham
Halifax T v Crawley T
Kidderminster H v Dagenham & Red
Southport v Hereford U
Tamworth v Accrington Stanley
Woking v Aldershot T
York C v Stevenage B

Saturday, 10 December 2005
Accrington Stanley v Kidderminster H
Aldershot T v Southport
Altrincham v Woking
Burton Alb v Gravesend & N
Canvey Island v Halifax T
Crawley T v Tamworth
Dagenham & Red v Cambridge U
Hereford U v York C
Morecambe v Grays Ath
Scarborough v Exeter C
Stevenage B v Forest Green

Monday, 26 December 2005
Cambridge U v Stevenage B
Exeter C v Aldershot T
Forest Green v Hereford U
Gravesend & N v Dagenham & Red
Grays Ath v Canvey Island
Halifax T v Accrington Stanley
Kidderminster H v Altrincham
Southport v Morecambe
Tamworth v Burton Alb
Woking v Crawley T
York C v Scarborough

Saturday, 31 December 2005
Cambridge U v Canvey Island
Exeter C v Hereford U
Forest Green v Aldershot T
Gravesend & N v Crawley T
Grays Ath v Stevenage B
Halifax T v Scarborough
Kidderminster H v Burton Alb
Southport v Accrington Stanley
Tamworth v Altrincham
Woking v Dagenham & Red
York C v Morecambe

Monday, 2 January 2006
Accrington Stanley v Halifax T
Aldershot T v Exeter C
Altrincham v Kidderminster H
Burton Alb v Tamworth
Canvey Island v Grays Ath
Crawley T v Woking
Dagenham & Red v Gravesend & N
Hereford U v Forest Green
Morecambe v Southport
Scarborough v York C
Stevenage B v Cambridge U

Saturday, 7 January 2006
Altrincham v Stevenage B
Cambridge U v Forest Green
Canvey Island v Accrington Stanley
Crawley T v York C
Exeter C v Gravesend & N
Grays Ath v Burton Alb
Halifax T v Morecambe
Scarborough v Hereford U
Southport v Dagenham & Red
Tamworth v Aldershot T
Woking v Kidderminster H

Saturday, 21 January 2006
Accrington Stanley v Cambridge U
Aldershot T v Halifax T
Burton Alb v Woking
Dagenham & Red v Tamworth
Forest Green v Altrincham
Gravesend & N v Canvey Island
Hereford U v Crawley T
Kidderminster H v Scarborough
Morecambe v Exeter C
Stevenage B v Southport
York C v Grays Ath

Tuesday, 24 January 2006
Accrington Stanley v Altrincham
Aldershot T v Canvey Island
Burton Alb v Halifax T
Dagenham & Red v Crawley T
Forest Green v Tamworth
Gravesend & N v Grays Ath
Hereford U v Cambridge U
Kidderminster H v Exeter C
Morecambe v Scarborough
Stevenage B v Woking
York C v Southport

Saturday, 28 January 2006
Altrincham v Aldershot T
Cambridge U v Gravesend & N
Canvey Island v Burton Alb
Crawley T v Morecambe
Exeter C v Accrington Stanley
Grays Ath v Hereford U
Halifax T v Forest Green
Scarborough v Dagenham & Red
Southport v Kidderminster H
Tamworth v Stevenage B
Woking v York C

Saturday, 4 February 2006
Aldershot T v Accrington Stanley
Cambridge U v Grays Ath
Canvey Island v Woking
Crawley T v Forest Green
Dagenham & Red v York C
Exeter C v Stevenage B
Gravesend & N v Hereford U
Halifax T v Kidderminster H
Morecambe v Burton Alb
Scarborough v Altrincham
Tamworth v Southport

Saturday, 11 February 2006
Accrington Stanley v Dagenham & Red
Altrincham v Cambridge U
Burton Alb v Exeter C
Forest Green v Scarborough
Grays Ath v Crawley T
Hereford U v Halifax T
Kidderminster H v Gravesend & N
Southport v Canvey Island
Stevenage B v Morecambe
Woking v Tamworth
York C v Aldershot T

Saturday, 18 February 2006
Aldershot T v Burton Alb
Cambridge U v Southport
Canvey Island v Hereford U
Crawley T v Altrincham
Dagenham & Red v Stevenage B
Exeter C v York C
Gravesend & N v Accrington Stanley
Halifax T v Grays Ath
Morecambe v Forest Green
Scarborough v Woking
Tamworth v Kidderminster H

Tuesday, 21 February 2006
Accrington Stanley v Morecambe
Altrincham v Halifax T
Burton Alb v Cambridge U
Forest Green v Gravesend & N
Grays Ath v Dagenham & Red
Hereford U v Aldershot T
Kidderminster H v Crawley T
Southport v Scarborough
Stevenage B v Canvey Island
Woking v Exeter C
York C v Tamworth

Saturday, 25 February 2006
Accrington Stanley v Burton Alb
Aldershot T v Morecambe
Cambridge U v Exeter C
Canvey Island v Crawley T
Dagenham & Red v Altrincham
Gravesend & N v Scarborough
Hereford U v Stevenage B
Kidderminster H v Grays Ath
Southport v Woking
Tamworth v Halifax T
York C v Forest Green

Saturday, 4 March 2006
Altrincham v York C
Burton Alb v Dagenham & Red
Crawley T v Accrington Stanley
Exeter C v Southport
Forest Green v Kidderminster H
Grays Ath v Tamworth
Halifax T v Gravesend & N
Morecambe v Hereford U
Scarborough v Canvey Island
Stevenage B v Aldershot T
Woking v Cambridge U

Saturday, 11 March 2006
Aldershot T v Dagenham & Red
Altrincham v Canvey Island
Crawley T v Scarborough
Forest Green v Southport
Grays Ath v Woking

Halifax T v Exeter C
Hereford U v Accrington Stanley
Morecambe v Kidderminster H
Stevenage B v Burton Alb
Tamworth v Cambridge U
York C v Gravesend & N

Saturday, 18 March 2006
Accrington Stanley v Stevenage B
Burton Alb v Hereford U
Cambridge U v Halifax T
Canvey Island v York C
Dagenham & Red v Morecambe
Exeter C v Crawley T
Gravesend & N v Tamworth
Kidderminster H v Aldershot T
Scarborough v Grays Ath
Southport v Altrincham
Woking v Forest Green

Saturday, 25 March 2006
Aldershot T v Scarborough
Altrincham v Burton Alb
Crawley T v Cambridge U
Forest Green v Dagenham & Red
Grays Ath v Southport
Halifax T v Woking
Hereford U v Kidderminster H
Morecambe v Canvey Island
Stevenage B v Gravesend & N
Tamworth v Exeter C
York C v Accrington Stanley

Saturday, 1 April 2006
Accrington Stanley v Grays Ath
Burton Alb v York C
Cambridge U v Morecambe
Canvey Island v Forest Green
Dagenham & Red v Halifax T
Exeter C v Altrincham
Gravesend & N v Aldershot T
Kidderminster H v Stevenage B
Scarborough v Tamworth
Southport v Crawley T
Woking v Hereford U

Saturday, 8 April 2006
Aldershot T v Cambridge U
Altrincham v Gravesend & N
Crawley T v Burton Alb
Forest Green v Accrington Stanley
Grays Ath v Exeter C
Halifax T v Southport
Hereford U v Dagenham & Red
Morecambe v Woking
Stevenage B v Scarborough
Tamworth v Canvey Island
York C v Kidderminster H

Saturday, 15 April 2006
Altrincham v Hereford U
Cambridge U v York C
Canvey Island v Kidderminster H
Crawley T v Aldershot T
Exeter C v Dagenham & Red
Grays Ath v Forest Green
Halifax T v Stevenage B
Scarborough v Burton Alb
Southport v Gravesend & N
Tamworth v Morecambe
Woking v Accrington Stanley

Monday, 17 April 2006
Accrington Stanley v Scarborough
Aldershot T v Grays Ath
Burton Alb v Southport
Dagenham & Red v Canvey Island
Forest Green v Exeter C
Gravesend & N v Woking
Hereford U v Tamworth
Kidderminster H v Cambridge U
Morecambe v Altrincham
Stevenage B v Crawley T
York C v Halifax T

Saturday, 22 April 2006
Accrington Stanley v Tamworth
Aldershot T v Woking
Altrincham v Grays Ath
Burton Alb v Forest Green
Canvey Island v Exeter C
Crawley T v Halifax T
Dagenham & Red v Kidderminster H
Hereford U v Southport
Morecambe v Gravesend & N
Scarborough v Cambridge U
Stevenage B v York C

Saturday, 29 April 2006
Cambridge U v Dagenham & Red
Exeter C v Scarborough
Forest Green v Stevenage B
Gravesend & N v Burton Alb
Grays Ath v Morecambe
Halifax T v Canvey Island
Kidderminster H v Accrington Stanley
Southport v Aldershot T
Tamworth v Crawley T
Woking v Altrincham
York C v Hereford U

OTHER FIXTURES — SEASON 2005–2006

JULY 2005

Sat 2 UEFA Intertoto Cup 2 (1)
Sun 3 UEFA Intertoto Cup 2 (1)
Sat 9 UEFA Intertoto Cup 2 (2)
Sun 10 UEFA Intertoto Cup 2 (2)
Wed 13 UEFA Champions League 1Q (1)
Thur 14 UEFA Cup 1Q (1)
Sat 16 UEFA Intertoto Cup 3 (1)
Sun 17 UEFA Intertoto Cup 3 (1)
Wed 20 UEFA Champions League 1Q (2)
Sat 23 UEFA Intertoto Cup 3 (2)
Wed 27 UEFA Champions League 2Q (1)
UEFA Intertoto Cup SF (1)
Thur 28 UEFA Cup 1Q (2)
Fri 29 UEFA Champions League 3Q Draw
UEFA Cup 2Q Draw

AUGUST 2005

Wed 3 UEFA Champions League 2Q (2)
UEFA Intertoto Cup SF (2)
Sat 6 Start of Football League
Sun 7 FA Community Shield
Tue 9 UEFA Intertoto Cup Final (1)
UEFA Champions League 3Q (1)
Wed 10 UEFA Champions League 3Q (1)
Thur 11 UEFA Cup 2Q (1)
Sat 13 Start of FA Premier League
Tue 16 Russia v England – U/20 Friendly
Wed 17 Denmark v England – Copenhagen – Friendly
Sat 20 FA Cup EP
Tue 23 UEFA Intertoto Cup Final (2)
UEFA Champions League 3Q (2)
Wed 24 UEFA Champions League 3Q (2)
FL Carling Cup 1
Thur 25 UEFA Cup 2Q (2)
UEFA Champions League Group Stage Draw
Fri 26 UEFA Super Cup
UEFA Cup 1st Rd Draw
Sat 27 FA Cup P
Mon 29 Bank Holiday

SEPTEMBER 2005

Fri 2 Wales v England – venue tbc – U21 UEFA Qualifier
Sat 3 Wales v England – Cardiff – FIFA World Cup Qualifier
Tue 6 Germany v England – venue tbc – U21 UEFA Qualifier
Wed 7 Northern Ireland v England – Belfast – FIFA World Cup Qualifier
England v tbc – U/19 Friendly
Sat 10 FA Cup 1Q
Sun 11 FA Women's Cup 1Q
Mon12 FA Youth Cup P**
Tue 13 UEFA Champions League Match Day 1
Wed 14 UEFA Champions League Match Day 1
Thur 15 UEFA Cup 1 (1)
Sat 17 FA Vase 1Q
Wed 21 FL Carling Cup 2
Sat 24 FA Cup 2Q
Sun 25 FA Women's Cup 2Q
Mon 26 FA Youth Cup 1Q**
Tue 27 UEFA Champions League Match Day 2
Wed 28 FA National League System Cup 1*
UEFA Champions League Match Day 2
Thur 29 UEFA Cup 1 (2)

OCTOBER 2005

Sat 1 FA Vase 2Q
Sun 2 FA Sunday Cup 1
Tue 4 UEFA Cup Group Stage Draw
Fri 7 England v Austria venue tbc – U21 UEFA Qualifier
Sat 8 England v Austria – Manchester United FC – FIFA World Cup Qualifier
FA Cup 3Q
Sun 9 FA County Youth Cup 1*
Mon 10 FA Youth Cup 2Q**
Tue 11 England v Poland – venue tbc – U21 UEFA Qualifier
Wed 12 England v Poland – Manchester United FC – FIFA World Cup Qualifier
Fri 14 England v Wales – U/16 Victory Shield
Sat 15 FA Trophy 1Q
Tue 18 UEFA Champions League Match Day 3

Wed 19	UEFA Champions League Match Day 3 LDV Vans Trophy 1
Thur 20	UEFA Cup Match Day 1
Sat 22	FA Cup 4Q
Sun 23	FA Women's Cup 1P
Mon 24	FA Youth Cup 3Q**
Wed 26	FL Carling Cup 3
Sat 29	FA Vase 1P
Sun 30	FA Sunday Cup 2 British summer time ends

NOVEMBER 2005

Tue 1	UEFA Champions League Match Day 4
Wed 2	UEFA Champions League Match Day 4
Thur 3	UEFA Cup Match Day 2
Fri 4	England v Northern Ireland – U16 Victory Shield
Sat 5	FA Cup 1P
Sun 6	FA County Youth Cup 2*
Sat 12	FA Trophy 2Q FA Youth Cup 1P* FIFA World Cup Play Off's
Sun 13	FA Women's Cup 2P Remembrance Sunday
Wed 16	Holland v England – Friendly FIFA World Cup Play Off's England v Switzerland – U/19 Friendly
Sat 19	FA Vase 2P
Sun 20	FA Sunday Cup 3
Tue 22	UEFA Champions League Match Day 5
Wed 23	UEFA Champions League Match Day 5 LDV Vans Trophy 2
Thur 24	UEFA Cup Match Day 3
Fri 25	Scotland v England – U16 Victory Shield
Sat 26	FA Trophy 3Q FA Youth Cup 2P*
Wed 30	UEFA Cup Match Day 4 *(English Clubs seeded with a 'bye' on this date)* FL Carling Cup 4

DECEMBER 2005

Sat 3	FA Cup 2P FA National League System Cup 2*
Sun 4	FA Women's Cup 3P
Tue 6	UEFA Champions League Match Day 6
Wed 7	UEFA Champions League Match Day 6 LDV Vans Trophy Area QF
Sat 10	FA Vase 3P
Sun 11	FA County Youth Cup 3*
Wed 14	UEFA Cup Match Day 5
Fri 16	UEFA Champions League 1st Knock-out Rd Draw UEFA Cup Last 32/16 Rd's Draws
Sat 17	FA Trophy 1P FA Youth Cup 3P*
Wed 21	FL Carling Cup 5
Sat 24	Christmas Eve
Sun 25	Christmas Day
Mon 26	Boxing Day
Tue 27	Bank Holiday
Sat 31	

JANUARY 2006

Sun 1	New Years Day
Mon 2	Bank Holiday
Sat 7	FA Cup 3P
Sun 8	FA Women's Cup 4P
Wed 11	FL Carling Cup SF 1
Sat 14	FA Trophy 2P
Sun 15	FA Sunday Cup 4
Sat 21	FA Vase 4P FA Youth Cup 4P*
Wed 25	FL Carling Cup SF 2 LDV Vans Trophy Area SF
Sat 28	FA Cup 4P
Sun 29	FA County Youth Cup 4* FA Women's Cup 5P

FEBRUARY 2006

Sat 4	FA Trophy 3P FA Youth Cup 5P*
Sat 11	FA Vase 5P
Sun 12	FA Women's Cup 6P
Wed 15	UEFA Cup 32 (1) LDV Vans Trophy Area Final 1
Sat 18	FA Cup 5P FA Youth Cup 6P*
Sun 19	FA Sunday Cup 5
Tue 21	UEFA Champions League 16 (1)
Wed 22	UEFA Champions League 16 (1) LDV Vans Trophy Area Final 2
Thur 23	UEFA Cup 32 (2)
Sat 25	FA Trophy 4P FA National League System Cup 3*
Sun 26	FL Carling Cup Final

MARCH 2006

Wed 1	International Friendly
Sat 4	FA Vase 6P
Sun 5	FA County Youth Cup SF*

Tue 7	UEFA Champions League 16 (2)
Wed 8	UEFA Champions League 16 (2)
Thur 9	UEFA Cup 16 (1)
Sat 11	FA Youth Cup SF (1)*
Sun 12	FA Women's Cup SF
Wed 15	UEFA Cup 16 (2)
Fri 17	UEFA Champions League QF/SF Draws UEFA Cup QF/SF Draws
Sat 18	FA Trophy SF (1)
Sun 19	FA Sunday Cup SF
Wed 22	FA Cup 6P+
Sat 25	FA Trophy SF (2) FA Youth Cup SF (2)*
Sun 26	British summer time begins
Tue 28	UEFA Champions League QF (1)
Wed 29	UEFA Champions League QF (1)
Thur 30	UEFA Cup QF (1)

APRIL 2006

Sat 1	FA Vase SF (1)
Sun 2	LDV Vans Trophy Final
Tue 4	UEFA Champions League QF (2)
Wed 5	UEFA Champions League QF (2)
Thur 6	UEFA Cup QF (2)
Sat 8	FA Vase SF (2)
Fri 14	Good Friday
Sat 15	
Mon 17	Easter Monday
Tue 18	UEFA Champions League SF (1)
Wed 19	UEFA Champions League SF (1)
Thur 20	UEFA Cup SF (1)
Sat 22	FA Cup SF FA National League System Cup SF*
Tue 25	UEFA Champions League SF (2)
Wed 26	UEFA Champions League SF (2)
Thur 27	UEFA Cup SF (2)
Sat 29	FA County Youth Cup Final (prov)
Sun 30	FA Sunday Cup Final (prov) End of Football League Championship

MAY 2006

Mon 1	Bank Holiday FA Women's Cup Final
Sat 6	FA Vase Final (prov) FA National League System Cup Final (prov) Play Off SF (1) – League Championship End of FA Premier League End of Football League 1 & 2
Sun 7	FA Vase Final (prov) FA National League System Cup Final (prov)
Wed 10	UEFA Cup Final Play Off SF (2) – League Championship
Sat 13	FA Cup Final Play Off SF (1) – League 1 & 2
Sun 14	FA Trophy Final
Wed 17	UEFA Champions League Final Play Off SF (2) – League 1 & 2
Sun 21	Play Off Final – League Championship
Sat 27	Play Off Final – League 1
Sun 28	Play Off Final – League 2
Mon 29	Bank Holiday
Wed 31	Start of close season at midnight

JUNE 2006

Fri 9	World Cup Commences
Fri 30	World Cup Quarter Finals End of close season at midnight

JULY 2006

Sat 1	World Cup Quarter Finals
Tue 4	World Cup Semi-Finals
Wed 5	World Cup Semi-Finals
Sat 8	World Cup 3rd Place
Sun 9	World Cup Final

** closing date of round*

*** ties to be played in the week commencing*

+ actual dates of ties to be decided

STOP PRESS

Summer transfers completed and pending: **Premier Division: Arsenal:** Alexander Hleb (Stuttgart) Undisclosed. **Aston Villa:** Aaron Hughes (Newcastle U) £1,500,000; Kevin Phillips (Southampton) £1,000,000; Patrik Berger (Portsmouth) Free; Stuart Taylor (Arsenal) Undisclosed. **Birmingham C:** Mikael Forssell (Chelsea) £3,000,000; Mehdi Nafti (Santander) Undisclosed. **Blackburn R:** Shefki Kuqi (Ipswich T) Free. **Bolton W:** El-Hadji Diouf (Liverpool) Undisclosed. **Charlton Ath:** Darren Bent (Ipswich T) £3,000,000. **Chelsea:** Asier Del Horno (Athletic Bilbao) £8,000,000; Scott Sinclair (Bristol R) Undisclosed. **Everton:** Per Kroldrup (Udinese) £5,000,000. **Fulham:** Heidar Helguson (Watford) £1,300,000; Jaroslav Drobny (Panionios) Undisclosed; Ahmad Elrich (Pusan Icons) Undisclosed. **Liverpool:** Jose Reina (Villarreal) £6,000,000; Antonio Barragan (Sevilla) Free; Mark Gonzalez (Albecete) Undisclosed; Boudewijn Zenden (Middlesbrough) Free. **Manchester U:** Park Ji-Sung (PSV Eindhoven) £4,000,000; Edwin Van der Sar (Fulham) Undisclosed. **Middlesbrough:** Ayegbeni Yakubu (Portsmouth) £7,500,000; Emanuel Pogatetz (Leverkusen) £1,800,000. **Newcastle U:** Scott Parker (Chelsea) £6,500,000. **Portsmouth:** Andy O'Brien (Newcastle U) £2,000,000; Laurent Robert (Newcastle U) Loan; John Viafara (Once Caldas) Undisclosed. **Sunderland:** Jon Stead (Blackburn R) £1,800,000; Kelvin Davis (Ipswich T) £1,250,000; Tommy Miller (Ipswich T) Free; Daryl Murphy (Waterford U) Undisclosed; Nyron Nosworthy (Gillingham) Free; Martin Woods (Leeds U) Free. **Tottenham H:** Tom Huddlestone (Derby Co) £2,500,000; Aaron Lennon (Leeds U) Undisclosed; Wayne Routledge (Crystal Palace) Undisclosed; Paul Stalteri (Werder Bremen) Free; Teemu Tainio (Auxerre) Free. **West Bromwich Albion:** Darren Carter (Birmingham C) £1,500,000; Steve Watson (Everton) Free. **West Ham U:** Paul Konchesky (Charlton Ath) £1,500,000; Roy Carroll (Manchester U) Free; James Collins (Cardiff C) Undisclosed; Danny Gabbidon (Cardiff C) Undisclosed. **Wigan Ath:** Mike Pollitt (Rotherham U) £200,000.

Football League Championship: Brighton & HA: Jason Dodd (Southampton) Free; Colin Kazim-Richards (Bury) Undisclosed. **Burnley:** Wade Elliott (Bournemouth) Free; Daniel Karbassiyoon (Arsenal) Free; Gareth O'Connor (Bournemouth) Free; Wayne Thomas (Stoke C) Free. **Cardiff C:** Jeff Whitley (Sunderland) Free. **Coventry C:** Richard Duffy (Portsmouth) Loan; Clayton Ince (Crewe Alex) Free; James Scowcroft (Ipswich T) Free. **Crystal Palace:** Jonathan Macken (Manchester C) £1,100,000; Jobi McAnuff (Cardiff C) Undisclosed. **Derby Co:** Marc Edworthy (Norwich C) Free. **Hull C:** Stephen McPhee (Beira Mar) £220,000; Keith Andrews (Wolverhampton W) Free. **Ipswich T:** Nicky Forster (Reading) Free; Dean McDonald (Arsenal) Free; Sam Parkin (Swindon T) Undisclosed. **Leeds U:** Dan Harding (Brighton & HA) Tribunal; Eddie Lewis (Preston NE) Free; Steve Stone (Portsmouth) Free. **Leicester C:** Rab Douglas (Celtic) Free; Nils-Eric Johansson (Blackburn R) Free; Momo Sylla (Celtic) Free. **Luton T:** Rowan Vine (Portsmouth) £250,000. **Norwich C:** Matthieu Louis-Jean (Nottingham F) Undisclosed; Peter Thorne (Cardiff C) Undisclosed. **Plymouth Arg:** Rufus Brevett (West Ham U) Free; Akos Buzsaki (Porto) Undisclosed; Taribo West (Al-Arabi) Undisclosed. **Preston NE:** Joe Anyinsah (Bristol C) Free. **QPR:** Simon Royce (Charlton Ath) Free. **Reading:** Kevin Doyle (Cork C) Undisclosed; Steve Hunt (Brentford) Free; Shane Long (Cork C) Undisclosed. **Sheffield U:** Danny Webber (Watford) £500,000; Gary Mulligan (Wolverhampton W) Free; Lilian Nalis (Leicester C) Free; Karl Nix (Aston Villa) Free; Craig Short (Blackburn R) Free. **Sheffield W:** John Hills (Gillingham) Free. **Southampton:** Darren Powell (Crystal Palace) Free; Dennis Wise (Millwall) Free. **Stoke C:** Mamady Sidibe (Gillingham) Free; Peter Sweeney (Millwall) Undisclosed. **Wolverhampton W:** Rohan Ricketts (Tottenham H) Free.

Football League 1: Barnsley: Paul Hayes (Scunthorpe U) Tribunal; Brian Howard (Swindon T) Free; Richard Kell (Scunthorpe U) Free. **Blackpool:** John Doolan (Doncaster R) Free; Scott Vernon (Oldham Ath) Free. **Bournemouth:** Stephen Cooke (Aston Villa) Free. **Bradford C:** Russell Howarth (Tranmere R) Free; Bobby Petta (Darlington) Free; Andrew Taylor (Middlesbrough) Loan. **Brentford:** Paul

Brooker (Reading) Free; DJ Campbell (Yeading) Nominal; Ricky Newman (Reading) Free; Olafur Ingi Skulason (Arsenal) Free; Sam Tillen (Chelsea) Free. **Bristol C:** Matt Heywood (Swindon T) Free; Alex Russell (Torquay U) Free; Grant Smith (Swindon T) Free; Marcus Stewart (Sunderland) Free. **Chesterfield:** Paul Hall (Tranmere R) Free. **Colchester U:** Chris Iwelumo (Aachen) Free. **Doncaster R:** Paul Heffernan (Bristol C) £100,000; Jan Budtz (Nordsjaelland) Free; Tonny Nielsen (Fremad) Free; Steve Roberts (Wrexham) Free. **Gillingham:** Tony Bullock (Dundee U) Free. **Hartlepool U:** Chris Llewellyn (Wrexham) Undisclosed. **Huddersfield T:** Martin McIntosh (Rotherham U) Free. **Milton Keynes Dons:** Craig Morgan (Wrexham) Undisclosed; Aaron Wilbraham (Hull C) Free. **Nottingham F:** Ian Breckin (Wigan Ath) £350,000; Nicky Eaden (Wigan Ath) Free; Gary Holt (Norwich C) Undisclosed. **Oldham Ath:** Richard Butler (Lincoln C) Free; Paul Edwards (Blackpool) Free; Terrell Forbes (Grimsby T) Free; Andy Liddell (Sheffield U) Free; Gareth Owen (Stoke C) Undisclosed; Chris Porter (Bury) Undisclosed; Rob Scott (Rotherham U) Free; Chris Swailes (Rotherham U) Free; Paul Warne (Rotherham U) Free; Richard Wellens (Blackpool) Free. **Port Vale:** Tony Dinning (Bristol C) Free; Mark Innes (Chesterfield) Free; Danny Sonner (Peterborough U) Free. **Rotherham U:** Colin Murdock (Crewe Alex) Free; Jon Otsemobor (Liverpool) Free; Gregor Robertson (Nottingham F) Free; Lee Williamson (Northampton T) Free; David Worrell (Plymouth Arg) Free. **Scunthorpe U:** Jim Goodwin (Stockport Co) Free; Ritchie Ryan (Sunderland) Free. **Swansea C:** Marc Goodfellow (Bristol C) Free. **Tranmere R:** Sam Aiston (Shrewsbury T) Free; Steve Wilson (Macclesfield T) Free. **Walsall:** Daniel Fox (Everton) Free; Anthony Gerrard (Everton) Free; Chris Westwood (Hartlepool U) Free. **Yeovil T:** Matt Harrold (Brentford) Nominal; Nathan Jones (Brighton & HA) Free; Luke Oliver (Woking) Nominal; David Poole (Manchester U) Free.

Football League 2: Boston U: Lee Canoville (Torquay U) Free; Ben Futcher (Lincoln C) Free; Julian Joachim (Leeds U) Free; Gavin Johnson (Colchester U) Free; Stuart Talbot (Brentford) Free; Noel Whelan (Aberdeen) Free. **Bury:** Stuart Barlow (Stockport Co) Free; Craig Dootson (Stalybridge C) Free; Neil Edwards (Rochdale) Free; John Fitzgerald (Blackburn R) Free; Jake Sedgemore (Shrewsbury T) Free. **Carlisle U:** Zigor Aranalde (Sheffield W) Free; Anthony Williams (Grimsby T) Free. **Chester C:** Scott McNiven (Mansfield T) Free; Marcus Richardson (Yeovil T) Free. **Grimsby T:** Terry Barwick (Scunthorpe U) Free; Paul Bolland (Notts Co) Free; John Lukic (Nottingham F) Free; Steve Mildenhall (Oldham Ath) Free; Jermaine Palmer (Stoke C) Free. **Leyton Orient:** Joe Dolan (Millwall) Free; Glyn Garner (Bury) Free; Joe Keith (Colchester U) Free; Shane Tudor (Cambridge U) Free. **Lincoln C:** Danny Bacon (Hucknall T) Free; Omari Coleman (Watford) Free; Colin Cryan (Scarborough) Undisclosed; Dean Keates (Kidderminster H) Free; Scott Kerr (Scarborough) Undisclosed; Paul Mayo (Watford) Free; Steve Robinson (Swindon T) Free. **Macclesfield T:** Kevin Townson (Rochdale) Free. **Mansfield T:** Adam Birchall (Arsenal) Free; Jason Talbot (Bolton W) Free; Matthew Tipton (Macclesfield T) Free; Gus Uhlenbeek (Wycombe W) Free. **Northampton T:** Chris Doig (Nottingham F) Free; Eoin Jess (Nottingham F) Free; Bradley Johnson (Cambridge U) Free; Brett Johnson (Aldershot T) Nominal; Ian Taylor (Derby Co) Free. **Notts Co:** Kevin Pilkington (Mansfield T) Free. **Oxford U:** Stuart Gray (Rushden & D) Free; Chris Hargreaves (Brentford) Free; Lee Mansell (Luton T) Free; Billy Turley (Rushden & D) Free; Chris Willmott (Northampton T) Free. **Peterborough U:** Paul Carden (Chester C) Free; Lee Harrison (Leyton Orient) Free; Dean Holden (Oldham Ath) Free. **Rochdale:** Jon Boardman (Woking) Free. **Rushden & D:** Neil McCafferty (Charlton Ath) Free; Greg Pearson (West Ham U) Free. **Shrewsbury T:** Jay Denny (Stoke C) Free; Ben Herd (Watford) Free; Neil Sorvel (Crewe Alex) Free; Mark Stallard (Barnsley) Free. **Stockport Co:** Rob Clare (Blackpool) Free; Jermaine Easter (Boston U) Free; Mark Robinson (Hereford U) Free. **Torquay U:** Darren Garner (Rotherham U) Free; Matt Villis (Plymouth Arg) Free. **Wrexham:** Dave Bayliss (Luton T) Free; Michael Ingham (Sunderland) Free; Lee Roche (Burnley) Free; Jonathan Walters (Hull C) Free. **Wycombe W:** Will Antwi (Aldershot T) Free; Kevin Betsy (Oldham Ath) Free; Tommy Mooney (Oxford U) Free; Stefan Oakes (Notts Co) Free.